THE GLOSSARY OF
STARTUP
ENTREPRENEURSHIP

Compiled & Edited By:
Megha Nair

Rhythm

Independent
Publication

THE GLOSSARY OF STARTUP ENTREPRENEURSHIP

Compiled & Edited By:
Megha Nair

ISBN:9798862448665

9798862448665

Published by:

Rhythm Independent Publication,

Jinkethimmanahalli, Varanasi, Bengaluru, Karnataka, India - 560036

For all types of correspondence, send your mails to the provided address above.

The information presented herein has been collated from a diverse range of sources, comprehensive perspective on the subject matter.

A/B Testing Platforms

A/B testing platforms are tools used by startups and entrepreneurs to test and optimize their website or mobile app's performance and effectiveness. These platforms allow businesses to compare two versions of a webpage or app screen (referred to as variant A and variant B) to determine which version leads to better user engagement and conversion rates. By randomly splitting their audience into two groups, with one group experiencing variant A and the other group experiencing variant B, startups and entrepreneurs can collect quantitative data to make informed decisions about design elements, content, and user experience. This process helps optimize conversion rates, increase user engagement, and improve overall business performance.

A/B Testing

A/B testing is a method used in startup and entrepreneurship to compare two versions of a webpage or app to determine which one performs better in terms of user engagement, conversions, or other predetermined metrics. This testing is conducted by randomly dividing users into two groups, with each group being shown a different version of the webpage or app. The purpose of A/B testing is to identify which version of the webpage or app leads to more desirable outcomes, such as higher click-through rates, increased purchases, or longer user engagement. It allows startups and entrepreneurs to make data-driven decisions and optimize their products or services based on the results obtained from the test.

Accelerator Program

An accelerator program is a highly focused and intensive mentorship-driven program designed to accelerate the growth and development of early-stage startups and entrepreneurs. It is specifically tailored to provide valuable resources, guidance, and support to entrepreneurs during the crucial initial stages of their ventures.Accelerator programs typically operate over a fixed period of time, usually ranging from three to six months, during which participating startups receive a range of benefits and support. These programs are usually run by experienced mentors, industry experts, and successful entrepreneurs who have a strong track record in building and scaling successful startups.The primary objective of an accelerator program is to help startups achieve rapid growth and scale their businesses effectively. To accomplish this, accelerator programs offer a comprehensive curriculum that covers various vital aspects of entrepreneurship, such as product development, market validation, business strategy, fundraising, marketing, and sales.Through a combination of structured coaching sessions, workshops, networking events, and access to a vast network of investors and potential customers, accelerator programs provide startups with unparalleled opportunities for learning, growth, and collaboration. These programs help entrepreneurs refine their business ideas, validate market demand, and create a solid foundation for sustainable growth.A key feature of accelerator programs is the provision of seed funding in exchange for equity. Participating startups receive a predetermined amount of capital investment, which helps fuel their growth and provides them with the necessary financial runway to pursue their business objectives. In addition to funding, accelerator programs often provide startups with co-working spaces, access to industry-specific mentors, and other valuable resources.Accelerator programs typically culminate in a demo day, where participating startups have the opportunity to showcase their progress and achievements to a wide audience of potential investors, partners, and customers. This event serves as a platform for startups to secure follow-on funding, forge strategic partnerships, and gain market visibility.In summary, an accelerator program is an immersive and results-oriented initiative that empowers startups and entrepreneurs with knowledge, tools, and resources needed to accelerate their growth trajectory and increase their chances of long-term success in the competitive startup ecosystem.

Accelerator

An accelerator, in the context of startup and entrepreneurship, is a program or initiative designed to support early-stage companies in their growth and development. It provides these startups with essential resources and guidance to accelerate their progress, increase their chances of success, and overcome common challenges and obstacles. The primary goal of an accelerator is to help startups become investable and scalable, ultimately leading to sustainable growth and profitability. Accelerators typically offer a combination of capital, mentorship, education, and networking opportunities, creating an environment conducive to learning, innovation, and collaboration.

Accredited Investor

An accredited investor, in the context of startup and entrepreneurship, refers to an individual or entity that meets certain financial criteria set by securities regulations, allowing them to invest in private offerings or startups. The criteria are designed to ensure that the investor has the experience and financial capacity to assume the risks associated with these types of investments. The definition of an accredited investor may vary depending on the jurisdiction, but it typically includes high net worth individuals, corporations, or nonprofit organizations that meet specific income or net worth thresholds. In the United States, for example, an individual is considered an accredited investor if they have an annual income of at least $200,000 (or $300,000 for joint income with a spouse) for the past two years and have a reasonable expectation of reaching the same income level in the current year. Alternatively, an individual can be classified as an accredited investor if they have a net worth of at least $1 million, excluding the value of their primary residence. Being an accredited investor provides certain advantages and opportunities in the startup and entrepreneurial ecosystem. Startups often rely on funding from accredited investors to finance their growth and development. By investing in private offerings or startups, accredited investors can potentially earn substantial returns on their investment if the company is successful. These investments also offer the possibility of participating in the company's growth and success, as well as the opportunity to support innovative ideas and contribute to job creation and economic growth. However, it is important to note that investing in startups and private offerings carries significant risks. Startups are inherently risky ventures, with a high likelihood of failure. Accredited investors are expected to have a thorough understanding of these risks and the ability to bear potential financial losses. They should conduct due diligence, evaluate the business model, team, and market potential before making any investment decisions. In conclusion, an accredited investor, in the context of startup and entrepreneurship, is an individual or entity that meets specific financial criteria to invest in private offerings or startups. This designation allows them to participate in the high-risk, high-reward world of startups and potentially contribute to innovation, job creation, and economic growth. However, it is crucial for accredited investors to carefully evaluate investment opportunities and be prepared for the inherent risks associated with investing in startups.

Acquisition Strategy

An acquisition strategy, in the context of startup and entrepreneurship, refers to a planned approach or set of actions undertaken by a company to acquire other businesses or assets in order to achieve specific objectives or goals. The main purpose of an acquisition strategy is to enable a company to grow and expand its business, market share, or resources more quickly and efficiently than it could through organic growth alone. It can provide startups with access to new markets, technologies, products, customers, talent, or synergistic opportunities, among others. An effective acquisition strategy involves careful analysis, planning, and execution. It begins with clearly defining the objectives and criteria for potential acquisitions, such as the specific industry, market segment, geographic location, or size of target companies. This helps in identifying suitable acquisition targets that align with the company's strategic goals and complement its existing business model and capabilities. Once potential targets are identified, the next step is to conduct a thorough due diligence process to assess their financial, operational, legal, and cultural aspects. This helps the acquiring company to evaluate the risks, synergies, value, and potential challenges associated with the acquisition. It also enables the company to negotiate and structure the deal in a way that maximizes value and minimizes risks for both parties involved. After the acquisition is completed, the acquiring company needs to have a well-defined integration plan to ensure a smooth transition and realization of the expected benefits. This may involve integrating systems, processes, teams, or cultures to achieve synergies, economies of scale, or cross-selling opportunities. It also requires effective communication, coordination, and leadership to ensure alignment and minimize disruptions. In conclusion, an acquisition strategy is a vital tool for startups and entrepreneurs to fuel growth, access new opportunities, and enhance competitiveness. It requires a systematic approach and careful consideration of various factors to identify, evaluate, and integrate potential acquisitions successfully.

Acquisition Target

Acquisition target refers to a company that is considered as a desirable and strategically valuable asset for another company or investor to acquire. In the context of startup and entrepreneurship, an acquisition target is a company that is seen as a potential candidate for acquisition by a larger, more established company or investor, often with the goal of expanding their market reach, diversifying their product offerings, or gaining a competitive advantage. Entrepreneurs and startups often strive to position themselves as attractive acquisition targets by demonstrating consistent growth, innovation, and the potential for future profitability. Being an acquisition target can offer numerous benefits for startups, such as access to additional financial resources, expertise, and a broader customer base. It can also provide an exit strategy for founders and early investors to monetize their investment and move on to new ventures or pursuits.

Acquisition

Acquisition refers to the process of one company purchasing another company or its assets to gain control, ownership, or access to its resources, products, technologies, customers, or markets. In the context of startup and entrepreneurship, acquisition plays a significant role in driving growth, providing strategic advantages, and expanding market presence. Startup acquisitions occur when a larger and established company, known as the acquirer, purchases a startup company, known as the target. This acquisition can take various forms, including full buyouts, partial stake purchases, mergers, or asset acquisitions. The ultimate goal of an acquisition is to create synergies, enhance competitiveness, and accelerate the acquirer's growth trajectory.

Action Learning

Action Learning is a problem-solving methodology that promotes continuous learning and development within the context of a startup and entrepreneurship. It is an effective approach for startups and entrepreneurs to address complex challenges, enhance critical thinking, and foster collaboration among team members. In the startup and entrepreneurship context, Action Learning involves a process of identifying and analyzing real-life problems, developing and implementing solutions, and reflecting on the outcomes. It encourages individuals and teams to take ownership of their learning and progress, while actively engaging in hands-on experiences.

Affiliate Marketing Networks

Affiliate Marketing Networks are platforms or networks that connect businesses (merchants) with individual marketers (affiliates) to promote and sell their products or services. These networks provide a way for entrepreneurs and startups to generate revenue and increase brand awareness without the need for significant upfront investment or a large sales team. Entrepreneurs and startups can join an affiliate marketing network to find affiliates who are willing to promote their products or services. The network acts as a mediator, facilitating the relationship between the merchant and the affiliate. Merchants provide the affiliates with unique links or codes to track their sales and performance. When customers purchase a product or service through these links, the affiliate earns a commission.

Agile Development

Agile development is a methodology commonly used in the context of startups and entrepreneurship. It is an iterative and collaborative approach to software development that emphasizes flexibility, adaptability, and frequent customer feedback. The core principles of agile development and its application within startups revolve around continuous improvement and rapid delivery of valuable, working software. Instead of following a rigid, predefined plan, agile teams prioritize the ability to quickly respond to change and learn from each iteration of development. The key characteristics of agile development in the startup and entrepreneurship context can be summarized as follows: 1. Iterative and incremental development: Agile teams break down the development process into small iterations, typically referred to as "sprints," that result in the creation of a functional and potentially releasable piece of software. This incremental approach allows startups to quickly release a minimum viable product (MVP) and gather valuable user feedback. 2. Cross-functional and self-organizing teams: Agile teams consist of members with diverse skills who collaborate closely throughout the development process. These teams are self-organizing, meaning they have the freedom and responsibility to make decisions regarding how to best achieve their goals. 3. Continuous customer collaboration: Agile development encourages regular and active involvement of customers or end-users throughout the development cycle. By obtaining feedback and insights directly from the target market, startups can ensure that their product aligns with customer needs and expectations. 4. Adaptive planning and flexibility: In agile development, plans are fluid and subject to change as requirements evolve or new insights emerge. Startups embrace the idea that change is a positive and necessary aspect of the development process, enabling them to respond quickly to market shifts. 5. Emphasis on technical excellence and simplicity: Agile teams prioritize delivering high-quality software through continuous integration, automated testing, and other technical practices. They strive for simplicity in both their processes and the design and implementation of their software, allowing for better maintainability and scalability. Overall, agile development provides startups and entrepreneurs with a framework that promotes adaptability, collaboration, and customer-centricity. By following agile principles, startups can accelerate their development cycles, minimize risks, and ultimately increase the chances of building successful and market-oriented products.

Agile Entrepreneurship

Agile entrepreneurship can be defined as a mindset and approach to startup and entrepreneurship that emphasizes adaptability, flexibility, and continuous improvement. It is a methodology that allows entrepreneurs to respond quickly to changing market conditions, customer needs, and technological advancements. Agile entrepreneurship is rooted in the Agile methodology, which originally emerged in the software development industry. It emphasizes iterative and incremental development, cross-functional teams, customer collaboration, and a focus on delivering value early and often. In the context of startups and entrepreneurship, agile entrepreneurship involves applying the principles of Agile to the entire business process. This includes everything from product development and marketing to sales and customer support. The goal is to create a startup that can quickly and effectively respond to changes in the market, customer feedback, and competitive landscape. One of the key aspects of agile entrepreneurship is the use of feedback loops. This means constantly gathering feedback from customers, partners, and stakeholders, and using that feedback to make informed decisions and adjustments to the business strategy. This iterative approach allows entrepreneurs to test assumptions, validate ideas, and pivot if necessary. Agile entrepreneurship also promotes cross-functional teamwork and collaboration. Rather than operating in silos, team members from various disciplines work together to solve problems and deliver value. This promotes creativity, innovation, and a shared sense of ownership and responsibility. Another important characteristic of agile entrepreneurship is the focus on delivering value early and often. Rather than waiting until a product or service is perfect, agile entrepreneurs aim to deliver a minimum viable product (MVP) as quickly as possible. This allows them to gather feedback and learn from real-world usage, enabling them to make improvements and iterate rapidly. In conclusion, agile entrepreneurship is a mindset and approach to startup and entrepreneurship that promotes adaptability, flexibility, and continuous improvement. It involves applying the principles of Agile to the entire business process, including product development, marketing, sales, and customer support. By embracing feedback, teamwork, and delivering value early and often, agile entrepreneurs can increase their chances of success in a rapidly changing and competitive business environment.

Agile Methodology

Agile Methodology is a project management approach that prioritizes flexibility, collaboration, and continuous improvement in the development and delivery of products or services. It is particularly relevant in the context of startups and entrepreneurship, as it allows for rapid adaptation to market changes, minimizes risk, and fosters innovation. In the startup and entrepreneurship world, where adaptability is crucial, Agile Methodology provides a framework that enables businesses to respond quickly and effectively to market demands. Unlike traditional project management methods that follow a linear and sequential process, Agile embraces an iterative and incremental approach. One of the cornerstones of Agile Methodology is early and regular delivery of working products or services. Instead of waiting for a fully developed solution, startups and entrepreneurs break down their projects into smaller, manageable increments called "sprints." Each sprint typically has a duration of two to four weeks and aims to deliver a minimum viable product (MVP) or an iteration that adds value to the end-users. Another fundamental aspect of Agile is collaboration. It fosters regular communication and close collaboration between stakeholders, including team members, customers, and investors. By involving stakeholders throughout the development process, startups can gather feedback, validate assumptions, and make necessary adjustments early on. This iterative feedback loop ultimately leads to better products, improved customer satisfaction, and increased chances of success. Agile Methodology also emphasizes adaptability and continuous improvement. Rather than rigidly sticking to a predefined plan, startups have the flexibility to adjust their priorities and goals as new information emerges or market conditions change. Regular meetings, such as daily stand-ups or sprint reviews, allow for constant assessment and adaptation, ensuring that the product or service aligns with evolving customer needs. Overall, Agile Methodology has become an essential tool for startups and entrepreneurs due to its ability to enable rapid development, encourage collaboration, and drive innovation. By implementing Agile principles, startups can navigate uncertainties, reduce time to market, and achieve a competitive edge in today's dynamic business landscape.

Agile Project Management

Agile Project Management in the context of Startup & Entrepreneurship refers to a flexible and iterative approach to managing projects, enabling entrepreneurs and startups to adapt and respond quickly to changing circumstances and requirements. Unlike traditional project management methodologies that follow a linear and sequential process, Agile Project Management emphasizes collaboration, communication, and feedback. It aims to deliver value to customers early and continuously by breaking the project down into smaller, manageable tasks called "user stories," which are then prioritized and tackled in short iterations called "sprints." One of the key principles of Agile Project Management is the ability to embrace change. In the startup and entrepreneurship world, where uncertainty and ambiguity are prevalent, being able to pivot and adapt quickly is critical. Agile methodologies allow entrepreneurs to gather feedback from customers, investors, and stakeholders early on, analyze the data, and make necessary adjustments to the project's direction and scope. Another essential aspect of Agile Project Management is the emphasis on collaboration and self-organization. Entrepreneurs and startups work closely with cross-functional teams that include individuals from various disciplines, such as development, design, marketing, and finance. By fostering a collaborative environment, Agile Project Management promotes effective communication, knowledge sharing, and collective decision-making. Additionally, Agile Project Management uses regular and frequent meetings, known as "stand-ups" or "scrum meetings," to keep the team in sync, identify and address any potential issues, and provide a platform for transparent and open communication. These meetings also allow for the celebration of achievements and the acknowledgment of challenges, fostering a culture of continuous improvement and learning. In conclusion, Agile Project Management in the context of Startup & Entrepreneurship is about embracing flexibility, collaboration, and adaptability to effectively manage projects in an ever-changing and uncertain environment. By breaking projects down into smaller iterations, gathering frequent feedback, and fostering a collaborative team environment, Agile methodologies enable entrepreneurs and startups to successfully navigate the challenging landscape of entrepreneurship.

Agile Startups

Agile startups refer to entrepreneurial ventures that adopt the principles and methodology of Agile in their operations and decision-making processes. Agile, originally a software development framework, has gained recognition as a versatile and efficient approach to managing projects and teams in various industries. In the context of startups and entrepreneurship, the Agile methodology provides a systematic and iterative approach to product development, allowing for flexibility and adaptability in response to changing market conditions and customer feedback. Agile startups prioritize collaboration, continuous learning, and customer-centricity. They work in short, time-bound cycles known as sprints, where cross-functional teams collaborate closely to deliver small, incremental releases of their product or service. Each sprint concludes with a review and retrospective, enabling the team to reflect on their progress and make improvements for the next iteration. One of the key aspects of Agile startups is the emphasis on customer feedback and validation. These startups incorporate customer input early in the development process, conducting experiments, collecting data, and using that feedback to shape and refine their product. By delivering value to customers in small increments, Agile startups can quickly adapt and pivot their strategy based on market response. Agile startups also prioritize transparency and effective communication within their teams. They leverage various Agile tools and techniques, such as daily stand-up meetings, Kanban boards, and user stories, to ensure that everyone is aligned and on track. This fosters a culture of collaboration, accountability, and continuous improvement. The Agile approach is well-suited for startups, especially those operating in rapidly changing markets or industries with high uncertainty. It allows founders and teams to validate assumptions, minimize risks, and optimize resource allocation. Additionally, by embracing Agile principles, startups can create a culture that values innovation, adaptability, and resilience, which are crucial for long-term success in today's dynamic business landscape.

Angel Funding

Angel funding, in the context of startup and entrepreneurship, refers to the financial investment provided by affluent individuals, commonly known as angel investors or angel backers, to early-stage businesses. These investors typically fund startups in exchange for an equity stake or convertible debt, supporting entrepreneurs in their efforts to launch and grow their ventures. Angel funding serves as the first external source of capital for startups, bridging the gap between self-funding and seeking larger investments from venture capitalists. Unlike traditional funding from banks or financial institutions, angel funding offers a more flexible and patient approach, reflecting the investor's belief in the startup's potential for growth.

Angel Investing

An angel investor, in the context of startup and entrepreneurship, refers to an individual who provides financial support to early-stage and high-potential startups in exchange for equity ownership or convertible debt. These investors are typically wealthy individuals or successful entrepreneurs themselves, and they use their personal funds to invest in promising ventures. Angel investing plays a crucial role in the startup ecosystem, as it helps bridge the gap between the initial development stages of a startup and the point where it can attract larger investments from venture capitalists or other institutional investors. Startups often turn to angel investors for funding when they are too new or too risky to secure traditional bank loans or attract interest from professional investors. In addition to financial support, angel investors also bring valuable expertise and guidance to startups. Due to their experience and industry knowledge, they can mentor and advise entrepreneurs, providing them with valuable insights, connections, and strategic guidance. This hands-on involvement sets angel investors apart from other types of investors, making them highly valuable to startups beyond just their financial contributions. Angel investors typically invest in industries and sectors they are familiar with, leveraging their domain expertise to identify potential winners and assess the viability of a startup. They often form part of an angel network or syndicate, pooling their resources to invest in a broader range of startups and minimize risk. Angel networks also provide a platform for collaboration and knowledge sharing among angel investors, further enhancing the support they can provide to startups. Unlike venture capitalists who tend to focus on later-stage startups and larger investments, angel investors are willing to take on higher risks and smaller investments. While they hope for significant returns on their investment, they understand that many startups may fail, and they diversify their portfolios accordingly. In conclusion, angel investing is an essential component of the startup ecosystem, providing early-stage startups with much-needed funding, expertise, and mentorship. By taking on higher risks and offering smaller investments, angel investors play a crucial role in fueling innovation and supporting the growth of promising startups.

Angel Investor Network

An Angel Investor Network is a group of high-net-worth individuals who provide financial support and guidance to startups and entrepreneurs. Operating as a collective, these angel investors pool their resources and expertise to identify promising early-stage companies and invest in them. Unlike traditional venture capitalists or banks, angel investors are typically individuals who have achieved success in their own businesses and now wish to support and nurture new ventures. They often invest their own personal funds, seeking not only financial returns but also the satisfaction of helping the next generation of entrepreneurs succeed.

Angel Investor

An angel investor is an individual who provides financial backing and support to early-stage or start-up companies, typically in exchange for equity ownership in the company. Unlike venture capitalists, angel investors are usually investing their own personal funds rather than managing a large pool of capital from institutional or corporate investors. Angel investors play a critical role in the early stages of a company's growth, when traditional funding sources like banks and venture capitalists may be hesitant to invest. They are often willing to take on higher levels of risk in exchange for the potential of greater returns in the future. In addition to providing capital, angel investors also bring valuable expertise, industry connections, and mentorship to the companies they invest in.

Angel Network

An Angel Network refers to a group of individual investors who collectively provide financial support and guidance to startups and entrepreneurs in exchange for equity or other forms of ownership in the company. These investors, known as angel investors or angel funders, are typically high-net-worth individuals who seek to make early-stage investments in promising business ventures. The primary role of an angel network is to bridge the funding gap that many startups face during their initial stages of development. These networks often operate as intermediaries, connecting entrepreneurs with potential investors who are interested in investing in their respective industries or business ideas. By pooling their financial resources and expertise, angel networks are able to provide startups with the necessary capital and mentorship to help them grow, scale, and achieve their business objectives. Angel networks offer a range of benefits for both startups and angel investors. For startups, securing funding from angel networks can be a critical milestone in their entrepreneurial journey. In addition to the financial investment, angel investors often bring valuable industry knowledge, experience, and networks to the table. This can help startups gain access to new markets, connections with potential customers, and strategic guidance to navigate the challenges of building a successful business. On the other hand, angel investors also benefit from being part of a network. By pooling their investments with other angels, they are able to diversify their portfolios and spread their risk across multiple startups. Additionally, angel networks provide angel investors with the opportunity to collaborate, learn from one another, and leverage their collective knowledge and resources to identify and invest in the most promising startups. Overall, angel networks play a fundamental role in the startup ecosystem by connecting early-stage companies with the necessary capital and expertise to fuel their growth. These networks serve as a vital bridge between entrepreneurs and investors, fostering innovation, job creation, and economic development in the entrepreneurial landscape.

Angel Syndicate

An angel syndicate, in the context of startup and entrepreneurship, refers to a group of individual angel investors who come together to pool their financial resources, knowledge, and expertise to invest in early-stage companies. Angel investors are typically high-net-worth individuals who provide capital to startups in exchange for equity ownership. They play a crucial role in providing funding and mentorship to early-stage companies that may not yet have access to traditional sources of financing, such as venture capital firms or banks. By forming a syndicate, angel investors can combine their resources and increase their investing power. This allows them to invest larger amounts of capital and fund a more diverse portfolio of startups. Additionally, syndicates provide a platform for investors to collaborate and share due diligence efforts, investment opportunities, and insights into emerging trends and industries. Angel syndicates may operate in different ways, depending on the specific agreements and structures established among the members. Some syndicates may have a lead investor or syndicate manager who takes the lead in sourcing deals, conducting due diligence, and negotiating terms with the startup. Other syndicates may operate on a more democratic basis, with all members having equal say in investment decisions. One of the key benefits of angel syndicates is that they offer startups access to a broader network of investors. This can provide startups with increased visibility, as well as a greater chance of securing follow-on funding from other members of the syndicate or their extended networks. Syndicates also allow investors to share the risk associated with early-stage investing, as investments are typically made on a shared basis rather than individually. In conclusion, an angel syndicate brings together individual angel investors to collectively invest in and support early-stage startups. By pooling their resources and expertise, syndicates provide startups with access to capital and mentorship, while offering investors the opportunity to diversify their investment portfolios and collaborate with like-minded individuals.

Angel Tax

Angel Tax refers to a tax imposed by the government on the funding received by startups through angel investors. In the context of startup and entrepreneurship, angel investors play a vital role in providing early-stage funding to startups in exchange for equity or ownership in the company. Angel Tax is a term commonly used in India, where it has been a subject of controversy and concern among entrepreneurs and investors. The concept of Angel Tax emerged as a measure to prevent money laundering and the misuse of funds through shell companies. The main aim was to scrutinize the investments made by angel investors in startups and determine whether they were genuine or a means to evade taxes. However, the stringent implementation of this tax has had unintended consequences for startups and has been viewed as a barrier to entrepreneurial growth. Under Angel Tax regulations, if the valuation of a startup during its fundraising exceeds its fair market value, the excess is considered income and taxed as per regular income tax rates. The fair market value is determined based on the net asset value of the shares of the startup as on the date of the issue of shares. This means that if a startup receives funding at a higher valuation than its net asset value, it will be liable to pay Angel Tax on the excess amount. The issue with the Angel Tax lies in its arbitrary implementation and the challenge of accurately determining the fair market value of a startup. Startups often have a high valuation due to their potential for growth and future profitability, which may not be reflected in their net asset value. This leads to disputes between startups and the tax authorities, resulting in unnecessary burdens and legal battles. Entrepreneurs and industry experts have been advocating for the removal or relaxation of Angel Tax to create a more favorable environment for startups and encourage investment. They argue that the tax hampers the inflow of funds into startups, discouraging innovation and hindering economic growth. The government has taken steps to address these concerns and simplify the Angel Tax regulations, but further reforms are still needed to make it more entrepreneur-friendly.

AngelList

AngelList is a renowned online platform that connects startups, investors, and job seekers in the field of entrepreneurship. It serves as a bridge between startup companies and individuals interested in investing or working in the startup ecosystem. With a mission to democratize the investment process and support early-stage startups, AngelList facilitates fundraising, job hunting, and networking within the startup community. Founders can create a profile on AngelList to showcase their company, while investors can browse through the platform to discover potential investment opportunities.

Anti-Dilution Clause

An anti-dilution clause, in the context of startup and entrepreneurship, is a provision included in investment agreements or shareholder agreements that protects investors or shareholders from the dilution of their ownership stake in the company. Dilution refers to the reduction in the

8

ownership percentage of existing shareholders or investors when new shares are issued. The purpose of an anti-dilution clause is to preserve the value of an investor's or shareholder's ownership stake by adjusting the conversion ratio of their preferred shares in the event of a subsequent financing round at a lower price per share than their initial investment. This adjustment is typically made through a mechanism known as "anti-dilution protection." The two main types of anti-dilution protections commonly used in startup and entrepreneurship agreements are: 1. Full ratchet: Under a full ratchet anti-dilution clause, if new shares are issued at a price per share lower than the original price paid by the investor, the conversion price of the investor's preferred shares is adjusted downward to reflect the new, lower price. This results in a higher number of shares being issued to the investor, effectively minimizing the dilution of their ownership stake. 2. Weighted average: In this type of anti-dilution protection, the adjustment to the conversion price of the preferred shares is based on a weighted average of the new share price and the original share price. The weighted average takes into account the number of new shares issued and the respective prices paid for those shares. This approach is considered more favorable to the company and can help strike a balance between protecting the investor's ownership stake and allowing for the company's future financing needs. Anti-dilution clauses are important for investors and shareholders as they provide a mechanism to protect their ownership stake from being significantly diluted in subsequent financing rounds. This protection can help maintain their proportional ownership and influence in the company, as well as preserve the economic value of their investment. However, it's important for entrepreneurs to carefully consider the potential effects and implications of including anti-dilution clauses in investment agreements, as they can impact the company's ability to raise future capital and attract new investors.

Artificial Intelligence (AI) Chatbots

Artificial Intelligence (AI) Chatbots, in the context of startup and entrepreneurship, refer to computer programs designed to simulate intelligent conversation with human users. These chatbots utilize advanced machine learning algorithms and natural language processing techniques to understand and respond to user inputs in a human-like manner. AI chatbots are becoming increasingly popular among startups and entrepreneurs as they offer numerous benefits. Firstly, they provide a cost-effective solution for customer support and assistance. By automating the customer service process, startups can minimize the need for human agents, resulting in significant cost savings. Additionally, AI chatbots can handle multiple customer interactions simultaneously, improving response times and enhancing customer satisfaction. Furthermore, AI chatbots can be integrated into various communication channels, including websites, messaging apps, and social media platforms. This versatility allows startups to engage with their customers on their preferred platforms, ultimately enhancing brand visibility and customer reach. Startup founders and entrepreneurs can leverage AI chatbots for lead generation and marketing purposes as well. These intelligent bots can qualify leads, provide personalized recommendations, and offer product information. By automating these processes, startups can streamline their sales and marketing efforts, allocate resources more efficiently, and ultimately boost revenue. Moreover, AI chatbots can analyze and gather valuable data from customer interactions, enabling startups to gain insights into consumer preferences, behavior patterns, and market trends. This data-driven approach empowers entrepreneurs to make informed decisions, refine their products or services, and adapt to changing market dynamics. However, it is essential for startups and entrepreneurs to design and train their AI chatbots effectively. The success of these chatbots relies on their ability to understand and respond accurately to various user queries. Regular updates and improvements based on user feedback are crucial in maintaining the effectiveness of the chatbot and ensuring a positive user experience. In summary, AI chatbots offer startups and entrepreneurs a powerful tool for automating customer support, lead generation, marketing, and data analysis. By harnessing the capabilities of artificial intelligence and natural language processing, these chatbots have the potential to enhance efficiency, reduce costs, and drive business growth.

Asset Sale

An asset sale refers to the transfer of ownership of specific assets from one party, known as the seller, to another party, known as the buyer. In the context of startups and entrepreneurship, an asset sale typically involves the sale of tangible and intangible assets owned by a startup or entrepreneur. These assets can include equipment, inventory, intellectual property, customer lists, contracts, and goodwill. Asset sales are commonly used in startup and entrepreneurial ventures for various reasons. One primary reason is that asset sales allow the seller to monetize their assets, generating much-needed cash for the business. This can be particularly beneficial for startups that may not yet be generating significant revenue or profits. Selling assets can provide the necessary funds to fuel growth, invest in new projects, or meet financial obligations. From the buyer's perspective, asset sales offer distinct advantages as well. By purchasing specific assets rather than acquiring the entire business, buyers can choose which assets they want to acquire and avoid any unwanted liabilities or obligations of the seller. This selective approach allows buyers to focus on acquiring assets that align with their strategic goals and can potentially enhance their own business operations. Asset sales can take various forms, depending on the nature of the assets being transferred and the agreement between the buyer and seller. The terms and conditions of an asset sale are typically outlined in a purchase agreement, which specifies the assets being sold, the purchase price, any warranties or representations, and any relevant terms of the transaction. It is worth noting that asset sales are distinct from stock sales, where the ownership of the business itself is transferred. In stock sales, the buyer acquires the entire company, including all of its assets, liabilities, contracts, and legal obligations. In contrast, asset sales allow for a more focused transfer of specific assets, giving both parties more flexibility and control in the transaction.

Automatic Conversion Clause

An automatic conversion clause refers to a provision in a startup's investment agreement that outlines the conditions under which convertible notes will convert into equity at a predetermined valuation or upon the occurrence of certain events. Typically, when a startup raises funds through a convertible note, the investors' funds are treated as debt and the note is structured to convert into equity at a later date or upon the startup's next funding round. The purpose of an automatic conversion clause is to provide clarity and transparency regarding the conversion process, ensuring that both the startup and the investors are aware of the conditions and triggers that will lead to the conversion of the debt into equity.

Automatic Conversion

Automatic Conversion refers to the process of transforming a startup idea or concept into a functioning and sustainable business entity, often driven by technology or innovative solutions. In the context of startups and entrepreneurship, automatic conversion involves the systematic and efficient transition from the initial stages of a business venture to a fully operational and scalable enterprise. It encompasses various steps and actions that help entrepreneurs convert their ideas into tangible products, services, or business models. The process of automatic conversion typically begins with the identification of a problem or an opportunity in the market. Entrepreneurs then formulate an idea or concept that can address this problem or capitalize on the opportunity. This idea may involve developing a new product, service, or technology, or it could involve improving existing offerings. Once the idea is conceptualized, entrepreneurs need to evaluate its feasibility and potential for success. This evaluation includes conducting market research, analyzing the competitive landscape, and assessing the potential demand for the proposed solution. It also involves developing a comprehensive business plan that outlines the value proposition, target market, revenue streams, and marketing strategies to be pursued. After the initial evaluation, entrepreneurs must focus on building a Minimum Viable Product (MVP) or a prototype that demonstrates the core functionalities and viability of their idea. This step often involves leveraging technology or innovative solutions to create a scalable and cost-effective product or service. Once the MVP is developed, entrepreneurs can test and validate their idea in the market. This involves gathering user feedback, iterating on the product, and refining the business model based on customer needs and market dynamics. This iterative process is crucial for adapting to market changes, refining the offering, and ensuring product-market fit. Finally, automatic conversion involves scaling the business and establishing a sustainable revenue model. This may include securing funding through investments or loans, expanding the customer base, optimizing operational processes, and implementing effective marketing and sales strategies. The goal is to transform the startup into a profitable and growth-oriented venture.

B Corporation (B-Corp)

A B Corporation, commonly referred to as a B-Corp, is a type of for-profit company that has been certified by the nonprofit organization B Lab. B Corps are committed to meeting rigorous standards of social and environmental performance, transparency, and accountability. They are distinguishable from traditional corporations because they seek to achieve a positive impact through their business activities. Startup companies and entrepreneurs can benefit from obtaining B Corporation certification. By becoming a B Corp, startups can demonstrate their commitment to sustainable business practices, which can help them attract socially-minded investors, customers, and employees. B Corp certification provides a clear signal to stakeholders that the company is taking both financial and non-financial factors into consideration in its decision-making processes. In order to become a B Corp, companies must undergo a thorough evaluation of their business practices and meet specific performance requirements established by B Lab. The assessment process scrutinizes a company's social and environmental impact, as well as its corporate governance and employee practices. B Corps are required to consider the interests of a wide range of stakeholders, including employees, customers, suppliers, and the communities in which they operate. By obtaining B Corp certification, startups and entrepreneurs gain access to a global network of like-minded businesses. This community of B Corps engages in collaborative efforts to drive positive change and share best practices. B Corps also benefit from increased visibility and recognition in the marketplace, which can lead to new business opportunities and partnerships. Furthermore, B Corp certification is not limited to any specific industry or sector. Startups from a wide range of sectors, including technology, healthcare, and consumer goods, can pursue B Corp certification. This allows entrepreneurs to showcase their commitment to social and environmental responsibility, regardless of the nature of their business. In summary, a B Corporation is a for-profit company that has been certified by B Lab as meeting rigorous standards of social and environmental performance. Startup companies and entrepreneurs can benefit from obtaining B Corp certification by demonstrating their commitment to sustainable business practices, accessing a global network of like-minded businesses, and attracting socially-minded stakeholders.

B2B (Business-To-Business)

B2B (Business-to-Business) refers to a type of commerce that involves the exchange of goods, services, or information between two businesses rather than between a business and a consumer. In the context of startup and entrepreneurship, B2B interactions play a crucial role in facilitating the growth and success of companies. Startups and entrepreneurs often engage in B2B transactions to acquire necessary resources, establish partnerships, and meet their business objectives. These interactions can occur at various stages of the entrepreneurial journey and involve different types of products or services.

B2B2C (Business-To-Business-To-Consumer)

B2B2C, which stands for business-to-business-to-consumer, is a business model in which a company sells products or services to other businesses, who then sell those products or services to consumers. In this model, the company acts as a middleman, facilitating the sale between the two parties. Startups and entrepreneurs often adopt the B2B2C model because it allows them to leverage the existing customer base of their partner businesses, while also gaining access to new markets and customers. By partnering with another business, the startup or entrepreneur can tap into their partner's distribution channels, customer relationships, and marketing expertise, which can greatly accelerate their growth and success.

B2C (Business-To-Consumer)

B2C (Business-to-Consumer) refers to a type of business model in which a company sells its products or services directly to individual customers. This model is commonly associated with startups and entrepreneurship as it offers a way for entrepreneurs to capitalize on market opportunities and establish new ventures. In a B2C model, the primary focus of the business is to attract and engage with consumers, aiming to fulfill their specific needs and desires. Startups operating in the B2C space typically develop innovative products or services that cater to a specific target market, leveraging technology and customer-centric strategies to gain a competitive advantage.

B2E (Business-To-Employee)

B2E (Business-to-Employee) is a business model that refers to the provision of goods, services, or information from a company to its employees. This concept is particularly relevant in the context of startups and entrepreneurship, as it focuses on meeting the unique needs and requirements of employees in these dynamic and fast-paced environments. Startups often face numerous challenges when it comes to managing and supporting their workforce. B2E solutions aim to address these challenges by streamlining internal processes, enhancing employee productivity, and improving overall satisfaction and engagement. These solutions can encompass a wide range of offerings, including employee self-service portals, training and development programs, communication tools, and employee wellness initiatives. One key aspect of B2E in the startup and entrepreneurship space is the use of technology to facilitate communication and collaboration between employees. Startups often have remote teams or geographically dispersed employees, making it crucial to have effective digital platforms to connect and engage with the workforce. B2E solutions can provide employees with access to real-time project updates, task management tools, and team collaboration platforms, enabling seamless communication and enhancing productivity. B2E also encompasses initiatives aimed at supporting employees' personal and professional growth. Startups recognize the importance of investing in their employees' development to foster a culture of continuous learning and improvement. This can include offering training programs, mentoring opportunities, and career progression pathways. By prioritizing employee development, startups can enhance employee satisfaction, reduce turnover rates, and attract top talent in the competitive entrepreneurial ecosystem. Furthermore, B2E solutions can incorporate employee wellness initiatives, which are increasingly important as startups often operate in high-pressure and demanding environments. Startups can provide access to wellness resources, such as fitness programs, mental health support, and work-life balance initiatives, to ensure the well-being of their employees. Prioritizing employee wellness not only promotes a positive work culture but also contributes to increased productivity and overall business success. In conclusion, B2E in the context of startup and entrepreneurship refers to the provision of goods, services, and information to employees, with the goal of enhancing productivity, engagement, and employee well-being. By investing in B2E solutions, startups can create a supportive and inclusive work environment, foster employee development, and ultimately thrive in the competitive startup landscape.

B2G (Business-To-Government)

B2G (Business-to-Government) refers to the commercial transactions and relationships between a business or startup and government bodies or agencies. It involves the provision of goods, services, or solutions to government entities, which may include federal, state, or local governments. In the context of entrepreneurship and startups, B2G encompasses various activities and opportunities for businesses to engage with government organizations. These interactions can include bidding on government contracts, providing specialized services or products, or collaborating with government agencies to develop innovative solutions. Startups and entrepreneurs often view B2G as an avenue for growth, as government entities have significant buying power and can offer stable and long-term contracts. Additionally, the government sector presents unique challenges and opportunities that can fuel innovation and drive social impact. Engaging in B2G transactions requires businesses to understand the complexities of government procurement processes, regulations, and compliance. Startups need to familiarize themselves with government policies and requirements, as well as identifying the specific needs and pain points of government agencies. Successful B2G engagement requires startups to tailor their products or services to meet government specifications and ensure they align with broader public goals or requirements. This may involve customization, localization, or integration with existing government systems or infrastructure. By doing so, startups can position themselves as reliable partners and providers of value-added solutions. Collaboration with government agencies can also provide startups with credibility and validation, as government endorsements or partnerships can serve as strong signals of quality and trustworthiness in the market. B2G activities may also open doors to additional business opportunities beyond the government sector, as success in these contracts can act as a reference or testimonial for other potential clients. In conclusion, B2G in the context of startup and entrepreneurship refers to the commercial interactions between businesses or startups and government bodies. It represents an opportunity for startups to provide goods, services, or solutions to government entities and requires an understanding of government procurement processes and compliance. Successful B2G engagement can lead to long-term contracts, credibility, and potential business growth.

B2G2C (Business-To-Government-To-Consumer)

B2G2C (Business-to-Government-to-Consumer) refers to a business model in which a startup or entrepreneur directly engages with both the government and consumers in order to offer products or services. This approach involves three distinct entities: the startup, the government, and the end consumers. Firstly, the startup or entrepreneur acts as the central figure, providing innovative products or services. Their aim is to address the needs and preferences of consumers or end users in a specific market. They must develop a clear understanding of the target audience, identify their pain points, and create offerings that solve their problems or fulfill their desires. Secondly, the government plays a crucial role in the B2G2C model. Startups and entrepreneurs need to establish a direct connection and collaborate with government agencies or departments relevant to their industry. This collaboration is essential, as it enables them to understand government regulations, policies, and initiatives that can impact their business operations and the industry as a whole. Startups may also seek government support, funding, or partnerships to facilitate their growth and success. Lastly, the end consumers are the ultimate recipients of the startup's products or services. The startup must effectively market and promote their offerings to attract and engage consumers. This requires developing a deep understanding of consumer preferences, conducting market research, and implementing effective marketing strategies. By connecting directly with consumers, startups can gather feedback, improve their offerings, and enhance customer satisfaction and loyalty. Additionally, startups may leverage digital platforms and technologies to reach a broader consumer base, expand their market share, and achieve sustainable growth. In summary, B2G2C is a business model that involves startups or entrepreneurs engaging with both the government and end consumers. By directly collaborating with the government, startups can understand regulations and policies, seek support, and build strategic partnerships. Simultaneously, by focusing on the needs of end consumers and delivering innovative products and services, startups can achieve market success and drive sustainable growth.

Balance Scorecard

A balance scorecard is a performance management tool that provides a comprehensive view of a startup or entrepreneurship's performance in achieving its strategic objectives and goals. It helps evaluate and measure various aspects of the business, including financial, customer, internal processes, and learning and growth perspectives. In the context of a startup or entrepreneurship, the balanced scorecard helps assess the overall health and performance of the business across multiple dimensions. It goes beyond traditional financial measures and considers other critical factors that contribute to the long-term success of the organization.

Blockchain Technology

Blockchain technology is a decentralized and distributed digital ledger that records transactions across multiple computers or nodes. It allows participants to securely and transparently interact with each other without the need for intermediaries, such as banks or governments. In the context of startups and entrepreneurship, blockchain technology offers several unique advantages. First and foremost, it can provide a more efficient way of conducting business by eliminating the need for intermediaries and reducing transaction costs. This can be particularly beneficial for startups that are working on disrupting traditional industries or creating new business models. Furthermore, blockchain technology has the potential to enhance trust and security in startup ecosystems. The transparent and immutable nature of blockchain records allows for greater accountability and reduces the risk of fraud or manipulation. This can be crucial for startups seeking to attract investors, partners, or customers who value transparency and integrity. Another potential application of blockchain technology in the startup space is in the area of fundraising and capital formation. Through the use of initial coin offerings (ICOs) or token sales, startups can raise funds directly from a global pool of interested investors. This can provide greater access to capital and democratize the investment process, allowing smaller investors to participate in early-stage funding rounds. Moreover, blockchain technology can enable startups to create decentralized applications (dApps) or platforms that operate without a central authority. This opens up new possibilities for innovation and disruption, as entrepreneurs

13

can build decentralized solutions that challenge the status quo and empower users.In conclusion, blockchain technology has the potential to revolutionize the startup and entrepreneurship landscape by providing a decentralized, transparent, and efficient way of conducting business. Its benefits include reduced transaction costs, enhanced trust and security, new fundraising opportunities, and the ability to create decentralized applications. Entrepreneurs who embrace blockchain technology can gain a competitive edge and drive innovation within their respective industries.

Blue Ocean Strategy

The Blue Ocean Strategy refers to a concept in startup and entrepreneurship that focuses on creating new market spaces or industries, instead of competing in existing ones. It involves developing innovative business models and value propositions to capture uncontested market shares. Typically, in traditional competitive markets, entrepreneurs and startups face intense competition, leading to price wars, limited differentiation, and profit erosion. In contrast, the Blue Ocean Strategy aims to break free from this red ocean of competition by identifying untapped market opportunities with little or no competition. This strategy encourages entrepreneurs to think outside the box and create a value proposition that stands out from existing offerings. By discovering new customer segments or creating demand for a unique product or service, startups can carve out a blue ocean for themselves, away from the intense competition of red oceans. Implementing a Blue Ocean Strategy requires careful analysis of customer needs and preferences, along with a deep understanding of industry trends. Instead of simply improving on existing products or services, entrepreneurs need to identify and solve pain points that are currently unaddressed, creating new and compelling value for customers. Successful execution of this strategy can lead to significant advantages for startups and entrepreneurs. By entering a market space with little or no competition, they have the opportunity to establish a dominant position, set higher profit margins, and secure customer loyalty. Blue Ocean Strategy allows entrepreneurs to differentiate themselves from competitors and avoid commoditization, resulting in sustained growth and success. However, it is important to note that identifying and creating a blue ocean is not without risks. It requires thorough market research, innovative thinking, and effective execution. Moreover, as new market spaces are created, there is always the possibility of imitation and subsequent competition. Therefore, continuous innovation and adaptation are crucial for sustainable success in a blue ocean.

Bootcamp

A bootcamp, in the context of startup and entrepreneurship, is an intensive and immersive training program designed to provide aspiring entrepreneurs with the necessary knowledge, skills, and resources to kickstart their own business ventures. These programs are typically structured as short-term, intensive workshops or courses that focus on various aspects of starting and running a business, such as ideation, market research, product development, marketing and sales strategies, financial management, and pitching to investors. Bootcamps often bring together a diverse group of participants, including aspiring entrepreneurs, industry professionals, and subject matter experts, who collaborate and learn from each other through hands-on exercises, group discussions, case studies, and real-world simulations. The goal is to create a dynamic and interactive learning environment that fosters creativity, critical thinking, and problem-solving skills. One of the key features of bootcamps is the emphasis on experiential learning. Participants are encouraged to apply the concepts and techniques they learn directly to their own startup ideas or projects. This hands-on approach allows them to gain practical experience, overcome challenges, and develop a deep understanding of the entrepreneurial process. In addition to the educational component, bootcamps also provide valuable networking opportunities. Participants have the chance to connect and collaborate with like-minded individuals, mentors, industry experts, and potential investors. These connections can be instrumental in building a supportive network, accessing resources, and creating partnerships that can help propel their startup ventures forward. Overall, a bootcamp serves as a catalyst for aspiring entrepreneurs, providing them with the necessary tools, knowledge, and network to turn their business ideas into reality. It offers a structured and intensive learning experience, combining theory with practice, and equipping participants with the skills and mindset needed to navigate the challenges of the startup world.

Bootstrap Financing

Bootstrap financing refers to the process of starting and growing a startup or entrepreneurship venture with limited financial resources or external funding. It involves using personal savings, revenue generated from the business, and other creative means to fund the various needs of the business. Entrepreneurs who opt for bootstrap financing often do so to maintain control over their business and avoid diluting ownership by taking on external investors. Additionally, it allows them to test and validate their ideas or business model before seeking external investment.

Bootstrapper

A bootstrapper, in the context of startup and entrepreneurship, refers to an individual or a team of individuals who start and operate a business venture with minimal external capital or resources. Bootstrapping is a self-funded approach to entrepreneurship that relies on personal savings, revenues generated from the business, and strategic cost-cutting measures to sustain and grow the venture. Instead of seeking external funding, bootstrappers focus on maximizing their existing resources and leveraging their creative problem-solving skills to overcome challenges and achieve their goals.

Bootstrapping

Bootstrapping refers to the process of starting and building a business or company with minimal external funding or resources, typically relying on the personal finances, skills, and ingenuity of the entrepreneur. In the context of startups and entrepreneurship, bootstrapping is seen as an alternative to seeking external investment or funding from venture capitalists, angel investors, or banks. Instead of relying on these traditional sources of capital, bootstrapping involves self-funding and utilizing available resources to get a business off the ground.

Brand Ambassador Programs

A Brand Ambassador Program is a marketing strategy employed by startups and entrepreneurs to leverage the influence and reach of individuals who are passionate about their brand. These individuals, known as brand ambassadors, are often customers, employees, or influencers who promote the brand's products or services to their networks through various channels, such as social media, word-of-mouth, and events. The main objective of a Brand Ambassador Program is to create brand awareness, build brand credibility, and increase customer engagement. By establishing a network of brand ambassadors, startups and entrepreneurs can tap into the power of personal recommendation and endorsement, which are proven to be more effective in gaining customers' trust and driving purchasing decisions compared to traditional marketing techniques. Brand ambassadors play a crucial role in shaping the brand perception and driving brand loyalty. They act as the face of the brand, embodying its values, and sharing their experiences and insights with their networks. Through their authentic and relatable content, brand ambassadors help startups and entrepreneurs connect with their target audience on a deeper level, fostering a sense of community and fostering trust. To establish an effective Brand Ambassador Program, startups and entrepreneurs need to develop a comprehensive strategy. This includes identifying potential brand ambassadors who align with the brand's values and target audience, providing them with the necessary resources and training to effectively represent the brand, and incentivizing their efforts through rewards and recognition. In conclusion, a Brand Ambassador Program is an essential component of a startup or entrepreneur's marketing strategy. By leveraging the influence and passion of brand ambassadors, startups can amplify their reach, build credibility, and foster customer loyalty. Through strategic planning and execution, a Brand Ambassador Program can be a powerful tool in driving the growth and success of a startup or entrepreneur's brand.

Brand Identity

A brand identity refers to the collection of visual and verbal elements that represent a startup or entrepreneurship venture. It encompasses the company's name, logo, tagline, color palette, typography, and overall design style. The brand identity plays a crucial role in establishing a startup's image, conveying its values, and setting it apart from competitors in the market. Logo: The logo is a symbol or graphic mark that serves as a visual representation of the startup. It should be simple, memorable, and relevant to the business. The logo often appears on various marketing materials, such as business cards, websites, and packaging, acting as a visual cue that instantly identifies the startup. Tagline: The tagline is a short phrase or slogan that accompanies the logo and conveys the startup's value proposition or key message. It should be catchy, concise, and memorable. The tagline reinforces the startup's positioning and helps customers understand what sets it apart from competitors. Color Palette: The color palette consists of a set of colors chosen to represent the startup. These colors should align with the brand's personality and evoke the desired emotions in its target audience. The consistent use of colors across all visual elements helps create a cohesive and recognizable brand identity. Typography: The typography refers to the typefaces or fonts used in the startup's communication materials. The choice of typography should reflect the brand's character and enhance readability. Using a consistent set of typefaces across different marketing channels creates a sense of unity and professionalism. Overall Design Style: The overall design style encompasses the visual elements, such as layouts, graphics, and imagery, used in the startup's marketing materials. It should be consistent with the brand's personality and target audience. A well-defined design style creates a cohesive and recognizable visual identity across all platforms. In conclusion, a brand identity is a combination of visual and verbal elements that represent a startup or entrepreneurship venture. It includes the startup's logo, tagline, color palette, typography, and overall design style. A strong and consistent brand identity helps establish the startup's image, communicate its values, and differentiate it from competitors in the market.

Bridge Financing

Bridge financing is a form of short-term financing that helps startups and entrepreneurs cover the gap between the need for immediate funds and the availability of long-term financing options. It typically involves obtaining a loan or investment to provide temporary financial support until a more permanent funding solution, such as a venture capital investment or a traditional bank loan, is secured. In the context of startups and entrepreneurship, bridge financing plays a crucial role in addressing the financial challenges faced during different stages of business development. In the early stages, startups often require capital to fund research and development, prototype development, and market testing. However, traditional lenders and venture capitalists may be hesitant to invest in these early-stage ventures due to the high level of uncertainty and risk involved. Bridge financing serves as a lifeline for startups during these initial stages, helping them bridge the gap between their need for funds and the time it takes to attract more substantial investments. It enables entrepreneurs to access the necessary capital to continue their operations and progress towards the next milestone, whether it is developing a minimum viable product or securing a market opportunity. Furthermore, bridge financing can also be beneficial during periods of rapid growth or expansion. Startups that experience sudden, exponential growth may find themselves in need of additional capital to scale up their operations, hire more employees, invest in marketing campaigns, or penetrate new markets. However, securing larger rounds of funding can take time, and bridge financing can provide the necessary flexibility and immediate funding required to sustain and leverage this growth spurt. Bridge financing is often considered a short-term and temporary solution, as it typically comes with higher interest rates and stricter terms compared to long-term financing options. Startups and entrepreneurs must carefully evaluate the cost and terms associated with bridge financing to ensure that the benefits outweigh the risks and costs involved.

Bridge Loan

A bridge loan is a short-term financing option typically used by startups and entrepreneurs to provide immediate capital while waiting for a more permanent and long-term funding solution. It serves as a financial bridge between the immediate need for resources and securing a larger funding round. In the context of startup and entrepreneurship, bridge loans enable companies to overcome temporary cash flow gaps or unexpected expenses without disrupting operations or delaying critical projects. This type of financing is especially valuable when startups need to quickly capitalize on growth opportunities or cover urgent expenses, such as payroll, equipment purchases, or marketing campaigns.

Burn Rate Analysis

Burn Rate Analysis is a financial metric used in the context of startups and entrepreneurship to measure the rate at which a company is spending its available funds or capital. It provides insights into how quickly a startup is depleting its cash reserves and helps in determining the estimated timeframe within which the company will run out of funds. The burn rate is calculated by dividing the total amount of money a startup has spent over a specific period by the remaining cash balance. This period is typically measured on a monthly basis. The burn rate analysis helps entrepreneurs and investors evaluate the financial health and sustainability of a startup, as well as make informed decisions regarding budgeting, fundraising, and investment strategies. A high burn rate indicates that a startup is spending its resources at a rapid pace, which could be a sign of aggressive growth strategies or inefficiencies in managing expenses. On the other hand, a low burn rate suggests that a startup is able to sustain its operations and extend its runway, providing a longer timeframe to reach profitability or secure additional funding. By monitoring the burn rate, entrepreneurs can assess the efficacy of their business model, identify areas of potential cost optimization, and adjust their spending patterns accordingly. It also helps in setting realistic revenue and growth targets, as well as forecasting the amount of capital needed to support the business until it becomes self-sustainable. Burn rate analysis is especially crucial for startups that heavily rely on external funding, such as venture capital or angel investments, as it allows them to demonstrate responsible financial management and present a clear plan for achieving profitability. It is essential for entrepreneurs to strike a balance between growth and financial sustainability by optimizing their burn rate and making strategic decisions based on the available resources.

Burn Rate Management

Burn rate management is a crucial aspect of startup and entrepreneurship, as it refers to the rate at which a company is utilizing its cash reserves or investment funding to cover its operating expenses. It measures the amount of money a startup is spending each month or year and helps determine if the business is on track financially or if adjustments are needed to ensure its sustainability. Startups often have limited resources and rely on external funding sources, such as venture capital or angel investors, to fuel their growth. However, these funds are finite and must be managed strategically to maximize their impact. Burn rate management involves closely monitoring and controlling the company's spending to optimize the available resources and extend the runway before additional funding is required. The burn rate can be calculated by subtracting the total expenses from the total revenue generated over a specific period, usually monthly or annually. By comparing the burn rate to the available funds, entrepreneurs can assess how long the business can operate without running out of money. This information is essential for making critical business decisions, such as scaling operations, hiring employees, or adjusting pricing strategies. Effective burn rate management involves a combination of cost-cutting measures and revenue generation strategies. Startups may explore various tactics to reduce expenses, such as negotiating better deals with suppliers, optimizing operational processes, or even downsizing the team if necessary. On the revenue side, entrepreneurs focus on increasing customer acquisition and retention, improving the product or service offering, or exploring new market opportunities. Failure to effectively manage the burn rate can lead to the premature demise of a startup. Running out of money without generating sufficient revenue to sustain the business is a common reason why startups fail. Therefore, entrepreneurs must constantly monitor the burn rate and take proactive measures to align expenses with revenue and extend the company's financial runway.

Burn Rate

Burn Rate refers to the rate at which a startup or entrepreneurial venture is consuming its available cash resources. It measures the speed at which a startup is spending its capital to cover various expenses such as employee salaries, rent, marketing, and research and development costs. The burn rate is a critical metric for startups as it helps evaluate and monitor the financial health and sustainability of the business. It provides insights into whether the startup is spending its capital at a sustainable pace or if it is burning through its funds too quickly. By tracking the burn rate, entrepreneurs can make informed decisions about their spending and adjust their strategies to ensure the longevity of their venture.

Burnout

Burnout in the context of startups and entrepreneurship refers to a state of physical and emotional exhaustion that occurs when an individual is overwhelmed by work-related stress and pressure. It is a syndrome characterized by chronic fatigue, cynicism, and a sense of inefficacy or reduced professional accomplishment. Startup founders and entrepreneurs often face a high level of demands and responsibilities as they strive to establish and grow their ventures. The intense workload, long hours, and constant pressure to succeed can lead to burnout, which can have detrimental effects on both personal and professional well-being. Burnout is typically caused by a combination of factors, including excessive work hours, heavy workloads, lack of control over work, insufficient support from colleagues or superiors, and a misalignment between personal values and the goals of the startup. The lack of work-life balance and the constant need to juggle multiple roles and tasks can also contribute to burnout. Signs and symptoms of burnout may include chronic fatigue, both physical and emotional, feelings of detachment or cynicism towards work, increased irritability or impatience, decreased productivity and effectiveness, and a weakened immune system. Burnout can also manifest in psychological symptoms such as depression, anxiety, or a loss of motivation and enthusiasm. Preventing and addressing burnout in the startup and entrepreneurship context is crucial for maintaining well-being and ensuring the long-term success of the venture. It involves implementing strategies such as setting realistic goals and expectations, prioritizing self-care and work-life balance, seeking social support from peers and mentors, and creating a positive and supportive work environment. In conclusion, burnout in the context of startups and entrepreneurship is a state of exhaustion and reduced professional accomplishment that occurs as a result of work-related stress and pressure. It can have detrimental effects on both personal and professional well-being. Taking proactive steps to prevent and address burnout is essential for the overall success and sustainability of startups and entrepreneurial ventures.

Business Acceleration

Business acceleration refers to the process of rapidly achieving growth and success for a startup or entrepreneurial venture. It involves implementing various strategies and tactics to expedite the development, launch, and scaling of a business, with the aim of achieving profitability and market dominance in a shorter timeframe. The primary goal of business acceleration is to help startups and entrepreneurs achieve accelerated growth by leveraging resources, expertise, and networks. It encompasses a range of activities that facilitate rapid progression, including but not limited to: mentoring, networking, access to finance, market research, product development, and marketing. Through business acceleration, startups can overcome common challenges such as limited funding, lack of market awareness, and scalability issues. By engaging with accelerator programs or seeking guidance from experienced mentors and industry experts, entrepreneurs can gain valuable insights, refine their business models, and enhance their chances of success. Accelerators and incubators play a crucial role in business acceleration by providing startups with tailored support, access to capital, and a network of like-minded individuals. These programs often involve structured curriculum, intensive mentorship, and opportunities to pitch to potential investors. By participating in accelerator programs, startups can fast-track their growth and increase their chances of securing investment. In addition to accelerator programs, other strategies for business acceleration include strategic partnerships, rapid product development, targeted marketing campaigns, and customer acquisition initiatives. By adopting a growth-oriented mindset and employing agile methodologies, startups can navigate the challenges of scaling and achieve rapid growth. In summary, business acceleration is the process of expediting growth and success for startups and entrepreneurs through the utilization of various strategies, resources, and support systems. It enables startups to overcome obstacles, gain market traction, and achieve scalability in a shorter timeframe, paving the path towards profitability and market dominance.

Business Accelerator

A business accelerator is a program designed to support and fast-track the growth of early-stage startups and entrepreneurship. It provides a range of resources, mentorship, and networking opportunities to help startups scale their business operations and increase their chances of success. The main aim of a business accelerator is to expedite the growth process of startups by providing them with the necessary tools and guidance. This is typically done through a structured and intensive program that lasts for a fixed period, usually ranging from a few months to a year. Business accelerators typically work by selecting a cohort of startups and providing them with a range of benefits. These benefits can include seed funding, office space, access to a network of mentors and investors, and specialized training and workshops. Accelerators often take an equity stake in the startups they support, providing an incentive for both parties to work together towards the startup's success. During the program, startups are exposed to a range of resources and expertise that can help them overcome common challenges and barriers to growth. They receive mentorship and guidance from experienced entrepreneurs and executives, who help them refine their business model, develop their product or service, and create a solid growth strategy. Startups also have the opportunity to network with potential partners, customers, and investors, which can open doors to new opportunities and collaborations. Additionally, business accelerators often provide startups with access to a community of like-minded entrepreneurs. This allows for peer-to-peer learning and support, as startups can learn from and collaborate with each other. The sense of community and shared experiences can help entrepreneurs navigate the ups and downs of building a business and provide a support system throughout their entrepreneurial journey.

Business Agility

Business Agility in the context of Startup & Entrepreneurship refers to the ability of a business to quickly adapt and respond to changes in the market and industry in order to maintain a competitive advantage. A startup or entrepreneurial venture operates in a highly dynamic and uncertain environment. New market trends, customer preferences, and disruptive technologies can emerge at any moment, forcing businesses to rapidly adjust their strategies, products, and operations. Business agility is the key to survival and success in this fast-paced landscape. Being agile involves several elements: 1. Continuous learning and improvement: Startups and entrepreneurs need to be open to acquiring new knowledge and skills, constantly learning from their experiences and incorporating feedback to enhance their performance. This includes experimenting with different approaches, accepting failures as valuable learning opportunities, and iterating on their products and services based on customer feedback. 2. Flexibility and adaptability: Entrepreneurs must be willing to pivot their business models or reinvent themselves entirely in response to market shifts and changes in customer demand. This requires staying attuned to customer needs and preferences, closely monitoring industry trends and competitors, and being willing to make bold and decisive changes to stay ahead of the curve. 3. Agile processes and decision-making: Startups should adopt agile methodologies and frameworks, such as Scrum or Lean Startup, to enable rapid decision-making, effective collaboration, and quick execution of projects. This involves breaking down work into small, manageable chunks, prioritizing tasks based on their value and impact, and regularly reviewing and adapting plans to ensure alignment with business objectives. 4. Embracing technology and automation: Leveraging technology and automation tools can significantly enhance business agility. Startups and entrepreneurs should embrace digital transformation, utilizing cloud-based solutions, data analytics, artificial intelligence, and other technological advancements to streamline processes, improve efficiency, and respond quickly to market changes. Overall, business agility is essential for startups and entrepreneurs to navigate the unpredictable and competitive landscape they operate in. By continuously learning, embracing change, adopting agile processes, and leveraging technology, they can stay ahead of the curve and effectively respond to market dynamics, positioning themselves for long-term success.

Business Angels

A Business Angel, also known as an Angel Investor, is an individual who provides financial support to early-stage startups and entrepreneurs in exchange for equity ownership or convertible debt. These individuals are typically high-net-worth individuals with a strong background in business and entrepreneurship. Business Angels play a crucial role in the startup ecosystem by providing capital and mentorship to help startups grow and succeed. They often bring more than just financial support to the table, as they also provide guidance, industry expertise, and valuable connections that can help startups overcome challenges and accelerate their growth.

Business Continuity Plan

A Business Continuity Plan (BCP) is a strategic framework designed to ensure the continued operation and sustainability of a startup or entrepreneurial venture, even in the face of unforeseen disruptions or crisis situations. The primary objective of a BCP is to minimize the impact of any disruption on the organization's critical business functions and processes, allowing it to maintain its operations and serve its customers, partners, and stakeholders effectively. By implementing a BCP, startups can effectively manage risks and safeguard their reputation, revenue, and overall survival.

Business Continuity Planning (BCP)

Business Continuity Planning (BCP) in the context of Startup & Entrepreneurship refers to the process of creating and implementing strategies and procedures that aim to ensure the ongoing operation of a startup in the face of potential threats and disruptions. These threats can include natural disasters, cyber attacks, economic downturns, or any other event that could hinder the normal functioning of a business. The purpose of BCP is to anticipate and prepare for unforeseen circumstances that may impede a startup's ability to carry out its critical functions. By proactively developing resilience and response plans, startups can minimize the impact of disruptive events and quickly recover to maintain operations and minimize losses. The BCP process typically involves several key steps. Firstly, an assessment is conducted to identify potential risks and vulnerabilities. This assessment helps entrepreneurs understand the potential impact and likelihood of various threats and prioritize their focus areas. With this information, startups can then develop strategies and procedures to address these risks effectively. The next step involves establishing a comprehensive backup and recovery plan. This plan should outline how critical data, infrastructure, and resources will be protected and restored in the event of a disruption. It should include considerations such as alternative workspaces, backup power sources, and cloud-based data storage to ensure that operations can continue seamlessly. Communication and coordination form another crucial aspect of BCP. Startups need to establish clear channels of communication both internally and externally, enabling effective communication during times of crisis. This includes establishing a crisis management team, defining roles and responsibilities, and establishing protocols for notifying employees, customers, and stakeholders about potential disruptions and actions being taken. Regular testing and reviewing of the BCP is also essential. Startups should conduct drills and simulations to evaluate the effectiveness and efficiency of their plans. This process helps identify areas of improvement and ensures that the BCP remains up-to-date and relevant as the business evolves.

Business Development Manager

A Business Development Manager is a professional responsible for the growth and expansion of a startup or entrepreneurship venture. This role involves identifying potential business opportunities, establishing strategic partnerships, and driving overall business development initiatives. The main goal of a Business Development Manager is to create and implement effective strategies that enhance the startup's market presence, increase revenue, and drive sustainable growth. They are responsible for analyzing market trends and customer needs to identify areas for business expansion and development. Key responsibilities of a Business Development Manager include conducting market research, identifying potential clients and partners, and developing relationships with key stakeholders. They collaborate with internal teams, such as sales and marketing, to develop and execute effective business plans. This role also involves networking and attending industry events to establish the startup's presence in the market. A successful Business Development Manager possesses strong analytical and strategic thinking skills. They have a deep understanding of market dynamics and are able to identify growth opportunities for the startup. They are excellent communicators and negotiators, able to build and maintain relationships with clients, partners, and stakeholders. In summary, a Business Development Manager plays a crucial role in the success of a startup or entrepreneurship venture. They are responsible for driving business growth through strategic planning, relationship building, and market analysis. Their expertise in identifying and capitalizing on business opportunities is vital for the startup's long-term success.

Business Development Services (BDS)

Business Development Services (BDS), in the context of startups and entrepreneurship, refer to a range of support services that are aimed at helping businesses grow and expand. These services play a crucial role in assisting startups and entrepreneurs in overcoming various challenges and obstacles that they may encounter during the early stages of their business journey. BDS can encompass a wide range of activities, including market research, marketing and sales strategies, product development, financial management, legal and regulatory compliance, and access to funding and investment opportunities. These services are typically provided by specialized consultants, professionals, or organizations that have expertise in specific areas of business development. The main objective of BDS is to provide startups and entrepreneurs with the tools, resources, and knowledge they need to effectively scale their business and achieve long-term sustainability. By leveraging these services, startups can gain a competitive advantage in the market, attract customers and investors, and optimize their operations for growth. Market research is a key component of BDS, as it helps startups gain insights into their target market, identify customer needs and preferences, and assess the competitive landscape. This information is crucial for developing effective marketing and sales strategies that can drive customer acquisition and revenue growth. Product development is another critical area of focus in BDS, as startups need to continually innovate and improve their offerings to stay competitive. This involves conducting research and development, prototyping, testing, and refining products or services to ensure they meet customer expectations and market demands. Financial management is also an essential aspect of BDS, as startups need to effectively manage their cash flow, budgeting, and financial reporting to make informed business decisions. This includes financial planning, forecasting, and analysis, as well as access to finance options, such as loans, grants, or investment opportunities. Lastly, BDS can also provide startups and entrepreneurs with guidance on legal and regulatory compliance to ensure they operate within the boundaries of the law. This may include assistance with business registration, intellectual property protection, contracts, and data privacy.

Business Development

Business development is a crucial aspect of startup and entrepreneurship, referring to the activities and strategies implemented to create sustainable growth and generate new business opportunities. It encompasses various processes, including market research, sales and marketing, partnerships, and customer acquisition, with the ultimate goal of expanding the business's reach, profitability, and customer base. In the context of startups, business development plays a vital role in securing initial funding, laying the foundation for growth, and establishing a strong position in the market. It involves identifying target markets, understanding customer needs and pain points, and developing innovative solutions that meet those requirements. Through market research and analysis, startups can identify unique selling propositions and market differentiators that will give them a competitive edge. Business development also encompasses sales and marketing activities. Startups need to create effective sales strategies and develop marketing campaigns that will attract customers and establish a strong brand presence. This includes identifying key customer segments, crafting compelling messaging, and employing various marketing channels and tactics to reach and engage with potential customers. In addition, business development involves building strategic partnerships and collaborations. Startups can leverage partnerships with established companies or industry influencers to gain access to new markets, technologies, or resources. By forging strong relationships with key stakeholders, startups can enhance their credibility, expand their network, and tap into new opportunities for growth. Furthermore, customer acquisition is a pivotal part of business development. Startups need to implement strategies to attract customers, convert leads, and retain their user base. This may involve developing referral programs, offering incentives, providing exceptional customer support, and continuously improving the product or service based on customer feedback and insights. In summary, business development in the context of startup and entrepreneurship involves conducting market research, implementing sales and marketing strategies, building strategic partnerships, and acquiring and retaining customers. It is a multifaceted process aimed at driving growth, increasing profitability, and establishing a strong market position.

Business Diversification

Business diversification refers to the strategy of expanding a startup or entrepreneurship venture by entering new markets or developing new products or services. It involves minimizing risk and maximizing potential opportunities by spreading investments and resources across different business areas or industries. Startups and entrepreneurs often pursue diversification as a means to achieve long-term growth and sustainability. By diversifying their business, they can reduce their reliance on a single market or product, thereby mitigating the impact of market fluctuations, changing consumer preferences, or competitive pressures.

Business Ethics

Business ethics in the context of startup and entrepreneurship refers to the moral principles and values that guide the decision-making and conduct of individuals and organizations in the pursuit of their entrepreneurial activities. Startups and entrepreneurs operate in a dynamic and rapidly evolving business environment that often poses complex ethical challenges. In this context, business ethics plays a crucial role in shaping their behavior and building a sustainable and socially responsible business.

Business Exit

A business exit refers to the process in which an entrepreneur or startup owner transitions out of their business by selling it, closing it down, or transferring it to new management. This can occur for a variety of reasons, such as achieving a desired financial outcome, pursuing new opportunities, or responding to changing market conditions. When an entrepreneur decides to exit their business, they must carefully consider the best approach based on their individual goals and circumstances. The most common types of business exits include: 1. Sale of the Business: In this scenario, the entrepreneur sells their business to another party, which can be an individual buyer, a competitor, or a larger corporation. The terms of the sale may involve a complete transfer of ownership or a partial sale where the entrepreneur retains a minority stake in the business. 2. Liquidation: When a business is liquidated, its assets are sold off to cover any outstanding debts or liabilities. Any remaining funds are then distributed to the owner(s) or shareholders. Liquidation is typically pursued when the business is no longer viable or the entrepreneur wishes to pursue other ventures. 3. Merger or Acquisition: In some cases, an entrepreneur may opt to merge their business with another company or be acquired by a larger organization. This can provide opportunities for synergies, access to new markets, or increased economies of scale. 4. Management Buyout: A management buyout occurs when the existing management team or employees of the business purchase the entire or a significant portion of the company. This type of exit allows the entrepreneur to transfer ownership and leadership to individuals familiar with the business. The process of a business exit involves careful planning, negotiation, and consideration of legal, financial, and operational implications. Additionally, entrepreneurs often seek the assistance of advisors, such as lawyers, accountants, or business brokers, to navigate the complexities of the exit process.

Business Expansion

Business expansion in the context of startup and entrepreneurship refers to the process of growing and scaling a business beyond its current size or market presence. It involves increasing the company's operations, reach, and resources to capture new customers, tap into new markets, or offer additional products or services. Expanding a startup or entrepreneurial venture is important for several reasons. Firstly, it allows the business to capitalize on new opportunities and take advantage of market trends. By expanding into new markets or offering new products, the business can attract a broader customer base and generate additional revenue streams. Secondly, business expansion helps to increase the company's competitiveness and market share. With a larger scale of operations, the business can achieve economies of scale, which leads to cost savings and a more competitive pricing strategy. It also enables the company to leverage its brand and reputation to gain a stronger foothold in the market, making it more difficult for competitors to enter or compete effectively. Furthermore, expanding a startup or entrepreneurial venture can provide access to new talent, resources, and partnerships. It allows the business to attract skilled individuals and tap into new networks or ecosystems, which can contribute to innovation and growth. It also enables the company to secure additional funding or investment, which is crucial for supporting the expansion initiatives and fueling further growth. However, business expansion also presents challenges and risks. It requires careful planning, strategic decision-making, and effective execution. The business needs to consider factors such as market demand, competition, regulatory requirements, and financial feasibility. Poorly planned or executed expansion efforts can result in financial losses, reputation damage, or even business failure. In conclusion, business expansion in the context of startup and entrepreneurship is the process of scaling a business to capture new markets, customers, or revenue streams. It offers opportunities for growth, increased competitiveness, and access to new resources, but also entails risks and challenges that need to be carefully managed. Ultimately, successful expansion can lead to sustainability, profitability, and long-term success for the startup or entrepreneurial venture.

Business Growth

Business Growth, in the context of Startup and Entrepreneurship, refers to the gradual but sustainable development and expansion of a startup venture or entrepreneurial endeavor. It encompasses the overall progress, development, and evolution of a business in terms of revenue, customer base, market reach, product/service offerings, and other key performance indicators. Business Growth is a crucial objective for startups and entrepreneurs as it indicates the success and effectiveness of their business strategies, marketing efforts, and operational capabilities. It is a reflection of the ability of a startup or entrepreneurial venture to generate profits, create value, and attract and satisfy customers.

Business Idea

A startup is a newly established business, typically driven by an individual or a small team of entrepreneurs, with the aim of bringing innovative ideas, products, or services to the market. Startups are often characterized by their fast-paced and dynamic nature, as well as their focus on scalability and high growth potential. Entrepreneurship, on the other hand, refers to the act of starting and managing a new business venture, usually with the objective of creating value and generating profit. It involves the identification of business opportunities, the ability to take risks, and the willingness to shoulder responsibilities. Entrepreneurs are individuals who possess a strong drive to create value and possess the necessary skills and mindset to navigate the challenges and uncertainties that come with starting and running a business.

Business Incubation Center

A Business Incubation Center is a program or facility that provides support and resources to startup companies and entrepreneurs. Its main objective is to help these new ventures grow and succeed by providing them with access to mentorship, training, and networking opportunities. The Business Incubation Center serves as a catalyst for the growth of innovative business ideas. It offers a supportive and nurturing environment where entrepreneurs can receive guidance and assistance in developing their business plans, securing funding, and navigating the challenges of starting a new venture. The center typically provides physical office space, shared facilities, and access to essential resources such as high-speed internet, meeting rooms, and technology infrastructure. This helps startups save on initial costs and allows them to focus on their core business activities. Furthermore, being surrounded by like-minded individuals and other startups fosters a spirit of collaboration and knowledge-sharing. In addition to physical infrastructure, the Business Incubation Center offers a range of business support services. This includes mentorship from experienced entrepreneurs and industry experts who can provide valuable guidance and advice. Regular workshops, training programs, and networking events are also organized to enhance the entrepreneurial skills and knowledge of the participants. Another crucial aspect of a Business Incubation Center is the access to funding and investment opportunities. The center often acts as a bridge between startups and potential investors, connecting them through networking events or facilitating introductions. It may also offer seed capital or assist in the process of securing funding from external sources. The ultimate goal of a Business Incubation Center is to accelerate the growth and success of startups, ensuring their long-term viability. Successful companies that graduate from the program often become more attractive to investors, customers, and potential partners. By providing the necessary support and resources, the center plays a vital role in nurturing the entrepreneurial ecosystem and fostering economic growth.

Business Incubation

Business incubation is a process that supports the growth and development of startup companies and entrepreneurs. It involves providing a range of resources, services, and support to help these businesses succeed in their early stages. Business incubators are organizations or programs that offer a nurturing environment for startups to thrive. They typically provide office space, access to equipment and technology, mentoring and coaching, networking opportunities, and access to funding sources. The goal of incubators is to accelerate the growth of startups and increase their likelihood of long-term success.

Business Incubator Program

A business incubator program is a structured and supportive environment designed to nurture and accelerate the growth of startups and early-stage entrepreneurial ventures. It provides a range of resources, support services, and mentorship to help entrepreneurs turn their ideas into viable and successful businesses. The primary goal of a business incubator program is to create an ecosystem that fosters innovation and entrepreneurship. It aims to reduce the barriers and challenges faced by startups by providing them with an infrastructure and a network of support. Through the program, entrepreneurs gain access to a variety of resources, including physical workspace, equipment, technology, and business support services such as legal, financial, and marketing advice. One of the key features of a business incubator program is the provision of mentorship and guidance. Experienced business professionals and industry experts work closely with the startups, offering their expertise and knowledge to help them navigate the challenges and hurdles of starting and growing a business. These mentors provide valuable insights, advice, and support that help entrepreneurs make informed decisions and avoid common pitfalls. In addition to physical resources and mentorship, a business incubator program also facilitates networking and collaboration opportunities. Entrepreneurs within the program have the chance to connect with like-minded individuals, potential partners, investors, and customers. This allows them to build crucial relationships and expand their network, which can be instrumental in accessing funding, expertise, and market opportunities. Moreover, a business incubator program often offers educational and training programs tailored to the specific needs of startups. These programs cover various aspects of business development, including product development, market research, sales and marketing, financial management, and legal and regulatory compliance. By providing targeted training, the program equips entrepreneurs with the skills and knowledge necessary to run a successful business. Overall, a business incubator program plays a vital role in supporting the growth and sustainability of startups. By providing essential resources, mentorship, and education, it helps entrepreneurs overcome obstacles and increase their chances of success. It serves as a crucial stepping stone for early-stage ventures, enabling them to flourish and contribute to the economy through job creation, innovation, and increased competitiveness.

Business Incubator

A business incubator is a program or organization that provides support and resources to startup companies and entrepreneurs to help them grow and succeed. The main goal of a business incubator is to accelerate the development and growth of these early-stage ventures, with the aim of graduating them into financially viable and sustainable businesses. Business incubators typically offer a range of services and facilities that are tailored to meet the specific needs of startups and entrepreneurs. These may include physical office spaces, access to networking opportunities, mentorship and coaching, funding and investment support, legal and financial advice, as well as access to specialized equipment and technologies. By providing these resources and support, business incubators create an ecosystem that fosters innovation, collaboration, and knowledge sharing. They create an environment where startups can thrive and overcome the common challenges and hurdles that they face during their early stages of development. One of the key benefits of joining a business incubator is access to a network of experienced mentors and advisors. These individuals have often been successful entrepreneurs themselves and can provide valuable guidance and insights to startups. They can help entrepreneurs refine their business models, develop effective marketing strategies, navigate the complexities of legal and regulatory compliance, and make connections with potential investors and customers. Furthermore, business incubators often facilitate access to funding and investment opportunities. They may have partnerships with venture capitalists, angel investors, and other financial institutions that are interested in supporting early-stage businesses. This can greatly increase the chances of startups securing the necessary capital to fuel their growth and expansion. In addition, business incubators also play a crucial role in fostering collaboration and knowledge sharing among startups. By bringing together entrepreneurs from different industries and backgrounds, they create an environment where ideas can be exchanged, partnerships can be formed, and innovation can flourish. This collaborative atmosphere often leads to the emergence of new ideas, products, and services that have the potential to disrupt and reshape industries.

Business Innovation

Business innovation refers to the process of introducing new ideas, products, services, or processes to improve or create value within a startup or entrepreneurial venture. It involves developing and implementing novel approaches, strategies, or tools to address existing challenges or to capitalize on emerging opportunities in the market. Innovation plays a vital role in the success and growth of startups and entrepreneurial ventures. It helps these businesses to differentiate themselves from competitors, attract customers, and drive financial performance. By continuously seeking innovative solutions, startups can stay agile and relevant in dynamic market environments and adapt to changing customer needs and preferences.

Business Intelligence (BI) Tools

Business Intelligence (BI) tools are software applications and technologies that help startups and entrepreneurs to analyze and interpret large volumes of data to make informed business decisions. These tools enable users to collect, manage, and analyze data from various sources, transforming it into actionable insights and valuable knowledge. BI tools are crucial for startups and entrepreneurs as they provide a holistic view of the business, allowing them to identify patterns, trends, and relationships within data. By leveraging these insights, startups can gain a competitive edge, improve operational efficiency, optimize resource allocation, and drive growth.

Business Mentor

A business mentor in the context of startup and entrepreneurship is an experienced and successful professional who guides and advises entrepreneurs on various aspects of starting and growing a business. The role of a business mentor is to provide knowledge, expertise, and support to entrepreneurs, helping them navigate the challenges and uncertainties of starting and running a business. A mentor acts as a trusted advisor, offering valuable insights and wisdom gained through their own experience in entrepreneurship.

Business Model Canvas

The Business Model Canvas is a strategic management tool used in the context of start-ups and entrepreneurship. It provides a visual representation of a company's business model, illustrating how the various components of the business work together to create value for customers and generate revenue. The Business Model Canvas consists of nine key building blocks that encapsulate the fundamental aspects of a business. These building blocks include: 1. Customer Segments: The specific groups of customers that a company targets to serve. 2. Value Propositions: The unique bundle of products, services, or experiences that address the needs and desires of the target customer segments. 3. Channels: The channels through which a company delivers its value propositions to customers. 4. Customer Relationships: The types of relationships a company establishes and maintains with its customers to enhance the overall customer experience. 5. Revenue Streams: The ways in which a company generates revenue from its value propositions. 6. Key Resources: The essential assets and resources required to deliver the value propositions and operate the business. 7. Key Activities: The crucial activities that a company must perform to deliver its value propositions effectively. 8. Key Partnerships: The external entities and collaborations that a company relies on to enhance its business model. 9. Cost Structure: The costs and expenses associated with operating the business and delivering the value propositions. By visualizing and analyzing these building blocks, the Business Model Canvas allows entrepreneurs and start-ups to assess the viability and profitability of their business ideas. It helps them identify potential gaps, challenges, and opportunities, enabling them to develop strategies to enhance their business model and achieve success. Additionally, the Business Model Canvas serves as a communication tool, facilitating discussions and collaborations among team members, investors, and other stakeholders.

Business Model Disruption Techniques And Strategies

A business model disruption is a strategic process that involves identifying and implementing innovative techniques and strategies to radically transform or overthrow existing business models within a particular industry or market. This approach is typically adopted by startups and entrepreneurs seeking to create new value propositions, exploit untapped opportunities, and challenge established players. There are several techniques and strategies that startups and entrepreneurs can employ to disrupt traditional business models: 1. Technology Disruption:

Leveraging advancements in technology to create new products, services, or platforms that offer superior value propositions compared to existing solutions. Examples include Uber, which disrupted the taxi industry through its innovative app-based ride-hailing platform, and Airbnb, which disrupted the hospitality industry by providing a peer-to-peer accommodation marketplace powered by technology. 2. Market Segmentation: Identifying underserved or overlooked segments within a market and tailoring products or services to meet their unique needs. This strategy involves focusing on niche markets that are currently overlooked by established players. For example, Dollar Shave Club disrupted the razor industry by targeting budget-conscious consumers who were dissatisfied with the high prices of traditional razor brands. 3. Business Model Innovation: Rethinking and redesigning traditional business models to create new sources of competitive advantage. This involves identifying new ways to create, deliver, and capture value. For instance, Netflix disrupted the video rental industry by transitioning from a brick-and-mortar rental model to a subscription-based streaming service. 4. Disintermediation: Eliminating middlemen or intermediaries in the value chain to reduce costs, improve efficiency, and enhance the customer experience. This strategy involves directly connecting customers with suppliers or providers, bypassing traditional distribution channels. For example, online travel agencies like Expedia disrupted the travel industry by enabling customers to book flights and accommodations directly, without the need for traditional travel agents. Overall, business model disruption is a strategic approach that allows startups and entrepreneurs to challenge established norms, create innovative solutions, and gain a competitive edge in the market. By leveraging techniques and strategies such as technology disruption, market segmentation, business model innovation, and disintermediation, startups can disrupt traditional business models and gain a foothold in the market.

Business Model Disruption Techniques

A business model disruption technique refers to the innovative strategies or approaches that startups and entrepreneurs use to challenge and revolutionize traditional business models within an industry. These techniques often involve the rethinking of existing norms and practices, aiming to create new value propositions, exploit untapped market opportunities, and outperform established competitors. One common business model disruption technique is the platform-based model. Startups leverage technology to create online platforms that connect different groups of users, facilitating interactions and transactions. These platforms often benefit from network effects, where the value increases as more users join, leading to a rapid scaling of business operations. Examples of successful platform-based disruptions include Airbnb, Uber, and Alibaba. Another technique is the freemium model, which offers basic services for free and charges a premium for additional features or enhanced versions of the product. By enticing users with a free offering, startups can quickly acquire a large user base and then convert a portion of them into paying customers. This approach has been employed by companies such as Dropbox, Evernote, and Spotify. Additionally, disruptive startups may adopt a subscription-based model, where customers pay a recurring fee to access a service or use a product. This approach offers a recurring revenue stream and fosters customer loyalty. Companies like Netflix and Dollar Shave Club have disrupted industries by offering affordable subscriptions compared to traditional pay-per-use models. Some startups disrupt established business models through a direct-to-consumer (D2C) approach. By eliminating intermediaries and selling products or services directly to customers, these startups can offer lower prices, better customer experiences, and greater control over the entire value chain. Warby Parker and Casper are examples of D2C disruptors in the eyewear and mattress industries, respectively. Overall, business model disruption techniques allow startups and entrepreneurs to challenge and reshape industry dynamics, introducing new ways of creating and delivering value. By identifying unmet needs, leveraging technology, and adopting innovative business models, startups can create sustainable competitive advantages and potentially dominate markets once dominated by incumbents.

Business Model Disruption

Business model disruption refers to a significant change or transformation in the way a business creates, delivers, and captures value within its industry. It is a concept closely linked to the fields of startup and entrepreneurship, where disruptive business models are often the driving force behind successful new ventures. At its core, business model disruption entails challenging and potentially displacing existing industry norms and practices by introducing innovative approaches to solve customer problems or create new markets. This disruption can stem from various factors, such as technological advancements, changes in customer behavior, or shifts in market dynamics.

Business Model Experimentation Techniques And Best Practices

The business model experimentation techniques and best practices within the context of startups and entrepreneurship refer to the systematic and iterative process of testing and refining different aspects of a business model to optimize its effectiveness and viability. This process involves exploring new strategies, products, customer segments, value propositions, revenue streams, and distribution channels, among other elements, to determine the most suitable and sustainable approach for generating revenue and delivering value to customers. Startups and entrepreneurs often face high levels of uncertainty and risk, making it crucial to adopt a proactive and experimental approach to business model development. By experimenting with different components of the business model, entrepreneurs can gather valuable insights that help them adjust their strategies, investments, and resources to increase their chances of success. Some of the commonly used techniques for business model experimentation include: - Lean Startup Methodology: This approach involves quickly developing a minimum viable product (MVP) to test assumptions and gather feedback from early adopters. It aims to minimize waste and optimize learning through rapid iterations and validated learning. - A/B Testing: This technique involves creating variations of certain elements within the business model, such as website design or pricing models, and testing them simultaneously to identify the most effective option based on data-driven insights. - Customer Journey Mapping: This practice involves visualizing and understanding the end-to-end experience of a customer, from the moment they discover a product or service to their ongoing engagement and loyalty. It helps entrepreneurs identify pain points, opportunities for improvement, and potential areas for innovation in their business model. - Business Model Canvas: This tool provides a visual representation of the various building blocks of a business model, allowing entrepreneurs to easily explore and iterate different configurations. It helps in identifying dependencies and relationships between different elements and facilitates collaboration and communication within a startup team or with investors. In order to make the most out of business model experimentation, entrepreneurs should follow some best practices: - Clearly define hypotheses and desired outcomes before conducting experiments. - Start with small-scale experiments to minimize potential risks and costs. - Use data and metrics to measure the success and impact of experiments. - Collaborate and seek feedback from customers and stakeholders throughout the experimentation process. - Iterate and pivot based on the insights gained from experiments. Overall, business model experimentation techniques and best practices enable startups and entrepreneurs to navigate the uncertain landscape of business development, mitigate risks, and increase their chances of creating sustainable and successful ventures.

Business Model Experimentation Techniques

A business model experimentation technique is a systematic and iterative approach used by startups and entrepreneurs to validate and refine their business models. It involves testing different assumptions, hypotheses, and strategies to identify the most viable and sustainable model for their venture. Entrepreneurs use various techniques to experiment with their business models, such as: 1. Customer Development: This technique involves engaging with potential customers early on to understand their needs, pain points, and preferences. By gathering feedback and data directly from customers, entrepreneurs can validate or pivot their initial assumptions and build a product or service that truly solves a problem. 2. Lean Startup Methodology: The lean startup methodology emphasizes rapid iteration and experimentation. It encourages entrepreneurs to develop a minimum viable product (MVP) and test it with real customers as quickly as possible. Through continuous testing and learning, startups can make informed decisions about their business model and iterate accordingly. 3. A/B Testing: A/B testing involves comparing two versions of a product, service, or feature to determine which one performs better. By isolating specific variables, entrepreneurs can collect data on user behavior, preferences, and conversion rates. This allows them to optimize their business model by making data-driven decisions and delivering a better user experience. 4. Business Model Canvas: The business model canvas is a visual tool that helps entrepreneurs map out and analyze their business model components. It allows them to identify key partners, resources, activities, and revenue streams, and facilitates brainstorming and experimentation. By iteratively updating the canvas based on feedback and insights, entrepreneurs can refine their business model and increase its effectiveness. 5. Minimum Viable Product (MVP): The MVP is a scaled-down version of a product or service that enables entrepreneurs to test their value proposition with real customers. By launching an MVP early on, startups can gather valuable user feedback, validate their assumptions, and make iterative improvements to their business model based on real-world usage and customer input. These techniques enable startups and entrepreneurs to validate and refine their business models through experimentation and data-driven decision-making. By continuously testing and iterating, they can increase their chances of building a successful and sustainable business.

Business Model Experimentation

A business model experimentation is a strategic approach used by startups and entrepreneurs to test and refine their business models in order to achieve sustainable growth and success in the market. It involves the systematic exploration of different hypotheses and assumptions about various aspects of the business, such as target customers, value proposition, revenue streams, and cost structure. The goal is to validate or invalidate these hypotheses through real-world experiments and feedback from customers and stakeholders. Startups and entrepreneurs often face high levels of uncertainty and ambiguity in the early stages of their ventures. Their business models may not be fully developed or optimized, and they may lack sufficient information about the market and customer preferences. Business model experimentation helps them to overcome these challenges by providing a structured and iterative process for learning and adaptation. The process of business model experimentation typically involves four main steps: 1. Hypothesis formulation: Startups identify the key assumptions and hypotheses underlying their business model. These may include assumptions about customer needs, pricing, distribution channels, and revenue generation. 2. Experiment design: Startups design experiments to test these hypotheses in a controlled and systematic manner. This may involve conducting surveys, interviews, or prototype testing with potential customers and stakeholders. 3. Data collection and analysis: Startups collect relevant data from the experiments and analyze the results. They use various metrics and indicators to measure the performance and validity of their hypotheses. 4. Learning and adaptation: Startups reflect on the results of the experiments and use the insights gained to refine and iterate their business model. They make necessary adjustments and modifications to improve their value proposition, target market, revenue streams, or cost structure. By continuously experimenting and adapting their business models, startups and entrepreneurs can reduce the risk of failure, increase their chances of success, and create sustainable competitive advantages in the market.

Business Model Generation

Business Model Generation is a concept used in the context of startups and entrepreneurship to describe the process of designing and refining a business model. It focuses on creating a clear and concise framework that outlines how a company creates, delivers, and captures value. A business model describes how an organization creates and delivers value to its customers, as well as how it generates revenue and sustains its operations. It is the blueprint that defines how all the different elements of a business work together to create a profitable venture. The process of business model generation involves identifying and analyzing key elements such as the target customer segment, value proposition, channels of distribution, customer relationships, revenue streams, key activities, key resources, and cost structure. These elements are represented visually using a tool called the Business Model Canvas, which provides a visual map of all the different components of a business model. Startup entrepreneurs use the Business Model Generation concept to refine their ideas, test assumptions, and identify potential risks and opportunities. By mapping out their business model, entrepreneurs are able to gain a better understanding of how all the different pieces of their venture fit together and whether there are any gaps or inconsistencies that need to be addressed. The flexibility of the Business Model Generation approach allows entrepreneurs to iterate and experiment with different business models and value propositions until they find one that is desirable, feasible, and viable. It encourages creative thinking and problem-solving, enabling entrepreneurs to think outside the box and come up with innovative solutions to customer needs. In conclusion, Business Model Generation is a strategic tool that helps startups and entrepreneurs design and refine their business models. By mapping out the different elements of a business and identifying how they work together, entrepreneurs are able to create a solid foundation for their ventures and increase their chances of success.

Business Model Innovation Process

A business model innovation process refers to the systematic, structured approach a startup or entrepreneur takes to develop and implement new and innovative business models that can offer unique value propositions and generate sustainable revenue streams. At its core, this process involves identifying and understanding customer needs, analyzing market trends and competition, and creating opportunities to address unmet needs or pain points in the market. It requires creativity, critical thinking, and strategic decision-making to design a business model that can effectively capture value, differentiate from competitors, and establish a strong market position.

Business Model Innovation

Business Model Innovation refers to the process of creating new and unique ways of generating value and revenue within a startup or entrepreneurial venture. It involves rethinking and redesigning fundamental aspects of a business, such as its target market, value proposition, revenue streams, cost structure, and distribution channels, in order to achieve sustainable competitive advantage and drive growth. In the context of startups and entrepreneurship, business model innovation is particularly crucial as it enables new and emerging ventures to differentiate themselves from established competitors and disrupt existing industries. It involves challenging traditional assumptions and norms, and developing innovative approaches to creating and delivering value to customers.

Business Model Validation

A business model validation is a process of testing and evaluating the viability and effectiveness of a startup's business model in the context of startup and entrepreneurship. It involves analyzing and scrutinizing the key components of the business model to validate its potential to generate revenue and sustain a competitive advantage in the market. During business model validation, entrepreneurs gather and analyze feedback from various stakeholders, including customers, investors, and industry experts, to assess the validity and feasibility of their business model. This process helps in identifying potential risks and challenges that the startup may face in the market, as well as opportunities for improvement and optimization.

Business Opportunity

A business opportunity refers to a promising possibility or chance for entrepreneurial individuals to develop and grow a successful business venture. It involves identifying a gap or a need in the market and creating a unique solution to address it. Startups and entrepreneurs play a vital role in recognizing business opportunities and taking the initiative to seize them. They are constantly on the lookout for innovative ideas or untapped markets where they can introduce new products or services. Entrepreneurs are driven by the desire to bring their vision to life and create value for customers. They are willing to take risks, invest resources, and put in the necessary effort to turn their business opportunity into a profitable venture. Startups typically start small and operate with limited resources, but they have the potential for rapid growth and scalability. Successful entrepreneurs understand the importance of thorough market research and analysis to validate their business opportunity. This includes assessing the demand for their product or service, understanding the competitive landscape, and identifying their target market. Once a business opportunity is identified, entrepreneurs must develop a comprehensive business plan to outline their strategies, objectives, and financial projections. This plan serves as a roadmap for the startup, guiding its operations and providing a framework for decision-making. A business opportunity can arise from various sources. It could be a result of technological advancements, changes in consumer behavior, market trends, or even personal experiences and skills. Entrepreneurs need to be observant and proactive in identifying these opportunities and capitalizing on them. In conclusion, a business opportunity represents a chance for entrepreneurs to create and develop a successful business venture by addressing a market need with a unique solution. It requires market research, careful planning, and a willingness to take risks. Startups and entrepreneurs play a crucial role in identifying and seizing these opportunities, driving innovation and economic growth.

Business Pitch

A business pitch is a concise and compelling presentation that outlines the core elements of a startup or entrepreneurial venture. It is a carefully crafted and delivered message aimed at capturing the attention and interest of potential investors, partners, and customers. The purpose of a business pitch is to effectively communicate the value proposition of a business idea or product, and to generate support, funding, or collaboration opportunities. The pitch serves as a way to showcase the innovative aspects, market potential, and unique selling points of the startup or entrepreneurial endeavor. The structure of a business pitch typically includes an introduction, problem statement, solution proposed, target market, market opportunity, competitive analysis, business model, revenue streams, marketing strategy, team composition, and financial projections. These elements need to be presented in a clear, concise, and compelling manner to captivate the audience and garner favorable responses. In addition to the content, delivering a business pitch also requires effective communication skills, including confident body language, clear speech, and the ability to engage the audience. Confidence in the pitch can be built through thorough preparation, practice, and a deep understanding of the business idea and its potential impact. A successful business pitch can lead to various outcomes, such as securing funding, attracting key business partners, obtaining mentorship, generating media coverage, or acquiring initial customer traction. It is a crucial tool for startup founders and entrepreneurs to convey their vision, passion, and ability to execute their business idea effectively. Business pitches are commonly delivered in formal settings such as pitch competitions, investor meetings, demo days, or networking events. They can also be shared through digital platforms, such as video presentations, slide decks, or executive summaries. Regardless of the format, a compelling pitch should inspire confidence and excitement, leaving the audience eager to learn more about the startup or entrepreneurial venture.

Business Pivot

A business pivot, in the context of startup and entrepreneurship, refers to a strategic change made by a company to adapt to new market conditions, improve its performance, and increase its chances of success. Startups often face unpredictable and rapidly changing business environments, where their initial business models or strategies may not yield the desired results. In such scenarios, a pivot becomes necessary to steer the company in a different direction and address emerging challenges. A business pivot can take various forms, such as changing the target market, altering the product or service offering, modifying the revenue model, or adjusting the overall business strategy. The main objective of a pivot is to find a better fit between the startup's offerings and the needs of its target customers. One of the common reasons for a business pivot is market feedback and customer insights. Startups may receive feedback indicating that their initial product or service does not adequately meet customer needs or does not generate enough demand. In response, they may pivot by refining the product, adding new features, or even completely changing their offering to better align with market demands. Another trigger for a business pivot can be changes in the competitive landscape. If a startup faces intense competition or struggles to differentiate itself from existing players, it may need to pivot to find a unique selling proposition or explore a new market niche that offers better growth prospects. Financial considerations can also lead to a business pivot. If a startup faces challenges in generating sufficient revenue or securing funding, it may need to pivot to develop new revenue streams, explore partnerships, or even change its pricing model to improve financial sustainability. Successful business pivots require a deep understanding of the market, customer needs, and the startup's own capabilities. Entrepreneurs need to conduct thorough market research, gather data, and analyze trends to identify opportunities for change. They must also be open to experimentation, as pivoting often involves trial and error before finding the right direction for the business. In conclusion, a business pivot is a strategic change made by a startup or entrepreneur to adapt to market dynamics, improve performance, and increase the likelihood of success. It involves altering aspects of the business model, strategy, or product offering to achieve a better fit with customer needs and market conditions.

Business Plan Competition

A business plan competition is an event or program organized for entrepreneurs and startups to showcase their business ideas and plans to a panel of judges, investors, and fellow entrepreneurs. It is an opportunity for entrepreneurs to receive valuable feedback, gain exposure, and potentially secure funding for their business ventures. The competition typically follows a structured format, with participants submitting their business plans and then presenting them in a formal pitch to the judges. The business plans outline the goals, strategies, and financial projections for the proposed startup or business expansion. The participants may also be required to develop a comprehensive marketing and sales strategy, operational plan, and an analysis of the competitive landscape. During the competition, the judges evaluate the business plans based on various criteria, including the viability of the idea, the market potential, the clarity and feasibility of the business model, and the team's ability to execute the plan. They may also assess the entrepreneurs' presentation skills and their ability to effectively communicate their ideas and vision. Business plan competitions often provide valuable networking opportunities for entrepreneurs, as they get to interact with other participants, judges, mentors, and potential investors. These interactions can lead to new partnerships, collaborations, and mentorship opportunities that can further enhance the development and growth of the startup. In addition to potential funding and networking benefits, participating in a business plan competition can also help entrepreneurs refine their business concepts, identify potential challenges and risks, and develop strategies to mitigate them. The feedback and insights provided by the judges and other participants can be invaluable in improving the overall feasibility and competitiveness of the business idea. Overall, a business plan competition serves as a platform for startups and entrepreneurs to validate their ideas, gain exposure, receive feedback, and potentially secure funding. It is a valuable opportunity for aspiring entrepreneurs to showcase their innovation, creativity, and business acumen, and to connect with key stakeholders in the entrepreneurial ecosystem.

Business Plan Template

A business plan is a formal document that outlines the goals of a startup or entrepreneurial venture and provides a roadmap for achieving those goals. It is often created by entrepreneurs or business owners seeking investment, partners, or to guide the growth and development of their businesses. The purpose of a business plan is to communicate the vision and strategy of the startup or entrepreneurial venture to stakeholders such as investors, employees, and potential partners. It serves as a blueprint for the organization's operations, marketing, and financial activities, helping to guide decision-making and measure progress towards the stated objectives. The structure of a business plan typically includes several key sections. The executive summary provides a high-level overview of the venture, highlighting its unique value proposition and market opportunity. This section is usually written last, but appears first in the document to capture the reader's attention. The company overview section provides background information about the organization, its mission, and the problem it aims to solve. It outlines the industry landscape, target market, and competitive advantage, setting the context for the rest of the plan. The market analysis section delves deeper into the target market, including demographics, trends, and customer needs. It also assesses the competitive landscape, identifying potential competitors and analyzing their strengths and weaknesses. The marketing and sales strategies section outlines how the organization plans to reach and attract customers. It describes the marketing channels, pricing strategies, and promotional activities that will be employed to generate sales and achieve market penetration. The operations and management section provides details on the day-to-day operations of the business and the team behind it. It includes information on the operational processes, key personnel, and organizational structure, highlighting the qualifications and experience of the management team. The financial projections section presents the financial forecast for the venture, including revenue, expenses, and profitability over a certain period of time. It also includes projected cash flow statements, balance sheets, and income statements, providing a comprehensive financial outlook for the business. In summary, a business plan is a formal document that outlines the goals, strategies, and financial projections of a startup or entrepreneurial venture. It serves as a roadmap for the organization, communicating its vision and strategy to stakeholders and guiding decision-making.

Business Plan

A business plan is a comprehensive document that outlines the goals, strategies, and financial projections for a new business or venture. It acts as a roadmap for the startup, providing a detailed blueprint of how the business will be structured, operated, and positioned in the market. The purpose of a business plan is to communicate the vision and potential of the startup to investors, lenders, and other stakeholders. It showcases the entrepreneur's understanding of the industry, target market, and competitive landscape, as well as their ability to strategically navigate these challenges and opportunities. A well-developed business plan typically includes several key sections. The executive summary provides a concise overview of the entire plan, highlighting the most important aspects and enticing the reader to continue. The company description provides background information about the startup, including its mission, values, and legal structure. The market analysis section delves into the industry and target market, analyzing factors such as customer needs, trends, and competition. This helps the entrepreneur determine how the startup can differentiate itself and position its products or services effectively. The organization and management section outlines the structure of the startup, including key team members and their roles. It demonstrates the entrepreneur's ability to assemble a capable and experienced team to execute the business plan successfully. The product or service line section provides a detailed description of the startup's offerings, highlighting their unique selling points and value proposition. It explains how these offerings meet customer needs and solve their pain points, ultimately driving demand and revenue. The marketing and sales strategy section outlines the startup's plans for promoting and selling its products or services. It includes market research, pricing, distribution, and promotional strategies, as well as an overview of the sales process and channels to be used. The financial projections section provides an analysis of the startup's financial performance and potential. It includes income statements, cash flow projections, and balance sheets, helping investors or lenders assess the startup's profitability, sustainability, and potential return on investment. A well-crafted business plan demonstrates the entrepreneur's commitment, expertise, and ability to turn an idea into a successful business venture. It serves as a roadmap for the startup, guiding its operations and decision-making processes while attracting support from investors and stakeholders.

Business Process Optimization

Business process optimization involves identifying and improving the various processes within a startup or entrepreneurship venture to increase efficiency, productivity, and overall effectiveness. It aims to streamline workflows, eliminate unnecessary steps, reduce costs, and enhance the quality and speed of operations. Startups and entrepreneurs often face resource constraints, tight deadlines, and the need to rapidly scale their business. Therefore, optimizing their processes becomes crucial to ensure sustainable growth and competitiveness in the market. The first step in business process optimization is to thoroughly analyze and map out the existing processes. This requires identifying each step, task, and decision point involved in the workflow and understanding the interactions between different departments and stakeholders. Once the current processes are understood, the next step is to identify bottlenecks, inefficiencies, and areas for improvement. This can be done through data analysis, performance metrics, customer feedback, and employee input. By pinpointing the areas that need optimization, startups can prioritize their efforts and focus on the most impactful changes. After identifying the areas for improvement, startups and entrepreneurs can then implement changes to streamline their processes. This may involve automating manual tasks, reassigning responsibilities, improving communication channels, adopting new technologies, or redesigning workflows. The goal is to simplify and standardize the processes, reducing the chances of errors, delays, and miscommunications. Once the process changes are implemented, it is essential to continuously monitor and evaluate their effectiveness. Regularly collecting and analyzing data on key performance indicators (KPIs) allows startups to assess the impact of the optimizations and identify any new areas for improvement. Overall, business process optimization is a continuous cycle of analyzing, improving, implementing, and evaluating processes within a startup or entrepreneurship venture. By consistently striving for efficiency and effectiveness, startups can enhance their operations, capitalize on opportunities, and stay ahead in today's competitive business landscape.

Business Process Reengineering (BPR)

Business Process Reengineering (BPR) is a fundamental approach implemented in startups and entrepreneurship to analyze and redesign existing business processes to achieve substantial improvements in operational efficiency, effectiveness, and overall productivity. In a startup or entrepreneurial setting, BPR aims to identify and eliminate redundant, time-consuming, and resource-intensive activities that hinder the smooth flow of operations and impede growth. It involves rethinking and reevaluating the entire business process landscape to achieve radical improvements in performance and generate competitive advantage.

Business Risk Management

Business Risk Management in the context of startups and entrepreneurship refers to the process of identifying, evaluating, and mitigating potential risks that could impact a startup's ability to achieve its objectives. It involves a systematic approach to understanding and managing risks that are inherent in the business environment. Risk is an inherent part of any business venture, especially in the startup phase where uncertainties and challenges are high. Effective risk management is crucial for startups to navigate these uncertainties and increase their chances of success. It involves proactively identifying potential risks, assessing their potential impact, and implementing strategies to minimize or eliminate them.

Business Strategy

A business strategy in the context of startup and entrepreneurship refers to a set of actions and decisions undertaken by an entrepreneur to achieve the long-term goals and objectives of their startup. It encompasses a comprehensive plan that outlines the direction, focus, and competitive advantage of the company. The business strategy serves as a roadmap for the startup, guiding its operations, resource allocation, and decision-making processes. It involves analyzing the market, understanding customer needs, and positioning the startup in a way that differentiates it from competitors. The first step in developing a business strategy is conducting market research to identify target customers, their preferences, and the existing competition. This information helps the entrepreneur understand the market landscape and determine how their startup can meet customer needs more effectively. By identifying the target market segment, the entrepreneur can tailor their offerings to suit the specific needs and desires of their customers. Once the market is analyzed, the entrepreneur can define the value proposition of their startup. This refers to the unique benefits and advantages that their product or service offers to customers. The value proposition should be a clear and compelling statement that highlights why customers should choose the startup over competitors. In addition to defining the value proposition, the business strategy must also outline the business model. This includes determining the revenue streams, cost structure, and key partnerships required to make the startup profitable. The entrepreneur must decide whether their startup will generate revenue through sales, subscriptions, advertising, or other means, and determine the cost structure to ensure profitability. Once the business model is established, the entrepreneur can define the marketing and sales strategies. This involves identifying the channels through which the startup will reach customers and developing a plan to promote and sell the products or services. The marketing strategy may include online and offline advertising, social media marketing, content marketing, public relations, and other techniques that help the startup build brand awareness and attract customers. Lastly, the business strategy should also address operational matters such as hiring and managing talent, acquiring necessary resources, and establishing efficient processes. The entrepreneur must ensure that the startup is equipped with the right team, infrastructure, and tools to execute the business strategy effectively. In summary, a business strategy in the context of startup and entrepreneurship is a comprehensive plan that outlines the direction, focus, and competitive advantage of the startup. It involves market analysis, defining the value proposition and business model, and developing marketing, sales, and operational strategies to achieve long-term goals.

Business Valuation

Business valuation in the context of startups and entrepreneurship refers to the process of determining the economic value of a new business venture. It involves assessing the worth of a startup by considering various factors such as its assets, revenue, growth potential, market position, intellectual property, and the overall economic and industry trends. The valuation of a startup is crucial for several reasons. Firstly, it helps entrepreneurs and investors to understand the financial value of the business at a given point in time. This information is vital for making informed decisions regarding investment opportunities, funding rounds, and potential exit strategies. Startups are typically valued using various methods, including the market approach, income approach, and asset-based approach. The market approach involves comparing the startup to recently sold similar businesses in the industry. This method relies on market multiples and transaction data to estimate the startup's value. The income approach, on the other hand, focuses on the projected future cash flows of the startup. It considers the expected revenue, expenses, and growth rates to estimate the present value of these future cash flows. This method is suitable for startups that have already generated significant revenue or have a solid business model. Lastly, the asset-based approach determines the value of the startup by considering its tangible and intangible assets. Tangible assets may include physical property, equipment, inventory, while intangible assets encompass intellectual property, patents, brand value, and customer relationships. This approach is useful when a startup has valuable assets that contribute significantly to its overall value. It is important to note that business valuation is not an exact science and can vary depending on the specific circumstances and assumptions made during the process. Startups are inherently risky, and their valuations may change rapidly as they evolve and grow. Therefore, regular reassessment of a startup's value is necessary to stay up to date with the changing market conditions and underlying business factors.

Buyer Persona Development

A buyer persona is a fictional representation of an ideal target customer for a startup or an entrepreneurial venture. It is a detailed description of the characteristics, preferences, and behaviors of the target customer segment. Creating buyer personas is an essential task for startups and entrepreneurs as it helps them understand their customers better, tailor their products or services to meet their needs, and effectively reach out to them with targeted marketing strategies.

Buyout

A buyout is a transaction in which one company or individual purchases a controlling stake in another company, effectively gaining control over its operations, assets, and decision-making processes. In the context of startups and entrepreneurship, a buyout often refers to the acquisition of a startup by a larger, more established company. This type of buyout typically occurs when the startup has demonstrated potential for growth and innovation, but requires additional resources and support to scale its operations. Entrepreneurs may choose to sell their startup to a larger company through a buyout for several reasons. Firstly, the buyout can provide the necessary capital to fund further growth and expansion. By joining forces with a larger company, the startup can access a wider customer base, distribution channels, and other resources that might have been otherwise unattainable. Additionally, the buyout can offer entrepreneurs an exit strategy, allowing them to cash out on their investment and potentially start new ventures or pursue other interests. The buyout may also provide stability and security for the startup's employees, as they become part of a larger organization with established processes and structures. However, it is important to note that buyouts can also present challenges and risks. The acquiring company may seek to integrate the startup into its existing operations, which can lead to changes in the startup's culture, management style, and strategic direction. This integration process can be complex and time-consuming, requiring both parties to navigate potential conflicts and differences in organizational values. In conclusion, a buyout in the context of startups and entrepreneurship refers to the acquisition of a startup by a larger company, providing the startup with resources and support for growth, while also offering entrepreneurs an exit strategy. It is a transaction that requires careful consideration and negotiation to ensure alignment between the two entities and successful integration of the startup into the acquiring company's operations.

C Corporation (C-Corp)

A C Corporation, also known as a C-Corp, is a type of business entity that is formed under state law and is recognized as a separate legal entity from its owners or shareholders. This means that the corporation can enter into contracts, own property, incur debts, and be held liable for its actions. One of the main advantages of a C Corporation is that it provides limited liability protection to its shareholders. This means that the shareholders are generally not personally liable for the debts and obligations of the corporation. In the event that the corporation is sued or cannot pay its debts, the shareholders' personal assets are typically protected. Another key feature of a C Corporation is its ability to raise capital. Unlike other business structures, such as sole proprietorships or partnerships, a C Corporation can easily bring in investors by selling shares of stock. This allows the corporation to raise funds for growth and expansion. In addition, a C Corporation has perpetual existence. This means that the corporation can continue to operate even if there are changes in ownership or management. The corporation can also continue its operations after the death or departure of its shareholders. When it comes to taxation, C Corporations are subject to what is known as "double taxation." This means that the corporation itself is subject to income tax on its profits, and then any dividends or distributions made to shareholders are also taxed at the individual level. However, C Corporations can take advantage of various tax deductions and credits to minimize their tax liability. Overall, a C Corporation is often the preferred choice for startups and entrepreneurs who plan to seek funding from investors or eventually go public. Its limited liability protection, ability to raise capital, and perpetual existence make it an attractive option for those looking to grow and scale their businesses.

Cannibalization

Cannibalization in the context of startups and entrepreneurship refers to the phenomenon where the introduction of a new product or service from a company negatively impacts the sales or market share of its existing products or services. In other words, when a startup or entrepreneur introduces a new offering that competes directly or indirectly with their own existing products, it can cannibalize the sales of those established products. This can occur due to various reasons, such as the new offering being more innovative, affordable, or simply more appealing to customers.

Cap Table (Capitalization Table)

A cap table, short for capitalization table, is a financial document that outlines the ownership stakes and the value of each stake in a startup or company. It provides a comprehensive overview of the company's equity structure by detailing the ownership percentages, types of securities issued, and the various shareholders or stakeholders involved. The cap table serves as a crucial tool for entrepreneurs, investors, and other stakeholders to understand and manage the ownership and equity distribution within the company. It is often used during fundraising rounds, mergers, acquisitions, or any significant event that may impact the company's ownership structure or valuation.

Capital Injection

Capital Injection refers to the process of providing additional funds or financial resources to a startup or entrepreneurial venture in order to support its growth and operations. It involves the infusion of capital into the business by external parties, such as investors or financial institutions, with the aim of increasing the company's financial capacity and facilitating its expansion. This injection of capital can take various forms, including equity investments, loans, or grants. Equity investments involve the purchase of shares or ownership in the company by the investor, entitling them to a portion of the company's profits and assets. Loans, on the other hand, involve providing funds to the startup with the expectation of repayment over a specified period of time, usually with interest. Grants are non-repayable funds provided by government or non-profit organizations to support specific projects or initiatives. Capital injection plays a vital role in the startup and entrepreneurship ecosystem. It serves as a catalyst for growth and allows startups to pursue their business goals and objectives. The additional funds can be used for a variety of purposes, such as hiring and retaining talented employees, developing new products or services, expanding marketing and sales efforts, upgrading infrastructure, or entering new markets. Furthermore, capital injection also helps startups to overcome financial obstacles and manage cash flow challenges. Many startups face difficulties in generating sufficient revenue during their early stages, and external funding can provide the necessary resources to bridge this gap. It enables startups to meet their financial obligations, pay operating expenses, and invest in the necessary resources to sustain and scale their operations.

Capital Investment

Capital investment, in the context of startup and entrepreneurship, refers to the funds allocated to acquire or upgrade physical assets, such as machinery, equipment, and property, that are essential for the growth and operation of a business venture. It is a crucial aspect of starting and scaling a startup, as it provides the necessary resources to bring ideas into reality, develop prototypes, and establish a solid foundation for future growth. A capital investment typically involves a significant amount of money and represents a long-term commitment to a particular project or business. Startups and entrepreneurs seek capital investments to finance various activities, such as research and development, product manufacturing, infrastructure development, marketing efforts, and expanding operational capacities. This financial injection helps startups to hire talent, purchase necessary technology, and invest in activities that create value and generate revenue.

Capital Management

Capital management refers to the strategic planning and efficient allocation of financial resources in a startup or entrepreneurial venture. It involves identifying, acquiring, and utilizing capital in a manner that maximizes the long-term value and growth potential of the business. In the context of startups and entrepreneurship, capital management plays a crucial role in ensuring the sustainability and success of a new business. Startups typically face challenges related to limited financial resources, uncertain revenue streams, and high growth expectations. Effective capital management enables entrepreneurs to navigate these challenges and optimize their use of funds. Capital management begins with the identification and evaluation of various sources of capital, such as personal savings, loans, grants, or venture capital. Entrepreneurs need to assess the pros and cons of each source and choose the most appropriate option based on factors like cost, availability, and flexibility. They must also consider the potential dilution of ownership and control associated with external funding sources. Once capital is obtained, entrepreneurs must allocate it efficiently to different areas of the business. This includes funding product development, marketing and sales, hiring and training employees, and establishing operational infrastructure. Effective capital allocation requires strategic decision-making and prioritization, considering the core objectives of the startup and the potential return on investment in each area. Regular monitoring and evaluation of capital utilization are essential to ensure that funds are being used effectively and in line with the business's financial goals. Entrepreneurs need to track key financial metrics and performance indicators, such as revenue growth, profitability, and cash flow. This allows them to make timely adjustments or reallocations of capital if necessary. Additionally, capital management involves managing risks associated with financial decisions. Entrepreneurs must identify and mitigate potential risks, such as credit risk, liquidity risk, or market risk. They may also consider implementing risk management strategies, such as diversification, insurance, or hedging, to protect the business's capital and financial stability.

Capital Markets

Capital Markets refer to the financial market where companies, governments, and entrepreneurs raise funds by selling securities such as stocks, bonds, and financial derivatives. These markets play a crucial role in fueling the growth and development of startups and entrepreneurship. In the context of startups and entrepreneurship, capital markets provide a platform for raising capital through various channels such as initial public offerings (IPOs), venture capital, private equity, and crowdfunding. Startups often rely on these markets to secure the necessary funds to finance their business operations, expand their market presence, develop new products or services, and support innovation. Capital markets enable startups and entrepreneurs to access a wide range of investors, including individual and institutional investors, who are willing to invest their money in exchange for ownership stakes or future returns. By selling securities, startups can attract investments and raise substantial amounts of capital, allowing them to take their business to the next level. Furthermore, capital markets provide startups with liquidity. This liquidity ensures that startup owners and early-stage investors can exit their investments by selling the securities they hold in the market. This ability to sell securities helps in generating returns on investment, providing a mechanism for exiting and reallocating funds to new entrepreneurial endeavors. Capital markets also serve as a barometer of a startup's performance and potential. The stock prices and valuations of publicly-traded startups reflect market sentiments and investors' confidence in the company's growth prospects. This valuation is crucial for raising additional capital, attracting strategic partnerships, and enhancing the startup's credibility in the industry. In summary, capital markets provide the necessary infrastructure and mechanisms for startups and entrepreneurs to raise capital, gain liquidity, and establish their worth in the market. They serve as a vital financial foundation that supports the growth, innovation, and sustainability of startup ventures.

Capital Raising Strategies

Capital Raising

Capital raising, in the context of startup and entrepreneurship, refers to the process of obtaining funds or financial resources from various sources to support the growth, development, and operations of a new business venture. Startup companies often require significant amounts of capital to fund their initial operations and expansion plans. Capital raising can be achieved through different methods, including equity financing, debt financing, and alternative financing options.

Capital Structure Analysis

A capital structure analysis refers to the evaluation and assessment of how a startup or entrepreneurial venture finances its operations and growth. It involves examining the mix of debt, equity, and other financial instruments used by the company to fund its activities and achieve its strategic goals. Capital structure analysis is an important aspect of financial planning and management, as it helps entrepreneurs understand the impact of different financing options on the company's risk and return. By analyzing the capital structure, entrepreneurs can make informed decisions about the optimal blend of debt and equity financing that aligns with the company's objectives and maximizes its long-term value.

Capital Structure Management Strategies And Optimization

Capital structure management strategies and optimization refer to the process of determining and managing the mix of debt, equity, and other financial instruments in a startup or entrepreneurial venture. It involves making decisions about how to raise funds, allocate those funds, and structure the ownership of the business. A startup or entrepreneurial venture typically requires significant capital to fund its operations, finance growth, and invest in future opportunities. However, limited resources and high levels of uncertainty often make it difficult for startups to access traditional sources of funding such as bank loans or public offerings. As a result, capital structure management becomes crucial for startups to ensure their financial health and sustainability. The primary goal of capital structure management in startups and entrepreneurship is to strike a balance between risk and return. Entrepreneurs must weigh the costs and benefits of different financing options and determine an optimal mix of debt and equity to maximize their value and minimize risks. This includes considerations such as the cost of debt, the potential dilution of ownership, and the impact on the company's ability to grow and attract future investors. Capital structure management strategies can vary depending on the startup's growth stage, industry, and specific circumstances. Early-stage startups, for example, may rely heavily on equity financing from angel investors or venture capitalists, trading ownership for capital. As the startup grows and matures, it may consider incorporating debt instruments such as bank loans or bonds to supplement equity financing and reduce the cost of capital. In addition to raising funds, capital structure management involves optimizing the allocation of capital within the startup. This includes decisions about how much capital should be allocated to different departments or projects, as well as managing the trade-off between short-term profitability and long-term growth. By effectively managing its capital structure, a startup can enhance its financial performance, improve its creditworthiness, and increase its ability to attract future investors or secure additional funding.

Capital Structure Management Strategies

Capital structure management strategies refer to the deliberate and proactive decisions made by startups and entrepreneurs to finance their business operations through a combination of debt and equity. It involves determining the proportionate mix of debt and equity that will provide the most optimal and sustainable financing structure for the long-term success of the business. The primary goal of capital structure management is to strike a balance between the cost of financing and the risk associated with it. By carefully examining different sources of capital and their implications, startups can design a capital structure that minimizes the cost of capital while ensuring adequate funds for growth and stability.

Capital Structure Management

Capital structure management refers to the decisions and strategies implemented by a startup or entrepreneur to determine the mix of debt and equity financing used to fund the business operations and pursue growth opportunities. This critical aspect of financial management involves determining the proportion of debt and equity in the overall capitalization of the startup, as well as how to raise and manage these funds. The capital structure directly impacts the financial risk, cost of capital, and the value of the business.

Capital Structure Optimization

Capital structure optimization refers to the strategic management and allocation of financial resources within a startup or entrepreneurial venture to maximize its value and optimize its overall cost of capital. It involves determining the ideal mix of equity and debt financing, as well as the proportion of each, to ensure the business can meet its financial obligations while simultaneously generating the highest possible return for its shareholders. In the context of startups and entrepreneurship, capital structure optimization plays a crucial role in ensuring long-term sustainability and growth. It requires a careful evaluation of various factors such as risk tolerance, cost of capital, cash flow projections, and growth prospects to determine the most efficient allocation of financial resources. The process of capital structure optimization typically begins with assessing the startup's current financial position, including its existing debt and equity obligations. Entrepreneurs need to analyze the potential benefits and drawbacks of different financing options, considering factors such as interest rates, repayment terms, and ownership dilution. By striking the right balance between debt and equity, startups can minimize their cost of capital while maintaining an optimal level of financial flexibility. Moreover, capital structure optimization involves continuous monitoring and adjustment as a startup evolves and matures. As a venture progresses through different growth stages, its financial needs and risk profile may change. Entrepreneurs should regularly reassess their capital structure and consider refinancing or altering their financing mix to meet the evolving requirements of the business.

Capital Structure Planning Strategies And Implementation

Capital structure planning strategies refer to the process of determining the mix of debt and equity financing that a startup or entrepreneur will utilize to fund their operations and growth. It involves making decisions regarding the proportion of debt and equity in the company's overall financing structure. The implementation of capital structure planning strategies is crucial for startups and entrepreneurs as it directly impacts their ability to raise funds, manage risks, and optimize their cost of capital. By carefully planning the capital structure, startups can ensure that they have sufficient funds to support their growth initiatives while minimizing the financial risk associated with excessive debt or dilution of equity.

Capital Structure Planning Strategies

Capital structure planning strategies refer to the deliberate and thoughtful allocation of funds across various sources of capital, such as equity and debt, to achieve optimal financial outcomes for a startup or entrepreneurial venture. The choice of capital structure is crucial for startups and entrepreneurs as it influences the overall financial health and success of the business. It involves determining the ideal mix of equity and debt financing, as well as deciding on the appropriate levels of each, to maximize the company's value and minimize its cost of capital. There are several key capital structure planning strategies that startups and entrepreneurs can employ: 1. Equity Financing: This strategy involves raising funds by selling shares of ownership in the company to investors. Equity financing provides capital without incurring debt, and it distributes the financial risk among multiple investors. It can be an attractive option for startups with high growth potential, but it often dilutes the ownership stake of the founders. 2. Debt Financing: This strategy involves borrowing funds from lenders, such as banks or financial institutions, with an obligation to repay the principal amount and interest. Debt financing allows startups to maintain full ownership control but comes with the risk of defaulting on loan payments. Startups need to carefully manage their debt levels to ensure they can meet their financial obligations. 3. Hybrid Financing: This strategy combines elements of both equity and debt financing. It involves issuing hybrid securities, such as convertible debt or preferred shares, which can be converted into equity at a later stage. Hybrid financing offers flexibility and can be structured to align with the specific needs and goals of the startup. 4. Bootstrapping: This strategy involves self-funding the startup through personal savings, credit cards, or revenue generated from initial sales. Bootstrapping allows entrepreneurs to retain complete control and ownership over the business but can limit the company's growth potential due to limited resources. 5. Capital Rationing: This strategy involves allocating capital to different projects or business units based on their expected return on investment. By prioritizing investments and selectively allocating resources, startups can maximize their overall profitability and minimize risk. Effective capital structure planning is essential for startups and entrepreneurs to optimize their financial resources, manage risk, and attract external funding. It requires careful consideration of the company's growth prospects, cash flow needs, and risk tolerance. By implementing the appropriate capital structure planning strategies, startups can position themselves for long-term success and sustainability.

Capital Structure Planning

The capital structure planning is a crucial aspect of startup and entrepreneurship that involves determining how a company will finance its operations and growth through a combination of equity and debt. At the core, capital structure refers to the mix of different sources of funding that a company utilizes to support its activities. This mix typically includes equity, which represents ownership in the company, and debt, which represents borrowed funds that need to be repaid. In the context of startups and entrepreneurship, capital structure planning becomes particularly important due to the unique challenges and opportunities these ventures face. Startups often have limited financial resources and may require substantial capital to develop and scale their business ideas. When planning the capital structure, entrepreneurs need to carefully consider various factors. One crucial element is the cost of capital. Equity financing, such as investments from venture capitalists or angel investors, may result in dilution of ownership but usually does not have a fixed repayment schedule. Debt financing, on the other hand, often involves borrowing from banks or other lenders and requires regular interest payments and eventual repayment of principal. Another consideration is the level of risk associated with the business. Startups typically have higher risk profiles, and taking on excessive debt could lead to financial distress if the company faces challenges in generating sufficient cash flows. Balancing the amount of equity and debt in the capital structure can help manage this risk and provide a more stable financial foundation. Furthermore, the stage of development and growth potential of the startup should also be taken into account. Early-stage startups may rely more heavily on equity financing to fund their research, development, and market entry. As the company progresses and starts generating revenue, it may be more feasible to incorporate debt to support expansion and capital expenditures. In conclusion, capital structure planning in the context of startups and entrepreneurship involves determining the optimal mix of equity and debt financing to support the company's operations and growth. It requires careful consideration of factors such as cost of capital, risk, and stage of development. By strategically planning the capital structure, entrepreneurs can ensure adequate funding while managing risk and maximizing the company's long-term success.

Capital Structure

Capital structure refers to the way a startup or entrepreneurial venture finances its operations and growth by utilizing a mix of debt and equity. It represents the combination of different sources of funding that a company utilizes to finance its activities. The composition of the capital structure can have a significant impact on the company's financial position, risk profile, and overall ability to generate returns. In the context of startups and entrepreneurship, capital structure plays a crucial role in determining the financial health and sustainability of the venture. Typically, startups rely on a variety of funding sources to meet their capital requirements and fuel their growth. These funding sources can include equity investments from founders, angel investors, venture capitalists, crowdfunding platforms, and government grants, as well as debt financing from banks, financial institutions, or even personal loans. The decision regarding the optimal capital structure for a startup involves striking a balance between risk and return. Equity financing provides funds in exchange for ownership stakes in the company, which dilutes the ownership of existing shareholders but does not create a repayment obligation. On the other hand, debt financing involves borrowing money that needs to be repaid with interest, but it does not dilute ownership. Striking the right mix of equity and debt financing is essential for startups, as it affects the cost of capital, the company's ability to attract investors, and its risk exposure. Finding an optimal capital structure requires careful consideration of various factors, such as the company's growth prospects, industry dynamics, cash flow patterns, and risk tolerance. Startups often face unique challenges in determining their capital structure due to the inherent uncertainties and risks associated with early-stage ventures. A capital structure that is too heavily reliant on debt may increase the financial risk and burden the company with fixed interest payments, while a capital structure that is too equity-heavy may lead to excessive dilution of ownership and control. Overall, the capital structure of a startup or entrepreneurial venture represents the way it finances its activities through a mix of debt and equity. The proportion of debt and equity funding sources used by the company affects its financial position, risk profile, cost of capital, and ability to attract investors. Striking the right balance in the capital structure is crucial for the long-term success and sustainability of a startup.

Capitalization Table (Cap Table)

The Capitalization Table (Cap Table) is a fundamental financial tool used in the context of startup and entrepreneurship. It provides a detailed breakdown of the ownership and capital structure of a company, including the distribution of shares among stakeholders and the different classes of equity. The Cap Table serves as a visualization of the ownership dynamics within a company, showcasing the percentage of ownership held by each shareholder and the corresponding value of their shares. This information is crucial for both the founders and investors, as it helps in understanding the current ownership situation and predicting the future dilution of ownership.

Case Study Analysis

A case study analysis is a methodical examination of a specific case or situation in the context of startup and entrepreneurship. It involves analyzing and interpreting data, facts, and information related to the case to gain a deeper understanding of the challenges, successes, and lessons learned. In startup and entrepreneurship, case studies are often used to explore real-world examples of business ventures, innovative projects, or entrepreneurial endeavors. They provide valuable insights into the strategies, decision-making processes, and outcomes of these cases. By studying these cases, entrepreneurs and aspiring business owners can learn from both the achievements and failures of others, enabling them to make more informed decisions and improve their own chances of success.

Cash Burn

Cash burn refers to the rate at which a startup or entrepreneur spends their available cash to fund their operations before they become profitable. It represents the net cash flow of a business, which is the difference between the cash inflows (such as revenue, investments, and loans) and the cash outflows (such as operating expenses, marketing costs, and salaries). Cash burn is a critical metric for startups because it helps determine how long a company can sustain its operations without the need for additional funding. It provides insights into the financial health of a business and its ability to generate enough revenue to cover its expenses. Startup founders often focus on increasing their cash burn rate in the early stages of their venture to invest in product development, marketing, and scaling their operations. This aggressive spending is aimed at gaining market share, attracting customers, and creating a competitive advantage. However, it also means that the startup is consuming its cash reserves at a faster pace. It is crucial for entrepreneurs to carefully manage their cash burn rate to ensure their startup remains financially viable. If the cash burn is too high and the startup fails to generate sufficient revenue or raise additional funding, it may run out of cash and be forced to shut down. On the other hand, if the cash burn is too low, the startup may not be investing enough in growth opportunities, which can hinder its long-term success. Investors closely monitor a startup's cash burn rate when evaluating its potential for investment. A high burn rate may be viewed as a sign of growth and ambition, but it also comes with a higher risk of failure. Startups with a low burn rate may be seen as more financially cautious, but they might also face challenges in attracting customers and scaling their business. In summary, cash burn is a financial metric that measures how quickly a startup uses up its available cash to finance its operations. Managing the cash burn rate effectively is crucial for the long-term success and sustainability of a startup.

Cash Flow Management

Cash flow management in the context of startup and entrepreneurship refers to the process of monitoring, analyzing, and controlling the flow of money within a business. It involves tracking the inflow and outflow of funds to ensure that the company has enough cash on hand to meet its financial obligations and support its ongoing operations. A key aspect of cash flow management is the ability to accurately forecast and project future cash flows. This allows startups and entrepreneurs to anticipate potential cash shortages or surpluses and take proactive measures to address them. By maintaining a solid understanding of their cash position, businesses can make informed decisions regarding investments, expenses, and funding options. Cash flow management is crucial for startups and entrepreneurs because cash is the lifeblood of any business. Without sufficient cash flow, even the most innovative ideas and promising ventures can quickly fail. It is important to balance the timing of cash inflows and outflows to ensure that the company has enough liquidity to cover its day-to-day expenses, such as payroll, rent, inventory, and supplier payments. In addition, effective cash flow management allows startups and entrepreneurs to strategically plan for future growth and expansion. By aligning cash flow projections with business goals and objectives, businesses can allocate resources wisely, seize opportunities, and mitigate potential risks. Furthermore, proper cash flow management allows startups and entrepreneurs to build credibility and maintain good relationships with stakeholders, including investors, lenders, suppliers, and employees. Demonstrating financial stability and discipline instills confidence and trust in the business, which can lead to increased investment, better credit terms, and stronger partnerships. In summary, cash flow management is a critical aspect of startup and entrepreneurial success. It entails monitoring and controlling the flow of money within a business to ensure sufficient cash on hand, accurately forecasting future cash flows, making informed decisions, planning for growth, and fostering strong relationships with stakeholders.

Cash Flow Projection

A cash flow projection is a financial tool that helps startups and entrepreneurs forecast the amount of money flowing in and out of the business over a specific period of time. It provides a detailed estimate of the cash inflows (revenue) and outflows (expenses) based on projected sales, expenses, and other cash transactions. The cash flow projection is an essential component of a startup's business plan, helping entrepreneurs evaluate the financial health of their business and make informed decisions. By analyzing the projected cash inflows and outflows, entrepreneurs can assess whether their business will have enough cash to cover expenses, meet financial obligations, and sustain operations in the long run.

Cash Flow Statement

The cash flow statement is a financial statement that provides information on the flow of cash in and out of a startup or entrepreneurial venture. It is an important tool for analyzing the liquidity and financial health of a business. The cash flow statement consists of three sections: operating activities, investing activities, and financing activities. These sections allows entrepreneurs to understand the sources and uses of cash within the business. The operating activities section of the cash flow statement shows the cash flows resulting from the primary activities of the startup or entrepreneurial venture. This includes cash generated from sales of products or services, as well as cash paid for operating expenses such as rent, wages, and utilities. By examining this section, entrepreneurs can assess the company's ability to generate cash from its core operations. The investing activities section of the cash flow statement provides information on the cash flows related to the purchase and sale of long-term assets, such as property, plant, and equipment. It also includes cash flows from investments in other companies or any proceeds from the sale of investments. Entrepreneurs can use this section to determine the extent to which the startup or entrepreneurial venture is investing in its future growth. The financing activities section of the cash flow statement shows the cash flows resulting from the financing activities of the startup or entrepreneurial venture. This includes cash received from issuing shares or borrowing, as well as cash paid for dividends or debt repayment. Entrepreneurs can use this section to evaluate the company's ability to raise capital and manage its debt obligations. By analyzing the cash flow statement, entrepreneurs can assess the financial stability and viability of their startup or entrepreneurial venture. It provides insights into the company's ability to generate cash, invest in growth opportunities, and meet its financial obligations. Furthermore, it helps entrepreneurs make informed decisions regarding cash management, financing, and investment strategies.

Cash Flow

Cash flow refers to the movement of money in and out of a startup or entrepreneurial venture. It is a measure of the financial health of a business and plays a crucial role in its sustainability and growth. Cash flow can be divided into three categories: operating activities, investing activities, and financing activities. Operating activities include the day-to-day operations of a business, such as revenue generation and expenses related to operations. Investing activities involve the purchase or sale of long-term assets, such as property, equipment, or investments. Financing activities are related to the inflow or outflow of cash from financing sources, such as loans or equity investments. Positive cash flow indicates that a startup is generating more cash inflows than outflows, which is essential for meeting financial obligations, such as paying suppliers, employees, and lenders. It also provides the necessary funds for growth and expansion. Negative cash flow, on the other hand, means that a startup is spending more cash than it is generating, which can lead to financial difficulties and may require external financing to cover the shortfall. Managing cash flow is crucial for startups and entrepreneurs to ensure the smooth operations and sustainability of their ventures. It involves forecasting and monitoring cash inflows and outflows, and implementing strategies to improve cash flow. This may include optimizing revenue generation, reducing expenses, negotiating favorable payment terms with suppliers, and closely managing inventory levels. In addition to managing day-to-day cash flow, startups and entrepreneurs must also consider the timing of cash flows. For example, they may have seasonal fluctuations in cash flow that require careful planning and budgeting. Additionally, unexpected events, such as economic downturns or changes in market conditions, can impact cash flow and require contingency plans to manage the financial impact. In conclusion, cash flow is a critical aspect of startup and entrepreneurship as it provides the necessary funds for operations, growth, and sustainability. Effective management of cash flow is vital for financial stability and success in the competitive business environment.

Churn Analysis

Churn analysis, in the context of startups and entrepreneurship, refers to the process of examining and evaluating customer attrition or defection from a business. It involves analyzing patterns and trends related to customer behavior with the objective of identifying factors that contribute to the loss of customers. Startup businesses rely heavily on acquiring and retaining customers to drive growth and sustainability. However, it is estimated that acquiring new customers can cost up to five times more than retaining existing ones. Therefore, understanding and reducing customer churn is crucial for startups to maximize their revenue and profitability. Churn analysis typically involves analyzing a variety of data sources, such as customer interactions, purchase history, and feedback, to identify key indicators that are linked to customer churn. By examining these indicators, startups can gain insights into potential reasons why customers are leaving and take proactive measures to mitigate churn. Through churn analysis, startups can identify common characteristics or behaviors shared by customers who have churned. This information can help in building predictive models or developing strategies to proactively engage with customers who exhibit similar behaviors, ultimately reducing churn rates. Moreover, churn analysis enables startups to understand the lifetime value of customers and the impact of churn on revenue. By quantifying the financial implications of churn, entrepreneurs can prioritize efforts and allocate resources to customer retention strategies that offer the highest return on investment.

Churn Rate

Churn rate, in the context of startup and entrepreneurship, refers to the rate at which customers or subscribers stop using a product or service over a given period of time. It is an essential metric for startups as it measures the sustainability of their customer base and the effectiveness of their customer retention strategies. The churn rate is calculated by dividing the number of customers who have stopped using the product or service by the total number of customers at the beginning of the specified period. The result is typically expressed as a percentage, representing the proportion of customers lost. A high churn rate can be detrimental to the success and growth of a startup. It indicates that customers are not finding enough value in the product or service to continue using it, leading to a loss of revenue and market share. It can also increase the cost of acquiring new customers, as the startup has to constantly replace those lost due to churn. Reducing churn rate is an important goal for startups, as it signifies a higher level of customer satisfaction and loyalty. By effectively managing customer relationships and continuously improving the product or service, startups can reduce churn and increase customer lifetime value. Some common strategies to reduce churn rate include implementing proactive customer support, offering incentives for continued usage, analyzing customer feedback, and providing regular updates and improvements to the product or service. It is also crucial for startups to closely monitor and analyze their churn rate, as it can reveal valuable insights into customer behavior and product-market fit. In conclusion, churn rate is a significant metric for startups in understanding customer attrition and evaluating the effectiveness of their customer retention efforts. By actively addressing and reducing churn, startups can improve their long-term viability and success in the competitive entrepreneurial landscape.

Co-Founder

A Co-Founder, in the context of startup and entrepreneurship, is one of the individuals who initiates the establishment of a new business venture alongside one or more individuals. Co-Founders are essential figures in the early stages of a startup and play a fundamental role in shaping its vision, strategy, and execution. Co-Founders typically bring complementary skill sets, expertise, and resources to the table, pooling their collective knowledge and experiences to build a successful venture. They share in the responsibilities, risks, and rewards associated with the startup, fostering a sense of shared ownership and commitment to its growth and success.

Common Stock

Common Stock refers to the basic type of ownership in a corporation that represents the equity ownership interest held by shareholders. In the context of Startup and Entrepreneurship, common stock is a vital instrument for both founders and investors. Entrepreneurs use common stock to raise capital and establish ownership in their startup. They typically issue common stock to initial investors in exchange for funding, which helps finance the company's operations and growth. Common stock allows founders to retain control over their business while also providing investors with the potential for a return on their investment.

Community Building

Community building refers to the intentional process of creating and nurturing a group of individuals who share similar interests and goals within the context of startup and entrepreneurship. It involves fostering a sense of belonging, trust, and collaboration among members of the community, ultimately working towards achieving common objectives. In the startup and entrepreneurship world, community building plays a pivotal role in establishing a strong foundation for success. By building a community around a startup, entrepreneurs are able to tap into a network of like-minded individuals who can offer support, knowledge, and resources.

Community Management

Community Management in the context of Startup & Entrepreneurship refers to the strategic planning and execution of activities aimed at building, growing, and engaging a community around a particular product, service, or brand. It involves fostering meaningful connections, facilitating communication, and creating a sense of belonging among community members. Effective community management is essential for startups and entrepreneurs as it plays a crucial role in establishing and maintaining a positive reputation, driving customer acquisition, and fostering customer loyalty. By actively engaging with the community, startups can gain valuable insights, gather feedback, and build strong relationships with their target audience.

Competitive Advantage

A competitive advantage in the context of startups and entrepreneurship refers to the unique qualities, resources, or positioning strategies that enable a company to outperform its competitors and achieve superior performance in the market. Startups constantly face intense competition and challenges in the marketplace. Having a competitive advantage is crucial for their survival and growth. It allows startups to differentiate themselves from competitors and create value for their target customers.

Competitive Analysis

43

A competitive analysis is a process that involves researching and evaluating the strengths and weaknesses of current and potential competitors in the market. It helps startups and entrepreneurs understand their competitors' strategies, products, and market position, allowing them to make informed decisions and develop effective business plans. Through a competitive analysis, startups and entrepreneurs can identify their competitors' target markets, customer segments, and pricing strategies. This information can be used to refine their own target market and customer segmentation, develop competitive pricing strategies, and differentiate their products or services from those of their competitors.

Competitive Benchmarking

Competitive benchmarking is a strategic process used by startups and entrepreneurs to analyze and compare their performance, strategies, and offerings against their direct competitors in the industry. It involves identifying and evaluating the strengths and weaknesses of competitors in order to gain insights and formulate strategies to enhance their own competitive advantage. By conducting competitive benchmarking, startups and entrepreneurs can better understand market trends, customer preferences, and industry best practices. The process typically includes assessing competitor products, pricing, marketing strategies, customer service, and overall business performance.

Competitive Intelligence Tools

Competitive Intelligence Tools refer to a set of strategies and tools used by startups and entrepreneurs to gather and analyze data about their competitors' activities, enabling them to make informed business decisions. These tools help in understanding the competitive landscape, identifying market trends, and gaining insights into competitor strategies and tactics. The main objective of using competitive intelligence tools is gaining a competitive advantage by staying ahead of competitors. By monitoring competitors' actions, such as pricing strategies, product launches, marketing campaigns, and customer satisfaction levels, startups and entrepreneurs can devise effective strategies to differentiate their offerings and outperform their competition.

Competitive Intelligence

Competitive Intelligence refers to the systematic gathering, analysis, and interpretation of data and information about competitors, market trends, and industry dynamics. It plays a crucial role in the strategic decision-making process for startups and entrepreneurs. By understanding their competitors, startups can identify opportunities, assess threats, and make informed decisions to gain a competitive advantage in the market. Competitive Intelligence involves various activities, including monitoring competitor activities, collecting and analyzing data on competitors' products, pricing, marketing strategies, and customer feedback. Startups and entrepreneurs can utilize both primary and secondary research methods to gather this information. Primary research involves gathering data firsthand through surveys, interviews, and focus groups, while secondary research involves analyzing existing data from sources such as market reports, industry publications, and online databases. The information obtained through Competitive Intelligence allows startups and entrepreneurs to assess the strengths and weaknesses of their competitors, understand customer preferences, and identify market trends. This knowledge enables them to develop effective marketing strategies, optimize their product offerings, and identify untapped market opportunities. Furthermore, Competitive Intelligence helps startups to anticipate and respond to market changes and emerging trends. It provides insights into the competitive landscape, allowing startups to benchmark their performance against competitors and identify areas for improvement. By tracking competitor activities and market trends, startups can proactively identify potential threats and adapt their strategies to stay ahead in the market. In conclusion, Competitive Intelligence serves as a critical tool for startups and entrepreneurs to navigate the complexities of the market. By gathering and analyzing data on competitors, market trends, and industry dynamics, startups can make informed decisions, identify opportunities, and gain a competitive advantage. It ensures that startups are well-positioned to respond to market changes and make strategic decisions that drive their growth and success.

Competitive Landscape

A competitive landscape refers to the overall structure of an industry or market in which startups and entrepreneurs operate. It encompasses all the existing players, including direct and indirect competitors, and describes their position, strategies, and market share. In the context of startup and entrepreneurship, understanding the competitive landscape is crucial for success. It helps entrepreneurs identify their target market, evaluate the demand for their products or services, and tailor their business strategies accordingly. One key aspect of the competitive landscape is the identification of direct competitors. These are companies that offer similar products or services and target the same customer segment. Analyzing direct competitors allows startups to differentiate themselves, highlight their unique value proposition, and capture market share. Indirect competitors, on the other hand, may offer substitute products or services that fulfill the same customer need. These competitors might not be obvious at first glance but can significantly impact the startup's success. For example, ride-sharing companies like Uber and Lyft compete indirectly with traditional taxi services. Furthermore, the competitive landscape includes an assessment of the competitive intensity within the industry. This analysis helps entrepreneurs understand the level of competition they will face and adjust their strategies accordingly. High competition may require startups to differentiate themselves further, invest in aggressive marketing, or innovate to stay ahead. Market share analysis is another critical element of the competitive landscape. It defines the relative position of startups and their competitors in the market. Startups can assess their market share to determine their traction and identify opportunities for growth. Moreover, understanding the market share of established players can help startups identify gaps or underdeveloped areas that can be exploited. In conclusion, a thorough understanding of the competitive landscape is essential for startups and entrepreneurs. By analyzing direct and indirect competitors, assessing competitive intensity, and evaluating market share, entrepreneurs can develop effective strategies, differentiate themselves from the competition, and ultimately succeed in their chosen market.

Content Management Systems (CMS)

A Content Management System (CMS) is a software application or a set of software tools that enable startups and entrepreneurs to create, manage, and publish digital content such as websites, blogs, and online stores, without the need for technical expertise or extensive coding knowledge. A CMS provides a user-friendly interface that allows users to easily create and edit content, organize and categorize it, customize the design and layout of their website, and control access and permissions for multiple users.

Content Marketing Strategy

Content marketing strategy refers to the systematic planning and implementation of creating, distributing, and promoting valuable and relevant content to a targeted audience, with the ultimate goal of driving profitable customer action and building brand loyalty. In the context of startups and entrepreneurship, content marketing strategy plays a crucial role in building brand awareness, establishing expertise, and driving customer engagement, all of which are essential for the success and growth of new businesses. A well-defined content marketing strategy for startups includes a comprehensive understanding of the target audience, their needs, and pain points. This knowledge allows startups to create content that provides solutions, educates, or entertains their audience, positioning themselves as a reliable source of information and building trust. Startups need to identify the most appropriate channels to distribute their content, whether it's through their website, blog, social media platforms, or email newsletters. Each channel may require a different approach and format to effectively engage with their target audience. Ultimately, the main goal of a content marketing strategy for startups and entrepreneurship is to attract the attention of potential customers, nurture relationships, and ultimately convert them into paying customers. By consistently delivering valuable and relevant content, startups can establish themselves as industry leaders, gain credibility, and strengthen their brand positioning. It is important for startups to continuously assess the effectiveness of their content marketing strategy by analyzing key metrics such as website traffic, engagement rates, and conversion rates. This analysis allows them to identify what is working and what needs improvement, enabling them to adjust their strategy accordingly. In conclusion, having a well-planned and executed content marketing strategy is vital for startups and entrepreneurship. It allows them to differentiate themselves from competitors, connect with their target audience, and drive growth and success in a highly competitive market.

Convertible Debt

Convertible debt refers to a financial instrument commonly used in the context of startup and entrepreneurship. It is a type of debt that can be converted into equity or ownership in a company at a later stage, typically during a future funding round or an exit event such as an acquisition or an initial public offering (IPO). The main purpose of convertible debt is to provide an alternative form of financing to startups and entrepreneurs who may have difficulty accessing traditional sources of capital, such as bank loans or venture capital. It allows these companies to raise funds from investors without immediately determining a specific valuation for the company.

Convertible Note

A convertible note is a financial instrument commonly used in the context of startups and entrepreneurship. It is a type of short-term debt that can be converted into equity at a future date, typically during a future financing round. Startups often use convertible notes to raise funds in their early stages, when it may be difficult to determine the company's valuation. Instead of setting a specific valuation for the company upfront, the convertible note allows investors to defer the valuation until a later date when the company is more established and has a clearer valuation. When a startup issues a convertible note, investors provide capital to the company, usually in the form of a loan. However, instead of receiving interest payments or fixed repayment terms, the investors hold a promissory note that can be converted into equity in the company at the occurrence of certain triggering events. These triggering events typically include a subsequent equity financing round, such as a Series A funding round. Convertible notes offer several advantages for both startups and investors. For startups, they provide a way to raise funds quickly without the need for an immediate valuation. This can be especially beneficial in the early stages when valuing a startup can be challenging. For investors, convertible notes offer the potential for a greater return on investment if the company's value increases significantly between the issuance of the note and the conversion into equity. When the triggering event occurs, the convertible note converts into equity, usually at a discount to the valuation established in the subsequent financing round. The discount is a way to compensate early investors for the additional risk they took by investing in the company at an earlier stage. The conversion rate may also be subject to a valuation cap, which sets a maximum valuation at which the note can convert into equity. In summary, a convertible note is a financial instrument used in startup financing that allows investors to provide capital to a company in the form of a loan that can be converted into equity at a later date. It offers advantages for both startups and investors, providing a flexible way to raise funds without an immediate valuation and potentially generating a higher return on investment for investors.

Corporate Culture

The corporate culture of a startup or entrepreneurship refers to the shared values, beliefs, attitudes, and behaviors that shape the working environment and guide the actions of individuals within the company. In a startup or entrepreneurship, the corporate culture plays a crucial role in defining the organization's identity, attracting and retaining talent, and ultimately driving its success. It encompasses various aspects, including the company's mission, vision, and core values, as well as its leadership style, communication practices, and employee engagement initiatives. The corporate culture of a startup or entrepreneurship is typically characterized by its innovative and fast-paced nature. Startups often prioritize agility, adaptability, and risk-taking, as they operate in highly dynamic and competitive markets. They value creativity, fresh ideas, and a willingness to challenge the status quo. In such environments, employees are encouraged to think outside the box, experiment, and learn from failures. Collaboration and teamwork are also emphasized, as startups understand the importance of cross-functional collaboration and leveraging diverse perspectives to drive innovation. Transparency and open communication are other key elements of the corporate culture in startups. Entrepreneurs often foster a culture of trust and honesty, encouraging employees to voice their opinions, share feedback, and participate in decision-making processes. This creates a sense of empowerment and ownership among the team members, fostering a positive and inclusive work environment. Furthermore, startup cultures often prioritize work-life balance, employee well-being, and personal development. Entrepreneurs recognize the importance of taking care of their employees' holistic needs and offer flexible working arrangements, wellness programs, and opportunities for professional growth. This helps in attracting top talent and nurturing a motivated and satisfied workforce. In summary, the corporate culture of a startup or entrepreneurship encompasses the shared values, attitudes, and behaviors that shape the working environment. It is characterized by innovation, agility, collaboration, transparency, and a focus on employee well-being and personal development. This culture plays a crucial role in attracting and retaining talent, fostering creativity and innovation, and driving the success of the organization.

Corporate Entrepreneurship

Corporate Entrepreneurship refers to the process by which established companies, also known as corporations, foster and promote innovation, creativity, and entrepreneurial activities within their existing organizational structures and cultures. It involves the development and implementation of new ideas, products, services, and business models, as well as the identification and exploitation of new market opportunities. Corporate Entrepreneurship aims to combine the entrepreneurial mindset and agility of startups with the resources, capabilities, and stability of established companies. By encouraging and supporting entrepreneurship within their ranks, corporations can stay competitive in rapidly changing markets, drive growth, and enhance their overall performance. Instead of solely relying on external startups, corporations can create an internal ecosystem that fosters and supports entrepreneurial initiatives. This internal entrepreneurial ecosystem usually consists of various elements, such as corporate venture capital, incubators, accelerators, innovation labs, and cross-functional teams. These elements provide the necessary resources, guidance, and support for employees to develop and implement their entrepreneurial ideas and projects within the corporate context. Corporate Entrepreneurship also involves creating a culture that encourages risk-taking, experimentation, and learning from failures. It requires a shift in mindset, from a focus on stability and risk aversion to embracing uncertainty and embracing calculated risks. Companies need to empower their employees, provide them with autonomy and ownership, and create an environment conducive to creativity and innovation. Successful corporate entrepreneurship can result in benefits such as increased product and service offerings, improved customer satisfaction, enhanced operational efficiency, and the ability to enter new markets. It can also lead to the creation of new business units and spin-off companies. In summary, Corporate Entrepreneurship is the process by which corporations promote and support entrepreneurial activities within their organizational structures, with the aim of driving innovation, growth, and overall performance.

Corporate Innovation

Corporate Innovation in the context of startup and entrepreneurship refers to the process of introducing and implementing new ideas, strategies, products, or business models within an established corporation or organization. It involves the creation and development of innovative solutions that can improve existing products or processes, explore new business opportunities, and drive growth and competitiveness in the market. Corporate innovation enables established companies to adapt to the rapidly changing business landscape, stay ahead of competition, and maintain their relevance and success in the long term. It involves fostering a culture of creativity, experimentation, and risk-taking within the company, as well as establishing mechanisms and processes to identify, evaluate, and implement new ideas.

Corporate Social Responsibility (CSR) Programs

Corporate Social Responsibility (CSR) Programs refer to initiatives undertaken by a startup or entrepreneur to create a positive impact on society and the environment while also generating business value. These programs are designed to go beyond the traditional business objectives of profitability and growth, and incorporate social and environmental considerations into the core business strategy. Startups and entrepreneurs recognize the importance of CSR programs as they can enhance their reputation, attract and retain talented employees, build trust among stakeholders, and contribute to sustainable development. These programs typically involve activities such as philanthropy, environmental conservation, employee volunteering, and ethical business practices.

Corporate Social Responsibility (CSR)

Corporate Social Responsibility (CSR) is a concept that is closely tied to the principles of

47

sustainability and ethical business practices. In the context of startups and entrepreneurship, it refers to the voluntary actions and initiatives undertaken by these enterprises to address and take responsibility for their social, environmental, and economic impacts. Startups and entrepreneurs that embrace CSR recognize that their operations can have a profound effect on society and the environment. They understand that they have a duty to contribute positively to the well-being of the communities in which they operate, as well as to minimize any negative impacts resulting from their activities. This extends beyond mere compliance with legal obligations and reflects a commitment to going above and beyond to make a difference.

Corporate Venture Capital (CVC)

Corporate Venture Capital (CVC) refers to the practice of established corporations investing in early-stage startup companies in order to gain strategic and financial benefits. It is a form of corporate investment activity that focuses on funding innovative startups that have the potential to create synergies with the corporate investor's own business. CVC is a way for corporations to tap into the entrepreneurial ecosystem and stay ahead of market disruptions by investing in promising startups. These investments can take the form of equity financing, convertible notes, or other financial instruments and typically involve a minority stake in the startup. One of the primary motivations for corporations to engage in CVC is the pursuit of strategic objectives. By investing in startups, corporations can access new technologies, business models, and talent that can supplement or enhance their existing operations. This allows corporations to stay competitive in rapidly evolving markets and adapt to changing customer demands. CVC also offers corporations the opportunity to diversify their portfolios and generate financial returns. While financial gains may not be the primary goal of CVC investments, they can provide a hedge against market uncertainties and contribute to the overall financial performance of the corporation. For startups, CVC can provide more than just funding. It offers access to the corporate investor's expertise, resources, and network, which can be invaluable for early-stage companies. These partnerships can lead to collaborations, joint ventures, and commercialization opportunities that can significantly accelerate the growth and success of the startup. However, CVC investments also come with challenges for both startups and corporate investors. Startups may face conflicts of interest with their corporate investors, loss of control over their operations, or barriers to accessing additional funding. Corporate investors, on the other hand, need to navigate the complexities of working with startups, manage potential conflicts with their own business units, and ensure a balanced approach to risk-taking.

Corporate Venture Capital Investment

Corporate Venture Capital (CVC) Investment refers to the financial support provided by established corporations to early-stage startups in order to foster innovation, gain strategic advantages, and explore emerging markets. It is a form of equity investment where a corporation directly invests in startups that align with their strategic objectives and have the potential to disrupt or complement their existing business operations. CVC investment offers several benefits for both startups and corporations involved. For startups, it provides access to capital, industry expertise, and valuable resources that can accelerate their growth and increase their chances of success. Corporations, on the other hand, benefit from CVC investment by gaining insights into disruptive technologies, expanding their product portfolios or service offerings, and enhancing their competitiveness in the market. CVC investments can take various forms, including direct equity investments, venture capital funds, or incubator programs. Unlike traditional venture capitalists or angel investors, corporations engaging in CVC investments typically have a strategic interest in the startup's success beyond financial returns. They may seek to create synergies between their existing operations and the startup's innovative technologies or leverage the startup's products or services to enhance their own offerings. Furthermore, CVC investments differ from traditional mergers and acquisitions (M&A) as they usually involve a minority stake in the startup rather than outright ownership. This allows startups to maintain their autonomy and entrepreneurial spirit while benefiting from the support and resources of a large corporate entity. However, CVC investments also present challenges and risks. Startups may face potential conflicts of interest between their corporate investor and other stakeholders, such as existing investors or customers. They may also experience difficulty in aligning their strategic goals with those of the corporate investor, especially if the startup's vision changes during its growth journey. In conclusion, Corporate Venture Capital (CVC) Investment is a form of equity investment where established corporations provide financial support and resources to early-stage startups that align with their strategic objectives. It offers both startups and corporations the opportunity to foster innovation, gain market advantages, and explore emerging technologies or markets. However, it also presents unique challenges and risks related to the alignment of strategic goals and potential conflicts of interest.

Corporate Venture Fund

A corporate venture fund is a strategic investment fund established by a larger corporation with the primary purpose of investing in early-stage or high-growth startups. Its aim is to achieve financial returns on investment as well as obtain strategic benefits for the parent company. A corporate venture fund differs from traditional venture capital funds in that it is operated and funded by a corporation rather than independent investors. This distinction is important because it allows the corporate venture fund to leverage the resources, expertise, and networks of the parent company to support its portfolio startups. The parent company may provide access to its existing customer base, distribution channels, manufacturing facilities, or technical know-how, among other resources, to help the startups accelerate their growth. The motivation for establishing a corporate venture fund can vary depending on the parent company's objectives. Some companies use it as a means of scouting for new technologies, markets, or business models that could disrupt or enhance their core business. They invest in startups that align with their strategic goals and have the potential to drive innovation in their industry. By keeping a finger on the pulse of the startup ecosystem, these corporations can stay ahead of the curve and remain competitive. Additionally, a corporate venture fund can provide the parent company with a window into emerging trends, customer preferences, and market dynamics. Through their investments, they gain insights about the startup's target market, competition, and consumer behavior, which can be valuable in informing their own product development, marketing strategies, or market expansion plans. For entrepreneurs and startups, securing investment from a corporate venture fund brings several advantages. Firstly, the association with a well-established corporation can enhance their credibility and reputation, making it easier for them to attract additional funding from other investors. Secondly, the corporate venture fund can provide guidance and mentorship through its network of industry experts, helping the startups refine their business strategies, scale their operations, and navigate challenges. In conclusion, a corporate venture fund is a specialized investment vehicle operated by a corporation to invest in startups. It offers strategic and financial benefits to both the parent company and the portfolio startups, fostering innovation, collaboration, and growth in the startup ecosystem.

Corporate Venturing

Corporate venturing refers to the practice of established companies investing in and partnering with startups or early-stage ventures to gain access to new technologies, markets, and business models. It involves a strategic collaboration between a large corporation and a small, innovative company.Startup and entrepreneurship are closely linked to corporate venturing as they often seek external funding and partnership opportunities to fuel their growth and development. Corporate venturing provides startups with access to financial resources, industry expertise, and valuable networks, while offering established companies the opportunity to tap into new ideas and disruptive innovations that can help them remain competitive in a rapidly changing business landscape.

Cost-Benefit Analysis

Cost-Benefit Analysis is a systematic process used by startups and entrepreneurs to evaluate the potential costs and benefits of a proposed business decision or project. It involves comparing and quantifying both the positive and negative aspects associated with a particular course of action. In the context of startups and entrepreneurship, cost-benefit analysis is crucial in making informed decisions that can contribute to the success and sustainability of a venture. It helps entrepreneurs assess the financial, social, and environmental implications of their choices, allowing them to make decisions that maximize the overall value and return on investment. The first step in conducting a cost-benefit analysis is to identify and list all the costs and benefits associated with the proposed decision or project. Costs may include both direct expenses (such as purchasing equipment, hiring employees, or acquiring licenses) and indirect costs (such as training, maintenance, or operational expenses). On the other hand, benefits can be financial gains (such as increased revenue or cost savings), improvements in productivity, enhanced brand reputation, or even positive environmental impacts. Once all the costs and benefits are identified, they need to be assigned monetary values or estimated as accurately as possible. This allows for a more objective comparison and evaluation of the potential return on investment. Entrepreneurs may rely on market research, expert opinions, and historical data to estimate the values associated with the various costs and benefits. After assigning values to costs and benefits, entrepreneurs can then analyze and compare the two. This can be done by subtracting the total costs from the total benefits to determine the net benefit or profit. If the net benefit is positive, it indicates that the benefits outweigh the costs, suggesting that the proposed decision or project is likely to be financially viable. Conversely, a negative net benefit suggests that the costs are likely to outweigh the benefits, indicating that the decision may not be advisable or that adjustments need to be made to improve the return on investment. In conclusion, cost-benefit analysis serves as a crucial tool for startups and entrepreneurs to evaluate the financial, social, and environmental impacts of business decisions. By quantifying the costs and benefits associated with a proposed action, entrepreneurs can make more informed choices that maximize value, mitigate risks, and contribute to the long-term success of their ventures.

Creative Destruction

Creative Destruction is a concept in the context of startup and entrepreneurship that refers to the continuous process of innovation and transformation within an industry. It is a fundamental principle that drives economic growth and development by replacing outdated products, technologies, and business models with new ones. In this dynamic process, startups and entrepreneurs play a crucial role by disrupting traditional markets, challenging established players, and introducing novel ideas and solutions. They identify gaps and inefficiencies in the existing market and develop innovative products or services to address those needs.

Crisis Management

Crisis Management in the context of Startup and Entrepreneurship refers to the strategic planning and execution of policies and procedures to handle unexpected events or situations that can potentially harm the business. Startups and entrepreneurs often face various crises that can disrupt the normal operations and pose significant threats to their survival and growth. These crises can arise from internal factors such as financial issues, product failures, operational failures, or external factors such as economic downturns, regulatory changes, or even natural disasters. The objective of crisis management is to minimize the negative impact of these crises on the business and its stakeholders. It involves quick decision-making, effective communication, and resource allocation to efficiently respond to the crisis and mitigate its consequences. Crisis management in startups and entrepreneurship typically follows a step-by-step approach. The first step is identification, where potential crises are identified through risk assessment and analysis. This helps in understanding the nature and severity of the crisis and allows entrepreneurs to prepare in advance. After identification, the next step is preparation. This involves creating crisis management plans, protocols, and procedures. Startups need to form crisis management teams, define their roles and responsibilities, and establish communication channels to ensure a swift and coordinated response during a crisis.

Crowd Equity

Crowd equity, also known as equity crowdfunding, is a form of fundraising in which a large number of individuals, known as the crowd, make small investments in a startup or entrepreneurial venture in exchange for equity ownership. This type of funding allows startups to raise capital from a pool of investors who are interested in supporting and investing in early-stage businesses. In the context of startups and entrepreneurship, crowd equity has emerged as an alternative to traditional funding sources such as venture capitalists or angel investors. It offers several advantages for both startups and investors. For startups, crowd equity provides access to a larger pool of potential investors who may be willing to invest smaller amounts of capital compared to traditional funding sources. This wider reach allows startups to tap into a diverse range of investors who may have a specific interest in their industry or product. Additionally, crowd equity enables startups to leverage the collective wisdom and support of their investor base, as these investors often bring valuable expertise, insights, and connections to the table. On the other hand, crowd equity offers investors the opportunity to diversify their investment portfolios by participating in a variety of startups across different industries. It allows individual investors to support innovative ideas and promising ventures that they believe in, even if they do not have the financial resources to invest large amounts. By investing smaller amounts in multiple startups, investors can spread their risk and potentially benefit from the success of one or more ventures. However, it is important to note that crowd equity investments come with risks. Startups typically have a high failure rate, and there is no guarantee of a return on investment. Investors should carefully evaluate the business model, financials, and team behind a startup before making an investment decision. Due diligence and research are crucial to mitigate risks and make informed investment choices. In conclusion, crowd equity is a form of fundraising that allows startups to raise capital from a large pool of individual investors in exchange for equity ownership. It offers advantages such as access to a diverse investor base and potential expertise, while also providing investors with the opportunity to support innovative ideas and diversify their investment portfolios. However, it is important for both startups and investors to carefully consider the risks and conduct due diligence before entering into a crowd equity arrangement.

Crowd Funding

Crowd Funding is a strategy used by startups and entrepreneurs to raise funds from a large number of individuals, typically through online platforms. It involves reaching out to a wide network of potential investors, customers, or supporters, who contribute small amounts of money towards the venture. The concept of crowd funding relies on the cumulative power of many small investments to provide the necessary capital for a project or business to get off the ground. Instead of relying on a single or limited number of investors, crowd funding enables entrepreneurs to tap into the collective resources of a larger group.

Crowd-Sourced Funding

Crowd-Sourced Funding, also known as crowdfunding, is a financing method utilized by startups and entrepreneurs to raise funds for their ventures. It involves soliciting contributions from a large number of individuals, typically through an online platform, in exchange for rewards or ownership stakes in the company. In this funding model, entrepreneurs present their business ideas and investment opportunities to a diverse audience, often engaging potential backers through social media networks, email campaigns, or personal connections. By leveraging the power of the crowd, entrepreneurs can gather funds from a wide range of sources, including friends, family, acquaintances, and strangers who are interested in supporting innovative projects. The process of crowdfunding typically follows a few key steps. First, the entrepreneur creates a detailed pitch that effectively communicates their vision, explaining the problem they aim to solve and how their idea can make a positive impact. The pitch may include videos, images, and written descriptions to provide a comprehensive overview of the venture. Once the pitch is complete, the entrepreneur identifies a suitable crowdfunding platform to host their campaign. These platforms act as intermediaries, facilitating the connection between entrepreneurs and potential investors. Entrepreneurs select a funding goal and set a deadline for their campaign, determining the amount of money they aim to raise within a specified timeframe. After launching the campaign, entrepreneurs embark on a promotional journey to spread the word about their venture to as many people as possible. They leverage their personal networks and social media presence to create awareness and generate interest in their project. Supporters can then visit the crowdfunding platform and make financial contributions to the campaign, often in exchange for tiered rewards based on their level of investment. If the campaign reaches its funding goal within the designated timeframe, the entrepreneur receives the collected funds and can proceed with executing their business plan. However, if the campaign falls short of the target, most crowdfunding platforms return the funds to the contributors. This ensures that entrepreneurs only receive the full funding they require if there is sufficient interest from the crowd. Crowd-sourced funding provides emerging startups and entrepreneurs with an alternative to traditional financing sources, such as bank loans or venture capital investments. By tapping into the collective support of a large number of individuals, entrepreneurs can overcome capital barriers, validate their ideas, and gain a loyal base of supporters who are emotionally invested in their success.

Crowdfunding Campaign

A crowdfunding campaign is a method used by startups and entrepreneurs to raise funds for their business or project by reaching out to a large number of individuals or potential investors through an online platform or social media channels. The main purpose of a crowdfunding campaign is to gather financial support from a diverse group of people who are interested in the idea, product, or service being offered by the startup or entrepreneur. This method allows them to bypass traditional funding channels such as banks, venture capitalists, or angel investors. In a crowdfunding campaign, the startup or entrepreneur typically sets a funding goal, which represents the amount of money they need to bring their idea or project to fruition. They then create an online campaign page on a crowdfunding platform, where they provide detailed information about their business, goals, and rewards for the backers. The campaign page serves as a communication tool to showcase the unique features of the idea, product, or service, and to engage potential backers to make financial contributions. The startup or entrepreneur may use various media, such as videos, images, and written content, to effectively convey the value proposition and generate interest in the campaign. Backers, or those who contribute to the crowdfunding campaign, can be individuals, businesses, or organizations. They are motivated by different factors, such as the potential for a financial return on investment, a belief in the product or service, or a desire to support innovation and entrepreneurship. Once the campaign is launched, the startup or entrepreneur actively promotes it through various online marketing channels, including social media, email marketing, and influencer collaborations. They aim to reach a wide audience and encourage them to visit the campaign page, learn more about the offering, and make a financial contribution. In return for their support, backers receive rewards based on the amount of money they contribute. These rewards can range from product samples, exclusive discounts, or early access to the product or service, depending on the campaign. This incentivizes potential backers to contribute and creates a sense of community and engagement around the campaign.

Crowdfunding Investor

A crowdfunding investor refers to an individual or entity that financially contributes to a startup or entrepreneurial venture through a crowdfunding platform. Crowdfunding has gained popularity as an alternative means for entrepreneurs to secure funding and bring their ideas to fruition, without relying solely on traditional investment sources such as banks or venture capitalists. In this model, the crowdfunding investor acts as a source of capital, providing funds to the entrepreneur in exchange for a stake in the venture. Crowdfunding platforms, such as Kickstarter or Indiegogo, facilitate the connection between entrepreneurs and potential investors. Entrepreneurs present their business ideas or prototypes on these platforms, and individuals interested in supporting these ventures can contribute funds. The funds collected can then be used by the entrepreneur to finance product development, marketing efforts, or other operational expenses necessary for startup growth. The role of the crowdfunding investor goes beyond providing financial support. By contributing to a venture, these investors also become advocates for the entrepreneur and their business idea. They have a vested interest in the success of the startup and often serve as a valuable network of contacts or provide guidance based on their expertise or experience. Investing through crowdfunding platforms offers various benefits for both entrepreneurs and investors. For entrepreneurs, crowdfunding provides an opportunity to validate their business idea and gain exposure to a wider audience. It allows them to leverage the power of crowds and create a community of supporters who believe in their vision. Furthermore, crowdfunding can serve as a marketing tool, as entrepreneurs have the chance to showcase their product or service to potential customers, facilitating market validation. On the other hand, crowdfunding investors can access a diverse range of investment opportunities that were traditionally reserved for venture capitalists or angel investors. They can support projects they find interesting or align with their own passions and values. Additionally, crowdfunding allows for smaller investment amounts, lowering the barrier to entry for individuals who may not have substantial capital available for investment. It enables investors to diversify their investment portfolio and take part in the early stages of startups that have the potential for high growth and profitability. In summary, a crowdfunding investor plays a crucial role in the world of startups and entrepreneurship by providing capital and support to innovative ventures through crowdfunding platforms. Their investment not only brings financial resources to the entrepreneur but also acts as an endorsement for the viability and market potential of the business idea. Through crowdfunding, both entrepreneurs and investors can reap the benefits of a more inclusive and democratic approach to funding startups.

Crowdfunding Platform Fee

Crowdfunding Platform Fee refers to the percentage or amount charged by a crowdfunding platform to entrepreneurs or startups for utilizing their platform to raise funds from a large number of individuals or investors. Crowdfunding has become an increasingly popular method for startups and entrepreneurs to raise capital for their business ventures, and platforms have emerged as intermediaries facilitating this process. These platforms offer entrepreneurs and startups a way to showcase their projects or business ideas and attract potential investors who are interested in supporting them. In return for providing this service, crowdfunding platforms charge a fee, which can vary depending on the platform and the specific terms and conditions of the agreement. The crowdfunding platform fee can be structured in different ways. Some platforms may charge a fixed percentage of the total funds raised, typically ranging from 5% to 10%. This means that if an entrepreneur successfully raises $100,000 through the platform, they would pay a fee of $5,000 to $10,000. Others may charge a flat fee or have a tiered fee structure based on the size of the funding goal. For example, a platform may charge a higher fee for projects aiming to raise $1 million compared to those aiming to raise $100,000. It is important for entrepreneurs and startups to carefully consider the platform fees when deciding on a crowdfunding platform. They should evaluate the value provided by the platform, such as the level of exposure, the quality of the investor network, and any additional services or support offered. Evaluating the fee structure in relation to the expected funding goals and potential return on investment is also crucial in order to determine the most suitable platform for their crowdfunding campaign. In conclusion, crowdfunding platform fee refers to the charge imposed by crowdfunding platforms on entrepreneurs and startups for utilizing their platform to raise funds. It is important for entrepreneurs to consider the fee structure and evaluate the value provided by the platform when deciding on the most appropriate crowdfunding platform for their fundraising needs.

Crowdfunding Platform

A crowdfunding platform is a digital platform that allows entrepreneurs and startups to raise funds from a large number of individuals or organizations. It serves as an intermediary between the entrepreneurs and the supporters, providing a way for the supporters to contribute money towards the development of a business idea or project. The platform typically operates by hosting fundraising campaigns, where entrepreneurs create a detailed description of their business idea or project and set a funding goal. Supporters can then browse through the available campaigns and choose which ones they want to support by making a financial contribution. This type of funding model is often referred to as "crowdfunding" because it harnesses the power of a large crowd of people to pool their financial resources and support projects they believe in. It is particularly appealing to entrepreneurs and startups because it offers an alternative to traditional funding sources, such as bank loans or venture capital investments. One of the key advantages of using a crowdfunding platform is that it allows entrepreneurs to tap into a wide network of potential supporters who may be interested in their business idea or project. This can help them gain exposure and attract funding from individuals or organizations that they may not have been able to reach through traditional fundraising methods. In addition to providing a platform for fundraising, many crowdfunding platforms also offer other tools and resources to help entrepreneurs and startups succeed. These may include features such as project management tools, marketing support, and access to a network of mentors and experts. Overall, crowdfunding platforms play a crucial role in the startup and entrepreneurship ecosystem by providing a scalable and accessible way for entrepreneurs to raise funds and bring their ideas to life. They provide a level playing field for individuals and small businesses to compete with larger players and access the funding and support they need to turn their innovative ideas into reality.

Crowdfunding Platforms

A crowdfunding platform is an online platform that enables entrepreneurs and startups to raise funds from a large pool of individuals or organizations. It provides a digital space where project creators can showcase their ideas and campaigns, and potential backers can contribute financially to support these initiatives. Entrepreneurs and startups often face challenges when it comes to securing funding for their ventures. Traditional sources of financing, such as banks and investors, may be difficult to access or require significant collateral or equity. In contrast, crowdfunding platforms offer an alternative method of raising capital that can be more accessible, democratic, and efficient. By leveraging the power of the internet and social media, crowdfunding platforms enable entrepreneurs to reach a wide audience of potential backers. These platforms provide project creators with the tools and resources to create compelling campaigns and showcase their products or services. This includes the ability to create a pitch video, upload images and descriptions, and set funding goals and rewards for different contribution levels. Backers, on the other hand, have the opportunity to support projects they believe in and receive various incentives in return for their contributions. These incentives can include early access to the product, exclusive merchandise, or special recognition. Additionally, crowdfunding platforms often incorporate social sharing features, allowing backers to promote the campaigns they support to their networks, further expanding the project's reach. Crowdfunding platforms typically operate on a reward-based, donation-based, or equity-based model. In reward-based crowdfunding, backers receive non-financial rewards or pre-purchase a product or service. In donation-based crowdfunding, backers contribute funds without expecting any financial return. Equity-based crowdfunding, on the other hand, allows backers to become shareholders in the venture, offering the potential for financial returns if the startup succeeds. Overall, crowdfunding platforms have revolutionized the way entrepreneurs and startups raise funds. They provide a democratized funding mechanism that allows individuals and organizations of all sizes to support innovative ideas and projects. By eliminating traditional barriers to financing, crowdfunding platforms have empowered entrepreneurs to bring their visions to life and have created new opportunities for investment and collaboration in the world of startup and entrepreneurship.

Crowdfunding

Crowdfunding is a method of raising funds for a startup or entrepreneurial project by receiving small amounts of money from a large number of people, typically through an online platform. This approach allows entrepreneurs to bypass traditional sources of funding, such as banks or venture capitalists, and instead, rely on the collective contributions of a broad network of individuals. Through crowdfunding, entrepreneurs present their project or idea to the public and set a funding target. Interested individuals, known as backers or investors, can then choose to contribute any amount to the project, usually in exchange for a reward or a stake in the venture. The collective effort of numerous backers enables entrepreneurs to raise the necessary capital to kickstart their venture, often without resorting to loans or sacrificing equity.

Crowdsale

A crowdsale, also known as an initial coin offering (ICO), is a fundraising method used by startups and entrepreneurs in the field of cryptocurrency and blockchain technology. It allows them to raise capital by selling tokens or digital assets to a large number of individuals, typically investors or supporters, in exchange for funding. The process of a crowdsale involves the issuance and distribution of these tokens to interested participants, who can then store, trade, or use them within the network or platform developed by the startup. The tokens can represent various things, such as utility within a specific application, ownership in a project, or even a form of cryptocurrency itself. Unlike traditional methods of fundraising, such as seeking venture capital or bank loans, a crowdsale offers a more accessible and decentralized approach. It allows startups to directly engage with their community and potential users, enabling them to gather support, establish a user base, and generate funding all at once. In this sense, a crowdsale merges the concepts of crowdfunding and cryptocurrency, offering a unique way for startups to access capital and grow their projects. One of the main advantages of a crowdsale is that it provides entrepreneurs with a means of raising funds without giving up equity or control over their venture. Instead of selling shares in their company, startups offer tokens that may have future value as the project develops and gains popularity. This decentralization of ownership and control aligns with the fundamental principles of blockchain technology, as it enables participants to have a stake and influence in the project's direction. However, it is crucial to note that crowdsales also come with their share of risks and challenges. Due to the relatively nascent and unregulated nature of the cryptocurrency market, individuals participating in crowdsales must exercise caution and thorough research. They should assess the viability and legitimacy of the project, evaluate the team's credentials, analyze the token's utility and potential value, and consider the associated legal and regulatory factors. In conclusion, a crowdsale is a fundraising mechanism within the domain of cryptocurrency and blockchain technology. It enables startups and entrepreneurs to raise funds by offering tokens or digital assets to a wide range of individuals, who can then use or trade these tokens within the developed network. While it presents opportunities for direct engagement and decentralization, participating individuals must also be aware of the risks and consider various factors before investing in a crowdsale.

Crowdsourced Equity Funding

Crowdsourced Equity Funding (CSEF) refers to a method of raising capital for a startup or entrepreneurial venture through the collective effort of a large number of individuals, typically via an online platform. Unlike traditional forms of fundraising, such as venture capital or bank loans, CSEF allows entrepreneurs to obtain funding directly from a large pool of individual investors, commonly referred to as the "crowd". These investors contribute relatively small amounts of money in exchange for equity in the startup, becoming shareholders and having a potential financial stake in the venture's success.

Crowdsourced Financing

Crowdsourced financing, also known as crowdfunding, is a method of raising capital for a startup or entrepreneurial venture by soliciting financial contributions from a large number of individuals, typically through an online platform. This approach is particularly beneficial for startups that have difficulty accessing traditional forms of financing, such as bank loans or venture capital. The concept behind crowdsourced financing is to leverage the power of the crowd to collectively contribute small amounts of money, which collectively add up to a significant sum. Instead of relying on a single investor or a few sources of funding, entrepreneurs can tap into a diverse group of individuals who are interested in supporting innovative ideas and business ventures.

Crowdsourced Funding Platform Development And Optimization

Crowdsourced Funding Platform Development and Optimization is the process of creating and enhancing a digital platform that allows entrepreneurs and startups to raise funds from a large number of individuals who are interested in supporting innovative business ideas. A crowdsourced funding platform, also known as a crowdfunding platform, provides a virtual space for entrepreneurs to showcase their projects and attract potential backers or investors. These platforms can take various forms, such as websites or mobile applications, and typically offer a range of features and functionalities to facilitate the fundraising process. The development phase of a crowdsourced funding platform involves designing and building the technological infrastructure of the platform, including its user interface, database management system, and payment processing capabilities. The platform must be user-friendly, visually appealing, and intuitive to use, ensuring a seamless experience for both entrepreneurs and backers. Once the platform is developed, optimization comes into play. This phase focuses on improving the platform's performance, usability, and conversion rates. Optimization efforts may include A/B testing, analyzing user data and feedback, and implementing changes to enhance the user experience and increase the likelihood of successful funding campaigns. The ultimate goal of crowdsourced funding platform development and optimization is to create a secure and efficient online ecosystem that connects entrepreneurs with potential investors, enabling them to raise the necessary funds to bring their innovative ideas to life. By leveraging the power of the crowd, these platforms democratize access to capital and provide an alternative to traditional funding sources such as banks or venture capitalists.

Crowdsourced Funding Platform Development

A crowdsourced funding platform, in the context of startup and entrepreneurship, refers to an online platform that allows individuals and businesses to raise funds from a large number of people, typically through small contributions. It serves as an alternative method of financing compared to traditional methods such as loans or venture capital. The concept of crowdsourced funding, also known as crowdfunding, relies on the power of the crowd to support and invest in innovative ideas and emerging enterprises. Entrepreneurs can present their projects or business proposals on the platform, providing details about their objectives, strategies, and potential impact. They set a funding goal, specifying the amount of money they need to implement their venture or idea successfully. Individuals interested in supporting these projects can browse through the various offerings on the platform and choose the ones they wish to contribute to. They can usually contribute any amount they desire, depending on the restrictions set by the platform. These contributions can range from small donations to larger investments, and may come with different types of rewards or incentives, depending on the specific crowdfunding model being used. One of the key aspects of a crowdsourced funding platform is the emphasis on collaboration and community engagement. It allows entrepreneurs to not only access funds but also gain visibility and market validation. By presenting their ideas to a wide audience and gathering support from potential users or customers, entrepreneurs can demonstrate demand for their product or service, which can be beneficial for future growth and development. Furthermore, this funding approach enables individuals who may not have access to traditional financing options to support projects they believe in and contribute to the success of new ventures. It democratizes the investment process, allowing anyone to participate and potentially benefit from early-stage investments that were previously exclusive to angel investors or venture capitalists.

Crowdsourced Funding Platform

A crowdsourced funding platform is a digital platform that enables startups and entrepreneurs to raise capital from a large number of individuals, typically through small monetary contributions. These platforms leverage the power of the crowd, connecting entrepreneurs with potential investors who are interested in supporting their ventures. By pooling together small amounts of money from numerous backers, startups can access the necessary capital to fund their businesses, launch new products or services, or expand their operations. Startups and entrepreneurs typically create profiles and pitch their business ideas on crowdsourced funding platforms, outlining their goals, strategies, and estimated funding requirements. They often offer rewards or incentives to attract backers, such as early access to new products, exclusive discounts, or even equity in the company. One of the advantages of using a crowdsourced funding platform is that it allows startups to tap into a wide network of potential investors who may be interested in their niche or industry. Moreover, it offers entrepreneurs a platform to showcase their innovative ideas and gain publicity, potentially attracting attention from venture capitalists or other sources of funding. Crowdsourced funding platforms also provide a level of transparency and accountability in the fundraising process. Backers can review the business plans, financial projections, and other relevant information shared by the entrepreneurs, allowing them to make informed decisions about where to invest their money. Additionally, these platforms often have mechanisms in place to ensure that the funds are used for their intended purpose, providing a certain level of security to the backers. Overall, crowdsourced funding platforms are an essential tool for startups and entrepreneurs looking to raise capital in a non-traditional way. They offer a democratic approach to fundraising, enabling individuals from all backgrounds to support innovative ideas and contribute to the growth of promising businesses.

Crowdsourced Product Development Platforms And Implementation

A crowdsourced product development platform is a digital platform that enables startups and entrepreneurs to engage a community of individuals to collaboratively contribute to the development of a product or service. It leverages the power of collective intelligence and diverse perspectives to ideate, design, and refine the offering. These platforms provide a collaborative space where entrepreneurs can submit their ideas or projects and receive input, suggestions, and feedback from a large community of individuals. Members of the community can contribute their expertise, skills, and ideas in various areas such as product design, marketing strategy, market research, and user experience.

Crowdsourced Product Development Platforms

Crowdsourced product development platforms are online platforms that connect startups and entrepreneurs with a community of individuals who contribute their ideas, skills, and resources to help develop and refine new products or services. These platforms utilize the collective intelligence and expertise of the crowd to bring innovative ideas to life, while also providing opportunities for individuals to showcase their talent and potentially earn rewards or recognition. Startups and entrepreneurs can leverage crowdsourced product development platforms to access a diverse pool of talent, including designers, engineers, marketers, and more. By posting their project or idea on these platforms, they can attract individuals who have the relevant skills and knowledge to contribute to the development process. This allows startups to tap into a wider range of expertise than they might have within their own team, helping to improve the quality and competitiveness of their product or service.

Crowdsourced Product Development

Crowdsourced Product Development is a strategy employed by startups and entrepreneurs to engage a community of individuals or a crowd to contribute ideas, feedback, and resources in the process of developing a new product or service. This approach is driven by the belief that a diverse and collective intelligence can lead to better and more innovative outcomes. In this model, the startup or entrepreneur leverages the power of the internet and various online platforms to solicit ideas and feedback from the crowd. This can be done through open innovation platforms, online communities, social media channels, or dedicated crowdsourcing websites. The process typically involves sharing information about the product idea or concept with the crowd and inviting them to participate in various activities such as brainstorming, ideation, design, testing, and funding. The crowd is encouraged to contribute their knowledge, skills, and expertise to help refine and improve the product. Crowdsourced Product Development offers several advantages for startups and entrepreneurs. Firstly, it provides access to a vast pool of talent and resources that may not be available within the organization. This can lead to greater creativity, diversity of perspectives, and a wider range of ideas. Secondly, it promotes a sense of ownership and engagement among the crowd, as they feel invested in the success of the product. This can result in a loyal and supportive user base. Thirdly, it enables rapid and cost-effective iteration and development of the product, as the startup can tap into the collective intelligence of the crowd. However, there are also challenges associated with this approach. Managing and coordinating the contributions of a large crowd can be complex and time-consuming. Ensuring quality control and intellectual property protection can also be a concern. Additionally, not all products or industries may be suitable for crowdsourced development, as some may require specialized expertise or confidentiality. In conclusion, Crowdsourced Product Development is a valuable strategy for startups and entrepreneurs looking to tap into the collective intelligence and resources of a crowd. By engaging the crowd in the product development process, startups can benefit from diverse perspectives, rapid iteration, and a sense of community ownership. While challenges exist, the potential for innovation and success makes this approach worth exploring.

Crowdsourcing Campaign

Crowdsourcing is a modern business practice commonly utilized in the context of startup and entrepreneurship. It involves obtaining ideas, services, or products by soliciting contributions from a large group of individuals or an online community, typically via the internet. This innovative approach enables startups and entrepreneurs to tap into the collective intelligence, expertise, and skills of a diverse crowd, often consisting of experts and enthusiasts in various fields. By harnessing the power of the crowd, entrepreneurs can access a vast pool of resources, knowledge, and creativity that might otherwise be difficult to acquire through traditional means.

Crowdsourcing Innovation

Crowdsourcing innovation is a collaborative and participatory approach in which entrepreneurs or startups seek ideas, solutions, and feedback from a large group of individuals, typically through an online platform or community. It involves harnessing the collective intelligence and creativity of the crowd, tapping into a diverse range of perspectives and expertise to generate innovative ideas and solutions to problems or challenges. The process of crowdsourcing innovation typically begins by defining a specific problem or challenge that the entrepreneur or startup is facing. This problem is then shared with the crowd, who are invited to submit their ideas and solutions. The crowd can consist of employees, customers, experts, or simply anyone with a relevant interest or expertise. These individuals can contribute their ideas, feedback, and insights through various means, such as online forums, surveys, or open innovation platforms. One of the key advantages of crowdsourcing innovation is the ability to tap into a large and diverse pool of talent and expertise. By involving a wide range of individuals, the entrepreneur or startup can access a vast array of different perspectives, experiences, and insights. This can lead to the generation of more creative and innovative ideas that may have otherwise been missed or overlooked. It also increases the likelihood of finding novel and effective solutions to problems or challenges. Furthermore, crowdsourcing innovation offers benefits in terms of cost-effectiveness and scalability. Unlike traditional innovation approaches that rely on a small internal team, crowdsourcing allows for a much larger number of individuals to contribute their ideas and insights. This not only reduces the time and costs associated with innovation but also enables the entrepreneur or startup to scale up their innovation efforts more easily. Overall, crowdsourcing innovation can be a powerful tool for startups and entrepreneurs looking to generate innovative ideas and solutions. By leveraging the collective intelligence and creativity of the crowd, they can tap into a diverse range of perspectives and expertise, leading to more creative and effective outcomes.

Crowdsourcing Platform Development

A crowdsourcing platform is a digital platform that enables individuals, businesses, and organizations to engage and collaborate with a large group of people in order to obtain information, ideas, funding, or services. Startups and entrepreneurs can leverage crowdsourcing platforms to access a diverse pool of talent, resources, and perspectives, without the need for extensive in-house capabilities or resources. Such platforms allow entrepreneurs to tap into the collective intelligence and creativity of the crowd, enabling them to solve problems, generate innovative ideas, validate concepts, and even raise funding.

Crowdsourcing Platform

A crowdsourcing platform is an online platform that connects entrepreneurs and startups with a large group of individuals to gather ideas, funds, expertise, and feedback to support and develop their projects or businesses. Startups and entrepreneurs often face various challenges, such as limited resources, lack of a support network, and the need for diverse skill sets. A crowdsourcing platform addresses these challenges by enabling them to tap into a crowd of people who can contribute to their projects or businesses in various ways. One of the key functionalities of a crowdsourcing platform is idea generation. Startups and entrepreneurs can present their ideas or business concepts on the platform, inviting the crowd to provide feedback, suggestions, and improvements. This feedback can help refine and shape the idea into a more viable and marketable product or service. In addition to idea generation, a crowdsourcing platform also facilitates fundraising. Startups and entrepreneurs can showcase their projects or businesses on the platform and appeal to the crowd for financial support. Through various mechanisms such as crowdfunding, individuals can contribute funds to help bring these projects or businesses to fruition. Furthermore, a crowdsourcing platform serves as a hub for accessing expertise and skills. Entrepreneurs and startups can seek assistance from the crowd in areas where they lack expertise or resources. This can include finding mentors, advisors, or volunteers who can provide guidance, industry knowledge, or specific skills to help propel their projects forward. Overall, a crowdsourcing platform offers startups and entrepreneurs a collaborative and inclusive approach to developing and growing their businesses. By harnessing the collective intelligence, creativity, and resources of a diverse crowd, these platforms offer a cost-effective and efficient way to overcome the challenges faced by startups and entrepreneurs.

Crowdsourcing

Crowdsourcing refers to the practice of obtaining ideas, solutions, or services from a large and diverse group of people, typically through the use of the internet. In the context of startup and entrepreneurship, it has become a popular method for sourcing funds, ideas, and tasks to support the growth and development of businesses. Startups often face limited resources, both in terms of capital and human capacity. Crowdsourcing provides an alternative approach to traditional funding and recruitment methods by tapping into the collective wisdom and resources of the crowd. This can be achieved through various crowdsourcing platforms, online communities, or social media channels. One of the main applications of crowdsourcing in startups is crowdfunding. Entrepreneurs can present their business ideas or initiatives on crowdfunding platforms and invite individuals or groups to contribute financially. This allows startups to access funding from a large number of people who are interested in supporting innovative projects or businesses they believe in. In return, backers may receive rewards, equity, or other forms of recognition. Crowdsourced innovation is another significant aspect of crowdsourcing in the startup ecosystem. Startups can involve the crowd in generating ideas, solving problems, or designing products and services through open innovation challenges or idea contests. By leveraging the collective intelligence of a diverse group of individuals, startups can gain fresh perspectives and uncover innovative solutions that may not have been discovered through internal resources alone. Crowdsourcing can also be used for various tasks that support startup operations. Startups often require help with tasks such as market research, content creation, or software development but may not have the capacity to hire full-time employees for these roles. Through crowdsourcing, startups can outsource these tasks to freelancers or individuals who have the necessary skills and are willing to contribute on a project basis. In summary, crowdsourcing in the context of startup and entrepreneurship refers to the practice of obtaining funds, ideas, or tasks from a large and diverse group of people through online platforms or communities. It provides startups with an alternative approach to funding, innovation, and task completion by leveraging the collective wisdom and resources of the crowd.

Crowdtesting

Crowdtesting, in the context of startup and entrepreneurship, refers to the practice of leveraging a diverse group of individuals, known as the crowd, to test software applications and products. Startups and entrepreneurs often face resource constraints, such as limited budget or access to a small testing team, which can hinder their ability to thoroughly test their software for bugs, usability issues, and overall functionality. This is where crowdtesting comes into play. By harnessing the power of the crowd, startups and entrepreneurs can tap into a vast pool of testers with different devices, operating systems, and backgrounds to ensure their product is rigorously tested under various conditions. The crowd consists of individuals who volunteer or are selected based on their demographic, geographic, or psychographic characteristics. They are compensated for their time and effort, usually under a pay-per-defect or pay-per-test model. These testers, who may range from tech-savvy professionals to ordinary users, follow predefined test scripts or explore the product under real-world scenarios, mimicking end-user behavior. Crowdtesting offers several advantages for startups and entrepreneurs. Firstly, it provides access to a large and diverse pool of testers, ensuring comprehensive test coverage that can uncover a wide range of issues that might go unnoticed with traditional testing methods. Additionally, the crowd offers a fresh perspective and unbiased feedback, helping startups identify potential usability, functionality, or design improvements. Moreover, crowdtesting enables cost-effectiveness by eliminating the need for hiring and maintaining a dedicated in-house testing team. Startups can leverage crowdtesting platforms that streamline the testing process, manage tester recruitment, and facilitate communication and feedback exchange. This minimizes overhead costs and allows startups to focus on core activities. Overall, in the fast-paced and competitive world of startups and entrepreneurship, crowdtesting plays an essential role in ensuring software quality and user satisfaction. By engaging a diverse crowd of testers, startups can mitigate potential risks, improve their product's performance, and ultimately gain a competitive edge in the market.

Customer Acquisition Cost (CAC)

Customer Acquisition Cost (CAC) is a key metric used in startups and entrepreneurship to measure the cost associated with acquiring a new customer. It represents the total amount of money a company needs to invest in marketing and sales activities to acquire each new customer. CAC helps startups and entrepreneurs analyze the efficiency and effectiveness of their customer acquisition strategies and campaigns. By calculating CAC, companies can determine the return on investment (ROI) of their marketing efforts, identify the most cost-effective channels for acquiring customers, and optimize their marketing budgets.

Customer Acquisition

Customer Acquisition refers to the process of identifying, targeting, and attracting new customers to a startup or entrepreneurial venture. It involves various marketing strategies and actions taken by the business to convert potential leads into paying customers. The ultimate goal of customer acquisition is to increase the customer base and generate revenue for the startup. It is a critical aspect of the business growth strategy as it directly impacts the company's profitability and sustainability. Customer acquisition starts with identifying the target market and understanding their needs, preferences, and pain points. This information helps in creating marketing campaigns and messages that resonate with the target audience. One of the key steps in customer acquisition is lead generation, which involves attracting potential customers and obtaining their contact information. This can be achieved through various channels such as social media, search engine optimization, content marketing, email marketing, and advertising. Once leads are generated, the next step is lead nurturing. This involves building relationships with leads and guiding them through the sales funnel. The startup needs to provide valuable information, address their concerns, and demonstrate the value of its products or services. Lead nurturing can be done through personalized communication, such as emails, phone calls, or direct messages. It is important to establish trust and credibility with the leads, as this increases the chances of conversion. The final stage of customer acquisition is the conversion of leads into customers. This involves convincing them to make a purchase or sign up for the startup's offerings. The startup may offer incentives, discounts, or limited-time promotions to encourage quick decisions. Customer acquisition is an ongoing process that requires continuous refinement and optimization. It is important for startups to track and analyze their customer acquisition efforts to identify what strategies are working and what can be improved. In conclusion, customer acquisition is a vital component of startup and entrepreneurial success. It involves various marketing activities aimed at attracting and converting leads into paying customers. By understanding the target market and implementing effective strategies, startups can achieve sustainable growth and profitability.

Customer Churn Analysis

Customer churn analysis refers to the process of examining and understanding the rate at which customers discontinue using a product or service provided by a startup or entrepreneur. It helps in identifying the reasons behind customer attrition and finding strategies to reduce churn and improve customer retention. Churn analysis involves analyzing historical data, such as customer demographics, purchase history, and behavioral patterns, to identify trends and patterns that may indicate potential churn. By understanding these patterns, startups and entrepreneurs can predict and forecast potential churning customers, allowing them to take proactive measures to retain customers.

Customer Development

Customer Development is a strategic process used by startups and entrepreneurs to gain a deep understanding of their target customers, validate their business assumptions, and refine their products or services to meet customer needs effectively. At its core, Customer Development involves four key steps: customer discovery, customer validation, customer creation, and company building. These steps are designed to help startups and entrepreneurs identify their target market, understand customer pain points, and develop products and services that solve these problems. 1. Customer Discovery: This initial phase involves identifying and understanding the target market and potential customers. Startups engage in conversations with potential customers, conduct interviews, and gather feedback to determine if their product or service addresses a real need or problem. The goal is to gain insights into customer preferences, pain points, and existing solutions in the market. 2. Customer Validation: Once the target customers and their needs are identified, startups must validate their assumptions by testing their product or service with early adopters. This phase involves building a Minimum Viable Product (MVP) or a prototype to gather customer feedback and measure market demand. Startups focus on acquiring initial paying customers and refining their value proposition based on customer feedback. 3. Customer Creation: This phase aims to scale customer acquisition and revenue generation strategies. Startups focus on optimizing their product or service based on early customer feedback and developing a repeatable sales and marketing process. The focus is on refining the business model, building customer relationships, and driving customer adoption and retention. 4. Company Building: In this final phase, startups transition from the discovery and validation process to building a scalable and sustainable business model. Startups focus on scaling operations, expanding their product or service offerings, optimizing their organizational structure, and building a strong customer base. The goal is to create a thriving business that continuously delivers value to its customers. Overall, Customer Development is a continuous process that helps startups and entrepreneurs gain customer insights, validate their assumptions, and build a successful business that meets market needs effectively. By focusing on the customer from the very beginning, startups can increase their chances of developing a product or service that resonates with their target market and drives long-term success.

Customer Feedback

Customer feedback is the valuable information and insights provided by customers regarding their experiences, satisfaction levels, and expectations with a startup or an entrepreneurial venture. It is a crucial element in the process of improving and developing products, services, and overall business operations. Customer feedback plays a significant role in shaping the success and growth of startups and entrepreneurial ventures. It provides entrepreneurs with important insights about their target market, enabling them to make informed decisions and tailor their offerings to better meet customer needs and preferences. By listening to customer feedback, startups can gain a competitive edge, build strong customer relationships, and enhance their overall brand image. Customer feedback can be obtained through various channels such as surveys, interviews, focus groups, online reviews, social media interactions, and direct communication with customers. It can cover a wide range of aspects, including product quality, pricing, customer service, user experience, and overall satisfaction. Entrepreneurs need to actively seek and collect customer feedback on a continuous basis to stay connected with their customer base and identify areas for improvement. Once customer feedback is collected, it needs to be carefully analyzed and interpreted. Startups can categorize feedback into positive, negative, or neutral sentiments, allowing them to identify areas of strength and weakness. Positive feedback can be used to reinforce and expand on successful strategies, while negative feedback can provide insights into areas of improvement and potential innovations. Entrepreneurs should consider customer feedback as a valuable source of inspiration and guidance for business growth. It can help them identify new market trends, uncover unmet customer needs, and explore opportunities for innovation. By incorporating customer feedback into their decision-making processes, startups can adapt to ever-changing market conditions and improve their chances of long-term success.

Customer Journey Mapping

Customer Journey Mapping is a strategic tool used in the context of startups and entrepreneurship to visually represent the various touchpoints and interactions that a customer has with a company from initial awareness to the final purchase and beyond. This mapping technique helps startups and entrepreneurs better understand and empathize with their customers' experiences and perspectives throughout their entire journey. By documenting and analyzing each step of the customer's interaction, startups can identify pain points, gaps, and areas of improvement in their customer service, marketing, and sales strategies.

Customer Lifetime Value (CLV)

Customer Lifetime Value (CLV) refers to the predicted net profit that a customer will generate throughout their relationship with a startup or entrepreneurial venture. It is a metric used to assess the long-term value of acquiring and retaining customers. The CLV concept is particularly crucial for startups and entrepreneurs as it helps them make informed decisions about marketing strategies, customer acquisition costs, and investment in customer relationship management. By estimating the CLV, startups can identify the most profitable customer segments and allocate resources effectively.

Customer Persona

A customer persona in the context of startup and entrepreneurship refers to a fictional representation of a target customer segment. It is created based on market research and real data to help startups and entrepreneurs understand the needs, preferences, and behaviors of their potential customers. A customer persona typically includes demographic information such as age, gender, location, and occupation. It also incorporates psychographic details such as interests, values, and lifestyle. By combining both quantitative and qualitative data, startups can develop a detailed and accurate representation of their target customers. The purpose of creating customer personas is to humanize the target audience and gain deep insights into their motivations and pain points. This enables startups to tailor their products or services to meet specific customer needs, enhance the customer experience, and build long-term relationships. Customer personas help in various aspects of startup and entrepreneurship, including product development, marketing, and customer acquisition. They provide startups with a clear understanding of who they are targeting and allow them to communicate more effectively with their potential customers. By having well-defined customer personas, startups can develop appropriate marketing strategies, create targeted and personalized marketing campaigns, and choose the most effective marketing channels to reach their target audience. This helps in optimizing marketing resources and increasing the chances of converting potential customers into actual buyers. Moreover, customer personas also assist in product development by providing startups with valuable insights into what features or functionalities their target customers desire. Startups can use these insights to prioritize product improvements or develop new products that align with the needs and preferences of their customer base.

Customer Relationship Management (CRM) Software

Customer Relationship Management (CRM) software refers to a tool or application used by startups and entrepreneurs to efficiently manage and analyze interactions with their customers. It provides a systematic approach to collect, organize, and utilize information related to sales, marketing, and customer service activities. By leveraging CRM software, startups and entrepreneurs can streamline their customer-centric operations, enhance customer satisfaction, and ultimately drive business growth. At its core, CRM software serves as a centralized database that stores relevant customer data, such as contact information, purchase history, and communication preferences. This information enables startups and entrepreneurs to better understand their customers' needs, preferences, and behaviors, allowing them to deliver personalized experiences and targeted marketing campaigns. CRM software also facilitates effective lead management, allowing startups and entrepreneurs to track and prioritize potential customers throughout the sales process. By automating lead nurturing and tracking, CRM software ensures that no opportunity is missed, enabling businesses to convert leads into loyal customers more efficiently. In addition to customer data management and lead tracking, CRM software provides features to enhance customer communication and support. It allows startups and entrepreneurs to manage and track customer interactions through various channels, such as email, social media, and phone calls. This functionality enables businesses to provide timely and relevant customer support, resulting in improved customer satisfaction and loyalty. Furthermore, CRM software offers robust reporting and analytics capabilities that help startups and entrepreneurs gain valuable insights into their customer base and business performance. It allows businesses to generate custom reports, visualize data trends, and measure key performance indicators. These insights enable startups and entrepreneurs to make data-driven decisions, identify opportunities for improvement, and optimize their overall customer relationship management strategies. In conclusion, CRM software is a crucial tool for startups and entrepreneurs in managing and fostering meaningful relationships with their customers. It provides a comprehensive suite of features, integrating customer data management, lead tracking, communication management, and analytics. By leveraging CRM software, startups and entrepreneurs can streamline their customer-centric operations, enhance customer satisfaction, and drive business growth in a competitive market.

Customer Relationship Management (CRM)

Customer Relationship Management (CRM) refers to a business strategy and set of practices aimed at managing and nurturing relationships with customers. In the context of startups and entrepreneurship, CRM plays a crucial role in acquiring new customers, retaining existing ones, and fostering long-term loyalty and satisfaction. The primary objective of implementing CRM in a startup is to develop strong and meaningful relationships with customers, which leads to increased sales, customer loyalty, and enhanced profitability. It involves utilizing various tools, processes, and technologies to gather and analyze customer data, understand their needs and preferences, and ultimately improve the overall customer experience. CRM enables startups to streamline their sales and marketing efforts by providing a centralized platform for managing customer interactions and communications. It helps entrepreneurs track and monitor the entire customer journey, from initial contact to post-purchase support and follow-up. By effectively managing customer interactions, startups can identify opportunities for cross-selling and upselling, tailor their marketing campaigns, and deliver personalized experiences. Furthermore, CRM platforms provide startups with the ability to segment their customer base, allowing them to target specific customer groups with customized messages and offers. By analyzing customer data, startups can identify their most valuable customers and allocate resources effectively. This data-driven approach ensures that startups invest their time and efforts in the right customers, leading to improved customer satisfaction and higher profitability. Another key aspect of CRM in startups involves customer service and support. By centralizing customer information and interactions, CRM systems enable startups to provide efficient and personalized support to their customers. Startups can track and resolve customer issues promptly, ensuring a positive customer experience and preventing customer churn. In conclusion, CRM is a vital business strategy for startups and entrepreneurs, helping them build and maintain strong relationships with customers. It enables startups to collect and analyze customer data, enhance customer experiences, and maximize customer retention. By implementing CRM practices, startups can improve their sales and marketing efforts, boost customer satisfaction, and ultimately achieve long-term business success.

Customer Satisfaction Surveys

A customer satisfaction survey is a formal assessment conducted by startups and entrepreneurs to gauge the level of satisfaction their customers have with their products, services, and overall experience. It involves obtaining feedback directly from customers through various methods, such as online surveys, phone interviews, or in-person questionnaires. The primary purpose of a customer satisfaction survey is to obtain valuable insights and data that can help businesses identify areas for improvement and enhance customer loyalty. By gathering feedback on different aspects of their offerings, startups and entrepreneurs can gain a better understanding of customer needs, preferences, and expectations.

Customer Segmentation

Customer segmentation is a practice utilized by startups and entrepreneurs to divide their target market into distinct groups or segments based on specific characteristics, behaviors, or needs. This strategy allows businesses to better understand their customers and tailor their marketing efforts, products, and services to meet the unique requirements of each segment. By identifying the different segments within their target market, startups can effectively allocate their resources and maximize their marketing impact. The process of customer segmentation involves analyzing various factors such as demographics, psychographics, buying behavior, and preferences to categorize customers into meaningful segments. Demographic factors may include age, gender, income, education, and geographic location, while psychographic factors take into account personality traits, values, interests, and lifestyles. Understanding buying behavior involves examining purchasing patterns, motivations, and decision-making processes. Preferences refer to customers' desires, preferences, and needs in terms of product features, pricing, convenience, and customer service expectations. Segmentation enables startups and entrepreneurs to create targeted advertising campaigns, develop products and services that cater to specific customer needs, and personalize the customer experience. It helps businesses identify their most valuable customer segments and focus their resources on attracting and retaining these customers. Startups can also identify new market opportunities that may have been previously overlooked by targeting niche segments or identifying unmet needs within existing segments. In addition to effectively reaching and engaging customers, customer segmentation also enables startups to improve their operational efficiency. By understanding the varying needs of different customer segments, businesses can optimize their supply chain, inventory management, and customer support processes. Startups can design distribution channels and delivery methods that align with specific segment preferences, leading to improved customer satisfaction and loyalty. Overall, customer segmentation plays a vital role in the success of startups and entrepreneurs. It helps businesses understand their target market on a deeper level, allows for tailored marketing efforts, improves operational efficiency, and ultimately leads to higher customer satisfaction and business growth.

Data Mining Tools

Data mining tools are software applications that are utilized by startups and entrepreneurs to extract useful and valuable information from large sets of data. These tools are designed to discover patterns, relationships, and hidden insights within the data that can be used to make informed business decisions and drive growth. The primary purpose of data mining tools in the context of startups and entrepreneurship is to leverage the power of data to gain a competitive advantage. Startups typically have limited resources and face numerous challenges in the early stages of their journey. By using data mining tools, startups can analyze vast amounts of data collected from various sources, such as customer interactions, website traffic, social media, and market trends. Data mining tools provide startups and entrepreneurs with the ability to transform raw data into actionable intelligence. These tools utilize different techniques, including statistical analysis, machine learning, clustering, and visualization, to identify patterns and trends within the data. By uncovering hidden insights, startups can make data-driven decisions and develop effective strategies to improve their products or services, target specific customer segments, optimize marketing campaigns, and enhance overall operational efficiency. One of the key advantages of data mining tools for startups is their ability to predict future outcomes based on historical data. By analyzing past trends and patterns, these tools can provide valuable insights into potential future scenarios, allowing startups to anticipate market shifts, mitigate risks, and seize new opportunities. This predictive analysis can be instrumental in achieving sustainable growth and maintaining a competitive edge in the highly dynamic startup ecosystem. In conclusion, data mining tools are invaluable assets for startups and entrepreneurs, enabling them to analyze large volumes of data, uncover hidden insights, and make data-driven decisions. By leveraging the power of these tools, startups can gain a competitive advantage, optimize their business operations, and drive growth in a data-centric world.

Debt Financing

Debt financing refers to the practice of raising capital for a startup or entrepreneurial venture by borrowing funds from external sources, typically in the form of loans or lines of credit. Unlike equity financing, where ownership shares are sold in exchange for funding, debt financing involves borrowing money that must be repaid over a specified period, often with interest. For startups and entrepreneurs, debt financing can be an attractive option for several reasons. First and foremost, it allows them to maintain full ownership and control over their company. By borrowing funds instead of selling equity, entrepreneurs can avoid diluting their ownership stake and retain decision-making authority. Additionally, debt financing provides startups with a predictable repayment structure. The terms of a loan or line of credit typically outline the amount to be repaid each month or quarter, as well as the interest rate applied to the borrowed funds. This allows entrepreneurs to plan and budget accordingly, giving them greater financial stability and confidence in managing their business. Furthermore, debt financing can help establish a credit history for the startup. By making regular, timely payments on their debt obligations, entrepreneurs can build a positive credit profile, which can facilitate future borrowing and potentially secure more favorable terms. This is particularly important for early-stage startups that may not yet have a proven track record or substantial assets to leverage. However, it's crucial to note that debt financing also carries certain risks and considerations. Taking on excessive debt can strain a startup's cash flow and restrict its ability to invest in growth initiatives. Repayment obligations can become burdensome, especially if a business is not generating sufficient revenue or facing unexpected challenges. In conclusion, debt financing can be an effective means for startups and entrepreneurs to raise capital while maintaining ownership and control over their company. It offers predictability in repayment, helps establish credit history, and enables strategic financial planning. However, entrepreneurs must carefully weigh the potential benefits against the risks associated with debt and ensure that the borrowed funds can be repaid without compromising the viability and growth potential of their startup.

Debt Round

Debt round refers to a specific stage of funding in startup financing where a company raises capital by taking on debt instead of selling equity. This form of financing allows startups to borrow money from lenders with the understanding that it will be repaid with interest over a predetermined period of time. During a debt round, entrepreneurs have the option to secure loans from various sources, including venture debt funds, banks, or even individual investors. The borrowed funds can be used to fuel growth initiatives, such as expanding operations, investing in research and development, or launching marketing campaigns. Unlike equity financing, where ownership stakes are sold in exchange for funding, debt financing does not dilute the ownership of the startup founders or existing shareholders.

Debt-To-Equity Conversion

Debt-to-Equity Conversion is a financial transaction in which a startup or entrepreneur converts their existing debt into equity shares in their company. This conversion allows the company to reduce its debt burden and potentially improve its financial stability. In the context of startups and entrepreneurship, debt financing is a common method used to obtain funding. Entrepreneurs often take on debt in the form of loans or borrowings from various sources such as banks, financial institutions, or private investors. While debt financing can provide immediate capital to fuel business growth, it also increases the company's financial obligations in terms of interest payments and repayment schedules. At times, a startup may encounter financial challenges or may prefer to reduce its debt burden. In such situations, debt-to-equity conversion can offer a viable solution. This conversion involves negotiating with the company's creditors to convert the outstanding debt into equity shares in the business. This conversion benefits both the startup or entrepreneur and the creditors. By converting debt into equity, the company can improve its financial standing by reducing the debt load and potentially enhancing profitability. Additionally, it allows the company to distribute the risk among various stakeholders and can attract new investors who may be more willing to invest in equity rather than debt. On the other hand, creditors may agree to the conversion if they believe that the company's prospects are improving and they have confidence in the entrepreneur's ability to generate returns on investment. However, it's important to note that not all debt can be converted into equity. The terms of the debt agreements, including covenants and restrictions, may impose limitations on the conversion process. Additionally, the conversion may dilute the existing ownership stake of the entrepreneur or other shareholders, which could impact their control and decision-making power within the company. In conclusion, debt-to-equity conversion is a financial strategy that allows startups and entrepreneurs to convert their existing debt into equity shares in their company. It can help improve the financial stability of the business and distribute risk among stakeholders. However, it's crucial to carefully evaluate the terms and implications of the conversion before proceeding.

Debt-To-Equity Ratio Analysis

The debt-to-equity ratio is a financial metric used in startup and entrepreneurship to assess the level of financial leverage or risk taken on by a company. It measures the proportion of a company's financing that comes from debt compared to equity. The debt-to-equity ratio is calculated by dividing the total debt of a company by its total equity. Debt refers to the amount of money borrowed or owed by the company, such as bank loans, bonds, or other forms of debt financing. Equity, on the other hand, represents the ownership stake or investment in the company by its shareholders or owners.

Debt-To-Equity Ratio

The debt-to-equity ratio is a financial metric used in startup and entrepreneurship to assess the proportion of debt and equity financing in a company's capital structure. Essentially, the debt-to-equity ratio provides insight into the company's leverage or reliance on borrowed funds compared to funds contributed by shareholders. It is a measure of financial risk and can help investors, creditors, and other stakeholders evaluate a company's solvency and ability to meet its financial obligations.

Debt-To-Equity Swap Agreement Terms Negotiation And Execution

A debt-to-equity swap agreement is a formal contract negotiated and executed between a startup and its creditors, typically in the context of financial distress or the need for capital restructuring. In this agreement, the startup and its creditors agree to convert a portion of the startup's outstanding debt into equity ownership. During the negotiation phase of the agreement, the startup and the creditors engage in discussions to determine the terms and conditions of the debt-to-equity swap. The key aspects of negotiation include the conversion ratio, which defines the number of equity shares the creditors will receive for each unit of debt converted, and any additional terms or conditions related to the equity ownership. Once the negotiation is complete, the agreement is executed, formalizing the terms agreed upon by both parties. The execution typically involves signing the agreement and filing the necessary legal forms to effectuate the debt-to-equity swap. From the perspective of the startup, a debt-to-equity swap agreement provides several potential benefits. Firstly, it allows the startup to reduce its debt burden, improving its financial position and potentially restoring viability. Secondly, it provides the startup with an opportunity to bring in new equity investors or align the interests of existing shareholders and creditors, fostering a stronger capital structure. Lastly, it enables the startup to potentially benefit from the expertise and networks of the creditors-turned-shareholders, facilitating future growth and development. On the other hand, creditors may view a debt-to-equity swap as a way to mitigate potential losses and convert their illiquid debt holdings into equity, which may provide them with an opportunity to recover the value of their investment in the long run. In conclusion, a debt-to-equity swap agreement is a crucial instrument in the realm of startups and entrepreneurship. It enables startups to restructure their capital and improve their financial position, while also providing creditors with an alternative avenue for potential recovery.

Debt-To-Equity Swap Agreement Terms Negotiation

A debt-to-equity swap agreement is a formal negotiation between a startup and its creditors regarding the terms of converting debt into equity. This type of agreement is typically pursued when a startup is struggling with its existing debt obligations and is seeking to improve its financial health by reducing its debt burden. The negotiation involves various key terms that both parties need to agree upon in order to execute the debt-to-equity swap. These terms include: 1. Conversion Ratio: The conversion ratio determines the number of equity shares that will be issued in exchange for a specific amount of debt. This ratio is often based on the fair market value of the startup's equity at the time of the agreement. 2. Valuation: The valuation of the startup is crucial in determining the fair market value of its equity. Both parties must agree on this valuation methodology to ensure a fair exchange of debt for equity. 3. Voting Rights: When debt is converted into equity, the creditors become shareholders and gain certain voting rights in the startup. The negotiation involves determining the extent of these voting rights, including any limitations or special rights given to the creditors. 4. Seniority: The negotiation also addresses the seniority of the converted debt. Creditors may negotiate to have their equity shares ranked higher in priority in case of liquidation or other events that trigger repayment. 5. Lock-up Period: A lock-up period refers to a specified length of time during which the creditors cannot sell or transfer their equity shares. This term protects the startup by ensuring stability and preventing any sudden influx of new shareholders. 6. Subordination: In some cases, creditors may agree to subordinate their equity to existing shareholders or new investors. This ensures that the startup can attract additional investment without affecting the rights of the existing shareholders. By negotiating and finalizing these terms, the startup and its creditors reach an agreement that allows for the conversion of debt into equity. This agreement provides the startup with the opportunity to improve its financial position and align the interests of its creditors with the success of the business.

Debt-To-Equity Swap Agreement Terms

A debt-to-equity swap agreement is a financial arrangement commonly used in the context of startups and entrepreneurship. It involves the conversion of debt, typically in the form of loans or bonds, into equity, which represents ownership in the company. Under this agreement, the startup or entrepreneur takes on debt from creditors, such as banks or investors, as a means of raising capital. However, in situations where the company faces financial difficulties or is struggling with its debt obligations, a debt-to-equity swap may be negotiated. A debt-to-equity swap agreement typically sets out the terms and conditions related to the conversion of debt into equity. These terms may include the conversion ratio, which determines the number of equity shares that will be issued in exchange for the debt. The conversion ratio is usually determined based on the fair market value of the company's shares or a predetermined formula agreed upon by the parties involved. In addition to the conversion ratio, the agreement may outline any additional rights or privileges associated with the equity shares issued through the swap. This may include voting rights, dividend entitlements, or any other benefits that come with being a shareholder in the company. Furthermore, the agreement may specify any conditions or restrictions on the conversion of debt into equity. This could include minimum thresholds for the amount of debt that must be converted, certain timelines for completion of the swap, or any regulatory or legal requirements that need to be met. Overall, a debt-to-equity swap agreement provides a mechanism for startups and entrepreneurs to restructure their debt obligations and strengthen their financial position. By converting debt into equity, the company can reduce its overall debt burden, potentially improve its creditworthiness, and provide an opportunity for creditors to become shareholders and participate in the company's future growth and success.

Debt-To-Equity Swap Agreement

A debt-to-equity swap agreement is a contractual agreement between a startup company and its creditors, whereby the company converts its outstanding debt into equity, or ownership shares, in the company. This agreement is commonly used in the field of startup and entrepreneurship when a company is facing financial challenges and needs to restructure its debt obligations in order to continue its operations. In a debt-to-equity swap agreement, the startup company enters into negotiations with its creditors, typically banks or financial institutions, to reach a mutual agreement on converting the debt into equity. The terms of the agreement are outlined in a legal contract that specifies the amount of debt that will be converted, the conversion ratio, and any other conditions or requirements that need to be met. The main purpose of a debt-to-equity swap agreement is to provide the startup company with a financial lifeline by reducing its debt burden and improving its cash flow. By converting debt into equity, the company can strengthen its capital structure and reduce its financial obligations, which can in turn attract new investors and increase the company's chances of raising additional funding. Furthermore, a debt-to-equity swap agreement can also provide benefits to the creditors. By converting debt into equity, the creditors become partial owners of the company and have the potential to earn profits through dividends or capital appreciation. This can be a more favorable outcome for the creditors compared to trying to recover the debt through other means, such as bankruptcy proceedings. It is important to note that a debt-to-equity swap agreement is a complex financial transaction that requires careful consideration and negotiation. Both the startup company and its creditors need to evaluate the risks and benefits, and ensure that the terms of the agreement are fair and equitable for all parties involved. Additionally, the legal and tax implications of the agreement should be thoroughly examined and understood. In conclusion, a debt-to-equity swap agreement is a strategic financial tool used by startups and entrepreneurs to restructure their debt obligations and improve their financial position. By converting debt into equity, the company can alleviate its debt burden and attract new investors, while providing potential benefits to its creditors. However, it is crucial to seek professional advice and conduct thorough due diligence before entering into such an agreement.

Debt-To-Equity Swap Process Flow And Execution

A debt-to-equity swap is a process in which a startup or entrepreneur converts their outstanding debt into equity, resulting in a change in the capital structure of the company. This swap is typically initiated when a company is facing financial difficulties and is unable to service its debt obligations. By converting debt into equity, the company can improve its financial position and reduce its debt burden. The debt-to-equity swap process flow typically involves the following steps: 1. Evaluation: The company evaluates its current financial situation and assesses whether a debt-to-equity swap is a viable solution. This includes analyzing the amount of debt, the company's cash flow, and the impact on existing shareholders. 2. Negotiation: The company enters into discussions with its creditors to negotiate the terms of the debt-to-equity swap. This includes determining the conversion ratio, which determines how much debt will be converted into equity. 3. Agreement: Once the terms of the debt-to-equity swap are agreed upon, the company and its creditors formalize the agreement through legal documentation. This includes drafting a debt-to-equity swap agreement and obtaining the necessary approvals from shareholders and regulatory authorities. 4. Conversion: The company converts the debt into equity as per the agreed terms. This may involve issuing new shares to the creditors or converting existing shares into equity. The conversion process may also involve adjustments to the company's capital structure and ownership rights. 5. Post-conversion: After the debt-to-equity swap is completed, the company's capital structure will be modified, with the creditors becoming shareholders. The company will have reduced debt obligations and improved financial stability, allowing it to focus on its operations and future growth. In conclusion, the debt-to-equity swap process is a strategic financial maneuver for startups and entrepreneurs to improve their financial position by converting debt into equity. It involves evaluating the financial situation, negotiating with creditors, formalizing the agreement, converting the debt, and adjusting the capital structure. This process can help alleviate financial difficulties and provide a more stable foundation for the company's growth and success.

Debt-To-Equity Swap Process Flow

A debt-to-equity swap process refers to a transaction where a company exchanges its existing debt obligations for equity ownership. This process is commonly used by startups and entrepreneurs to improve their financial position and reduce their debt burden. It typically involves negotiation and agreement between the company and its creditors, followed by the conversion of debt into shares of the company's common stock. The debt-to-equity swap process typically begins with a company facing financial difficulties or a high level of indebtedness. The company may approach its creditors to negotiate a debt restructuring or repayment plan. In some cases, the creditors may agree to convert a portion or all of the company's debt into equity. This can be an attractive option for both the company and its creditors, as it allows the company to reduce its debt obligations and improve its balance sheet, while the creditors have the potential to benefit from the future growth and profitability of the company.

Debt-To-Equity Swap Process

A debt-to-equity swap is a process in startup and entrepreneurship where a company exchanges its debt obligations for equity ownership. This strategy is usually employed when a company is facing financial distress or is burdened with high levels of debt that it cannot repay.During a debt-to-equity swap, the company negotiates with its creditors to convert a portion or all of its outstanding debt into shares of the company's stock. This swap allows the company to reduce its debt burden and improve its financial position by strengthening its equity base.

Debt-To-Equity Swap Ratio Analysis

A debt-to-equity swap ratio analysis is a financial tool used in the context of startup and entrepreneurship to assess the relative value of debt and equity in a company. It helps to determine the appropriate exchange ratio between debt and equity when converting debt into equity. The debt-to-equity swap ratio analysis takes into account various factors such as the financial health of the company, its future prospects, and the prevailing market conditions. It aims to strike a fair balance between the interests of the creditors and the shareholders while restructuring the company's capital structure.

Debt-To-Equity Swap Ratio

Debt-to-Equity Swap Ratio refers to the proportion at which a startup or entrepreneur converts its debt into equity shares. It is a financial transaction that occurs between a startup or entrepreneur and its creditors. In this swap, the startup or entrepreneur offers its creditors the option to convert their outstanding debt into equity ownership in the company. This ratio is a crucial decision-making tool for startups facing financial distress or difficulties in servicing their debt obligations. By offering the debt-to-equity swap, startups can reduce their debt burden, improve their liquidity position, and potentially attract new investors.

Debt-To-Equity Swap Terms

A debt-to-equity swap is a financial transaction commonly used in the context of startups and entrepreneurship. It involves converting a portion or all of a company's outstanding debt into equity ownership. This swap is typically negotiated between the company and its creditors as a means to improve the company's financial position and reduce its debt burden. The terms of a debt-to-equity swap can vary depending on the specific circumstances and agreement between the parties involved. However, some common elements can be observed. Firstly, the debt being converted into equity can consist of various forms, such as loans, bonds, or other forms of debt instruments. The amount of debt being converted is usually determined based on the agreed-upon terms of the swap and the company's financial needs. In some cases, all outstanding debt may be converted, while in others, only a portion may be swapped. Secondly, the equity being issued to the creditor or creditors participating in the swap represents ownership in the company. This can take the form of shares or other units of ownership, depending on the legal structure of the company. The value of the equity being issued is calculated based on factors such as the company's valuation, market conditions, and negotiations between the parties. Thirdly, the debt-to-equity swap may also involve additional terms and conditions. For example, the agreement may stipulate that the creditor is subject to certain restrictions or limitations in terms of selling or transferring their equity ownership. Additionally, the agreement may include provisions for the creditor's involvement in the company's decision-making processes, such as board representation or voting rights. In summary, a debt-to-equity swap in the context of startups and entrepreneurship is a financial transaction where a company converts some or all of its outstanding debt into equity ownership. The specific terms of the swap can vary but typically involve converting different forms of debt into shares or units of ownership. This transaction is often used to improve the company's financial position and reduce its debt burden, while providing the creditor with a stake in the company's future success.

Debt-To-Equity Swap Transaction

A debt-to-equity swap transaction in the context of startup and entrepreneurship refers to a financial arrangement where a company converts its existing debt obligations into equity ownership for its creditors. This transaction typically occurs when a startup or entrepreneur is facing financial distress and is unable to meet its debt obligations. During a debt-to-equity swap, the company negotiates with its creditors to agree on the terms of the conversion. The creditors, who are owed money by the company, agree to exchange their outstanding debt for shares or ownership in the company. This allows the creditors to become shareholders in the company, with the hope of realizing future gains and the potential for a return on their investment.

Debt-To-Equity Swap

A debt-to-equity swap refers to a financial transaction in the context of startup and entrepreneurship where a company's debt is converted into equity. This swap typically involves the company's creditors agreeing to cancel a portion or all of the outstanding debt in exchange for shares or ownership in the company. Startups and entrepreneurs often turn to debt-to-equity swaps as a strategic move to alleviate financial burdens, improve their balance sheets, and attract potential investors. By converting debt into equity, companies can reduce their overall indebtedness, enhance their creditworthiness, and strengthen their financial position.

Decacorn

A decacorn is a term used in the startup and entrepreneurship world to refer to a privately-held company that has reached a valuation of $10 billion or more. The concept of the decacorn was coined as the natural progression from the unicorn phenomenon, which refers to startups valued at $1 billion or more. Decacorns are extremely rare and represent the crème de la crème of the startup ecosystem. These companies have achieved rapid, exponential growth and have proven to be highly valuable and successful in a relatively short period of time. The term "decacorn" is derived from the words "decade" and "unicorn," illustrating the idea that these companies have taken less than a decade to achieve the remarkable valuation milestone.

Demand Generation

Demand generation refers to the strategic marketing process aimed at creating awareness and interest in a product or service, with the ultimate goal of turning prospects into customers. It encompasses a series of activities and tactics designed to generate and nurture leads, create brand recognition, and drive customer acquisition. In the context of startups and entrepreneurship, demand generation plays a crucial role in the initial growth and success of a new venture. Startups often face the challenge of building a customer base and establishing themselves in a competitive market. This is where demand generation comes into play, helping startups generate demand for their offering and create a pipeline of potential customers. The process of demand generation typically starts with identifying the target market and understanding the specific needs and preferences of potential customers. Startups need to conduct thorough market research and competitive analysis to gain insights into the market landscape and develop effective marketing strategies. Once the target market is identified, startups can utilize various tactics to generate demand. These may include content marketing, social media marketing, search engine optimization, email marketing, and online advertising. The key objective is to create compelling and relevant content that resonates with the target audience, educates them about the product or service, and addresses their pain points and challenges. Furthermore, startups can leverage lead generation techniques to capture the contact information of potential customers and nurture them through the sales funnel. This involves offering valuable content assets, such as whitepapers, ebooks, or webinars, in exchange for contact details. Startups can then use email marketing campaigns or personalized outreach to engage with leads and guide them towards making a purchase decision. In addition to acquiring new customers, demand generation also focuses on retaining existing customers and fostering brand loyalty. Startups can implement customer retention strategies, such as providing exceptional customer service, offering loyalty programs, and delivering a superior product experience, to ensure customer satisfaction and encourage repeat business. In conclusion, demand generation is a critical element of startup and entrepreneurial success. By effectively generating and nurturing demand, startups can build a loyal customer base, drive revenue growth, and establish a strong brand presence in the market.

Design Thinking

Design Thinking, in the context of startup and entrepreneurship, refers to a problem-solving approach that focuses on understanding and meeting the needs of customers in order to create successful and innovative products or services. At its core, Design Thinking is a human-centered methodology that promotes empathy, collaboration, and experimentation. It allows entrepreneurs to effectively tackle complex problems and challenges by emphasizing the importance of understanding and empathizing with the end-users or customers who will ultimately benefit from the startup's offerings.

Digital Advertising Platforms

Digital Advertising Platforms are online platforms that enable businesses and entrepreneurs to create, manage, and optimize their online advertising campaigns. These platforms provide a range of tools and functionalities to target specific audiences, track campaign performance, and maximize the return on investment (ROI) of advertising efforts. Startups and entrepreneurs can leverage digital advertising platforms to reach their target customers more effectively and efficiently. These platforms allow businesses to create ads using various formats, such as text, images, videos, or interactive media, and distribute them across multiple digital channels, including search engines, social media platforms, websites, and mobile apps. Digital advertising platforms offer advanced targeting options that allow startups and entrepreneurs to define specific demographics, interests, behaviors, and geographical locations of their target audience. This helps in delivering ads to the right people at the right time, increasing the chances of conversions and customer acquisition. These platforms also provide powerful analytics and reporting tools, enabling startups and entrepreneurs to monitor the performance of their advertising campaigns in real-time. They can track key metrics such as impressions, clicks, conversions, and cost per acquisition (CPA). This data-driven approach helps businesses to optimize their campaigns, identify underperforming areas, and make data-backed decisions to improve ROI. In addition, digital advertising platforms often offer built-in optimization features, such as automated bidding and ad placement algorithms. These features leverage machine learning and artificial intelligence to automatically adjust bidding strategies, target the most relevant audiences, and optimize ad placements for maximum visibility and engagement. Overall, digital advertising platforms play a crucial role in the success of startups and entrepreneurs by providing them with the necessary tools and capabilities to effectively advertise their products or services online. These platforms help businesses reach a wider audience, increase brand visibility, drive website traffic, generate leads, and ultimately grow their customer base.

Digital Entrepreneurship

Digital Entrepreneurship refers to the process of creating and managing a business in the digital realm, leveraging technology and the internet to develop innovative products, services, and strategies. It involves using digital platforms, tools, and techniques to reach a wider audience, streamline operations, and drive business growth. Startups and entrepreneurs who embrace digital entrepreneurship focus on harnessing digital technologies, such as mobile applications, e-commerce platforms, social media, and data analytics, to disrupt traditional industries or create entirely new markets. They capitalize on the opportunities offered by the digital economy, which is characterized by fast-paced innovation, global connectivity, and constant evolution. In the context of startups, digital entrepreneurship encompasses the utilization of digital channels to validate business ideas, build a customer base, and scale operations. Rather than relying solely on traditional brick-and-mortar establishments, startups create online platforms or mobile applications to showcase their products or services, interact with customers, and facilitate transactions. Additionally, digital entrepreneurship often involves the use of technology-driven business models, such as Software as a Service (SaaS), platform-based marketplaces, and subscription-based services. These models enable startups to provide scalable and flexible solutions, as well as generate recurring revenue streams. Furthermore, digital entrepreneurship is characterized by agility and adaptability. Startups constantly experiment with various digital marketing strategies to reach their target audience effectively. They analyze data to gain insights into customer preferences, behaviors, and market trends, allowing them to tailor their offerings and strategies accordingly. Overall, digital entrepreneurship is a dynamic and forward-thinking approach to startup and entrepreneurship. It embraces the opportunities and challenges of the digital era, leveraging technology and innovation to create, grow, and sustain businesses in the digital landscape.

Digital Marketing Analytics

Digital marketing analytics refers to the process of analyzing, measuring, and interpreting data from various digital marketing channels to gain insights and make informed decisions. It plays a crucial role in startup and entrepreneurship by enabling them to understand the effectiveness and impact of their online marketing efforts. Startup and entrepreneurial ventures often operate with limited resources and tight budgets. Therefore, it becomes important for them to allocate their marketing budgets effectively and efficiently. Digital marketing analytics helps in achieving this by providing valuable data and insights about the performance of different marketing campaigns, channels, and activities. By analyzing digital marketing data, startups can track key performance indicators (KPIs) such as website traffic, conversion rates, customer engagement, and return on investment (ROI). These insights help them identify what works and what doesn't in their marketing strategy, allowing them to make data-driven decisions and optimize their marketing efforts. Furthermore, digital marketing analytics provides startups with a deeper understanding of their target audience. Through data analysis, startups can segment their audience based on demographics, behaviors, and preferences. This knowledge allows them to create personalized and targeted marketing campaigns that resonate with their potential customers, increasing the chances of conversion and customer acquisition. In addition to monitoring ongoing marketing campaigns, digital marketing analytics also helps startups in assessing the overall health and growth of their business. They can evaluate key business metrics such as customer acquisition cost (CAC), customer lifetime value (CLV), and customer churn rate. By understanding these metrics, startups can make data-backed decisions on scaling their business, refining their product or service offerings, and maximizing customer lifetime value. In conclusion, digital marketing analytics is a vital tool for startups and entrepreneurs in today's digital landscape. By leveraging data and insights from various digital marketing channels, startups can optimize their marketing efforts, improve customer targeting, and make informed decisions that drive growth and success.

Digital Marketing

Digital marketing is a strategic approach used by startups and entrepreneurs to promote their products or services through online channels. It encompasses a wide range of tactics and techniques that leverage digital platforms and technologies to reach and engage a target audience, ultimately driving business growth and success. Startups and entrepreneurs understand the importance of digital marketing in today's highly competitive business landscape. It allows them to connect with potential customers, build brand awareness, and establish a strong online presence. Through various digital marketing channels such as search engines, social media platforms, email marketing, content marketing, and online advertising, startups can effectively market their offerings and generate leads. One of the key benefits of digital marketing for startups and entrepreneurs is its cost-effectiveness compared to traditional marketing methods. With limited budgets, startups can allocate their resources strategically and run targeted digital marketing campaigns to reach their specific target audience. This allows them to optimize their marketing spend, maximize return on investment, and achieve measurable results. Another advantage of digital marketing for startups is its ability to provide valuable insights and data. Through various digital marketing tools and analytics platforms, startups can track and measure the performance of their marketing efforts in real-time. They can gather data on website traffic, user engagement, conversion rates, and other key metrics to gain insights into customer behavior and preferences. This data-driven approach helps startups make informed decisions, refine their marketing strategies, and continuously optimize their campaigns for better results. In conclusion, digital marketing is an essential component of startup and entrepreneurial success. By leveraging digital platforms and technologies, startups can effectively reach their

71

target audience, promote their products or services, and drive business growth. With its cost-effectiveness, measurability, and data-driven approach, digital marketing enables startups to compete and thrive in today's digital age.

Digital Product Development

Digital product development refers to the process of creating and improving digital products, such as mobile applications, websites, and software, with the goal of meeting the needs and demands of customers in a digital market. It is a crucial aspect of startup and entrepreneurship as it involves the innovation and creation of digital solutions that can drive business growth and success in today's technology-driven world. A startup or entrepreneur embarks on a digital product development journey to identify, design, develop, and deliver digital solutions that can solve a problem or fulfill a market need. This process typically involves various stages, including market research, idea generation, prototyping, testing, and refinement, to ensure that the final product is user-friendly, scalable, and meets market expectations. The success of a startup or entrepreneur heavily depends on their ability to develop and launch innovative and competitive digital products that can capture the attention and interest of customers. Through digital product development, startups and entrepreneurs can differentiate themselves from competitors, attract users, generate revenue, and build a strong brand presence. One of the key aspects of digital product development is understanding and analyzing customer needs and behaviors. Startups and entrepreneurs must conduct thorough market research to identify target audiences, their pain points, and the features and functionalities that would add value to their lives. By gaining insights into customer preferences and behavior, startups can make informed decisions about product design, user experience, and marketing strategies. Additionally, digital product development involves the utilization of various technologies, tools, and frameworks to bring ideas to life. This includes programming languages, design software, project management tools, and agile development methodologies. Startups and entrepreneurs need to stay updated with the latest trends and advancements in the digital landscape to leverage these resources effectively and efficiently. In summary, digital product development plays a crucial role in the startup and entrepreneurial ecosystem. It involves the creation, improvement, and delivery of innovative digital products that can solve problems and meet market needs. By focusing on customer demands, leveraging technology, and staying up-to-date with industry trends, startups and entrepreneurs can develop successful digital products that drive business growth and profitability.

Dilution

Dilution is a concept in the context of startup and entrepreneurship that refers to the decrease in the ownership percentage of existing shareholders due to the issuance of new shares. When a startup requires additional capital to fund its growth, it often raises funds from external investors, such as venture capitalists or angel investors, by selling them a portion of the company's ownership in the form of shares. This issuance of new shares results in the dilution of the ownership percentage of existing shareholders, including the founders, early employees, and initial investors.

Disruption Strategy

A disruption strategy, in the context of startups and entrepreneurship, refers to a deliberate approach taken by companies to challenge and transform existing industries or markets through the introduction of innovative products, services, or business models. It involves identifying a gap or inefficiency in the current market landscape and developing solutions that not only meet customer needs but also outperform traditional industry players. Disruption strategies typically involve leveraging emerging technologies, changing consumer behaviors, or removing barriers to entry. Startups and entrepreneurs who employ this strategy seek to gain a competitive advantage by offering something new, different, or more affordable than what is currently available in the market. One key characteristic of a disruption strategy is the focus on exponential rather than incremental innovation. It aims to fundamentally change the way business is conducted within an industry, often leading to the displacement of well-established companies or business models. Disruptors often have a strong vision, a deep understanding of customer pain points, and the ability to anticipate and adapt to market shifts. Another aspect of disruption strategies is the reliance on agile and flexible operations. Startups and entrepreneurs need to be nimble and responsive to changes in the market or competitive landscape to effectively capitalize on disruptive opportunities. This may involve continuous experimentation, iteration, and a high tolerance for failure. A successful disruption strategy involves not just developing a groundbreaking product or service, but also creating a sustainable business model around it. Entrepreneurs need to consider factors such as scalability, revenue generation, and long-term viability to ensure the longevity of their disruptive venture. Overall, a disruption strategy in startup and entrepreneurship is a strategic approach that aims to transform industries by challenging existing norms, introducing innovative solutions, and capitalizing on emerging opportunities. It requires a combination of creativity, market insight, and execution excellence to effectively disrupt and reshape established markets.

Disruptive Innovation

Disruptive innovation, in the context of startups and entrepreneurship, refers to the introduction of a new product, service, or business model that fundamentally changes the traditional way of doing things in an industry. It often targets underserved or overlooked market segments and has the potential to create a significant impact on existing market leaders. A disruptive innovation typically begins as a small-scale venture with limited resources and challenges the status quo by offering a simpler, more accessible, or more affordable alternative to established products or services. It leverages emerging technologies, unique approaches, or unconventional business models to gain a competitive advantage and attract a different customer base. Unlike sustaining innovations that improve upon existing products or services, disruptive innovations have the potential to completely transform industries by creating new markets or reshaping existing ones. They often disrupt established players who have become complacent and focused on serving their existing customers and needs, rather than exploring new opportunities. Startups and entrepreneurs are particularly well-suited to driving disruptive innovation. With their agility and flexibility, they have the ability to quickly identify market gaps, experiment with novel ideas, and pivot their strategies based on early feedback and market realities. They often challenge conventional wisdom and industry norms, seeking to create breakthroughs that can revolutionize entire industries. Successful disruptive innovations often follow a disruptive cycle. They start by targeting low-end or niche markets with a product or service that is initially inferior to existing alternatives in terms of quality or performance. However, over time, as the disruptive innovation improves and gains more adoption, it begins to reach mainstream customers and eventually surpasses the capabilities of established solutions. This cycle represents a pattern of disruptive innovation disrupting incorporated incumbents. In conclusion, disruptive innovation is a powerful concept in the world of startups and entrepreneurship. It describes the introduction of new products, services, or business models that challenge established norms and create significant market disruptions. Startups and entrepreneurs play a crucial role in driving disruptive innovation, relying on their innovative thinking, agility, and ability to identify market opportunities that others may overlook.

Disruptive Technology

A disruptive technology refers to an innovation that creates a significant shift in an existing market by introducing a new product or service that disrupts the established players. This term is commonly used in the context of startups and entrepreneurship as disruptive technologies often provide unique opportunities for new ventures to gain a competitive advantage and challenge incumbents. Disruptive technologies can transform industries by fundamentally altering the way products or services are created, delivered, or consumed. They typically offer improved functionality, greater convenience, lower costs, or a combination of these factors compared to existing solutions. In many cases, disruptive technologies leverage advancements in areas such as computing power, connectivity, data analysis, or materials science.

Drag-Along Rights

Drag-Along Rights, in the context of startup and entrepreneurship, refer to a provision typically included in a company's shareholder agreement or the articles of association. These rights grant majority shareholders, commonly the founders or the venture capitalists, the power to "drag-along" minority shareholders, such as other investors or early-stage employees, in the event of an acquisition or sale of the company. When a drag-along right is exercised, it compels the minority shareholders to sell their shares on the same terms and conditions as the majority shareholders. This provision aims to protect the majority shareholders' interest by ensuring that a potential buyer acquires the entire company rather than dealing with multiple shareholders separately. Additionally, it streamlines the acquisition process and reduces the potential for conflicts among the shareholders.

Drag-Along Tag-Along

The terms "drag-along" and "tag-along" are commonly used in the context of startup and entrepreneurship to refer to clauses in shareholder agreements that dictate how shares can be sold or transferred in the event of certain transactions. A drag-along clause is a provision that allows majority shareholders to force minority shareholders to sell their shares in the event that a significant transaction occurs, such as the sale of the company. This provision is designed to protect the interests of majority shareholders by ensuring that they can sell their shares without being impeded by minority shareholders who may not want to sell. It is typically used to facilitate the acquisition or consolidation of a startup by a larger company or investor. On the other hand, a tag-along clause is a provision that gives minority shareholders the right to "tag along" with majority shareholders and sell their shares on the same terms and conditions as the majority shareholders. This provision protects the interests of minority shareholders by allowing them to participate in the same transaction and receive the same price per share as the majority shareholders. It is typically used to prevent minority shareholders from being left behind or disadvantaged in the event of a sale or transfer of shares. Both drag-along and tag-along clauses are important in startup and entrepreneurial ventures as they help ensure fairness and protect the interests of shareholders. These provisions provide a mechanism for majority shareholders to sell their shares and for minority shareholders to receive a fair price and not be forced into unfavorable transactions. They also provide a level of certainty and transparency in the event of a sale or transfer of shares, which can be critical in attracting investors and securing financing for the startup. In summary, drag-along and tag-along clauses are provisions in shareholder agreements that dictate how shares can be sold or transferred in certain transactions. A drag-along clause allows majority shareholders to force minority shareholders to sell their shares, while a tag-along clause allows minority shareholders to sell their shares on the same terms as the majority shareholders. These clauses are important in ensuring fairness and protecting the interests of shareholders in startup and entrepreneurial ventures.

Due Diligence Checklist

Due diligence is a process performed by entrepreneurs and investors to thoroughly investigate and assess the viability and potential risks of a startup before making any investment or partnership decisions. This comprehensive evaluation involves conducting a detailed analysis of various aspects of the business, including financials, operations, legal and regulatory compliance, intellectual property, and market potential. The due diligence checklist serves as a guideline to ensure that all relevant information is gathered and assessed during the due diligence process. It helps entrepreneurs and investors systematically review and verify essential information about the startup, identify any potential red flags or obstacles, and make an informed decision based on the findings.

Due Diligence Process

Due diligence process refers to a comprehensive investigation and assessment of a startup or entrepreneurial venture that potential investors, partners, or acquirers undertake to gather relevant information and evaluate the business's viability, potential risks, and financial prospects. This process involves conducting a thorough examination of various aspects of the startup or entrepreneurship, including its operations, financials, legal and regulatory compliance, intellectual property, market position, competitive landscape, and management team. The purpose is to gather sufficient information to make informed decisions and mitigate potential risks before entering into any business deal or investment.

Due Diligence

Due diligence in the context of startup and entrepreneurship refers to the comprehensive research and analysis conducted by investors or entrepreneurs to evaluate a business opportunity before making a financial commitment. It is a process of thoroughly examining the potential risks, opportunities, and challenges associated with a startup or an entrepreneurial venture. Diligence in this context involves scrutinizing various aspects of the business such as the market, industry trends, competition, business model, financials, intellectual property, management team, and legal and regulatory compliance. This examination helps investors or entrepreneurs make informed decisions about investing in or pursuing a specific startup opportunity.

E-Commerce

E-commerce, short for electronic commerce, refers to the buying and selling of goods and services over the internet. It involves conducting business transactions electronically, allowing entrepreneurs to reach a wider audience, streamline processes, and create new revenue streams. E-commerce has become increasingly popular among startups and entrepreneurs due to its numerous advantages. By setting up an online store or platform, startups can efficiently cater to customers' needs without the limitations of physical locations. This eliminates the need for a traditional brick-and-mortar store and reduces associated costs such as rent and utilities. Furthermore, e-commerce enables entrepreneurs to reach a global market. With internet access prevalent in many parts of the world, businesses have the opportunity to connect with customers from different regions, expanding their customer base and potential for growth. This international presence also allows startups to adapt to changing market trends and customer preferences, leveraging their agility to succeed. One of the key advantages of e-commerce for startups and entrepreneurs is the ability to personalize the customer experience. Through data analytics and targeted marketing strategies, businesses can provide personalized recommendations and offers, enhancing customer satisfaction and loyalty. Moreover, e-commerce platforms enable entrepreneurs to gather valuable insights about customer preferences, behaviors, and purchasing patterns, facilitating effective decision-making and informed business strategies. In addition, startups can leverage e-commerce to streamline their supply chain and inventory management processes. By utilizing advanced inventory management software and automation tools, entrepreneurs can optimize operations, reduce costs, and improve overall efficiency. This not only helps ensure product availability but also minimizes the risk of overstocking and stockouts, enhancing customer satisfaction. Moreover, e-commerce platforms offer startups various payment options, providing convenience and promoting secure transactions. By incorporating secure payment gateways and encryption technologies, entrepreneurs can protect sensitive customer information, gaining trust and confidence from their target audience. In conclusion, e-commerce plays a pivotal role in the startup and entrepreneurship ecosystem. It allows startups to establish an online presence, connect with a global audience, personalize the customer experience, optimize supply chain management, and provide secure payment options. By embracing e-commerce, startups can leverage these advantages to foster growth, increase profitability, and remain competitive in today's digital landscape.

Early Adopters

Early adopters, in the context of startup and entrepreneurship, refer to individuals or organizations that are among the first to adopt and embrace a new product, service, or technology introduced by a startup or an entrepreneur. Early adopters are crucial to the success of startups as they play a significant role in the product development, feedback, and marketing process. They are often characterized by their willingness to take risks, their openness to trying new things, and their ability to recognize the potential of a new innovation before it becomes mainstream.

Early Growth Stage

An early growth stage is a phase in the life cycle of a startup where the company has successfully passed the initial startup phase and is experiencing significant growth in terms of revenue, customer acquisition, and market presence. During the early growth stage, startups have typically validated their business model and product-market fit and are now focused on scaling their operations and expanding their market share. This stage is characterized by a rapid increase in sales, as well as the need for additional funding and resources to support the growth.

Early Stage Investment

Early stage investment refers to the financial backing provided to startups and entrepreneurs in the early stages of their business development. It is a crucial component of the entrepreneurial ecosystem, as it enables startups to access the necessary capital and resources to grow and succeed. Early stage investment typically occurs during the seed or angel funding stages, when startups are in the early phases of product development and market validation. At this stage, startups often do not have a fully developed product or consistent revenue, making it difficult for them to secure traditional forms of financing, such as bank loans.

Early-Stage Entrepreneur

Early-stage entrepreneur refers to an individual who is at the beginning stages of starting their own business venture, commonly known as a startup. This term is typically used in the context of entrepreneurship, which involves the process of creating, launching, and managing a new business idea or concept. An early-stage entrepreneur is someone who has recognized a potential opportunity in the market, and has taken the initial steps to turn their idea into a viable business venture. Early-stage entrepreneurs often face numerous challenges and uncertainties as they navigate the early stages of their startup. They may be in the process of conducting market research, developing a business plan, or seeking funding and investment opportunities. These entrepreneurs are typically driven by their vision and passion for their business idea, and are willing to take risks in order to achieve their goals. They possess a strong entrepreneurial mindset, characterized by traits such as creativity, resilience, and resourcefulness.

Early-Stage Financing

Early-Stage Financing refers to the initial investment of capital in a startup or entrepreneurial venture. It is a crucial stage of funding that occurs during the early phases of the company's development and is typically provided by angel investors, venture capitalists, or early-stage funding firms. During the early stages of a startup or entrepreneurial venture, companies often lack the financial resources needed to fund their operations, product development, and market expansion. Early-Stage Financing plays a pivotal role in bridging this funding gap and enabling the company to turn its ideas into reality. Early-Stage Financing is characterized by its risk and high potential for return on investment. Investors providing early-stage funding take on a significant level of risk by investing in startups that have little to no operating history, limited revenue streams, and uncertain market traction. However, they are attracted to this stage of investment due to the potential for high returns if the company succeeds and achieves significant growth. Investors engaged in Early-Stage Financing typically evaluate startups based on their business plan, market potential, team strength, and scalability. They assess the viability of the business model and the potential for the company to generate revenue, capture market share, and attract future rounds of funding. In return for their investment, early-stage investors usually acquire an equity stake in the company, giving them ownership and a proportionate share of future profits. This equity stake acts as an incentive for investors to support the growth and success of the startup. Early-stage investors often play an active role in advising and mentoring the entrepreneurs, leveraging their experience and network to contribute to the company's development. Early-Stage Financing is a critical phase for startups as it provides the necessary resources to develop and refine their products, validate market demand, attract talent, and expand their operations. It sets the foundation for future growth and subsequent rounds of financing, such as Series A, B, and C funding.

Early-Stage Funding

Early-Stage Funding refers to the initial round of financing that a startup or entrepreneur obtains to launch and grow their business venture. This funding is crucial for startups in their early stages of development, as it allows them to cover the costs associated with product development, market research, hiring key personnel, and other operational expenses. During the early-stage of a startup, entrepreneurs often seek funding from various sources, including angel investors, venture capitalists, friends and family, and crowdfunding platforms. These investors provide the necessary capital in exchange for equity or ownership stake in the company. The amount of funding secured during this stage varies significantly and is usually based on the startup's business model, market potential, and growth prospects.

Early-Stage Investment

Early-stage investment refers to the financial backing provided to start-ups and entrepreneurs in the initial phases of their business. It is a crucial source of funding that helps these early-stage companies to develop and grow their ideas into viable businesses. Early-stage investment usually occurs in the seed stage or early stage of a start-up's development, when the business is still in its infancy and has not yet generated significant revenue. At this stage, the start-up typically requires funds to refine its product or service, build a strong team, establish market presence, and secure further investments.

Early-Stage Startup

An early-stage startup refers to a newly established venture that is in its initial phase of development. It is an entrepreneurial project that is at its early stage of ideation, planning, and execution. These startups are typically characterized by their focus on innovation, scalability, and rapid growth potential. Early-stage startups are driven by entrepreneurs who are passionate about bringing their ideas to life. They are often fueled by a vision to disrupt existing markets or create entirely new ones. At this stage, startups are exploring business models, conducting market research, and building their core team. One of the key features of early-stage startups is their limited financial resources. These ventures often rely on seed funding or investments from angel investors or venture capitalists to support their operations and secure their future growth. The primary goal during this phase is to validate their business concept, attract more investors, and gather the necessary resources to move forward. Early-stage startups face various challenges and uncertainties. They need to be adaptable, agile, and open to feedback as they navigate through the unpredictable startup ecosystem. The founders need to iterate on their ideas, continuously refine their product or service, and pivot if needed to find the right market fit. Success for early-stage startups is often measured by achieving key milestones, such as launching a minimum viable product (MVP), acquiring initial customers, generating revenue, and gaining investor interest. These milestones demonstrate the startup's potential and attract further investment, which is crucial for scaling the business. In conclusion, early-stage startups are the foundation of the entrepreneurial ecosystem. They represent the innovative and disruptive ideas that have the potential to shape industries and drive economic growth. These ventures require determination, resilience, and a strategic approach to navigate the complexities of entrepreneurship and successfully emerge as sustainable businesses in the long run.

Early-Stage Venture Capital Investment Strategies And Enhancement

Early-Stage Venture Capital Investment Strategies and Enhancement Early-stage venture capital investment refers to the funding and support provided by investors to startups and entrepreneurs in their initial stages of development. This type of investment focuses on companies with significant growth potential but limited operating history and market traction. Venture capitalists who engage in early-stage investments have specific strategies to navigate the unique challenges and risks associated with startups and entrepreneurship. Firstly, these investors conduct thorough due diligence to assess the viability and potential of the startup. This involves evaluating the market size, competition, management team, technology, and financial projections. By conducting in-depth research and analysis, venture capitalists can make informed investment decisions. Secondly, early-stage venture capitalists often adopt a diversified portfolio approach. They invest in multiple startups across different industries, thereby spreading the risk and increasing the chances of success. This strategy recognizes that not all startups will achieve significant growth or generate substantial returns. By diversifying their investments, venture capitalists can maximize their overall portfolio performance. Furthermore, venture capitalists actively play a role in enhancing the startups' chances of success. They provide more than just capital; they offer expertise, mentorship, and access to valuable networks. Through their experience and industry connections, venture capitalists can help startups navigate challenges, refine their business strategies, and accelerate growth. They often take board seats or advisory roles and work closely with the management team to drive the company's progress. In addition to these strategies, venture capitalists may also use various enhancement techniques to increase the value and growth potential of their portfolio companies. This can include assisting with business development, facilitating strategic partnerships or introductions, and helping to secure follow-on funding. By leveraging their networks and resources, venture capitalists can provide startups with the necessary support to scale their operations and reach their full potential.

Early-Stage Venture Capital Investment Strategies

Early-stage venture capital investment strategies refer to the approaches and methodologies employed by venture capital firms when investing in startups at their early stages of development. These strategies are designed to identify and support promising entrepreneurs with innovative and scalable business ideas, providing them with the necessary funding and resources to grow and succeed. One common early-stage venture capital investment strategy is the "spray and pray" approach, where investors make a large number of relatively small investments in a portfolio of startups, hoping that a few will become successful and generate high returns. This strategy spreads the investment risk across multiple startups and relies on the potential for a few "unicorns" to deliver significant financial gains. Another strategy is the "follow-on" approach, where venture capital firms continue to invest in startups over multiple funding rounds as the companies progress and achieve key milestones. This approach allows investors to provide ongoing support and funding to startups with proven potential and reduces the risk associated with investing in unproven early-stage companies. Additionally, some venture capital firms adopt a "hands-on" approach, actively participating in the management and strategic decision-making of the startups they invest in. These firms provide entrepreneurs with not only capital but also valuable industry expertise, coaching, and networking opportunities to accelerate the growth and success of the startups. Moreover, some early-stage venture capital firms focus on specific industries or sectors, such as technology, healthcare, or renewable energy. By specializing in a particular niche, these firms develop domain expertise, network connections, and market knowledge that enables them to make informed investment decisions and provide tailored support to startups operating in those sectors. Overall, early-stage venture capital investment strategies aim to identify and support high-potential startups, while mitigating the inherent risks associated with early-stage investing. By leveraging their financial resources, industry expertise, and networking capabilities, venture capital firms play a critical role in fostering entrepreneurship and innovation, driving economic growth, and generating substantial returns for their investors.

Early-Stage Venture Capital Investment

Early-stage venture capital investment refers to the funding provided to startup companies in their initial stages of development, typically in exchange for an equity stake in the company. This type of investment is made by venture capital firms or individual investors known as angel investors. The main objective of early-stage venture capital investment is to support and nurture promising startups with high growth potential. The funds are typically used for product development, market research, hiring key personnel, and expanding the company's operations. In addition to financial support, early-stage venture capitalists often provide mentorship, guidance, and industry connections to help the startup succeed.

Early-Stage Venture Investment Process Enhancement

The early-stage venture investment process enhancement refers to the improvement and optimization of the various activities and steps involved in investing in startups during their early stages of development. This process involves evaluating and selecting promising startup opportunities, conducting due diligence, negotiating deal terms, and providing financial and non-financial support to the selected startups. In the context of entrepreneurship, early-stage venture investment is a critical step that provides startups with the necessary capital, expertise, and network to grow their business and achieve their goals. However, the investment process can be complex and challenging, requiring careful analysis and decision-making to identify high-potential startups and align investment strategies with the goals and risk appetite of the investors. The enhancement of the early-stage venture investment process aims to streamline and improve the efficiency and effectiveness of each stage of the process. This can be achieved through the use of data-driven analysis and decision-making, leveraging technology and digital tools, collaborating with various stakeholders such as accelerators and incubators, and adopting best practices and frameworks in investment evaluation and due diligence. One key area of enhancement is in the identification and selection of startups with high growth potential. This can involve the use of data analytics and market research to identify emerging trends and market opportunities, as well as leveraging networks and relationships to find promising startups with innovative business models and scalable products or services. Once potential startups have been identified, a thorough due diligence process is conducted to assess the feasibility and attractiveness of the investment opportunity. This may include evaluating the market potential, analyzing the startup's technology and intellectual property, assessing the strength and experience of the founding team, and conducting financial analysis to gauge the company's financial health and growth prospects. Negotiating deal terms is another important aspect of the early-stage venture investment process. This involves determining the valuation of the startup, defining the investment structure and rights, and setting expectations and milestones for future funding rounds and exit strategies. Effective negotiation requires a deep understanding of the startup's business and market dynamics, as well as the ability to balance the interests of both the investors and the entrepreneurs. Finally, the process of providing ongoing support and guidance to the invested startups plays a crucial role in their growth and success. This includes providing mentorship, strategic guidance, access to networks and resources, and monitoring the startup's progress and milestones. By enhancing this support system, investors can increase the likelihood of their investments generating positive returns and creating long-term value.

Early-Stage Venture Investment Process

The early-stage venture investment process in the context of startups and entrepreneurship refers to the series of steps taken by investors to identify, evaluate, and fund early-stage startups with high growth potential. This process involves careful consideration of various factors, including the startup's business model, market potential, team, and financial projections. The first step in the early-stage venture investment process is deal sourcing. Investors actively seek out startups through various channels such as networking events, pitch competitions, referrals, and startup databases. They may also receive pitches directly from entrepreneurs seeking investment. The goal is to identify promising startups that align with the investor's investment thesis and objectives. Once potential investment opportunities are identified, the next step is due diligence. This involves conducting a thorough analysis of the startup's market, competitors, product or service offering, financials, intellectual property, and team. Investors assess the startup's potential for success and evaluate the risks associated with the investment. Due diligence is a critical step to ensure that the startup has a scalable business model and a solid foundation for growth. After completing the due diligence process, investors negotiate the terms of the investment. This includes determining the valuation of the startup, the amount of funding to be provided, and the rights and obligations of both the investor and the entrepreneur. Negotiations aim to strike a fair and mutually beneficial agreement that aligns the interests of both parties. Once the investment terms are agreed upon, the final step is to close the deal and provide the funding to the startup. This typically involves legal documentation, such as investment agreements, shareholders' agreements, and any necessary regulatory filings. Once the deal is closed, the investor becomes a shareholder in the startup, and the funds are transferred to support the startup's growth and development.

Early-Stage Venture Investment Strategies

Early-stage venture investment strategies refer to the specific tactics and approaches that investors use when funding and supporting startups in their early stages of development. These strategies aim to maximize the potential for long-term growth and profitability while minimizing the risks associated with investing in early-stage companies. There are several key elements that define early-stage venture investment strategies. Firstly, investors typically focus on startups that are in their seed or early stages of development. These companies are often pre-revenue or have only just begun generating revenue. By investing early, investors hope to secure favorable terms and prices for their investments, as well as the potential for significant returns as the startup grows. Another important aspect of early-stage venture investment strategies is the emphasis on due diligence. Investors conduct thorough research and analysis of the startup's business model, products or services, market opportunities, competitive landscape, and the experience and capabilities of its founders. This due diligence helps investors assess the startup's potential for success and determine whether it aligns with their investment criteria and objectives. Once an investment is made, early-stage venture investors often provide ongoing support to startups. This support can take various forms, such as mentorship, strategic guidance, and access to networks and resources. Mentoring and guidance from experienced investors can help startups navigate challenges and make important strategic decisions. Early-stage venture investors also play an active role in helping startups secure additional funding as they progress. They leverage their networks and connections to introduce the startup to other potential investors, such as angel investors, venture capital firms, or strategic partners. This additional funding can fuel the startup's growth and enable it to reach key milestones, such as product development, market expansion, or customer acquisition. In summary, early-stage venture investment strategies involve investing in startups at a stage where they are still in their early developmental phase. These strategies emphasize thorough due diligence, ongoing support, and facilitation of additional funding to maximize the startup's potential for success. By adopting these strategies, investors aim to identify and invest in promising startups with the goal of generating significant returns in the long run.

Early-Stage Venture Investment

Early-stage venture investment refers to the funding provided to startups and entrepreneurs during the early stages of their businesses. It involves financial support and resources offered to new business ideas that are still in the development or exploration phase. This type of investment typically occurs during the pre-seed, seed, and early-stage funding rounds. At this stage, startups are seeking capital to validate their business ideas, develop prototypes, conduct market research, and refine their business models. Early-stage venture investment plays a crucial role in the startup ecosystem by fueling innovation and providing the necessary resources for entrepreneurs to transform their ideas into viable businesses. This investment supports the growth and scalability of startups, enabling them to bring their products or services to market. Early-stage investors can include angel investors, venture capital firms, and institutional investors who have a high tolerance for risk and a keen interest in discovering new ideas with high growth potential. They provide funding in exchange for equity ownership in the early-stage ventures, which offers the investors the potential for substantial returns on their investment. Aside from financial investment, early-stage venture investors often provide mentorship, guidance, and industry connections to support the startups they invest in. This support goes beyond capital, helping entrepreneurs navigate the challenges of starting and growing a business. The investment process for early-stage venture capital often involves a thorough evaluation of the startup's team, business model, market potential, competitive advantage, and scalability. Investors seek businesses that demonstrate the potential to disrupt existing markets or create new ones, as well as those with a clear path to revenue generation and profitability. In summary, early-stage venture investment is a crucial component of the startup ecosystem, providing startups with the necessary funding, guidance, and resources to validate their ideas and bring their products or services to the market. This investment fuels innovation, supports entrepreneurial growth, and has the potential for significant returns for investors.

Early-Stage Venture

An early-stage venture refers to a startup or entrepreneurial endeavor that is in its initial stages of development and growth. It typically involves a new business idea, product, or service that is being brought to market and has not yet reached the point of generating significant revenue or achieving profitability. Entrepreneurs who are involved in early-stage ventures are often focused on testing and refining their business model, acquiring customers and users, and securing funding to fuel their growth. These ventures are characterized by high levels of uncertainty, as the entrepreneurs navigate through the challenges and risks associated with building a successful business from scratch.

Early-Stage Investor

An early-stage investor, in the context of startups and entrepreneurship, refers to an individual or a company that provides funding to a startup in its early stages of development. This funding is typically used to cover the initial costs of starting a business, such as product development, hiring initial team members, and marketing activities. Early-stage investors are often referred to as angel investors, seed investors, or venture capitalists. Early-stage investors play a crucial role in the startup ecosystem by providing the necessary capital that allows entrepreneurs to turn their innovative ideas into viable businesses. These investors not only provide financial support but also bring valuable expertise, strategic guidance, and industry connections to the table. Their involvement goes beyond just writing a check and hoping for a return on investment; they actively participate in the growth and success of the startups they invest in.

Earnout

An earnout is a financial arrangement between the buyer and seller in a business acquisition, especially in the context of startups and entrepreneurship. It is often used when there is uncertainty about the future performance or value of the acquired company. Under an earnout agreement, a portion of the purchase price is agreed upon, and the remaining amount is tied to the future performance of the acquired company. This allows the buyer to defer a portion of the payment and align the interests of the buyer and seller in achieving certain performance objectives. The earnout is typically based on pre-defined financial metrics such as revenue, profitability, or customer growth. For example, the earnout may be structured so that the seller receives additional payments if the acquired company achieves certain revenue targets over a specified period of time. This incentivizes the seller to continue working towards the success of the business even after the acquisition is completed. Earnout agreements can be beneficial for both buyers and sellers. Buyers are able to reduce their risk by linking a portion of the payment to the future performance of the acquired company. This can be particularly valuable in the context of startups, where there may be greater uncertainty about the future profitability and growth potential. For sellers, earnouts provide an opportunity to receive a higher purchase price if their company performs well after the acquisition. They may also benefit from continued involvement in the business or access to additional resources and expertise from the buyer. However, earnouts also introduce potential challenges and risks. There may be disagreements between the buyer and seller regarding the achievement of the earnout targets, leading to disputes and legal battles. Sellers may also feel pressured to prioritize short-term revenue or profitability goals at the expense of long-term growth. In conclusion, an earnout is a financial arrangement that allows a buyer to defer a portion of the payment for an acquired company and tie it to the future performance of the business. It is commonly used in the startup and entrepreneurship context to align the interests of the buyer and seller, reduce risk, and incentivize continued success after the acquisition.

Economic Feasibility Study

An economic feasibility study in the context of startup and entrepreneurship is a comprehensive analysis that evaluates the financial and commercial potential of a new business venture. It aims to determine whether the proposed business idea is economically viable and can generate sufficient profit to cover its expenses and ensure sustainable growth. The economic feasibility study involves assessing various aspects of the potential venture, including market demand, competition, pricing dynamics, cost structure, revenue projections, and financial risks. By conducting this study, entrepreneurs can gain valuable insights into the viability and profitability of their business concept, enabling them to make informed decisions and develop an effective business strategy.

Economic Value Added (EVA) Analysis

Economic Value Added (EVA) Analysis is a financial measurement tool used in the context of startup and entrepreneurship to assess the value created by a business in excess of its cost of capital. It focuses on determining the true economic profit generated by a company, taking into account both its operating earnings and the opportunity cost of the capital invested. EVA is calculated by subtracting the company's cost of capital from its net operating profit after taxes (NOPAT). The cost of capital includes the weighted average cost of debt and equity, representing the minimum return expected by the capital providers. The resulting EVA value demonstrates the extent to which a company is generating value for its investors and shareholders. For startups and entrepreneurs, EVA analysis can provide valuable insights into the financial performance and profitability of their business ventures. By analyzing EVA, entrepreneurs can determine if their business is generating economic value and whether they are effectively utilizing their capital. Positive EVA indicates that a startup is creating value for its stakeholders, while negative EVA signifies that the business is failing to generate returns above its cost of capital. Furthermore, EVA analysis can help startups and entrepreneurs identify areas for improvement and make informed decisions to enhance their financial performance. By evaluating the components contributing to EVA, such as operating profits, tax rate, and capital employed, entrepreneurs can pinpoint areas of inefficiency and take appropriate actions to optimize their business operations. For instance, they may identify cost reduction opportunities, explore strategies to increase revenue, or allocate resources more effectively. Overall, EVA analysis is a useful tool for startups and entrepreneurs to evaluate their financial performance and measure the value they generate. It provides a comprehensive perspective on a company's profitability by considering the cost of capital, enabling entrepreneurs to make informed decisions to optimize their business operations and enhance shareholder value.

Elevator Pitch Workshops

Elevator Pitch Workshops are short and focused training sessions designed to help startups and entrepreneurs craft a compelling and concise pitch to communicate their business idea or concept effectively in a limited amount of time. The purpose of these workshops is to provide participants with the necessary skills and knowledge to deliver a clear and impactful elevator pitch that captures the attention of potential investors, partners, or customers. The elevator pitch is a brief, persuasive speech that can be delivered in the time it takes to ride an elevator, typically less than two minutes. In the startup and entrepreneurship context, the elevator pitch is crucial for attracting interest, generating excitement, and ultimately securing support or funding for a new business venture. During the Elevator Pitch Workshops, participants learn essential techniques for articulating their value proposition, defining their target audience, and conveying the unique features and benefits of their product or service. They are guided through a step-by-step process of refining their pitch, starting with understanding the problem they are solving and the market opportunity they are addressing. Participants are also taught how to structure their pitch effectively, incorporating a compelling hook or opening statement, clear and concise problem statement, explanation of their solution, and key differentiators that set them apart from competitors. They learn to highlight the market potential, target customers, and how their business addresses a specific pain point or need. Specific examples and case studies are often used to illustrate effective pitch elements. Additionally, Elevator Pitch Workshops provide participants with opportunities for practice and feedback. They engage in interactive exercises and role-playing scenarios to refine their delivery skills, improve their body language, and enhance their ability to engage with their audience effectively. Feedback sessions allow participants to receive constructive criticism and suggestions for improvement from experienced mentors and instructors. By completing an Elevator Pitch Workshop, startups and entrepreneurs gain valuable skills and insights that can greatly enhance their ability to attract attention and make a lasting impression in a fast-paced and competitive business environment. The workshops not only provide participants with the tools and knowledge to craft a persuasive pitch but also empower them to confidently communicate their business idea and secure the support needed to turn their vision into a successful reality.

Elevator Pitch

An elevator pitch is a concise and compelling summary of a startup or business idea, designed to quickly and effectively communicate its value proposition to potential investors, partners, or customers. It is called an "elevator pitch" because it should be short enough to deliver during the time it takes for an elevator ride, typically between 30 seconds to two minutes. The purpose of an elevator pitch is to grab the attention of the listener and leave a lasting impression, generating interest and opening the door for further conversation or opportunities. It should clearly articulate what problem the startup is addressing, how it solves that problem, and why it is unique or superior to existing solutions in the market.

Employee Stock Options (ESOPs)

Employee Stock Options (ESOPs) are a type of equity compensation that startups and entrepreneurial companies grant to their employees as a form of incentive to attract and retain talent. ESOPs enable employees to buy a specified number of shares of the company's stock at a predetermined price, typically lower than the market price. ESOPs are usually granted to employees as part of their compensation package, and the granting of stock options is often based on factors such as the employee's job performance, tenure, or role within the company. These options serve as a motivational tool for employees, aligning their interests with the long-term success of the company and giving them a sense of ownership.

Employee Stock Ownership Plans (ESOPs)

An Employee Stock Ownership Plan (ESOP) is a type of employee benefit plan that provides employees of a company with an ownership interest in the company. This ownership interest is typically in the form of company stocks or shares. ESOPs are commonly used by startups and entrepreneurs as a way to attract and retain talented employees, promote employee motivation and loyalty, and provide employees with a stake in the company's success. In an ESOP, employees are given the opportunity to acquire ownership in the company through various means such as stock options, restricted stock units (RSUs), or direct stock purchases. The ownership interest is usually granted to employees as a reward for their contributions to the company or as part of their compensation package. ESOPs offer several advantages to both startups/entrepreneurs and employees. For startups and entrepreneurs, ESOPs can be a cost-effective way to offer employees a stake in the company's success without using precious cash resources. This can help attract top talent and incentivize employees to work hard to drive the company's growth. Additionally, ESOPs can provide tax benefits to the company, as contributions made to the plan are generally tax-deductible. For employees, ESOPs can be a valuable financial asset and a powerful motivator. By owning company stocks, employees have the potential to benefit from the company's growth and success. This can create a sense of ownership and loyalty among employees, as they have a direct stake in the company's performance. ESOPs also provide a means for employees to accumulate wealth over time and can serve as a retirement benefit if the company's stock value increases.

Entrepreneurial Community

An entrepreneurial community refers to a group of individuals who are actively engaged in entrepreneurial activities and are connected through shared interests, goals, and resources. This community consists of entrepreneurs, business owners, investors, mentors, advisors, and other stakeholders who support and collaborate with each other to foster an environment of innovation, growth, and success. Within an entrepreneurial community, individuals come together to exchange ideas, knowledge, and experiences, as well as provide support, encouragement, and guidance to one another. These interactions take place through various channels, such as networking events, workshops, conferences, online platforms, and co-working spaces. The community acts as a hub for those seeking to start or grow their own ventures, enabling them to connect with like-minded individuals, access valuable resources, and gain insights from those who have already experienced the challenges and triumphs of entrepreneurship. The entrepreneurial community plays a vital role in fueling the startup ecosystem. It provides a supportive and nurturing environment for aspiring entrepreneurs, helping them overcome obstacles, develop key skills, and access the necessary resources to turn their ideas into successful ventures. In addition to networking opportunities, the community also offers access to funding sources, business development programs, industry connections, and mentorship, which are crucial for the sustainable growth of startups. Moreover, an entrepreneurial community fosters a culture of collaboration and innovation. It encourages individuals to collaborate on projects, share expertise, and leverage collective knowledge to tackle complex challenges in an ever-changing business landscape. Through these collaborations, entrepreneurs can tap into diverse perspectives and skills, find potential co-founders or team members, and validate their ideas through constructive feedback and market insights. In summary, an entrepreneurial community is a cohesive network of individuals who are committed to supporting and promoting entrepreneurship. It serves as a platform for collaboration, shared learning, and resource-sharing, ultimately contributing to the success and growth of startups and entrepreneurs.

Entrepreneurial Ecosystem

An entrepreneurial ecosystem refers to the network of various actors and elements that collectively contribute to the growth and development of startups and entrepreneurs in a specific geographical area or industry. It is a complex system comprising multiple interconnected components, which include entrepreneurs, investors, mentors, government bodies, educational institutions, and support organizations. The entrepreneurial ecosystem is characterized by a dynamic and interactive environment that fosters the creation, growth, and success of startups. It provides a platform for entrepreneurs to connect, collaborate, and exchange ideas, resources, and expertise. The ecosystem plays a crucial role in nurturing innovation, promoting entrepreneurship, and driving economic growth. One of the key elements of a thriving entrepreneurial ecosystem is a pool of talented and motivated entrepreneurs. These entrepreneurs possess the drive, passion, and skills necessary to transform their innovative ideas into successful businesses. They are the driving force behind the creation and growth of startups and play a crucial role in attracting talent, capital, and other resources to the ecosystem. In addition to entrepreneurs, the ecosystem also relies on a network of investors who provide financial resources and support to startups. These investors can be angel investors, venture capitalists, or corporate investors who are willing to take calculated risks in exchange for potential high returns. Their involvement is crucial as it provides startups with the necessary capital to fund their operations, research and development, and scale their business. Mentors and support organizations are other important components of an entrepreneurial ecosystem. Mentors are experienced entrepreneurs, industry experts, or professionals who provide guidance, advice, and support to early-stage startups. They offer valuable insights, help startups navigate challenges, and connect them to relevant networks and resources. Support organizations, such as incubators, accelerators, and co-working spaces, provide startups with physical infrastructure, access to resources, and educational programs. Government bodies and policies also play a significant role in shaping the entrepreneurial ecosystem. They create an enabling environment through regulations, incentives, and policies that promote entrepreneurship, innovation, and investment. Government support can range from funding programs for startups to creating favorable tax policies, simplifying regulations, and fostering collaboration between academia, industry, and the startup community. In conclusion, an entrepreneurial ecosystem is a complex and interconnected network of entrepreneurs, investors, mentors, support organizations, and government bodies that collectively contribute to the growth and success of startups. It provides the necessary support, resources, and infrastructure for entrepreneurs to transform their ideas into thriving businesses, driving innovation and economic growth.

Entrepreneurial Leadership

Entrepreneurial leadership refers to the ability of an entrepreneur to lead and manage a startup or entrepreneurial venture effectively. It entails taking charge, making decisions, and guiding the organization towards its goals and objectives. An entrepreneurial leader possesses certain key traits that set them apart from traditional leaders. They are highly motivated and driven individuals who exhibit a strong passion for their business idea or concept. They are risk-takers and have the ability to identify new opportunities and act upon them. They are proactive and innovative in their approach, constantly seeking ways to improve and differentiate their venture. The role of an entrepreneurial leader is multifaceted. They are responsible for setting the vision and direction of the startup, defining its goals and objectives, and formulating strategies to achieve them. They play a crucial role in building and managing a team, attracting and retaining talent, and creating a positive organizational culture. They are accountable for allocating resources effectively, managing finances, and ensuring the overall success and sustainability of the venture. Entrepreneurial leadership is characterized by certain essential skills and competencies. Effective communication is vital, as the leader must clearly articulate the startup's vision and goals to stakeholders, investors, employees, and customers. Adaptability and flexibility are crucial, as startups operate in a dynamic and uncertain environment. The leader must be able to adapt to changing market conditions, pivot when necessary, and make informed decisions in a rapidly evolving landscape. Furthermore, entrepreneurial leaders must possess strong problem-solving and decision-making abilities. They must be able to identify issues and obstacles, and develop creative solutions to overcome them. They must also be able to take calculated risks and make tough decisions, often with limited information or resources. In summary, entrepreneurial leadership is the ability to lead and manage a startup or entrepreneurial venture effectively. It requires a unique combination of traits, skills, and competencies that enable the leader to drive innovation, navigate challenges, and create a successful and sustainable venture.

Entrepreneurial Mindset

An entrepreneurial mindset refers to a set of attitudes, behaviors, and thinking patterns that are often associated with successful startup founders and entrepreneurs. It is characterized by a proactive and innovative approach to business and a willingness to take risks and embrace uncertainty. Entrepreneurs with an entrepreneurial mindset demonstrate a strong belief in their ability to identify and seize opportunities, and they are driven by a desire to create value and make a positive impact in the world. They are persistent and resilient, willing to learn from failure and adapt their strategies in the face of challenges. One key aspect of an entrepreneurial mindset is a strong sense of initiative and self-motivation. Entrepreneurs take ownership of their goals and actively seek out opportunities rather than waiting for them to come their way. They are proactive in identifying problems and developing innovative solutions, constantly looking for ways to improve and differentiate their products or services. Another important characteristic of an entrepreneurial mindset is comfort with risk and uncertainty. Entrepreneurs understand that starting and running a business involves inherent risks, and they are willing to take calculated risks to achieve their goals. They are not deterred by failure or setbacks but rather view them as learning opportunities and stepping stones to success. An entrepreneurial mindset also entails a strong ability to think critically and creatively. Entrepreneurs are constantly seeking new ways to solve problems and identify opportunities. They are open-minded and adaptable, willing to challenge conventional wisdom and think outside the box. They are able to envision possibilities that others may overlook and are not afraid to take unconventional paths to achieve their goals. In summary, an entrepreneurial mindset is a set of attitudes, behaviors, and thinking patterns that enable individuals to approach business and entrepreneurship with an innovative and proactive mindset. It is characterized by a strong sense of initiative, comfort with risk and uncertainty, and the ability to think critically and creatively. Entrepreneurs with an entrepreneurial mindset are driven by a desire to create value and make a positive impact in the world, and they are willing to embrace challenges and adapt their strategies along the way.

Entrepreneurial Network

An entrepreneurial network is an interconnected group of individuals, organizations, and resources that support and facilitate the development, growth, and success of startups and entrepreneurs. These networks are composed of various stakeholders including entrepreneurs, investors, mentors, advisors, service providers, and government agencies, among others. They collaborate and exchange knowledge, capital, expertise, and connections to help startups and entrepreneurs navigate the challenges and uncertainties of the business world. An entrepreneurial network plays a crucial role in creating an ecosystem conducive to startup and entrepreneurial activities. It fosters innovation and entrepreneurship by providing access to critical resources and opportunities that entrepreneurs need to succeed. The network provides a platform for networking and collaboration, enabling entrepreneurs to connect with like-minded individuals, potential co-founders, investors, and partners. Through these connections, entrepreneurs can access valuable advice, guidance, and financial support to launch and grow their ventures. Furthermore, an entrepreneurial network offers various programs, events, and workshops aimed at developing entrepreneurial skills, knowledge, and capabilities. These initiatives provide education, training, and mentorship to entrepreneurs, helping them enhance their business acumen and increase their chances of success. The network also facilitates access to capital by connecting entrepreneurs with potential investors, including angel investors, venture capitalists, and crowdfunding platforms. This financial support allows startups to secure funding for product development, marketing, operations, and expansion. In addition, an entrepreneurial network offers access to specialized services and resources, such as legal and accounting advice, marketing and branding support, technology infrastructure, and incubation and co-working spaces. These resources are crucial for startups to overcome challenges and build a strong foundation for their businesses. Overall, an entrepreneurial network plays a vital role in supporting and nurturing the growth of startups and entrepreneurs. By providing access to knowledge, capital, networks, and resources, these networks contribute to the development of a vibrant and sustainable entrepreneurial ecosystem.

Entrepreneurial Skills

Entrepreneurial skills refer to the specific capabilities and qualities that enable individuals to identify and seize business opportunities, as well as effectively manage and grow a startup venture. They encompass a range of attributes, knowledge, and behaviors that are vital for entrepreneurs to navigate the challenges and complexities of the startup ecosystem. One of the key entrepreneurial skills is creativity. Entrepreneurs are often required to think outside the box, come up with innovative ideas, and find unique solutions to problems. They need to be able to generate new concepts and approaches that differentiate their startup from competitors and attract customers or investors. Another significant entrepreneurial skill is risk-taking. Startups often involve uncertainties and potential failures. Entrepreneurs must be willing to take calculated risks, make decisions in uncertain environments, and be comfortable with the possibility of failure. They need to develop a mindset that embraces risk as an opportunity for growth and learning. Entrepreneurs also need to possess strong leadership skills. They should be able to effectively communicate their vision, inspire and motivate team members, and make tough decisions. Leadership skills help entrepreneurs build a strong team, create a positive and productive work environment, and align the efforts of everyone towards the startup's goals. Furthermore, resourcefulness is a crucial entrepreneurial skill. Startups often face limited resources, such as financial capital and human resources. Entrepreneurs need to be resourceful in finding creative ways to overcome these challenges and make the most out of the available resources. They should be able to efficiently utilize their network, negotiate partnerships, and identify opportunities for cost-saving or revenue-generating activities. Additionally, adaptability is an essential skill for entrepreneurs. The startup environment is dynamic and constantly changing. Entrepreneurs must be able to adapt to market trends, technological advancements, and shifts in consumer preferences. They need to be open to feedback, continuously learn and improve, and be willing to pivot their business strategy when necessary. In conclusion, entrepreneurial skills encompass creativity, risk-taking, leadership, resourcefulness, and adaptability. These skills enable entrepreneurs to identify opportunities, navigate challenges, and successfully manage and grow their startups. Developing and honing these skills is critical for aspiring entrepreneurs to increase their chances of building a sustainable and successful venture.

Entrepreneurial Spirit

The entrepreneurial spirit refers to the mindset, characteristics, and attitude possessed by individuals who embark on entrepreneurial endeavors. It is a combination of traits and qualities that drive individuals to take risks, innovate, and create new ventures. Entrepreneurship is the process of identifying, developing, and launching new business ideas or ventures. It involves recognizing opportunities, organizing resources, and taking calculated risks to achieve business success. At its core, the entrepreneurial spirit embodies a strong desire for autonomy and the ability to take initiative. Entrepreneurs are driven by a passion to bring their ideas to life, challenge the status quo, and make a positive impact on the world. Key traits of the entrepreneurial spirit include creativity, resilience, determination, and a willingness to learn and adapt. Entrepreneurs are often innovative thinkers who are constantly looking for ways to improve existing products, services, or processes. They embrace failure as a learning opportunity and are persistent in the face of setbacks. An entrepreneurial spirit is also characterized by a high level of self-motivation and perseverance. Entrepreneurs are willing to work long hours, take on multiple roles, and make sacrifices in pursuit of their goals. They are not afraid to take calculated risks and are comfortable with uncertainty. In addition to being self-motivated, entrepreneurs are also adept at managing and leveraging resources. They are skilled at identifying and attracting talented individuals, building strong networks, and securing financial backing for their ventures. Overall, the entrepreneurial spirit is a fundamental driving force behind the startup culture. It is the catalyst for innovation, economic growth, and job creation. Through their vision, passion, and determination, entrepreneurs bring new ideas to market, disrupt industries, and reshape the business landscape.

Entrepreneurship Development

Entrepreneurship development refers to the process of cultivating and enhancing the skills, qualities, and mindset necessary to start and grow a successful startup or business venture. It involves the acquisition of knowledge, attitudes, and behaviors that enable individuals to identify and seize entrepreneurial opportunities, effectively manage risks, and create innovative solutions to address market needs. Entrepreneurship development encompasses a wide range of activities and initiatives aimed at promoting and supporting the growth of startups and entrepreneurs. This includes providing access to resources, such as capital, networks, mentors, and training programs, that can help entrepreneurs turn their ideas into viable businesses. It also involves fostering an entrepreneurial ecosystem and creating an enabling environment that encourages the development and scaling of innovative ventures. Successful entrepreneurship development involves the cultivation of certain key competencies and attributes. These include the ability to identify and evaluate business opportunities, think creatively and critically, take calculated risks, and adapt to changing market conditions. It also requires strong leadership skills, effective communication and negotiation abilities, and a strong passion and drive for success. Entrepreneurship development plays a crucial role in economic growth and development. Startups and entrepreneurs are often at the forefront of technological advancements, job creation, and innovation, all of which contribute to the overall prosperity of a nation. By nurturing and supporting entrepreneurial talent, entrepreneurship development can help stimulate economic activity, create employment opportunities, and drive sustainable development. In summary, entrepreneurship development is the process of equipping individuals with the knowledge, skills, and mindset needed to start and grow successful businesses. It involves providing support, resources, and opportunities for aspiring entrepreneurs to turn their ideas into reality, and is integral to fostering economic growth and innovation.

Equity Crowdfunding Platform

Equity Crowdfunding Platform refers to an online platform that allows startups and entrepreneurs to raise funds from a large number of individuals in exchange for equity shares or ownership stakes in their business. This alternative method of fundraising has gained popularity in recent years as a way to secure capital for early-stage ventures. An equity crowdfunding platform acts as an intermediary between the entrepreneurs seeking funds and the investors looking to invest in promising startups. It provides a virtual marketplace where entrepreneurs can showcase their business ideas, products, and potential growth prospects, while investors can browse through various investment opportunities and choose to invest in businesses that align with their interests and investment criteria. The platform enables startups to create fundraising campaigns, wherein they set a specific target amount they aim to raise and determine the percentage of equity they are willing to offer in return for the investment. The campaigns typically outline the business model, current financials, growth projections, and the specific use of funds. Additionally, they may include other relevant information such as the background and expertise of the founders, competitive analysis, and market opportunities. Investors, on the other hand, can assess these campaigns and make informed decisions based on the available information. They can evaluate the potential of the business, the viability of the product or service, the market size and competition, and other factors that may influence the success of the venture. Once an investor decides to invest, they can directly contribute funds through the equity crowdfunding platform. The platform typically handles the financial transactions and ensures the compliance with legal and regulatory requirements, such as anti-money laundering regulations and investor accreditation. Equity crowdfunding platforms offer benefits to both startups and investors. For startups, it provides access to a wider pool of potential investors who may be interested in supporting innovative ideas and early-stage ventures. It enables them to raise capital without relying solely on traditional funding sources, such as banks or venture capitalists, which may be inaccessible or less willing to take risks on unproven concepts. For investors, equity crowdfunding platforms offer the opportunity to diversify their investment portfolios by allocating funds to high-potential startups. They can participate in the early stages of a company's growth and potentially benefit from its success in the form of capital appreciation and dividends.

Equity Crowdfunding

Equity crowdfunding is a form of funding that allows startups and entrepreneurs to raise capital by offering equity in their company to a large number of investors through an online platform. It provides an alternative to traditional funding methods such as bank loans, venture capital, or angel investors. In this model, the entrepreneurs set a funding goal and a valuation for their company, and then invite individuals or institutional investors to invest in their company by purchasing shares. The investors, in return for their investment, receive an equity stake in the company proportionate to the amount they have invested. This means that they become shareholders and have a potential financial return if the company is successful. Equity crowdfunding offers several advantages for startups and entrepreneurs. Firstly, it allows them to access a larger pool of potential investors. By using online platforms, they can reach a broader audience and attract investors who may not have been traditionally involved in early-stage investments. Secondly, equity crowdfunding can provide a more efficient and streamlined process for raising capital. Unlike traditional methods, entrepreneurs can pitch their idea and request funding directly to the online community, saving time and effort in seeking out individual investors. Another benefit of equity crowdfunding is that it provides a platform for entrepreneurs to validate their product or service in the market. By presenting their business model to a large number of investors, entrepreneurs can gauge interest, gather feedback, and potentially attract strategic investors or partners. However, it is important to note that equity crowdfunding also comes with some challenges. Startups and entrepreneurs must comply with regulations set by securities regulators to protect investors from fraud or misleading information. They need to provide transparent and accurate information about their company's financials, potential risks, and growth prospects to the investors.

Equity Financing Agreement

An equity financing agreement is a formal legally binding contract between a startup company and an investor, typically in the context of entrepreneurship. This agreement outlines the terms and conditions under which the investor provides funds to the startup in exchange for equity ownership in the company. The agreement usually contains several key elements, including the amount of investment, the percentage of equity the investor will receive in return, and any conditions or requirements the investor may have. The terms of the agreement can vary depending on the specific needs and goals of both the startup and the investor. Equity financing is a common method for startups to raise capital and fuel their growth. Unlike debt financing, which involves borrowing money that needs to be repaid with interest, equity financing involves selling a portion of the company's ownership to investors in exchange for funding. Startups often opt for equity financing because it offers several advantages. Firstly, it provides access to capital without the burden of debt repayments, allowing the company to allocate more resources towards research, development, and growth. Additionally, equity financing allows startups to leverage the expertise and networks of the investors, who often provide guidance and support beyond just the financial investment. However, equity financing also comes with some drawbacks. One major disadvantage is the dilution of the founders' ownership and control over the company. As more equity is issued to investors, the founders' percentage of ownership decreases, potentially leading to a loss of decision-making power. Furthermore, equity financing may require the startup to disclose sensitive information and grant certain rights to the investors, which could limit the company's flexibility in certain areas. In conclusion, an equity financing agreement is a crucial contract for startups seeking capital. It allows them to secure funding in exchange for selling equity to investors, providing resources for growth and access to investor expertise. However, founders must carefully consider the terms and potential drawbacks of equity financing before entering into such an agreement.

Equity Financing

Equity financing in the context of startup and entrepreneurship refers to the process of raising capital for a business by selling shares of ownership, or equity, in the company to investors. This type of funding is commonly sought by startups and early-stage companies as a way to acquire the necessary capital to fuel growth and expansion. When a startup seeks equity financing, it typically creates and issues new shares of stock to investors in exchange for their investment. These shares represent a percentage of ownership in the company, and the investors become shareholders. The amount of equity a company is willing to offer in exchange for investment depends on various factors, such as the valuation of the company, the potential for growth, and the level of interest from investors.

Equity Investment

Equity investment in the context of startups and entrepreneurship refers to the process of obtaining funding for a new business in exchange for ownership stake or shares in the company. It is a form of financing that allows individuals or entities to invest their capital into a startup with the expectation of receiving a return on their investment. When a startup seeks equity investment, they are essentially offering a portion of their ownership in the company to investors in exchange for financial support. This means that investors become shareholders and have a claim on the future profits and value of the company.

Equity Stake

Equity stake refers to the ownership interest that an individual or entity holds in a startup or entrepreneurial venture. It represents the portion or percentage of the company's shares that an investor or founder possesses, enabling them to participate in the company's success and potential financial returns. When a startup is formed, founders often rely on external funding sources, such as venture capitalists or angel investors, to finance their business operations and growth. In exchange for their investment, these investors acquire an equity stake in the company. The equity stake can be in the form of common stock, preferred stock, or other securities, depending on the agreement between the startup and the investor. The equity stake serves as a measure of the investor's or founder's ownership in the company and determines their influence over decision-making processes. It entitles the stakeholder to a portion of the company's earnings and assets, which are typically distributed in the form of dividends or capital gains when the company achieves a liquidity event, such as an initial public offering (IPO) or acquisition. An equity stake not only provides a financial interest in the company but also grants certain rights and privileges to the holder. These rights may include voting rights, board representation, and participation in major company decisions. The equity stake can also act as an incentive for the stakeholders to actively contribute to the growth and success of the startup, as they will directly benefit from the company's performance. It's crucial for entrepreneurs and startups to carefully consider the amount of equity they offer to external investors when seeking funding. While equity stake dilution is a common occurrence in a startup's lifecycle, excessive dilution can result in founders losing control over their own company. Therefore, maintaining a balance between attracting investment and preserving founder control is essential.

Equity

Equity refers to the ownership stake or share in a startup company that an entrepreneur or investor holds. It represents the portion of the company that is owned by the shareholders, including founders, employees, and investors. Equity can be acquired through various means, such as investing money, contributing assets, or providing services to the startup. In return for their investment or contribution, shareholders receive equity in the form of shares or stock options, which represent their ownership and potential future profits in the company.

Ethical Hacking Services

Ethical Hacking Services refers to the range of cybersecurity services offered by professionals who possess extensive knowledge and expertise in identifying and exploiting vulnerabilities within an organization's computer systems. In the context of Startup & Entrepreneurship, ethical hacking services play a crucial role in ensuring the security and integrity of a startup's digital assets and infrastructure. With the increasing reliance on technology and the ever-growing threat of cyber attacks, startups and entrepreneurs face significant risks to their sensitive data and intellectual property. Ethical hacking services help them identify and address these vulnerabilities before malicious actors can exploit them.

Ethnographic Research

Ethnographic research in the context of startup and entrepreneurship is a qualitative research method used to gain an in-depth understanding of a particular target market or customer segment by studying their behaviors, attitudes, beliefs, and cultural norms. It involves immersing oneself within the community or group being studied to observe and document their daily activities and interaction patterns. This research method aims to uncover insights and identify unmet needs that can inform the development of new products, services, or business models. Through ethnographic research, entrepreneurs and startups can gain a deeper understanding of their potential customers' lives, experiences, and challenges. It allows them to see the world from the perspective of their target market, enabling them to empathize with their customers and identify opportunities to create value. By observing and engaging with customers in their natural setting, researchers can uncover underlying motivations, social dynamics, and cultural influences that shape their behaviors and decision-making processes.

Exclusivity Agreement

An exclusivity agreement, in the context of startup and entrepreneurship, refers to a legally binding contract between two parties that restricts one party from entering into similar agreements with other parties during a specified period of time.The purpose of an exclusivity agreement is to provide protection and assurance to the party that is offering or investing resources, such as time, money, or proprietary information, to the other party. This agreement ensures that the receiving party does not engage in similar ventures or partnerships with competitors or other entities that could potentially undermine the interests of the initiating party.Startups often seek exclusivity agreements with investors, suppliers, vendors, or partners to gain a competitive advantage, secure resources, or maintain control over crucial assets or business relationships. Such agreements foster trust, minimize risks, and create a sense of commitment between the parties involved.Typically, exclusivity agreements outline specific terms and conditions that bind the receiving party. These terms may include provisions regarding the duration of exclusivity, geographical restrictions, intellectual property rights, confidentiality obligations, and any defined milestones or deliverables. The agreement may also stipulate the consequences of breaching the exclusivity clause, such as financial penalties, termination, or legal action.For startups, exclusivity agreements can be vital in protecting their innovative ideas, technologies, or market strategies from being shared or capitalized upon by competing or unauthorized entities. They provide a measure of security when disclosing confidential information or when engaging in strategic collaborations that involve the sharing of proprietary knowledge.However, while exclusivity agreements may offer advantages, they can also impose limitations on the receiving party. They may hinder their ability to explore alternative opportunities, seek more favorable terms, or pursue potential partnerships that could be more beneficial or aligned with their business goals.In conclusion, an exclusivity agreement plays a pivotal role in the startup ecosystem as it enables entrepreneurs to establish proprietary relationships, safeguard intellectual property, and minimize risks. These agreements help nurture trust, secure resources, and create a framework for collaborations that can contribute to the growth and success of startups.

Exit Event

An Exit Event, in the context of startup and entrepreneurship, refers to a key milestone or event that marks the successful exit of an entrepreneur or investor from a startup venture. It signifies the moment when the entrepreneur or investor realizes their return on investment by selling their stake in the company or taking it public through an initial public offering (IPO). An exit event is a strategic move for both entrepreneurs and investors alike. For entrepreneurs, it represents the culmination of their hard work and dedication, as well as the opportunity to reap the rewards of their efforts. It may also signal the end of their involvement with the startup, allowing them to move on to new ventures or opportunities. On the other hand, for investors, an exit event provides the chance to achieve a successful return on their investment. By selling their shares or taking the company public, they can monetize their investment and potentially earn a significant profit. This event also allows investors to reallocate their resources and reinvest in other startups or ventures. The most common types of exit events are acquisitions and IPOs. In an acquisition, a larger company acquires all or a majority of the shares of the startup, usually resulting in a payout for the entrepreneur and investors. An IPO, on the other hand, involves taking the startup public by offering shares for purchase on the open market. This event allows the entrepreneur and investors to sell their shares to the public and potentially realize substantial gains. Exit events are often the primary goal for entrepreneurs and investors in the startup ecosystem. They provide validation of the business model and its potential for growth, while also offering a financial reward for the risks and challenges undertaken. Additionally, successful exit events can attract future investors and entrepreneurs to the startup ecosystem, fueling innovation and economic growth.

Exit Interview

An exit interview in the context of startup and entrepreneurship refers to the process of conducting a formal conversation with an employee who is leaving the company, with the purpose of gathering valuable feedback and insights about their overall experience at the startup. The exit interview serves as a platform for the departing employee to express their thoughts, opinions, and suggestions about the organization, its culture, management, policies, and practices. During an exit interview, the entrepreneur or relevant personnel typically pose a series of open-ended questions to the departing employee, encouraging them to share details about their reasons for leaving, their views on the work environment, and any challenges or concerns they may have faced. The interview may also provide an opportunity for the employee to provide constructive criticism, suggestions for improvement, or to voice any grievances they may have. The primary objective of conducting an exit interview in a startup or entrepreneurial setting is to gain valuable feedback that can be used to enhance the company's operations, management, and overall employee experience. By actively listening to the departing employee's insights, entrepreneurs can uncover areas for improvement, identify trends or patterns in employee dissatisfaction, and make informed decisions to address issues that may impact employee retention, engagement, and performance. Exit interviews can also serve as a means to understand the reasons behind employees leaving the startup, providing an opportunity for entrepreneurs to evaluate and refine their recruitment and retention strategies. Insights gathered from exit interviews can help entrepreneurs identify any potential weaknesses or areas of improvement within the organization, which can then be addressed to enhance employee satisfaction and reduce turnover in the future. In summary, an exit interview in the context of startup and entrepreneurship is a formal conversation held with a departing employee, aimed at gathering feedback, identifying areas for improvement, and gaining insights that can help enhance the company's operations, culture, and overall employee experience.

Exit Interviews

An exit interview in the context of startup and entrepreneurship refers to a structured conversation or questionnaire conducted when an employee or founder is leaving the company. It is a formal process that aims to gather feedback, insights, and opinions from the departing individual regarding their experience working in the startup. The main purpose of an exit interview is to gain valuable insights that can help the startup improve its operations, culture, and overall performance. By analyzing the feedback received from departing employees or founders, the startup can identify areas of improvement, address any existing issues, and make necessary changes to enhance employee satisfaction and retention.

Exit Multiple Analysis

Exit Multiple Analysis is a valuation method used in the context of startups and entrepreneurship to determine the potential worth of a company or business at the time of its exit, such as during an acquisition or an initial public offering (IPO). This analysis takes into consideration various financial factors and metrics to estimate the expected return on investment for investors and shareholders. The exit multiple, also known as the valuation multiple, is derived by comparing the financial performance of similar companies in the market that have recently been acquired or gone public. It is calculated by dividing the sale price or market capitalization of those comparable companies by their respective financial metrics, such as revenue, earnings, or cash flow. The resulting multiple represents the market's perception of the company's value in relation to its financial performance. Exit multiple analysis requires careful research and analysis of the market and industry in which the startup operates. It involves identifying and studying comparable companies that have recently undergone an exit event and extracting relevant financial data. This data is then used to calculate the exit multiple and apply it to the startup's own financial metrics to estimate its potential valuation at the time of exit. This valuation method is particularly useful in the context of startups and entrepreneurship because it allows entrepreneurs and investors to establish a potential target valuation for their business. It provides a benchmark for negotiation and decision-making regarding investment, acquisition, or exit strategies. By comparing the startup's financial performance to that of similar companies that have already exited, stakeholders can gain insights into the market's assessment and expectations of the company's value. However, it's important to note that exit multiple analysis is just one of many valuation methods available, and it should be used in conjunction with other approaches to obtain a comprehensive understanding of a company's value. Additionally, the accuracy of the analysis depends on the availability and reliability of relevant financial data from comparable companies, which may vary across industries and markets.

Exit Multiple

An exit multiple is a financial valuation metric used in the context of startup and entrepreneurship to determine the potential return on investment (ROI) for investors or founders when they exit their venture. It is calculated by dividing the exit value of a startup by a specific financial metric such as earnings, revenue, or book value. When startups are acquired or go public, investors and founders often need to assess the value of their investment. The exit multiple is a helpful tool as it provides a standardized measure to compare and evaluate different exit opportunities. It allows investors and founders to understand the potential ROI and make informed decisions regarding their exit strategy.

Exit Multiples

Exit multiples refer to the valuation multiple that investors use to determine the price at which a startup or entrepreneurial venture can be sold or acquired. It is a measure of the venture's potential value in the market and is often calculated based on similar business transactions or market comparables.Exit multiples are usually expressed as a multiple of certain financial metrics such as revenue, earnings before interest, tax, depreciation, and amortization (EBITDA), or net income. These financial metrics serve as a basis for estimating the venture's future profitability and cash flows, thereby determining its value in the eyes of potential buyers or investors.The use of exit multiples in startup and entrepreneurship contexts is essential as it helps entrepreneurs and investors make informed decisions regarding potential exits or acquisitions. By analyzing similar industry transactions, exit multiples can provide a benchmark for valuing a startup and understanding the potential returns a venture can generate in the future.When determining the appropriate exit multiple, several factors need to be considered, such as industry dynamics, market conditions, growth potential, competitive advantages, and risk factors. These factors influence the valuation multiple and can vary significantly between different sectors and stages of startups.An exit multiple can be influenced by the startup's growth rate and scalability. Startups with high growth prospects and scalable business models are typically valued at higher multiples due to their potential for generating substantial returns in the future.Furthermore, the level of competition in the market can also impact the exit multiple. In highly competitive industries, exit multiples may be lower as investors perceive higher risks and uncertainties, which can reduce the perceived value of a startup.

Exit Plan

An exit plan, in the context of startup and entrepreneurship, refers to a strategic plan that outlines the ways in which a founder or investor intends to exit their business venture and realize a return on their investment. It serves as a roadmap for how the entrepreneur plans to exit the startup, whether through a sale, merger, acquisition, or by taking the company public through an initial public offering (IPO).An exit plan is an essential component of a startup's overall business strategy and is typically developed early on in the company's lifecycle, often during the formation or funding stages. It provides clarity and direction for the entrepreneur and potential investors, as it demonstrates a clear understanding of how the startup will generate returns and create value.The primary purpose of an exit plan is to maximize the value of the startup and its stakeholders' investments. It helps the entrepreneur establish goals and milestones to work towards, ensuring that the business is on track for a successful exit. Additionally, having a well-defined exit plan can attract potential investors or buyers, as it provides them with confidence in the entrepreneur's vision and strategic thinking.There are several common exit strategies that entrepreneurs may consider when developing their plan. One option is a strategic acquisition, where the startup is acquired by a larger company that sees value in incorporating the startup's products, technology, or talent into their own operations. Another possibility is a merger, in which the startup joins forces with another company to enhance its market position and competitiveness.Alternatively, the entrepreneur might choose to take the startup public through an IPO, allowing the company's shares to be traded on a stock exchange. This can provide liquidity for early investors and potentially generate significant returns if the company's value increases over time.Regardless of the chosen exit strategy, the entrepreneur should also consider preparing for circumstances where the business may not succeed as originally planned. In such cases, the exit plan should outline alternative options, such as selling the company's assets or winding down operations in an orderly manner.In conclusion, an exit plan is a crucial strategic document for startup founders and investors, outlining the intended pathways for exiting the business and maximizing the return on investment. It helps guide decision-making, attract potential stakeholders, and ensures the long-term success of the startup.

Exit Planning

Exit planning is a strategic process undertaken by startup founders and entrepreneurs to prepare and manage the exit from their business. It involves creating and implementing a comprehensive plan to maximize the value of the business and ensure a smooth transition of ownership or leadership. The primary objective of exit planning is to create a profitable exit strategy that aligns with the entrepreneur's goals and objectives. This process often starts at the early stages of a startup's development and continues throughout its lifecycle. The exit plan is designed to provide a clear roadmap for when and how the entrepreneur intends to exit the business, whether through a sale, merger, acquisition, or other means. Exit planning involves several key steps. First, the entrepreneur must assess the current state of the business and its market value. This includes conducting a thorough analysis of financials, operations, and market conditions to determine the company's strengths, weaknesses, opportunities, and threats. Based on this assessment, the entrepreneur can then develop strategies to enhance the value of the business and address any areas of weakness. This may involve implementing operational improvements, developing a strong management team, diversifying revenue streams, or expanding into new markets. Furthermore, exit planning involves identifying potential buyers or investors and establishing relationships with them. This process may include networking, attending industry events, and engaging in direct outreach to interested parties. By building relationships with potential buyers or investors well in advance, the entrepreneur can increase the likelihood of a successful exit. Additionally, exit planning also addresses legal and financial matters that are crucial for a smooth transition. This involves working with legal and financial professionals to ensure compliance with applicable regulations, minimize tax liabilities, and structure the transaction in the most advantageous way. In conclusion, exit planning plays a vital role in startup and entrepreneurship. It allows founders and entrepreneurs to strategically prepare for and execute their exit from the business, maximizing its value and ensuring a seamless transition. By following a comprehensive exit plan, entrepreneurs can optimize their chances of achieving their financial and personal objectives.

Exit Strategies

An exit strategy refers to a plan that an entrepreneur or startup founder develops to exit from their business or investment in a way that maximizes financial return and minimizes potential risks. It is essentially a proactive approach taken by founders to anticipate and plan for the various scenarios that could lead to their departure from the business. The primary purpose of an exit strategy is to ensure that the entrepreneur or startup founder can exit the business in a manner that meets their personal and financial goals. This includes strategies for selling the business, going public through an initial public offering (IPO), or merging with another company. The choice of the exit strategy may depend on factors such as market conditions, the company's growth trajectory, industry trends, and the founder's long-term objectives. One common exit strategy is a merger or acquisition, where a larger company acquires the startup or its assets. This allows the entrepreneur to cash out their investment and potentially continue their involvement in the business under the new ownership. Another option is an IPO, which involves listing the company's shares on a public stock exchange, allowing the founder to sell their shares to the public. However, an IPO can be a complex and costly process, requiring significant resources and compliance with regulatory requirements. Selling the business to a strategic buyer or an individual investor is another exit strategy. This may involve negotiating a sale agreement, conducting due diligence, and transferring ownership of the business. Alternatively, the entrepreneur may choose to liquidate the business, selling off its assets and distributing the proceeds to stakeholders. In addition to financial considerations, an exit strategy also takes into account the impact on employees, customers, and other stakeholders. A well-planned and executed exit strategy can help ensure a smooth transition of ownership and minimize any disruptions to the business operations.

Exit Strategy Implementation

An exit strategy implementation refers to the process of executing a specific plan to withdraw or divest from a startup or entrepreneurial venture. This strategy is typically developed and implemented by the founders or stakeholders of a startup with the goal of maximizing returns and minimizing risk. Exit strategies are crucial for entrepreneurs as they provide a clear framework for the eventual sale, merger, or liquidation of the business. By having a well-defined exit strategy in place, entrepreneurs can effectively align their short-term and long-term goals, secure funding, attract investors, and establish a roadmap for the evolution of their business.

Exit Strategy Planning

Exit strategy planning refers to the process of devising a strategic plan for a startup or entrepreneurial venture to facilitate its eventual exit from the market. It involves careful evaluation of various options and designing a structured approach to maximize returns and minimize risks for the stakeholders involved. The purpose of exit strategy planning is to provide a clear direction and roadmap for the founders and investors of a startup, ensuring that they have a well-defined path to realize their investments and achieve their desired goals. It involves determining the right timing and method to exit the business, which may include options such as mergers and acquisitions, IPOs (Initial Public Offerings), or liquidation. One of the key reasons for developing an exit strategy is to mitigate risks associated with the startup's lifespan. Many startups fail to become profitable or sustainable, and without an exit strategy, the founders and investors may face significant financial losses. By having a well-thought-out exit plan, entrepreneurs can have a contingency plan in case their startup does not meet their expected goals or faces challenges in the market. Another important aspect of exit strategy planning is ensuring the smooth transition of ownership and control. Whether it is through a merger, acquisition, or IPO, the exit strategy should outline the steps and processes required to transfer ownership and operations to the new entity or shareholders. This includes considerations such as negotiating agreements, conducting due diligence, and addressing legal and financial obligations. Furthermore, exit strategy planning also plays a crucial role in attracting investors and partners. Potential investors are often interested in knowing how and when they can realize their investments, and a well-defined exit strategy can provide the necessary reassurance and increase the likelihood of securing funding. Likewise, strategic partners may be more inclined to collaborate with a startup that has a clear roadmap for potential exits, as it demonstrates a focus on long-term growth and profitability. In conclusion, exit strategy planning is a vital component of the startup and entrepreneurial journey. It helps mitigate risks, provides a clear roadmap for founders and investors, facilitates the smooth transition of ownership, and enhances the attractiveness of the venture to potential investors and partners. By carefully considering and planning for the eventual exit, startups can position themselves for success and maximize their returns in the long run.

Exit Strategy

Exit Strategy is a predetermined plan or course of action employed by entrepreneurs and startup founders with the aim of liquidating or divesting their ownership interests in the company. It is a strategic plan designed to provide an avenue for founders and other stakeholders to exit the startup and potentially generate a return on their investment. The primary goal of an exit strategy is to maximize the value of the startup and provide an opportunity for founders and investors to monetize their ownership stakes. There are several common exit strategies that entrepreneurs may consider: The most commonly recognized exit strategy is an Initial Public Offering (IPO), where the company goes public and offers its shares to the public on a stock exchange. This strategy allows founders, early employees, and investors to sell their shares at market prices and potentially realize significant financial gains. Another widely used exit strategy is an acquisition or merger. This involves selling the startup to a larger company that sees value in integrating the startup's products, services, or technology into its own operations. The acquiring company typically pays a premium for the startup, providing a return on investment to the founders and investors. In some cases, entrepreneurs may opt for a management buyout as an exit strategy. This involves selling the company to the existing management team, allowing them to take over ownership and control. This strategy is often used when founders are ready to retire or pursue other ventures. Other exit strategies may include a strategic sale to a competitor, a private equity buyout, or a leveraged buyout. Each strategy has its own set of considerations and potential benefits, depending on the specific circumstances of the startup. It is important for entrepreneurs to have an exit strategy in place from the early stages of the startup. This helps guide decision-making and ensures that the company is structured and positioned in a way that is attractive to potential acquirers or investors. It also provides a clear path for founders and stakeholders to eventually exit the business and realize a return on their investment.

Exit Valuation

An exit valuation in the context of startup and entrepreneurship refers to the estimated value of a startup company at the time of an exit event, such as an initial public offering (IPO) or acquisition. It is a critical measure for both the startup founders and potential investors as it determines the return on investment and can greatly impact the future trajectory of the company. The exit valuation is typically calculated based on various factors and methodologies, including the company's financial performance, market potential, industry comparables, and the overall investor sentiment. It is a complex process that involves the careful analysis of multiple variables and requires the expertise of professionals such as investment bankers and valuation experts. For entrepreneurs, the exit valuation is crucial as it helps them understand the potential value they can realize from their startup in the future. It acts as a benchmark for setting their fundraising goals, as well as determining the viability of various exit strategies. A higher exit valuation indicates a greater potential for financial success and encourages investors to provide funding. However, it also means higher expectations and pressure to deliver on the promises made to investors. Investors, on the other hand, consider the exit valuation as a key factor in their investment decisions. They assess the potential return on investment based on the projected exit valuation and evaluate the startup's growth prospects, market competitiveness, and the current valuation multiples of similar companies in the industry. A higher exit valuation increases the likelihood of investors achieving a significant return on their investment. It is important to note that the exit valuation is not a fixed or guaranteed amount. It can fluctuate significantly based on the performance of the startup, market conditions, and investor sentiment. Startups often go through multiple financing rounds, and the exit valuation can change with each funding round as new investors enter and existing investors reevaluate their investments. In conclusion, the exit valuation plays a crucial role in startup and entrepreneurship as it determines the potential financial success and return on investment. It helps entrepreneurs set goals and make informed decisions, while investors rely on it to assess the viability of their investment. The exit valuation is a dynamic and ever-changing measure that reflects the market perception of a startup's value.

Exits And Acquisitions

Exits and Acquisitions are two important terms in the context of startup and entrepreneurship. An exit refers to the process in which a startup or entrepreneur realizes their investment and leaves the venture. It can be achieved through various means such as selling the startup, going public through an initial public offering (IPO), or merging with another company. The ultimate goal of an exit is to provide a return on investment for the startup's founders and investors. On the other hand, an acquisition occurs when one company purchases another company, either fully or partially. In the startup ecosystem, acquisitions are often seen as a viable exit strategy for startups, as they allow the founders and investors to monetize their efforts and realize their returns on investment. Acquisitions can take several forms, such as asset acquisitions, stock acquisitions, or mergers.

Experiential Learning

Experiential learning in the context of startups and entrepreneurship is a process of gaining knowledge, skills, and understanding through hands-on experiences and active engagement with real-world challenges and problems encountered in the startup ecosystem. Instead of relying solely on traditional classroom instruction, experiential learning emphasizes learning by doing, where entrepreneurs actively participate in practical activities and projects to develop and refine their entrepreneurial competencies. It involves embracing real-life situations, taking calculated risks, and learning from both successes and failures.

FOMO (Fear Of Missing Out)

FOMO (Fear of Missing Out) can be defined as a psychological feeling of anxiety or unease that occurs when entrepreneurs or individuals perceive that they are missing out on opportunities, experiences, or events within the startup ecosystem. In the context of startups and entrepreneurship, FOMO often arises due to the fast-paced and dynamic nature of the industry. Entrepreneurs are constantly exposed to a plethora of new ideas, technologies, and trends that have the potential to create significant impact and success. The fear of missing out drives individuals to constantly stay connected and engaged, fearing that they may miss out on a groundbreaking idea, a valuable networking opportunity, or an influential industry event. FOMO can manifest in various ways within the startup community. Entrepreneurs may feel pressured to constantly attend startup events, conferences, and meetups in order to stay updated and connected with the latest developments. They may fear that by not being present at these events, important connections may be missed, partnerships may go unrealized, or valuable knowledge and insights may be overlooked. Similarly, FOMO can also extend to the digital realm, where entrepreneurs are overwhelmed by the constant influx of information and updates from various sources such as social media, industry blogs, and startup communities. The fear of missing out on the latest news, trends, or opportunities can lead individuals to tirelessly browse through online platforms, attempting to stay ahead of the curve and not miss out on any potentially valuable information. While some level of FOMO can be motivating and beneficial in driving entrepreneurs to seek out new opportunities, excessive fear of missing out can have negative consequences. Constantly chasing after every opportunity can lead to burnout, decision paralysis, and a lack of focus on the core objectives of the startup. It can also result in a superficial understanding of the industry, as individuals may spread themselves too thin trying to keep up with everything rather than diving deep into specific areas of expertise. Ultimately, managing FOMO in the startup ecosystem requires entrepreneurs to strike a balance between staying informed and connected, while also prioritizing their time and resources effectively. It's important for entrepreneurs to consciously evaluate the potential value and impact of each opportunity or event, and make informed decisions about their involvement based on their unique goals and circumstances.

Fail-Fast Approach

The Fail-Fast approach in the context of startup and entrepreneurship refers to a mindset and strategy that encourages entrepreneurs to quickly identify and acknowledge failures and shortcomings in their business model or product, allowing them to make necessary adjustments or pivot before investing significant time and resources. Instead of viewing failure as something to be avoided or feared, the fail-fast approach embraces it as a learning opportunity. By actively seeking out potential failures, entrepreneurs can gather valuable feedback and data that can inform their decision-making and ultimately increase the chances of success in the long run.

Family And Friends Round

Startup: A startup is a newly-established company or organization that is in the early stages of development and growth. It is typically founded by one or more individuals with the aim of bringing a unique product, service, or solution to the market. Startups often operate in innovative and disruptive industries, and their success is driven by their ability to identify and exploit new business opportunities. Entrepreneurship: Entrepreneurship refers to the process of designing, launching, and running a new business venture. It involves taking risks and leveraging resources to create a viable and profitable enterprise. Entrepreneurs are individuals who identify opportunities, develop innovative ideas, and take on the responsibility of managing and growing their businesses. They possess a combination of skills, such as creativity, vision, leadership, and resilience, which are essential for navigating the challenges and uncertainties of the business world.

Feasibility Analysis

Feasibility analysis, in the context of startup and entrepreneurship, refers to the evaluation and assessment of the potential success and viability of a new business idea or venture. It is a critical process that allows entrepreneurs to determine whether their proposed business concept is feasible and has the potential to be profitable and sustainable in the long run. The analysis involves assessing various aspects of the startup idea, including market demand, competition, financial resources, technical feasibility, and operational requirements. The first aspect of feasibility analysis involves examining the market demand and potential customer base for the product or service. This includes conducting market research to understand the target market, their needs, and preferences. It also involves identifying the size of the market and determining if there is enough demand to support the business. In addition to market demand, entrepreneurs need to evaluate the level of competition in the industry. This involves researching and analyzing existing competitors, their market share, and the strategies they employ. Understanding the competitive landscape helps entrepreneurs identify potential challenges and develop strategies to differentiate their business and attract customers. Financial feasibility is another crucial aspect of feasibility analysis. Entrepreneurs need to assess the financial resources required to start and operate the business. This includes estimating the startup costs, such as equipment, inventory, and marketing expenses. It also involves projecting the potential revenues and expenses to determine if the business can generate profits and sustain itself financially. Furthermore, entrepreneurs need to evaluate the technical feasibility of their startup idea. This involves assessing whether the necessary technology, infrastructure, and resources are available or can be acquired to support the business operations. Finally, operational feasibility examines the resources, logistics, and operational processes required to run the business smoothly. Entrepreneurs need to consider factors such as staffing, supply chain management, production capacity, and distribution channels. The aim is to determine if the startup idea can be implemented and operated effectively. Ultimately, feasibility analysis is an essential tool for entrepreneurs to assess the viability and potential success of their startup idea. It helps identify potential risks, challenges, and opportunities, enabling entrepreneurs to make informed decisions and develop effective strategies to launch and grow their business.

Financial Modeling Software

Financial modeling software refers to a specialized tool that enables startups and entrepreneurs to create, manipulate, and analyze financial models. It is designed to aid in strategic decision-making by providing accurate forecasts and projections based on various financial variables and assumptions. This software is crucial for startups as it helps them in assessing the financial viability of their business ideas and developing realistic financial plans. This software typically incorporates features such as built-in templates, financial formulas, and scenario analysis, which allow users to input relevant data and create comprehensive financial models. These models are based on key financial statements, including income statements, balance sheets, and cash flow statements. By utilizing these tools, startups and entrepreneurs can assess the potential impact of various business strategies and make informed decisions that align with their goals.

Financial Projections

Financial projections refer to the estimated future financial performance of a startup or entrepreneurial venture. They are prepared based on a thorough analysis of the company's past financial data and market conditions, as well as assumptions about future growth, trends, and the implementation of specific strategies. These projections are typically presented in the form of financial statements, such as income statements, balance sheets, and cash flow statements, for a specific period, usually three to five years. They serve as a tool for entrepreneurs and investors to assess the financial viability and potential profitability of a startup or new venture.

Fintech (Financial Technology)

Fintech, short for Financial Technology, refers to the application of technological innovations in the financial services industry. It can be defined as an entrepreneurial field that focuses on developing and implementing innovative solutions to improve financial processes and services, using advanced software, mobile applications, and other digital tools. Startups and entrepreneurs in the fintech space aim to disrupt traditional financial systems and create new business models that are more efficient, flexible, and customer-centric. They leverage advancements in artificial intelligence, big data analytics, blockchain technology, and cloud computing to offer innovative products and services that address the evolving needs of consumers, businesses, and financial institutions. The fintech industry encompasses a wide range of areas, including payments and remittances, lending and borrowing, asset management, insurance, personal finance, and regulatory technology. Startups and entrepreneurs in these areas develop and offer digital solutions that make financial transactions and processes faster, cheaper, and more secure. For example, payment platforms like PayPal and Square revolutionized the way people send and receive money, making it easier and more convenient to make online transactions. Furthermore, fintech startups often target underserved segments of the population by providing access to financial services that were previously limited or unavailable. Through innovative technologies and business models, they aim to bridge the gap between traditional financial institutions and the unbanked or underbanked population. This can include offering microloans and credit to individuals and small businesses with limited credit history or access to traditional banking services. In conclusion, fintech is a rapidly growing sector in the startup and entrepreneurship ecosystem, driven by technological advancements and the demand for more efficient and accessible financial services. Startups and entrepreneurs in this space are at the forefront of creating innovative solutions that simplify financial processes, increase financial inclusion, and disrupt traditional financial institutions. As the adoption of digital technologies continues to expand, the fintech industry is expected to further transform the way we interact with money, investments, and financial institutions.

Fintech Platforms

A fintech platform refers to a digital platform that offers financial services and solutions using technology. These platforms leverage the power of technology to provide innovative and convenient financial services to individuals, businesses, and other stakeholders. Startups and entrepreneurs can benefit from fintech platforms in various ways. Firstly, these platforms often provide a cost-effective alternative to traditional financial institutions, allowing startups and entrepreneurs to access financial services without the need for extensive physical infrastructure or high fees. This can be especially beneficial for early-stage startups that have limited resources. Secondly, fintech platforms offer increased accessibility and convenience. By providing services through digital channels such as websites or mobile applications, startups and entrepreneurs can access financial services anytime and from anywhere. This flexibility is crucial for agile and fast-growing startups that require quick and efficient access to funds, payment processing, or other financial solutions. Furthermore, fintech platforms often utilize advanced technologies such as artificial intelligence and machine learning to improve the accuracy and efficiency of financial services. These technologies can automate processes such as credit scoring, risk assessment, or fraud detection, allowing startups and entrepreneurs to make data-driven decisions and reduce the risk of human error. In addition, many fintech platforms offer a range of financial services, including but not limited to, payment processing, lending, investment management, insurance, and accounting. This comprehensive approach provides startups and entrepreneurs with a one-stop solution for their financial needs, reducing the need to work with multiple providers and streamlining financial operations. In conclusion, fintech platforms are digital platforms that leverage technology to provide innovative and convenient financial services to startups and entrepreneurs. These platforms offer cost-effective alternatives to traditional financial institutions, increased accessibility and convenience, advanced technologies for improved efficiency, and comprehensive financial solutions.

Fintech Startup

Fintech startup refers to a new venture that leverages technology to provide financial products or services in innovative ways, disrupting traditional financial systems. Entering the fintech space requires a combination of entrepreneurial skills, knowledge of the financial industry, and technological know-how. As an entrepreneur, launching a fintech startup involves identifying opportunities for disruption in the financial sector and developing solutions that address specific pain points or inefficiencies. These pain points could range from slow and complex payment systems to limited access to financial services for underserved populations. By harnessing the power of technology, fintech startups aim to streamline processes, increase accessibility, and deliver enhanced user experiences. The success of a fintech startup largely depends on the ability to identify and target a specific niche market, develop a robust business model, and secure appropriate funding. Startup founders must conduct thorough market research to understand the competitive landscape and assess potential demand for their solution. They must also take into account regulatory requirements and compliance, as the financial industry is highly regulated to ensure consumer protection and stability. In order to navigate the complex financial landscape, fintech startups often collaborate with established banking institutions or partner with other fintech companies to leverage expertise, resources, and customer networks. Building strategic partnerships allows startups to scale their operations and reach a broader audience, while also gaining credibility in the industry. Fintech startups also face challenges related to data security, privacy, and data analytics. Protecting sensitive financial information is of utmost importance to establish trust and compliance with regulations. Additionally, startups need to effectively collect, analyze, and utilize data to gain actionable insights that drive business growth and improve offerings. In conclusion, fintech startups are dynamic entrepreneurial ventures that disrupt the traditional financial industry by leveraging technology to deliver innovative financial products or services. These startups rely on a combination of industry expertise, technological advancements, strategic partnerships, and effective data utilization to gain a competitive edge and create value in the market.

Focus Group Discussions

Focus Group Discussions are a qualitative research method that involves bringing together a small group of individuals to discuss specific topics or issues relevant to a startup or entrepreneurship context. These discussions typically last for a predetermined period of time and are guided by a moderator who facilitates the conversation. The main purpose of conducting focus group discussions in the startup or entrepreneurship field is to gather in-depth insights, opinions, and experiences from participants regarding a particular product, service, or concept. This method allows startups and entrepreneurs to gain a deeper understanding of their target audience's needs, preferences, and behaviors, consequently helping them make informed decisions and refine their business strategies. During a focus group discussion, participants are encouraged to express their thoughts openly and share their perspectives with the group. The moderator's role is to ensure that the conversation stays on track, while also allowing for spontaneous and free-flowing discussion. They may use various probing techniques, such as follow-up questions or prompts, to elicit further insights from participants. Focus group discussions provide startups and entrepreneurs with several advantages. Firstly, they enable direct interaction and real-time exploration of participants' attitudes and perceptions towards a product or service. This direct feedback can offer valuable insights, helping businesses identify potential issues, strengths, and areas for improvement. Additionally, focus group discussions allow for the exploration of underlying motivations and reasons behind participants' opinions and behaviors. By probing deeper into participants' thoughts, startups and entrepreneurs can uncover hidden insights and uncover potential gaps in their understanding of their target market. However, it is important to note that focus group discussions may also have limitations. The small sample size may not be representative of the entire target market, and participants' responses may be influenced by group dynamics or social desirability bias. Therefore, startups and entrepreneurs should interpret the findings from focus group discussions cautiously and consider conducting further research or using other methods to validate the insights gathered.

Follow-On Funding

Follow-On Funding refers to the additional funding that is provided to a startup or entrepreneur at a later stage of their business journey, after they have already received an initial round of funding. This type of funding is typically secured to support the continued growth and development of the company. Startups and entrepreneurs often require additional funding beyond their initial round of investment to further scale their operations, expand into new markets, or develop new products or services. This is where follow-on funding becomes crucial. It allows these companies to access the financial resources needed to sustain their growth trajectory and achieve their long-term goals.

Follow-On Investment Round

A follow-on investment round, in the context of startup and entrepreneurship, refers to a subsequent funding round that takes place after the initial round, typically referred to as the seed round or Series A funding. Follow-on investment rounds are usually undertaken to provide additional capital to fuel the growth and expansion of a startup. During the initial rounds of funding, startup companies often secure funds from venture capitalists, angel investors, or other sources to launch their business and develop their product or service. However, as the startup progresses and demonstrates promise and traction in the market, it may require additional funds to scale its operations, hire more staff, invest in R&D, expand into new markets, or enhance its infrastructure. In such cases, the startup's existing investors or new investors may participate in a follow-on investment round. These subsequent funding rounds could take the form of Series B, C, D, and so on, depending on the startup's growth trajectory and funding needs. The objective of a follow-on investment round is to provide the necessary capital for the startup to continue its growth and achieve its strategic goals. Follow-on investment rounds are often larger in scale compared to the initial rounds, as they aim to support the startup's expansion plans. The valuation of the startup may increase with each subsequent round, reflecting its progress, market potential, and ability to execute its business plan. Throughout the follow-on investment round, startup entrepreneurs must showcase their company's achievements, market potential, and growth prospects to investors. The due diligence process will be repeated, and negotiations regarding investment terms, equity dilution, and board representation may take place. Securing follow-on investment rounds is crucial for startups aiming to scale and establish themselves in the market. It serves as a vote of confidence from investors, signaling that they believe in the company's future prospects and are willing to provide additional funds to fuel its growth.

Follow-On Investment

Follow-on investment refers to a subsequent round of funding that an established startup or entrepreneur seeks after receiving an initial investment. It is essentially an additional injection of capital from existing or new investors to support the growth and expansion of the startup. This type of investment typically occurs when a startup has achieved certain milestones or demonstrated potential for further growth. It is often sought at critical stages when the initial funding is being depleted and more resources are required to scale operations, enter new markets, develop new products or services, or acquire key assets.

Follow-On Round

A startup is a young company founded by one or more entrepreneurs with the goal of developing and commercializing a unique product or service. Startups are characterized by their innovative and scalable business models, their ability to disrupt established industries, and their potential for rapid growth.Entrepreneurship, on the other hand, refers to the process of starting, managing, and growing a business venture. It encompasses the activities of identifying opportunities, mobilizing resources, taking risks, and creating value through innovation and the successful operation of a new enterprise.

Founder Vesting

Founder vesting is a contractual agreement that outlines the timeframe and conditions under which founders of a startup can earn their ownership equity. It is a mechanism that serves to incentivize founders to remain committed and loyal to the startup over the long term. Typically, founder vesting is implemented through vesting schedules, which detail the specific milestones or time periods that founders must meet in order to fully own their equity. This means that the founders' shares are subject to a vesting period, during which their ownership gradually accrues. If a founder leaves the startup before the vesting period is complete, they may lose a portion of their equity.

Founder

A founder is an individual who initiates and establishes a startup or business venture. They are responsible for conceiving and envisioning the idea behind the startup, creating the initial business plan, securing funding, and assembling a team to bring the idea to life. The role of the founder in the context of startups and entrepreneurship is crucial. Their vision and leadership provide the guiding force that determines the direction and success of the company. They are typically driven by a passion for their idea and possess a deep understanding of the industry they are operating in.

Founders' Agreement

A Founders' Agreement is a formal document that outlines the terms and conditions agreed upon by the founders of a startup or entrepreneurial venture. It serves as a valuable tool in establishing the rights, obligations, and responsibilities of each founder, helping to prevent misunderstandings and disputes in the future. The Founders' Agreement typically covers a wide range of important aspects related to the startup, including the division of ownership and equity among the founders, the roles and responsibilities of each founder, the decision-making process, and the allocation of profits and losses. It also addresses potential scenarios such as the departure or death of a founder, outlining the procedures for transferring ownership and resolving any disputes that may arise. By setting clear guidelines and expectations, the Founders' Agreement helps create a solid foundation for the startup and ensures that all founders have a shared understanding of key issues. This can be especially crucial in situations where founders have different levels of involvement, expertise, or financial contributions. The agreement provides a fair and transparent framework for decision-making, promoting a harmonious working relationship and reducing the likelihood of conflicts among the founders. Additionally, the Founders' Agreement can include provisions related to intellectual property rights, non-disclosure agreements, and non-compete clauses to protect the startup's proprietary information and prevent founders from engaging in competing ventures during their involvement with the startup. This helps safeguard the startup's innovations and gives the founders confidence in sharing important ideas and strategies with one another. In conclusion, a Founders' Agreement is an essential document for startups and entrepreneurs as it establishes the foundation for the working relationship among the founders. It clarifies ownership, responsibilities, and decision-making processes, while also protecting the startup's intellectual property and addressing potential conflicts. By having a well-drafted and comprehensive Founders' Agreement, founders can mitigate risks and ensure a smoother journey towards their entrepreneurial goals.

Franchise Agreement

A franchise agreement is a legally binding contract between a franchisor and a franchisee that outlines the terms and conditions of a business relationship. It defines the rights and obligations of both parties and governs the operations of the franchise.In the context of startups and entrepreneurship, a franchise agreement allows an entrepreneur (franchisee) to establish and operate a business using the established brand, trademarks, and business model of an existing successful company (franchisor). This agreement allows the entrepreneur to leverage the reputation, customer base, and operational expertise of the franchisor to start and run their own business.

Franchise Business

A franchise business is a type of business arrangement where an entrepreneur (the franchisee) purchases the rights to open and operate a business based on an existing successful model and brand (the franchisor). The franchisor grants the franchisee the license to use their trademarks, business methods, and sell their products or services. This business model is popular in startup and entrepreneurship because it allows individuals to start a business with a proven concept and established brand recognition. The franchisee benefits from the support, training, and guidance provided by the franchisor, which increases the chances of success compared to starting a business from scratch.

Franchise Model

A franchise model is a system in which an entrepreneur purchases the rights to operate a business under an established brand and proven business model. It is a popular approach for startups as it allows them to leverage the success and reputation of an existing brand, reducing the risks associated with starting a new business from scratch. Under the franchise model, the franchisor, or the owner of the established brand, grants the franchisee, or the entrepreneur, the right to use their brand name, trademarks, and business processes. In return, the franchisee pays an initial franchise fee and ongoing royalties or a percentage of their revenue to the franchisor. This fee provides the franchisee with access to a range of benefits, including training, marketing support, and the use of established supply chains. The franchise model offers several advantages for startups and entrepreneurs. Firstly, it provides a proven business concept, allowing the entrepreneur to skip the trial and error phase of developing a business idea. The franchisor has already tested their business model, identified their target market, and established effective marketing strategies. This significantly reduces the risks associated with starting a new business. Secondly, the franchise model offers the support and guidance of the franchisor. Franchisees receive comprehensive training on the brand's business processes, ensuring they have the necessary knowledge and skills to operate the business successfully. The franchisor also provides ongoing support in areas such as marketing, operations, and customer service. This support system can be invaluable to startups and entrepreneurs, particularly those who may have limited business experience. Additionally, the franchise model allows entrepreneurs to tap into an established customer base. By operating under a well-known brand, the franchisee can benefit from the existing reputation and customer loyalty associated with the brand. This can lead to a faster and smoother entry into the market, as customers are already familiar with the brand and its products or services. In conclusion, the franchise model offers startups and entrepreneurs a structured and low-risk approach to starting a business. By purchasing the rights to operate under an established brand, entrepreneurs can leverage the brand's success, benefit from ongoing support, and tap into an existing customer base.

Franchise

A franchise is a business model in which the creator of a successful business (known as the franchisor) grants an individual or company (known as the franchisee) the right to operate a replica of the original business in a specified location or territory. In this arrangement, the franchisor provides the franchisee with a proven and well-established business concept, along with extensive support, training, and ongoing assistance. The franchisee, in turn, pays the franchisor an initial fee and ongoing royalties in exchange for the right to use the franchisor's brand name, trademarks, business systems, and intellectual property. The franchise model offers several benefits to both the franchisor and the franchisee. For the franchisor, it provides an opportunity to expand their business quickly and efficiently, leveraging the resources and capital of individual franchisees. It allows the franchisor to maintain control over the brand and the quality of products or services offered, while also generating additional revenue through franchise fees and royalties. For the franchisee, the franchise model presents a lower risk compared to starting a new business from scratch as they are building upon a proven concept with a established customer base. They receive support and guidance from the franchisor, which includes assistance with site selection, lease negotiation, marketing, and ongoing training. The franchisee also benefits from the credibility and recognition associated with the established brand. However, while the franchise model offers many advantages, it also comes with certain limitations. The franchisee is expected to adhere to the franchisor's rules, policies, and operational guidelines, limiting their flexibility and decision-making autonomy. They are also required to pay ongoing fees to the franchisor, which can impact their profitability. Additionally, the success of the franchise is dependent on various factors including market conditions, location, competition, and the franchisee's commitment and skills. In summary, a franchise is a business arrangement in which the franchisor grants the franchisee the right to operate a replica of their successful business. It offers benefits such as a proven concept and support from the franchisor, but also comes with limitations and ongoing fees. Ultimately, the success of a franchise depends on the execution of the business model by both the franchisor and the franchisee.

Franchisee

A franchisee is an individual or a group of individuals who purchase the rights to operate a business under a recognized brand name and established business model. The franchisee enters into a contractual agreement with the franchisor, the company that owns the brand, to operate a business using the franchisor's trademark, products, and services. Unlike starting a business from scratch, becoming a franchisee offers several advantages. First and foremost, the franchisee benefits from the recognition and reputation that the brand has already established. This eliminates the need for extensive marketing efforts and helps attract customers who are already familiar with the brand. Additionally, the franchisee receives ongoing support and training from the franchisor, which can include assistance with site selection, staff training, marketing campaigns, and operational guidance. The franchisor typically charges a franchise fee and ongoing royalties from the franchisee. The franchise fee is a one-time payment made by the franchisee to the franchisor, granting them the right to operate the business under the franchise brand. The ongoing royalties are a percentage of the franchisee's sales that are paid to the franchisor for continued use of the brand name, products, and support services. As a franchisee, one must adhere to the established operating procedures and standards set by the franchisor. This ensures consistency across all franchise locations and helps maintain the brand's reputation. The franchisee is responsible for day-to-day operations, including managing employees, maintaining inventory, and providing customer service. Franchising offers a lower risk option for entrepreneurs who want to start their own business. The established brand, proven business model, and ongoing support provided by the franchisor increase the chances of success. However, it is important for potential franchisees to thoroughly research and evaluate the franchise opportunity before making a commitment. This includes understanding the costs involved, evaluating the franchisor's track record, and considering market demand and competition in the chosen industry.

Franchisor

A franchisor is a company or individual that owns a business concept or brand and grants the right to third-party individuals or entities, known as franchisees, to operate a business using that concept or brand in exchange for payment of fees or royalties. The relationship between a franchisor and franchisee is governed by a legally binding agreement, called a franchise agreement, which outlines the rights and obligations of each party. As a franchisor, the primary objective is to expand the reach of the business concept or brand by leveraging the resources and efforts of independent franchisees. Franchisors provide franchisees with the necessary support, training, and guidance to ensure the successful operation of their franchises. This support may include assistance with site selection, marketing and advertising programs, ongoing training and updates, access to proprietary systems and technologies, and a proven operational model.

Freelancing

Freelancing is a form of self-employment where individuals offer their services to multiple clients on a contractual basis rather than being employed by a single company. It is commonly practiced in the context of startup and entrepreneurship as it provides a flexible and cost-effective way to obtain specialized skills and resources. In this arrangement, freelancers, also known as independent contractors or consultants, work independently to complete projects or tasks assigned by their clients. They have the freedom to choose their clients, negotiate rates and terms, and manage their workload and schedule. This flexibility allows freelancers to create a work-life balance that suits their preferences and enables them to pursue various opportunities simultaneously. Startups and entrepreneurs often rely on freelancers to fill skill gaps or supplement their existing teams without the need for long-term employment commitments. They can leverage the expertise of freelancers in areas such as graphic design, software development, content writing, marketing, and more. Freelancers bring specialized skills, experience, and fresh perspectives to the table, enabling startups to access talent that may not be available or affordable in-house. Furthermore, freelancing offers entrepreneurs a cost advantage as they only pay for the specific services they require. They are not burdened with the costs associated with hiring and maintaining a full-time employee, such as salaries, benefits, and office space. The ability to bring in freelancers as needed allows startups to be more agile and responsive to changing market conditions, while keeping their operational costs under control. With the increasing availability of online platforms and marketplaces dedicated to freelancing, the practice has become more accessible and widespread. Freelancers can create profiles, showcase their skills, and connect with potential clients from around the world. On the other hand, startups and entrepreneurs can easily find and hire freelancers who align with their project requirements and budget. In summary, freelancing in the context of startup and entrepreneurship refers to the arrangement where independent contractors provide their services to multiple clients on a contractual basis. It offers flexibility, specialized skills, and cost advantages to startups while providing freelancers with the opportunity to work on diverse projects and maintain a flexible lifestyle.

Freemium Model

The freemium model is a business strategy commonly used by startups and entrepreneurs in the software industry. It involves offering a basic version of a product or service for free, while charging customers for additional premium features or enhanced functionality. The freemium model aims to attract a large user base by providing a valuable product or service at no cost. This helps startups and entrepreneurs generate brand awareness, acquire new customers, and increase market penetration. By offering a free version, they remove the barrier to entry for potential users who may be hesitant to pay for an unfamiliar product. This enables them to reach a wider audience and build a customer base that can later be monetized. Once the freemium product gains traction and establishes a user base, startups and entrepreneurs can introduce premium features or advanced functionalities that provide additional value to the users. These premium features are typically offered through paid subscriptions or one-time purchases, allowing the business to generate revenue from a portion of their user base. The revenue generated from the premium offerings helps sustain the business and supports further product development, marketing efforts, and customer support. The freemium model also offers startups and entrepreneurs the opportunity to upsell and cross-sell to their existing user base. By offering a free version, they can demonstrate the value and benefits of the product or service, making it easier to convince users to upgrade to the premium offerings. Additionally, they can leverage the user data obtained from the free users to personalize marketing messages and target specific customer segments effectively. While the freemium model can be an effective strategy for startups and entrepreneurs, it does come with challenges. It requires careful planning and execution to balance the free and premium offerings, ensuring that the basic version remains valuable enough to attract new users while the premium features provide substantial value to justify the cost. The freemium model also requires ongoing innovation and product development to keep users engaged and entice them to upgrade to the paid version.

Funding Cycle

A funding cycle in the context of startup and entrepreneurship refers to the process by which a startup secures financing from external sources. This cycle involves various stages, each with its own requirements and objectives, that entrepreneurs need to navigate in order to raise the necessary capital to launch and grow their business. The first stage of the funding cycle is often referred to as the pre-seed stage, where entrepreneurs use their personal savings or funds from friends and family to finance their idea or prototype. At this stage, startups may also seek support from angel investors or participate in pitch competitions to secure additional funding. The objective is to develop a compelling business plan and gather proof of concept to attract potential investors. The next stage is the seed stage, in which startups seek larger investments to support the development of their product or service. This may involve presenting their business plan to venture capitalists or angel investor networks. The seed stage funding is typically used to refine the product, conduct market research, and build the initial team. Investors at this stage assess the startup's potential for growth and profitability. If the startup successfully progresses through the seed stage, it may proceed to the next stage known as the Series A funding. This stage involves raising a significant amount of capital to scale up operations, expand market reach, and drive customer acquisition. The focus is on building a robust business model and demonstrating traction in the market. Venture capital firms and institutional investors are often the key players at this stage, with rigorous due diligence and negotiations to determine the terms of investment. Subsequent funding rounds, such as Series B, C, and beyond, may follow as the startup continues to grow. These rounds typically involve larger investments and are aimed at further scaling the business, enter new markets, or strengthen the team. Each funding round requires entrepreneurs to showcase their progress, business metrics, and future plans to attract new investors or secure follow-on investments from existing ones.

Funding Options

Funding options in the context of startup and entrepreneurship refer to the various methods and sources through which entrepreneurs can secure financial resources to start or grow their business ventures. These funding options play a crucial role in helping startups turn their ideas into reality and fuel their growth and expansion. There are several funding options available to entrepreneurs, each with its own advantages and considerations. One of the most common funding options for startups is bootstrapping, where the entrepreneur uses their personal funds or relies on friends and family to finance the initial stages of the business. Bootstrapping allows entrepreneurs to maintain complete control over the business but may limit the amount of capital available. Another popular funding option is crowdfunding, which involves raising funds from a large number of individuals, typically through online platforms. Crowdfunding allows entrepreneurs to generate capital while also testing market demand for their product or service. However, entrepreneurs must carefully plan and execute their crowdfunding campaigns to attract sufficient interest and secure the necessary funding. Venture capital is a funding option commonly pursued by startups with high growth potential. Venture capitalists provide financial backing in exchange for equity or a stake in the business. This funding option can bring not only capital but also industry expertise and networks, but it often requires entrepreneurs to relinquish some control and ownership of their company. Angel investors are affluent individuals who invest their personal funds in startups in exchange for equity. Unlike venture capitalists, angel investors typically invest in early-stage startups and provide mentorship and guidance alongside their financial support. Securing angel investment can provide startups with crucial capital and valuable industry connections. Traditional bank loans and lines of credit are also funding options for entrepreneurs. These options may require collateral or a proven track record of profitability but can provide startups with stable and flexible financing options. Additionally, grants and government funding programs can also support startups, particularly those with innovative or social impact-focused ventures. In conclusion, funding options are key considerations for entrepreneurs looking to start or grow their businesses. Selecting the most appropriate funding options requires careful evaluation of the business's stage, growth potential, and the entrepreneur's goals and preferences. Each funding option has its own benefits and considerations, and entrepreneurs must thoroughly research and plan their funding strategy to secure the necessary capital for their startup.

Funding Pipeline

A funding pipeline refers to the process through which startups and entrepreneurs secure financial resources to support the growth and development of their business ventures. It encompasses the various stages and sources of funding that entrepreneurs rely on to obtain the necessary capital for their operations. The funding pipeline typically begins with the initial stage, known as seed funding or early-stage financing. At this stage, entrepreneurs often seek funds from their personal savings, family, friends, or angel investors. These initial funds help startups launch their business ideas, conduct market research, and develop prototypes or minimum viable products. As startups progress and demonstrate potential for growth, they move into the next stage of funding, referred to as venture capital financing. Venture capital firms or individual investors provide capital in exchange for equity or ownership stakes in the startup. This infusion of funds helps startups scale their operations, expand their customer base, and execute their growth strategies. Once the startup has achieved significant growth and validation, it may consider additional funding options such as private equity or strategic partnerships. Private equity firms invest in more mature businesses, aiming to increase their value over time and eventually exit the investment with a substantial return. Strategic partnerships involve collaboration with established companies to leverage their resources, market access, and expertise. The funding pipeline also includes the possibility of obtaining funds through debt financing. This form of funding involves borrowing money from banks, financial institutions, or alternative lending platforms. Startups may choose to utilize debt financing when they have a clear plan for generating consistent revenue streams that can support the repayment of the borrowed funds. In summary, the funding pipeline in the context of startup and entrepreneurship encompasses the journey entrepreneurs undertake to secure financial support for their ventures. From seed funding to venture capital financing, and potentially private equity or strategic partnerships, startups explore various sources and stages of funding to fuel their growth and achieve their business objectives.

Funding Platform

A funding platform is a type of online platform that connects startups and entrepreneurs with potential investors or funders. It acts as an intermediary between these two groups, facilitating the process of raising funds for startups and providing investment opportunities for interested parties. For startups and entrepreneurs, a funding platform offers a convenient and efficient way to access capital. Instead of relying solely on traditional methods such as bank loans or personal savings, they can present their business ideas or projects on the platform and attract potential investors. These investors can be individuals or institutions, including angel investors, venture capitalists, or even crowdfunding contributors. By showcasing their business ideas or projects on the platform, startups can gain visibility and increase their chances of securing funding. The funding platform typically provides a range of services to facilitate the fundraising process. This may include tools for creating and maintaining fundraising campaigns, conducting due diligence on potential investors, and facilitating communication between startups and investors. The platform may also offer resources and guidance to startups in preparing their pitches, developing business plans, and conducting market research. For investors, a funding platform offers a variety of investment opportunities. They can browse through the available startups and projects on the platform and select those that align with their investment criteria and interests. The platform may provide information such as the startup's business model, market potential, and financial projections to help investors make informed investment decisions. Additionally, a funding platform may offer features to mitigate the risks associated with startup investments. This may include investor protection mechanisms, such as escrow accounts or investment guarantees. The platform may also facilitate the negotiation and documentation of investment terms, ensuring transparency and clarity for both startups and investors. In summary, a funding platform plays a crucial role in connecting startups and entrepreneurs with potential investors, enabling the process of raising funds for innovative projects. It provides a convenient and efficient platform for startups to access capital and for investors to discover investment opportunities. By providing various services and features, a funding platform aims to streamline the fundraising process and enhance the success rate for both startups and investors.

Funding Round

A funding round in the context of startup and entrepreneurship refers to a specific period or phase in which a startup company seeks to raise capital from external investors. It is a crucial step for startups to secure the necessary financial resources to grow and develop their business. During a funding round, startup founders and entrepreneurs typically approach venture capitalists, angel investors, or other funding sources to pitch their business idea and secure investment. The funding round can be divided into different stages or rounds, such as seed round, series A, series B, and so on, depending on the startup's funding needs and growth stage.

Funding Rounds In Startups

A funding round in the context of startups and entrepreneurship refers to a specific stage in the process of securing external capital or funding for a startup company. Startups often require financial resources to fuel their growth, develop their products or services, and expand their operations. They typically seek funding from external investors to support these efforts, as the internal resources of the company are often limited. A funding round can be seen as a structured and organized effort by a startup to raise a specific amount of capital from investors. These rounds are usually planned and executed at different stages of a startup's life cycle, and each round is aimed at raising a specific amount of funding. The amounts sought in each round can vary greatly, depending on the needs and growth trajectory of the startup. Funding rounds are commonly categorized into different types or stages, such as seed round, Series A, Series B, and so on. Seed rounds usually take place at the early stages of a startup, when the business is in its infancy and has a limited track record. These rounds focus on raising capital to validate the startup's concept, develop a minimum viable product, and test the market demand. As the startup progresses and achieves certain milestones, it may seek additional rounds of funding, such as Series A, B, C, and beyond. These subsequent rounds are often aimed at scaling the business, expanding the customer base, or entering new markets. Each funding round typically involves a new valuation of the startup, which determines how much equity or ownership stake the investors receive in exchange for their investment. Funding rounds are crucial for startups as they enable them to access the necessary capital to fund their operations and growth plans. The successful completion of a funding round not only provides the startup with the financial resources it needs but also validates its business model and attracts attention from potential customers, partners, and other investors.

Funding Sources

The term "funding sources" refers to the various avenues through which startups and entrepreneurs can obtain financial support for their business ventures. These sources typically provide the necessary capital to fuel the growth and development of a startup, allowing it to meet its day-to-day operational expenses, invest in new technologies, hire talent, and expand its market reach. There are several types of funding sources available to startups and entrepreneurs, including: 1. Bootstrapping: Bootstrapping is a self-funding method in which entrepreneurs finance their ventures using personal savings or by borrowing money from family and friends. This approach is often considered as the initial step to get a startup off the ground, as it allows entrepreneurs to retain full control over their business without diluting ownership. 2. Angel Investors: Angel investors are individuals who provide financial backing to early-stage startups in exchange for equity or convertible debt. These investors are typically seasoned entrepreneurs or high-net-worth individuals who possess industry expertise, networks, and a willingness to take risks. In addition to capital, angel investors often offer mentorship and guidance to startups. 3. Venture Capital: Venture capital firms invest in startup companies with high-growth potential. These firms raise capital from various sources, such as institutional investors and wealthy individuals, to create a fund. They then invest this capital in startups in exchange for equity. Venture capitalists often bring significant industry knowledge, market connections, and management expertise to help startups scale rapidly. 4. Crowdfunding: Crowdfunding platforms allow entrepreneurs to raise funds from a large number of individuals who are interested in supporting their project. Entrepreneurs present their business ideas on these platforms and individuals can contribute money in exchange for rewards, products, or equity. Crowdfunding offers startups an opportunity to validate their ideas and gain market exposure while securing financial support. 5. Grants and Government Programs: Many governments and organizations offer grants, subsidies, or funding programs specifically designed to support startups and entrepreneurship. These programs aim to promote innovation, job creation, and economic growth. Startups can access these funds by participating in competitions, submitting proposals, or meeting specific criteria set by the granting organizations. Other funding sources may include bank loans, accelerators, incubators, strategic partnerships, and corporate investments. The choice of funding sources depends on factors such as the stage of the startup, its growth potential, industry dynamics, and the preferences and goals of the entrepreneurs.

Funding Stages

Funding stages in the context of startup and entrepreneurship refer to the various rounds of financing that a startup goes through in order to raise capital for growth and development. There are typically several funding stages that startups progress through, each with its own characteristics and goals: 1. Pre-Seed Stage: This is the earliest stage of funding where entrepreneurs use their own savings or funds from friends and family to develop their startup idea and create a minimum viable product (MVP). Funding at this stage is typically minimal and used to validate the business concept. 2. Seed Stage: At this stage, startups have a working prototype or MVP and are seeking external funding to scale their operations. Seed funding is usually provided by angel investors or early-stage venture capital firms. Funding obtained in the seed stage is used to refine the product, develop a customer base, and create a market presence. 3. Series A: Once a startup has demonstrated market traction and growth potential, they seek a Series A round of funding. This funding round is led by venture capital firms and is used to further develop the product, expand the team, and penetrate the market. Series A funding is typically used to finance the initial stages of scaling a startup. 4. Series B, C, D, etc.: Additional funding rounds, referred to as Series B, C, D, etc., are conducted as a startup achieves further milestones and requires more capital to grow. These funding rounds involve larger investments from venture capital firms and potentially strategic investors. The funds raised at each subsequent stage are used for product development, market expansion, and potentially, mergers and acquisitions. 5. IPO or Acquisition: The final stage of funding for a startup is an initial public offering (IPO) or an acquisition by another company. An IPO involves selling shares of the startup to the public, allowing it to raise significant funds for future growth. Alternatively, a startup may be acquired by a larger company, which provides an exit opportunity for the founders and early investors. Funding stages play a crucial role in the growth and success of startups, providing the necessary capital to bring their ideas to life and fuel their expansion. The specific funding stages a startup goes through depend on its growth trajectory and the amount of external investment it requires to achieve its business goals.

Funding Strategies

Funding strategies can be defined as the specific plans and approaches that startups and entrepreneurs use to secure financial resources to support the development, growth, and sustainability of their businesses. These strategies involve the identification, evaluation, and pursuit of various funding options, including both traditional and alternative sources of capital. Startups and entrepreneurs must carefully consider their specific business needs, goals, and market conditions to determine the most appropriate funding strategy for their venture.

Funding Strategy

A funding strategy in the context of startup and entrepreneurship refers to the plan and approach that a company or individual follows to secure and manage the necessary financial resources for their business venture. It involves identifying and evaluating various sources of funding, determining the optimal mix of funding options, and developing a roadmap to raise and utilize the funds effectively. The funding strategy is a crucial aspect of the startup and entrepreneurial journey, as it directly impacts the company's ability to grow, innovate, and sustain its operations. A well-defined funding strategy not only helps in meeting immediate capital requirements but also lays the groundwork for long-term financial sustainability and success.

Funding Types

Funding types refer to the different sources of capital that startups and entrepreneurs can access to finance their business ventures. These funding options are crucial for starting and growing a business, as they provide the necessary financial resources to fuel innovation, develop products or services, hire employees, and scale operations. There are various funding types available to startups and entrepreneurs, each with its own characteristics and requirements: 1. Self-Funding: This refers to using personal savings, assets, or borrowing against personal assets to finance a business. Self-funding allows entrepreneurs to retain full control and equity in their venture but requires personal financial stability and may limit the available capital. 2. Friends and Family: Friends and family members can provide initial capital in the form of loans or investments. This type of funding is often considered the initial round of financing for startups but comes with potential strains on personal relationships and limited capital availability. 3. Angel Investors: Angel investors are individuals or groups who provide capital in exchange for equity or convertible debt. They often have entrepreneurial experience and industry knowledge, and can offer valuable mentorship in addition to financial support. Angel investors typically invest in the early stages of a startup. 4. Venture Capital: Venture capital (VC) firms invest in startups with high growth potential in exchange for equity. They typically invest larger amounts of capital compared to angel investors and may require a seat on the company's board of directors. Venture capital funding is typically sought by startups in the early to later stages of development. 5. Crowdfunding: Crowdfunding platforms allow entrepreneurs to pitch their ideas or products to a wide audience and raise funds from individual contributors. This type of funding can take various forms, such as pre-orders, donations, or investments, and usually happens through online platforms. 6. Grants: Grants are non-repayable funds provided by government agencies, non-profit organizations, or research institutions. Startups and entrepreneurs can access grants to support specific projects, research, or development in areas such as technology, healthcare, or social innovation. 7. Bank Loans: Traditional bank loans are a common funding option for startups and entrepreneurs. These loans usually require collateral, a strong credit history, and a well-developed business plan. Bank loans can provide a stable source of capital but may have higher interest rates and stricter repayment terms compared to other funding types. 8. Accelerators and Incubators: Accelerator and incubator programs provide startups with funding, mentorship, and resources needed to accelerate business growth. In exchange for these services, the programs often require equity in the startup. These programs are typically short-term and aim to support early-stage startups in specific industries.

Fundraising Approaches And Execution

Fundraising Approaches and Execution refers to the strategies and actions taken by startups and entrepreneurs to secure financial support for their business ventures. It involves the implementation of various methods and techniques to attract funding from different sources, such as investors, venture capitalists, banks, and crowdfunding platforms. Successful fundraising requires careful planning and execution, as it is crucial for the growth and sustainability of a startup or entrepreneurial endeavor. The following are some common approaches that startups and entrepreneurs use to raise funds: - Equity Financing: This approach involves selling a percentage of ownership in the company in exchange for capital. It is often used to attract angel investors or venture capitalists who are willing to take a stake in the business in hopes of earning a return on their investment. - Debt Financing: Startups and entrepreneurs can also borrow funds from banks or other financial institutions through loans or lines of credit. Debt financing requires the repayment of the borrowed funds plus interest within a specified period. - Grants and Subsidies: Some startups and entrepreneurs may qualify for grants or subsidies provided by government agencies, non-profit organizations, or industry-specific programs. These funds do not need to be repaid, but typically come with specific terms and conditions. - Crowdfunding: This approach involves raising funds from a large number of individuals through online platforms. Startups and entrepreneurs can present their business idea or product to potential backers who can choose to contribute funds in exchange for rewards, equity, or simply to support the project. - Bootstrapping: Bootstrapping refers to self-funding or using personal savings to finance a startup. This approach allows entrepreneurs to retain full control of their business but may limit the growth potential due to financial constraints. Execution of fundraising approaches involves a series of steps and actions. Startups and entrepreneurs need to identify their funding needs, create a compelling business plan and pitch deck, and target potential funders based on their industry, stage, and investment preferences. They need to effectively communicate their value proposition, market potential, and growth strategy to attract investors or secure financing. This often includes conducting thorough market research, building relationships with potential investors, attending networking events, and leveraging online platforms to reach a wider audience. In conclusion, fundraising approaches and execution are vital for startups and entrepreneurs to secure the necessary capital to launch and grow their businesses. By strategically selecting the appropriate fundraising methods and effectively implementing them, startups can increase their chances of securing funding and fueling their growth.

Fundraising Approaches

Fundraising approaches in the context of startups and entrepreneurship refer to the various methods and strategies that entrepreneurs use to secure financial resources for their businesses. These approaches are critical in enabling startups to expand, develop new products or services, and sustain their operations. There are several fundraising approaches that startups can utilize based on their specific needs and circumstances: 1. Equity Financing: This approach involves raising funds by selling shares or equity stakes in the company to investors. Startups often seek equity financing from venture capitalists, angel investors, or through crowdfunding platforms. In exchange for their investment, these investors become partial owners of the company and share in its potential profits. 2. Debt Financing: Startups can secure funds through debt financing, which involves borrowing money from lenders or financial institutions. This could include bank loans, lines of credit, or bonds. Unlike equity financing, debt financing requires the company to repay the borrowed amount plus interest over a predetermined period. 3. Bootstrapping: Bootstrapping is a self-funding approach where entrepreneurs use their own savings or personal resources to finance their startup. This approach allows entrepreneurs to maintain full control and ownership of their business but may limit the available funds for growth and expansion. 4. Grants and Subsidies: Startups can explore grants and subsidies provided by government organizations, non-profit entities, or corporate foundations. These funding opportunities are typically awarded based on specific criteria and can support startups in specific sectors or with innovative ideas. 5. Strategic Partnerships: Startups can form strategic partnerships with other companies or individuals who provide financial support in exchange for mutually beneficial collaborations. These partnerships can provide startups with funding, mentorship, access to resources, and market opportunities. 6. Revenue Generation: Rather than relying on external funding sources, startups can focus on generating revenue from their products or services to fuel their growth. This approach may involve adopting a freemium model, licensing intellectual property, or implementing a subscription-based business model. Fundraising approaches are crucial for startups and entrepreneurs to secure the necessary funds to launch or scale their businesses. Each approach comes with its own advantages and considerations, and entrepreneurs must carefully consider their business goals, financial needs, and investor requirements to determine the most suitable fundraising approach for their startup.

Fundraising Strategies And Tactics

Fundraising strategies and tactics in the context of startup and entrepreneurship refer to the various approaches and methods employed by entrepreneurs to secure funding for their ventures. These strategies are crucial for startup founders to raise capital and support the growth and development of their businesses. Fundraising strategies typically involve identifying potential sources of funding, cultivating relationships with investors, and presenting a compelling case for investment. Entrepreneurs must understand the different types of fundraising options available, such as bootstrapping, crowdfunding, venture capital, angel investing, and government grants, and determine which ones are most suitable for their specific needs and goals. Tactics, on the other hand, focus on the specific actions and techniques entrepreneurs use to execute their fundraising strategies effectively. This may include conducting research to identify potential investors or donors, preparing a comprehensive business plan and financial projections, creating a compelling pitch deck or presentation, and engaging in networking events and industry conferences to connect with potential investors. Entrepreneurs may also employ various tactics during the actual fundraising process, such as negotiating funding terms and conditions, leveraging their network of professional contacts for introductions to investors, and utilizing online platforms and social media to reach a broader audience and generate interest in their venture. Successful fundraising strategies and tactics require entrepreneurs to have a deep understanding of their target market, competitive landscape, and unique value proposition. They must effectively communicate their business vision, growth potential, and how the investment will be used to drive the success of their venture. In summary, fundraising strategies and tactics are crucial for startup founders and entrepreneurs to secure the financial resources necessary to support the growth and development of their businesses. By employing a variety of approaches and techniques, entrepreneurs can increase their chances of attracting investment and creating sustainable success.

Fundraising Strategies

Fundraising strategies refer to the specific plans, techniques, and tactics that startups and entrepreneurs employ to raise capital or financial support for their business ventures. These strategies are crucial for startups and entrepreneurs as they often lack the resources and funding necessary to turn their ideas into profitable businesses. One commonly used fundraising strategy is the traditional method of seeking investment from external sources such as venture capitalists and angel investors. This involves pitching the business idea to potential investors in order to secure financial support. Startups and entrepreneurs often prepare detailed business plans, financial projections, and pitch decks to convince investors of the viability and potential profitability of their ventures. Another fundraising strategy is crowdfunding, which has gained significant popularity in recent years. Crowdfunding platforms allow individuals, known as backers or contributors, to pledge money to support a startup or entrepreneur's idea. This strategy often involves creating an engaging campaign page, offering rewards or incentives to backers, and engaging with potential supporters through social media and other channels. In addition to external fundraising methods, startups and entrepreneurs can also employ internal fundraising strategies. These strategies involve utilizing the resources and networks within their own organizations to raise capital. For example, entrepreneurs may seek investment from family and friends, or utilize personal savings or credit to finance their ventures. Some startups also opt for bootstrapping, which involves funding the business using minimal resources and revenue generated from early sales. Furthermore, fundraising strategies may also involve engaging in strategic partnerships with larger companies or organizations. Startups and entrepreneurs may seek collaborations or sponsorships from established industry players to gain access to funding, expertise, or resources. These partnerships can provide startups with a valuable platform to showcase their products or services, as well as leverage the reputation and network of the larger company. In summary, fundraising strategies in the context of startup and entrepreneurship encompass the various methods and approaches employed to raise capital and financial support. Whether through traditional investment pitches, crowdfunding campaigns, internal funding sources, or strategic partnerships, startups and entrepreneurs must carefully plan and execute these strategies in order to secure the funding necessary for growth and success.

Fundraising Tactics

Fundraising Tactics in the context of startup and entrepreneurship refer to specific strategies, techniques, and approaches employed by founders and business owners to raise capital for their ventures. These tactics are crucial for startups as they allow them to secure the necessary funding to fuel their growth, support initial operations, and invest in product development, marketing, and other critical areas of their business. There are numerous fundraising tactics that entrepreneurs can adopt to attract investors and potential backers. One common tactic is the creation and presentation of a compelling pitch deck, which is a concise and visually appealing overview of the startup's mission, market opportunity, business model, team, and financial projections. A well-crafted pitch deck can captivate the interest of angel investors, venture capitalists, and other potential sources of funding. Additionally, entrepreneurs often engage in networking activities as part of their fundraising tactics. Building relationships with industry influencers, experienced entrepreneurs, and investors can provide valuable connections and insights that may lead to funding opportunities. Attending startup events, industry conferences, and pitch competitions can also help founders showcase their ventures and attract the attention of potential investors. Crowdfunding has emerged as a popular fundraising tactic in recent years, leveraging online platforms to raise small amounts of money from a large number of individuals. Founders can offer various incentives or rewards to encourage individuals to contribute to their campaigns. Crowdfunding can not only provide financial support but also serve as a validation of the startup's concept and market potential. For startups seeking larger investments, equity financing and venture capital are often pursued. Entrepreneurs may craft detailed business plans and financial models to demonstrate the potential return on investment for venture capitalists. Furthermore, engaging in strategic partnerships and collaborations with established companies can be an effective tactic to secure both funding and valuable industry expertise. Ultimately, fundraising tactics play a crucial role in the success of startups and entrepreneurship. By carefully selecting and executing the right strategies, entrepreneurs can secure the capital needed to bring their ideas to life and accelerate the growth of their ventures.

Gamification

Gamification, in the context of startup and entrepreneurship, refers to the implementation of game-like elements and mechanics into non-game situations, with the aim of enhancing engagement, motivation, and participation. Entrepreneurs adopt gamification strategies to make business processes more enjoyable and interactive, ultimately increasing user involvement, loyalty, and productivity. By leveraging principles commonly used in games, such as challenges, rewards, competitions, and social interaction, startups can create meaningful experiences for their customers, employees, and stakeholders.

Global Entrepreneurship

Global entrepreneurship refers to the practice of starting and managing businesses on a global scale, with a focus on innovation, risk-taking, and the creation of new products, services, and markets. Entrepreneurs who engage in global entrepreneurship are not limited by geographical boundaries and seek opportunities beyond their domestic markets. They leverage technology, networks, and resources to create and expand their ventures internationally.

Global Market Expansion

Global Market Expansion refers to the strategic process undertaken by startups and entrepreneurs to establish and grow their business operations internationally. It involves taking the existing products or services that are successful in the domestic market and expanding their reach to new countries or regions. For startups and entrepreneurs, global market expansion presents numerous opportunities for growth and increased profitability. By venturing into new markets, they can tap into a larger customer base, access new channels of distribution, and capitalize on emerging trends and demands on a global scale. Additionally, expanding internationally can help diversify the business and mitigate risks associated with overreliance on a single market.

Go-To-Market Strategy (GTM)

A go-to-market strategy (GTM) refers to the plan and approach that a startup or entrepreneur follows to introduce and deliver their product or service to the market. It encompasses all the activities and tactics that are required to successfully launch and promote the product in the target market. The purpose of a go-to-market strategy is to establish a strong market presence, generate sales, and ultimately achieve business growth. It involves a comprehensive analysis of the market, target customers, competition, and overall business objectives. A successful go-to-market strategy typically includes several key components: 1. Market Analysis: This involves understanding the market dynamics, trends, and customer needs. It includes identifying the target market segment and evaluating the potential demand for the product or service. 2. Value Proposition: This refers to the unique value or benefit that the product or service offers to the target customers. It is important to clearly articulate the value proposition and differentiate the product from competitors in order to attract customers. 3. Pricing Strategy: Determining the right pricing strategy is crucial in order to ensure profitability and remain competitive in the market. The pricing should take into consideration factors such as production costs, value provided to customers, and price sensitivity. 4. Distribution Channels: Selecting the appropriate distribution channels is essential for reaching the target customers effectively and efficiently. This may include direct sales, e-commerce platforms, partnerships, or third-party retailers. 5. Marketing and Promotion: Developing a strong marketing and promotion plan is essential for creating awareness and driving customer acquisition. This may involve various tactics such as advertising, public relations, social media marketing, and content marketing. 6. Sales and Customer Support: Setting up effective sales processes and customer support mechanisms is crucial for converting leads into sales and ensuring customer satisfaction. This may involve hiring and training sales teams, implementing CRM systems, and providing ongoing support to customers. A well-executed go-to-market strategy can significantly increase the chances of success for startups and entrepreneurs. It helps in effectively positioning the product or service in the market, attracting customers, and generating revenue. Additionally, a GTM strategy allows businesses to adapt and evolve based on market feedback and changing customer needs.

Golden Handcuffs

Golden Handcuffs is a term used in the context of startups and entrepreneurship to describe a situation where employees or founders are enticed to stay with a company or project due to financial incentives or rewards. These incentives can come in the form of high salaries, stock options, bonus structures, or other perks that are designed to keep talented individuals from leaving the company or pursuing other opportunities. However, while these financial rewards may initially seem attractive, they can also create a sense of dependency and can prevent individuals from exploring new ventures or taking risks. The term "golden handcuffs" implies that although the rewards may be tempting, they can also limit an individual's freedom and inhibit their ability to pursue new opportunities or personal aspirations.

Google Ads

Google Ads is an online advertising platform developed by Google for businesses and individuals looking to promote their products or services. It operates on a pay-per-click (PPC) model, where advertisers bid on specific keywords and pay only when their ad is clicked. For startups and entrepreneurs, Google Ads presents a powerful tool to drive targeted traffic to their websites and increase their visibility in the online space. With Google Ads, businesses can create and manage their own advertising campaigns, allowing them to reach a wider audience and attract potential customers.

Green Entrepreneurship

Green entrepreneurship refers to the practice of creating and managing a startup or business with a focus on sustainability, environmental impact, and social responsibility. It involves the development and implementation of innovative solutions to environmental challenges, while also aiming to generate profit and create a positive impact on society. Green entrepreneurs are individuals who identify opportunities to address environmental problems and develop business ideas around them. These entrepreneurs are driven by a passion for sustainability and are committed to finding ways to reduce the negative impact of business activities on the environment. They often leverage technology, research, and collaboration to create products, services, or processes that are more environmentally friendly and contribute to a more sustainable future.

Growth Capital Funding

Growth capital funding refers to the financial resources provided to startups and entrepreneurs to support their expansion and growth. This type of funding is specifically designed to fuel the development of promising ventures and maximize their potential. Startups and entrepreneurs require growth capital funding to scale their operations, develop new products or services, enter new markets, or strengthen their market position. This funding is typically sought in the early stages of a business's life cycle when it has demonstrated potential for rapid growth but requires additional resources to capitalize on its opportunities.

Growth Hacking Tools

Growth hacking tools refer to various software, platforms, and techniques that startups and entrepreneurs use to rapidly and efficiently grow their businesses. These tools play a crucial role in driving customer acquisition, increasing user engagement, and ultimately boosting revenue. Startups and entrepreneurship are characterized by limited resources, tight budgets, and the need for quick and scalable growth. Therefore, growth hacking tools are essential for startups to maximize their impact with minimal investment. These tools can be categorized into different areas, such as marketing, analytics, customer engagement, and automation. Marketing tools, for instance, help startups reach their target audience effectively through channels such as social media, content marketing, email marketing, and search engine optimization. Analytics tools are vital for startups to track and measure their key performance indicators (KPIs) and gain insights into user behavior. These tools enable entrepreneurs to understand which marketing strategies and channels are most effective, allowing them to optimize their efforts and improve their conversion rates. Customer engagement tools, on the other hand, help startups build and nurture relationships with their user base. This can include tools for managing customer support, email automation, live chat, and social media management. By actively engaging and communicating with their customers, startups can increase customer loyalty, drive referrals, and improve customer satisfaction. Automation tools are also a crucial part of growth hacking, as they enable startups to streamline and scale their operations. These tools automate repetitive tasks, such as email campaigns, social media posting, lead nurturing, and data analysis. By automating these processes, startups can save time and resources, allowing them to focus on more strategic growth initiatives. In conclusion, growth hacking tools are essential for startups and entrepreneurs to achieve rapid and efficient growth. These tools encompass a wide range of software and techniques that help startups with marketing, analytics, customer engagement, and automation. By leveraging these tools effectively, startups can maximize their impact, acquire and retain customers, and ultimately drive revenue growth.

Growth Hacking

Growth hacking refers to a set of strategies and techniques used by startups and entrepreneurs to rapidly and efficiently grow their business. It focuses on finding innovative and unconventional ways to attract and retain customers, increase revenue, and achieve sustainable growth. This approach emphasizes the use of data-driven experiments and analytics to iterate and refine marketing, product development, and sales strategies. Growth hackers often leverage platforms and tools such as social media, SEO, email marketing, A/B testing, and customer feedback to identify and capitalize on opportunities for growth.

Growth Marketing

Growth marketing, in the context of startups and entrepreneurship, refers to a marketing strategy that focuses on driving rapid and scalable growth for a business. It goes beyond traditional marketing techniques by employing a data-driven and experimentation-based approach, with the aim of continuously optimizing and improving marketing efforts to maximize results. Unlike traditional marketing, which often follows a linear and predictable process, growth marketing embraces a dynamic and iterative approach. It involves constantly testing and learning from various marketing tactics and channels, and then scaling up the ones that prove to be successful in driving growth. This iterative process allows startups to identify the most effective strategies for acquiring and retaining customers, while eliminating the ones that do not yield satisfactory results. At the core of growth marketing is the use of data and analytics to make informed decisions. By leveraging data from various sources such as user behavior, customer feedback, and market trends, growth marketers gain valuable insights to drive their marketing strategies. These insights enable them to identify opportunities for growth, understand customer preferences and pain points, and personalize marketing efforts to deliver more targeted and relevant messages to their audience. Another key element of growth marketing is rapid experimentation. Growth marketers often run multiple marketing experiments simultaneously, testing different variables such as messaging, channels, targeting criteria, and creative elements. This enables them to quickly identify what works and what doesn't, allowing for quick optimization and iteration to achieve better results. Growth marketing also emphasizes the importance of collaboration and cross-functional alignment within a startup. It involves close collaboration between marketing teams, product teams, and other relevant departments to ensure that marketing efforts are aligned with the overall business objectives and customer needs. This cross-functional collaboration enables startups to deliver a seamless and cohesive customer experience, which is essential for driving growth and building a strong brand.

Growth Metrics

Growth Metrics in the context of Startup and Entrepreneurship refer to the quantitative measurements used to evaluate the progress and success of a startup or entrepreneurial venture. These metrics provide insights into various aspects of the business, such as customer acquisition, revenue generation, user engagement, and operational efficiency. One commonly used growth metric is Customer Acquisition Cost (CAC), which measures the amount of money spent on acquiring a new customer. This metric helps entrepreneurs determine the efficiency and effectiveness of their marketing and sales efforts. A lower CAC indicates that the startup is acquiring customers at a relatively low cost, which is essential for sustainable growth. Another important growth metric is Lifetime Value (LTV), which estimates the total revenue that can be expected from a single customer during their entire relationship with the business. By comparing the LTV to the CAC, entrepreneurs can evaluate the profitability of acquiring and retaining customers. A higher LTV than CAC suggests that the business is generating sufficient revenue from each customer, leading to potential long-term success. User Engagement metrics are also crucial for startups and entrepreneurs. Metrics such as Monthly Active Users (MAU) and Daily Active Users (DAU) help evaluate the number of users actively engaging with the product or service. These metrics provide insights into the level of customer satisfaction and the

113

effectiveness of the product in addressing their needs. Additionally, metrics like Retention Rate measure the percentage of users who continue to use the product or service over a specific period, indicating the level of customer loyalty and satisfaction. Furthermore, Revenue Growth Rate is a key metric that indicates the speed at which a startup is generating revenue. This metric helps entrepreneurs assess the scalability and sustainability of their business model. A high revenue growth rate implies that the business is successfully attracting new customers and increasing sales, which is fundamental for long-term success. In conclusion, growth metrics play a vital role in measuring and evaluating the progress of a startup or entrepreneurial venture. These quantitative measurements provide valuable insights into customer acquisition, revenue generation, user engagement, and overall business performance. By constantly monitoring and analyzing these metrics, entrepreneurs can make informed decisions and develop strategies to drive sustainable growth.

Hackathon

A hackathon is a competitive event typically held over a short period of time, such as 24 to 48 hours, where individuals or teams of participants come together to collaboratively work on innovative projects or solutions. Focused on fostering creativity, problem-solving, and entrepreneurship, hackathons bring together people from diverse backgrounds such as developers, designers, entrepreneurs, and subject matter experts. The participants typically work in a fast-paced and intense environment to brainstorm ideas, develop prototypes, and create functional solutions.

Hackathons

Hackathons are intensive events where groups of individuals, typically developers, designers, and entrepreneurs, come together to collaboratively work on innovative projects within a short period of time, often ranging from a few hours to a few days. These events are often organized to foster creativity, problem-solving, and resourcefulness, while providing a platform for individuals to showcase their skills and ideas. The primary goal of a hackathon is to encourage participants to rapidly conceive and develop new solutions, products, or services, typically in the field of technology. These events are particularly popular in the startup and entrepreneurship ecosystem, where the emphasis is on building prototypes, validating ideas, and iterating quickly. During a hackathon, participants form teams (which can be pre-formed or randomly assigned) and work together to develop their ideas into tangible outcomes. These outcomes can range from software applications, websites, or mobile apps to physical prototypes or business models. It is common for participants to work continuously for the duration of the event, often sacrificing sleep and personal comfort to focus on their projects. Hackathons are characterized by their fast-paced and competitive nature. Participants are typically given a specific challenge or problem to solve, known as a "prompt" or "theme," which serves as a starting point for their projects. However, participants are free to interpret and approach the prompt in their own unique ways, allowing for a wide range of creativity and innovation. Hackathons also provide opportunities for networking and collaboration. Participants often have the chance to interact with industry professionals, mentors, and potential investors who can provide guidance, support, and even funding for their projects. Additionally, hackathons usually culminate in a presentation or demo session, where teams showcase their work to a panel of judges or the wider audience. This provides a platform for participants to receive feedback, gain exposure, and potentially attract further support or investment for their projects. Overall, hackathons have become a key component of the startup and entrepreneurship ecosystem, facilitating rapid prototyping, fostering innovation, and creating opportunities for collaboration and networking among like-minded individuals with diverse skill sets.

Hockey Stick Growth

Hockey Stick Growth refers to a rapid and exponential increase in a startup's revenue or user base after a period of steady growth. It is a term commonly used in the context of startup and entrepreneurship to describe a significant shift in a company's trajectory, marked by a sudden surge in success and profitability. Typically, in the early stages of a startup, growth is gradual and linear, with revenue or user numbers increasing steadily over time. However, when a company experiences hockey stick growth, there is a sudden and dramatic spike in growth, resulting in a sharp upward curve that resembles the shape of a hockey stick. There are several factors that can contribute to hockey stick growth. It often occurs when a startup successfully identifies and taps into a large market opportunity or when it gains traction through a viral product or marketing campaign. Additionally, disruptive technologies or innovative business models can also fuel rapid growth and attract significant investment. While hockey stick growth can bring tremendous success and financial gains to a startup, it also presents unique challenges. Startups must be prepared to scale their operations rapidly to meet increased demand and maintain high levels of customer satisfaction. They may need to adjust their business strategies, hire additional staff, or secure additional funding to support the sudden surge in growth. Entrepreneurs and investors often strive for hockey stick growth as it represents a significant milestone in a startup's journey. It demonstrates the potential for massive success and can attract further investment, partnership opportunities, and increased market share.

Human-Centered Design

Human-Centered Design (HCD) in the context of startup and entrepreneurship refers to an approach that prioritizes the needs, preferences, and experiences of human users throughout the design and development process of a product or service. It involves understanding and empathizing with users, involving them in the design process, and continuously iterating and refining the solution based on their feedback and behavior. HCD recognizes that successful startups and entrepreneurial ventures are built upon the ability to identify and solve real problems faced by the target audience. It goes beyond a technology-driven or market-driven approach by placing the user at the center of the design process. By understanding the users' needs, behaviors, and motivations, startups can create solutions that effectively meet their requirements and deliver a positive user experience.

IPO (Initial Public Offering)

An Initial Public Offering (IPO) refers to the process through which a private company offers its shares to the public for the first time, allowing the company to become publicly traded. It is a significant milestone for startups and entrepreneurs as it opens up new opportunities for growth and capital infusion. During an IPO, a company offers a portion of its ownership in the form of shares to the public. This enables individuals and institutional investors to become shareholders and own a stake in the company. By going public, startups and entrepreneurs can raise substantial amounts of capital that can be used for various purposes, such as expanding operations, investing in research and development, and acquiring other companies. Before the IPO process can begin, a company needs to meet certain requirements. These requirements may vary depending on the jurisdiction, but they generally include having a minimum number of shareholders, a certain level of revenue or assets, and meeting regulatory obligations. Once a company meets these criteria and decides to pursue an IPO, it will typically engage with investment banks or underwriters who assist in the process. The IPO process itself involves several stages. First, the company and its underwriters determine the valuation and price at which the shares will be offered to the public. Then, a registration statement, including financial information and other relevant disclosures, is filed with the regulatory authorities. This document, known as the prospectus, provides potential investors with information about the company's business, strategy, and financials. Once the prospectus is approved by the regulatory authorities, the company embarks on a roadshow to market its shares to potential investors. The roadshow typically involves presentations by the company's management team to institutional investors and analysts, showcasing the company's growth prospects and investment potential. After the roadshow, the IPO culminates in the "pricing" stage where the final offer price and the number of shares to be sold are determined. Subsequently, the shares are allocated to investors, and trading usually begins on a stock exchange. This newfound liquidity allows the original shareholders, including the founders and early investors, to sell their shares if they choose to do so. IPOs can provide numerous benefits for startups and entrepreneurs, including increased visibility, access to capital, and liquidity for existing shareholders. However, the process also entails costs and obligations, such as regulatory compliance, ongoing reporting, and the potential loss of control for the founders. Therefore, the decision to go public should be carefully considered and aligned with the company's long-term growth objectives.

IPO Roadshow

IPO Roadshow An IPO (Initial Public Offering) Roadshow refers to the process of presenting a startup company's investment opportunity to potential investors in order to generate interest and attract funding for the company's initial public offering. During an IPO Roadshow, entrepreneurs and startup representatives travel to different cities, meeting with institutional investors, analysts, and potential shareholders. The purpose of these presentations is to provide detailed information about the company's business model, financials, growth potential, competitive advantages, and market strategy. The goal is to convince investors that investing in the company's shares would be a lucrative and worthwhile opportunity. The IPO Roadshow typically involves a series of meetings, presentations, and Q&A sessions with potential investors, where the company's management team discusses the company's vision, its unique value proposition, and its future plans. These meetings are highly structured and usually follow a predefined script and PowerPoint presentation. The entrepreneurs aim to convey the company's objectives and strategies effectively, answering any queries from investors and addressing any concerns they may have. The primary objective of an IPO Roadshow is to generate investor interest and secure investments that will contribute to the successful completion of the IPO process. The roadshow serves as an opportunity for the company to showcase its business potential and attract long-term investors who believe in the company's growth prospects. Successful roadshows result in a higher demand for the company's shares, potentially leading to a higher valuation and increased proceeds from the IPO. The IPO roadshow is a critical phase in the IPO process, as it provides entrepreneurs and startup representatives the chance to build relationships with potential investors and understand their perspectives on the company's offering. It also allows investors to evaluate the company's management team, assess its credibility, and gain insights into its ability to execute plans and deliver on its promises. In summary, an IPO Roadshow is a strategic and structured presentation process undertaken by entrepreneurs and startup representatives to attract potential investors and generate interest in the company's IPO. Through these presentations, entrepreneurs aim to convince investors about the company's growth potential, secure investments, and achieve a successful IPO.

Idea Validation Surveys

Idea Validation Surveys in the context of Startup & Entrepreneurship are systematic methods used to assess the viability and potential success of a business concept or idea before investing significant time and resources into its development. These surveys serve as a crucial tool to collect feedback, gather insights, and validate assumptions of entrepreneurs or startup founders regarding their proposed products or services. By conducting idea validation surveys, entrepreneurs aim to gather reliable data and evidence to evaluate the market demand, product-market fit, target audience preferences, and overall feasibility of their business idea. This information helps them make informed decisions and mitigate risks associated with starting a new venture.

Ideation Workshop

An ideation workshop is a structured session in the context of startup and entrepreneurship, designed to generate and refine new ideas for potential business ventures. It serves as a platform for individuals or teams to collaborate, brainstorm, and explore innovative concepts that have the potential to solve a specific problem or meet a market demand. The workshop typically involves a diverse group of participants with different backgrounds, skills, and perspectives, encouraging the generation of a wide range of ideas. The facilitator plays a crucial role in guiding the participants through various exercises and techniques to stimulate creativity and foster an open and supportive environment. The primary objective of an ideation workshop is to generate a significant number of ideas that have the potential for further development and implementation. The participants are encouraged to think outside the box, challenge existing assumptions, and explore unconventional approaches to problem-solving. During the workshop, participants engage in activities such as brainstorming, mind mapping, rapid prototyping, and role-playing to stimulate their creative thinking and generate new ideas. The focus is on quantity rather than quality, aiming to generate a large volume of ideas, regardless of their feasibility or practicality at the initial stage. Once the ideation phase is complete, the ideas are evaluated and refined based on criteria such as market potential, feasibility, scalability, and alignment with the startup's goals and vision. The most promising concepts are selected for further analysis and development, leading to the creation of a business plan or the initiation of a minimum viable product (MVP). An ideation workshop is a critical step in the entrepreneurial journey as it helps entrepreneurs and startup teams to identify market opportunities, come up with innovative solutions, and create a competitive advantage. It encourages a culture of innovation and creativity within the organization, enabling entrepreneurs to stay ahead of the curve and adapt to changing market dynamics.

Ideation

Startup: A startup is a newly established business venture with the primary goal of bringing an innovative product or service to market and achieving rapid growth. Startups often operate in emerging industries and aim to disrupt traditional markets with their unique solutions. They are characterized by their focus on scalability, agility, and disruption. Startups are typically founded by entrepreneurs who possess a strong vision for their business and are willing to take risks to achieve their goals. Entrepreneurship: Entrepreneurship refers to the process of identifying, creating, and pursuing opportunities to start and grow a business. It involves the willingness to take risks, the ability to innovate, and the drive to solve problems. Entrepreneurs are individuals who possess these traits and embark on the entrepreneurial journey to build and develop successful businesses. They are often characterized by their passion, resilience, and determination to overcome obstacles.

Inbound Marketing Strategies

Inbound marketing is a strategy used by startups and entrepreneurs to attract and engage potential customers by providing valuable and relevant content to them. Unlike traditional outbound marketing, which involves interrupting and pushing advertisements to a wide audience, inbound marketing focuses on creating a connection and building a relationship with customers through various online channels. With inbound marketing, startups and entrepreneurs aim to attract customers organically by offering informative and educational content that addresses their pain points and solves their problems. This content can take the form of blog posts, eBooks, videos, podcasts, and social media updates. Inbound marketing is a cost-effective strategy for startups and entrepreneurs as it allows them to target a specific audience and measure the effectiveness of their efforts. By creating valuable content that resonates with their target customers, startups can establish themselves as thought leaders in their industry and build trust with their audience. Inbound marketing involves several key elements: - Attract: This involves creating compelling content that appeals to the target audience and draws them to the startup's website or social media channels. - Convert: Once visitors are on the startup's website, the goal is to convert them into leads by offering something of value in exchange for their contact information, such as a free eBook or webinar. - Close: After converting leads, startups need to nurture them further through personalized communication and targeted offerings to turn them into paying customers. - Delight: Once a customer has made a purchase, inbound marketing continues by providing ongoing support and valuable content to build customer loyalty and encourage repeat purchases. Inbound marketing allows startups and entrepreneurs to build a strong online presence, increase brand awareness, generate qualified leads, and ultimately drive revenue growth. By consistently delivering quality content that addresses their target customers' needs, startups can build a loyal customer base and establish themselves as trusted industry leaders.

Incubation Center

An incubation center is a dedicated facility or organization that provides support, resources, and guidance to early-stage startups and entrepreneurs. It acts as a nurturing environment for these new ventures to grow and develop. Typically, an incubation center offers a range of services and amenities to its members, which can include physical office space, access to mentors and experts, networking opportunities, funding assistance, and educational programs. These resources are designed to address the various challenges that startups face in their initial stages, helping them overcome obstacles and increase their chances of success.

Incubation Period

The incubation period is a crucial phase in the life cycle of a startup or entrepreneurial venture. It is the initial period of development where the idea for a new business is conceived, refined, and tested before it is launched into the market. During this phase, entrepreneurs work on validating their business concept, creating a business plan, and building the necessary infrastructure to support their venture. This period is characterized by intense research, planning, and development activities. Entrepreneurs conduct market research to assess the viability of their idea and identify potential customers. They analyze competitors, market trends, and consumer preferences to gain insights that can shape their business strategy. They also engage in product or service development, refining their offerings to meet the identified needs and wants of their target market. The incubation period serves as a critical incubator for ideas, allowing entrepreneurs to fine-tune their concept and strategy. This phase provides the necessary time and space for entrepreneurs to assess the feasibility of their venture and make informed decisions. It is a time to refine and iterate on the initial idea, incorporating feedback and adjusting the business model accordingly. During this phase, entrepreneurs may also seek support from external resources such as mentors, advisors, or incubator programs. These resources can provide guidance, expertise, and access to networks that can help entrepreneurs navigate the challenges of starting a business. They can offer valuable insights, help entrepreneurs avoid common pitfalls, and provide a nurturing environment for entrepreneurial growth. Overall, the incubation period is a critical stage in the startup journey. It is a time of exploration, learning, and preparation, where entrepreneurs lay the foundation for their business. By investing time and effort into this phase, entrepreneurs increase their chances of building a successful and sustainable venture.

Incubation Services

Incubation services in the context of startup and entrepreneurship refer to the support, guidance, and resources provided to early-stage businesses or entrepreneurs during their initial development phases. These services are typically offered by incubators or accelerators, which are organizations that specialize in facilitating the growth and success of startups. Incubation services aim to provide startups with a nurturing environment where they can receive mentorship, access to networks, funding opportunities, and various business development services. The purpose is to assist startups in overcoming the numerous challenges they face during their early stages and maximize their chances of success.

Incubator Program

An incubator program in the context of startup and entrepreneurship refers to a supportive and collaborative environment that helps early-stage startups and entrepreneurs to grow and develop their business ideas. It is typically a structured program designed to provide various resources, mentorship, networking opportunities, and guidance to help startups overcome the challenges they may face in their early stages of development. Incubator programs aim to accelerate the growth and success of startups by offering a range of support services. These services may include office space, access to equipment and technology, legal and accounting assistance, marketing and branding guidance, as well as access to funding opportunities. The incubator program can span over a specific period, usually several months to a few years, during which the startups receive intensive support from experienced mentors and industry experts. The primary goal of an incubator program is to facilitate the growth and development of startups by providing them with the necessary resources, skills, and knowledge. By participating in the program, startups can benefit from the collective expertise and guidance of mentors who have experience in building successful businesses. The program also offers startups the opportunity to connect with like-minded entrepreneurs, investors, and potential partners through networking events and workshops. In addition to providing resources and mentorship, incubator programs often require startups to meet certain milestones and objectives. These milestones may include the development of a minimum viable product, achieving specific revenue targets, or securing funding from investors. By establishing these milestones, the incubator program ensures that startups stay focused and make progress towards their goals. Overall, incubator programs play a critical role in the startup ecosystem by nurturing and supporting early-stage startups. They provide a platform where entrepreneurs can transform their ideas into viable businesses by leveraging the expertise, resources, and connections available through the program. Through the guidance and support of the incubator, startups have a higher chance of succeeding and becoming sustainable businesses in the long term.

Incubator And Accelerator Programs

An incubator program is a structured program designed to support the growth and development of early-stage startup companies. It typically provides physical workspace, mentoring, networking opportunities, access to funding, and other resources necessary for the success of these startups. Incubators aim to accelerate the growth of startups by offering a supportive environment and a range of services to help entrepreneurs navigate the challenges of starting and growing a business. Accelerator programs, on the other hand, are intensive programs that aim to accelerate the growth and development of startups in a relatively short period of time, usually three to six months. Accelerators provide a tailored curriculum, mentorship, and access to a network of investors, mentors, and industry experts. They often culminate in a demo day, where startups present their progress and pitch to potential investors.

Incubator

Incubator, in the context of startup and entrepreneurship, refers to an organization that provides support and resources to early-stage businesses or individuals with innovative ideas. The primary goal of an incubator is to nurture and accelerate the growth of startups by offering a variety of services and infrastructure. An incubator typically offers a physical space where startups can operate, collaborate, and access necessary facilities. This shared workspace allows entrepreneurs to interact with like-minded individuals, fostering a sense of community and collaboration. By providing a conducive environment, incubators seek to maximize the chances of success for their resident startups. Furthermore, incubators provide mentorship and guidance to startups, typically through a network of experienced entrepreneurs and industry professionals. Mentors offer insights and expertise, helping founders navigate the challenges of building and scaling their businesses. This invaluable guidance helps entrepreneurs avoid common pitfalls and make more informed decisions. Additionally, incubators often offer access to a wide range of resources and services that startups may not have on their own. This includes access to funding opportunities, connections to investors and venture capitalists, legal and accounting support, market research, and business development assistance. These resources are designed to provide startups with the necessary infrastructure and knowledge to accelerate their growth. Incubators also often organize events, workshops, and networking sessions for startups to connect with industry experts, potential partners, and customers. These events enhance the visibility of startups and help them build their professional network, which can be crucial for their long-term success. In exchange for the support and resources provided, incubators may require startups to give up a percentage of equity or pay a fee. This arrangement aligns the interests of the incubator with those of the startup, as the success of the startup directly impacts the incubator's reputation and potential returns. Overall, incubators play a vital role in the startup ecosystem by offering an environment conducive to growth, mentorship, resources, and networking opportunities. Their support helps startups overcome challenges more efficiently, increasing their chances of success in the competitive entrepreneurial landscape.

Influencer Marketing Platforms

Influencer Marketing Platforms refer to online tools or platforms that connect brands or businesses with influential individuals, known as influencers, who have a substantial online following. These platforms allow startups and entrepreneurs to collaborate with influencers to promote their products or services to a larger audience. Typically, influencer marketing platforms provide a marketplace where brands can search and connect with influencers who align with their target audience and brand values. These platforms streamline the process of finding and partnering with influencers, making it easier for startups and entrepreneurs to leverage the power of influencer marketing.

Initial Angel Investor

An initial angel investor, in the context of startup and entrepreneurship, refers to an individual or group who provides financial support during the early stages of a startup's growth. These investors are often high-net-worth individuals or experienced entrepreneurs who are willing to take on the risk associated with investing in a new and unproven venture. The role of an initial angel investor is crucial for startups as they provide seed funding that enables the founders to bring their idea to life. This funding is typically used to cover initial expenses such as product development, market research, hiring employees, and marketing efforts. By investing in the early stages, angel investors help entrepreneurs bridge the gap between their idea and securing more substantial funding from venture capitalists or other institutional investors. Unlike venture capitalists who invest larger sums of money in more mature startups, angel investors typically invest smaller amounts in return for equity or convertible debt. They often provide mentorship, guidance, and connections to help the startup succeed. Additionally, angel investors may use their own industry expertise and experience to support the entrepreneur in refining their business model, identifying potential markets, and navigating challenges. Angel investors play a critical role in the startup ecosystem by providing not only capital but also valuable resources and networks. Their early-stage investments can help entrepreneurs turn their ideas into viable businesses, creating jobs and driving innovation. However, investing in startups is inherently risky, and angel investors understand that many startups fail. Therefore, they often diversify their investment portfolio by funding multiple startups, hoping that a few successful investments will outweigh any losses. In conclusion, initial angel investors are individuals or groups who provide early-stage funding and support to startups. Their contributions are essential in helping entrepreneurs bring their ideas to life and navigate the challenges of the early stages of their business. While these investments come with risks, the potential rewards can be substantial, both for the investor and the startup.

Initial Coin Offering (ICO) Token

An Initial Coin Offering (ICO) token in the context of startup and entrepreneurship refers to a type of digital asset that is created and sold to investors in order to fund the development of a new project or business. ICOs have gained popularity in recent years as a way for startups to raise capital without going through traditional methods such as venture capital funding or obtaining loans from financial institutions. ICOs are usually conducted by blockchain-based startups that utilize cryptocurrencies and blockchain technology. The process works by the startup issuing tokens, which are essentially digital assets or digital representations of a stake in the project or platform being developed. These tokens are typically created using smart contract protocols on a blockchain network, such as Ethereum. Investors who are interested in supporting the startup can participate in the ICO by purchasing the tokens using established cryptocurrencies like Bitcoin or Ethereum. The purchased tokens represent a form of ownership or utility within the project or platform. The value of the tokens may appreciate if the project is successful or if there is high demand for the platform's services or products. ICOs offer several advantages to startups and entrepreneurs. Firstly, they provide a decentralized and democratic way of raising funds, allowing anyone with an internet connection and the required cryptocurrency to participate. This opens up investment opportunities to a global audience of potential investors. Secondly, ICOs provide a cost-effective and efficient fundraising method, as they eliminate the need for intermediaries like investment banks or venture capital firms. Lastly, ICOs allow startups to build a community of early adopters and supporters who believe in the project's vision and are invested in its success. However, there are also potential risks and challenges associated with ICOs. One of the main concerns is the lack of regulatory oversight and investor protection. The cryptocurrency market is highly volatile, and there have been cases of ICO scams and fraudulent activities. It is essential for investors to conduct thorough due diligence and research before participating in any ICO to minimize the risk of loss. In conclusion, an ICO token is a digital asset created and sold by startups through a decentralized and democratic fundraising method. It allows startups to raise capital for their projects or platforms by issuing tokens to investors in exchange for established cryptocurrencies. While ICOs offer advantages such as global accessibility and cost-effectiveness, there are also risks involved, emphasizing the importance of investor diligence.

Initial Coin Offering (ICO)

An Initial Coin Offering (ICO) is a fundraising method used by startups and entrepreneurs to raise capital by issuing a new digital token or cryptocurrency. It is often used as an alternative to traditional methods such as venture capital funding or initial public offerings (IPOs). In an ICO, a company or project creates and sells a certain number of its own digital tokens or coins in exchange for existing cryptocurrencies such as Bitcoin or Ethereum. These tokens are typically based on blockchain technology, which is a decentralized and transparent digital ledger that records all transactions across multiple computers or nodes. The main purpose of an ICO is to raise funds for the development and implementation of a specific project or product. Startups and entrepreneurs use ICOs to gather capital at an early stage when traditional funding may be limited or not readily available. By selling their own tokens, companies can bypass the often rigorous and time-consuming process of seeking traditional investment from venture capitalists or angel investors. One of the key advantages of ICOs is that they offer a quick and efficient way for companies to raise capital in a relatively short period of time. This can be particularly beneficial for startups that require immediate funding to accelerate their development and bring their products or services to market. Additionally, ICOs provide an opportunity for both early-stage investors and enthusiasts of the project to become stakeholders and potentially reap significant returns if the project is successful. However, ICOs also carry risks and uncertainties. Due to their decentralized nature and lack of comprehensive regulations, ICOs can be susceptible to fraud, scams, and market manipulation. Investors should thoroughly research and assess the legitimacy and credibility of an ICO project before participating. Furthermore, the value of ICO tokens can be highly volatile, and there is no guarantee that the tokens will appreciate in value over time. In conclusion, an Initial Coin Offering is a method used by startups and entrepreneurs to raise capital through the issuance and sale of their own digital tokens or coins. It offers a quick and efficient way to gather funds for projects and products, but also carries risks and uncertainties that investors should be aware of.

Initial Funding

Initial Funding refers to the capital or financial resources obtained by a startup or entrepreneur at the beginning stages of their business venture. It serves as the initial injection of funds that allows the startup to establish its operations, develop its products or services, and pave the way for future growth and sustainability. The purpose of initial funding is to cover various expenses that arise during the initial stages of a business, including but not limited to market research, product development, branding, marketing, legal fees, hiring staff, office space, equipment, and inventory. It provides the necessary resources to kickstart the business and turn the entrepreneur's vision into a tangible reality.

Initial Public Offering (IPO) Underwriting

Initial Public Offering (IPO) underwriting is a process in which investment banks or underwriters help a startup or entrepreneurial company to go public by offering its shares to the general public for the first time. This process involves several steps, including valuation, due diligence, pricing, marketing, and distribution of the shares. Valuation is the first step in an IPO underwriting process. Investment banks work with the company to determine the value of its shares based on its financial performance, market conditions, and growth prospects. This valuation helps the company and underwriters to determine the number of shares to be sold and the price at which they will be offered to the public. Once the valuation is determined, due diligence is conducted to assess the company's financial statements, operations, and legal compliance. This step is crucial in ensuring that the company meets the regulatory requirements and has accurate and reliable financial information for potential investors. Pricing is the next step in the IPO underwriting process. The underwriters work with the company to set the initial price at which the shares will be offered to the public. This price is usually based on the valuation, market conditions, and investor demand. After the pricing is finalized, the underwriters begin marketing the IPO to potential investors. They utilize a range of marketing strategies, such as roadshows, investor presentations, and media coverage, to attract interest and generate demand for the shares. The final step in the IPO underwriting process is the distribution of the shares. The underwriters coordinate with stock exchanges and brokerage firms to facilitate the sale and allocation of the shares to individual and institutional investors.

Initial Public Offering (IPO)

An Initial Public Offering (IPO) is a process through which a private company offers its shares to the public for the first time, converting itself into a publicly-traded company. In the context of startup and entrepreneurship, an IPO represents a significant milestone for a company as it allows them to raise capital by selling ownership stakes in the company to public investors. This capital infusion enables the company to fund its growth, expand operations, invest in research and development, pay off debts, and make strategic acquisitions. By going public, a startup gains access to a broader pool of potential investors. These investors can include institutional investors such as mutual funds, pension funds, and hedge funds, as well as individual retail investors who can buy and sell the company's shares on stock exchanges. Through an IPO, startups can enhance their brand recognition, reputation, and credibility in the market. Going public often increases a company's visibility and provides opportunities for attracting key partnerships, talented employees, and potential customers. It can also serve as a platform for future fundraising activities, such as secondary offerings. However, the IPO process can be complex, time-consuming, and costly for startups. It involves thorough preparation, extensive documentation, and regulatory compliance with securities and exchange commissions. Companies need to disclose detailed financial information, including their financial statements, business operations, risks, and management team in a prospectus, which is reviewed by regulatory bodies. In addition, going public exposes the company to greater scrutiny from the public, analysts, and the media. The company's financial performance, decision-making processes, and future prospects become subject to high levels of transparency and disclosure requirements. Overall, an IPO can be a significant milestone for startups and entrepreneurs, enabling them to access capital, gain visibility, and unlock new growth opportunities. However, it is essential for companies to carefully evaluate the advantages and disadvantages of going public and consider alternative funding options before deciding to embark on the IPO journey.

Initial Token Offering (ITO)

Initial Token Offering (ITO) refers to a fundraising method utilized by startups and entrepreneurs in the field of blockchain technology. It is a process in which a company issues and sells its own tokens or coins to investors in exchange for other forms of cryptocurrencies, such as Bitcoin or Ethereum, or in some cases, fiat currencies like USD or EUR. The ITO concept is inspired by the Initial Public Offering (IPO) model in traditional capital markets, where companies offer shares to the public to raise funds. However, in the context of ITOs, instead of offering shares, startups offer tokens or coins that are typically built on blockchain platforms like Ethereum. The primary purpose of conducting an ITO is to secure funding for startups without the need to rely on traditional venture capital firms or banks. It allows startups to access a global pool of potential investors and raises capital quickly and efficiently. During an ITO, a startup typically releases a whitepaper that outlines the details of the project, including its purpose, roadmap, team members, and technical specifications. Investors interested in the project can then purchase tokens by sending the required amount of cryptocurrency to a designated address provided by the startup. ITO participants receive tokens in proportion to their investment, which can serve various purposes within the startup ecosystem. These tokens can represent ownership or equity in the company, grant access to specific services or products, or be used as a medium of exchange within the startup's platform. ITO investors are attracted by the potential growth and profitability of the startup, as well as the opportunity to be part of an emerging technology trend. However, it is crucial for investors to conduct thorough due diligence and assess the credibility and viability of the startup before investing in an ITO, as the crypto market can be highly volatile. In conclusion, an Initial Token Offering (ITO) is a fundraising method where startups issue and sell tokens or coins in exchange for cryptocurrencies or fiat currencies. It enables startups to access global investment opportunities and raise capital quickly, while investors have the opportunity to support innovative projects and potentially profit from their growth.

Initial Token Sale (ITS)

An Initial Token Sale (ITS), also known as an Initial Coin Offering (ICO), is a fundraising method used by startups and entrepreneurs to raise capital for their project or business. It involves the sale of cryptographic tokens or coins to investors in exchange for funds, typically in cryptocurrencies such as Bitcoin or Ethereum. The ITS process begins with the startup or entrepreneur issuing a whitepaper that outlines their project, its goals, and how the funds raised will be utilized. This whitepaper serves as a prospectus, providing potential investors with information regarding the project's technology, team, and token allocation. It also includes details on the token sale, including the start and end dates, the number of tokens available for sale, and the price per token. Investors interested in participating in the ITS can typically contribute funds by sending the required amount of cryptocurrency to the startup's designated wallet address. In return, they receive a specific number of tokens based on the exchange rate set by the startup. These tokens are often ERC-20 tokens created on the Ethereum blockchain but can also be tokens built on other blockchain platforms. The tokens sold during an ITS usually serve a specific purpose within the project's ecosystem. They may represent a stake in the project, granting holders certain rights or privileges, or they may function as a utility token, providing access to the project's products or services. The value of these tokens will depend on various factors, including the project's success, adoption, and market demand. While ITSs offer startups and entrepreneurs an alternative method of raising funds without going through traditional venture capital channels, they also come with risks. Due to the unregulated nature of the cryptocurrency market, investing in ITSs carries a higher level of risk compared to traditional investments. The lack of oversight and the potential for fraudulent projects highlights the importance of conducting thorough research and due diligence before participating in an ITS.

Initial Traction Stage

The initial traction stage in the context of startups and entrepreneurship refers to the early phase of building a business where founders aim to validate their product or service idea and gain initial customer interest and adoption. During this stage, startups focus on obtaining their first set of customers or users and gathering feedback to iterate and improve their offerings. The primary goal is to prove that there is demand for the product or service, and that it solves a specific problem or fills a gap in the market. To achieve initial traction, entrepreneurs employ various strategies such as: 1. MVP Development: Startups often develop a Minimum Viable Product (MVP) to quickly build a version of their product that demonstrates its core value proposition. By focusing on the essential features, entrepreneurs can test the market and gather feedback without significant resources. 2. Targeted Marketing: Startups identify their target audience and develop marketing campaigns to reach and engage potential customers. This may involve online advertising, social media campaigns, content marketing, or partnerships with influencers and industry leaders. 3. Customer Validation: Entrepreneurs engage with potential customers to validate their product's value proposition and collect feedback. This can be done through surveys, interviews, focus groups, or beta testing programs. The insights gained help refine the product and understand the market better. 4. Iteration and Improvement: Startups use the feedback received to iterate and improve their product or service. This involves implementing changes and enhancements based on customer preferences and pain points. The iterative process continues until the product reaches a level of market fit and customer satisfaction. By gaining initial traction, startups can demonstrate proof of concept to potential investors, partners, and stakeholders. This validation helps build credibility and increases the chances of securing funding, attracting talent, and scaling the business. In conclusion, the initial traction stage in startups and entrepreneurship is the critical phase where founders aim to gain customer interest, validate their product idea, and refine their offering based on customer feedback. It involves developing an MVP, targeted marketing, customer validation, and continuous iteration to achieve market fit and build the foundation for future growth.

Initial Traction

Initial Traction refers to the early signs of market acceptance and validation that a startup or entrepreneurial venture receives. It represents the initial success and progress made in gaining customers, generating revenue, and delivering value to the target market. For startups and entrepreneurs, initial traction is a crucial milestone that demonstrates the viability of their business model, product, or service. It provides proof that there is a demand for what they are offering and that they are heading in the right direction.

Initial Validation

Initial Validation refers to the process of gathering evidence and feedback to determine the viability of a startup or entrepreneurial idea. It involves testing assumptions, gathering data, and seeking validation from potential customers or users. This stage is crucial for startups and entrepreneurs because it helps to minimize risks and increase the chances of success. By conducting initial validation, entrepreneurs can gather information to make informed decisions and pivot their strategies if necessary.

Initial Venture Capital

Initial Venture Capital refers to the first round of financing that a startup company raises from external investors. It is a form of private equity investment, where venture capitalists provide funds to early-stage or high-growth startups in exchange for an equity stake in the company. This type of capital is crucial for startups as it provides the necessary funds to develop and launch their products or services, scale their operations, hire key personnel, and execute their business strategies. The funds raised through initial venture capital enable startups to accelerate their growth and achieve their milestones.

Innovation Accelerator

An innovation accelerator in the context of startup and entrepreneurship is a program or organization that provides support, resources, and guidance to individuals or teams with innovative and groundbreaking business ideas. It aims to accelerate the growth and development of these startups by offering various services and opportunities. The primary goal of an innovation accelerator is to help startups bring their ideas to fruition and become successful businesses. They typically provide a range of services, including mentorship, funding, networking opportunities, and access to specialized expertise. The support offered by an accelerator is tailored to the specific needs of each startup, helping them overcome common challenges and maximize their chances of success. One of the main advantages of joining an innovation accelerator is the mentorship and guidance provided by experienced entrepreneurs and industry experts. These mentors can offer valuable advice based on their own experiences, helping startups navigate obstacles and make informed decisions. In addition, accelerators often provide access to a network of potential investors, which can greatly enhance the chances of securing funding. Another key aspect of innovation accelerators is their focus on providing resources and tools to help startups refine their business models and develop their products or services. This can range from workshops and training sessions to access to specialized equipment or facilities. By leveraging these resources, startups can iterate and improve their offerings, increasing their competitiveness and market potential. Moreover, innovation accelerators often provide startups with exposure and networking opportunities. They typically organize events, such as pitch competitions or demo days, where startups can showcase their ideas to potential investors, partners, and customers. This exposure can help startups attract attention and generate interest in their business, potentially leading to partnerships, funding, and growth opportunities. In summary, an innovation accelerator plays a crucial role in supporting startups and promoting entrepreneurship. By offering mentorship, funding, resources, and networking opportunities, accelerators help startups overcome challenges and accelerate their growth, ultimately increasing their chances of long-term success.

Innovation Culture

Innovation Culture refers to the set of attitudes, behaviors, and practices that prioritize and support the creation and implementation of new and valuable ideas within a startup or entrepreneurial environment. Within the context of startups and entrepreneurship, innovation culture is crucial for fostering creativity and driving growth. It encompasses the collective mindset and values of the organization, promoting an environment where experimentation, risk-taking, and learning from failures are embraced.

Innovation Ecosystem

An innovation ecosystem, in the context of startup and entrepreneurship, refers to the interconnected network of organizations, individuals, resources, and processes that collaborate to foster and support innovative activities. At its core, an innovation ecosystem provides a conducive environment that encourages the generation, diffusion, and commercialization of new ideas, products, and services. It brings together various stakeholders, such as startups, entrepreneurs, investors, universities, research institutions, government agencies, and support organizations, to create a dynamic and vibrant ecosystem that promotes innovation and economic growth.

Innovation Hub

An Innovation Hub is a collaborative and dynamic ecosystem that serves as a platform for startups and entrepreneurs to network, collaborate, and innovate in order to bring new ideas, products, and services to market. Within an Innovation Hub, startups and entrepreneurs have access to a wide range of resources, support, and expertise. This includes access to funding opportunities, mentorship programs, shared office spaces, specialized equipment and technology, and access to a network of investors, industry experts, and potential partners. The primary goal of an Innovation Hub is to foster and promote innovation and entrepreneurship. It provides a supportive environment where startups and entrepreneurs can connect with like-minded individuals, learn from each other, and collaborate on projects or initiatives that have the potential to disrupt traditional industries or create new markets. By bringing together startups, entrepreneurs, investors, and industry experts, Innovation Hubs aim to facilitate the exchange of knowledge, ideas, and resources. This collaborative environment encourages creativity, experimentation, and risk-taking, as well as provides opportunities for startups to validate their ideas, refine their business models, and receive feedback and guidance from experienced professionals. In addition to creating a supportive and collaborative community, Innovation Hubs often host events, workshops, and conferences to facilitate knowledge-sharing and promote the development of entrepreneurial skills. These events provide opportunities for startups and entrepreneurs to learn from successful founders, industry leaders, and subject matter experts, as well as network with potential investors, partners, and customers. Overall, an Innovation Hub plays a critical role in driving entrepreneurial growth and economic development. It acts as a catalyst for innovation and provides startups and entrepreneurs with the necessary resources, support, and networks to thrive in a competitive business landscape. Whether it's through access to funding, mentorship, or collaborative workspaces, Innovation Hubs are instrumental in fueling the success and growth of startups and entrepreneurs.

Innovation Lab

An innovation lab is a dedicated space or unit within a startup or entrepreneurship ecosystem that fosters creativity, collaboration, and experimentation in order to drive innovation and develop new ideas, products, or solutions. Innovation labs are designed to be agile and flexible, providing an environment that encourages the generation of new ideas and facilitates the exploration and testing of these ideas through various methods such as design thinking, rapid prototyping, and user-centered research. They serve as a hub for innovation within the startup or entrepreneurship ecosystem, aiming to transform innovative concepts into tangible outcomes. The main objective of an innovation lab is to foster a culture of innovation and entrepreneurship by providing resources, support, and guidance to startups and entrepreneurs. The lab may offer a range of services and facilities, including co-working spaces, mentorship programs, access to industry experts and investors, as well as technical resources like state-of-the-art equipment, software, and prototyping tools. Innovation labs often follow an iterative and collaborative approach, encouraging interdisciplinary collaboration and knowledge sharing among participants. They promote a mindset of continuous learning and improvement, allowing startups and entrepreneurs to experiment, fail, and learn from their experiences in a safe and supportive environment. The outcomes of innovation labs can vary, but they typically aim to develop innovative products, services, or business models that have the potential to disrupt existing markets or create new ones. These outcomes are often driven by market insights, user feedback, and a deep understanding of customer needs and pain points. Overall, innovation labs play a crucial role in the startup and entrepreneurship ecosystem by nurturing a culture of innovation, empowering startups and entrepreneurs, and driving economic growth through the development of breakthrough ideas and solutions.

Innovation Management Software

Innovation Management Software is a tool designed to help startups and entrepreneurs streamline and optimize their innovation processes. It provides a digital platform for managing and organizing various aspects of innovation, such as idea generation, evaluation, implementation, and tracking. Through this software, startups and entrepreneurs can effectively manage their innovation projects, collaborate with team members, and monitor the progress of their innovation initiatives. The primary goal of Innovation Management Software is to facilitate the systematic and structured management of innovation within a startup or entrepreneurial environment. It offers a range of features and functionalities that support the entire innovation lifecycle, from ideation to execution. These features typically include: 1. Idea capture and management: The software allows startups and entrepreneurs to capture, record, and organize ideas that emerge within the organization. It offers a centralized repository for storing and categorizing ideas based on different criteria, such as relevance, feasibility, and strategic fit. 2. Idea evaluation and selection: The software provides tools for evaluating and selecting the most promising ideas for further development. It may include features like scoring, ranking, and reviewing ideas based on predefined criteria and parameters. This helps startups and entrepreneurs make informed decisions about which ideas to pursue and invest resources in. 3. Project management: Innovation Management Software facilitates the planning, execution, and monitoring of innovation projects. It allows startups and entrepreneurs to create project plans, allocate resources, define milestones, and track progress. It also enables effective collaboration among team members, ensuring coordination and alignment throughout the project lifecycle. 4. Knowledge management: The software helps startups and entrepreneurs capture, share, and leverage knowledge and insights gained from innovation activities. It allows for the storage and retrieval of relevant information, best practices, and lessons learned. This helps in building a knowledge base that can support future innovation endeavors and avoid reinventing the wheel. 5. Performance measurement and reporting: Innovation Management Software provides startups and entrepreneurs with tools to measure and track the performance and impact of their innovation initiatives. It generates reports and analytics on key metrics, such as the number of ideas generated, time-to-market, success rate, and return on investment. This enables decision-makers to assess the effectiveness and efficiency of their innovation processes and make data-driven improvements.

Innovation Management

Innovation management in the context of startup and entrepreneurship refers to the systematic process of identifying, developing, and implementing new ideas, products, services, or business models with the aim of creating value and achieving a competitive advantage. It encompasses the strategic and operational activities that are necessary to foster and facilitate innovation within a startup or entrepreneurial venture. Innovation management involves various stages and activities, including idea generation, idea screening, concept development, prototype building, pilot testing, commercialization, and continuous improvement. It requires effective leadership, resource allocation, collaboration, and the adoption of innovation-friendly organizational structures and processes. In the context of startups and entrepreneurship, innovation management plays a critical role in driving growth and sustainability. Startups are typically characterized by their disruptive and innovative nature, as they seek to introduce new solutions to existing problems or create entirely new markets. Effective innovation management enables startups to harness their entrepreneurial spirit and convert ideas into viable and profitable ventures. One key aspect of innovation management is the creation of an environment that fosters creativity and encourages the generation of new ideas. This can be achieved through the establishment of cross-functional teams, the promotion of open communication and knowledge-sharing, and the provision of resources and incentives that incentivize innovation. By nurturing a culture of innovation, startups can tap into the collective intelligence of their employees and stakeholders to generate novel solutions and drive continuous improvement. Furthermore, innovation management involves the identification and assessment of potential risks and obstacles that may hinder the successful implementation of innovative ideas. Startups need to thoroughly analyze market trends, customer needs, technological advancements, and competitive landscapes to ensure that their innovative solutions align with market demand and have a competitive advantage.

Innovation Pipeline

The innovation pipeline is a strategic process employed by startups and entrepreneurs to continuously develop, refine, and implement new ideas and solutions within their businesses. It is a systematic approach that allows these entities to maintain a steady flow of innovative products, services, or processes to meet market demands and achieve long-term success. The innovation pipeline typically consists of several stages or phases that startups and entrepreneurs navigate through as they conceive, explore, and commercialize new ideas. These stages can vary depending on the specific industry, business model, or market, but commonly include: 1. Ideation: This initial stage involves brainstorming and generating a wide range of ideas and concepts. Startups and entrepreneurs evaluate the feasibility and potential impact of each idea, considering factors such as market trends, customer needs, and business capabilities. 2. Evaluation: In this stage, startups and entrepreneurs assess the feasibility and viability of their ideas. They conduct market research, analyze competition, and evaluate the potential risks and rewards associated with each idea. This evaluation process helps prioritize and select the most promising concepts to move forward. 3. Development: Once an idea is selected, startups and entrepreneurs move on to the development stage. This involves transforming the concept into a tangible product, service, or process. They conduct prototyping, testing, and refinement to ensure the idea meets quality standards and fulfills customer needs. 4. Commercialization: In this stage, startups and entrepreneurs aim to bring the developed idea to market. They create marketing strategies, establish distribution channels, and launch promotional campaigns to generate awareness and attract customers. The focus shifts towards scaling the innovation and generating revenue. 5. Continuous improvement: The innovation pipeline is not a linear process; it is iterative and requires constant improvement. Startups and entrepreneurs gather feedback, analyze performance data, and make necessary adjustments to enhance the innovation and address any shortcomings. This stage ensures the innovation remains relevant and competitive in the dynamic business landscape. The innovation pipeline is crucial for startups and entrepreneurs as it enables them to stay ahead of the competition, adapt to market changes, and seize opportunities. It fosters a culture of innovation and enables the organizations to deliver novel solutions that create value for customers and drive growth in the long run.

Innovation Strategy Development And Execution

Innovation strategy development and execution in the context of startup and entrepreneurship refers to the process of creating and implementing a plan to introduce new and innovative ideas, products, or business models that provide unique value to customers, and ultimately, drive the growth and success of the startup. This involves a systematic approach to identify and evaluate opportunities for innovation, define a clear direction and objectives, and outline the necessary steps and resources required to bring those ideas to life. The strategy should align with the startup's overall vision and goals, and take into account its target market, competitive landscape, and internal capabilities. At the core of innovation strategy development is the understanding that innovation is not just limited to technological advancements, but can also stem from improvements in processes, customer experiences, or business models. It requires thinking creatively and critically about how to solve problems, meet unmet needs, or tap into new markets. The execution of the innovation strategy involves translating the plan into action, mobilizing resources, and implementing the necessary initiatives to bring the innovative ideas to market. This includes conducting research and development, designing and prototyping, testing and iterating, and eventually scaling and commercializing the innovations. Successful execution of the innovation strategy requires collaboration and coordination across various functions within the startup, such as product development, marketing, operations, and finance. It also involves continuously monitoring and evaluating the progress and impact of the innovation initiatives, and making adjustments and improvements as needed. In summary, innovation strategy development and execution in the context of startup and entrepreneurship is about creating and implementing a plan to introduce new and unique ideas, products, or business models that provide value to customers and drive startup growth. It involves a systematic approach to identify opportunities, define objectives, and outline the necessary steps and resources to bring those ideas to life. Execution involves translating the plan into action, mobilizing resources, and implementing initiatives to bring innovations to market.

Innovation Strategy Development

Innovation Strategy Development is the process of formulating a plan or approach to create and implement innovative ideas and solutions within a startup or entrepreneurial venture. It involves identifying and analyzing opportunities for innovation, evaluating the potential impact and feasibility of different ideas, and designing a strategic roadmap to guide the implementation and execution of innovative initiatives. The objective of innovation strategy development is to enable startups and entrepreneurs to differentiate themselves from competitors, create sustainable value, and achieve long-term growth and success. It is a proactive and systematic approach that combines creativity, market insights, and business acumen to foster a culture of innovation and drive organizational transformation. At the core of innovation strategy development is the identification of key areas or domains where innovation can be applied to address customer needs, optimize operations, or develop new business models. This involves conducting market research, gathering customer feedback, and analyzing industry trends to gain a deep understanding of the market landscape and potential opportunities. Once potential areas for innovation have been identified, the next step in the process is to generate a range of innovative ideas. This can be done through brainstorming sessions, idea generation workshops, or by leveraging external sources such as open innovation platforms or partnerships with other organizations. The objective is to foster a culture of creativity and encourage the exploration of unconventional and disruptive ideas. Following idea generation, the next phase in innovation strategy development is idea evaluation and selection. This involves assessing the potential impact, feasibility, and viability of different ideas through various criteria such as market demand, technical feasibility, financial viability, and strategic fit. The goal is to identify the most

127

promising ideas that align with the overall business objectives and have the highest potential for success. Once the promising ideas have been selected, the next step is to design a strategic roadmap for implementing and executing the innovation initiatives. This includes defining the specific actions, resources, and timelines required to bring the ideas to life, as well as establishing performance metrics and milestones to track progress and measure the success of the innovation efforts. In conclusion, innovation strategy development is a critical process for startups and entrepreneurs to create and implement innovative ideas and solutions that can enable them to differentiate themselves, create value, and achieve sustainable growth. It involves identifying opportunities, generating ideas, evaluating potential impact, feasibility, and viability, and designing a strategic roadmap for implementation and execution.

Innovation Strategy Implementation And Management

Innovation Strategy Implementation and Management refers to the process of implementing and managing an innovation strategy in the context of startup and entrepreneurship. It involves the execution of a set of deliberate actions and the allocation of necessary resources to bring about innovative ideas and technologies into practice. Startups and entrepreneurs often face the challenge of developing and implementing innovative solutions to address market needs and stay ahead of the competition. Innovation strategy implementation and management provides a systematic approach to transform innovative ideas into tangible outcomes.

Innovation Strategy Implementation

Innovation strategy implementation in the context of startups and entrepreneurship refers to the process of translating innovative ideas into tangible products, services, or processes that create value for the market and drive business growth. It involves executing a well-defined plan to transform innovative concepts into actionable outcomes that address customer needs, disrupt existing markets, and create competitive advantages. Successful innovation strategy implementation requires a systematic approach that balances creativity and execution. It begins with identifying and understanding the target market and customer needs to ensure that the innovation aligns with market demand. This involves conducting market research, analyzing trends, and gathering customer insights to guide the development and refinement of the innovation. Once the innovation concept is defined, the next step in implementation is to develop a detailed strategy and roadmap that outlines the required resources, activities, and milestones. This includes identifying the necessary technological, financial, and human resources needed to bring the innovation to life. The strategy should also consider potential risks and challenges, as well as contingencies and mitigation plans. With a clear strategy in place, the execution phase begins. This involves mobilizing the necessary resources, assembling a team, and coordinating the various activities and tasks to bring the innovation to fruition. Effective project management and communication are crucial during this phase to ensure that everyone is aligned and working towards the same goals. Regular monitoring and evaluation of progress are also essential to identify and address any roadblocks or deviations from the plan. Innovation strategy implementation requires a culture that embraces experimentation, iteration, and learning from failures. It involves creating an environment that encourages creativity, collaboration, and risk-taking. This can be achieved by fostering a culture of open communication, providing resources for continuous learning and development, and recognizing and celebrating innovative achievements. In conclusion, innovation strategy implementation in startups and entrepreneurship is the process of translating innovative ideas into tangible outcomes that create value and drive business growth. It involves understanding market needs, developing a detailed strategy, mobilizing resources, and executing the plan while fostering a culture of innovation. By effectively implementing innovation strategies, startups and entrepreneurs can differentiate themselves, disrupt markets, and achieve sustainable success.

Innovation Strategy

Innovation Strategy - Definition in the Context of Startup & Entrepreneurship Innovation strategy, in the context of startup and entrepreneurship, refers to the systematic approach utilized by individuals or organizations to foster and implement innovation within their businesses. It involves developing a clear plan and framework that enables the generation, evaluation, and execution of innovative ideas to drive growth, competitiveness, and sustainability. An innovation strategy is essential for startups and entrepreneurs as it allows them to differentiate themselves from competitors, adapt to changing market trends, and create unique value propositions. A successful innovation strategy aims to identify new opportunities, disrupt existing markets, and transform ideas into tangible products, services, or business models to meet evolving customer needs. There are several key components that make up an effective innovation strategy: 1. Focus: This entails identifying specific areas or domains where innovation efforts will be concentrated. By focusing on specific sectors or markets, startups can allocate their limited resources efficiently and increase the chances of success. 2. Research and Analysis: Thoroughly understanding the target market, industry trends, and customer preferences is crucial for formulating a solid innovation strategy. This involves conducting extensive market research, analyzing competitors, and identifying unmet needs or pain points that can be addressed through innovative solutions. 3. Idea Generation: This stage involves actively seeking out and generating creative ideas through brainstorming sessions, customer feedback, collaborations, or other means. It is crucial to encourage a diverse range of perspectives and foster a culture that promotes ideation and experimentation. 4. Idea Evaluation: Once a pool of ideas has been generated, it is vital to evaluate and select the most viable options. This involves assessing the feasibility, potential impact, scalability, and alignment with the overall business objectives. Only the most promising ideas should be further developed and implemented. 5. Implementation: Transforming innovative ideas into reality requires effective planning, resource allocation, and project management. Close collaboration between various stakeholders, including employees, partners, and investors, is crucial to ensure the successful execution of the chosen innovation initiatives. 6. Continuous Improvement: An innovation strategy is an ongoing process that requires continuous monitoring, evaluation, and iteration. Startups and entrepreneurs must be nimble and adaptable, incorporating feedback and learning from both successes and failures to continuously improve their offerings and capture new opportunities. In conclusion, an innovation strategy provides a strategic roadmap for startups and entrepreneurs to foster and implement innovation effectively. It involves various stages from idea generation to implementation, emphasizing the importance of focus, research, ideation, evaluation, implementation, and continuous improvement. By embracing innovation and developing a robust strategy, startups can navigate uncertainty, create value, and gain a competitive edge in the dynamic entrepreneurial landscape.

Innovation Workshops

Innovation workshops refer to interactive sessions or sessions where participants, typically startups and entrepreneurs, come together to brainstorm, generate ideas, and explore creative solutions to address business challenges or create new opportunities. These workshops are designed to foster a collaborative and open environment that promotes innovative thinking and allows participants to tap into their creativity. The structure of innovation workshops may vary, but they usually involve various exercises and activities aimed at stimulating idea generation and problem-solving.

Innovation

Innovation refers to the process of creating and developing new ideas, products, services, or technologies that bring about significant changes or improvements in various aspects of society, industry, or market. It is a fundamental aspect of startup and entrepreneurship, as it drives the creation of unique value propositions and differentiation in a highly competitive market. Innovation is the manifestation of entrepreneurial and creative efforts, where individuals or teams identify and leverage opportunities to address existing problems, needs, or desires in new and more effective ways. It involves the exploration and exploitation of novel ideas, often resulting in the generation of disruptive or incremental innovations. Startups, by nature, thrive on innovation. They are characterized by their ability to take risks, challenge the status quo, and introduce groundbreaking solutions to meet the evolving demands of customers and markets. The pursuit of innovation enables startups to capture untapped market opportunities, create competitive advantages, and drive sustainable growth. Entrepreneurs, as catalysts of innovation, play a pivotal role in the process. They possess a unique combination of vision, creativity, and determination to turn ideas into reality. Entrepreneurs identify market gaps, design innovative business models, and assemble resources to transform their ideas into viable and scalable ventures. Innovation within the startup and entrepreneurial context is not limited to creating revolutionary products or technologies. It also encompasses the development of innovative processes, organizational structures, marketing strategies, and value delivery methods. It involves continuously seeking new ways to solve problems, improve efficiency, enhance customer experience, and stay ahead of the competition. Effective innovation requires a supportive ecosystem that fosters collaboration, experimentation, and learning. Startups and entrepreneurs often interact with various stakeholders, such as investors, mentors, customers, and industry experts, to gain insights, validation, and resources. They embrace a culture of openness, adaptability, and resilience to navigate through uncertainties and challenges in their innovation journey. In summary, innovation is the driving force behind startups and entrepreneurship. It involves the creation and development of new ideas, products, services, and strategies that bring about significant improvements or disruptions in the market. Entrepreneurs play a vital role in pursuing and implementing innovation, aiming to create unique value propositions and achieve sustainable growth in a competitive landscape.

Innovative Business Models

Innovative business models refer to unique and novel approaches adopted by startups and entrepreneurs to create, deliver, and capture value in the market. These models are designed to disrupt traditional industries, solve existing problems, and create new opportunities. Startups and entrepreneurs often face fierce competition and limited resources, making it essential for them to find innovative ways to differentiate themselves and stand out in the market. Innovative business models enable them to do exactly that.

Innovator's Dilemma

In the context of startup and entrepreneurship, the Innovator's Dilemma refers to a phenomenon where successful startups or entrepreneurs face a difficult decision between sustaining their current business model or pursuing disruptive innovations that may ultimately lead to their own downfall. When a startup or entrepreneur initially enters the market, they often introduce a groundbreaking product or service that satisfies an underserved or unmet need. This innovation allows them to gain a competitive advantage and rapidly grow their customer base, establishing themselves as market leaders. However, as the startup evolves and becomes more successful, it faces certain challenges. The success and growth of the startup create a natural tendency to focus on sustaining and optimizing the existing business model. This involves refining the current product, expanding market share, and catering to the needs of existing customers. This focus on sustaining the current business model may lead to a state of complacency, where the startup becomes resistant to change and less willing to explore new technologies or ideas. At the same time, disruptive technologies or new market entrants start to emerge, offering alternative solutions that are initially inferior in terms of performance or functionality but hold the potential to disrupt the market in the future. Here lies the Innovator's Dilemma. Should the startup or entrepreneur continue to focus on sustaining its current business model and risk being overtaken by disruptive innovations in the future? Or should they be proactive in self-disrupting and embracing the new technologies or approaches that may undermine their existing success? This dilemma arises because sustaining innovations, which improve existing products and services, are often easier to execute and have a proven market demand. On the other hand, disruptive innovations, which initially cater to niche markets or unmet needs, may face skepticism and uncertainty, making it difficult to justify pursuing them over the short-term profitability of sustaining the current business model. In conclusion, the Innovator's Dilemma in the context of startup and entrepreneurship revolves around the decision to sustain the current business model or pursue disruptive innovations. This decision requires careful consideration of the potential risks and rewards associated with both approaches, as well as a willingness to adapt and embrace change in order to remain competitive in a rapidly evolving market.

Intellectual Property (IP) Licensing

Intellectual Property (IP) licensing refers to the legal agreement between a startup or entrepreneur (the licensee) and the owner of intellectual property rights (the licensor) for the authorized use or exploitation of the intellectual property. This agreement grants the licensee certain rights to use, sell, or develop the licensed intellectual property, while the licensor retains ownership and control over the IP. Intellectual property can include a wide range of intangible assets, such as patents, trademarks, copyrights, trade secrets, and designs. These types of IP provide exclusive rights to their owners and can be valuable assets for startups and entrepreneurs. Licensing allows a startup or entrepreneur to leverage the intellectual property of others without having to invest in developing their own, enabling them to access new technologies, products, or services.

Intellectual Property Management Tools

Intellectual Property Management Tools refer to various resources and strategies used by startups and entrepreneurs to effectively manage their intellectual property assets. Intellectual property (IP) includes creations of the mind such as inventions, designs, trademarks, and literary or artistic works, and it is crucial for startups and entrepreneurs to protect and manage their IP assets in order to secure a competitive advantage and avoid infringement. These tools provide step-by-step guidance and organized frameworks for the identification, protection, valuation, and commercialization of intellectual property. They help startups and entrepreneurs navigate the complex landscape of IP laws and regulations, enabling them to make informed decisions regarding the creation, acquisition, and exploitation of their IP assets. One key aspect of intellectual property management tools is the assistance they provide in conducting thorough IP searches. These searches involve examining existing patents, trademarks, and copyrights to ensure that the startup's proposed IP is novel and not already owned by someone else. By conducting comprehensive IP searches, startups can avoid potential legal disputes in the future. Another important function of these tools is IP protection. They assist in the application process for patents, trademarks, and copyrights, ensuring that the necessary documentation and requirements are met. These tools may also provide alerts and reminders for IP renewal deadlines, helping startups maintain ongoing protection for their assets. Furthermore, intellectual property management tools often include features for IP valuation and portfolio management. These features enable startups and entrepreneurs to assess the value of their IP assets and understand their potential for commercialization. By tracking and organizing their IP portfolio, startups can strategize and prioritize their IP assets for licensing, partnerships, or potential investment opportunities. In summary, intellectual property management tools are essential resources for startups and entrepreneurs to effectively manage their intellectual property assets. By utilizing these tools, they can protect and leverage their IP assets, mitigate the risk of infringement, and maximize their competitive advantage in the market.

Intellectual Property Rights (IPR)

Intellectual Property Rights (IPR) refer to the legal rights that are granted to individuals or organizations to protect their intellectual creations, inventions, or innovations. These rights play a crucial role in the context of startups and entrepreneurship as they provide a framework to safeguard and monetize the ideas, products, or services that entrepreneurs develop and bring to market. IPR encompasses various forms of protection, including patents, trademarks, copyrights, trade secrets, and industrial designs. Patents, for instance, offer exclusive rights to inventors for a specified period, preventing others from using, making, or selling their patented technology without permission. This enables startups to establish a competitive advantage in the market by ensuring that their innovative solutions cannot be easily replicated or copied by competitors. Trademarks are another essential component of IPR, as they provide entrepreneurs with the exclusive right to use a specific name, logo, or symbol to distinguish their products or services from others in the market. This helps build brand recognition and loyalty, allowing startups to differentiate themselves and establish a strong identity in the minds of consumers. Copyrights protect original works of authorship, such as literary, artistic, or musical creations. Startups can use copyrights to protect their software code, website content, graphic designs, or written materials. By securing these rights, entrepreneurs can prevent others from reproducing or distributing their works without authorization, ensuring that their creative efforts are not unfairly exploited. Trade secrets play a unique role in IPR, particularly in the realm of startups. These rights protect confidential and proprietary information that provides a competitive edge to a business. Startups often rely on trade secrets to safeguard their business models, customer data, manufacturing processes, or marketing strategies. By keeping this information secret, startups can maintain a distinct advantage over their competitors. Industrial designs refer to the aesthetic or visual aspects of a product, such as its shape, pattern, or color. Registering and protecting these designs through IPR grants startups exclusive rights to prevent others from copying or imitating their unique product designs, enabling them to establish a distinctive visual appeal and differentiate their offerings in the market.

Intellectual Property

Intellectual property is a legal term that refers to creations of the mind, such as inventions, designs, logos, trade secrets, and artistic works, which are protected by laws including patents, trademarks, copyrights, and trade secrets. In the context of startups and entrepreneurship, intellectual property plays a crucial role in safeguarding and promoting innovation, creativity, and competitiveness. It provides a legal framework for entrepreneurs to protect their unique ideas, inventions, and brand identity, enabling them to have a competitive edge in the market and attract investments.

Intrapreneurship

Intrapreneurship is a term derived from the combination of "intra" and "entrepreneurship" and refers to the practice of entrepreneurial activities within a larger organization or company. It describes individuals within the organization who exhibit characteristics similar to those of entrepreneurs, taking risks and innovating to create new products, services, or processes. Intrapreneurship involves fostering an entrepreneurial mindset and encouraging employees to think and act like entrepreneurs. Intrapreneurs are given the freedom and resources to explore new ideas and create value within the organization. They are encouraged to challenge the status quo, identify opportunities for growth and improvement, and take ownership of their projects. One of the primary objectives of intrapreneurship is to drive innovation and promote the development of new business lines or ventures within the existing company structure. Intrapreneurs are often tasked with identifying new market trends, researching and developing new products or services, and exploring untapped areas for growth. They are given the responsibility to take calculated risks, learn from failures, and continuously adapt and refine their ideas. Intrapreneurship is closely tied to the concept of corporate entrepreneurship, as it promotes entrepreneurial thinking and behavior within established organizations. It encourages employees to take initiative, be proactive, and think outside the box to generate new value and drive the organization forward. Intrapreneurial activities may result in the creation of new revenue streams, the improvement of existing processes or products, or the development of innovative solutions to solve organizational challenges.

Investment Thesis

An investment thesis is a formal written statement that outlines a startup entrepreneur's investment strategy and criteria. It serves as a framework for making investment decisions and guides the entrepreneur in identifying and evaluating potential business opportunities. The investment thesis typically includes the entrepreneur's vision and goals for the startup, as well as the specific industries, markets, or technologies they plan to focus on. It outlines the entrepreneur's knowledge and expertise in these areas and highlights the key trends and market dynamics that contribute to their investment strategy. The investment thesis also outlines the entrepreneur's criteria for selecting investment opportunities. This may include factors such as the target company's stage of development, revenue potential, competitive advantage, and management team. The thesis may also specify the desired investment size and expected return on investment. By developing an investment thesis, the startup entrepreneur is able to articulate their investment strategy and criteria to potential stakeholders, including venture capitalists, angel investors, and other funding sources. It provides a clear and concise overview of the entrepreneur's investment focus and rationale, helping to attract the right investors who align with the startup's goals and vision. Furthermore, the investment thesis serves as a guide for the entrepreneur in evaluating potential investment opportunities. It provides a framework for conducting due diligence and assessing the potential risks and rewards associated with each opportunity. This allows the entrepreneur to make informed investment decisions that align with their investment strategy and maximize the chances of success. In summary, an investment thesis is a formal written statement that outlines a startup entrepreneur's investment strategy and criteria. It serves as a guide for making investment decisions and communicates the entrepreneur's vision and goals to potential stakeholders. By developing an investment thesis, the entrepreneur can attract the right investors and make informed investment decisions that align with their investment strategy.

Investor Pitch

Investor Pitch is a concise and compelling presentation that startup entrepreneurs use to showcase their business idea, growth potential, and convince investors to provide financial support. It is a critical tool for entrepreneurs to secure funding and build a strong foundation for their startup. The goal of an investor pitch is to convey the unique value proposition of the startup, demonstrate market potential, outline business strategies, and convince investors about the profitability and scalability of the venture. It is typically delivered through a formal presentation or pitch deck, accompanied by a well-crafted verbal narrative. An effective investor pitch starts with a captivating opening that grabs the attention of investors. It should clearly and succinctly define the problem that the startup is addressing and highlight its market demand. By providing a compelling solution, entrepreneurs can demonstrate the opportunity and generate interest from potential investors. The presentation should also emphasize the competitive advantage of the startup, such as technology, intellectual property, or unique expertise, which sets it apart from existing solutions. Demonstrating a deep understanding of the target market and a clear execution strategy strengthens the case for investment. Entrepreneurs should also present a solid financial plan, showcasing revenue models, growth projections, and potential return on investment. By substantiating the financial viability and potential profitability, entrepreneurs can instill confidence in investors and make the venture more appealing. The credibility and expertise of the entrepreneur and the team are crucial aspects of the investor pitch. Highlighting relevant experience, industry knowledge, and track record creates trust and credibility. An investor needs to feel confident in the ability of the entrepreneur to execute the business plan and overcome challenges. Lastly, a persuasive investor pitch should have a clear call to action, indicating the funding requirement and the terms sought from potential investors. Entrepreneurs should be prepared to answer questions, address concerns, and negotiate terms during and after the presentation. In summary, an investor pitch is a strategic communication tool that provides entrepreneurs with an opportunity to attract investors and secure funding for their startup. By effectively presenting the value proposition, market potential, financial viability, and the capabilities of the team, entrepreneurs can increase their chances of securing financial support and driving the success of their venture.

Job To Be Done (JTBD) Framework

The Job To Be Done (JTBD) framework is a strategic approach used in startup and entrepreneurship to identify and understand customer needs and motivations. It focuses on the underlying goals and desires that customers are trying to achieve when they use a product or service. The JTBD framework recognizes that customers "hire" products or services to get a specific job done in their lives. This job can range from everyday tasks to more complex goals. By understanding the job, entrepreneurs can develop innovative solutions that fulfill those unmet needs or improve upon existing offerings.

Joint Venture Agreements

A joint venture agreement is a formal legal agreement between two or more parties to collaborate and pool their resources, expertise, and capital in order to achieve a specific business objective. It is commonly used in the context of startups and entrepreneurship to leverage each party's strengths and create a mutually beneficial partnership. The joint venture agreement outlines the terms and conditions of the collaboration, including the goals, responsibilities, and contributions of each party. Key elements typically included in the agreement are: 1. Purpose and goals: The agreement clearly defines the purpose of the joint venture and the specific goals it aims to achieve. This could be the development of a new product, expansion into a new market, or the sharing of resources to increase operational efficiency. 2. Contributions: Each party's contributions in terms of capital, assets, intellectual property, or expertise are detailed in the agreement. This ensures that all parties have a clear understanding of what they are expected to bring to the joint venture. 3. Roles and responsibilities: The agreement outlines the roles and responsibilities of each party involved in the joint venture. This includes decision-making authority, management responsibilities, and any specific tasks or duties assigned to each party. 4. Profit and loss sharing: The agreement specifies how profits and losses will be allocated among the parties. This could be based on the proportion of capital contributed or any other agreed-upon formula. 5. Duration and termination: The agreement includes the duration of the joint venture and the conditions under which it can be terminated. This could be based on the achievement of specific milestones, expiration of a certain time period, or the occurrence of other specified events. A well-drafted joint venture agreement is essential in minimizing potential conflicts and ensuring that the interests of all parties involved are protected. It establishes a clear framework for collaboration, outlines expectations, and provides mechanisms for dispute resolution. This helps startups and entrepreneurs mitigate risks, share resources, and capitalize on opportunities that would be difficult to achieve independently.

Joint Ventures

Joint Ventures are strategic partnerships formed between two or more entities, typically companies or organizations, with the purpose of working together on a specific project or business opportunity.The main objective of a joint venture is to combine the resources, expertise, and market presence of the participating entities in order to achieve mutual benefits, such as shared costs, increased market share, access to new markets or technologies, and risk mitigation.

Kaizen (Continuous Improvement)

Kaizen, also known as continuous improvement, is a concept in the context of startups and entrepreneurship that focuses on making incremental changes to processes, products, and services to enhance efficiency and drive growth. It is rooted in the philosophy of constantly seeking opportunities for improvement and engaging all employees in the process. In the startup and entrepreneurship domain, kaizen plays a critical role in fostering innovation, maintaining competitiveness, and achieving long-term success. Rather than pursuing radical changes or drastic overhauls, kaizen promotes a gradual and relentless commitment to improvement. It encourages entrepreneurs and startup teams to identify and eliminate inefficiencies, streamline workflows, optimize resource allocation, and enhance customer experiences.

Kanban Boards

A Kanban board is a visual project management tool that helps startups and entrepreneurs organize and track their tasks and projects. It provides a clear, real-time overview of the progress and status of each task, making it easier to manage workflows and improve productivity. The board typically consists of columns that represent different stages of work, such as "To Do," "In Progress," and "Done." Each task is represented by a card or sticky note, which moves across the board as it progresses through the various stages. This visual representation allows team members to see at a glance what tasks are in progress, what needs to be done next, and what has been completed.

Key Performance Indicator (KPI) Tracking

Key Performance Indicator (KPI) Tracking is an essential component in the context of Startup and Entrepreneurship. It refers to the process of monitoring and measuring the performance of key metrics or indicators that are critical to the success and growth of a startup or entrepreneurial venture. KPI tracking involves the identification of specific goals and objectives that align with the overall business strategy, and then measuring the progress and achievements towards those goals. It provides valuable insights into the performance and efficiency of various business processes, allowing entrepreneurs to make data-driven decisions and optimize their operations.

Knowledge Management Systems

A knowledge management system (KMS) refers to a set of processes, tools, and technologies that enable a startup or entrepreneurship venture to capture, organize, and share knowledge effectively within the organization. It aims to enhance collaboration, foster innovation, and improve decision-making by ensuring that valuable knowledge and information are easily accessible and usable. A KMS typically consists of various components, such as a knowledge repository, knowledge sharing platforms, and knowledge transfer mechanisms. The knowledge repository serves as a centralized storage system, where information and knowledge assets, including documents, reports, best practices, and expert insights, are collected and organized. This allows employees and stakeholders to locate and retrieve relevant information quickly and efficiently. The knowledge sharing platforms facilitate the exchange of knowledge and ideas among individuals and teams. These platforms can take multiple forms, such as intranets, social collaboration tools, or online forums, providing spaces for discussions, knowledge sharing, and problem-solving. By promoting communication and information sharing, startups and entrepreneurs can tap into the expertise and experiences of their employees, leading to enhanced innovation and improved outcomes. Knowledge transfer mechanisms, another crucial component of a KMS, enable the smooth transfer of knowledge from one individual or team to another. This can be achieved through various means, such as mentoring programs, training sessions, and communities of practice. These mechanisms help to disseminate tacit knowledge, which is often deeply rooted in individuals' experiences and expertise, and convert it into explicit knowledge that can be shared and utilized by others. Implementing a KMS in a startup or entrepreneurship venture can bring several benefits. It helps to avoid rework and duplication of efforts by allowing employees to access existing knowledge and learn from previous experiences. It also promotes continuous learning and improvement by capturing lessons learned and creating a culture of knowledge sharing and innovation. Ultimately, a well-designed KMS contributes to the overall success and competitiveness of a startup or entrepreneurship venture by leveraging the collective intelligence and knowledge assets of the organization.

Landing Page

A landing page refers to a single web page that is specifically designed to promote or market a product, service, or business to a target audience. It is typically the first page that visitors see when they click on a link from an advertisement, search engine, or other sources of web traffic. The main purpose of a landing page is to convert visitors into leads or customers by encouraging them to take a specific action, such as making a purchase, signing up for a newsletter, or requesting more information. A well-designed landing page focuses on delivering a clear and concise message that resonates with the target audience. It should be visually appealing, easy to navigate, and optimized for converting visitors. The content on a landing page is usually limited to key information that highlights the value proposition and key benefits of the product or service being promoted. This can include compelling headlines, persuasive copy, engaging visuals, customer testimonials, and trust indicators such as security badges or social proof.

Launchpad

A Launchpad is a platform that provides support and resources to startups and entrepreneurs in their early stages of development. It serves as a launching point for new businesses, offering guidance, mentorship, funding opportunities, and a network of like-minded individuals.

Lead Generation Tools

Lead generation tools are essential resources for startups and entrepreneurs, as they facilitate the process of finding and acquiring potential customers or clients. These tools help businesses identify individuals or companies who have shown interest in their products or services and gather relevant information to nurture them into becoming paying customers. Startup and entrepreneurship can be highly competitive industries, where identifying and reaching out to the right target audience is crucial for success. Lead generation tools provide a systematic approach to finding and engaging with potential prospects, eliminating the need for manual and time-consuming methods.

Lean Analytics Tools

Lean analytics tools are software or platforms that assist startups and entrepreneurs in collecting and analyzing data to gain insights into their business operations, customer behavior, and market trends. These tools enable lean startups to make data-driven decisions and adapt their strategies quickly and efficiently. One of the key principles of lean startup methodology is the concept of "build, measure, learn." Lean analytics tools play a crucial role in the "measure" phase by providing startups with the necessary tools to track, measure, and analyze key performance indicators (KPIs) and metrics. These tools help startups in identifying and measuring the success or failure of their experiments, marketing campaigns, product features, or any other business initiative. Startups and entrepreneurs use lean analytics tools to track various types of metrics, such as acquisition metrics (e.g., website traffic, conversion rates, cost per acquisition), retention metrics (e.g., churn rate, user engagement, customer lifetime value), and revenue metrics (e.g., average revenue per user, conversion rates, customer acquisition cost). By continuously monitoring and analyzing these metrics, startups can gain valuable insights into their business performance, customer behavior, and market trends. In addition to tracking and measuring metrics, lean analytics tools also provide startups with features to visualize and analyze data. These features include dashboards, charts, graphs, and reports that enable startups to interpret data effectively and identify patterns, trends, and insights. Startups can use these insights to make data-driven decisions, adjust their strategies, and optimize their business processes. Some popular lean analytics tools used by startups and entrepreneurs include Google Analytics, Mixpanel, Kissmetrics, Amplitude, and Heap Analytics. These tools offer a wide range of functionalities, such as event tracking, funnel analysis, cohort analysis, A/B testing, and user segmentation. Startups can choose the most suitable tool based on their specific needs, budget, and technical requirements.

Lean Analytics

Lean Analytics is a systematic and data-driven approach to measuring and analyzing key metrics in the context of startup and entrepreneurship. It provides startups and entrepreneurs with a framework to make informed decisions based on real-time data, allowing them to optimize their product development and growth strategies. The concept of Lean Analytics is derived from the Lean Startup methodology, which emphasizes the importance of rapid experimentation, validated learning, and continuous improvement. It is based on the belief that startups should focus on measuring and testing their assumptions, rather than relying on intuition or guesses. Lean Analytics involves the identification and tracking of key performance indicators (KPIs) that are critical to the success of a startup. These KPIs vary depending on the nature of the business, but commonly include metrics such as user engagement, customer acquisition cost, conversion rates, and revenue growth. By regularly monitoring these metrics, startups can gain insights into the effectiveness of their strategies and make data-driven decisions to optimize their business model or pivot if necessary. The process of implementing Lean Analytics involves setting clear and measurable goals, collecting relevant data, analyzing the data using various techniques, and taking action based on the insights gained. Startups often use a variety of tools and technologies, such as web analytics platforms, A/B testing frameworks, and customer feedback systems, to gather and analyze data. The benefits of Lean Analytics for startups and entrepreneurs are numerous. It helps them avoid wasting time and resources on unproven assumptions, enables them to identify and address potential problems or bottlenecks early on, and allows for iterative improvements to their products or services based on user feedback. By using Lean Analytics, startups can achieve faster growth, higher customer satisfaction, and increased profitability.

Lean Canvas Workshops

A Lean Canvas Workshop is a specific type of workshop designed to help startups and entrepreneurs develop and refine their business models using the Lean Canvas tool. The workshop typically involves a group of participants who come together to collaborate and brainstorm ideas, analyze their business concepts, and identify potential areas of opportunity and improvement.The purpose of the Lean Canvas Workshop is to provide a structured and collaborative environment for startups and entrepreneurs to assess the viability and potential of their business ideas. It aims to help them gain a clear understanding of their target market, customer segments, value propositions, revenue streams, cost structures, and key resources and activities required to deliver their products or services.

Lean Canvas

Lean Canvas is a strategic management tool used in the context of startups and entrepreneurship. It serves as a visual framework designed to guide entrepreneurs through the process of outlining and validating their business concept. The Lean Canvas is similar to a business plan but is more concise and flexible, focusing on key elements that are essential for the success of a startup. It provides a simplified way to plan, test, and refine a business model by breaking it down into nine important building blocks. The first block on the Lean Canvas is the Problem, where entrepreneurs identify the pain points or unmet needs that their target customers face. Next is the Solution block, which describes how the startup aims to solve the identified problem. It lays out the value proposition and unique selling points that differentiate the product or service from competitors. The next block is Key Metrics, which defines the key performance indicators that the startup will track to measure its progress and success. The

Unique Value Proposition block describes the compelling reason why customers should choose the startup's solution over their competitors. It highlights the product's benefits and advantages. The next three blocks in the Lean Canvas deal with the startup's unfair advantage, channels, and customer segments. Unfair Advantage refers to the distinctive factors that give the startup an edge over competitors, such as proprietary technology, exclusive partnerships, or deep industry knowledge. Channels are the paths through which the startup will reach and engage with its target customers. Customer Segments identify the specific groups of people or organizations that the startup aims to serve. The final three blocks in the Lean Canvas consist of Cost Structure, Revenue Streams, and Key Activities. Cost Structure outlines the startup's expenses and cost drivers, while Revenue Streams identify the different ways the startup intends to generate income. Key Activities describe the critical actions and processes necessary to deliver the product or service and create value for customers. In summary, the Lean Canvas is a strategic planning tool that assists entrepreneurs in developing and validating their startup ideas. By focusing on the essential elements required for success, it offers a streamlined framework for business modeling and facilitates the iterative process of improving and refining the business concept.

Lean Product Development

Lean Product Development is a methodology used in the context of startups and entrepreneurship, aimed at minimizing waste and maximizing value in the process of developing new products. It emphasizes iterative experimentation, customer feedback, and continuous improvement to reduce the risk of developing products that do not meet customer needs or do not have a viable market. In Lean Product Development, the focus is on creating a minimal viable product (MVP) - a version of the product that has enough features to satisfy early adopters and gather feedback for further development. This approach allows startups and entrepreneurs to validate their ideas, assumptions, and hypotheses early on, before investing significant resources in building a fully-featured product that may not be well-received by the target market. Key principles of Lean Product Development include: 1. Iterative Development: Instead of trying to develop the perfect product from the beginning, Lean Product Development involves building a basic version quickly and then improving it through multiple iterations. This allows for faster learning, adaptation, and validation of ideas. 2. Customer Involvement: Engaging customers early and frequently throughout the development process is crucial in Lean Product Development. By gathering feedback and insights from customers, startups can better understand their needs, preferences, and pain points, and make informed decisions about product features and improvements. 3. Continuous Improvement: Lean Product Development encourages a culture of continuous learning and improvement. Startups and entrepreneurs should regularly review and analyze the feedback and data collected from customers, stakeholders, and market research, and use it to iterate and refine their product. 4. Waste Reduction: The Lean methodology advocates for eliminating any activities or processes that do not add value to the product or the customer. By minimizing waste, such as unnecessary features, excessive documentation, or lengthy development cycles, startups can optimize their resources and focus on delivering a product that meets customer needs efficiently. In conclusion, Lean Product Development is a customer-centric approach to product development that helps startups and entrepreneurs create innovative, market-driven products by embracing iterative development, customer involvement, continuous improvement, and waste reduction.

Lean Startup Methodology

The Lean Startup methodology is a framework for developing and launching startup businesses, with a focus on minimizing waste and maximizing learning. It was popularized by Eric Ries in his book "The Lean Startup" and has since become a widely adopted approach in the world of entrepreneurship. At its core, the Lean Startup methodology is about iterative experimentation and feedback loops. It advocates for a process of testing hypotheses, learning from the results, and then adjusting course based on those learnings. The goal is to build a sustainable business model by continually refining and improving the product or service based on real-world feedback. One of the key principles of the Lean Startup methodology is the concept of a Minimum Viable Product (MVP). An MVP is a basic version of the product or service that delivers enough value to early customers while also allowing the startup to learn from their usage and feedback. By releasing an MVP early on and gathering feedback, startups can avoid investing time and resources into building something that customers may not want or need. The

Lean Startup methodology also emphasizes the use of metrics and data to drive decision-making. Startups are encouraged to define specific key metrics, known as Key Performance Indicators (KPIs), that align with their goals and monitor them closely. By tracking these metrics, entrepreneurs can gain insights into what is working and what needs adjustment, enabling them to make data-driven decisions. Furthermore, the Lean Startup methodology promotes a culture of continuous learning and adaptation. It recognizes that startups operate in an environment of uncertainty and rapid change, and therefore encourages a mindset of experimentation and flexibility. Rather than sticking to rigid plans, startups are encouraged to embrace the "build-measure-learn" feedback loop and be willing to pivot or change direction if necessary. In summary, the Lean Startup methodology is a systematic approach to building startup businesses that emphasizes iterative experimentation, learning from customer feedback, and data-driven decision-making. It provides a framework for startups to minimize waste, maximize learning, and ultimately increase their chances of building successful and sustainable businesses.

Lean Startup

The Lean Startup is an approach to building and growing a startup that focuses on iterative development, validated learning, and continuous experimentation. It was popularized by Eric Ries in his book "The Lean Startup" and has since become a widely accepted methodology for entrepreneurs and startups. At the core of the Lean Startup methodology is the Build-Measure-Learn feedback loop. Instead of spending months or even years developing a product or service without any real customer feedback, the Lean Startup encourages entrepreneurs to build a minimum viable product (MVP) as quickly as possible. This MVP is a basic version of the product/service that can be tested with real customers to gather feedback. Once the MVP is released, the startup then measures how customers respond to it. These measurements can include various metrics such as user engagement, conversion rates, and customer satisfaction. The goal is to gather data that will help validate or invalidate the assumptions made during the development of the MVP. Based on the learnings from the measurements, the startup can then make informed decisions about the next steps. This might involve making improvements to the MVP, pivoting to a different customer segment or market, or even abandoning the idea altogether. The key is to use the data and insights gained from the measurements to drive decision-making. By continuously iterating through this Build-Measure-Learn feedback loop, startups can reduce wasted time and resources on ideas that don't resonate with customers. It allows them to navigate uncertainty and adapt their strategy based on real-world feedback. This approach is particularly beneficial in fast-paced and highly competitive startup environments where speed and agility are crucial for success. In summary, the Lean Startup is a methodology that emphasizes rapid experimentation, validation through data, and iterative development. It helps entrepreneurs and startups build successful businesses by focusing on what customers really want and need.

Lean Thinking

Lean Thinking is a mindset and methodology that focuses on creating value for the customer while minimizing waste and inefficiencies in the startup and entrepreneurship context. It is based on the principles of Lean Manufacturing, which were pioneered by Toyota in the 1950s, and have since been applied successfully in various industries. The goal of Lean Thinking for startups and entrepreneurs is to achieve operational excellence, improve efficiency, and increase customer satisfaction. It is a systematic approach that encourages continuous improvement, innovation, and learning, while keeping costs low and delivering value quickly.

Leverage

Leverage in the context of startup and entrepreneurship refers to the strategic use of available resources and advantages to maximize the potential for success and growth. Startups often face limited resources and significant challenges. In order to overcome these obstacles, entrepreneurs need to leverage their unique strengths and opportunities to gain a competitive advantage in the market. This involves identifying and utilizing existing assets, such as intellectual property, relationships, and skills, effectively. One of the key ways to leverage resources is through relationships and partnerships. Startups can leverage the expertise and networks of their team members, investors, advisors, and business partners to gain access to valuable resources, knowledge, and support. By building strong relationships and partnerships, entrepreneurs can tap into a wider pool of expertise, resources, and opportunities, which can significantly enhance their chances of success. In addition to networking and partnerships, startups can also leverage technology and innovation to their advantage. By adopting emerging technologies and leveraging the latest tools and platforms, entrepreneurs can streamline their operations, reduce costs, and gain a competitive edge. This can include leveraging artificial intelligence, big data analytics, cloud computing, and other digital solutions to optimize processes, improve customer experience, and drive growth. Furthermore, startups can leverage their intellectual property and proprietary assets to create barriers to entry for competitors. By patenting inventions, trademarking brand names, and protecting unique knowledge, startups can establish a strong market position and prevent others from replicating their products or services easily. This strategic use of intellectual property can provide startups with a competitive advantage and enhance their chances of long-term success. In conclusion, leveraging resources is essential for startups and entrepreneurs to achieve growth and success. By strategically utilizing available resources, building strong relationships and partnerships, harnessing technology and innovation, and protecting intellectual property, startups can maximize their potential and increase their chances of thriving in the competitive business landscape.

Leveraged Buyout Analysis

A leveraged buyout (LBO) analysis is a financial assessment conducted within the context of startup and entrepreneurship to evaluate the feasibility of acquiring a company using a significant amount of borrowed money. In an LBO, an entrepreneur or startup seeks to acquire a controlling stake in a target company by leveraging the company's assets and cash flow potential. The entrepreneur or startup typically borrows a large portion of the acquisition cost, often using a combination of debt and equity, and uses the target company's future cash flows to repay the debt. The LBO analysis involves assessing various financial aspects to determine the viability and profitability of the potential acquisition. This analysis helps the entrepreneur or startup assess the potential risks and rewards associated with acquiring the target company using borrowed funds. Key factors considered in an LBO analysis include the target company's financial performance, market position, growth potential, and ability to generate cash flows. The entrepreneur or startup evaluates the target company's historical and projected financial statements, including its income statement, balance sheet, and cash flow statement, to understand its financial health and performance. The LBO analysis also involves evaluating the capital structure of the potential acquisition, which includes assessing the level of debt to be used and the expected interest rates on the borrowed funds. This analysis helps the entrepreneur or startup understand the potential impact of the debt on the target company's future cash flows and profitability. Furthermore, the LBO analysis focuses on estimating the potential return on investment (ROI) that the entrepreneur or startup can achieve through the acquisition. This involves calculating the expected cash flows generated by the target company, considering the debt repayments, and determining the profitability of the investment. Overall, the LBO analysis is a crucial tool for entrepreneurs and startups to assess the financial feasibility of acquiring a company using borrowed funds. By evaluating the target company's financial performance and projecting its future cash flows, the analysis provides insights into the potential risks and rewards associated with an LBO transaction, enabling informed decision-making.

Leveraged Buyout (LBO)

A leveraged buyout (LBO) is a financial transaction where a startup or entrepreneur acquires another company, primarily using borrowed funds or debt to finance the acquisition. In an LBO, the acquiring party typically uses a small amount of their own capital and leverages it with borrowed money from banks or other financial institutions. This type of acquisition allows startups and entrepreneurs to take control of a company without committing substantial amounts of their own capital. The borrowed funds are secured by the assets of the acquired company, and the cash flows generated by the acquired company are used to repay the debt over time.

Lifestyle Business

A lifestyle business in the context of startup and entrepreneurship refers to a venture that is primarily designed to support the personal goals and needs of the entrepreneur, rather than solely focusing on financial growth or market expansion. It is a business model that allows the entrepreneur to maintain a desired lifestyle while still generating enough income to sustain and support their chosen lifestyle. Unlike traditional startup models that prioritize rapid growth, scalability, and exit strategies, a lifestyle business is often built around the personal interests, values, and passions of the entrepreneur. The primary goal is to create a business that aligns with their desired lifestyle, allowing them to have greater control over their time, flexibility, and work-life balance. Entrepreneurs who pursue a lifestyle business often prioritize factors such as personal fulfillment, autonomy, and happiness over the pursuit of exponential growth or competitive market dominance. They aim to build a business that supports their desired way of life, whether it's more flexible working hours, spending more time with family, pursuing hobbies or leisure activities, or living in a specific location. Lifestyle businesses can span a wide range of industries and sectors, and their success is often measured based on the entrepreneur's ability to achieve their desired lifestyle rather than traditional business indicators such as revenue growth or market share. While financial sustainability is still important, the focus is on maintaining a profitable business that enables the entrepreneur to live a balanced and fulfilling life. In summary, a lifestyle business in the context of startup and entrepreneurship is a business model designed to support the personal goals and aspirations of the entrepreneur. It allows them to create a business that aligns with their desired lifestyle, providing them with greater control over their time, flexibility, and work-life balance. The success of a lifestyle business is measured based on the entrepreneur's ability to achieve their desired lifestyle, rather than purely financial or market-based metrics.

Lifestyle Entrepreneur

A lifestyle entrepreneur is a type of entrepreneur who builds a business with the goal of creating a lifestyle that aligns with their personal interests and values. Rather than simply pursuing financial success, lifestyle entrepreneurs prioritize flexibility, creativity, and fulfillment in their work. Unlike traditional entrepreneurs who may be solely focused on growing their business and maximizing profits, lifestyle entrepreneurs prioritize achieving a balance between their work and personal life. They aim to create a business that allows them to have more control over their schedule, giving them the freedom to pursue their passions and spend time with family and friends. One of the key characteristics of a lifestyle entrepreneur is the pursuit of a business that reflects their interests and hobbies. These entrepreneurs often choose to start businesses in industries and niches that they are passionate about, allowing them to integrate their work with their personal life seamlessly. Flexibility is a major aspect of the lifestyle entrepreneur's approach, allowing them to work on their own terms. They may choose to work remotely or set their own hours, enabling them to have more control over their daily routine and achieve a better work-life balance. Creativity is another essential element of the lifestyle entrepreneur's journey. They seek opportunities to express their unique talents and ideas through their businesses, often choosing innovative and unconventional approaches to stand out from their competitors. Lastly, lifestyle entrepreneurs prioritize personal fulfillment. They aim to create a business that brings them joy and a sense of purpose. Rather than being solely driven by financial profits, they measure their success by the level of satisfaction and happiness they derive from their work. In conclusion, a lifestyle entrepreneur is an individual who creates a business that aligns with their personal interests, values flexibility and creativity in their work, and prioritizes personal fulfillment over solely financial success. This type of entrepreneur strives to achieve a balance between their work and personal life, aiming to create a lifestyle that brings them joy and allows them to pursue their passions.

Liquidation Event

A liquidation event, in the context of startup and entrepreneurship, refers to the process of terminating a business by selling off its assets to generate funds for distribution among its creditors and shareholders. It often occurs when a startup fails to become profitable or faces insurmountable financial challenges, leading to the decision to cease operations. During a liquidation event, the assets of the startup are sold in order of priority, with secured creditors having the first claim. These creditors hold security interests in specific assets of the business, such as property or equipment, which they can seize and sell to recover their debts. Any proceeds from these sales go towards satisfying their claims. Once secured creditors have been satisfied, any remaining funds are then used to fulfill other outstanding debts, such as loans, unpaid bills, and employee wages. After the distribution of funds to creditors, the remaining assets (if any) are distributed among the shareholders of the startup. Shareholders typically own equity in the company and may be entitled to a portion of the proceeds from asset sales. However, their claims often rank lower in priority compared to secured creditors and other debt holders. As a result, shareholders may not receive any funds if the liquidation process does not generate enough money to cover all debts. A liquidation event can take different forms depending on the specific circumstances. It may involve an outright sale of the startup's assets to a third party, such as another company or liquidation firm. Alternatively, it could involve a wind-up process, where the company is gradually wound down by selling off assets over time. In some cases, a liquidation event may also result in the dissolution of the startup, whereby its legal existence ceases altogether.

Liquidation Preference Multiple

Liquidation Preference Multiple is a term commonly used in the context of startup entrepreneurship and refers to the monetary preference given to certain investors in the event of a company's liquidation or sale. It specifies the amount of return these investors will receive before any other shareholders, such as common stockholders, receive their proceeds. When a company is liquidated or sold, the proceeds are typically distributed to various stakeholders based on their ownership percentage. However, investors with a Liquidation Preference Multiple are entitled to receive their investment amount back, along with a multiple of that amount, before other shareholders receive anything. This multiple is typically expressed as a number, such as 1x, 2x, or even higher.

Liquidation Preference

Liquidation Preference is a term commonly used in the context of startup and entrepreneurship. It refers to the rights and privileges given to certain investors in the event of a liquidation event, such as the sale of the company or its assets. This preference determines the order in which investors are entitled to receive their investments back, along with any accrued dividends or interest, before other shareholders receive any distribution. Typically, liquidation preference is granted to investors who have provided early-stage funding to the startup, such as angel investors, venture capitalists, or private equity firms. These investors take on higher risks by investing in startups that may have a higher probability of failure, hence they negotiate for certain protections to ensure their capital is safeguarded in the event of an exit or liquidation.

Liquidity Event

A liquidity event is a significant event in the life of a startup or entrepreneurial venture that results in the conversion of investments into cash or other liquid assets. It can be seen as a milestone that marks the exit of investors and provides a financial return for the founders and stakeholders involved in the business. There are several types of liquidity events that can occur in the startup and entrepreneurship ecosystem. One common example is an initial public offering (IPO), where a private company offers its shares to the public for the first time. This allows the company to raise significant capital and provides an exit opportunity for early investors and founders who may choose to sell their shares. Another type of liquidity event is a merger or acquisition (M&A), where a larger company acquires a startup or entrepreneurial venture. This often occurs when the acquiring company sees potential synergies or growth opportunities in the target company and is willing to pay a premium to acquire it. The liquidity event in this case comes in the form of the cash or stock that the acquiring company offers as consideration for the deal. Liquidation events are also considered liquidity events, although they typically occur when a startup or entrepreneurial venture fails to achieve its objectives and decides to wind down its operations. In this case, the assets of the company are sold off to repay its debts and investors may receive some portion of their initial investment back. Overall, liquidity events play a crucial role in the startup and entrepreneurship ecosystem as they provide a mechanism for investors and founders to realize the returns on their investments and efforts. They also often serve as a validation of the success and potential of the business, attracting further investment and encouraging innovation in the industry.

MVP (Minimum Viable Product)

A minimum viable product (MVP) is the most basic version of a product that can be released to the market to validate the core idea and gather feedback from early users. It is a strategy often used by startups and entrepreneurs to test their hypotheses, minimize development costs, and quickly learn from users' reactions. The concept of MVP is rooted in the lean startup methodology, which advocates for building products iteratively and incrementally. By focusing on delivering the minimum set of features required to solve the core problem, an MVP allows entrepreneurs to validate their assumptions without investing excessive time and resources into building a complete product that may not meet user needs.

Market Analysis Techniques

Market analysis techniques refer to the various methods and tools used by startups and entrepreneurs to evaluate and understand their target market, competition, and potential opportunities. These techniques play a crucial role in determining the feasibility and viability of a business idea, developing a solid business plan, and making informed decisions that drive growth and success. One commonly used market analysis technique is the SWOT analysis, which stands for Strengths, Weaknesses, Opportunities, and Threats. This technique involves identifying and analyzing the internal strengths and weaknesses of the startup, as well as the external opportunities and threats in the market. It allows entrepreneurs to assess their competitive advantages, pinpoint areas for improvement, and identify potential obstacles or risks. By understanding these factors, startups can develop strategies that capitalize on their strengths and opportunities while minimizing weaknesses and threats. Another essential technique is market segmentation, which involves dividing the target market into distinct groups based on demographic, geographic, psychographic, and behavioral characteristics. By segmenting the market, startups can better understand the specific needs, preferences, and behaviors of different customer groups. This knowledge enables entrepreneurs to tailor their marketing, product development, and customer acquisition strategies to effectively reach and serve their target segments. Furthermore, startups and entrepreneurs often utilize competitor analysis to gain insights into their competitors' strategies, strengths, weaknesses, and market position. This technique involves researching and analyzing the competitive landscape, including direct and indirect competitors, their products or services, pricing, distribution channels, and marketing tactics. By understanding the competition, startups can identify opportunities for differentiation, determine pricing and positioning strategies, and develop marketing campaigns that resonate with their target customers. In addition to these techniques, startups and entrepreneurs may employ market research methods such as surveys, focus groups, and interviews to gather valuable insights from potential customers. This primary research can provide in-depth information about customer preferences, needs, and pain points, which can guide product development, marketing messaging, and customer service efforts.

Market Analysis

Market analysis is a critical process in the field of startup and entrepreneurship that involves evaluating and understanding various aspects of a target market in order to make informed business decisions. It involves gathering and analyzing relevant data related to the market, including its size, growth potential, competition, customer behavior, and trends. Through market analysis, startups and entrepreneurs gain insights into the demand and potential profitability of a product or service in a specific market. This helps them identify and evaluate opportunities, determine their target audience, and develop effective marketing strategies. By understanding the market dynamics, they can make informed decisions regarding pricing, distribution channels, and promotional activities.

Market Assessment

A market assessment is an evaluation of the characteristics, trends, and dynamics of a specific market or industry. It involves gathering and analyzing data to determine the potential opportunities and challenges that exist within the market, as well as the level of demand for a product or service. For startups and entrepreneurs, conducting a market assessment is crucial for making informed decisions about the viability and potential profitability of their business idea. It helps them understand the target market, competition, customer needs, and market trends, which are essential for developing a successful business strategy. In a market assessment, several key factors are considered. These include the market size, which refers to the total addressable market and the potential customer base. The assessment also looks at the market growth rate, which indicates the rate at which the market is expanding and the potential for future demand. Competitor analysis is another important aspect of a market assessment. It involves studying the strengths and weaknesses of existing competitors, their market share, pricing strategies, and customer base. This helps startups and entrepreneurs identify opportunities for differentiation and gain a competitive advantage. Moreover, a market assessment assesses customer needs and preferences. It includes understanding customer demographics, their purchasing behavior, and their preferences regarding product features, pricing, and distribution channels. This information is crucial for developing products or services that meet customer demands and creating effective marketing strategies. Market trends and dynamics are also examined in a market assessment. This involves analyzing factors such as technological advancements, regulatory changes, and economic conditions that could impact the market. Understanding these trends helps entrepreneurs anticipate future opportunities and challenges and adapt their business model accordingly. In conclusion, a market assessment is a comprehensive evaluation of a specific market or industry. It provides startups and entrepreneurs with essential insights into their target market, competition, customer needs, and market trends. By conducting a market assessment, entrepreneurs can make informed decisions, develop effective strategies, and increase their chances of success in the competitive business landscape.

Market Disruption

Market disruption refers to the process in which a startup or entrepreneurial venture introduces a new product, service, or business model that significantly changes the existing market landscape and displaces established incumbents. It involves the creation of innovative ideas, technologies, or approaches that challenge the status quo and revolutionize the way industries operate. When a market is disrupted, the traditional ways of doing business are replaced by more efficient, cost-effective, and customer-centric alternatives. Disruptive startups often target underserved or overlooked segments of the market, offering solutions that are more accessible, affordable, or convenient compared to existing options. This can lead to a fundamental shift in consumer preferences and behaviors, forcing established companies to adapt or risk becoming obsolete. One of the key characteristics of market disruption is the ability to create and capture new demand. Disruptive startups often tap into latent needs or create entirely new markets by addressing pain points or unmet customer desires. By offering superior value propositions, they can attract customers away from traditional competitors, challenging their market position and profitability. In addition, market disruption often relies on disruptive innovation. This concept, introduced by Clayton Christensen, involves the development of technologies or business models that initially cater to niche markets but gradually improve to compete with established players. Disruptive innovation enables startups to enter and disrupt markets that were previously inaccessible due to high costs or strong competition. Market disruption can have far-reaching implications for both startups and incumbents. While disruptive startups have the potential for rapid growth and high profitability, they also face numerous challenges, including resource constraints, regulatory barriers, and resistance from established players. Incumbents, on the other hand, must be vigilant and adaptable to respond to disruptive threats. Failure to do so can result in significant losses in market share and revenue.

Market Entry Strategy

A market entry strategy is a plan developed by a startup or entrepreneur to enter a new market with their product or service. It involves a careful analysis of the target market, identifying the best possible entry point, and implementing strategies to gain a competitive advantage. The first step in developing a market entry strategy is to conduct thorough market research. This involves gathering information about the target market, such as its size, growth potential, competition, consumer preferences, and regulatory environment. The purpose of this research is to gain insights into the market and identify opportunities and challenges. Based on the market research, the next step is to choose the most suitable entry point. This could involve launching the product or service in a specific geographic market, targeting a particular customer segment, or partnering with existing market players. The choice of entry point depends on various factors, such as market demand, competition, resources, and business objectives. Once the entry point is identified, the startup or entrepreneur needs to develop a value proposition that differentiates their offering from competitors. This could be achieved through product innovation, superior customer service, competitive pricing, or a unique distribution model. The goal is to provide customers with a compelling reason to choose the startup's product or service over existing alternatives. In addition to a strong value proposition, a market entry strategy also involves developing a marketing and sales plan. This includes determining the most effective channels to reach the target market, creating promotional strategies, and setting sales targets. The startup or entrepreneur needs to carefully design its marketing and sales efforts to attract and retain customers in the new market. Finally, evaluating and adjusting the market entry strategy is essential for long-term success. The startup or entrepreneur needs to continuously monitor market trends, consumer feedback, and competitor activities to identify any necessary adjustments or refinements to the strategy. This iterative process ensures that the startup remains competitive and responsive to changing market conditions.

Market Expansion Strategy

A market expansion strategy in the context of startups and entrepreneurship refers to the plan and actions taken by a business to enter new markets or expand their presence in existing markets. This strategy is aimed at increasing the customer base, generating more sales, and ultimately growing the business. Market expansion strategies can take various forms, depending on the specific goals and resources of the startup. One common approach is geographical expansion, where the startup identifies and enters new geographic markets. This can involve opening new physical locations, establishing partnerships with local distributors or retailers, or leveraging digital platforms to reach customers in different regions.

Market Expansion

Market expansion refers to the strategic growth process where a startup or entrepreneur aims to extend their reach into new markets, either geographically or by targeting different customer segments. It involves analyzing market opportunities, identifying target markets, and planning and implementing effective marketing strategies to penetrate and establish a foothold in these new markets. In the context of startups and entrepreneurship, market expansion plays a crucial role in achieving sustainable growth and long-term success. Startups often begin by focusing on a niche market or a specific customer segment to validate their business idea and gain traction. However, to scale their operations and maximize their potential, they need to explore new markets beyond their initial target audience. Geographical market expansion involves entering new regions or countries, often with different cultural, economic, and regulatory landscapes. It requires conducting comprehensive market research to understand the local demand, competitive landscape, customer behavior, and market potential. Startups need to adapt their products or services to meet the specific needs and preferences of these new markets. Expanding into new customer segments involves identifying and targeting different groups of customers who may have distinct needs, preferences, or purchasing behaviors. Startups may need to modify their marketing strategies, messaging, pricing, or distribution channels to effectively reach and engage these new customer segments. Market expansion requires careful planning and execution. Startups need to allocate resources, set clear objectives, and develop tailored marketing plans. They may use various strategies such as partnerships, alliances, acquisitions, or opening new sales channels to enter new markets. It is essential to monitor and evaluate the results continuously, adjusting strategies as necessary to optimize market penetration and maximize growth potential.

Market Feasibility Analysis

A market feasibility analysis in the context of startups and entrepreneurship refers to the evaluation of the potential success of a new product or service in a specific market. This analysis is conducted to determine whether there is a viable market for the product or service, and if so, to identify the key factors that will contribute to its success. The market feasibility analysis involves gathering and analyzing relevant data, such as market size, competition, target audience, and industry trends. It helps the startup or entrepreneur understand the demand for their offering, as well as the potential barriers or challenges they may face in entering and growing in the market.

Market Fit

Market Fit in the context of startup and entrepreneurship refers to the alignment between a product or service and its target market. It signifies the degree to which a product or service satisfies the needs and demands of its intended customers, resulting in strong customer traction and sustainable business growth. When a startup achieves product-market fit, it essentially means that it has discovered a winning combination of product features, pricing, distribution channels, and marketing strategies that resonates with its target audience. The startup has identified a genuine problem or need in the market and has successfully developed and positioned its offering as the solution. This alignment creates a strong product-market fit, allowing the startup to attract and retain customers, gain a competitive edge, and drive revenue growth.

Market Insight

Market insight, in the context of startup and entrepreneurship, refers to the knowledge and understanding gained about the target market and industry through research, analysis, and observation. It involves gathering information about potential customers, competitors, trends, and market dynamics to make informed business decisions and develop effective strategies. Market insight is crucial for startups and entrepreneurs as it helps them identify needs, opportunities, and challenges in the market. It provides a foundation for developing products or services that meet customer demands and stand out from competitors. By understanding the market landscape, startups can make informed decisions about pricing, positioning, and marketing strategies to maximize their chances of success.

Market Intelligence

Market intelligence refers to the information and insights that entrepreneurs and startups gather and analyze in order to make informed decisions about their business strategies and operations. It involves collecting and evaluating data about the market, customers, competitors, and industry trends to gain a deeper understanding of the business environment and make more informed decisions. Market intelligence plays a crucial role in the success of a startup or entrepreneurship venture. It helps entrepreneurs identify opportunities for growth, understand customer needs and preferences, and assess the competitive landscape. By gathering and analyzing relevant data, startups can make informed decisions about product development, marketing, pricing, and distribution strategies.

Market Niche

A market niche refers to a specific segment or subset of a larger market that is characterized by specific needs, preferences, or behaviors of its customers. It represents a small, well-defined group of individuals or businesses that share common characteristics or interests. Startups and entrepreneurs often target a market niche as a strategy to differentiate themselves from competitors and to cater to the unique needs of a specific customer base. By focusing on a niche market, startups can better understand and address the specific pain points and requirements of their target audience.

Market Opportunity Assessment

The market opportunity assessment is a crucial process for startups and entrepreneurs to evaluate the potential for success in a specific market. It involves analyzing various factors, trends, and conditions to determine the viability and profitability of a business venture. During the market opportunity assessment, entrepreneurs gather and analyze data related to market size, growth rate, competition, customer needs, and purchasing behavior. By understanding these key aspects, entrepreneurs can identify opportunities and assess the potential demand for their products or services. The assessment begins with identifying the target market and conducting in-depth market research. This includes studying the demographics, psychographics, and behavior patterns of potential customers. Entrepreneurs also examine the market dynamics, such as customer preferences, trends, and regulatory factors, which can impact business operations. Once the market research is completed, entrepreneurs assess the competitive landscape by studying existing players in the market. This helps them understand their strengths, weaknesses, distribution channels, pricing strategies, and customer loyalty. By analyzing the competition, entrepreneurs can position their products or services uniquely and create a competitive advantage. Furthermore, entrepreneurs evaluate the market's growth potential and demand. This involves analyzing historical market trends, economic indicators, and technological advancements. By understanding the market's growth rate, entrepreneurs can determine if the opportunity is sustainable and profitable in the long run. Financial feasibility is another critical aspect of market opportunity assessment. Entrepreneurs analyze the costs associated with product development, manufacturing, marketing, and distribution. They also assess potential revenue streams, pricing strategies, and profit margins. This analysis helps entrepreneurs determine if the business venture is financially viable. Ultimately, the market opportunity assessment provides entrepreneurs with valuable insights and data to make informed decisions. It helps them identify market gaps, target customer segments, and develop effective marketing strategies. By conducting a thorough assessment, entrepreneurs can minimize risks, optimize resources, and increase the chances of business success.

Market Opportunity

A market opportunity refers to a favorable set of circumstances that allows entrepreneurs and startups to create and capture value by meeting the needs and wants of a specific customer segment. Market opportunities arise from various factors, such as changes in consumer preferences, technological advancements, shifts in regulatory policies, or emerging societal trends. These factors create gaps in the market, providing entrepreneurs with the chance to identify and exploit untapped potential. By understanding these market gaps, entrepreneurs can develop innovative solutions, products, or services that address the needs of customers in a unique and valuable way. Identifying and evaluating market opportunities is a crucial step for startups and entrepreneurs. It involves conducting market research to gather insights about customer needs, preferences, and market trends. This research helps entrepreneurs to understand the size of the potential customer base, the competitive landscape, and the viability of their proposed venture. Once a market opportunity has been identified, entrepreneurs need to assess their own capabilities and resources to determine if they have the necessary skills, expertise, and access to the required resources to capitalize on the opportunity. They need to establish a sustainable competitive advantage that sets them apart from existing competitors and attracts customers to their offering. Entrepreneurs also need to develop a viable business model that outlines how they will create, deliver, and capture value from the market opportunity. This includes defining the target customer segment, understanding the value proposition, choosing the appropriate distribution channels, and establishing pricing strategies. Successful entrepreneurs continuously monitor and adapt to changes in the market to exploit new opportunities and stay ahead of the competition. They remain agile and proactive in identifying and responding to emerging trends, shifts in consumer behavior, and technological advancements that could impact their business.

Market Penetration

Market penetration refers to the strategy employed by a startup or entrepreneur to gain a larger share of an existing market. It involves increasing market share by selling more products or services to the existing customer base or by attracting new customers to the market. This is done by effectively promoting and marketing the products or services, offering competitive pricing, and ensuring widespread distribution. Market penetration is a crucial element of a startup's growth strategy as it allows them to achieve rapid growth by capturing a larger market share. It is particularly beneficial when entering an established market where competitors already exist. By focusing on market penetration, startups can differentiate themselves from the competition and establish a strong foothold in the industry.

Market Research Analysis

Market research analysis is the process of examining data and information related to a specific market in order to gain insights and develop strategies for a startup or entrepreneurship venture. It involves collecting and analyzing various types of data, such as customer demographics, market trends, competitor analysis, and consumer behavior. The purpose of market research analysis is to gather relevant and reliable information that can help entrepreneurs make informed decisions and minimize risks. By understanding the market dynamics and identifying potential opportunities, entrepreneurs can develop effective marketing strategies, improve their product or service offerings, and establish a competitive edge in the market. Market research analysis typically involves several key steps. First, entrepreneurs need to define their research objectives and determine the specific information they need to gather. This could include identifying target markets, understanding customer preferences, or evaluating the competitive landscape. Next, entrepreneurs must collect data from a variety of sources, such as surveys, interviews, and secondary research. Primary research involves gathering new data directly from customers or potential customers, while secondary research involves analyzing existing data from various sources, such as government reports, industry publications, or online databases. Once the data is collected, it is analyzed using various quantitative and qualitative techniques. Quantitative analysis involves statistical methods to analyze numerical data, such as calculating market share or conducting regression analysis. Qualitative analysis involves interpreting non-numerical data, such as customer feedback or consumer reviews, to identify patterns and trends. Finally, entrepreneurs use the insights gained from the analysis to make informed decisions and develop strategies. These strategies could include pricing decisions, product development plans, marketing campaigns, or expansion strategies. Market research analysis is an ongoing process that requires regular monitoring and updating as market conditions and consumer preferences change over time.

Market Research Methods

Market research methods refer to the systematic process of collecting, analyzing, and interpreting relevant data to gain insights and understand market dynamics. For startups and entrepreneurs, market research methods play a crucial role in evaluating the viability of their business idea, identifying target markets, understanding customer preferences, and assessing the competitive landscape. The primary goal of using market research methods in the context of startup and entrepreneurship is to minimize risks, make informed decisions, and optimize resource allocation. By understanding the market demand, startups can tailor their products or services to meet customer needs, differentiate themselves from competitors, and increase their chances of success.

Market Research Techniques And Analysis

Market research techniques and analysis, in the context of startup and entrepreneurship, refer to the systematic methods and tools used to gather, analyze, and interpret information about a specific market or industry. This process helps startup founders and entrepreneurs make informed decisions regarding their business strategy, product development, customer targeting, and overall market positioning. Market research techniques involve collecting primary and secondary data. Primary data is obtained directly from potential customers, competitors, suppliers, and industry experts through surveys, interviews, focus groups, and observations. This data helps startups understand customer preferences, market size, demand, and trends. Secondary data, on the other hand, is collected from existing sources such as market reports, industry publications, government publications, and online databases. This data provides insights into market segmentation, competitor analysis, market share, and other relevant statistics. Market research analysis involves processing and interpreting the collected data to extract meaningful insights. Statistical analysis techniques such as regression analysis, correlation analysis, and customer segmentation analysis can be used to identify patterns, relationships, and correlations within the data. This helps startups identify target customer segments, understand the factors influencing customer behavior, and assess market opportunities and threats. The outcomes of market research techniques and analysis provide valuable information that can guide startups and entrepreneurs in making informed business decisions. These insights help identify market gaps and customer needs, which can be used to develop innovative products or services. Market research also helps assess the competitive landscape, allowing startups to position themselves effectively against their rivals. Additionally, the gathered data can aid in pricing strategies, marketing campaigns, and sales projections, enabling startups to optimize their resources and maximize profitability.

Market Research Techniques

Market research techniques are systematic methods used by startups and entrepreneurs to gather and analyze information about their target market, industry trends, customer preferences, and competitors. These techniques help startups make informed decisions, identify opportunities, minimize risks, and develop effective marketing strategies. One commonly used market research technique is surveys. Surveys involve asking a series of questions to gather data from a sample of the target market. Startups can use online surveys, paper-based surveys, or telephone interviews to collect information about customer demographics, preferences, purchasing behaviors, and satisfaction levels. Surveys can provide startups with insights into customer needs, market trends, and potential demand, helping them refine their products or services and target specific customer segments. Another effective market research technique is interviews. Interviews involve one-on-one or group conversations with customers, industry experts, or key stakeholders. Startups can conduct structured or semi-structured interviews to gain deeper insights into customer motivations, pain points, and behaviors. By listening to customers' experiences and feedback, startups can identify areas for improvement, uncover unmet needs, and develop products or services that truly address customer problems. Observation is another valuable market research technique. It involves systematically watching and recording behaviors, interactions, and trends in the target market or industry. Startups can observe customers in real-life situations, such as in stores or during product trials, to understand how they interact with products, make purchasing decisions, or use competing solutions. By observing customer behaviors and preferences, startups can uncover hidden insights and opportunities, refine their marketing strategies, and develop more effective sales approaches. Data analysis is a crucial market research technique that startups use to make sense of the gathered information. Startups can collect quantitative data, such as customer demographics or sales figures, or qualitative data, such as customer feedback or focus group discussions. By analyzing this data, startups can identify patterns, trends, correlations, and outliers that provide valuable insights into market dynamics, customer preferences, and competitive landscape. Data analysis enables startups to make data-driven decisions, measure the success of their marketing efforts, and adjust their strategies accordingly.

Market Research

Market research in the context of startup and entrepreneurship refers to the systematic gathering, analyzing, and interpreting of information about a specific target market, industry, or consumer segment. It involves collecting data about customers, competitors, and market trends in order to make informed decisions and develop effective strategies to launch and grow a successful business. The purpose of market research is to gain a deep understanding of the market dynamics, identify potential opportunities and threats, and validate the viability of a business idea or concept. It provides entrepreneurs with valuable insights to customer preferences, needs, and buying behavior, which helps in designing products or services that meet their demands. Market research is crucial for startups and entrepreneurs as it allows them to identify their target audience and position their offerings effectively. By conducting research, entrepreneurs can determine the size of their potential market, assess the level of competition, and identify any gaps or unmet needs that can be capitalized on. There are several methods and techniques used to conduct market research, such as surveys, interviews, focus groups, and data analysis. Surveys involve gathering information through questionnaires or online forms, while interviews and focus groups provide qualitative data through direct interaction with potential customers or industry experts. Data analysis involves processing and interpreting the collected data to identify patterns, trends, and key insights. This analysis helps in understanding customer preferences, identifying market segments, and making informed decisions about pricing, branding, and marketing strategies. The findings of market research are used to develop a comprehensive business plan, determine the optimal marketing mix, and make strategic decisions regarding product development, distribution channels, and target markets. It helps startups and entrepreneurs minimize risks and maximize the chances of success by providing a solid foundation of knowledge and evidence to support business decisions. In conclusion, market research is a critical component of startup and entrepreneurship as it helps in understanding the market landscape, identifying customer needs, and developing effective strategies for business growth. It enables entrepreneurs to make informed decisions, minimize risks, and maximize the chances of building a successful and sustainable business.

Market Saturation

Market saturation refers to a situation in which a market is nearly or completely filled with similar products or services, reaching a point where it becomes difficult for new entrants to find a viable position. It typically occurs when there is a high level of competition and a limited number of potential customers. For startups and entrepreneurs, market saturation poses significant challenges. When a market is saturated, it becomes harder to differentiate and stand out from the competition. Customers have numerous options to choose from, making it difficult for a new entrant to attract attention and gain a substantial market share. In such a scenario, startups often face intense price competition, leading to lower profit margins. In order to overcome market saturation, startups and entrepreneurs need to develop unique value propositions and find innovative ways to differentiate their products or services from existing offerings. This could involve targeting niche markets that are underserved by existing competitors or identifying unmet customer needs and developing solutions that address them effectively. Furthermore, it is crucial for startups to thoroughly analyze the competitive landscape and understand the strengths and weaknesses of existing players. This knowledge can help entrepreneurs identify gaps in the market and carve out a unique space for their venture. In addition to differentiation, startups need to focus on building strong customer relationships and creating brand loyalty. By providing exceptional customer experiences and delivering superior value, startups can create a loyal customer base even in a saturated market. This customer loyalty can become a competitive advantage that helps the startup weather the challenges of market saturation.

Market Segmentation Analysis

Market segmentation analysis is a strategic process that involves dividing a broad market into distinct groups of customers who have similar characteristics, needs, or behavior. In the context of startups and entrepreneurship, market segmentation analysis is essential for identifying specific target markets and aligning business strategies accordingly. Startups and entrepreneurs often operate in highly competitive markets where resources are limited. Therefore, having a deep understanding of the target market is crucial for success. Market segmentation analysis allows startups to identify and prioritize specific customer segments that they can effectively cater to, ensuring optimal resource utilization and maximizing the chances of success.

Market Segmentation

Market segmentation is a strategic practice employed by startups and entrepreneurs to divide and target their potential customers into distinct groups based on certain characteristics or traits. It involves analyzing the market and identifying specific segments or subgroups that share similar needs, preferences, or behaviors. This process allows startups and entrepreneurs to tailor their products, marketing strategies, and messaging to better cater to the unique needs and interests of each segment. By understanding the diverse characteristics and behaviors of their target market, startups can develop more effective marketing campaigns, build stronger relationships with their customers, and gain a competitive advantage in the marketplace.

Market Share

Market share refers to the portion or percentage of total sales within a specific industry that a particular company or product holds. In the context of startups and entrepreneurship, market share is a crucial metric used to measure the success and competitiveness of a new venture in relation to the overall market. For startups, gaining market share is essential as it demonstrates the company's ability to attract and retain customers in a competitive landscape. Establishing a significant market share is an indication that the startup's product or service is meeting customer needs and outperforming its competitors. Conversely, a low market share suggests that the startup may be facing challenges in differentiating its offering or attracting a customer base. Market share can be calculated by dividing a company's total sales revenue by the total sales of the industry in which it operates, and then multiplying the result by 100 to convert it to a percentage. This calculation provides an understanding of how much of the market a company controls. Having a high market share can provide several benefits for startups and entrepreneurs. Firstly, it can lead to increased brand recognition and customer loyalty, as a larger market share generally indicates a higher level of trust and credibility. This can result in a positive feedback loop, where satisfied customers become brand advocates and help attract new customers. Secondly, a higher market share often translates to economies of scale, enabling startups to enjoy cost advantages when negotiating with suppliers and subcontractors. This can lead to reduced production costs, increased profit margins, and the ability to invest in research and development or marketing initiatives, fueling further growth. Lastly, a substantial market share can act as a barrier to entry for potential competitors. It becomes more difficult for new entrants to gain traction and compete effectively against established players when they already dominate a significant portion of the market. This presents an opportunity for startups to solidify their position and defend against potential threats.

Market Size Analysis

Market Size Analysis refers to the process of assessing the total potential market value of a specific product or service within a given industry or target market segment. It involves gathering and analyzing relevant data to estimate the size and growth potential of the market, which helps startups and entrepreneurs make informed decisions regarding their business strategies, investment planning, and resource allocation. The primary objective of conducting a market size analysis is to understand the market's potential and the demand for a particular product or service. By determining the size of the market, entrepreneurs can evaluate the feasibility of their business ideas and identify the profit potential. It provides valuable insights into the market's existing and future opportunities, allowing startups to identify their target customers and create effective marketing and sales strategies. Market size analysis involves several key steps, such as identifying the total addressable market (TAM), segmenting the market based on relevant factors like demographics, geography, or customer behavior, and calculating the potential market share and growth rates. Startups can use various methods and data sources to gather relevant information, such as primary market research surveys, secondary data from industry reports, government databases, or competitor analysis. By conducting a comprehensive market size analysis, startups and entrepreneurs can assess the market's growth potential and potential barriers to entry. It helps in understanding the competitive landscape, identifying key competitors, and evaluating their market share. This knowledge enables startups to position themselves effectively and differentiate their products or services to gain a competitive advantage. Additionally, a market size analysis also helps in forecasting revenue projections, making financial plans, attracting investors, and securing funding for business growth.

Market Sizing

Market sizing refers to the process of determining the potential size and value of a target market or segment. It involves estimating the total addressable market (TAM) and the served available market (SAM) for a particular product or service. This analysis helps entrepreneurs and startups understand the size of the opportunity and make informed decisions regarding market entry, resource allocation, and growth strategies. The first step in market sizing is to define the target market or segment based on various criteria such as demographics, geography, behavior, or industry. This can be done by conducting market research, analyzing industry reports, and studying customer profiles. Once the target market is defined, entrepreneurs can estimate the TAM by calculating the total potential demand for their product or service. This can be done by considering factors such as the number of potential customers, their purchasing power, and the frequency of purchase. After estimating the TAM, the next step is to determine the SAM, which represents the portion of the TAM that the business can realistically serve. This involves identifying the specific customer segments that the product or service is best suited for and assessing the competition or alternatives in the market. By understanding the SAM, entrepreneurs can assess the revenue potential and market share they can realistically achieve. Market sizing is a critical step in the business planning process as it helps entrepreneurs and startups evaluate the viability of their business idea and assess the potential for success. It allows them to understand the size of the market opportunity, identify potential risks and challenges, and make informed decisions regarding their business strategy. By having a clear understanding of the market size, entrepreneurs can allocate resources effectively, tailor their marketing and sales efforts, and develop a competitive advantage.

Market Validation Process

Market validation is a crucial process in the realm of startups and entrepreneurship. It involves conducting comprehensive research and analysis to determine the viability and potential success of a new product or service in the market. This process helps entrepreneurs avoid costly mistakes and make informed decisions by gathering feedback and data directly from their target audience. During the market validation process, entrepreneurs engage in various activities to ensure that their business idea aligns with market demand. They start by defining their target market and identifying their ideal customer. This involves understanding the demographics, behaviors, and preferences of potential customers, as well as their pain points and unmet needs. Entrepreneurs then validate their business idea by collecting feedback from potential customers through surveys, interviews, and focus groups. This allows them to gain insights into customer preferences, validate product features, and determine pricing strategies.

By utilizing online platforms, social media, and other channels, entrepreneurs can reach a larger audience and gather diverse perspectives. In addition to gathering customer feedback, market validation also involves analyzing the competition. Entrepreneurs study their competitors' products, pricing strategies, and marketing tactics to identify gaps in the market that their product or service can fill. This analysis helps entrepreneurs differentiate their offerings and develop unique selling propositions to attract customers. Furthermore, market validation is an ongoing process that includes conducting market tests and experiments. Entrepreneurs may create prototypes or offer pilot versions of their product or service to evaluate customer response and gather relevant data. This iterative approach allows entrepreneurs to make necessary adjustments and improvements before fully launching their product or service. In conclusion, market validation is a fundamental process for startups and entrepreneurs to determine the feasibility and potential success of their business idea. By engaging in research, gathering customer feedback, analyzing competition, and conducting market tests, entrepreneurs can gain valuable insights that inform their strategy and increase their chances of success in the competitive market.

Market Validation

Market validation in the context of startups and entrepreneurship refers to the process of testing and evaluating a business idea, product, or service to determine its potential for success in the target market. It involves gathering feedback and data from potential customers, industry experts, and other stakeholders to validate the market demand, assess the competitive landscape, and refine the value proposition. Market validation is a crucial step in the startup journey as it helps entrepreneurs assess the viability of their business concept before investing significant time, resources, and money in development and commercialization. It provides insights into the market size, customer needs and preferences, competitive advantages, pricing strategies, and potential revenue streams. The market validation process typically involves several key activities: 1. Identifying the target market: Startups need to clearly define their target market segment and identify the specific customer groups they aim to serve. This includes understanding the demographics, psychographics, and purchasing behavior of the target customers. 2. Conducting market research: Entrepreneurs need to gather relevant market data to assess the market potential and identify any existing gaps or opportunities. This may involve analyzing industry reports, conducting surveys, interviews, and focus groups, and studying competitor products or services. 3. Developing a minimum viable product (MVP): An MVP is a simplified version of the product or service that is developed and launched quickly to gather feedback from early adopters. The feedback helps in improving the product or service based on customer needs and preferences. 4. Testing and iterating: Startups need to continuously test and iterate their products or services based on customer feedback and market insights. This involves making necessary adjustments, enhancements, or pivots to align with market demands. 5. Proof of concept: Entrepreneurs need to provide evidence that their business concept is feasible and can generate value for customers. This may involve demonstrating successful pilot tests, securing initial customers or partnerships, or achieving early revenue milestones. By going through the market validation process, startups can reduce the risks associated with launching a new business and increase their chances of success. It allows entrepreneurs to make informed decisions, refine their value proposition, and validate their business model before scaling up operations and pursuing further funding opportunities.

Market Viability Analysis

The market viability analysis is a thorough examination conducted by entrepreneurs and startup founders to assess the market potential of their products or services. It helps them determine whether their business idea is feasible and has the potential for success in the target market. In this analysis, various factors are taken into consideration to evaluate the viability and sustainability of the business venture. These factors include the market size, target customer segment, competition, market trends, and potential demand for the product or service.

Marketing Attribution Models

Marketing attribution models refer to the processes and methodologies used by startups and entrepreneurs to determine the value and impact of their marketing efforts on the overall success of their business. These models analyze and evaluate the various marketing channels, campaigns, and touchpoints that contribute to driving customer acquisition, conversions, and revenue generation. By attributing specific outcomes or customer actions to different marketing activities, entrepreneurs can gain valuable insights into the effectiveness and return on investment (ROI) of their marketing strategies.

Marketing Automation Software

Marketing Automation Software refers to a system or software platform that assists startups and entrepreneurs in automating and streamlining their marketing processes. It enables businesses to effectively manage, automate, and analyze various marketing tasks and activities, ultimately enhancing efficiency, productivity, and overall marketing performance. Marketing automation software provides a comprehensive set of tools and functionalities that allow startups and entrepreneurs to automate repetitive marketing tasks, such as email marketing, social media posting, lead generation, segmentation, customer relationship management (CRM), data analysis, and more. By automating these activities, businesses can save time and resources, enabling them to focus on other crucial aspects of their operations.

Marketing Funnel

A marketing funnel, in the context of startup and entrepreneurship, refers to the series of steps or stages that a potential customer goes through before making a purchase or conversion. It is a strategic model that entrepreneurs use to guide their marketing efforts and optimize their sales process. The marketing funnel follows a linear path, starting from creating awareness and generating interest in the product or service, then guiding the potential customer through the consideration and evaluation stage, and finally leading to the decision to make a purchase. Each stage of the funnel requires specific marketing tactics and messaging to effectively move the potential customer closer to the desired outcome. The first stage of the marketing funnel is the awareness stage, where the entrepreneur focuses on creating awareness and capturing the attention of potential customers. This can be achieved through various marketing channels, such as social media, content marketing, advertising, and public relations. The goal is to make the target audience aware of the existence and value of the product or service. The next stage is the interest stage, where the potential customer shows interest in the product or service. This can be indicated by actions such as signing up for a newsletter, attending a webinar, or engaging with the brand through social media. The entrepreneur must nurture this interest by providing more information, highlighting the benefits, and addressing any concerns or objections the potential customer may have. In the consideration and evaluation stage, the potential customer is actively considering the product or service as a potential solution to their problem. They are comparing different options and evaluating the benefits and features. The entrepreneur needs to provide extensive information, testimonials, case studies, and demonstrations to convince the potential customer that their product or service is the best choice. Finally, in the decision stage, the potential customer makes a purchase or conversion. This can be done through an online transaction, signing up for a subscription, or booking a service. The entrepreneur must make the process as seamless and convenient as possible to encourage the potential customer to take action. After the conversion, the entrepreneur can continue to engage and nurture the customer to build brand loyalty and encourage repeat purchases. The marketing funnel is a vital framework for entrepreneurs to plan and execute their marketing strategies effectively. By understanding the different stages and the corresponding marketing tactics, entrepreneurs can optimize their efforts and increase the likelihood of converting potential customers into loyal advocates.

Mature Startup

A mature startup refers to a stage in the life cycle of a startup company that has moved beyond its initial stages of development and has achieved a certain level of stability and growth. It is characterized by a more established business model, a solid customer base, and a sustainable revenue stream. At this stage, a mature startup has typically overcome the challenges associated with the early stages of a company's growth, such as developing a minimum viable product, acquiring initial customers, and securing funding. The company has proven its concept and demonstrated its ability to deliver value to customers. Mature startups often have a larger team and a more defined organizational structure. They have hired key personnel and have a clear division of roles and responsibilities. The company is no longer solely reliant on the founders' vision and skills but is driven by a team with diverse expertise and experience. Furthermore, a mature startup has usually expanded its market presence and may have entered new markets or established partnerships with other companies. It has built a reputation and brand recognition that helps to attract new customers and partners. In terms of funding, a mature startup may have completed multiple rounds of financing, including seed, angel, and venture capital investments. It may also have generated revenue through sales and marketing efforts, making it less dependent on external funding. To sustain its growth and continue to thrive, a mature startup focuses on scaling its operations, improving its products or services, and expanding its customer base. It seeks to increase market share, introduce new features or offerings, and optimize its business processes. The company may also explore opportunities for strategic partnerships or acquisitions to further enhance its market position.

Mentor Matching Platforms

A mentor matching platform is a digital platform that connects startup founders or entrepreneurs with experienced mentors who can provide guidance, support, and advice throughout the startup journey. These platforms aim to facilitate the mentorship process by leveraging technology to match mentors and mentees based on their specific needs, expertise, and goals. Startup founders and entrepreneurs often face numerous challenges and uncertainties, especially in the early stages of their ventures. While they may have a vision and passion for their business idea, they may lack the necessary knowledge, skills, or network to navigate the complex startup landscape successfully. This is where mentorship plays a crucial role. Mentor matching platforms act as intermediaries, connecting entrepreneurs with mentors who have relevant industry experience, domain expertise, or a successful track record in entrepreneurship. Through these platforms, entrepreneurs can find mentors who can provide valuable insights, guidance, and feedback to help them overcome challenges, make informed decisions, and accelerate their startup's growth. The matching process on these platforms typically involves entrepreneurs creating profiles, specifying their areas of interest, industry, stage of their startup, and the specific areas in which they seek guidance. Mentors, on the other hand, provide information about their own expertise, experience, and availability. The platform then uses algorithms or manual matching processes to pair entrepreneurs with mentors based on compatible attributes and goals. Once the mentor and mentee are connected, they can initiate a mentorship relationship, often through virtual or in-person meetings, email exchanges, or video calls. The frequency and format of the interactions may vary depending on the availability and preferences of both parties. In addition to facilitating mentor-mentee connections, these platforms may also offer additional resources, such as articles, webinars, or networking events, to further support the growth and development of startups and entrepreneurs.

Mentorship Program

A mentorship program in the context of Startup & Entrepreneurship refers to a structured and organized relationship where an experienced individual, known as a mentor, provides guidance, support, and knowledge to a less experienced entrepreneur, known as a mentee, in order to assist them in their personal and professional development. The goal of a mentorship program is to facilitate the mentee's growth by leveraging the mentor's expertise and experience in the startup and entrepreneurship industry. This relationship is typically built on trust, mutual respect, and open communication between the mentor and the mentee.

Mentorship

Mentorship in the context of startup and entrepreneurship can be defined as a mutually beneficial relationship between a more experienced individual (the mentor) and a less experienced individual (the mentee) in which the mentor offers guidance, support, and knowledge to help the mentee navigate through the challenges and uncertainties of starting and growing a business. The mentor, who typically has a successful background in entrepreneurship or business, shares their expertise and wisdom with the mentee, providing valuable insights, advice, and feedback. The mentor acts as a sounding board for the mentee, helping them refine their business ideas, develop strategies, and make informed decisions. Through regular meetings, conversations, and interactions, the mentor contributes to the mentee's professional and personal development, fostering their entrepreneurial skills, leadership abilities, and business acumen. The mentor not only imparts knowledge and experience but also provides emotional support, encouragement, and motivation, helping the mentee overcome obstacles and stay focused on achieving their goals. The role of a mentor goes beyond providing guidance and support; they also serve as role models for the mentee, demonstrating the behaviors, attitudes, and values necessary for success in entrepreneurship. By sharing their own successes and failures, mentors inspire and motivate the mentee to push their boundaries, take calculated risks, and persevere in the face of challenges. Effective mentorship plays a crucial role in the growth and success of startups and entrepreneurs. It accelerates the learning curve for mentees, helping them avoid costly mistakes and navigate the complexities of the business landscape. The mentor's expertise and insights enable the mentee to make informed decisions, identify opportunities, and adapt their strategies to effectively address market demands. Furthermore, mentorship provides mentees with access to the mentor's networks, connections, and resources, opening doors to potential partnerships, investors, customers, and other valuable opportunities. This network can significantly enhance the mentee's chances of success and contribute to the growth of their startup. In summary, mentorship in the context of startup and entrepreneurship is a relationship in which a more experienced individual guides, supports, and shares their knowledge and expertise with a less experienced individual to help them navigate the challenges, make informed decisions, and accelerate their personal and professional growth in the business world.

Mergers And Acquisitions (M&A) Advisor

A mergers and acquisitions (M&A) advisor in the context of startup and entrepreneurship is a professional who provides guidance and assistance to startups and entrepreneurs during the process of merging with or acquiring other businesses. When a startup or entrepreneur is considering expanding their business or entering a new market, they may decide to do so through mergers or acquisitions. However, navigating through the complexities of such transactions can be challenging, especially for those who may not have prior experience in this area. An M&A advisor brings valuable expertise and knowledge to the table, helping startups and entrepreneurs effectively execute their M&A strategies. They assist in evaluating potential target companies, conducting due diligence, negotiating terms and conditions, and finalizing the deal. One of the key roles of an M&A advisor is to conduct thorough research and analysis to identify suitable acquisition targets or merger opportunities that align with the strategic goals of the startup or entrepreneur. They assess factors such as market potential, competition, financial performance, and synergy potential to determine the best fit for the client's objectives. Furthermore, an M&A advisor plays a vital role in the due diligence process. They ensure that all the necessary information is gathered and analyzed to verify the accuracy of the target company's financial statements, contracts, legal compliance, intellectual property rights, and any potential risks or liabilities that may impact the deal. This ensures that the startup or entrepreneur can make an informed decision before proceeding with the transaction. During negotiations, the M&A advisor acts as a mediator between the startup or entrepreneur and the target company. They help structure the deal, determine the purchase price, negotiate favorable terms, and resolve any disagreements that may arise. Their expertise and experience in negotiating M&A transactions can greatly influence the outcome and ensure that the interests of the client are well-represented. Finally, the M&A advisor assists in the finalization of the deal, including drafting and reviewing legal documents, coordinating with lawyers and other professionals involved, and ensuring a smooth transition post-transaction. In summary, an M&A advisor in the context of startup and entrepreneurship provides invaluable guidance and support throughout the entire process of merging with or acquiring other businesses, helping startups and entrepreneurs navigate the complexities of these transactions and maximize their chances of success.

Mergers And Acquisitions (M&A) Due Diligence

Mergers and Acquisitions (M&A) Due Diligence is a crucial process in the context of Startup & Entrepreneurship. It refers to the comprehensive examination and evaluation of a potential merger or acquisition target to assess its financial, legal, operational, and strategic aspects. During an M&A transaction, startups and entrepreneurs perform due diligence to gather important information about the target company in order to make well-informed decisions. This involves conducting a thorough analysis of the target company's financial statements, tax records, contracts, intellectual property, customer base, competitive position, and other relevant areas.

154

Mergers And Acquisitions (M&A)

Mergers and acquisitions (M&A) refer to the strategic activities in which one company combines with another company or acquires another company to achieve specific business goals. In the context of startups and entrepreneurship, M&A plays a crucial role in shaping the growth and development of companies. Mergers occur when two separate entities come together to form a new organization that is often stronger and more competitive in the market. This can happen for various reasons, such as expanding market share, gaining access to new technologies or products, or achieving cost synergies by combining resources and operations. On the other hand, acquisitions involve one company purchasing another company, usually to gain control over its assets, technology, or customer base. The acquiring company may integrate the acquired company's operations into its own or operate it as a separate entity. For startups and entrepreneurs, participating in M&A activities can offer numerous benefits. It can provide an opportunity to accelerate growth and scale up operations by combining resources, expertise, and market reach. Startups often seek acquisitions to access new markets, acquire intellectual property, or gain a competitive edge in their industry. M&A activities also allow startups to respond to market dynamics, stay competitive, and achieve their strategic objectives. It can help startups expand their product or service offerings, diversify revenue streams, or enter new markets that may have been difficult to penetrate independently. However, M&A transactions can be complex and challenging for startups. They require careful planning, due diligence, and negotiation to ensure the success of the integration process. Startups must evaluate the cultural fit, compatibility of business models, and potential synergies between the companies involved. In conclusion, M&A activities in the context of startups and entrepreneurship involve the strategic combination or acquisition of companies to achieve specific business objectives. These activities can provide startups with opportunities for growth, access to new markets, and the ability to respond to market dynamics. However, they also pose challenges and require thorough planning and evaluation to ensure successful integration.

Mezzanine Financing

Mezzanine financing is a form of funding that is commonly used in the world of startups and entrepreneurship. It sits between traditional debt financing and equity financing, providing a hybrid solution that offers benefits for both the startup and the investor. Mezzanine financing is typically used when a startup needs additional capital to grow and expand, but does not want to dilute existing ownership by issuing more equity. It allows startups to borrow money that can be converted into equity at a later stage, under certain conditions. This flexibility is highly attractive for startups who are looking to raise capital without giving up too much control or ownership.

Microloans

Microloans are small loans that are typically provided to startup businesses or entrepreneurs with limited access to traditional forms of financing. They are designed to help these individuals or businesses overcome financial barriers and launch or expand their operations. The concept of microloans originated from the belief that providing small amounts of capital to aspiring entrepreneurs can have a significant impact on poverty alleviation and economic development. Microloans are often offered by microfinance institutions (MFIs), which are organizations that specialize in providing financial services to low-income individuals or communities.

Milestone Financing

Milestone financing refers to a funding approach in the context of startups and entrepreneurship. It involves the provision of capital to a startup company or entrepreneur in stages or milestones based on the achievement of predetermined goals or objectives. In milestone financing, the funding is distributed incrementally as the startup reaches specific milestones or key performance indicators (KPIs) agreed upon by the investor and the entrepreneur. These milestones typically include the completion of certain product development stages, achieving specific revenue targets, reaching a certain number of customers or users, or securing key partnerships or collaborations.

Milestone-Based Financing

Milestone-Based Financing is a funding strategy commonly used in the context of startups and entrepreneurship. It involves providing financial resources to a startup or entrepreneur in stages, based on the achievement of predetermined milestones. Instead of receiving a large sum of money upfront, milestone-based financing allows startups to secure funding incrementally as they meet specific objectives or milestones. These milestones can be defined based on various factors such as product development, market validation, revenue generation, or user acquisition. This financing approach offers several advantages for both investors and startups. For investors, it reduces the risk of funding a startup that may fail to deliver on its promises. By linking the disbursement of funds to milestones, investors can ensure that the startup is making progress and achieving tangible results before providing additional capital. For startups, milestone-based financing provides a structured approach to funding that aligns with their growth trajectory. It allows them to focus on achieving important milestones, which can provide validation and attract further investment. Additionally, startups can use milestone-based financing as a way to build trust and credibility with potential investors, as the achievement of milestones serves as evidence of progress and success. This financing model also encourages startups to be more disciplined and resourceful in managing their finances. Knowing that funding is contingent on achieving specific milestones, startups are incentivized to use their resources efficiently and make strategic decisions that maximize their chances of success. However, milestone-based financing can also present challenges. Startups may face pressure to achieve milestones within specific timeframes, which can lead to rushed decision-making or sacrificing long-term sustainability for short-term gains. Additionally, defining meaningful and measurable milestones can sometimes be subjective and open to interpretation, requiring clear communication and alignment between investors and startups. In conclusion, milestone-based financing is a funding approach that provides startups with funding in stages, based on the achievement of predetermined milestones. It offers benefits such as reduced risk for investors, structured funding for startups, and increased accountability. However, it also comes with challenges related to timing, decision-making, and milestone definition. Overall, milestone-based financing can be an effective tool for supporting startup growth and success.

Minimum Lovable Product (MLP)

Minimum Lovable Product (MLP) is a term commonly used in the context of startups and entrepreneurship. It refers to the development and release of a product with the bare minimum features required to make it attractive and loveable to the target audience. The concept of MLP is derived from the well-known Minimum Viable Product (MVP) approach, which focuses on developing a product with the bare minimum features necessary to test its viability in the market. However, whereas the MVP approach primarily emphasizes on viability, the MLP approach goes a step further by incorporating the element of desirability.

Minimum Viable Audience (MVA) Analysis

A Minimum Viable Audience (MVA) Analysis is a strategic approach employed by startups and entrepreneurs to identify and target a specific group of potential customers who are most likely to benefit from and engage with their product or service. This analysis allows startups to focus their limited resources and efforts on a defined audience, increasing their chances of successful market entry and sustainable growth. The MVA Analysis involves several key steps. Firstly, startups need to understand their product or service and its unique value proposition. This helps in determining the target audience's problem or need that the startup's offering aims to solve. By identifying the pain points, startups can evaluate the overall market size and potential demand for their solution. Once the market potential is assessed, startups should analyze the available customer segments and identify the most appropriate segment to target. This involves evaluating factors such as customer demographics, psychographics, behavior patterns, and preferences to determine which segment aligns best with the startup's offering and value proposition. By focusing on a specific segment, startups can tailor their marketing efforts and resources to effectively reach and engage their target customers. Furthermore, the MVA Analysis includes identifying early adopters within the target segment. Early adopters are the individuals or organizations who are quick to embrace new technologies or innovations. They often provide valuable feedback and insights for startups, helping them improve their offerings and refine their messaging. By understanding the characteristics and needs of early adopters, startups can design their products and marketing strategies to effectively appeal to this influential group. Overall, the MVA Analysis plays a crucial role in shaping a startup's go-to-market strategy and identifying its key audience. By understanding their target audience's needs, preferences, and behavior, startups can position their products or services in a way that resonates with their customers and offers a compelling value proposition. This targeted approach increases the chances of gaining early traction, building a loyal customer base, and achieving long-term success in the competitive entrepreneurial landscape.

Minimum Viable Audience (MVA)

Minimum Viable Audience (MVA) is a concept in the context of startups and entrepreneurship that refers to the smallest group of target customers for a product or service that the startup can initially focus on to test and validate its assumptions and value proposition. The MVA approach recognizes that startups have limited resources, including time, money, and personnel. Instead of trying to target a broad audience from the beginning, the focus is on identifying a niche segment that has a pressing problem or need that the startup can solve. This niche segment becomes the MVA, and the startup designs and develops its product or service specifically for this audience. The MVA strategy is based on the idea that by targeting a smaller audience, startups can minimize risk and optimize their chances of success by gaining early adopters and generating initial revenue. By focusing on a specific group of customers, startups can gather valuable feedback and learn about the market, its needs, and the viability of the product or service. This iterative process allows startups to evolve and adapt their offering based on real customer insights, leading to a better product-market fit. When determining the MVA, startups consider various factors, such as the size and accessibility of the audience, their willingness to pay, and their potential for growth. The MVA is often defined based on demographics, psychographics, and other specific criteria that align with the startup's value proposition. Once the MVA is identified, startups then focus their efforts on building relationships, acquiring customers, and delivering value to this audience. As the startup gains traction and validates its business model, it can gradually expand its target audience to larger market segments.

Minimum Viable Audience

A Minimum Viable Audience (MVA) refers to the smallest target demographic or group of customers that a startup or entrepreneur aims to serve with their product or service. This concept is closely related to the Minimum Viable Product (MVP), which focuses on creating a basic version of a product that meets the core needs of early adopters. Identifying and understanding the MVA is crucial for startups and entrepreneurs as it helps them narrow down their target market and focus their resources and efforts on a specific group of customers. By catering to this smaller audience, entrepreneurs can gather valuable feedback, validate their ideas, and iterate their products or services to better meet the needs of their customers. The MVA approach involves taking a lean and iterative approach to product development. Rather than trying to please a broad range of customers or creating a product with extensive features from the start, entrepreneurs concentrate on serving a specific segment of the market. This allows them to quickly test their ideas, learn from the feedback they receive, and make informed decisions about product development. By defining and engaging with their MVA, startups and entrepreneurs can also build a dedicated community around their brand. These early adopters become brand advocates, providing valuable word-of-mouth marketing and potentially attracting a larger customer base. It is important to note that the MVA is not permanent. As startups gain a foothold in the market, they may expand their target audience and develop additional features or offerings. However, the MVA serves as a starting point and serves to provide focus and direction during the early stages of a startup's journey.

Minimum Viable Experiment

A Minimum Viable Experiment (MVE) is a lean and structured approach used by startups and entrepreneurs to validate a specific hypothesis or assumption about their business model. It is designed to provide key insights and data that will guide decision-making and determine the viability of a product or service in the market. At its core, an MVE is an iterative process that involves designing and implementing an experiment with the minimal resources and time required to gather conclusive results. It is focused on obtaining the most essential information and feedback needed to evaluate the feasibility of an idea, while minimizing the risk and cost associated with traditional market research or product development.

Minimum Viable Product (MVP) Testing

A Minimum Viable Product (MVP) is a concept in startup and entrepreneurship that refers to the most basic version of a product or service that can be developed and released to the market. It is the initial version that allows entrepreneurs to test their assumptions, collect feedback, and learn from real user interactions. The MVP is designed to validate the underlying business idea or concept, with a focus on solving a particular problem or meeting a specific need of the target audience. The main purpose of an MVP is to gather insights and gather proof that the product or service is viable and has market potential before investing significant time, effort, and resources into further development. Typically, an MVP includes only the core features and functionalities necessary to offer a minimal solution to the problem at hand. It eliminates any unnecessary frills or extra features that are not essential for the initial validation stage. By keeping the MVP simple, startups can reduce development time and costs, making it easier to iterate and pivot if needed based on user feedback. The MVP testing phase involves getting the product in the hands of real users, whether through controlled experiments or by launching it in the market on a limited scale. This allows entrepreneurs to gather feedback, measure user engagement, and evaluate whether the product meets the expectations of the target audience. The insights gathered during this testing phase help in making informed decisions about the future direction of the product and any necessary adjustments or refinements. MVP testing is an iterative process, where the product is continuously refined based on user feedback, until it reaches a stage where it can be deployed at a larger scale. It is a crucial part of the lean startup methodology, as it allows entrepreneurs to validate their assumptions and build a product that truly solves a problem or fulfills a need in the market.

Minimum Viable Product (MVP)

Minimum Viable Product (MVP) is a term commonly used in the context of startups and entrepreneurship. It refers to a version of a product or service that has the bare minimum features necessary to address the needs of early adopters and gather valuable feedback for further development. The concept of MVP is rooted in the lean startup methodology, which emphasizes the importance of validating assumptions and reducing waste in the product development process. Instead of spending extensive time and resources building a fully-featured product, entrepreneurs aim to get an early version into the hands of users as quickly as possible.

Mobile App Prototyping

Mobile app prototyping, in the context of startup and entrepreneurship, refers to the creation of a simulated version of a mobile application that serves as a visual representation of its functionality and user interface. This process involves designing and developing a prototype that allows stakeholders to interact with the app's basic features and flows. The primary purpose of mobile app prototyping is to gather feedback and validate ideas before investing significant time and resources into building the actual app. It enables startup founders and entrepreneurs to test different concepts, user experiences, and design elements to identify potential issues and improve the overall user journey. Through app prototyping, entrepreneurs can explore various options and make informed decisions about the app's features and functionality, enhancing the likelihood of successful development. App prototyping typically involves creating wireframes and mockups that outline the app's structure, layout, and content. Wireframes serve as a basic blueprint, outlining the placement of different elements and defining the app's navigation flow. Mockups, on the other hand, provide a more detailed visual representation of the app, including colors, typography, and graphical assets. During the prototyping phase, entrepreneurs have the opportunity to gather user feedback and input to refine their app's features and user experience. They can conduct user testing sessions, where potential users interact with the prototype and provide valuable insights, helping identify pain points, usability issues, and areas for improvement. This iterative process allows startups to iterate on their product and align it with their target market's needs and preferences, creating a more compelling and user-friendly app. In conclusion, mobile app prototyping is an essential step in the startup and entrepreneurship journey. It enables entrepreneurs to visually represent their mobile app ideas, test different concepts, gather user feedback, and refine their app's features and design. By investing in prototyping, startups can reduce the risks associated with app development and increase the chances of creating a successful and user-centric product.

Monetization Models

158

Monetization Models refer to the various strategies and approaches that startups and entrepreneurs adopt to generate revenue from their products or services. These models provide a framework for turning a business idea into a profitable venture. One common monetization model is the Advertising model. Under this model, startups generate revenue by displaying advertisements on their website or mobile app. The advertisements can be in the form of banners, videos, or sponsored content. The revenue is typically generated through pay-per-click (PPC) or pay-per-impression (PPI) arrangements with advertisers. Advertising models are often used by content-based platforms such as news websites or social media platforms. Another monetization model is the Subscription model. Startups using this model provide their customers with access to a product or service for a recurring fee. This model is commonly used by software-as-a-service (SaaS) startups, where customers pay a monthly or annual subscription fee to use the software. Subscription models provide a predictable stream of revenue and encourage customer loyalty. E-commerce is a popular monetization model where startups sell physical or digital products online. The revenue is generated through the sale of products, and startups often use online marketplaces or their own e-commerce platforms to reach customers. This model requires careful management of inventory, logistics, and customer support. Freemium is another widely adopted monetization model in which startups offer a basic version of their product or service for free, while charging for premium features or additional functionalities. Startups implementing this model aim to attract a large user base with the free version and then convert a portion of these users into paying customers. Freemium models are commonly used by software applications and online platforms. In conclusion, monetization models play a crucial role in the success of startups and entrepreneurs. By choosing the right model for their business, startups can generate revenue, attract customers, and establish a sustainable and profitable venture.

Monetization Strategies

Monetization strategies refer to the various methods and techniques employed by startups and entrepreneurs to generate revenue and turn their ideas or businesses into profitable ventures. These strategies involve the identification and implementation of revenue streams that align with the core operations and value proposition of the startup or entrepreneurial endeavor. There are several monetization strategies that startups and entrepreneurs can consider. One common approach is through the adoption of a freemium model, which offers a basic product or service for free while charging a premium for additional features or enhanced functionality. This strategy allows the startup to attract a larger user base and then convert a percentage of those users into paying customers. Another popular monetization strategy is advertising, where the startup leverages its platform or user base to display targeted advertisements. Revenue is generated by charging advertisers for ad space or based on user engagement metrics such as clicks or impressions. In some cases, startups may choose to offer their product or service on a subscription basis. This model involves charging users a recurring fee in exchange for continued access to the offering. Startups can offer different subscription tiers or pricing options to cater to various customer segments and maximize revenue potential. Furthermore, partnerships and collaborations with other businesses can also be a lucrative monetization strategy. Startups can enter into strategic alliances or joint ventures to leverage each other's resources, networks, and customer bases. These collaborations can lead to revenue sharing or joint product offerings, creating a win-win situation for all parties involved. Additionally, startups can explore the possibility of licensing or selling their intellectual property, such as patents, trademarks, or software, to generate revenue. This strategy allows startups to monetize their intangible assets and tap into new markets or industries without directly engaging in the manufacturing or distribution of products. Ultimately, the choice of monetization strategy depends on various factors such as the nature of the startup's product or service, target market, competitive landscape, and growth objectives. Startups and entrepreneurs should carefully analyze these factors and adopt a monetization strategy that aligns with their business goals and creates sustainable revenue streams.

Monetization Strategy

A monetization strategy refers to a comprehensive plan implemented by a startup or entrepreneur to generate revenue from their products, services, or platform. It involves identifying and leveraging various sources and methods to generate income and sustain the business in the long run. Proper execution of a monetization strategy is crucial for startups and entrepreneurs as it enables them to cover their expenses, invest in growth, attract investors, and eventually achieve profitability. One common monetization strategy is the direct revenue model, where startups generate income by selling their products or services directly to customers. This can be done through one-time sales, subscriptions, or a freemium model where a basic version of the product is offered for free with additional features available for a fee. Startups can also generate revenue by offering premium services, add-ons, or upgrades to enhance the user experience or access to advanced functionalities. Another popular monetization strategy is the advertising model, where startups provide a platform for advertisers to reach their target audience and generate revenue through ad placements. This can include display ads, sponsored content, native advertising, or partnerships with brands. Startups may choose to use third-party advertising networks or develop their own in-house advertising solutions to maximize their revenue potential. In addition to direct sales and advertising, startups can adopt the subscription model, where customers pay a recurring fee to access and use the startup's products or services. This model provides a predictable and steady stream of revenue, typically on a monthly or annual basis. Startups may offer different subscription tiers with varying features and benefits to cater to different customer segments and increase revenue. Other monetization strategies include the freemium model, where a basic version of the product is offered for free to attract users, with a percentage of them converting to paid users for additional features and premium content. Startups can also explore partnerships and collaborations with other businesses to generate revenue through licensing, franchising, or joint ventures. Ultimately, the choice of a monetization strategy depends on the nature of the startup, the target market, and the competitive landscape. It requires careful analysis, experimentation, and adaptation to determine the most effective revenue streams that align with the startup's goals, values, and customer base.

Monetization

A startup is a newly established business that usually operates in a competitive and volatile environment, aiming to bring innovative products or services to market. It is characterized by uncertainty, limited resources, and a high level of risk. The primary objective of a startup is to achieve growth and profitability, ultimately leading to success and sustainability. In the context of entrepreneurship, monetization refers to the process of generating revenue or profits from a startup's products, services, or platforms. It involves converting the startup's offerings into a sustainable and scalable business model that can generate consistent and increasing income. Monetization strategies can vary depending on the nature of the startup, its target market, and the industry it operates in. Some common approaches include: Advertising: Generating revenue by displaying advertisements on websites, apps, or other digital platforms. This model relies on attracting a large user base to gain advertisers' interest and generate ad impressions or clicks. Subscription: Charging users a recurring fee in exchange for access to premium content, features, or services. This model often requires providing enough value to justify the ongoing expense for customers. E-commerce: Selling products or services directly to customers through an online platform. This model can involve inventory management, order fulfillment, and customer support. Affiliate marketing: Earning a commission by promoting and selling another company's products or services through referral links. This model leverages the startup's audience and marketing capabilities to drive sales for partner companies. Licensing or franchising: Granting other individuals or businesses the right to use the startup's intellectual property, brand, or technology in exchange for fees or royalties. This model can help expand the startup's reach without the need for significant investments in new markets. Data monetization: Analyzing and selling aggregated or anonymized user data to third parties for market research, targeted advertising, or other purposes. This model focuses on leveraging the valuable insights derived from user behavior or preferences. Effective monetization requires understanding and continuously evaluating the startup's target market, customer needs, and competitive landscape. It involves finding the right balance between generating revenue and providing value to customers, while also considering long-term sustainability and growth.

Multi-Variate Testing Tools

Multi-variate testing tools are technological solutions used by startups and entrepreneurs to optimize their websites or mobile applications. These tools allow businesses to test multiple variations of their digital assets simultaneously, such as different headlines, call-to-action buttons, or images, to determine which combination provides the best results in terms of user engagement, conversion rates, or other key performance indicators. As startups and entrepreneurs strive to generate maximum value from limited resources, multi-variate testing tools offer a cost-effective approach to improve their products or services. By running experiments that involve tweaking various elements of their digital platforms, businesses can gain insights into what aspects of their interface or content resonate most with their target audience.

Multichannel Marketing

Multichannel marketing in the context of startup and entrepreneurship refers to the strategic approach of businesses using multiple marketing channels to reach their target audience and promote their products or services. It involves the integration and coordination of various marketing channels, both online and offline, to create a seamless and consistent customer experience. This marketing strategy recognizes that consumers today engage with brands through multiple touchpoints, such as websites, social media platforms, email, physical stores, and mobile apps. Startups and entrepreneurs need to leverage these channels effectively to maximize their reach, engage with potential customers, and drive sales.

Net Promoter Score (NPS) Surveys

A Net Promoter Score (NPS) survey is a commonly used tool in the context of startups and entrepreneurship to measure customer satisfaction and loyalty. It is a quantitative assessment that seeks to determine the likelihood of customers recommending a company, product, or service to others. The NPS survey is typically conducted by asking customers a single question: "On a scale of 0 to 10, how likely are you to recommend our company/product/service to a friend or colleague?" Based on their response, customers are classified into three categories: Promoters (score 9-10), Passives (score 7-8), and Detractors (score 0-6).

Network Effect

A network effect, in the context of startup and entrepreneurship, refers to the phenomenon where the value and utility of a product or service increase as more people use it. It is a positive feedback loop that drives the growth and success of a startup by creating a barrier to entry for potential competitors. When a startup creates a product or service that benefits from network effects, every new user adds value to the entire network. As more users join, the network becomes more valuable, attracting even more users, and creating a virtuous cycle. This effect can be seen in various industries, especially in technology-driven startups.

Network Effects Strategies

A network effects strategy refers to a business approach that leverages the power of network effects to enhance the value and competitiveness of a startup or entrepreneurial venture.Network effects, also known as demand-side economies of scale, occur when the value of a product or service increases as more users or participants join the network. It is a phenomenon where the utility and benefits of a product or service grow exponentially with the number of users, creating a positive feedback loop that amplifies the growth and sustainability of the business.In the context of startup and entrepreneurship, network effects strategies can be a critical element of success. By focusing on building a strong network and fostering user participation, startups can gain a significant competitive advantage that becomes difficult for competitors to replicate.One common type of network effects strategy is the platform strategy, where a startup creates a platform that connects multiple users or participants. Platforms like Amazon, Uber, and Airbnb are prime examples of this approach. As more buyers and sellers, drivers, or hosts join the platform, the value of the platform increases for all participants, attracting even more users.Another network effects strategy is the data strategy. Startups that collect and analyze user data can use it to improve their products or services, personalize offerings, and create a better user experience. The more data they gather, the more effective and valuable their products become, leading to increased user adoption and retention.Additionally, startups can employ a compatibility strategy, aiming to create products that are compatible with existing networks or technologies. By aligning their offerings with popular platforms or widely used technologies, startups can tap into existing user bases and benefit from the network effects already in place.Network effects strategies are often complemented by other growth strategies, such as viral marketing, referral programs, and strategic partnerships. They require a focus on user acquisition, engagement, and retention, as well as continuous improvement of the product or service to sustain and enhance the network effects.Overall, network effects strategies play a pivotal role in startup and entrepreneurial success by capitalizing on the positive feedback loop created when more users or participants join the network, driving sustained growth and competitive advantage.

Networked Business

A networked business, in the context of startup entrepreneurship, refers to a company or organization that thrives on the power of connectivity and collaboration made possible by networking technologies. Networked businesses leverage the internet, social media platforms, and various communication tools to establish and maintain connections with customers, suppliers, employees, and other stakeholders. These businesses understand the value of building relationships, exchanging information, and facilitating transactions in a digital, interconnected world.

Networking Events

Networking events are formal gatherings organized within the context of startup and entrepreneurship, aiming to facilitate the exchange of ideas, foster connections, and create opportunities for collaboration among individuals and companies within the industry. These events provide a platform for entrepreneurs, investors, industry professionals, and other relevant stakeholders to come together, share their experiences, and build valuable relationships. During networking events, participants engage in conversations, discussions, and presentations, allowing them to gain insights, learn from each other, and explore potential partnerships or business opportunities. These gatherings often feature keynote speakers, panel discussions, workshops, and other activities designed to stimulate engagement and interaction among attendees.

Networking Skills

Networking skills, in the context of startup and entrepreneurship, refer to the ability to build and maintain connections and relationships with individuals and groups in order to exchange information, opportunities, and support for personal and professional growth. Successful entrepreneurs understand the value of networking skills as they provide a platform to meet potential investors, customers, strategic partners, and mentors who can contribute to the success of their startup. Networking allows entrepreneurs to tap into a wider pool of resources, knowledge, and expertise that can help them navigate the challenges of starting and growing a business. Networking skills involve effective communication, active listening, and the ability to establish rapport with others. It requires the ability to identify and connect with individuals who share similar interests, goals, or expertise and to cultivate and nurture these relationships over time. These skills also encompass the ability to leverage social media platforms, attend networking events, and participate in industry conferences or associations to enhance personal and professional connections. Networking skills can facilitate access to valuable resources such as potential investors, business partners, or suppliers. It enables entrepreneurs to gain insights into market trends, industry developments, and emerging opportunities. By connecting with individuals who have diverse backgrounds and experiences, entrepreneurs can also broaden their perspectives and gain new ideas and perspectives that can fuel innovation and creativity within their startup. In addition to exchanging information and resources, networking skills also play a crucial role in building a support system. Entrepreneurs often face numerous challenges and uncertainties, and having a strong network of like-minded individuals can provide emotional support, encouragement, and advice during difficult times. Networking allows entrepreneurs to connect with mentors or industry experts who can provide guidance, mentorship, and share their own experiences and insights. In conclusion, networking skills are of paramount importance in the context of startup and entrepreneurship. They provide opportunities to establish and nurture connections, access valuable resources, gain insights, and build emotional support systems. Developing and honing networking skills can significantly contribute to the success and growth of a startup.

Networking

Networking in the context of startup and entrepreneurship refers to the act of establishing and nurturing relationships with individuals and organizations for the purpose of gaining support, resources, and opportunities that can contribute to the growth and success of a startup. Networking plays a vital role in the entrepreneurial journey as it allows entrepreneurs to expand their reach, tap into knowledge and expertise of others, and access valuable resources that may otherwise be unavailable to them. It involves building relationships with potential investors, mentors, industry experts, customers, partners, and even competitors. The benefits of networking for startups and entrepreneurs are manifold. Firstly, networking provides access to a diverse range of perspectives and ideas. By connecting with individuals from different backgrounds and industries, entrepreneurs can gain fresh insights, alternative approaches, and innovative solutions to challenges they face. Networking also facilitates knowledge sharing, enabling entrepreneurs to stay up-to-date with industry trends, emerging technologies, and best practices. Furthermore, networking offers numerous opportunities for collaboration and partnership. By forging relationships with potential customers or clients, entrepreneurs can generate leads, acquire new customers, and increase sales. Networking also opens doors to partnerships with other startups or established companies, allowing for joint ventures, co-creation, and resource sharing. In addition, networking can lead to valuable mentorship and guidance. Seasoned entrepreneurs or industry experts can provide invaluable advice, feedback, and mentorship to emerging entrepreneurs, helping them navigate the challenges and complexities of entrepreneurship. Mentors can offer strategic guidance, connect entrepreneurs with relevant contacts, and share their own experiences and lessons learned. Overall, networking is a crucial component of success for startups and entrepreneurs. It enables the exchange of resources, knowledge, and opportunities that can propel a startup's growth and enhance its chances of success. By actively participating in networking events, conferences, and online communities, entrepreneurs can build a strong network of contacts, foster collaborations, and tap into the power of collective innovation and support.

Non-Disclosure Agreement (NDA)

A non-disclosure agreement (NDA) is a legally binding contract between two or more parties that outlines the confidential information they agree to share with each other while undertaking a specific business relationship or transaction. In the context of startup and entrepreneurship, NDAs are commonly used to protect sensitive or proprietary information, trade secrets, and other valuable assets that are crucial for the success of a startup. When starting a new venture, entrepreneurs often need to share their innovative ideas, business plans, customer lists, financial projections, or other confidential information with investors, potential partners, vendors, or employees. However, they want to ensure that such information remains confidential and is not misused or disclosed to unauthorized individuals or competitors. This is where an NDA comes into play. The NDA typically contains provisions that define what information is considered confidential, how it should be handled, and the obligations and responsibilities of the parties involved. It may include clauses related to the duration of the agreement, non-disclosure obligations, permitted disclosures, remedies for breach of confidentiality, and dispute resolution mechanisms. By signing an NDA, the parties are bound by its terms and promise not to disclose or use the confidential information for any purpose other than the specific business relationship or transaction outlined in the agreement. The NDA creates a legal framework that allows entrepreneurs to share sensitive information with confidence, knowing that their intellectual property and competitive advantage are protected. For startups, NDAs are particularly important during initial discussions with potential investors or partners. Investors often require entrepreneurs to disclose confidential information to evaluate the viability and potential returns of the startup. With an NDA in place, entrepreneurs can mitigate the risk of their ideas being stolen, replicated, or used by others without their consent.

Online Presence

An online presence refers to the digital footprint a startup or entrepreneur establishes on the internet through various online channels and platforms. It is the collective representation of a business or individual's identity, activities, and interactions on the web. Having a strong online presence is crucial for startups and entrepreneurs in today's digital age. It allows them to showcase their brand, products, or services to a larger audience and reach potential customers or clients beyond physical boundaries. With the internet becoming an integral part of people's lives, a well-established online presence can significantly contribute to the growth and success of a startup. A startup's online presence typically includes its website, social media profiles, online directories, blogs, and other digital platforms where it engages with its target audience. These channels serve as virtual storefronts, acting as touchpoints for potential customers looking for information, products, or services. Through these platforms, startups can establish their brand identity, share valuable content, provide customer support, and create meaningful connections with their audience. Furthermore, an online presence allows startups and entrepreneurs to leverage various digital marketing strategies to attract, engage, and convert leads into customers. These strategies include search engine optimization (SEO), social media marketing, email marketing, content marketing, and paid advertising. By optimizing their online presence and implementing these strategies effectively, startups can enhance their visibility, improve search engine rankings, and engage with their target audience in a more personalized way. In addition to promoting products or services, a well-crafted online presence can also help establish startups as thought leaders or industry experts. By sharing valuable and insightful content on their websites or blogs, entrepreneurs can position themselves as authoritative figures in their respective industries. This not only boosts their credibility but also strengthens their brand image and attracts potential partners, investors, or collaborators. In conclusion, an online presence is a vital component for startups and entrepreneurs to succeed in today's digital landscape. It enables them to showcase their brand, connect with their audience, promote their offerings, and establish themselves as industry experts. By effectively managing their online presence, startups can harness the power of digital marketing and expand their reach beyond geographical boundaries.

Online Reputation Management (ORM) Tools

Online Reputation Management (ORM) Tools Online Reputation Management (ORM) Tools are software platforms or services that help startups and entrepreneurs monitor, analyze, and influence their online reputation. In today's digital age, where a single negative review or social media comment can significantly impact a business's image and success, it is crucial for startups and entrepreneurs to actively manage their online reputation. ORM tools offer various functionalities and features to help startups and entrepreneurs effectively manage their online reputation. These tools monitor online platforms such as social media, review sites, and search engine results pages to identify any negative or damaging content related to the business. They provide real-time alerts and notifications, allowing entrepreneurs to respond promptly and address any issues before they escalate. The analysis aspect of ORM tools enables startups and entrepreneurs to gain insights into their overall online reputation. These tools generate reports and analytics that highlight trends, sentiment analysis, and customer feedback. By analyzing this data, startups can identify areas for improvement and make informed decisions about their marketing and customer service strategies. ORM tools also provide functionalities for influencing and improving online reputation. They allow entrepreneurs to actively engage with customers through social media management, review management, and customer feedback solutions. These features help startups build a positive online presence, address customer concerns, and manage their brand image effectively. In conclusion, Online Reputation Management (ORM) Tools are essential for startups and entrepreneurs to maintain a positive online reputation. They offer monitoring, analysis, and influencing capabilities that enable businesses to address potential issues, improve customer satisfaction, and enhance their brand image. By actively managing their online reputation, startups can build trust, attract customers, and achieve long-term success in today's competitive digital landscape.

Open Innovation Platforms

Open Innovation Platforms are collaborative platforms that facilitate the exchange of ideas, knowledge, and resources among startups, entrepreneurs, and other stakeholders in the entrepreneurial ecosystem. These platforms leverage technology and online communities to enable open innovation, a paradigm that encourages the sharing, co-creation, and commercialization of ideas and solutions. Startups and entrepreneurs can use open innovation platforms to connect with a network of diverse individuals, including other entrepreneurs, industry experts, investors, and potential customers. These platforms provide a virtual space where participants can share their ideas, seek feedback, and form partnerships to develop and launch innovative products and services.

Operational Efficiency Tools

Operational Risk Assessment

Operational Risk Assessment in the context of Startup & Entrepreneurship refers to the evaluation and identification of potential risks associated with the day-to-day operations of a new business venture. It involves the systematic analysis and mitigation of risks that may arise from various operational activities, processes, and procedures. When starting a new business, entrepreneurs face numerous operational risks that can significantly impact the success and sustainability of their venture. These risks can range from supply chain disruptions and equipment failure to human errors and cybersecurity threats. Conducting a thorough operational risk assessment enables entrepreneurs to identify potential hazards, assess their potential impact, and implement appropriate strategies to mitigate the risks.

Opportunity Cost

An opportunity cost, in the context of startup and entrepreneurship, refers to the potential benefit or value that is foregone or sacrificed when choosing one course of action over another. When starting a business or pursuing entrepreneurial ventures, individuals often face various options and decisions. Each decision involves different trade-offs, and the opportunity cost helps evaluate and quantify these trade-offs. For example, imagine an entrepreneur who has limited resources and is deciding between two potential business opportunities. Opportunity A offers the potential for rapid growth and a high return on investment, but it requires a significant upfront investment of time and money. Opportunity B, on the other hand, requires less initial investment but offers a slower growth trajectory and potential returns. By choosing to pursue Opportunity A, the entrepreneur incurs the opportunity cost of not pursuing Opportunity B. This cost includes both the potential financial benefits and the intangible benefits that could have been gained from Opportunity B. Opportunity cost is not limited to financial considerations. It also encompasses the time, effort, energy, and other resources that could have been allocated elsewhere. For instance, if an entrepreneur chooses to spend a significant amount of time developing a new product, the opportunity cost could involve the time that could have been used for marketing or building customer relationships. Understanding opportunity cost is essential for startups and entrepreneurs as it helps in making informed decisions and evaluating potential risks and benefits. By considering the opportunity cost, entrepreneurs can assess the alternatives and determine which option provides the greatest potential value and aligns with their goals and resources. In conclusion, opportunity cost in the context of startup and entrepreneurship refers to the potential benefit or value that is forfeited when choosing one course of action over another. It involves both financial and non-financial trade-offs, including resources such as time, effort, and energy. This concept helps entrepreneurs make informed decisions and evaluate the potential risks and benefits of different opportunities.

Organic Growth

Outsourcing Services

Outsourcing services in the context of startup and entrepreneurship refer to the practice of contracting out specific business functions or tasks to external service providers or individuals who are specialized in that particular area. The objective behind outsourcing services is to leverage the expertise and resources of third-party providers to efficiently and cost-effectively handle non-core activities, allowing the business to focus on its core competencies and strategic priorities. Startups and entrepreneurs often turn to outsourcing services as a means to reduce operational costs, enhance operational efficiency, access specialized skills and knowledge, and improve scalability. By outsourcing certain tasks, startups can avoid the need to hire and train additional in-house staff or invest in expensive infrastructure and equipment. This can save both time and money, enabling startups to allocate their limited resources more effectively. Outsourcing services can encompass a wide range of business functions, including but not limited to, IT services, customer support, marketing, accounting and finance, human resources, and administrative tasks. The choice of which functions to outsource depends on the specific needs and priorities of the startup or entrepreneur. Engaging outsourcing services also brings the advantage of accessing a global talent pool. Startups can tap into the expertise and skills of professionals from around the world, regardless of geographical boundaries. This allows for greater flexibility in meeting business requirements and obtaining specialized knowledge that may not be readily available internally. However, it is essential for startups and entrepreneurs to carefully consider the pros and cons of outsourcing services. While outsourcing can offer significant benefits, there are also potential challenges and risks involved, such as loss of control over certain aspects of the business, potential security and confidentiality issues, and the need for effective communication and coordination with external providers. In conclusion, outsourcing services in the context of startup and entrepreneurship involve delegating specific business functions to external service providers to achieve operational efficiency, cost savings, and access to specialized skills. Startups and entrepreneurs should carefully evaluate the potential benefits and risks before deciding to outsource specific tasks or functions.

Pain Point

Pain Point: In the context of Startup & Entrepreneurship, a pain point refers to a specific problem or challenge that a target market or customer segment is experiencing, which is recognized as an opportunity for a startup or entrepreneur to provide a solution. Pain points can arise from a variety of sources, including unmet needs, inefficiencies, inconveniences, or frustrations within a particular industry or market. These pain points often represent opportunities for startups to innovate and create products, services, or business models that address these challenges and provide value to customers. Identifying pain points is a crucial step in the startup and entrepreneurial process. It involves conducting thorough market research, gaining insights into customer behavior, and understanding the key problems or challenges that potential customers face within a specific niche or target market. Once a pain point has been identified, entrepreneurs and startups can develop solutions that effectively address and alleviate the problem. This may involve creating a new product or service, improving upon existing solutions, or implementing innovative business models that provide a more efficient and effective way for customers to solve their pain points. Successful entrepreneurs and startups focus on understanding and empathizing with their target customers to deeply understand their pain points and offer viable and valuable solutions. By addressing these pain points, startups can build a competitive advantage, differentiate themselves in the market, and gain customer loyalty and trust. In conclusion, a pain point in the context of startup and entrepreneurship refers to a specific problem or challenge that customers or target markets face. Identifying and addressing these pain points is essential for startup success and presents opportunities for entrepreneurs to develop innovative solutions that provide value to customers.

Pareto Principle (80/20 Rule)

The Pareto Principle, also known as the 80/20 Rule, is a concept widely applied in the context of startups and entrepreneurship. It states that approximately 80% of the effects or results are derived from 20% of the causes or inputs. This principle is named after the Italian economist Vilfredo Pareto, who observed this pattern in wealth distribution, discovering that 80% of the land in Italy was owned by 20% of the population. In the context of startups, the Pareto Principle suggests that a small portion of your efforts or activities will yield a large portion of the desired outcomes. For instance, around 80% of your revenue may come from just 20% of your customers, or 80% of your problems may be caused by 20% of the issues. This principle highlights the significance of identifying and focusing on the most valuable and impactful aspects of your business.

Participatory Design

Participatory Design in the context of Startup & Entrepreneurship refers to a collaborative approach to the design and development of products, services, or systems. It involves actively involving users, stakeholders, and designers in the decision-making process, ensuring that the end result meets their needs, preferences, and expectations. Startup and entrepreneurial ventures can greatly benefit from leveraging participatory design principles and methods. By involving stakeholders and users from the early stages of development, startups can gain valuable insights and feedback that can inform the design and development process. This not only helps in creating better products or services but also reduces the risk of investing time and resources in developing something that does not align with the target market.

Patent Application Services

Patent Application Services refer to the specialized services offered to startups and entrepreneurs to navigate the complex and time-consuming process of applying for a patent. Patents are legal rights granted by the government to inventors, giving them exclusive rights to their inventions and preventing others from making, using, or selling the claimed invention for a limited period of time. In the context of startup and entrepreneurship, patent application services are crucial for protecting innovative ideas, technologies, and valuable intellectual property. These services usually involve working with patent attorneys, agents, or consultants who have expertise in patent law and the application process. The process of obtaining a patent typically involves several stages, including conducting a patent search, drafting a patent application, and filing it with the appropriate patent office. Patent application services assist startups and entrepreneurs in each of these stages, ensuring that the application is prepared correctly and meets all the requirements set by the patent office. One of the primary services provided by patent application services is conducting a patent search. This involves thoroughly researching existing patents and publications to determine if a similar invention already exists. By conducting a comprehensive search, startups can assess the patentability of their ideas and make informed decisions on the patent application process. Another key service offered is the drafting of the patent application itself. Patent attorneys or agents work closely with the inventors to understand the technical details of the invention and translate it into a comprehensive, detailed, and legally sufficient patent application. This includes describing the invention's features, functions, and advantages in a clear and concise manner, along with providing the necessary diagrams and drawings. Furthermore, patent application services assist with navigating the intricacies of patent office procedures, rules, and deadlines. They help entrepreneurs prepare and file the patent application, including responding to any office actions or rejections from the patent examiner. Overall, patent application services are vital for startups and entrepreneurs to protect their intellectual property, gain a competitive advantage, and secure the rights to their innovations. By leveraging these specialized services, startups can streamline the patent application process and ensure the highest chances of obtaining a valuable patent for their inventions.

Patent Search Tools

Patent search tools refer to software or digital platforms that help startups and entrepreneurs conduct extensive searches within patent databases to identify existing patents in a specific field or technology area. These tools are designed to assist innovators in conducting a thorough analysis of the patent landscape, ensuring that their inventions or business ideas do not infringe upon existing patents and helping them gain insights for potential areas of innovation and differentiation. The primary purpose of patent search tools is to help startups and entrepreneurs assess the novelty and potential patentability of their inventions. By searching through extensive patent databases, these tools enable entrepreneurs to identify similar or related patents that may impact their ability to secure patent protection for their own innovative ideas. This process is crucial as it helps entrepreneurs avoid potential infringement issues and legal disputes, saving them valuable time and resources. These tools typically provide various advanced search features and filters to refine and narrow down search results based on specific criteria, such as keywords, patent classifications, inventors, assignees, and publication dates. Moreover, they often incorporate data visualization and analytics capabilities to help users interpret the results and identify relevant trends or patterns within the patent landscape. In addition to searching for existing patents, some patent search tools also provide additional features that can benefit startups and entrepreneurs. For instance, these tools may offer patent monitoring capabilities to track and receive updates on recently filed or granted patents in a particular technology domain. This functionality allows innovators to stay updated on the latest developments, identify potential competitors, and uncover new opportunities for collaboration or cross-licensing. Overall, patent search tools play a crucial role in the startup and entrepreneurship ecosystem by empowering innovators to make informed decisions about their inventions and business strategies. By providing access to comprehensive patent databases and advanced search functionalities, these tools help startups and entrepreneurs navigate the complex patent landscape, minimize infringement risks, and maximize their chances of securing patent protection for their innovative ideas.

Peer-To-Peer (P2P) Lending Platforms

Peer-to-Peer (P2P) lending platforms are online financial platforms that connect individual borrowers and lenders. These platforms facilitate loans between individuals, bypassing traditional financial institutions such as banks. P2P lending platforms act as intermediaries, allowing borrowers to request loans and lenders to fund these loans directly.Startups and entrepreneurs can leverage P2P lending platforms as an alternative funding source for their businesses. P2P lending provides an opportunity for startups and entrepreneurs to access capital that may be difficult to obtain through conventional means. These platforms offer several benefits for startups: P2P lending platforms provide a simplified and streamlined loan application process. Borrowers can create profiles and submit their loan requests online. This eliminates the need for extensive paperwork and multiple visits to traditional financial institutions, saving time and effort for startups and entrepreneurs. Additionally, P2P lending offers flexible loan terms and competitive interest rates. Startups can negotiate loan amounts, repayment periods, and interest rates directly with lenders, providing more flexibility compared to traditional lenders. This can be particularly beneficial for startups that may have unique financial needs or limited credit history. Furthermore, P2P lending platforms provide access to a wider range of potential lenders. Startups and entrepreneurs can attract individual investors who may be interested in supporting innovative business ideas and earning a return on their investment. This expands the pool of available funding sources, increasing the chances of securing financing. In conclusion, P2P lending platforms offer startups and entrepreneurs an alternative avenue for obtaining funding. These platforms provide a simplified loan application process, flexible loan terms, and access to a wider range of potential lenders. By leveraging P2P lending, startups and entrepreneurs can access the capital needed to fuel their ventures and achieve their business goals.

Pestle Analysis

A PESTLE analysis is a strategic business tool used by startups and entrepreneurs to analyze and evaluate the external factors that may impact their organization. It provides a framework for understanding the macro-environment forces that can shape the success or failure of a business venture. P stands for political factors, which include government policies, regulations, and political stability. Startups need to consider how changes in political landscape can affect their operations, such as new laws or shifts in government priorities. E represents economic factors, including economic growth, inflation rates, and exchange rates. Entrepreneurs need to understand the economic conditions in the market they operate, as it can influence their pricing strategies, purchasing power of customers, and cost of resources. S stands for sociocultural factors, which encompass social and cultural aspects of the market. Entrepreneurs need to evaluate demographics, lifestyle trends, consumer attitudes, and cultural norms that influence consumer behavior and shape demand for their products or services. T stands for technological factors, focusing on technological advancements and innovations that can impact startups and entrepreneurs. Entrepreneurs need to be aware of emerging technologies, changes in communication methods, automation, and digital disruption that may require them to adapt their business models. L represents legal factors, which encompass laws and regulations that businesses must comply with. Entrepreneurs need to understand the legal environment in which they operate, such as intellectual property rights, labor laws, product safety regulations, and data protection laws. E symbolizes environmental factors, referring to ecological and environmental considerations. Startups need to consider sustainability, climate change impacts, resource scarcity, and environmental regulations that affect their operations and may present new market opportunities. By conducting a PESTLE analysis, startups and entrepreneurs can identify opportunities and threats in the external environment. This analysis helps inform strategic decision-making, risk management, and the development of business plans and marketing strategies that align with the external forces influencing their startup.

Pilot Test

A pilot test is a method used in the startup and entrepreneurship field to assess the feasibility and effectiveness of a new product, service, or idea. It involves implementing a small-scale version of the business concept in a controlled environment to gather data and make informed decisions before full-scale implementation. During a pilot test, a startup or entrepreneur aims to validate key assumptions and gather real-world feedback to refine their business model and minimize the risk of failure. This process typically involves selecting a specific target market or segment, deploying a limited version of the product or service, and closely monitoring the results.

Pitch Competition

A pitch competition is an event where startup founders and entrepreneurs present their business concepts, products, or services to a panel of judges or investors in order to secure funding, partnerships, or recognition. The purpose of a pitch competition is to showcase the potential of a startup or entrepreneurial venture and convince the judges or investors of its viability, innovation, and market potential. It is a platform for entrepreneurs to present their ideas and receive feedback, mentoring, and potential funding or investment opportunities.

Pitch Deck

A pitch deck is a brief presentation created by an entrepreneur or startup to communicate their business idea and potential to investors, potential partners, or other stakeholders. It is typically delivered in person or as a slide deck, and aims to persuade the audience to invest in or support the venture. The purpose of a pitch deck is to concisely and effectively convey the value proposition of the startup, outlining its key features, market opportunity, business model, and competitive advantage. It serves as a visual aid to support the entrepreneur's verbal pitch, providing a framework for discussing the various aspects of the business.

Pitching

A pitch is a concise presentation or proposal made by an entrepreneur to potential investors or stakeholders in order to secure funding, partnerships, or support for their startup. It is usually delivered verbally, accompanied by visual aids such as slides or a pitch deck, and aims to effectively communicate the value proposition and potential of the business. The purpose of a pitch is to capture the attention and interest of the audience, compelling them to further explore and invest in the startup. It is a crucial tool in the early stages of the entrepreneurial journey, where founders often have limited resources and need to convince others of their idea's viability. Typically, a pitch consists of several key components. Firstly, entrepreneurs must clearly define the problem or need that their startup aims to address. This involves identifying the target market and explaining why the problem is significant and not adequately solved by existing solutions. It is important to articulate the pain points and challenges faced by potential customers to emphasize the necessity and demand for the startup's solution. Secondly, the pitch should outline the entrepreneur's proposed solution and unique value proposition. This entails describing the product or service, its features, and how it effectively solves the identified problem. Presenting any intellectual property or competitive advantages, such as patents, trademarks, or proprietary technology, can help differentiate the startup from competitors and demonstrate its potential for growth and profitability. The pitch should also include a clear business model, detailing how the startup plans to generate revenue and achieve profitability. This involves outlining the target market, customer acquisition strategy, pricing strategy, and projected financials. A key aspect of the business model is the scalability and potential for expansion, as investors are often looking for startups with a significant market opportunity and the potential to achieve high returns on investment. Additionally, the pitch should highlight the startup's team and their qualifications, expertise, and experience. This serves to instill confidence in the audience, showing that the founders have the necessary skills and abilities to execute the business plan successfully. Discussing any existing partnerships, advisors, or early customers can further validate and strengthen the startup's credibility and potential for success. In summary, a pitch is an essential tool for entrepreneurs to communicate their startup's vision, value proposition, and potential to investors and other stakeholders. It requires concise and compelling storytelling, effectively conveying the problem, solution, business model, and team. A successful pitch can lead to securing funding, partnerships, or support, propelling the startup towards growth and success.

Pivot

A pivot, in the context of startup and entrepreneurship, refers to a strategic shift made by a company in response to changing market conditions or customer feedback. It involves a deliberate change in the company's business model, product offering, or target market, with the aim of improving its chances of success and achieving sustainable growth. Pivoting is often necessary for startups and entrepreneurs as they navigate the unpredictable and competitive business landscape. It allows them to adapt to unforeseen challenges, capitalize on emerging opportunities, and maximize their chances of achieving product-market fit.

Pivoting Strategy

A pivoting strategy in the context of startup and entrepreneurship refers to the process of making significant changes in a startup's business model or approach in response to market feedback, shifts in the industry, or the discovery of new opportunities. It is a strategic decision made by entrepreneurs to adapt and adjust their business plans in order to achieve sustainable growth and success. Pivoting is often necessary for startups due to the unpredictable nature of markets and the constantly evolving business landscape. It allows entrepreneurs to remain flexible and responsive to changes in consumer needs, emerging trends, or unforeseen challenges. By recognizing when the original plan is not achieving the desired outcomes, entrepreneurs can pivot to a new direction that has a higher likelihood of success.

Portfolio Company

A portfolio company refers to a startup or entrepreneurial venture that is part of an investment portfolio held by a venture capital firm, private equity company, or other types of investors. These investors typically invest in multiple companies, pooling their resources to diversify their risk and increase their chances of successful returns. Portfolio companies are chosen based on their potential for growth and profitability. Investors carefully select companies that align with their investment strategy and have the potential to yield high returns on their investment. These companies are often in the early stages of development and require additional funding to scale their operations, expand their market reach, or develop new products and services. Once a company becomes a portfolio company, it receives not only financial support but also strategic guidance and operational expertise from the investor. The investor usually takes an active role in the company's management and decision-making processes, providing valuable insights and industry connections. This involvement helps the portfolio company navigate challenges, capitalize on opportunities, and ultimately drive growth. Portfolio companies may operate in various industries, including technology, healthcare, biotech, e-commerce, and many others. The investor's role is to identify promising startups within these sectors and provide the necessary resources to help them succeed. Successful portfolio companies often go on to achieve significant milestones, such as a successful initial public offering (IPO) or acquisition, resulting in the investor reaping substantial financial gains. In summary, a portfolio company is a startup or entrepreneurial venture that is part of an investor's portfolio. These companies receive financial support and strategic guidance from the investor to fuel their growth and development. By investing in multiple companies, investors aim to diversify their risk and maximize their returns in the dynamic world of entrepreneurship and startup investments. A portfolio company refers to a startup or entrepreneurial venture that is part of an investment portfolio held by a venture capital firm, private equity company, or other types of investors. These investors typically invest in multiple companies, pooling their resources to diversify their risk and increase their chances of successful returns. Portfolio companies are chosen based on their potential for growth and profitability. Investors carefully select companies that align with their investment strategy and have the potential to yield high returns on their investment. These companies are often in the early stages of development and require additional funding to scale their operations, expand their market reach, or develop new products and services.

Portfolio Management

Portfolio management in the context of startup and entrepreneurship refers to the strategic management of a collection of investments or projects with the goal of maximizing returns and minimizing risk for a startup or entrepreneur. It involves the allocation of resources, such as financial capital, human capital, and time, in a way that optimizes the overall performance and success of the portfolio of projects or investments.

Post-Market Surveillance

Post-Market Surveillance refers to the ongoing process of monitoring and evaluating a product or service after it has been launched into the market. It involves collecting and analyzing data related to customer feedback, product performance, safety, and compliance to ensure that the product continues to meet the expectations and requirements of the target market. For startups and entrepreneurs, post-market surveillance plays a critical role in delivering a successful product or service. It enables them to gather valuable insights and make informed decisions to improve their offering, build customer loyalty, and gain a competitive edge in the market.

Post-Money Valuation

A post-money valuation is the estimated worth of a startup company after it has received external funding, typically through a funding round or investment. This valuation is determined by assessing the company's financial position, growth potential, and market competitiveness. Once a startup receives external funding, the investors provide capital in exchange for a percentage of ownership in the company. The post-money valuation is calculated by adding the external investment amount to the pre-money valuation, which is the estimated worth of the company before receiving the investment. The pre-money valuation is often based on factors such as the startup's revenue, assets, intellectual property, customer base, and market potential. However, it is important to note that early-stage startups may have limited financial information available, making the pre-money valuation more speculative and subjective. The post-money valuation is significant in the context of startups and entrepreneurship as it determines the dilution of ownership for existing shareholders and the share of ownership for new investors. This valuation also influences the terms and conditions of the investment, including the amount of equity or preferred stock allocated to investors. A higher post-money valuation indicates a larger capital infusion into the company, reflecting confidence in its future growth potential. This can attract more investors and potentially lead to additional funding opportunities. On the other hand, a lower post-money valuation may indicate a higher level of risk or lower market appetite for the company, making it more challenging to secure future funding. It is important to note that post-money valuations are not fixed or permanent. As startups evolve and grow, their value can change, influenced by factors such as market conditions, revenue growth, profitability, and industry trends. Therefore, post-money valuations serve as a snapshot in time, reflecting the perceived value of the company based on the available information and investor sentiment.

Pre-Money Valuation

A pre-money valuation, in the context of startups and entrepreneurship, refers to the estimated value of a company prior to receiving any external investment or funding. It is a valuation metric that provides a benchmark for determining how much ownership an investor would receive in exchange for their investment. Calculating the pre-money valuation involves assessing various factors such as the company's assets, intellectual property, revenue projections, market potential, and comparable valuations of similar companies. Typically, startup founders and investors negotiate the pre-money valuation during the funding round, which helps determine the investment amount and the percentage ownership the investor will hold in the company.

Pre-Seed Funding

Pre-seed funding is the initial capital raised by a startup or entrepreneur to validate and develop a business concept or idea before seeking significant investments from external sources. It is often considered the first official round of funding for a startup. The main purpose of pre-seed funding is to support the initial stages of a startup's development, which typically involve conducting market research, building a minimum viable product (MVP), and identifying potential target markets. This funding is crucial for entrepreneurs to prove the viability and feasibility of their business model and attract further investments. Pre-seed funding is usually obtained from the founders' personal savings, friends, family, and early supporters who believe in the entrepreneur's vision. It is typically a smaller amount of money compared to later-stage funding rounds, as the focus is on validating the basic business concept and gathering initial market feedback. Entrepreneurs often use pre-seed funding to refine their business plans and clarify their value proposition before pitching to angel investors or venture capitalists. This early-stage funding helps entrepreneurs reach key milestones such as developing a prototype or securing initial customers or users, which can significantly increase their chances of securing further investments. While pre-seed funding is not as common or well-known as seed funding or series A funding, it is an essential stage in the startup funding lifecycle. It provides crucial support for entrepreneurs to test their ideas, gather feedback, and build a solid foundation for future growth. In summary, pre-seed funding is the initial capital raised by startups or entrepreneurs to validate and develop their business concepts before seeking larger investments. It plays a crucial role in the early stages of a startup's development and helps entrepreneurs refine their business plans and attract further investments from angel investors or venture capitalists.

171

Pre-Seed Round Financing

Pre-Seed Round Financing refers to the initial stage of funding that a startup receives in order to develop its product or service. It is the earliest form of financing a company can secure and typically takes place during the ideation and early development stages.During the Pre-Seed Round, entrepreneurs seek capital from a variety of sources, such as angel investors, friends and family, or the founders themselves. The goal of this funding round is to help the startup achieve key milestones, such as building a prototype or conducting market research, that will increase its chances of attracting further investment in the future.

Pre-Seed Round Investor

A pre-seed round investor is an individual or group of individuals who invests in startups during their early stages of development. This type of investment occurs before the seed round, which is typically the first formal funding round for startups. The purpose of a pre-seed round is to provide the necessary capital for entrepreneurs to validate their business ideas and develop a minimum viable product (MVP). Pre-seed investors are usually high-net-worth individuals, angel investors, or early-stage venture capital firms who are willing to take significant risks in exchange for potentially high returns. The amount of capital invested in a pre-seed round is often relatively small compared to later rounds, ranging from a few thousand dollars to a few hundred thousand dollars. The funds raised in this round are typically used to conduct market research, build prototypes, hire key team members, and cover other early-stage expenses. Pre-seed investors play a crucial role in the startup ecosystem by providing the initial financial support that entrepreneurs need to turn their ideas into reality. They help founders overcome the challenges associated with starting a business, such as limited resources and a lack of track record or traction. In addition to providing capital, pre-seed investors also offer valuable expertise, mentorship, and networking opportunities to startups. They bring industry knowledge, contacts, and experience that can help founders navigate the early stages of their entrepreneurial journey. This support can be instrumental in attracting follow-on funding and accelerating the growth of the startup. Overall, a pre-seed round investor is a key player in the startup ecosystem. They are willing to take on significant risk in exchange for the potential to be part of the next big success story. Their early-stage investment and support can make a critical difference in the success of a startup, setting the foundation for future growth and development.

Pre-Seed Round

Pre-Seed round, also known as Pre-Seed funding or Pre-Seed stage, is the first formal funding stage in the startup journey. This stage occurs before the Seed round and serves as the initial injection of capital to transform an idea into a viable business model. During the Pre-Seed round, entrepreneurs approach family, friends, and sometimes angel investors to secure the necessary funds for product development, market research, and validation. Unlike later funding rounds, where startups demonstrate significant traction or revenue, Pre-Seed funding is primarily based on the potential of the idea and the capability of the founding team. The capital raised in the Pre-Seed round is typically used to build a prototype or minimum viable product (MVP), conduct market research, validate the business model, and attract potential customers or partners. This stage allows founders to refine their idea and gather initial feedback before seeking larger investments. During the Pre-Seed stage, entrepreneurs often leverage their personal networks to secure funding, as institutional investors are typically not involved at this early stage. These personal connections may include friends, family, former colleagues, or mentors who believe in the founder and their idea. The amount of funding raised in the Pre-Seed round can vary significantly depending on the startup's needs and the industry it operates in. Some startups may secure a few thousand dollars, while others may raise hundreds of thousands or even millions. It is crucial for entrepreneurs to strike a balance between raising enough capital to execute their plans and avoiding excessive dilution of their ownership stake. In conclusion, the Pre-Seed round serves as an initial injection of capital for startups to transform an idea into a viable business model. It allows founders to build a prototype, conduct market research, and validate their idea before seeking larger investments. While typically funded by personal networks, the Pre-Seed round sets the foundation for future funding rounds that will drive the growth and scalability of the startup.

Pre-Seed Stage Funding

Pre-Seed stage funding refers to the initial round of funding that a startup receives in its early stages of development. It is the earliest stage of financing a new venture, typically occurring before the startup has a finished product, established customer base, or substantial revenue. At this stage, the startup is often in the idea or concept phase and requires capital to fund research, development, and initial operations. The purpose of pre-seed funding is to enable entrepreneurs to validate their ideas, secure necessary resources, and lay the groundwork for future growth. This type of funding is typically provided by angel investors, friends and family, or incubators and accelerators. Unlike later stages of funding, such as seed or venture capital, pre-seed financing is generally smaller in scale and is used to fund the startup's initial expenses such as market research, product development, and initial marketing efforts. Pre-seed stage funding is crucial for startups as it enables them to validate their business concept and refine their strategies before seeking additional investment. This funding allows entrepreneurs to conduct market research, build a minimum viable product (MVP), and engage potential customers to gather feedback. Additionally, pre-seed funding can be used to attract a more substantial investment in the future by demonstrating progress and growth potential. Entrepreneurs seeking pre-seed funding should be prepared to demonstrate a clear understanding of their target market, competitive landscape, and unique value proposition. They should also have a well-defined business plan outlining their objectives, strategies, and financial projections. Investors are more likely to provide funding to startups with a compelling vision, a strong team, and a viable plan for growth. In conclusion, pre-seed stage funding plays a crucial role in the early development of a startup. It is the initial capital injection that enables entrepreneurs to validate their ideas, build a product, and attract future investment. This funding is essential for startups to establish a strong foundation and increase their chances of success in the highly competitive startup ecosystem.

Pre-Seed Stage Investment Management And Planning

Pre-Seed Stage Investment Management and Planning in the context of Startup and Entrepreneurship refers to the strategic process of managing and planning investments during the earliest stages of a startup's development. This stage typically occurs before any product development or significant market traction has occurred. It encompasses activities aimed at securing initial funding, defining the startup's vision and goals, and establishing a solid foundation for future growth. During the Pre-Seed Stage, entrepreneurs must focus on identifying and securing initial sources of funding. This may involve pitching to angel investors, venture capitalists, or even friends and family. The investment management aspect of this stage involves effectively allocating these funds to ensure the startup can cover essential expenses like product development, marketing, and hiring key team members. Additionally, Pre-Seed Stage Investment Management and Planning also involves setting clear objectives, strategy, and milestones for the startup. This includes defining the startup's mission, vision, and values, as well as conducting market research to identify potential target customers and competitors. Entrepreneurs must also develop a comprehensive business plan that outlines the startup's value proposition, revenue model, and go-to-market strategy. Furthermore, this stage requires careful financial planning and budgeting to ensure adequate resources are allocated for different activities and to prevent unnecessary expenditures. Entrepreneurs must prioritize their spending to minimize risks and maximize the chances of success. This may involve making tough decisions about which expenses are necessary, outsourcing tasks to reduce costs, or seeking partnerships and collaborations to leverage resources. Overall, Pre-Seed Stage Investment Management and Planning are critical for startups as it provides a strategic framework for securing initial funding, defining the startup's vision and goals, and laying a solid foundation for future growth. Effective management and planning during this stage can significantly improve a startup's chances of success by ensuring the optimal utilization of resources and setting the stage for subsequent stages of funding and growth opportunities.

Pre-Seed Stage Investment Management

Pre-Seed Stage Investment Management refers to the activities and strategies utilized by investors to support early-stage startups and entrepreneurs in the initial phases of their businesses. The pre-seed stage is the earliest stage of a startup, where the founding team is still developing the business idea, conducting market research, and building a prototype or minimum viable product (MVP). At this stage, the company may not generate any revenue and typically lacks a proven business model. Investment management during the pre-seed stage is crucial for startups as it can provide them with the necessary financial resources, guidance, and connections needed to navigate the early challenges and establish a strong foundation. Pre-seed investors support startups by providing funding in exchange for equity ownership, enabling them to develop their product, validate their market fit, and prepare for subsequent funding rounds.

Pre-Seed Stage Investment Planning And Management

Pre-seed stage investment planning and management refers to the process of strategizing and overseeing the initial funding and operational activities of a startup or entrepreneurial venture. This stage typically occurs before the startup has obtained significant external funding or generated substantial revenue. The objective of pre-seed stage investment planning and management is to secure the necessary resources and set a strong foundation for the startup to progress towards its goals and milestones. During this stage, the entrepreneur or founding team is primarily focused on refining their business idea, validating the market potential, and building a minimum viable product (MVP) or prototype. Key activities in pre-seed stage investment planning and management include: 1. Business Planning: Startup founders need to create a comprehensive business plan that outlines their value proposition, target market, revenue model, and growth strategy. This plan serves as a roadmap to guide their activities and attract potential investors. 2. Financial Management: Entrepreneurs must carefully manage their financial resources during the pre-seed stage. This includes estimating costs, projecting revenues, and creating a budget to ensure that the startup can operate efficiently with limited funding. 3. Investor Relations: Startups in the pre-seed stage often rely on angel investors, friends, and family for funding. Entrepreneurs must build relationships with potential investors, present their business plan, and negotiate the terms of investment to secure the necessary capital. 4. Market Validation: Before scaling their operations, startups must validate their target market and ensure that there is sufficient demand for their product or service. This may involve conducting market research, gathering customer feedback, and iterating on their product or go-to-market strategy. 5. Team Building: As the startup grows, founders may need to recruit additional team members with specialized skills to support the development and execution of their business plan. Effective pre-seed stage investment planning involves identifying the key talents required and attracting them to join the team. Overall, pre-seed stage investment planning and management is crucial for startups to establish a solid foundation and secure the resources needed for future growth. It involves careful financial management, market validation, investor relations, and team building to position the startup for success in subsequent stages of fundraising and expansion.

Pre-Seed Stage Investment Planning

Pre-seed stage investment planning refers to the process of strategically allocating financial resources and securing funding for a startup venture in its earliest stages of development. It involves identifying and evaluating potential investment opportunities, creating a funding roadmap, and developing a comprehensive plan to secure the necessary capital to launch and grow the business.The pre-seed stage is one of the initial phases in a startup's journey, typically occurring before the company has a working prototype or generates any significant revenue. During this stage, entrepreneurs often rely on their personal savings or contributions from friends and family to fund initial operations. However, as the startup progresses and requires additional capital to support product development, market research, and operational expenses, seeking external investment becomes crucial.The primary objective of pre-seed stage investment planning is to attract external investors who are willing to provide funding in exchange for equity or future returns. These investors may include angel investors, venture capitalists, or early-stage funds, who are typically looking for high-potential startups with innovative ideas and scalable business models.To effectively plan for pre-seed stage investment, entrepreneurs need to conduct thorough market research, assess competitive landscapes, and clearly define their business goals and strategies. This involves identifying target markets, understanding customer needs, and determining the unique value proposition of the startup. By developing a compelling business plan and pitch deck, entrepreneurs can effectively communicate their vision, potential market opportunities, and growth projections to potential investors.In addition to attracting investors, pre-seed stage investment planning also involves exploring alternative funding sources such as grants, incubators, and crowdfunding platforms. These options can provide startups with non-equity funding or additional support services to accelerate their growth and increase their chances of attracting external investment.In summary, pre-seed stage investment planning is a critical process for startups seeking to secure funding and develop a strong foundation for growth. By strategically allocating financial resources and seeking external investment, entrepreneurs can increase their chances of success and lay the groundwork for future stages of development.

Pre-Seed Stage Investment

Pre-Seed Stage Investment refers to the initial round of funding that a startup receives from outside investors or angel investors in order to develop and validate its business idea before any product or service has been developed. This stage typically occurs before the startup has generated any revenue or obtained any significant customer traction. During the pre-seed stage, entrepreneurs and startup founders often rely on personal savings, loans, or assistance from friends and family to bootstrap their business ideas and create a prototype or minimum viable product (MVP) to demonstrate the potential of their concept. However, in many cases, these personal resources may not be sufficient to fully develop the idea or attract further investment. Pre-seed stage investment plays a critical role in providing the necessary capital to help startups bridge this gap between the initial concept and product development stage. Investors in this stage typically provide funds to cover the costs associated with market research, product validation, hiring key team members, developing a business plan, and building out the initial infrastructure. Unlike later stage investments, pre-seed investments are often smaller in size and come with higher risk due to the significant uncertainties associated with early-stage startups. In return for their investment, pre-seed investors typically receive equity or convertible notes, which entitle them to a percentage of ownership in the startup. The primary objective of pre-seed stage investment is to help startups reach a point where they are ready for seed stage investment or further funding. The funds raised during this stage are typically used to refine and validate the startup's business model, attract early adopters or beta customers, conduct market research, develop a minimum viable product, and build a strong founding team. In summary, pre-seed stage investment serves as a crucial catalyst for early-stage startups by providing the initial capital needed to transform their ideas into viable businesses. It allows entrepreneurs to build prototypes, validate their business models, and attract further investment to scale and grow their startups.

Pre-Seed Stage Investor Relations

Pre-Seed Stage Investor Relations refers to the management and communication activities between a startup and potential investors during the initial phase of its development. It focuses on building and maintaining relationships with investors who may provide funding to the startup in the pre-seed stage, which is the earliest phase of a startup's life cycle. During this stage, entrepreneurs and startup founders seek funding to develop or refine their business idea, build a prototype, or conduct market research. Pre-seed stage investors typically include angel investors, friends and family, and early-stage venture capital firms. These investors are willing to take high risks in exchange for potential high returns on their investments. The primary objective of pre-seed stage investor relations is to attract and secure funding for the startup. This involves various activities, such as creating a compelling investment proposition, preparing an investor pitch deck, and networking with potential investors. The entrepreneur or startup founder must effectively communicate their vision, business model, market potential, and growth strategies to capture the interest and confidence of investors. In addition to attracting funding, pre-seed stage investor relations also involve ongoing communication and relationship management with existing investors. This includes providing regular updates on the startup's progress, financial performance, and future plans. Effective investor relations can help entrepreneurs build trust and credibility, increasing the likelihood of continued support and potential follow-on investments. Overall, pre-seed stage investor relations play a crucial role in the success of a startup. It requires effective communication, networking, and relationship management skills. By engaging with potential investors and maintaining strong relationships with existing investors, startups can secure the necessary funding to grow and develop their businesses.

Pre-Seed Stage Investor

A pre-seed stage investor is an individual or organization that provides financial backing to startups and entrepreneurs in the earliest stages of their development. This type of investor typically invests before or at the very beginning of a company's fundraising journey, often in exchange for equity or ownership stakes in the business. Unlike other types of investors, such as angel investors or venture capitalists, pre-seed stage investors are focused specifically on supporting startups in their initial stages of formation. This means that they are willing to take on higher levels of risk, as these companies are often still in the ideation or product development phase. The role of a pre-seed stage investor goes beyond just providing funds. They often bring valuable expertise, mentorship, and connections to the table, helping entrepreneurs refine their business models, develop their products, and navigate the complexities of the startup ecosystem. Pre-seed stage investors evaluate startup opportunities based on a variety of factors, such as the uniqueness of the concept, the potential market size, the strength of the team, and the scalability of the business model. They aim to identify startups with high growth potential and provide them with the necessary resources to succeed. Typically, the amount of funding provided by a pre-seed stage investor is relatively small compared to later-stage investors, as the main objective at this stage is to help startups get off the ground and reach key milestones, such as building a prototype or securing initial customers. In summary, pre-seed stage investors play a crucial role in the startup ecosystem by providing early-stage funding and support to entrepreneurs. They are willing to take on higher risks and actively participate in the growth and development of the startups they invest in. Their contribution helps turn ideas into viable businesses and lays the foundation for future financing rounds.

Pre-Seed Stage

The pre-seed stage in the context of startup and entrepreneurship refers to the initial phase of a startup before it officially begins operations or generates any revenue. It is the earliest stage of the startup journey, where entrepreneurs and founders typically focus on developing and validating their business idea, gathering resources, and preparing for future rounds of funding.In the pre-seed stage, entrepreneurs often work on fine-tuning their business concept and conducting market research to identify their target customers, assess competition, and validate their product or service offering. This stage involves brainstorming, ideation, and feasibility studies to determine the viability of the startup idea.During the pre-seed stage, entrepreneurs also lay the groundwork for their startup by assembling a team of individuals with complementary skills and expertise who are dedicated to bringing the business idea to life. This includes finding co-founders, key employees, advisors, and potential partners who can contribute to the development and growth of the startup.Another essential aspect of the pre-seed stage is raising capital. While startups at this stage generally do not have a proven track record or revenue, entrepreneurs seek funding to cover initial expenses such as product development, market research, and building a minimum viable product (MVP). Funding sources for the pre-seed stage often come from personal savings, friends and family, angel investors, or early-stage venture capitalists who are willing to invest in promising startups with high growth potential.In summary, the pre-seed stage is the first phase of a startup's journey, where entrepreneurs focus on validating their business idea, assembling a team, and securing initial funding. It is a critical stage that sets the foundation for future growth and success.

Preferred Return

A preferred return, in the context of startup and entrepreneurship, refers to a specific type of financial arrangement between investors and entrepreneurs. When a startup seeks funding from investors, they may negotiate a preferred return as part of the investment terms. A preferred return guarantees that investors will receive a certain rate of return on their investment before any other distributions or profits are shared with other stakeholders. Under a preferred return structure, investors are entitled to receive their initial investment plus a predetermined percentage of profits or revenue generated by the startup, typically on an annual basis. This percentage is often set higher than market rates to compensate investors for taking on the risk associated with early-stage investments. The preferred return is calculated based on the investor's initial investment amount, which serves as the principal. For example, if an investor invested $100,000 with a preferred return of 8%, they would be entitled to receive $8,000 per year before any profits are shared with other stakeholders. In the event that the startup fails to generate sufficient profits to cover the preferred return, the unpaid portion accumulates as a deficit. This deficit must be repaid to investors once the startup becomes profitable or is sold. A preferred return can be seen as a way for investors to minimize their risk and ensure a baseline return on their investment. It provides a level of financial security and incentivizes investors to support early-stage startups despite the inherent risks involved. From an entrepreneur's perspective, offering a preferred return may attract more investors and help secure funding for their startup. However, it also means that a portion of the profits generated by the business will be allocated to investors before being distributed to the entrepreneurs or other stakeholders. In conclusion, a preferred return is a financial mechanism that guarantees investors a specified rate of return on their investment, ensuring they receive a certain share of profits or revenue before other stakeholders. It is a common feature in startup funding and provides investors with added protection and incentivizes them to support early-stage ventures.

Preferred Stock

Preferred stock refers to a type of equity security commonly used in the context of startup and entrepreneurship. It represents a form of ownership in a company, giving holders a claim on the company's assets and earnings ahead of common stockholders in the event of liquidation. However, unlike common stock, preferred stock typically does not carry voting rights. As the name suggests, preferred stockholders have preferences over common stockholders in certain aspects. One such preference is the payment of dividends. Preferred stockholders have a higher priority when it comes to receiving dividends, meaning that they are entitled to a fixed dividend payment before any dividends are distributed to common stockholders. This fixed dividend rate is usually stated as a percentage of the preferred stock's par value. Furthermore, in the event of liquidation, preferred stockholders have a priority claim over common stockholders when it comes to receiving the company's assets. They have the right to be repaid their initial investment, often referred to as the liquidation preference, before common stockholders can receive any remaining assets. Preferred stock is often attractive to investors due to its combination of debt and equity characteristics. It offers a fixed dividend payment, providing investors with a regular income stream, while also providing the potential for capital appreciation if the company's value increases. However, it lacks the potential for significant gains typically associated with common stock ownership. In startup and entrepreneurial contexts, preferred stock can be used as a means of raising capital. Companies can issue preferred stock to investors, allowing them to invest in the company and become part-owners. This can be an appealing option for startups as it does not require the immediate repayment of the invested capital, unlike debt financing options such as loans. In summary, preferred stock is a type of equity security that grants holders certain preferences over common stockholders, including priority for dividend payments and claims on the company's assets in case of liquidation. Its combination of debt-like characteristics, such as fixed dividends, and equity-like potential for capital appreciation makes it an attractive option for investors in the startup and entrepreneurship space.

Private Equity

Private equity refers to an investment strategy where funds are raised from institutional investors, high-net-worth individuals, and other financial institutions to invest in privately-owned companies. In the context of startup and entrepreneurship, private equity plays a crucial role in providing capital and support to early-stage and high-growth companies. Private equity firms typically invest in startups that have the potential for strong financial returns. These firms usually take a minority or majority ownership stake in the company and actively participate in its management and strategic decisions. The goal of private equity investment is to help the startup scale and grow rapidly, ultimately generating substantial profits for both the investors and the entrepreneurs.

Private Investment In Public Equity (PIPE)

Private Investment in Public Equity (PIPE) refers to a financing method commonly utilized in the context of startups and entrepreneurship. It involves the sale of shares or other securities by a publicly-traded company to private investors, including accredited investors and institutional investors. Startups and entrepreneurs often seek private investment to raise capital for various purposes, such as expanding their operations, developing new products or services, or funding research and development. PIPE transactions offer an alternative source of funding by allowing these companies to access private capital markets rather than relying solely on traditional avenues like venture capital or bank loans.

Private Placement Memorandum (PPM)

A Private Placement Memorandum (PPM) is a legal document that is used in the context of startup and entrepreneurship to raise capital from private investors. It serves as a detailed disclosure document that provides potential investors with information about the investment opportunity and helps them make informed decisions. The PPM outlines important information about the startup, such as its business model, financial projections, the management team, and any potential risks associated with the investment. It is a key component of the fundraising process and is typically used for larger rounds of financing, such as a Series A, B, or C funding.

Private Placement Offering

A private placement offering is a fundraising method commonly utilized by startups and entrepreneurs to secure financing for their business ventures. It involves offering securities, such as stocks or bonds, to a select group of accredited investors, typically institutional investors or high-net-worth individuals. Unlike public offerings, which are open to the general public, private placements are considered exempt from registration with regulatory authorities like the Securities and Exchange Commission (SEC) in the United States. This exemption allows startups and entrepreneurs to avoid certain compliance requirements and costs associated with a public offering.

Pro Rata Participation

Pro rata participation is a concept that is commonly used in the context of startup and entrepreneurship to determine how investors will share in the proceeds of a financing round or an exit event. It refers to the proportional allocation of shares or returns based on the amount of capital invested by each party. When a startup raises funding from investors, they typically issue shares or equity in exchange for the capital. Pro rata participation ensures that existing shareholders have the opportunity to maintain their ownership percentage in the company by allowing them the right to invest additional capital in subsequent financing rounds. By exercising their pro rata rights, existing investors can prevent their ownership from being diluted by new investors. For example, let's say a startup has three investors: Investor A, Investor B, and Investor C. Each investor has initially invested $100,000 for a total of $300,000. The company decides to raise another round of funding for $200,000, and all three investors have pro rata rights. If Investor A decides to exercise their pro rata rights, they will contribute an additional $66,667 to maintain their ownership percentage. The same applies to Investor B and Investor C. In the event of an exit, such as an acquisition or an IPO, pro rata participation determines how the proceeds will be distributed among the shareholders. Investors with pro rata participation rights will receive a proportionate share of the exit proceeds based on their ownership percentage in the company. This ensures that investors who have provided more capital have a greater stake in the returns generated by the startup. Pro rata participation is an important mechanism for investors to protect their ownership and maintain their proportional share of the company's equity or returns. It provides them with the flexibility to invest more capital in subsequent financing rounds and ensures that they are adequately compensated in the event of an exit. This concept is crucial in attracting and retaining investors in the highly competitive startup ecosystem, as it promotes fairness and transparency in the distribution of financial gains.

Pro Rata Rights

Pro rata rights in the context of startup and entrepreneurship refer to the rights that allow existing shareholders to maintain their ownership percentage in a company by being given the opportunity to invest in future rounds of financing on a pro rata basis. These rights are typically included in the terms of preferred stock agreements and give the existing shareholders the option to purchase additional shares of the company's stock at the same price and terms as the new investors. By exercising their pro rata rights, shareholders can avoid dilution of their ownership stake as the company raises additional capital.

Product Adoption

Product adoption in the context of startup and entrepreneurship refers to the process by which individuals and businesses adopt a new product or service offered by a startup or entrepreneur. It involves customers becoming aware of a product, understanding its value proposition, and making a decision to use or purchase it. In the early stages of a startup, product adoption is crucial for its success and growth. It is the key driver of revenue generation and market penetration. The level of product adoption can determine the viability and sustainability of a startup in the long run.

Product Design Sprints

A Product Design Sprint is a structured framework used by startups and entrepreneurs to quickly validate and iterate on product ideas. It is a time-bound process that allows teams to rapidly prototype, test, and gather user feedback in order to make informed decisions about product development. The purpose of a Product Design Sprint is to minimize risk and maximize learning in the early stages of product development. It helps startups and entrepreneurs validate their assumptions, identify potential problems, and make necessary adjustments before investing significant time and resources into building a product. The process typically involves a cross-functional team consisting of designers, developers, product managers, and other key stakeholders. It is conducted over a period of five days, with each day dedicated to a specific phase of the sprint. Day 1: Understanding - The team begins by aligning on the problem they are trying to solve and gaining a deep understanding of the target audience. They also explore potential solutions and generate various concepts through brainstorming sessions. Day 2: Diverge - The team sketches multiple solutions and explores different possibilities. They prioritize ideas and select the most promising ones to move forward with. Day 3: Decide - The team reviews and critiques the sketched solutions. They make decisions about which ideas to pursue and create a storyboard to define the user flow and interactions. Day 4: Prototype - Using the storyboard as a guide, the team creates a high-fidelity prototype of the product. This prototype is a simulation of the final product and should be realistic enough to test with potential users. Day 5: Validate - The team conducts user testing with the prototype, gathering feedback and insights from real users. They use this feedback to iterate on the design and make improvements. By the end of the five-day sprint, the team should have a clearer understanding of their users' needs and preferences. They will have validated or invalidated their assumptions and have a solid foundation for further product development. Overall, a Product Design Sprint is a valuable tool for startups and entrepreneurs to accelerate the product development process. It allows them to quickly test and validate ideas, reduce the risk of failure, and ultimately increase the chances of building a successful product.

Product Development Cycle

The product development cycle in the context of startups and entrepreneurship refers to the process of creating, refining, and bringing a new product or service to market. It encompasses the various stages involved in identifying market opportunities, designing and developing the product, testing and validating its market fit, and finally launching and scaling the product. The first stage of the product development cycle is the ideation phase. This involves identifying a problem or opportunity in the market that the product aims to address. Entrepreneurs conduct market research, analyze customer needs, and brainstorm ideas to come up with a concept for their product. Once an idea is generated, it needs to be evaluated for its feasibility and potential demand. The next stage is the design and development phase. Here, entrepreneurs translate the product concept into a tangible design. They create prototypes, wireframes, or beta versions to get feedback and iterate on the design. This stage also involves engineering and manufacturing considerations, where the product is refined and optimized for production. After the design and development phase, the testing and validation stage begins. This involves gathering feedback from potential customers or target market segments. Entrepreneurs conduct surveys, interviews, or focus groups to understand customer preferences, pain points, and expectations. This feedback helps in further refining and improving the product before taking it to market. Finally, the product is ready for the launch and scale stage. This involves creating a marketing and sales strategy, setting up distribution channels, and executing a go-to-market plan. Entrepreneurs focus on building brand awareness, acquiring customers, and generating revenue. As the product gains traction, entrepreneurs continuously gather customer feedback and make necessary adjustments or updates to meet evolving market needs.

Product Development

Product Development refers to the process of creating, designing, and introducing a new product or service into the market. It embodies the entire journey from the initial idea to the final product, incorporating various stages such as research, planning, development, testing, and launching. For startups and entrepreneurs, product development plays a crucial role in bringing their innovative ideas to life and turning them into viable and marketable products or services. It is a continuous and iterative process that aims to meet customer needs, enhance user experience, and achieve business objectives.

Product Fit

Product Fit refers to the level of alignment between a startup's product or service and the needs of its target market. It is a critical aspect of startup success, as a strong product fit helps to ensure that the product or service is able to effectively meet customer demands and preferences. Achieving product fit requires a deep understanding of the target market and the pain points that customers are experiencing. Startups must conduct thorough market research to identify the specific needs and desires of their target audience. This includes gathering data on customer preferences, behavior patterns, and existing solutions in the market. Once the target market has been identified and their needs have been analyzed, startups can begin developing a product or service that is tailored to meet those needs. This involves creating a value proposition that clearly communicates the unique benefits and features of the product. Additionally, startups must ensure that their product is superior to existing solutions in the market, either by offering better functionality, lower cost, or a combination of both. To validate product fit, startups often engage in customer discovery and validation processes. This involves conducting user interviews, focus groups, and alpha/beta testing to gather feedback and insights from potential customers. By involving the target market in the development process, startups can refine their product to better suit customer needs and preferences. Product fit is not a one-time accomplishment, but an ongoing process. As startups grow and evolve, they must continuously adapt their product to ensure that it remains relevant and valuable to customers. This may involve introducing new features, improving usability, or expanding the product's capabilities to address emerging market trends. In conclusion, product fit is a fundamental concept in the startup ecosystem. It represents the degree to which a startup's product or service aligns with the needs of its target market. By achieving a strong product fit, startups increase their chances of success and longevity in the market.

Product Hunt

Product Hunt is a platform that serves as a discovery platform for new products and startups in the field of entrepreneurship. It allows entrepreneurs to showcase their products and connect with potential investors, customers, and early adopters. The platform consists of a website and mobile app where users can browse through a curated list of products, vote for their favorites, and leave feedback. Product Hunt was founded in 2013 by Ryan Hoover and is based in San Francisco, California. It has grown to become one of the go-to platforms for startup enthusiasts, investors, and tech professionals looking for the next big thing. The platform is known for its highly engaged community of early adopters who actively participate in discussions, provide feedback, and help shape the future of the products listed on the platform. For startups and entrepreneurs, Product Hunt offers a unique opportunity to gain visibility and exposure for their products. By listing their products on the platform, entrepreneurs can reach a wider audience and attract potential customers and investors who are actively looking for new and innovative solutions. The voting system on Product Hunt allows products to gain traction and rise to the top of the curated list, increasing their chances of getting noticed by influential individuals and companies in the startup ecosystem. In addition to showcasing products, Product Hunt also features a community section where users can engage in discussions, ask questions, and seek advice from fellow entrepreneurs and experts. This fosters a sense of collaboration and knowledge sharing among the startup community. Entrepreneurs can leverage this feature to network, learn from others, and gain valuable insights into the challenges and opportunities in the startup world. Overall, Product Hunt serves as a launchpad for startups and entrepreneurs, enabling them to gain exposure, connect with potential stakeholders, and receive feedback from a highly engaged community. It has become an essential tool in the startup ecosystem, providing a platform for discovery, discussion, and growth.

Product Launch

A product launch refers to the process of introducing a new product into the market by a startup or an entrepreneur. It is a critical milestone in the development and growth of a company, as it represents the culmination of months or even years of effort in designing, manufacturing, and refining the product. The aim of a product launch is to create awareness, generate excitement, and ultimately drive sales of the new product. During a product launch, the startup or entrepreneur strategically plans and executes various marketing and promotional activities to create a buzz and attract the target customers. These activities may include press releases, media coverage, social media campaigns, influencer partnerships, and events such as product demos or launch parties. The goal is to capture the attention and interest of potential customers, investors, and industry stakeholders. Aside from marketing efforts, a successful product launch also involves meticulous planning and execution of other operational aspects. This includes ensuring that the product is ready for sale, with adequate inventory, pricing, packaging, and distribution channels in place. The startup or entrepreneur must also consider post-launch support such as customer service, technical troubleshooting, and continuous product improvement. Timing is crucial in a product launch. Startups and entrepreneurs carefully choose the right moment to introduce their product, considering factors such as market trends, competitor activity, and customer demand. By launching at the opportune time, they can gain a competitive edge and maximize their chances of success. A successful product launch can have significant positive impacts on a startup or entrepreneur. It can help establish credibility, build brand recognition, attract investors, and drive revenue growth. However, a poorly executed product launch can have adverse effects, including wasted resources, negative publicity, and missed market opportunities. In summary, a product launch is a crucial event for startups and entrepreneurs, symbolizing the introduction of their new product into the market. It involves strategic marketing efforts, operational planning, and careful timing to create awareness, excitement, and sales among the target customers. A successful product launch can propel the growth and success of a startup or entrepreneur, while a poorly executed one can lead to negative consequences.

Product Life Cycle Management (PLM)

Product Life Cycle Management (PLM) is a strategic process that aims to efficiently manage the entire lifespan of a product, from its conception to its withdrawal from the market. This process involves the continuous analysis, planning, and optimization of all aspects related to the product, including its design, development, production, marketing, and customer support. PLM plays a crucial role in the success of startups and entrepreneurship by enabling them to effectively navigate the challenges associated with product development, launch, growth, and eventual decline. At the startup stage, PLM helps entrepreneurs in accurately defining the target market and understanding the needs and preferences of potential customers. By conducting thorough market research and gathering valuable feedback, entrepreneurs can identify gaps in the market and develop innovative products that meet the demands of their target audience. PLM also involves careful planning and resource allocation to ensure timely and cost-effective product development. Startups can leverage PLM tools and techniques to streamline their design, prototyping, and manufacturing processes, thereby minimizing time-to-market and maximizing their competitive advantage. During the growth stage, PLM assists startups in scaling up their operations and meeting the increasing demand for their products. Entrepreneurs can use PLM to optimize their supply chain management, improve production efficiency, and enhance the quality and reliability of their products. By monitoring and analyzing key performance indicators, startups can identify areas for improvement and implement necessary changes to stay ahead of the competition. PLM also helps in effectively managing product variations and customization options to cater to diverse customer preferences. As products reach the maturity stage, PLM enables entrepreneurs to extend their product lifespan and maintain market share. By continuously innovating and introducing product enhancements, startups can counter the threat of obsolescence and keep their offerings relevant in a dynamic market. PLM facilitates efficient product lifecycle planning and assists in making informed decisions, such as when and how to introduce product line extensions or diversify into new markets. In the decline stage, PLM plays a crucial role in the orderly withdrawal of products from the market. Entrepreneurs can utilize PLM to manage inventory, optimize pricing strategies, and transition customers to newer products or alternatives. By effectively managing the decline phase, startups can minimize losses and reallocate resources towards new product development or other growth opportunities.

Product Life Cycle

The product life cycle is a concept in the context of startup and entrepreneurship which refers to the stages that a product goes through from its introduction to the market to its eventual decline and discontinuation. It is a useful framework for entrepreneurs and startups to understand and navigate the different phases that their product will go through. The first stage of the product life cycle is the introduction stage. During this phase, the product is launched and enters the market for the first time. The focus is on building awareness and generating initial sales. This stage is often characterized by high costs and limited profits as the startup invests in marketing and distribution to establish a customer base. The second stage is the growth stage. At this point, the product has gained traction in the market and sales are increasing. The focus shifts towards expanding market share and reaching a wider audience. In this stage, the startup may also face increased competition as other companies recognize the product's success. It is crucial for entrepreneurs to capitalize on the growth stage by scaling their operations and maximizing sales. In the third stage, the product enters the maturity stage. Sales growth starts to slow down as the product reaches its peak market penetration. The competition intensifies, and pricing may become more competitive. During this stage, entrepreneurs must focus on differentiating their product from competitors and maintaining customer loyalty. They may also consider introducing product variations or new features to prolong the product's life cycle. The final stage is the decline stage. Sales start to decline as the product becomes outdated or replaced by newer innovations. At this point, the startup must decide whether to continue investing in the product or discontinue it. If the product's decline is inevitable, entrepreneurs can explore options such as selling off remaining inventory or repurposing the product for a different market.

Product Lifecycle Management (PLM)

Product Lifecycle Management (PLM) refers to the strategic and systematic management of a product throughout its entire lifecycle, from ideation to disposal. In the context of startup and entrepreneurship, PLM plays a crucial role in ensuring the successful development, commercialization, and sustainability of a product or service. At its core, PLM involves the comprehensive management and integration of data, processes, and people across different stages of a product's lifecycle. It encompasses various dimensions, including product design, engineering, manufacturing, supply chain management, marketing, sales, and customer service. By effectively managing these aspects, PLM enables startups and entrepreneurs to optimize their resources, minimize costs, streamline operations, and maximize profitability. PLM begins with the ideation and conceptualization phase, where entrepreneurs identify potential opportunities and develop ideas for new products or enhancements to existing ones. It then progresses to the design and development stage, where detailed specifications and prototypes are created. This phase involves collaboration among designers, engineers, and other stakeholders to ensure the product meets customer needs and market demands. PLM facilitates efficient communication among team members, tracks design iterations, and manages documentation to ensure accuracy and adherence to specifications. Once the product design is finalized, PLM facilitates the smooth transition to the manufacturing phase. It helps coordinate the production processes, manage the sourcing of raw materials, monitor quality control procedures, and track inventory levels. By effectively managing these activities, PLM helps startups and entrepreneurs optimize their manufacturing operations and ensure timely delivery of products to customers. PLM also plays a pivotal role in the marketing and sales of a product. It provides a centralized platform for managing marketing campaigns, tracking customer feedback, and analyzing market data. By leveraging PLM, startups can gain valuable insights into customer preferences, identify market trends, and tailor their marketing strategies accordingly. Furthermore, PLM enables efficient after-sales service and support, allowing entrepreneurs to address customer concerns and gain customer loyalty. Finally, PLM encompasses the end-of-life phase, where products reach the end of their lifecycle or are phased out. This involves managing product discontinuation, disposal, and potential replacements or upgrades. Proper management of this stage ensures the efficient use of resources and minimizes environmental impact.

Product Lifecycle

The product lifecycle refers to the stages that a product goes through from its introduction to its eventual decline. It is a concept commonly used in the context of startups and entrepreneurship

182

to understand the progression of a product in the market and inform strategic decisions. The lifecycle is typically divided into four distinct stages: introduction, growth, maturity, and decline. The introduction stage is the initial phase when a product is introduced to the market. During this stage, the product is new and unfamiliar to consumers, and the company's primary focus is on creating awareness and generating demand. Startups and entrepreneurs often face numerous challenges at this stage, such as building brand recognition, attracting early customers, and refining the product based on initial feedback. The growth stage is characterized by a rapid increase in sales and market acceptance. Positive word-of-mouth, expanding distribution channels, and improved product features contribute to the product's growth. Startups and entrepreneurs in this stage need to focus on scaling their operations, expanding their customer base, and enhancing their marketing efforts to take advantage of the growing demand. The maturity stage is the longest and most stable phase of the product lifecycle. At this point, the product has reached its peak level of market acceptance, and competition may become more intense. Startups and entrepreneurs in the maturity stage often face the challenge of maintaining market share and product differentiation. They may need to introduce new features, explore new target markets, or offer competitive pricing to stay relevant and prolong the maturity stage. The decline stage marks the gradual decrease in sales and market interest for a product. This decline can be due to technological advancements, changing consumer preferences, or the emergence of newer and better alternatives. Startups and entrepreneurs in this stage need to carefully evaluate their options, whether to invest in product rejuvenation, diversify into new markets, or gracefully exit the market. The decline stage also presents opportunities for innovation and reinvention by identifying and addressing unmet needs. In conclusion, understanding the product lifecycle is crucial for startups and entrepreneurs to navigate the various stages of a product's lifespan. By recognizing which stage their product is in and adapting their strategies accordingly, they can maximize their chances of success and sustain their business in a dynamic market environment.

Product Manager

A Product Manager is a key role in the world of startups and entrepreneurship. This position is responsible for assessing market needs, defining product requirements, and overseeing the development and launch of new products. Product Managers must closely collaborate with stakeholders such as customers, designers, engineers, and executives to ensure that the product meets market demands and aligns with the overall business strategy. They must have a deep understanding of the market, competitors, and customer needs to make informed decisions and prioritize product features and enhancements.

Product Roadmap

A product roadmap is a strategic document that outlines the direction and vision for a product or service offered by a startup or entrepreneurship venture. It provides a high-level plan of action, detailing the goals and key milestones that the company aims to achieve over a specified time frame. The product roadmap serves as a blueprint for the development and growth of the product, guiding the decision-making process and setting priorities for the startup. It serves as a communication tool, enabling the entire team to understand the product strategy and align their efforts towards common objectives.

Product Roadmapping Tools

Product roadmapping tools are essential resources for startups and entrepreneurs to plan, visualize, and communicate the strategic direction and future development of their products or services. These tools enable businesses to align their internal and external stakeholders, such as developers, designers, marketers, investors, and customers, towards a common vision and set clear priorities for development efforts. By utilizing a product roadmapping tool, startups and entrepreneurs can prioritize and allocate resources efficiently, ensuring that their development efforts are focused on delivering the most value to their target market. These tools facilitate the creation of a roadmap, which serves as a strategic plan that outlines the product's evolution over time, including key milestones, features, and enhancements. Product roadmapping tools typically allow users to visually represent their roadmap using various formats, such as timelines, Gantt charts, or swimlanes. This visual representation provides a clear and concise overview of the product's long-term vision, as well as its short-term objectives and deliverables.

It helps entrepreneurs and their teams to visualize the larger picture and track progress as they work towards their goals. Furthermore, these tools enable startups and entrepreneurs to effectively communicate their product strategy to internal teams and external stakeholders. By sharing the roadmap with team members, everyone can understand the direction of the product and their role in achieving its goals. Additionally, by sharing the roadmap with external stakeholders, such as investors or customers, entrepreneurs can garner support and feedback that can further refine their product strategy. Overall, product roadmapping tools are vital for startups and entrepreneurs as they enable efficient resource allocation, strategic planning, and effective communication. These tools help align stakeholders, track progress, and ensure that the product's development is focused on delivering maximum value to the target market. By utilizing these tools, startups and entrepreneurs can navigate the complex journey of product development and increase their chances of success in the highly competitive startup ecosystem.

Product-Market Fit Validation

Product-market fit validation is a crucial process for startups and entrepreneurs to determine if their product or service satisfies the needs and demands of a target market. It involves gathering feedback and data to assess whether the product solves a problem and meets customer requirements. This validation process begins with identifying the target market and understanding their pain points, challenges, and desires. Startups need to deeply understand the problem they are trying to solve and who exactly is experiencing that problem. This helps in identifying the target audience and allows for better alignment between the product and market needs. After identifying the target market, entrepreneurs must create a minimum viable product (MVP), which is a basic version of the product that can be used for testing and gathering feedback. This allows for quick iterations and avoids spending resources on unnecessary features. The MVP is then released to a small group of target customers who provide feedback on their experience. This feedback is crucial in understanding whether the product resonates with the market and if any adjustments need to be made. Validation of product-market fit also involves measuring key metrics such as customer acquisition, retention, and satisfaction. Startups need to track and analyze these metrics to determine if their product is gaining traction and meeting customer expectations. They may also conduct surveys, interviews, and usability tests to gather qualitative feedback and understand the root causes of any issues or challenges. The goal of product-market fit validation is to ensure that the product or service creates enough value for customers and generates sustainable demand. This validation process helps entrepreneurs refine their product, identify market opportunities, and make informed decisions about their business strategy. Successful product-market fit validation increases the chances of long-term success and growth for startups, as it provides evidence that their product addresses a genuine need in the market.

Product-Market Fit

Product-Market Fit is a critical concept in the world of startups and entrepreneurship. It refers to the degree of alignment between a product or service and its target market. In simple terms, it signifies the extent to which a product satisfies a strong market demand, resulting in a successful and sustainable business. When a startup achieves product-market fit, it means that there is a substantial match between what the target market wants and what the product offers. This fit is crucial because it determines the potential success or failure of a startup. Without product-market fit, it becomes challenging for a business to attract and retain customers, generate revenue, and ultimately survive in the market. Product-market fit can be measured by certain key indicators, such as customer satisfaction, repeat purchases, positive reviews, and market share. These indicators reflect the level of customer acceptance and adoption of the product, demonstrating its value and relevance in the market. Reaching product-market fit typically involves an iterative process of testing, refining, and adapting the product to better meet the needs and preferences of the target market. This process often requires gathering and analyzing customer feedback, conducting market research, and making necessary adjustments to the product features, pricing, distribution channels, or marketing strategies. Entrepreneurs and startup founders strive to achieve product-market fit as early as possible in the life cycle of their business. This is because product-market fit determines the overall viability and growth potential of a startup. It enables the company to establish a competitive advantage, attract investors, and scale its operations. In conclusion, product-market fit is the alignment between a product or service and its target market, ensuring that the product fulfills a strong market demand. It is a key success factor for startups and entrepreneurs, as it determines the viability, growth, and long-term sustainability of a business.

Profit Sharing

Profit sharing is a financial strategy commonly used in the context of startups and entrepreneurship. It involves the distribution of a portion of a company's profits among employees or partners, based on a predetermined formula or agreed-upon terms. This distribution is typically made in addition to regular salaries or compensations. In the startup and entrepreneurship world, profit sharing serves several purposes. Firstly, it can be used as a tool to attract, motivate, and retain talented individuals within the organization. By offering the opportunity to share in the financial success of the company, it incentivizes employees to work harder, contribute more, and align their interests with those of the business. Furthermore, profit sharing can foster a sense of ownership and accountability among team members. By directly linking financial rewards to performance and profitability, it encourages individuals to take responsibility for their actions and decisions, as well as to actively contribute to the company's growth and success. Profit sharing arrangements can vary widely depending on the startup's goals, structure, and culture. Some common models include the distribution of a fixed percentage of profits among employees, the allocation of shares or stock options that can be sold later at a profit, and the establishment of bonus pools tied to specific performance metrics or milestones. It is important to note that profit sharing is generally subject to certain conditions and terms as agreed upon by the company and its employees or partners. These conditions may include a minimum tenure or contribution requirement, eligibility criteria, and forfeit provisions for individuals who leave the company before the profits are distributed. In summary, profit sharing in the context of startups and entrepreneurship refers to the distribution of a portion of a company's profits to employees or partners. It is a financial strategy aimed at attracting, motivating, and retaining talented individuals, while also fostering a sense of ownership and accountability within the organization. The specific terms and conditions of profit sharing arrangements may vary depending on the startup's goals and structure.

Profit And Loss (P&L) Analysis

Profit and Loss (P&L) analysis is a financial assessment tool used by startups and entrepreneurs to evaluate the financial performance of their businesses. It provides a comprehensive view of the company's revenue, expenses, and net profit or loss over a specific period of time, typically on a monthly, quarterly, or annual basis. The P&L statement, also known as an income statement or statement of earnings, is an essential component of a startup's financial reporting. It reflects the company's ability to generate revenue, control costs, and ultimately, achieve profitability. By analyzing the P&L statement, entrepreneurs can identify areas of strength and weakness in their business operations, make informed decisions, and take necessary actions to improve the overall financial health of the startup.

Project Management Software

Project management software refers to a technological tool or application that enables start-ups and entrepreneurs to effectively plan, organize, and execute their projects from initiation to completion. This software facilitates collaboration, communication, and coordination among team members, allowing for streamlined workflows and efficient resource allocation. Start-ups and entrepreneurs face unique challenges in managing their projects due to limited resources, tight budgets, and fast-paced environments. Project management software addresses these challenges by offering features such as task management, scheduling, budgeting, and reporting, thus empowering start-ups and entrepreneurs to effectively manage their projects within the constraints.

Proof Of Concept (POC)

A Proof of Concept (POC) is a short, preliminary demonstration or trial of an idea, product, or service that aims to validate its feasibility and potential success in the market. In the context of startups and entrepreneurship, a POC is commonly used to test the viability and potential scalability of a business concept before investing significant resources into its development. The purpose of a POC is to provide tangible evidence that a business idea or innovation has the potential to be successful and solve a particular problem or meet a market need. It helps entrepreneurs and startup founders gather empirical data and feedback to validate assumptions, refine their value proposition, and make informed decisions about the direction of their venture.

Proof Of Stake (PoS)

Proof of Stake (PoS) is an innovative consensus algorithm in the blockchain industry that provides a secure and efficient way for startups and entrepreneurs to validate and verify transactions on a decentralized network. Unlike traditional Proof of Work (PoW) systems, which require miners to solve complex mathematical puzzles to create new blocks and secure the network, PoS relies on the ownership of digital assets (cryptocurrencies) as a form of stake to participate in the consensus process. In a PoS system, individuals or groups that hold a certain amount of cryptocurrency are selected to create new blocks and validate transactions based on their stake. The higher the stake, the higher the chances of being chosen as a block creator. This mechanism incentivizes participants to maintain a high stake in the network, as it increases their chances of being selected and earning transaction fees as rewards. Compared to PoW, PoS offers several advantages for startups and entrepreneurs in the blockchain space. Firstly, PoS requires significantly less computational power and energy consumption, making it a more sustainable and cost-effective solution. This is particularly beneficial for startups with limited resources, as it reduces the barriers to entry and allows for greater participation in the network. Secondly, PoS promotes greater security and reduces the risk of centralization. Since PoS participants are selected based on their stake, they have a vested interest in the network's security and integrity. This encourages them to act honestly and validate transactions accurately to maintain the value of their digital assets. Furthermore, PoS provides a more scalable solution for startups and entrepreneurs, as it eliminates the need for expensive mining equipment and allows for faster block creation and transaction confirmation. This scalability is crucial for startups looking to build decentralized applications (DApps) or launch their own cryptocurrencies on the blockchain, as it ensures a smooth and efficient user experience. In conclusion, Proof of Stake (PoS) is a consensus algorithm that has significant benefits for startups and entrepreneurs in the blockchain industry. Its energy efficiency, security, and scalability make it an attractive option for building decentralized applications and launching new cryptocurrencies. By using their digital assets as stake, startups can participate in the consensus process and contribute to the growth and development of the decentralized ecosystem.

Prototype Development

A prototype is a preliminary version of a product or service that is created with the purpose of testing and validating its functionality and feasibility before full-scale production or development. It is typically developed in the early stages of a startup or entrepreneurial venture to provide a tangible representation of the idea or concept. The process of prototype development involves translating abstract ideas into a physical or digital form that can be interacted with and evaluated. This allows entrepreneurs to gather feedback, make necessary adjustments, and improve the product or service before investing significant time, resources, and capital into its final implementation.

Prototype Testing

Prototype testing is a crucial stage in the startup and entrepreneurship journey, where a preliminary version or early model of a product, service, or idea is evaluated by a select group of users or potential customers. It is a method used to validate and gather valuable feedback before fully developing the product or implementing the idea. During prototype testing, entrepreneurs typically create and refine a basic version of their product or service, focusing on the core functionalities and features. This initial prototype may not be fully polished or completed, but it serves as a tangible representation of the concept or solution. The purpose of prototype testing is to gather insights from the target audience regarding various aspects such as usability, desirability, functionality, and overall viability. The process of prototype testing involves presenting the prototype to a group of potential users or customers and observing their interactions, behaviors, and feedback. This can be done through various methods, such as interviews, surveys, usability tests, focus groups, or even direct observation. The feedback collected from participants helps entrepreneurs and startups understand what works well, what needs improvement, and what aspects may be missing or unnecessary. Prototype testing is an iterative process, often involving multiple rounds of testing and refinement. Based on the feedback received, entrepreneurs can make necessary adjustments, add or remove features, improve the user interface, or modify other elements to enhance the overall user experience and increase the chances of success. This iterative approach allows for quick adaptation and ensures that the final product or solution meets the needs and expectations of the target audience. Overall, prototype testing plays a vital role in reducing the risk and uncertainty associated with launching a new product or implementing a new idea. By involving users early on and gathering their feedback, startups and entrepreneurs can make informed decisions, prioritize their efforts and resources effectively, and increase the chances of creating a product or solution that meets market demand and fulfills user needs.

Prototyping

Prototyping in the context of Startup & Entrepreneurship refers to the process of creating a preliminary or experimental version of a product, service, or system. It involves developing a working model that showcases the basic features and functionality of the final offering. A prototype serves as a tangible representation of the idea or concept, allowing entrepreneurs to visually depict their vision to potential stakeholders, such as investors, partners, or customers. It is often used as a tool for validation, feedback gathering, and iteration before investing significant resources into full-scale production.

Quantitative Data Analysis Tools

Quantitative Data Analysis Tools refer to a set of software or applications that assist startups and entrepreneurs in analyzing and interpreting numerical data to make informed business decisions. These tools utilize statistical methods and techniques to gather, organize, and analyze large volumes of quantitative data, such as sales figures, customer data, website traffic, marketing metrics, financial records, and more. Quantitative data analysis is crucial for startups and entrepreneurs as it enables them to gain valuable insights into market trends, customer behavior, and various business aspects. By using these tools, startups can identify patterns, detect correlations, measure performance, and evaluate the effectiveness of their strategies and tactics. This process provides a solid foundation for evidence-based decision making, leading to increased efficiency, improved competitiveness, and greater chances of success. There are various types of quantitative data analysis tools available to startups and entrepreneurs. Statistical software like SPSS, SAS, and R offer extensive capabilities to conduct complex statistical analysis, regression modeling, data visualization, and predictive analytics. These tools often require a certain level of technical expertise but provide robust functionality for in-depth analysis. Data visualization tools like Tableau and Power BI allow startups to transform raw data into visually appealing charts, graphs, and dashboards. This visualization not only presents the data in a more digestible format but also facilitates the identification of trends, outliers, and anomalies. These tools enable entrepreneurs to communicate insights effectively and make data-driven decisions. Another category of quantitative data analysis tools includes survey and questionnaire software such as SurveyMonkey and Google Forms. These tools assist startups in collecting quantitative data directly from their customers or target audience. By designing and distributing surveys, startups can gather responses that can be analyzed to gain insights into customer preferences, satisfaction levels, and market trends. In summary, quantitative data analysis tools are essential resources for startups and entrepreneurs. These tools empower startups to extract meaningful information from numerical data, enabling them to make informed business decisions. By leveraging these tools, startups can enhance their competitiveness, optimize strategies, and maximize their chances of success in today's data-driven business environment.

Quantitative Research Surveys

Quantitative research surveys in the context of startup and entrepreneurship refer to a systematic approach of gathering data and insights in a structured format for analysis and decision-making. These surveys rely on the collection of numerical data to measure and quantify various aspects of a particular startup or entrepreneurial venture. Quantitative research surveys are designed to obtain specific information and metrics that can be analyzed statistically. These surveys typically involve the use of closed-ended questions, where respondents are presented with predefined response options to choose from. The aim is to gather data that can be analyzed using statistical methods to identify trends, patterns, and correlations.

Quiet Period

A quiet period in the context of startup and entrepreneurship refers to a predetermined period of time during which a company restricts the release of certain information, particularly related to its operations, financial status, and future plans. This period typically occurs around the time of an initial public offering (IPO) or other significant events that may have a material impact on the company. The purpose of a quiet period is to prevent the dissemination of potentially inaccurate or misleading information that could influence investors' decisions. By limiting the flow of information, companies aim to ensure that investors receive only reliable and verified data when making investment choices.

Rapid Prototyping

Rapid Prototyping is a crucial process in the field of Startup and Entrepreneurship, where a functional model or prototype is quickly developed to test and validate a concept or idea before investing significant time and resources into its full development. The aim of Rapid Prototyping is to gather user feedback, identify flaws, and refine the product or service early on in the development process. This iterative approach allows startups and entrepreneurs to make informed decisions and make necessary adjustments to increase the chances of success and reduce the potential for failure.

Real Options Valuation

The concept of Real Options Valuation in the context of Startup and Entrepreneurship refers to the evaluation of the potential opportunities and flexibility that an entrepreneur has to adapt and adjust their business strategies and decisions in response to changing market conditions or opportunities. The term "real options" is derived from the financial concept of options, which are financial instruments that give the holder the right, but not the obligation, to buy or sell an underlying asset at a specific price within a certain period of time. In a startup or entrepreneurial context, real options valuation recognizes that the entrepreneur faces uncertainties and risks in their business environment, and by adopting a flexible approach, they can capture value from these uncertainties. It emphasizes that startups and entrepreneurs should not only focus on the traditional financial metrics and static business plans but also consider the dynamic nature of their business and the potential for future strategic decisions. Real options valuation involves identifying and valuing the various options that an entrepreneur has in their business. These options can include the option to delay or abandon a project, the option to expand or contract operations, the option to enter or exit a market, and the option to adopt new technologies or business models. By valuing these options, the entrepreneur can make more informed decisions and assess the potential value and risk associated with their business opportunities. This valuation approach recognizes that entrepreneurship is a dynamic and uncertain process, and that the value of a startup or entrepreneurial venture is not solely determined by its current financial performance or projections. By considering the real options available, an entrepreneur can better capture the value of flexibility, adaptability, and future growth potential in their business.

Return On Assets (ROA)

The Return on Assets (ROA) is a financial ratio that measures the profitability of a startup or entrepreneurial venture by comparing its net income to its total assets. It is an important metric for investors, lenders, and stakeholders in assessing the efficiency and effectiveness of the company's asset utilization. ROA is calculated by dividing the net income of the startup by its average total assets. The net income is the revenue generated minus all expenses, including operating costs, taxes, and interest payments. Total assets include both current assets, such as cash, inventory, and accounts receivable, as well as long-term assets, such as property, equipment, and investments. A higher ROA indicates that the startup is effectively using its assets to generate income and is more efficient in its operations. It implies that the company is able to generate more profits with the given level of investment in assets. On the other hand, a lower ROA suggests that the startup is not utilizing its assets efficiently and may be facing issues such as low sales, high expenses, or poor asset management. ROA is a valuable metric for startups and entrepreneurs to assess their financial performance and make informed decisions about resource allocation and operating strategies. It helps them identify areas of improvement and devise strategies to increase profitability and asset utilization. Investors and lenders also use ROA to evaluate the financial health and growth potential of a startup before making investment or lending decisions. However, it is important to note that ROA is just one of many financial ratios and should be used in conjunction with other performance indicators to get a comprehensive view of the startup's financial performance. It should also be compared with industry benchmarks and peer companies to evaluate the company's relative performance and identify areas of competitive advantage or weakness.

Return On Investment (ROI)

Return on Investment (ROI) is a financial metric used to evaluate the profitability and efficiency of an investment in the context of startups and entrepreneurship. It measures the return or gain on an investment relative to its cost, providing insight into the profitability of the venture. In the startup and entrepreneurship space, where resources are often limited and risks are high, calculating ROI becomes crucial to make informed decisions. ROI allows entrepreneurs to assess the success or failure of an investment by comparing the amount gained or lost to the amount originally invested.

Revenue Generation

Revenue generation refers to the process of acquiring income or funds for a startup or entrepreneurial venture through various sources. It is the primary objective of any business to generate revenue, as it is essential for sustaining operations, achieving growth, and maximizing profitability. In the context of startups and entrepreneurship, revenue generation plays a crucial role in establishing a strong foundation and ensuring long-term success. Startups typically face unique challenges in generating revenue, as they often operate with limited resources and face fierce competition in the market. There are several strategies that startups and entrepreneurs can employ to generate revenue: 1. Sales and Marketing: Developing effective sales and marketing strategies is crucial for a startup to attract customers and generate revenue. This includes identifying target markets, creating compelling value propositions, and implementing sales channels and promotional activities. 2. Product or Service Pricing: Determining the optimal price for a product or service is essential for revenue generation. Startups must consider various factors, such as production costs, competitor pricing, market demand, and perceived value, to set prices that are both competitive and profitable. 3. Partnerships and Collaborations: Forming strategic partnerships and collaborations with other businesses can provide opportunities for revenue generation. This can involve joint marketing initiatives, cross-selling products or services, or sharing resources to reduce costs and expand market reach. 4. Business Model Innovation: Startups often need to explore innovative business models to differentiate themselves from competitors and create new revenue streams. This may include offering subscription-based services, implementing a freemium model, or utilizing the sharing economy. 5. Customer Retention and Upselling: Retaining existing customers and encouraging upselling is an effective way to generate revenue. Startups can focus on enhancing customer experiences, providing excellent customer service, and introducing new offerings to increase customer loyalty and drive additional sales. In conclusion, revenue generation is a critical aspect of startup and entrepreneurial success. By employing effective sales and marketing strategies, pricing products or services strategically, forming partnerships, embracing business model innovation, and focusing on customer retention, startups can generate the income necessary to sustain and grow their ventures.

Revenue Growth

Revenue growth refers to the increase in the income generated by a startup or entrepreneurship venture over a specific period of time. It is a key metric that indicates the financial performance and success of the business in generating revenue. For startups and entrepreneurs, revenue growth is of utmost importance as it demonstrates the ability of the business to attract customers, generate sales, and ultimately achieve profitability. A steady and consistent revenue growth is a positive sign, indicating that the business is on the right path and is gaining traction in the market.

Revenue Model Analysis

A revenue model analysis is a crucial component of any startup or entrepreneurship venture, which involves the evaluation and understanding of how a company generates revenue, and the impact it has on the overall business operations and profitability. It provides insight into the strategies and tactics required for sustainable growth and success in the competitive market. The revenue model represents the framework through which a company effectively monetizes its products or services. It outlines the specific channels, pricing structures, and methods employed to generate income. By analyzing the revenue model, entrepreneurs can identify potential revenue streams, assess the profitability of their offerings, and make informed decisions to optimize their business operations.

Revenue Model Development

Revenue model development is a crucial aspect of startup and entrepreneurship as it involves determining the strategies and methods by which a company generates income and sustains its operations. It encompasses the identification and implementation of various revenue streams, pricing strategies, and monetization models to generate consistent and profitable revenues. One key aspect of revenue model development is understanding the target market and customers' needs and preferences. This enables entrepreneurs to design products or services that cater to their customers' demands, ensuring a higher likelihood of sales and revenue generation. By conducting market research, analyzing competition, and understanding customer behavior, startups can identify market gaps and develop innovative solutions that resonate with their target audience. Another important consideration in revenue model development is the selection of the appropriate revenue streams. These streams can be classified into various categories such as sales revenue, subscription revenue, advertising revenue, and licensing or royalty fees. Startups need to evaluate their business model and determine the most suitable revenue streams that align with their core offerings and target market. By diversifying revenue streams, entrepreneurs can reduce the reliance on a single source and establish a more stable and sustainable revenue base. Pricing strategies also play a crucial role in revenue model development. Startups need to determine the optimal price point for their offerings that balances profitability, value proposition, and market competitiveness. This requires consideration of factors such as production costs, competitors' pricing, customers' willingness to pay, and perceived value. Pricing models can range from fixed pricing, subscription-based pricing, freemium models, tiered pricing, and dynamic pricing, among others. Moreover, revenue model development requires continuous monitoring and adaptation to market dynamics. Startups must regularly evaluate their revenue model performance, gather feedback from customers, and make necessary adjustments to optimize revenue generation. This iterative process allows entrepreneurs to refine their revenue model and ensure that it remains relevant and effective in a dynamic business environment.

Revenue Model Evaluation

A revenue model is a framework that outlines how a startup or entrepreneurial venture generates revenue and makes money. It is an essential component of a business plan, as it helps the entrepreneur understand how the business will be sustainable and profitable in the long term. The revenue model evaluates various sources of revenue and identifies the most effective and sustainable ways to monetize the startup's products or services. It takes into consideration the target market, customer segments, pricing strategy, and cost structure to maximize profitability.

Revenue Model Innovation

Revenue model innovation refers to the development of new and creative ways for a startup or entrepreneur to generate income and sustain their business. It involves finding innovative ways to monetize products or services, capture customer value, and earn revenue. In the context of startups and entrepreneurship, revenue model innovation plays a crucial role in attracting investors, achieving profitability, and gaining a competitive edge in the market. Startups often face challenges in generating revenue due to limited resources, market uncertainty, and intense competition. Therefore, they need to continuously explore and adapt their revenue models to drive sustainable growth. Revenue model innovation can take various forms, depending on the nature of the business and its target market. It involves identifying new revenue streams, exploring alternative pricing models, and finding inventive ways to deliver value to customers. Startups may experiment with different revenue models such as subscription-based pricing, freemium models, licensing and royalties, or a combination of these. One example of revenue model innovation is the introduction of the "freemium" model, which offers basic services for free while charging for premium features or additional services. This model allows startups to acquire a large user base and generate revenue by upselling or offering enhanced features to a premium segment of customers. Another example is the use of data monetization, where startups collect and analyze customer data to provide targeted advertising or sell insights to third parties. This revenue model enables startups to leverage their data assets and create additional revenue streams beyond their core products or services. Revenue model innovation requires a deep understanding of customer needs, market dynamics, and industry trends. It involves conducting market research, analyzing customer behavior, and staying updated with technological advancements. Startups need to be agile and flexible in adapting their revenue models to changing market conditions and customer preferences. In conclusion, revenue model innovation is a vital aspect of startup and entrepreneurial success. It involves finding innovative ways to generate revenue, sustain growth, and deliver value to customers. By continuously exploring and adapting their revenue models, startups can differentiate themselves in the market, attract investors, and achieve long-term profitability.

Revenue Model Optimization Tactics And Strategies

A revenue model refers to the strategy and plan a startup or entrepreneur uses to generate income and maximize profits. It outlines the ways in which a business generates revenue from its products or services. Revenue model optimization tactics and strategies involve analyzing and refining the existing revenue model to increase sales, improve profitability, and enhance overall business performance. One tactic for revenue model optimization is diversification. This involves expanding the range of products or services offered to appeal to a broader customer base. By diversifying their offerings, startups can attract new customers and generate additional streams of revenue. For example, an e-commerce startup selling clothing and accessories may choose to add home decor products to their inventory. Another strategy for revenue model optimization is pricing optimization. This involves adjusting the prices of products or services to maximize sales and profitability. Startups can conduct market research to determine the optimal price point that balances customer demand and business profitability. Pricing strategies include penetration pricing (setting lower prices to gain market share) and premium pricing (setting higher prices to position products as premium or exclusive). Effective customer segmentation is also an important tactic for revenue model optimization. Startups can analyze customer data and behavior to identify different customer segments and tailor their products or services accordingly. This allows them to effectively target specific customer groups with personalized offerings, ultimately increasing sales and customer loyalty. In addition, startups can explore partnerships and collaborations as a revenue model optimization tactic. By forming strategic alliances with other businesses, startups can leverage each other's resources and customer bases. For example, a food delivery startup may partner with a popular restaurant to offer exclusive menu items, attracting more customers and generating additional revenue. Overall, revenue model optimization involves continuous analysis, experimentation, and adaptation to ensure that a startup's revenue generation methods are efficient and effective. By implementing various tactics and strategies, startups and entrepreneurs can increase their chances of business success and sustainable profitability.

Revenue Model Optimization Tactics

Revenue model optimization refers to the process of refining and improving the strategies and models a startup or entrepreneurship employs to generate revenue and drive profitability. It involves analyzing, testing, and making data-driven decisions to enhance the effectiveness and efficiency of the business's revenue streams and maximize financial performance. Optimizing the revenue model is crucial for startups and entrepreneurs as their success depends on generating sufficient revenue for growth and sustainability. By fine-tuning the revenue model, startups can identify and capitalize on opportunities to increase sales and profits, mitigate risks, and improve overall business performance.

Revenue Model Optimization

Revenue Model Optimization refers to the process of refining and maximizing the revenue generation strategy of a startup or entrepreneurial venture. It involves analyzing and fine-tuning different elements of the revenue model, such as pricing, sales channels, customer acquisition, and cost structure, to increase profitability and sustainability. Startups and entrepreneurs often face the challenge of finding the most effective and efficient ways to generate revenue. Revenue Model Optimization aims to address this challenge by examining all aspects of the revenue model and making strategic adjustments to improve financial performance. The first step in Revenue Model Optimization is understanding the target market and identifying the most suitable pricing strategy. This involves analyzing customer needs, preferences, and willingness to pay, as well as evaluating competitor pricing strategies. By determining the right price points, startups can optimize revenue generation while remaining competitive. Another crucial aspect of Revenue Model Optimization is identifying the most effective sales channels. This involves evaluating various distribution channels, such as direct sales, online platforms, partnerships, or retail, and selecting the ones that are most likely to reach the target customers and generate revenue efficiently. Additionally, startups may explore alternative revenue streams, such as licensing or subscription models, to diversify their income sources. Customer acquisition is another vital aspect of Revenue Model Optimization. Startups need to identify cost-effective marketing and advertising strategies to attract and retain customers. This may involve using digital marketing channels, social media platforms, or influencer partnerships to reach the target audience effectively. Moreover, startups can leverage data analytics and customer insights to personalize marketing campaigns and enhance customer engagement. Furthermore, startups need to optimize their cost structure to maximize profitability. This includes identifying and reducing unnecessary expenses, negotiating better deals with suppliers or vendors, and optimizing operational processes to improve efficiency. By eliminating inefficiencies and controlling costs, startups can increase their profit margins. In conclusion, Revenue Model Optimization is a crucial process for startups and entrepreneurs to refine and maximize their revenue generation strategies. By analyzing and fine-tuning pricing, sales channels, customer acquisition, and cost structure, startups can enhance their financial performance, increase profitability, and achieve long-term sustainability.

Revenue Model Review

A revenue model refers to the strategy a startup or entrepreneur employs to generate income from their products or services. It outlines the various ways in which a business plans to make money and sustain itself financially. The revenue model is a vital component of a startup's overall business plan, as it determines the company's profitability and helps attract potential investors. It serves as a blueprint for how a startup intends to monetize its offerings and achieve financial success. There are several different types of revenue models that startups can adopt, depending on their specific goals and target market. Some common revenue models include: 1. Sales Revenue Model: The startup generates revenue by selling products or services directly to customers. This model is commonly used by e-commerce businesses and retail stores. 2. Subscription Revenue Model: The startup charges customers a recurring fee in exchange for access to its products or services on a regular basis. This model is often seen in software-as-a-service (SaaS) companies and media streaming platforms. 3. Advertising Revenue Model: The startup generates revenue by displaying advertisements to its users or customers. This model is commonly used by social media platforms and online content publishers. 4. Freemium Revenue Model: The startup offers a basic version of its product or service for free but charges for additional features or premium content. This model is often used by mobile app developers and online gaming companies. 5. Licensing Revenue Model: The startup generates revenue by granting other companies the right to use its intellectual property, such as patents or trademarks, in exchange for licensing fees. 6. Affiliate Revenue Model: The startup earns a commission by promoting and selling other companies' products or services through affiliate partnerships. 7. Transaction Fee Revenue Model: The startup charges a fee for facilitating transactions between buyers and sellers on its platform. This model is commonly used by online marketplaces and payment processors. It is important for startups and entrepreneurs to carefully choose the revenue model that aligns with their business objectives, target market, and competitive landscape. A successful revenue model should strike a balance between generating enough income to cover costs and providing value to customers. Additionally, startups should regularly review and adapt their revenue models as market conditions and customer preferences evolve. In conclusion, a revenue model serves as a roadmap for startups and entrepreneurs to generate income and build a sustainable business. It outlines the different ways in which the startup plans to monetize its offerings and achieve profitability. By selecting the right revenue model and regularly assessing its effectiveness, startups can increase their chances of long-term success in the competitive business landscape.

Revenue Model Testing

Revenue model testing refers to the process of evaluating and validating the various strategies and methods utilized by a startup or entrepreneur to generate income and sustain the business. It involves analyzing and experimenting with different revenue streams and approaches to determine their feasibility, profitability, and scalability. The primary objective of revenue model testing is to assess and refine the business's revenue-generating capabilities. This process is crucial for startups and entrepreneurs as it enables them to identify the most effective and sustainable ways to generate revenue, while also minimizing risks and maximizing profitability.

Revenue Model Validation Approaches

Revenue model validation is the process of testing and verifying the effectiveness and viability of a startup or entrepreneur's revenue generation methods. It involves evaluating and assessing the different strategies and channels through which the company aims to generate income and determining their potential for success in the market.This validation process helps to ensure that the chosen revenue model is aligned with the target audience, market conditions, and the overall business goals and objectives. By validating the revenue model, startups and entrepreneurs can gain confidence in their ability to generate revenue and attract customers.

Revenue Model Validation

A revenue model validates the way in which a startup or entrepreneurial venture generates income from its products or services. It outlines the specific strategies and tactics that the company will employ to generate revenue and achieve profitability. The revenue model is a crucial component of a startup's business plan, as it provides a roadmap for sustained growth and financial success. The validation of a revenue model involves several key steps. Firstly, the startup must clearly define its target market and identify the customers who will benefit from its products or services. This involves conducting market research and gathering data to understand the needs and preferences of potential customers. Once the target market is defined, the startup can proceed to develop its revenue streams. These streams may consist of various sources, such as product sales, subscription fees, licensing agreements, or advertising revenue. The revenue model must be designed in such a way that it aligns with the needs and purchasing behaviors of the target market, ensuring that customers are willing to pay for the value provided by the startup. After developing the revenue streams, the startup needs to test and validate its revenue model. This involves conducting market testing and gathering feedback from potential customers. The startup may offer its products or services on a limited scale or provide prototypes to gain insights into customer preferences and pricing sensitivity. Based on the feedback received, the revenue model may need to be revised and refined. This iterative process allows the startup to align its business model with market demand and optimize its revenue generation potential. The validation of the revenue model is an ongoing process, as it requires constant monitoring and adaptation to changing market dynamics and customer preferences. In conclusion, the validation of a revenue model is a critical step for startups and entrepreneurs. It involves defining the target market, developing revenue streams, and testing the model through market research and customer feedback. By validating the revenue model, startups can ensure their financial viability and create a sustainable path towards profitability and growth.

Revenue Model

A revenue model refers to the strategy or plan implemented by a startup or entrepreneur to generate income and sustain their business operations. It outlines the various sources and methods through which the company expects to generate revenue. The revenue model acts as a blueprint that guides the startup or entrepreneur on how to monetize their products or services. It helps them identify the target market, pricing strategies, and distribution channels that will enable them to maximize their revenue potential. The most common revenue models used by startups and entrepreneurs include: Product Sales: This model involves generating revenue by selling physical or digital products. The startup sets a price for its products based on factors such as production costs, market demand, and competition. Subscription or Membership Fees: Many startups adopt a subscription-based revenue model, where customers pay a recurring fee to access the company's products or services. This model often appeals to businesses in the software, media streaming, and online learning industries. Advertising: Startups and entrepreneurs can generate revenue through advertising by offering space on their website, app, or other platforms to advertisers. The revenue is typically generated through pay-per-click or pay-per-impression models. Freemium: This model involves offering a basic version of a product or service for free, while charging customers for premium features or enhanced versions. The goal is to attract a large user base with the free option and convert a portion of them into paying customers. Affiliate Marketing: This revenue model involves partnering with other businesses and earning a commission for referring customers to their products or services. Startups can integrate affiliate marketing into their website or app to generate income. These are just a few examples of revenue models that startups and entrepreneurs can explore. The selection of the most suitable revenue model depends on various factors, such as the nature of the business, target market, competition, and scalability. In conclusion, a revenue model serves as a crucial aspect of startup and entrepreneurship, outlining how the business will generate income and sustain itself. By carefully analyzing the market and adopting the most appropriate revenue model, startups and entrepreneurs can increase their chances of success and profitability.

Revenue Multiple

A revenue multiple is a financial metric used in the context of startups and entrepreneurship. It is a ratio that is calculated by dividing the enterprise value of a company by its revenue. The enterprise value represents the total value of a company, including its equity and debt, and is often used as a measure of its overall worth. The revenue multiple provides insight into how much investors are willing to pay for each dollar of a company's revenue. It is a valuation metric that is commonly used to compare the value of different startups or to assess the market value of a company in relation to its revenue. The higher the revenue multiple, the more investors are willing to pay for each dollar of revenue generated by the company. Entrepreneurs and investors often use revenue multiples to evaluate the health and potential of a startup. It can indicate the growth prospects and profitability of the company, as well as its ability to generate revenue. A high revenue multiple may suggest that the company is highly valued and has strong growth potential, while a low revenue multiple may indicate that the company is undervalued or that there are concerns about its financial performance. However, it is important to note that revenue multiples should not be viewed in isolation. Other factors such as industry trends, market conditions, and profitability should also be considered when using this metric. Additionally, revenue multiples may vary across different industries and sectors, so it is important to compare the ratio to similar companies or industry averages.

Revenue Run Rate

The revenue run rate is a metric commonly used in the context of startups and entrepreneurship to estimate the annual revenue based on the current or projected financial performance over a shorter period, such as monthly or quarterly. It is calculated by taking the revenue generated during a specific time period and multiplying it by the appropriate multiple to annualize the revenue. For example, if a startup earns $50,000 in a month, the revenue run rate would be $600,000, assuming a constant revenue generation rate throughout the year.

Revenue Strategy

Revenue strategy refers to the strategic approach taken by a startup or entrepreneur to generate income and sustain their business operations. It involves a set of actions and techniques designed to optimize the revenue generation potential of a business venture. Revenue strategy encompasses various aspects such as pricing, product positioning, target market identification, and sales and marketing efforts. This strategic framework aims to maximize the revenue streams of a startup, enabling it to achieve profitability and long-term sustainability. A well-defined revenue strategy helps startups and entrepreneurs effectively monetize their products or services. It requires a deep understanding of market dynamics, customer preferences, and competitive landscape. Firstly, a revenue strategy involves determining the right pricing strategy for the products or services offered by the startup. This includes analyzing the perceived value of the offering, considering the costs involved, and benchmarking against competitors' pricing. By finding the optimal balance between affordability and profitability, startups can attract customers while meeting their financial objectives. Secondly, revenue strategy involves identifying the most lucrative target market for the startup's offering. This requires conducting comprehensive market research and segmentation to identify potential customer segments with high purchasing power and a strong need for the product or service. By focusing marketing and sales efforts on these segments, startups can allocate resources efficiently and maximize their revenue generation potential. Furthermore, a revenue strategy includes product positioning and differentiation. Startups must identify and articulate their unique selling proposition (USP) that differentiates their offerings from competitors. This involves understanding customer needs, conducting competitive analysis, and highlighting the distinct features or benefits of their products or services. By effectively positioning their offerings, startups can attract customers and command premium prices. Lastly, revenue strategy incorporates sales and marketing efforts to drive customer acquisition and retention. This involves designing targeted marketing campaigns, building strategic partnerships, and implementing effective sales techniques. Startups need to leverage various channels such as digital marketing, social media, and traditional advertising to create awareness and generate leads. Additionally, they must focus on providing excellent customer service and building long-term relationships to maximize customer lifetime value and encourage repeat purchases.

Revenue Stream

A revenue stream refers to the source of income for a startup or an entrepreneur. It is the specific way in which a business generates revenue or earns money. Revenue streams are crucial for the success and sustainability of a startup, as they provide the necessary financial resources to cover expenses, invest in growth, and generate profit. In the context of startups and entrepreneurship, revenue streams can take various forms, depending on the nature of the business and its target market. Some common revenue streams include: 1. Product sales: This revenue stream involves selling physical or digital products to customers. It can be a one-time purchase, or it can involve recurring sales through subscriptions or consumables. 2. Service fees: Startups can generate revenue by providing services to clients or customers. These services can range from consulting and professional advice to technical support and maintenance. 3. Licensing and royalty fees: If a startup has developed intellectual property, such as patents, trademarks, or copyrights, it can generate revenue by licensing its rights to other businesses or individuals. Royalty fees are often paid based on the usage or sales of the licensed property. 4. Advertising and sponsorship: Startups can earn revenue by displaying advertisements or securing sponsorships. This revenue stream is commonly used by online platforms, media companies, and event organizers. 5. Subscription fees: Many online startups offer subscription-based services, where customers pay a recurring fee for access to exclusive content, additional features, or premium support. Subscription revenue streams can provide a stable and predictable source of income. 6. Affiliate marketing: This revenue stream involves earning commissions by promoting and selling products or services from other companies. Startups can join affiliate programs and earn a percentage of the sales they generate through their marketing efforts. It is essential for startups and entrepreneurs to identify and prioritize their revenue streams as part of their business model. Diversifying revenue streams can reduce risk and increase financial stability. It is also important to continually evaluate and adapt revenue streams based on market trends and customer preferences.

Revenue Streams

A revenue stream refers to the various sources of income that a startup or entrepreneur generates from their business activities. It is the money that flows into the company, contributing to its financial growth and sustainability. Revenue streams can come in different forms and can vary depending on the nature of the business. In a startup or entrepreneurial context, revenue streams are crucial for the success and survival of the business. They determine the company's ability to generate profits, cover expenses, and ultimately achieve its goals. Understanding and effectively managing revenue streams is essential for making informed decisions, driving growth, and attracting investors. There are several types of revenue streams that startups and entrepreneurs can explore, depending on their business model and target market. Some common examples include: - Selling products or services: This is the most traditional revenue stream, where a company sells physical products, digital goods, or provides services in exchange for money. - Subscription or membership fees: Businesses can offer subscription-based models where customers pay a recurring fee to access their products or services. - Licensing or franchising: Startups can generate revenue by licensing their intellectual property or business model to third parties in exchange for royalties or franchise fees. - Advertising and sponsorship: Companies can earn revenue by displaying advertisements or partnering with other businesses for sponsorships or endorsements. - Data monetization: Startups that collect and analyze data can generate revenue by selling insights, reports, or access to their data to other businesses. - Affiliate marketing: Businesses can earn commissions by promoting and selling products or services offered by other companies. It is important for startups and entrepreneurs to diversify their revenue streams to minimize risks and create a stable income foundation. By exploring different revenue opportunities, businesses can adapt to market changes, identify new growth areas, and stay competitive in the fast-paced startup ecosystem.

Reverse Merger

A reverse merger is a method by which a private company goes public by merging with a publicly traded company. In this process, the private company acquires the majority stake of the publicly traded company, essentially taking over its operations and becoming the controlling entity. This allows the private company to bypass the complex and expensive initial public offering (IPO) process. Typically, a reverse merger occurs when a private company wants to gain access to the public markets and secure the benefits of being a publicly traded company, such as increased liquidity and easier access to capital. The private company identifies a suitable publicly traded company that is already listed on a stock exchange and has a similar industry or business focus. Both companies negotiate and agree on the terms of the merger. Once the merger is finalized, the shareholders of the private company receive shares of the publicly traded company in exchange for their ownership stake in the private company. As a result, the private company's owners become the majority shareholders of the merged entity, effectively gaining control and the ability to influence its operations and strategic decisions. Reverse mergers are often viewed as a faster and more cost-effective way for private companies to become publicly traded compared to the traditional IPO process. This is because reverse mergers have fewer regulatory requirements and can be completed in a shorter timeframe. Additionally, the private company can benefit from the existing infrastructure and resources of the publicly traded company, including its listing on a stock exchange, established investor base, and financial reporting systems. However, reverse mergers also carry certain risks and challenges. The private company must thoroughly assess the financial condition and regulatory compliance of the publicly traded company before entering into the merger. There is also a potential for conflicts and disagreements between the existing shareholders of the publicly traded company and the private company's owners, which may impact the merged entity's governance and decision-making process.

Risk Assessment

Risk assessment in the context of startup and entrepreneurship refers to the process of identifying, analyzing, and evaluating potential risks that may hinder the success of a new business venture. It involves assessing both internal and external factors that could impact the startup's operations, financial stability, and overall growth. The aim of risk assessment is to proactively identify and understand the potential risks and their potential consequences, allowing entrepreneurs to develop strategies to mitigate or eliminate these risks. By doing so, startups can enhance their chances of success and prevent or minimize potential losses. There are various types of risks that startups need to assess. Market risks involve analyzing the target market's demand, competition, and potential market shifts that could affect the startup's product or service offering. Financial risks revolve around evaluating the startup's capital requirements, cash flow projections, and the potential impact of external economic factors on the business's financial health. Operational risks encompass assessing the startup's operational processes, technology infrastructure, and potential disruptions or system failures that may hinder its operations. Legal and regulatory risks involve understanding and complying with applicable laws, regulations, and licensing requirements to avoid legal complications or penalties. Additionally, startups must evaluate and manage human resource risks, such as hiring and retaining skilled employees, maintaining a positive organizational culture, and handling potential conflicts or labor issues. Reputation and brand risks involve safeguarding the startup's reputation and building a strong brand image, preventing negative publicity, and managing customer satisfaction. The risk assessment process typically involves identifying potential risks, analyzing their likelihood and potential impact, evaluating their significance to the startup's objectives, and prioritizing them based on their level of importance. Entrepreneurs use various methods and tools, such as SWOT analysis, scenario analysis, and risk matrices, to assess and categorize risks. Once risks are identified, entrepreneurs can develop risk mitigation strategies and contingency plans to minimize their impact or avoid them altogether. These strategies may include diversifying the startup's product offering, implementing robust financial controls, establishing backup systems, and conducting thorough market research and analysis.

Runway

Runway in the context of startup and entrepreneurship refers to the amount of time and resources a startup has before it runs out of money. It is the time period during which a startup must achieve profitability, secure additional funding, or sustain its operations through other means. Like an airplane runway, the startup's runway is the length of time it has to take off and gain enough altitude to sustain flight. The runway is calculated based on the startup's current cash flow and burn rate, which is the rate at which it is spending money.

SAFE Financing

SAFE Financing, short for Simple Agreement for Future Equity, is a type of financial instrument commonly used in startup and entrepreneurship ecosystems. It is a legal contract between a startup company and an investor, typically a venture capital firm or angel investor, that allows the investor to provide funding to the startup in exchange for the right to receive equity in the future. The main purpose of SAFE Financing is to provide a simplified and standardized approach to fundraising for startups. Unlike traditional equity financing, where investors receive shares in the company immediately, SAFE Financing defers the determination of the investor's ownership percentage until a future equity financing round occurs. This allows startups to receive the necessary funding without the complexities and negotiations associated with setting a valuation at the time of investment. A typical SAFE Financing agreement consists of several key clauses. The first clause outlines the amount of investment and the date it is made, establishing the financial terms of the agreement. The second clause defines the triggering events that determine when the SAFE Financing converts into equity, such as the occurrence of a qualified equity financing round or the sale of the company. The third clause specifies the terms of conversion, including the discount rate or valuation cap that may apply. SAFE Financing offers several advantages for both startups and investors. For startups, it provides a streamlined process for raising capital, allowing them to focus on business growth instead of prolonged negotiations. It also offers flexibility in determining the investor's ownership percentage, as the conversion terms can be customized to align with the company's anticipated future valuation. For investors, SAFE Financing allows them to invest in promising early-stage startups without immediately committing to a fixed valuation, reducing the risk associated with traditional equity investments. In conclusion, SAFE Financing is a simplified and standardized financial instrument that enables startups to raise capital from investors in exchange for future equity. It offers benefits such as streamlined fundraising processes and flexible valuation terms, making it an attractive option for both startups and investors in the dynamic world of entrepreneurship.

SAFE Note

In the context of startup and entrepreneurship, a SAFE (Simple Agreement for Future Equity) Note is a financial instrument commonly used by early-stage companies to raise seed capital. It is a type of convertible note that allows investors to lend money to a company with the expectation of converting the loan into equity at a later date. The SAFE Note offers a simplified and standardized approach to fundraising compared to traditional equity financing methods. Unlike traditional convertible notes, the SAFE Note does not carry an interest rate or maturity date. Instead, it offers the investor the right to convert their investment into equity when a specified triggering event occurs.

SAFE (Simple Agreement For Future Equity)

A SAFE (Simple Agreement for Future Equity) is a financial instrument commonly used in the startup and entrepreneurship ecosystem. It is a type of investment contract that allows investors to invest in early-stage companies in exchange for equity in the future. The SAFE is designed to be a simpler and quicker alternative to traditional equity financing options such as convertible notes or preferred stock. It was introduced by the startup accelerator Y Combinator as a way to address the complexity and cost associated with traditional fundraising methods. Under a SAFE, the investor provides a certain amount of capital to the startup, typically in the form of a cash investment. In return, the investor receives the right to convert their investment into equity at a later specified date or milestone event, such as a subsequent funding round or an acquisition of the company. One of the key features of a SAFE is its simplicity. Unlike traditional equity financing, a SAFE does not involve setting a valuation for the company at the time of investment. This simplifies the investment process and allows startups and investors to focus more on building the business rather than negotiating complex terms. By using a SAFE, startups can attract early-stage investors without the need to go through a lengthy and expensive valuation process. It also allows startups to defer the determination of valuation until a later stage when the company's value is likely to be higher and more accurately assessed. From the investor's perspective, a SAFE offers the potential for a high return on investment if the startup succeeds. If the company fails, the investor typically has no legal recourse to recover their investment, as the SAFE is not a debt instrument. Overall, a SAFE is a flexible and efficient financing option for startups and early-stage companies. It provides a simplified investment structure for both the entrepreneur and the investor, giving startups access to much-needed capital and investors the potential for future equity upside.

SME (Small And Medium-Sized Enterprises)

A Small and Medium-sized Enterprise (SME) refers to a business that falls within a certain size range and operates with limited resources and manpower, typically having fewer than 250 employees. In the context of startups and entrepreneurship, SMEs play a crucial role in driving economic growth, innovation, and job creation. Startups are often considered a subset of SMEs, characterized by their focus on scalable business models and disruptive technologies, aiming for rapid growth and high-profit potential. While all startups can be considered SMEs, not all SMEs are startups. SMEs encompass a wider range of businesses that may have been operating for an extended period and have established a stable presence in the market. SMEs are known for their flexibility and ability to adapt quickly to changing market conditions. They often operate with an entrepreneurial mindset, seeking growth opportunities and embracing innovation. As they operate with limited resources, SMEs must prioritize their activities and apply lean principles to maximize efficiency and productivity. Entrepreneurs frequently establish and operate SMEs, leveraging their entrepreneurial skills and vision to build successful businesses. They take calculated risks, identify market gaps, and develop innovative solutions to meet customer needs. Entrepreneurs often face various challenges in managing and growing their SMEs, such as limited access to financial resources, competition from larger firms, and regulatory hurdles. SMEs can serve as incubators for new ideas and technologies, creating a vibrant ecosystem for startups and innovation. Startups often collaborate with SMEs in various ways, including partnerships, supply chain integration, and knowledge sharing. SMEs can provide startups with valuable insights, market access, and resources, while startups bring fresh ideas, agility, and disruptive potential to SMEs. In conclusion, SMEs are vital components of the startup and entrepreneurship ecosystem, fueling economic growth, job creation, and innovation. They encompass a diverse range of businesses, from established SMEs to high-growth startups. Entrepreneurs play a significant role in establishing and managing SMEs, driving them forward with their vision, skills, and willingness to take risks.

SWOT Analysis Framework

The SWOT analysis framework is a strategic tool utilized by entrepreneurs and startups to assess the internal and external factors that may impact their business's success or failure. SWOT stands for strengths, weaknesses, opportunities, and threats, which represent the four categories of factors analyzed in this framework. Strengths are internal factors that provide a competitive advantage or unique advantage to the startup. These can include the expertise and skills of the founding team, proprietary technology or intellectual property, strong brand recognition, or access to key resources or distribution channels. By identifying and leveraging their strengths, startups can differentiate themselves from competitors and create value for their target market. Weaknesses, on the other hand, are internal factors that hinder the startup's growth or performance. These can include limited financial resources, lack of a strong brand presence, inexperienced team members, or an inadequate business model. By identifying and addressing their weaknesses, startups can improve their chances of success by developing strategies to mitigate or overcome these obstacles. Opportunities refer to external factors that could positively impact the startup's growth or profitability. These can include market trends, changes in consumer behavior, emerging technologies, or new legislation. By identifying and seizing opportunities, startups can capitalize on favorable conditions and gain a competitive advantage in the market. Finally, threats are external factors that may pose challenges or risks to the startup's viability. These can include intense competition, changing market dynamics, economic downturns, or legal and regulatory barriers. By identifying and preparing for potential threats, startups can develop contingency plans and minimize risks to their business. The SWOT analysis framework provides entrepreneurs and startups with a comprehensive overview of their internal strengths and weaknesses, as well as the external opportunities and threats they face. By conducting a SWOT analysis, startups can gain insights into their current market position, identify areas for improvement, and develop effective strategies to navigate the challenges and capitalize on their strengths.

SWOT Analysis Tools

A SWOT analysis is a tool used in the context of startup and entrepreneurship to assess the strengths, weaknesses, opportunities, and threats of a business venture or idea. It provides a comprehensive overview of the internal and external factors that may affect the success or failure of a startup. The strengths refer to the positive attributes or advantages that the startup possesses. These could include factors such as unique expertise, innovative products or services, strong brand reputation, or a talented team. By identifying and leveraging these strengths, startups can gain a competitive edge and differentiate themselves in the market. On the other hand, weaknesses are the areas where the startup may be lacking or facing challenges. These could be in terms of limited financial resources, lack of experience or skills, ineffective marketing strategies, or weak distribution channels. By acknowledging these weaknesses, startups can develop strategies to overcome them and improve their chances of success. Opportunities are external factors that could potentially benefit the startup. This could include emerging market trends, technological advancements, changing customer preferences, or new partnership opportunities. By capitalizing on these opportunities, startups can tap into new markets, increase their customer base, and drive growth. Lastly, threats are external factors that could potentially harm the startup. Examples of threats could be intense competition, economic downturns, regulatory changes, or lack of customer demand. By identifying and understanding these threats, startups can develop contingency plans to mitigate their impact and ensure long-term sustainability.

SWOT Analysis

A SWOT analysis is a strategic planning tool used by startups and entrepreneurs to evaluate their internal strengths and weaknesses, as well as external opportunities and threats. It helps businesses identify areas where they have a competitive advantage and areas that need improvement. The first step in conducting a SWOT analysis is to identify internal strengths. These are the positive aspects of the business that give it a competitive edge. This could include factors such as a unique product or service, proprietary technology, strong financial resources, or a talented team. By identifying these strengths, startups can determine what sets them apart from competitors and leverage them to their advantage. The next step is to identify internal weaknesses. These are the areas where the business is lacking or has room for improvement. This could include factors such as a limited budget, lack of experience or expertise, inefficient processes, or a weak brand. By recognizing these weaknesses, startups can work to address them and become more competitive in the market. Once the internal factors have been analyzed, startups and entrepreneurs can move on to evaluating external opportunities. These are factors in the industry or market that could potentially benefit the business. This could include factors such as emerging trends, changing customer needs, favorable market conditions, or strategic partnerships. By identifying these opportunities, startups can develop strategies to capitalize on them and gain a competitive advantage. The final step is to identify external threats. These are factors in the industry or market that could potentially harm the business. This could include factors such as intense competition, economic downturns, changing regulations, or new entrants to the market. By recognizing these threats, startups can develop strategies to mitigate the risks and stay ahead of the competition. In conclusion, a SWOT analysis is a valuable tool for startups and entrepreneurs to assess their internal strengths and weaknesses, as well as external opportunities and threats. By conducting a thorough analysis, businesses can develop strategies to maximize their strengths, address their weaknesses, capitalize on opportunities, and mitigate threats. This allows them to make informed decisions and set themselves up for success in the competitive startup and entrepreneurship landscape.

SaaS Business Model

A SaaS (Software as a Service) business model refers to a type of business that delivers software applications over the internet. In this model, instead of customers buying and installing software on their own computers or servers, they access and use the software through a web browser or a thin client. This approach eliminates the need for customers to maintain and upgrade the software, as all the maintenance and upgrades are managed by the SaaS provider. The SaaS business model typically involves a subscription-based pricing structure, where customers pay a recurring fee for the use of the software. This subscription fee often includes additional services such as technical support, training, and updates. The pricing structure may vary based on factors such as the number of users, the level of functionality, or the amount of data storage required. From the perspective of startups and entrepreneurs, the SaaS business model offers several advantages. Firstly, it allows for quick and relatively low-cost entry into the market, as the infrastructure and software development resources are often provided by the SaaS provider. This reduces the upfront investment required and enables startups to focus on developing a compelling software product or service. Secondly, the SaaS business model provides a scalable and flexible platform for growth. SaaS companies can easily add or remove features, customize the software for different customer needs, or scale the infrastructure to accommodate increasing user demand. This flexibility allows startups to adapt to market changes and quickly respond to customer feedback. Thirdly, the subscription-based pricing model of SaaS businesses offers a predictable and recurring revenue stream. This stability in revenue allows startups to plan and invest in future growth, attract investors, and build customer relationships based on long-term value rather than one-time purchases. In conclusion, the SaaS business model provides startups and entrepreneurs with a cost-effective and scalable way to deliver software applications to customers. By leveraging the subscription-based pricing structure and the advantages of cloud-based infrastructure, SaaS startups can focus on innovation, respond to market demand, and build sustainable businesses.

SaaS (Software As A Service) Business

SaaS, or Software as a Service, is a business model in which a company offers software applications to customers over the internet on a subscription basis. It is a cloud computing solution that allows users to access and use software applications without the need for physical installation or maintenance on their own hardware. In the context of startups and entrepreneurship, SaaS has gained significant traction due to its many advantages. One of the key benefits of a SaaS business model for startups is the lower barrier to entry. Compared to traditional software development, building and deploying a SaaS application is often less capital-intensive and faster, allowing startups to enter the market quickly and at a lower cost. Furthermore, the subscription-based pricing model of SaaS offers startups predictable and recurring revenue streams, enhancing financial stability and enabling better long-term planning and growth strategies. This is especially crucial for startups that may face challenges in securing one-time large sales or upfront payments. SaaS also offers startups the opportunity to scale their business rapidly. With a cloud-based infrastructure, SaaS companies can easily accommodate an increasing number of users without the need for substantial hardware investments or system upgrades. In addition, updates and new features can be rolled out seamlessly to all customers, eliminating the need for individual software installations and reducing support and maintenance costs. Moreover, SaaS provides a high level of flexibility for startups. Users can access the software from any device with an internet connection, enabling remote work and collaboration. This flexibility can be particularly advantageous for startups that have geographically dispersed teams or target global markets. In summary, SaaS offers numerous benefits to startups and entrepreneurs, including lower entry barriers, predictable revenue streams, scalability, and flexibility. By leveraging the power of cloud computing, SaaS businesses can deliver software applications efficiently, enabling startups to focus on innovation, customer acquisition, and growth.

SaaS (Software As A Service)

Software as a Service (SaaS) refers to a software distribution model in which applications are hosted by a third-party provider and made available to users over the internet. In this model, startups and entrepreneurs can access and use software applications without the need for extensive installation processes or the purchase of individual licenses. SaaS is a popular choice for startups and entrepreneurs due to its affordability and flexibility. Instead of having to invest in expensive hardware and software licenses, SaaS allows them to pay for software applications on a subscription basis. This subscription-based pricing model provides startups with more predictability in terms of costs and allows for scalability as their business grows.

Sales Funnel Automation

Sales Funnel Automation is the process of using technology and software to automate and streamline the sales journey of a startup or entrepreneurship venture. It refers to the systematic approach of automating various stages of the sales funnel, from lead generation to conversion, in order to optimize efficiency, increase sales, and enhance customer satisfaction. The sales funnel is a visual representation of the customer journey, illustrating the path from initial awareness to final purchase. It consists of several stages, including lead generation, lead nurturing, prospecting, sales, and customer retention. Each stage requires a different set of actions and strategies to move the customer closer to making a purchase. With sales funnel automation, startups and entrepreneurs can automate repetitive and time-consuming tasks, allowing them to focus on more important aspects of their business. This includes automating lead generation through targeted marketing campaigns, nurturing leads through personalized email sequences, tracking and analyzing sales data, and automating follow-ups and customer support. By implementing sales funnel automation, startups and entrepreneurs can benefit in numerous ways. Firstly, it saves time and effort by automating repetitive tasks, freeing up valuable resources to focus on high-value activities such as developing new products or improving customer experience. Secondly, it improves efficiency and scalability by streamlining the sales process, allowing businesses to handle a larger volume of leads and customers without sacrificing quality or personalized attention. Moreover, sales funnel automation provides valuable insights and data analytics that enable startups and entrepreneurs to make informed decisions and optimize their sales strategies. By tracking and analyzing customer behavior, businesses can identify bottlenecks in the sales funnel and implement targeted strategies to address them. This leads to improved conversion rates, increased revenue, and enhanced customer satisfaction.

Sales Funnel

A sales funnel is a systematic approach used by startups and entrepreneurs to guide potential customers through the buyer's journey, from the first point of contact to making a purchase. It is a visual representation of the various stages a prospect goes through before becoming a paying customer. The sales funnel consists of several stages, each with its own purpose and corresponding marketing strategies. The first stage is the awareness stage, where the primary goal is to make potential customers aware of your product or service. This is achieved through various marketing channels such as social media, content marketing, and advertising. Once a prospect is aware of your offering, they enter the second stage of the funnel, known as the interest stage. At this stage, the goal is to nurture the prospect's interest and provide them with more information about your product or service. This can be done through targeted email campaigns, webinars, or product demonstrations. The third stage of the sales funnel is the evaluation or decision stage. Here, the prospect is considering whether or not to make a purchase. The focus at this stage is to provide the prospect with the necessary information and resources to help them make an informed decision. This can include case studies, customer testimonials, or free trials. Finally, the last stage of the sales funnel is the action stage, where the prospect becomes a paying customer. This is the ultimate goal of the sales funnel, and it is achieved through effective closing techniques such as sales calls, negotiations, or online checkout processes. The sales funnel is an essential tool for startups and entrepreneurs as it helps them track and optimize their sales process. By understanding which stage of the funnel prospects are in, businesses can tailor their marketing efforts accordingly and increase their chances of converting leads into customers.

Scalability

Scalability in the context of Startup and Entrepreneurship refers to the ability of a business to handle growth and increased demand while maintaining or improving its performance. It is a crucial aspect for startups and entrepreneurs as they aim to build sustainable and successful ventures. When a business is scalable, it means that it has the potential to grow and expand its operations without experiencing significant hurdles or limitations. Scalability enables startups to meet the needs of a larger customer base, increase revenue, and potentially expand into new markets or industries.

Scalable Business Model

A scalable business model refers to a framework or strategy that enables a startup or entrepreneur to efficiently grow their business without being limited by resources or capacity constraints. It is an approach that focuses on creating a system or structure that can accommodate growth and expansion in a sustainable and profitable manner. In the context of startups and entrepreneurship, scalability is the ability of a business to grow its revenue and customer base exponentially, while keeping costs under control. A scalable business model is designed to achieve this growth by leveraging technology, streamlining operations, and maximizing resources.

Scale Out

Scale Out in the context of startups and entrepreneurship refers to the process of expanding a business by increasing its capacity to handle larger volumes of work and accommodate a growing customer base. This scaling strategy involves adding more resources, such as servers, employees, or physical locations, to the existing infrastructure to meet the demands of the growing business. When a startup experiences significant growth and demand for its product or service, it may become necessary to scale out in order to effectively handle the increasing workload. Scaling out allows the business to maintain efficiency and continue providing a high level of service to its customers.

Scale Up

Scale Up refers to the process of increasing the size and scope of a startup or entrepreneurial venture in order to achieve sustainable growth and maximize its potential impact in the market. It involves expanding key business aspects such as workforce, customer base, revenue, and operations, while maintaining profitability and efficiency. The scale-up phase typically occurs after the initial startup phase, during which the company has validated its product or service, gained traction in the market, and is now ready to take advantage of growth opportunities. Scaling up is a critical milestone for startups as it allows them to capitalize on their success and move towards becoming a more mature and sustainable business. Scaling up a startup requires careful planning and execution. It involves a series of strategic decisions and actions that aim to increase the company's capacity to deliver its product or service at a larger scale. This may involve expanding manufacturing facilities, enhancing distribution networks, hiring additional employees, and implementing efficient operations and management systems. One key aspect of scaling up is the ability to attract and retain more customers. Startups need to develop effective marketing and sales strategies to reach new markets, acquire new customers, and increase market share. This may involve investing in advertising, expanding online presence, and developing partnerships or distribution channels. Another important factor in scaling up is the ability to raise sufficient capital to fund growth initiatives. Startups may seek additional funding from venture capitalists, angel investors, or other sources to finance their expansion plans. The ability to raise funds is often dependent on the startup's track record, market potential, and ability to demonstrate a clear path to profitability. Scaling up also requires strong leadership and management capabilities. Entrepreneurs need to build a team that can effectively handle the increasing demands and complexities of a growing business. This may involve hiring experienced managers, delegating responsibilities, and fostering a culture of innovation and continuous improvement. In summary, scaling up is a critical phase in the journey of a startup or entrepreneurial venture. It involves expanding key aspects of the business to achieve sustainable growth and maximize its potential impact. Successful scaling up requires strategic planning, effective marketing and sales strategies, access to sufficient funding, and strong leadership and management capabilities.

Scale-Up Funding

Scale-Up funding is a form of financial support provided to startups and entrepreneurs who have successfully launched their businesses and now wish to expand and grow rapidly. This funding is specifically focused on helping startups scale up their operations, increase market reach, and accelerate growth.Scale-up funding is typically sought after by startups that have already established a solid business model and have shown promising traction in the market. Unlike seed funding or early-stage funding, which is used to launch a business idea or develop a product, scale-up funding is intended to fuel the growth of a business that is already operational and generating revenue.

Scale-Up Strategy

A scale-up strategy, in the context of startup and entrepreneurship, refers to a planned approach that helps a startup or a small business grow rapidly and efficiently. It is a set of focused actions and initiatives aimed at accelerating the business's growth trajectory, expanding its operations, and increasing its market share. The goal of a scale-up strategy is to take a startup from its initial stages to a more mature and profitable phase. This strategy is typically implemented when a startup has successfully proved its business model, gained some traction in the market, and has the potential to grow exponentially. A scale-up strategy involves several key elements: 1. Market expansion: The business identifies new target markets and develops strategies to reach and penetrate those markets. This may involve launching new products or services, entering new geographical regions, or targeting different customer segments. 2. Scalable operations: The company focuses on improving and optimizing its operational capabilities to handle increased demand and growth. This may include streamlining processes, investing in automation, enhancing supply chain management, and adopting efficient technologies. 3. Talent acquisition and development: Scaling up requires hiring and retaining the right talent to support the growth objectives. The business focuses on attracting skilled individuals, building a strong team, and investing in employee training and development to ensure they have the necessary skills and expertise to drive the company's growth. 4. Funding and financial management: Scaling up typically requires additional funding to support expansion efforts. The company may seek external investments, secure loans, or explore other sources of capital to fuel growth. Effective financial management is essential to ensure that resources are allocated efficiently and sustainably. 5. Customer acquisition and retention: The company develops strategies to attract new customers and retain existing ones. This may involve implementing marketing and advertising campaigns, improving customer service, fostering customer loyalty programs, and leveraging digital marketing channels. In conclusion, a scale-up strategy is a deliberate and structured approach that aims to propel a startup or small business towards rapid and sustainable growth. By focusing on market expansion, scalable operations, talent acquisition, funding, and customer acquisition, a startup can optimize its potential for success and achieve significant growth in a relatively short period of time.

Scale-Up

Scale-Up in the context of startups and entrepreneurship refers to the process of expanding and growing a business rapidly in order to increase its market presence, revenue, and profitability. It involves transitioning from a small-scale business model to a large-scale operation with the goal of achieving significant and sustainable growth. When a startup reaches the scale-up stage, it has already proved the viability of its business model and has achieved a certain level of success and growth. Scale-up often involves securing additional funding, expanding the team, and scaling the production or service delivery capabilities to meet the growing demand.

Scaling Up

Scaling up in the context of startup and entrepreneurship refers to the process of rapidly increasing the size, scope, and impact of a business. It involves expanding operations, increasing customer base, and growing revenue and profits on a considerable scale. Scaling up is a crucial phase for startups and entrepreneurs as it determines the sustainability and long-term success of their ventures. It requires careful planning, effective execution, and management of resources to ensure a smooth transition from a small or medium-sized operation to a large-scale enterprise.

Scaling

Scaling in the context of startup and entrepreneurship refers to the process of increasing a company's capacity to handle growth. It involves expanding the operations, resources, and capabilities of the business to meet the demands of a growing customer base and market. Scaling is crucial for startups as it enables them to grow and thrive in a competitive environment. It allows businesses to capitalize on opportunities, attract investors, and enhance their market share. However, scaling is not just about increasing the size of the company; it also involves maintaining the quality of products or services, improving operational efficiency, and managing growth effectively.

Scenario Analysis Software

Scenario Analysis Software is a tool used in the context of startup and entrepreneurship to analyze and evaluate different potential scenarios and their impact on the business. It allows entrepreneurs and startups to assess the potential outcomes of different decisions, strategies, and external factors in order to make informed and strategic decisions to mitigate risks and maximize opportunities. The software takes into consideration various factors such as market trends, competition, customer behavior, financial projections, and operational constraints to provide a comprehensive analysis of the potential scenarios. Startup and entrepreneurial ventures often operate in a dynamic and uncertain environment. They face numerous challenges such as limited resources, intense competition, changing market dynamics, and evolving customer preferences. It becomes essential for startups to anticipate and prepare for various possible future scenarios to adapt and respond effectively. This is where scenario analysis software becomes invaluable. The software allows startups to create multiple scenarios based on different assumptions and variables. These scenarios could involve changes in market conditions, financial performance, competitive landscape, technological advancements, and regulatory frameworks. By inputting different parameters and variables, entrepreneurs can simulate various hypothetical situations and visualize their potential impact on the business. Scenario analysis software provides startups with a quantitative and qualitative understanding of potential risks and opportunities associated with different scenarios. It helps entrepreneurs identify the key drivers and variables that significantly impact the business outcomes. By conducting scenario analysis, startups can assess the likelihood of various scenarios, determine the key risk factors, and develop contingency plans. Furthermore, the software allows for sensitivity analysis, which helps entrepreneurs understand the degree of sensitivity of their business to changes in different variables. This enables informed decision-making and better risk management strategies. It also helps startups prioritize their resources, investments, and strategic initiatives based on the potential impact of different scenarios.

Scenario Planning

Scenario Planning is a strategic management tool used in the context of startup and entrepreneurship to analyze potential future events and circumstances that may impact the business. It involves developing multiple scenarios or alternative futures based on different assumptions and factors, in order to anticipate and prepare for possible outcomes. By considering various scenarios, entrepreneurs can better understand the potential risks and opportunities that their startup may face. This helps in making informed decisions and developing effective strategies to navigate uncertain and complex business environments.

Search Engine Marketing (SEM) Tools

Search Engine Marketing (SEM) Tools are online marketing tools designed to help startups and entrepreneurs promote their businesses through search engine advertising. SEM tools enable businesses to optimize their online presence, increase visibility, and drive targeted traffic to their websites. SEM tools typically include keyword research tools, ad creation and management platforms, performance tracking and reporting, and analytics tools. These tools provide startups and entrepreneurs with valuable insights and data to improve their online marketing strategies and campaigns.

Secondary Market

A secondary market is a platform where previously issued securities, such as stocks, bonds, and other financial instruments, are bought and sold between investors, rather than being issued by the original issuer. In the context of startups and entrepreneurship, the secondary market refers to the trading of shares or equity stakes of privately held companies that are not listed on public stock exchanges. In the startup ecosystem, the secondary market plays a crucial role in providing liquidity to early investors, founders, and employees of privately held companies. It allows them to monetize their ownership in the company before a traditional exit event, such as an initial public offering (IPO) or acquisition, takes place.

Securities And Exchange Commission (SEC)

The Securities and Exchange Commission (SEC) is a regulatory organization in the United States that oversees and enforces securities laws to protect investors and maintain fair and efficient markets. It plays a crucial role in promoting transparency and investor confidence in the startup and entrepreneurship ecosystem. The SEC is responsible for administering and enforcing various laws, including the Securities Act of 1933 and the Securities Exchange Act of 1934. These laws require companies, including startups, to disclose certain information to the public when offering securities for sale. By doing so, the SEC ensures that potential investors have access to accurate and reliable information to make informed investment decisions. For startups and entrepreneurs, the SEC's role is significant in several ways. Firstly, if a startup plans to raise capital through the sale of securities, it must comply with the SEC's registration requirements unless an exemption applies. This means providing comprehensive and truthful disclosures about the business, its financial condition, risks, and the securities being offered. This information is typically included in a registration statement, which is subject to review by the SEC. The SEC also plays a critical role in preventing fraud and misconduct in the startup and entrepreneurship space. It investigates and takes enforcement actions against individuals or companies that violate securities laws, engage in insider trading, or manipulate the market. By ensuring compliance and punishing wrongdoers, the SEC promotes a level playing field and safeguards the long-term interests of investors and entrepreneurs alike.

Seed Capital Investment

Seed capital investment is a form of funding provided to startups and entrepreneurs in the early stages of their business ventures. This type of investment is characterized by its focus on financing the initial development and launch of a new business idea or concept. The main objective of seed capital investment is to provide entrepreneurs with the necessary financial resources to transform their ideas into viable businesses. This funding is typically sought by entrepreneurs who have a business plan and a vision for their startup but lack the necessary capital to bring their ideas to fruition. Seed capital investment typically comes from angel investors, venture capitalists, or specialized investment firms that specialize in funding early-stage startups. These investors are interested in supporting innovative and high-potential business ideas in exchange for equity or ownership in the startup. Unlike other forms of investment, seed capital investment is considered high-risk due to the early stage of the startup and the uncertainty surrounding its potential for success. As a result, investors in seed capital often expect a high return on their investment if the startup is successful. Seed capital investment is typically used by entrepreneurs to cover a variety of expenses in the early stages of their startup. These expenses may include market research, product development, hiring key team members, marketing and advertising, and initial operational costs. Overall, seed capital investment plays a crucial role in supporting the growth and development of startups and entrepreneurs. It provides the necessary funding to turn innovative ideas into vibrant businesses and helps startups navigate the challenges and risks associated with their early stages of development.

Seed Capital

205

Seed Capital refers to the initial funding provided to a startup or entrepreneur to help them get their business off the ground. It is often obtained from investors or venture capitalists who are willing to take a risk on a new and potentially innovative business idea. This type of capital is typically used to cover the early expenses of starting a business, such as product development, market research, and hiring key team members. It can also be used to establish a physical presence, acquire necessary equipment, and secure intellectual property rights.

Seed Funding Platforms

Seed funding platforms are online platforms or websites that connect startups and early-stage entrepreneurs with potential investors or funders. These platforms act as intermediaries, enabling startups to access financial support to develop their business ideas and bring their products or services to market. These platforms provide a variety of services and resources to startups and entrepreneurs. They typically have a database of investors or funders who are actively seeking investment opportunities in startup ventures. Startups can create a profile on the platform, outlining their business idea, market potential, and financial requirements. Investors can then browse through these profiles and choose to invest in startups that align with their investment criteria and interests. Seed funding platforms also often provide additional services to startups and entrepreneurs to help them create attractive investment propositions. This may include guidance on creating a compelling business plan, financial projections, and pitch decks. They may also offer networking opportunities, connecting startups with mentors, industry experts, and other entrepreneurs who can provide valuable advice and support. For startups and early-stage entrepreneurs, seed funding platforms offer several advantages. Firstly, they provide access to a large pool of potential investors who are specifically interested in funding innovative and high-growth ventures. This increases the chances of securing funding compared to traditional fundraising methods. Secondly, the platform's resources and guidance can help startups refine their business idea and develop a solid investment pitch, increasing their chances of success. Lastly, seed funding platforms often simplify the investment process, providing a streamlined and efficient way for startups to connect with potential investors and secure funding. In conclusion, seed funding platforms play a crucial role in the startup and entrepreneurship ecosystem by connecting startups with potential investors and providing them with resources and guidance to secure funding. These platforms help bridge the gap between investors looking for high-potential ventures and startups seeking financial support to bring their innovative ideas to life.

Seed Funding

Seed Investor

A seed investor is an individual or organization that provides financing to startup companies or entrepreneurs in their early stages of development. These investors typically invest a relatively small amount of money, known as seed capital, in exchange for equity or ownership in the company. Seed investors are one of the key sources of funding for startups, as they help bridge the gap between the founders' personal savings and the larger funding rounds provided by venture capitalists or angel investors. They are typically willing to take on higher risks in exchange for potentially higher returns on their investment.

Seed Round Financing

Seed round financing is an early stage funding round in the context of startups and entrepreneurship. It refers to the initial capital injection made by external investors, typically angel investors or venture capitalists, to support the development and growth of a startup company. This financing round usually takes place shortly after the founding of the company, aiming to provide the necessary funding to turn an idea or concept into a viable business. In the seed round, the startup is still in its infancy, often at the ideation or prototype stage. The funding received in this round is crucial for the entrepreneur to validate the business model, conduct market research, build a minimum viable product (MVP), and create a foundation for future growth. Seed financing allows the entrepreneur to bridge the gap between the initial self-funding stage and attracting larger rounds of funding in subsequent stages. During the seed round, investors generally assess the startup's potential for growth, evaluate its market viability, and determine its scalability. They consider factors such as the market size, competitive landscape, team composition, product or service uniqueness, and the entrepreneur's vision. Unlike later-stage funding rounds, where investors focus on the startup's financial performance and market traction, seed round investors often make their decision based on the potential of the idea, the entrepreneur's track record, and their ability to execute the business plan. Seed financing is typically provided in exchange for equity, meaning that investors receive shares in the startup in return for their investment. The valuation of the startup during the seed round can be challenging, as the company's financial and operational history is limited. Therefore, valuation methods such as comparable analysis or the use of convertible notes may be employed to determine the investment amount and the corresponding equity stake. In summary, seed round financing plays a crucial role in supporting early-stage startups and entrepreneurs. It provides the necessary capital to validate ideas, develop products or services, and lay the foundation for future growth. By attracting external investors, startups have the opportunity to gain not only financial resources but also valuable expertise and connections that can propel their business forward.

Seed Round

Seed Round refers to the initial stage of fundraising for a startup or entrepreneurial venture. It is the first official round of funding where the founders seek capital to support the development of their business idea or product. During the Seed Round, entrepreneurs approach individual investors, angel investors, or venture capital firms to secure the necessary funds to launch their startup. This funding is crucial for covering various expenses, including product development, market research, and initial marketing efforts.

Seed Stage Funding

Seed Stage Funding refers to the initial round of financing that a startup or entrepreneur receives to develop and launch their business. It is typically the first external funding that a startup raises, after it has exhausted its own resources and funds from family and friends. This type of funding is called "seed" because it is meant to help the business grow from a small seedling into a mature plant. It provides the necessary capital to cover the early-stage expenses such as market research, product development, hiring key team members, and creating a minimum viable product (MVP).

Seed Stage Investor

Seed Stage Investor refers to an individual or entity that invests capital into startups during their initial stages of development and growth. These investors typically provide funding in exchange for equity or ownership stakes in the startup. As the name suggests, seed stage investing happens at the earliest stage of a startup's life cycle, often when the entrepreneur has only an idea or minimal product development progress. Seed stage investors play a crucial role in supporting these early-stage companies by providing the necessary funds for them to develop their products, build their teams, and initiate their go-to-market strategies. Seed stage investors can be angel investors, venture capital firms, or even startup accelerator programs. Their investment decisions are based on various factors, such as the potential market size, the scalability of the business idea, the strength of the founding team, and the viability of the product or service offering. This type of investment comes with higher risk compared to later-stage investments, as the startup is still in the process of finding its product-market fit and establishing a sustainable business model. However, seed stage investors are often willing to take these risks in exchange for the potential for high returns on investment if the startup is successful. Seed stage investors not only provide financial support but also offer valuable guidance, mentorship, and networking opportunities to the entrepreneurs they back. They may leverage their industry expertise, connections, and experience to help the startup navigate challenges and achieve its growth objectives. In conclusion, seed stage investors are essential players in the startup ecosystem as they provide funding and support to early-stage companies, enabling them to transform their ideas into successful businesses. Through their investments, seed stage investors fuel innovation and contribute to the overall growth of the entrepreneurial landscape.

Seed Stage

Seed Stage is the initial phase of a startup, characterized by the early development and conceptualization of an entrepreneurial venture. It is the first stage in the startup life cycle, where the entrepreneur starts to transform their idea into a tangible business model. During this stage, the entrepreneur typically focuses on validating their idea, conducting market research, and developing a minimum viable product (MVP). The primary goal is to attract initial funding and gather early adopters or customers who are willing to try out the product or service. In the Seed Stage, entrepreneurs often rely on personal savings, family and friends, or angel investors to finance their startup. This funding is used to cover initial expenses such as product development, market research, and hiring a core team. The entrepreneur will also work on building a strong network, seeking mentorship, and refining their pitch to present their startup to potential investors. At this stage, the entrepreneur faces significant challenges and uncertainties. They must validate their assumptions about the market demand for their product or service and gather real-world feedback from early adopters. This feedback is crucial for making necessary iterations and improvements to their product or business model. In order to succeed in the Seed Stage, entrepreneurs need to have a clear vision, resilience, and adaptability. They must be willing to pivot and make necessary adjustments based on market feedback. The ability to build and nurture relationships also plays a vital role in attracting potential investors and advisors. Overall, the Seed Stage is a critical phase in the startup journey, where entrepreneurs lay the foundation for their business. It requires a strong entrepreneurial mindset, innovative thinking, and the ability to navigate the challenges and uncertainties that come with starting a new venture.

Seed-Stage Investment Round

A seed-stage investment round is the initial phase of funding that a startup or entrepreneur seeks to raise from external investors to support the development and growth of their business idea. This round typically occurs in the early stages of a startup's lifecycle when the concept is still in its nascent phase and lacks substantial traction or proven market validation. During the seed-stage investment round, startups typically approach angel investors, venture capital firms, or other early-stage investment sources to secure the necessary capital to bring their idea to fruition. These investors are willing to take on higher levels of risk compared to later-stage investors and are often attracted by the potential for significant returns on their investment. The purpose of a seed-stage investment round is to provide the necessary financial resources for the startup to fund key activities such as product development, market research, hiring key personnel, and marketing efforts. This funding enables the startup to reach critical milestones and demonstrate proof of concept, which is crucial for attracting further funding in subsequent stages. Seed-stage investments are typically smaller in size compared to later-stage rounds, as the startup is still in the early phases of its development and may lack a robust revenue stream or customer base. The valuation of the startup at this stage is also typically lower, reflecting the higher level of risk and uncertainty associated with early-stage ventures. In return for their investment, seed-stage investors often receive equity in the startup, allowing them to potentially benefit from the future success and growth of the business. Additionally, these investors may provide mentorship, advice, and access to their network and resources, which can be invaluable for the startup's growth trajectory. In conclusion, a seed-stage investment round serves as a crucial stepping stone for startups and entrepreneurs in their journey to bring their ideas to market. This funding round provides the necessary capital to kick-start the business and demonstrates the potential of the startup to attract subsequent rounds of investment.

Seed-Stage Investment

Seed-stage investment refers to the early stage of funding provided to startups or entrepreneurs to help them develop and launch their business idea. This initial investment is typically made by angel investors, venture capital firms, or even friends and family who believe in the potential of the startup. The purpose of seed-stage investment is to provide the necessary capital for startups to validate their business model, build a prototype or minimum viable product (MVP), and conduct market research. This initial funding is crucial for startups as it allows them to refine their product or service, understand their target market, and attract further investment. Seed-stage investors typically invest in exchange for equity in the startup. This means that they become partial owners of the company and stand to gain a portion of the company's future profits or potential sale. The amount of equity provided in exchange for the investment varies depending on factors such as the startup's valuation, growth potential, and the investor's appetite for risk. Seed-stage investments are considered high risk, high reward as most startups fail to reach their full potential. However, successful startups that have received seed-stage investments can experience exponential growth and generate substantial returns for investors. In addition to providing financial support, seed-stage investors often offer guidance and mentorship to entrepreneurs. They leverage their industry knowledge, experience, and network to help the startup navigate challenges, make strategic decisions, and connect with potential customers or partners. Overall, seed-stage investment plays a crucial role in the early development of startups. It provides the initial capital and support necessary for entrepreneurs to turn their innovative ideas into viable businesses. By taking a calculated risk on promising startups, seed-stage investors fuel innovation, job creation, and economic growth.

Seed-Stage Investor Engagement And Relations

Seed-stage investor engagement and relations refer to the process of establishing, maintaining, and nurturing relationships between start-up entrepreneurs and early-stage investors. This interaction is crucial for securing funding and aligning investors' interests with the start-up's goals. During the seed stage of a start-up, founders often seek external capital to finance their ventures. Engaging with seed-stage investors involves identifying potential investors, establishing initial contact, and showcasing the business potential of the start-up. The engagement process may involve activities such as pitching the business idea, discussing financial projections, and demonstrating the market viability of the product or service. Once initial interest is established, the start-up and the investor enter into a relationship that requires ongoing communication and collaboration. It is essential for entrepreneurs to build trust and transparency with investors by providing regular updates on the progress and challenges faced by the start-up. This includes timely and accurate reporting of financials, key milestones achieved, and any pivots or changes in the business strategy. In addition to financial support, seed-stage investors often bring valuable expertise and industry connections to start-ups. Entrepreneurs should actively seek the guidance and mentorship of investors to maximize the potential for success. This may involve seeking advice on strategic decisions, leveraging the investor's network for business development opportunities, or accessing their knowledge and experience in scaling operations. Effective seed-stage investor engagement and relations also encompass managing investor expectations and potential conflicts. As start-ups go through inevitable ups and downs, clear and open communication is crucial to maintaining a healthy relationship. Entrepreneurs should be proactive in addressing potential challenges and risks, and seek input from investors in overcoming obstacles. In conclusion, seed-stage investor engagement and relations are fundamental to the success of start-ups. By actively engaging with investors, start-up entrepreneurs can secure funding, leverage expertise, and establish a supportive network. Ongoing communication and collaboration with investors not only ensure financial support but also foster trust, transparency, and a shared vision for growth.

Seed-Stage Investor Engagement

Seed-stage investor engagement refers to the process of establishing and maintaining a relationship between a startup entrepreneur and potential investors during the early stages of a startup's development. It involves actively seeking and attracting seed-stage investors who are willing to provide the necessary funding and support to help the startup grow and succeed. During seed-stage investor engagement, entrepreneurs typically seek out angel investors or early-stage venture capital firms who are interested in investing in startups with high growth potential. The entrepreneur engages with these potential investors by presenting their business idea, showcasing their product or service prototype, and discussing their business model and growth strategy. The goal is to convince the investor that the startup is worth investing in and that it has the potential to generate significant returns on their investment. Seed-stage investor engagement is a critical stage in the startup journey as it can determine whether or not the startup receives the necessary funding to continue its operations and scale its business. It requires entrepreneurs to effectively communicate their vision, demonstrate market potential, and make a compelling case for investment. This often involves preparing a pitch deck, conducting meetings and negotiations, and providing detailed financial and market analysis to potential investors. Successful seed-stage investor engagement can provide startups with the financial resources, expertise, and network connections needed to accelerate growth, attract additional investors, and ultimately achieve long-term success. It can also help in building credibility and validation for the startup, as investors bring their experience and reputation to the table. Additionally, seed-stage investors often provide mentorship and guidance to entrepreneurs, helping them navigate the challenges of early-stage startup development. In conclusion, seed-stage investor engagement is a crucial aspect of startup entrepreneurship, involving the process of attracting and securing investment from early-stage investors. It requires effective communication, a strong business proposition, and the ability to convince potential investors of the startup's growth potential and value proposition. By engaging with seed-stage investors, startups can access the necessary funding, expertise, and support to drive growth and propel their business forward.

Seed-Stage Investor Meetings And Presentations

Seed-stage investor meetings and presentations are crucial steps in the startup and entrepreneurship journey. During this stage, founders and entrepreneurs seek funding from potential investors to turn their innovative ideas into viable businesses. Investor meetings involve face-to-face interactions between founders and potential investors. These meetings serve as an opportunity for founders to pitch their startup and convince investors of its potential. The goal is to secure funding to support the initial stages of growth and development. The presentations in these meetings are carefully crafted to highlight key aspects of the startup, such as the problem it is solving, its unique value proposition, the target market, and the business model. Founders need to effectively communicate their vision, strategy, and the market opportunity to captivate investors' interest. Typically, founders present a pitch deck, a concise and visual presentation that addresses critical questions investors may have. The pitch deck often includes a problem statement, market analysis, competitive landscape, product or service description, financial projections, and the funding requirements. The content should be persuasive, factual, and concise, keeping the investors engaged throughout the presentation. During the investor meetings, founders should be prepared to answer questions and provide further details on topics like the team's capabilities, marketing and distribution strategies, revenue streams, and potential barriers to entry or competition. Investors will scrutinize the startup's business model, scalability potential, and the founders' ability to execute the plan successfully. The outcome of these meetings can vary. Investors may express interest and proceed with due diligence, conducting further assessments to evaluate the startup. They may also provide feedback or guidance on improving the business model or strategy. Alternatively, investors may decide not to invest due to various reasons, such as misalignment with their portfolio or insufficient growth potential. Overall, seed-stage investor meetings and presentations are instrumental in attracting funding and shaping the future of a startup. Founders must approach these interactions with confidence, professionalism, and a thorough understanding of their business, industry, and target market.

Seed-Stage Investor Meetings

Seed-stage investor meetings refer to the initial interactions between startups and potential investors during the early stages of the startup's development. These meetings are crucial for startups to secure the necessary funding to launch and grow their businesses. During seed-stage investor meetings, entrepreneurs present their business ideas, products, or services to potential investors in the hopes of securing financial investment. Startups typically approach seed-stage investors, such as angel investors or seed-stage venture capital firms, who are willing to take higher risks in exchange for potential high returns.

Seed-Stage Investor Pitch

A seed-stage investor pitch is a formal presentation given by an entrepreneur or startup founder to potential investors in order to secure funding for their early-stage business. This pitch is typically delivered in a concise and persuasive manner, with the aim of communicating the unique value proposition and growth potential of the startup to the investors. The purpose of a seed-stage investor pitch is to showcase the business idea, demonstrate its market potential, and highlight the team's capabilities and vision. It provides an opportunity for the entrepreneur to articulate their business model, target market, competitive advantage, and go-to-market strategy. The pitch should also address the potential risks and challenges involved in executing the business plan, along with the proposed solutions or mitigations.

Seed-Stage Investor Presentation

A seed-stage investor presentation is a concise and comprehensive document that startup entrepreneurs use to pitch their business ideas and secure funding from potential investors during the early stages of their venture. This presentation is a critical tool for startups seeking initial capital to develop and grow their businesses. The primary purpose of a seed-stage investor presentation is to effectively communicate the startup's value proposition, market opportunity, competitive advantage, and growth potential to investors. It provides an overview of the business model, the product or service being offered, the target market, and the financial projections and investment requirements. The presentation typically starts with a brief introduction of the startup's founders, their background, and their expertise. It also outlines the problem or need the startup aims to address, along with a clear and compelling explanation of how the product or service solves that problem or satisfies that need. Moreover, the presentation highlights the startup's target market, identifying the size, demographics, and characteristics of the potential customers. It emphasizes the market opportunity by presenting relevant market research and industry trends to demonstrate the demand for the startup's offering. Additionally, the presentation explains the startup's competitive advantage, showcasing what sets it apart from existing competitors and how it plans to maintain or strengthen its position in the market. This may include differentiating features, intellectual property, strategic partnerships, or unique distribution channels. Furthermore, the financial aspect of the presentation includes the startup's financial projections, past performance (if applicable), and detailed breakdown of how the investment will be utilized. It should provide a clear understanding of the return on investment potential, the timeline for growth and profitability, and the exit strategy. In summary, a seed-stage investor presentation is a vital tool for startups to attract potential investors and secure early-stage funding. It should convey the startup's vision, value proposition, market opportunity, competitive advantage, and financial projections in a clear and concise manner. By effectively communicating these key aspects, entrepreneurs increase their chances of receiving the necessary funding to propel their business forward.

Seed-Stage Investor Relations

Seed-Stage Investor Relations refers to the strategic management and communication between startup companies and their early-stage investors. This process typically begins after a startup has secured seed funding and aims to establish and maintain a positive relationship with its investors. During the seed stage, startups often rely on individual angel investors or small venture capital firms for funding. These investors provide crucial capital to help the startup develop its product or service and scale its operations. In return for their investment, they typically receive equity in the company. The role of Investor Relations (IR) in the seed-stage is to ensure effective communication and alignment between the startup and its investors. This involves transparently sharing information and updates about the company's progress, financial performance, and overall strategy. By regularly updating investors, startups can build trust and credibility, which can lead to continued support and potential follow-on investments. Seed-Stage Investor Relations also involve managing expectations and addressing potential concerns or challenges that may arise during the early stages of a startup. By proactively addressing these issues, startups can mitigate risks and maintain investor confidence. In addition to communication, IR in the seed-stage may also involve facilitating networking opportunities between the startup and its investors. These connections can create additional value for the company, as investors may provide industry expertise, introductions to potential customers or partners, or access to further funding opportunities. Overall, Seed-Stage Investor Relations plays a crucial role in the success of a startup. By establishing open and proactive communication channels with early-stage investors, startups can cultivate strong partnerships, access valuable resources, and position themselves for continued growth and success.

Seed-Stage Investor

Seed-stage investor in the context of startup and entrepreneurship refers to an individual or firm that provides capital to startups in their early stages of development. These investors typically fund the initial stages of a business, where the company has a minimal viable product or prototype and is in need of financial resources to further develop their product or service. Seed-stage investors are crucial in the startup ecosystem as they take on significant risk by investing in companies that have not yet proven their market viability. These investors may include angel investors, venture capitalists, or specialized seed funds. They play a critical role in supporting entrepreneurs and fostering innovation by providing the necessary financial backing for early-stage startups.

Sensitivity Analysis

Serial Entrepreneur

A serial entrepreneur is an individual who continuously identifies opportunities, creates new ventures, and takes risks in order to build and grow businesses. They are driven by a desire for innovation and a passion for solving problems in the marketplace. Serial entrepreneurs are characterized by their ability to start and manage multiple businesses over their career, often in different industries or sectors. Serial entrepreneurs possess certain key traits that enable them to succeed in the startup ecosystem. Firstly, they have a high risk tolerance and are comfortable with uncertainty and ambiguity. They are willing to take calculated risks and are not deterred by failure, viewing it as a learning opportunity rather than a setback. Secondly, serial entrepreneurs have strong leadership and management skills. They are able to assemble a talented team, motivate and inspire them, and effectively delegate tasks to achieve the organization's goals. They are skilled communicators and have the ability to network and build relationships, which is crucial for securing funding and partnerships in the early stages of a startup. Thirdly, serial entrepreneurs possess a keen eye for identifying market gaps and potential opportunities. They are able to spot trends, anticipate customer needs, and innovate products or services that meet those needs. They are constantly scanning the business landscape, researching industry trends, and seeking out untapped markets. Finally, serial entrepreneurs are resilient and adaptable. They are not discouraged by setbacks or obstacles, but rather use them as fuel to find new ways to succeed. They embrace change and are willing to pivot their business strategies if necessary. In conclusion, a serial entrepreneur is a dynamic and driven individual who seizes opportunities, takes risks, and creates multiple ventures over their career. They possess a unique combination of traits and skills that enable them to navigate the challenging and ever-changing startup landscape.

Series A Funding

Series A funding is a crucial stage of funding in the startup and entrepreneurship world. It is the first significant round of financing that a startup receives from external investors, typically venture capitalists, after the initial seed funding stage. During the Series A funding round, the startup aims to secure the necessary capital to scale and grow its business operations. This funding is usually utilized to fuel expansion plans, develop the product or service further, build a strong team, and increase market reach. The process of securing Series A funding involves several stages. First, the startup needs to prepare a compelling business plan, including a detailed financial model and growth projections, to attract potential venture capital investors. Once the plan is ready, the startup pitches its business to venture capitalists who can evaluate the potential for high returns on their investments. A successful Series A funding round ensures that the startup receives the required funds to execute its growth strategy. It can provide the financial stability needed to navigate the challenges of scaling a business and achieve long-term success. Additionally, attracting reputable venture capitalists during Series A funding can bring valuable expertise, industry connections, and guidance to the startup. However, securing Series A funding is a highly competitive process. Investors analyze several factors before making their investment decisions, such as the market potential, the startup's competitive advantage, the quality of the team, and the overall growth prospects. Startups that can demonstrate a strong track record, market traction, and a clear path to profitability are more likely to attract investors during the Series A funding round. In conclusion, Series A funding is a critical milestone for startups, as it enables them to access the necessary capital to scale their operations and achieve growth. It provides the funding, expertise, and network needed to position the startup for long-term success in the highly competitive entrepreneurial landscape.

Series AA Preferred Stock

Series AA Preferred Stock refers to a class of stock that startup companies issue to investors during their early stages of fundraising. This type of stock represents ownership in the company and provides certain rights and privileges to its holders. Series AA Preferred Stock is typically offered to angel investors, venture capitalists, and other institutional investors who provide the necessary capital for the startup's growth and development. These investors are often looking for high-potential opportunities and are willing to assume a higher level of risk in exchange for potential returns. By issuing Series AA Preferred Stock, startups can raise capital without diluting the ownership and control of the founders. This means that the founders can retain a majority stake in the company while still securing the necessary funding. Holders of Series AA Preferred Stock usually have preferential rights over common stockholders. These preferential rights may include a priority claim on the company's assets and earnings in the event of liquidation or sale, priority in receiving dividends, voting rights on certain matters, and the ability to convert their preferred shares into common shares at a predetermined ratio. Series AA Preferred Stock is often structured with different features and terms compared to subsequent series of preferred stock. This is to accommodate the changing needs of the startup as it progresses through various stages of funding. In later rounds of financing, the startup may issue additional series of preferred stock, such as Series A, B, C, and so on, each with its own distinct features and rights. Series AA Preferred Stock provides early-stage investors with the potential for significant returns if the startup is successful. However, it also comes with higher risks compared to other forms of investments. Investors should carefully evaluate the startup's business model, market potential, and the experience and track record of the founding team before committing to invest in Series AA Preferred Stock. In conclusion, Series AA Preferred Stock is a class of stock that startups issue to early-stage investors in exchange for capital. It provides certain rights and privileges to its holders and allows startups to raise funds while maintaining founder control. Investors should assess the risks and potential returns before investing in Series AA Preferred Stock.

Series AA

Series AA is a specific funding round that typically takes place in the early stages of a startup's development. It is an important step in the process of raising capital for entrepreneurs to bring their business ideas to fruition.In the world of startup and entrepreneurship, Series AA is considered the first institutional funding round. This means that the funding comes from venture capital firms or angel investors rather than friends and family or personal savings.

Series B Funding

Series B funding refers to the second round of financing that a startup or entrepreneurial venture receives from investors. It typically occurs after the initial seed round (Series A funding) and is intended to further support the growth and development of the company. During this stage, the startup has usually demonstrated significant progress and traction in terms of product development, market validation, customer acquisition, and revenue generation. The funding raised in this round is often used to scale operations, expand into new markets, invest in additional research and development, and hire key talent.

Series B-1

A Series B-1 round of financing is a stage in the funding cycle of a startup company. It typically occurs after a successful Series A round and before a Series B round. In this stage, the startup raises additional capital to fund its growth and operations. The purpose of a Series B-1 round is to provide the startup with the necessary financial resources to further develop and scale its business. This round is often conducted when the company has achieved certain milestones and demonstrated positive growth potential, but requires additional funding to reach the next stage of its development. In a Series B-1 round, the startup typically seeks funding from venture capital firms, institutional investors, and sometimes existing investors who participated in previous rounds. These investors evaluate the startup's performance, market potential, and management team to determine if it is a worthwhile investment. During the Series B-1 round, the startup may use the funds for various purposes such as expanding its team, developing new products or services, improving its infrastructure and operations, and marketing and sales activities. The specific allocation of funds may vary depending on the company's business model and growth strategy. Typically, a Series B-1 round involves negotiations between the startup and potential investors regarding the terms of the investment, including valuation, ownership stake, voting rights, and other agreements. The startup's goal is to secure sufficient funding while maintaining a reasonable level of control and ownership. Ultimately, the success of a Series B-1 round depends on the ability of the startup to convince investors of its growth potential and the viability of its business model. The funds raised in this round are intended to propel the company towards achieving profitability and market dominance in its industry.

Series C Funding

Series C funding refers to the third round of financing that a startup receives from external investors. It is typically obtained when a startup has already achieved significant milestones, such as product development and market validation, and requires additional funds to scale its operations, expand into new markets, or prepare for an initial public offering (IPO). During Series C funding, startups aim to secure larger amounts of capital compared to the previous rounds (Seed, Series A, and Series B) to further accelerate their growth. The investors participating in this round are often venture capital firms, private equity firms, or strategic investors who believe in the startup's potential for future success. Companies seeking Series C funding must demonstrate a solid track record of performance and growth. They are expected to present a clear and compelling business plan, showcasing how the additional funding will be utilized to maximize shareholder value and achieve sustainable profitability. Series C funding rounds typically involve a more rigorous due diligence process than earlier rounds, as investors are more cautious and demanding at this stage. They thoroughly evaluate the startup's financials, market opportunity, competitive landscape, intellectual property, and overall operational capabilities to assess the risk and potential return on investment. In return for their investment, Series C investors receive equity or preferred shares in the startup, granting them ownership stakes and the potential for future returns. The valuations during Series C funding are usually higher than previous rounds, reflecting the startup's growth potential and market value. Overall, Series C funding plays a crucial role in the growth and development of startups, enabling them to scale rapidly, expand their market presence, and attract top talent. It serves as a bridge between the early-stage funding and potential exit opportunities, such as an IPO or acquisition, allowing startups to realize their long-term visions and objectives.

Series FF Preferred Stock

Series FF Preferred Stock refers to a type of preferred stock that is commonly issued to investors during the early stages of a startup company. Preferred stock represents ownership in the company, providing investors with certain rights and privileges that differ from those of common stockholders. The "FF" in Series FF Preferred Stock indicates that it is a later series of preferred stock issued by the company. As a startup or entrepreneur, issuing Series FF Preferred Stock can be an effective way to raise capital and attract investment. This type of stock is typically offered to angel investors, venture capitalists, or other institutional investors who are willing to take early-stage risks in return for potential high returns on their investment. Series FF Preferred Stock often carries certain advantages and preferences over common stock. Firstly, these shareholders usually have priority over common stockholders when it comes to receiving dividends. In the event of a liquidation or acquisition, preferred stockholders have a higher claim on the company's assets compared to common stockholders. Moreover, Series FF Preferred Stock may also provide investors with certain voting rights, allowing them to have a say in the company's major decisions. This can range from approving significant corporate actions, such as mergers or changes in the company's structure, to electing members of the board of directors. Additionally, Series FF Preferred Stock may have features like conversion options, which allow the stockholders to convert their preferred shares into common shares at a predetermined ratio in the future. This can be beneficial for investors if the company experiences significant growth and the value of the common stock increases substantially. Overall, Series FF Preferred Stock serves as a valuable tool for startups and entrepreneurs to secure investment and provide certain benefits to early-stage investors. The issuance of this stock allows the company to raise capital while providing investors with a potential return on their investment and a voice in the company's decision-making process.

Series FF Stock

Series FF stock refers to a specific type of financing instrument commonly used in the context of startups and entrepreneurship. It typically refers to a preferred stock class offered to early-stage investors in a startup company. Series FF stock is used when a startup has already gone through previous funding rounds, such as Series A, Series B, and so on, and requires additional funding to fuel its growth and expansion plans. This type of stock is typically issued to a select group of investors who show a strong belief in the startup's potential and are willing to invest a significant amount of capital.

Series G Preferred Stock

Series G Preferred Stock is a type of equity financing commonly used by startup companies to raise capital from investors. It represents a class of shares that have a higher claim on the company's assets and earnings compared to common stockholders in the event of liquidation. This funding round typically occurs after several previous rounds of financing, such as Series A, B, C, D, and so on, with each subsequent round denoted by a letter of the alphabet. Series G Preferred Stock is usually offered to investors who are willing to provide a large amount of capital to support the growth and expansion of the startup.

Series Seed Funding

Series Seed Funding is a type of investment that occurs in the early stages of a startup's development. It typically occurs after the founder or founders have raised initial funds from their own personal savings or from friends and family. This stage of funding is called the seed stage, as it is when the business idea is still in its infancy and has not yet generated significant revenue or traction. The purpose of Series Seed Funding is to provide the startup with the necessary capital to further develop its product or service and to validate its market potential. This funding is used to hire key team members, conduct further research and development, and execute marketing and sales strategies. It is also used to cover any operational expenses the startup may incur during this early stage. Series Seed Funding is usually provided by angel investors, venture capitalists, or early-stage investment firms. These investors provide the capital in exchange for equity in the startup. The terms of the funding, including the amount of capital raised and the equity stake given to the investors, are typically negotiated between the startup and the investors. The amount of capital raised during Series Seed Funding can vary widely, but it is typically in the range of $500,000 to $2 million. This funding is usually provided in multiple rounds, with each round providing additional capital as the startup achieves specific milestones or targets. These milestones may include reaching a certain level of revenue, acquiring a certain number of customers, or securing additional partnerships or contracts. Series Seed Funding is a critical stage of financing for startups, as it provides the necessary resources to take the business idea from concept to reality. It allows the startup to build its team, validate its product or service, and begin generating traction in the market. Without this funding, many startups would struggle to survive and scale their operations.

Series Seed

Series Seed refers to the initial stage of funding usually provided by investors to startup companies in exchange for equity or ownership in the company. This stage typically occurs after the founder or entrepreneur has used their own personal funds or raised money from friends and family, and is seeking additional financing to grow their business. During the Series Seed stage, startups are often pre-revenue or have minimal sales traction, and are in the process of developing and refining their product or service. The funding received at this stage is used to support key activities such as product development, hiring key team members, and marketing efforts necessary to bring the startup to the next level. Investors providing Series Seed funding are typically angel investors, early-stage venture capital firms, or other institutional investors who believe in the potential of the startup and its ability to grow and generate returns. In exchange for their investment, these investors receive equity in the company, often in the form of preferred stock. The terms of the Series Seed funding are negotiated between the startup and the investors, and can vary depending on factors such as the startup's industry, growth potential, and the investor's level of involvement. Common terms include the valuation of the company, the amount of equity offered, and any rights or protections given to the investors. Series Seed funding allows startups to continue developing their product or service, refine their business model, and prove their market viability. It also provides a crucial runway for startups to attract further funding in later rounds, such as Series A, B, and beyond. In summary, Series Seed funding is the initial stage of financing provided to startups, usually by angel investors or early-stage venture capitalists, in exchange for equity. This funding is used to support key activities and propel the startup towards further growth and success.

Shareholder Agreement

A shareholder agreement is a legally binding contract that outlines the rights, responsibilities, and obligations of the shareholders of a startup or entrepreneurial venture. It serves as a means to establish clear guidelines and protect the interests of the shareholders in the company. The agreement typically covers various aspects such as ownership percentages, voting rights, decision-making processes, dispute resolution mechanisms, and restrictions on the transfer of shares. It is designed to provide a framework for governance and ensure that the shareholders are aligned in their objectives and expectations.

Shareholder Equity

Shareholder equity, in the context of startup and entrepreneurship, refers to the residual interest in the assets of a company after deducting its liabilities. It represents the net worth of the company, or the amount of the business that belongs to its shareholders. Shareholder equity is an important metric for startups and entrepreneurs as it reflects the financial health and value of the business. Shareholder equity is calculated by subtracting a company's total liabilities from its total assets. Liabilities include any debts, loans, or other obligations that the company has, while assets include tangible and intangible resources, such as cash, inventory, property, intellectual property, and investments. The resulting figure, known as shareholder equity, represents the value that the shareholders have in the company. Shareholder equity is a key indicator of a company's financial strength and ability to generate profits. It is important for startups and entrepreneurs to monitor and track their shareholder equity over time, as it can impact their ability to attract investors, secure financing, and grow their business. A higher shareholder equity indicates a stronger financial position and can increase investor confidence, while a lower shareholder equity may raise concerns about the company's financial stability. Startup founders and entrepreneurs can increase shareholder equity by growing the company's assets and reducing its liabilities. This can be achieved through various strategies, such as increasing sales revenue, improving operational efficiency, controlling costs, finding new investment opportunities, and managing debt. By consistently focusing on increasing shareholder equity, startups and entrepreneurs can build a more valuable and sustainable business.

Shareholder Rights Agreement

A Shareholder Rights Agreement, in the context of Startup and Entrepreneurship, is a legally binding agreement between a company and its shareholders that outlines the rights and obligations of the shareholders. It is designed to protect the interests of the shareholders and promote transparency and fairness in corporate decision-making. The Shareholder Rights Agreement typically covers various aspects of shareholder rights, including voting rights, information rights, preemptive rights, and restrictions on transfer of shares. It establishes a clear framework for the shareholders' involvement in the company's affairs and helps in maintaining a proper balance of power between the management and the shareholders.

Shareholder Vote

A shareholder vote is a formal process in which the shareholders of a startup or entrepreneurial venture participate to make important decisions affecting the company. Shareholders are individuals who have invested capital into the company in exchange for ownership in the form of shares. They have the right to vote on matters that impact the company's operations, future direction, and overall governance. The purpose of a shareholder vote is to provide a democratic mechanism for decision-making within the company. It allows shareholders to have a say in key business decisions, ensuring transparency and accountability. Shareholders typically vote on various matters, such as electing the board of directors, approving major corporate actions, amending the company's bylaws, or making significant changes to the capital structure. During a shareholder vote, each shareholder has the opportunity to cast their vote based on their proportional ownership in the company. The voting process may be conducted in person at a shareholders' meeting or through proxy voting, where shareholders assign their voting rights to a designated representative. The voting may be done using physical ballots, by a show of hands, or electronically through online platforms. A successful outcome of a shareholder vote is determined by the majority rule. This means that a proposal or decision is approved if it receives more than 50% of the total votes cast. However, some decisions may require a supermajority vote, which means a higher threshold, such as two-thirds or three-fourths majority, depending on the company's bylaws or legal regulations. It is important for startup founders and entrepreneurs to respect the rights and opinions of shareholders during the voting process. Shareholder votes can significantly impact the direction and success of a company. By actively involving and engaging shareholders in decision-making processes, startup founders can build trust and establish a supportive relationship with their investors.

Social Capital

Social capital refers to the network of relationships, trust, and norms that exist within a startup or entrepreneurial ecosystem. It encompasses the value derived from social connections, collaborations, and interactions among individuals and organizations involved in the startup community. Within the context of startups and entrepreneurship, social capital plays a critical role in facilitating knowledge sharing, resource exchange, and business opportunities. It enables entrepreneurs to tap into a collective pool of expertise, insights, and support that can enhance their chances of success.

Social Entrepreneurship Platforms

Social entrepreneurship platforms are innovative online platforms that facilitate the development and growth of social enterprises. These platforms serve as a virtual space where individuals, organizations, and communities can connect, collaborate, and access resources and support to address social and environmental challenges. These platforms are specifically designed to support social entrepreneurs in launching and scaling their ventures by offering a range of services and tools. They provide a comprehensive ecosystem that combines networking opportunities, mentorship, funding options, educational resources, and access to a community of like-minded individuals and organizations. Social entrepreneurship platforms play a crucial role in bridging the gap between social entrepreneurs and the resources they need to succeed. They provide a centralized hub where startup founders can showcase their ideas, connect with potential investors, partners, and customers, and access tailored support and guidance to navigate the unique challenges faced by social enterprises. One of the key features of these platforms is the ability to connect stakeholders with shared goals and interests. Social entrepreneurs can network and collaborate with other individuals or organizations working on similar issues, forming partnerships and leveraging collective expertise to create sustainable social impact. Furthermore, social entrepreneurship platforms offer educational resources and training programs to equip social entrepreneurs with the necessary skills and knowledge to build and run successful ventures. These resources may include workshops, webinars, online courses, and mentorship programs tailored to the specific needs of social enterprises. Access to funding is also a critical aspect of social entrepreneurship platforms. They provide a platform for social entrepreneurs to showcase their ventures to potential investors and secure the necessary financial support to launch or expand their operations. In addition to traditional funding options, some platforms may also offer crowdfunding features that allow social entrepreneurs to raise funds from a wider community of supporters. In summary, social entrepreneurship platforms provide a virtual ecosystem that supports social entrepreneurs in realizing their visions for a better world. By offering a range of resources, services, and networking opportunities, these platforms empower social entrepreneurs to create sustainable and impactful ventures.

Social Entrepreneurship Ventures

Social entrepreneurship ventures are business initiatives that prioritize social impact and sustainable solutions to address societal problems. These ventures are driven by entrepreneurs who are passionate about creating positive change and improving the well-being of communities. Unlike traditional entrepreneurship, where the primary focus is on generating profits, social entrepreneurship focuses on using business principles and innovation to bring about social change. These ventures aim to tackle pressing issues such as poverty, inequality, environmental degradation, and lack of access to education or healthcare. Social entrepreneurship ventures employ innovative approaches and business models to address these challenges. They often operate in sectors that have been historically underserved or neglected, and partner with nonprofit organizations, governments, and other stakeholders to create sustainable and impactful solutions. One key characteristic of social entrepreneurship ventures is their dual bottom line focus. While financial sustainability is important, these ventures place equal emphasis on generating social value. They measure success not just in terms of profits, but also in terms of their contribution to social well-being and sustainable development.

217

Another important aspect of social entrepreneurship ventures is their emphasis on collaboration and inclusivity. These ventures often involve multiple stakeholders and seek to empower marginalized communities. They actively engage with the beneficiaries of their initiatives and work towards creating opportunities for them to become self-sufficient. In summary, social entrepreneurship ventures are business initiatives that aim to create positive social impact by using innovative approaches, business principles, and collaboration. They address pressing societal problems and prioritize sustainable solutions. These ventures exemplify the potential of business to drive positive change and create a more inclusive and equitable society.

Social Entrepreneurship

Social entrepreneurship is a concept that combines the innovative mindset of an entrepreneur with a focus on creating positive social and environmental impact. It involves leveraging business principles and strategies to address societal challenges and improve the well-being of communities. At the core of social entrepreneurship is the belief that businesses have the power to drive social change and tackle pressing problems. Social entrepreneurs are driven by a mission to create scalable and sustainable solutions to social issues, rather than purely pursuing financial gains.

Social Impact Entrepreneurship

Social Impact Entrepreneurship refers to a form of entrepreneurship wherein entrepreneurs create and scale business ventures that aim to address social and environmental challenges while also generating financial returns. This type of entrepreneurship goes beyond mere profit-making and focuses on creating positive social change, often targeting marginalized communities and addressing issues such as poverty, inequality, climate change, and access to education, healthcare, and clean energy. Social impact entrepreneurs are driven by a dual mission of both financial sustainability and social impact. They recognize that traditional business models have limitations in addressing complex societal issues and strive to create innovative solutions through their ventures. They adopt a holistic approach that considers the social, environmental, and economic implications of their actions, and aim to create sustainable value for all stakeholders involved. These entrepreneurs play a pivotal role in addressing social and environmental challenges that are often overlooked by governments and traditional economic actors. They bring fresh perspectives, innovative ideas, and entrepreneurial drive to create scalable solutions that can have a lasting and transformative impact on society. Through their ventures, they demonstrate that business and social good are not mutually exclusive, but can be mutually reinforcing. Furthermore, social impact entrepreneurship is not limited to a specific sector or industry. It can encompass a wide range of business models, from for-profit enterprises with a social mission to nonprofit organizations that leverage entrepreneurial approaches to generate revenue and achieve sustainable social impact. The focus is on leveraging entrepreneurial principles, such as innovation, risk-taking, and scalability, to address societal challenges effectively. In conclusion, social impact entrepreneurship is about using the power of entrepreneurship to create positive social change. It encompasses entrepreneurs who are driven by a dual mission of financial sustainability and social impact, employing innovative business models to address social and environmental challenges. These entrepreneurs play a critical role in driving transformative change and demonstrating that business can be a force for good.

Social Innovation

Social Innovation is a concept in the realm of startup and entrepreneurship that refers to the development and implementation of new ideas, strategies, and solutions to address social and environmental challenges in society. It encompasses the innovative application of technology, business models, and organizational processes to create positive social impact and generate sustainable change. This process involves identifying and understanding societal problems and then offering innovative solutions that go beyond traditional approaches. It focuses on transforming existing systems, practices, and mindsets to improve the well-being of individuals, communities, and the overall social fabric.

Social Media Marketing Tools

Social media marketing tools refer to the various software, platforms, and services that are used by startups and entrepreneurs to manage and enhance their presence on social media platforms. These tools provide a range of functionalities, including scheduling posts, analyzing engagement metrics, monitoring brand mentions, and facilitating social media advertising. In the context of startups and entrepreneurship, social media marketing tools play a crucial role in establishing and growing a brand's online presence. They enable startups to reach a wider audience, engage with potential customers, and build brand awareness, all of which are vital for business growth. One of the key features of these tools is post scheduling. Startups can use these tools to plan and automate their social media content, ensuring a consistent and regular presence on various platforms. This feature is particularly helpful for entrepreneurs who have limited resources and time, allowing them to manage multiple social media accounts more efficiently. Another important aspect of social media marketing tools is their ability to analyze engagement metrics. These tools provide startups with insights into their audience's behavior, helping them identify the type of content that resonates the most with their followers. By understanding which posts generate the most likes, comments, and shares, entrepreneurs can refine their social media strategy and optimize their content to drive better engagement. Furthermore, social media marketing tools offer features for monitoring brand mentions. Startups can track their brand's reputation on social media by monitoring keywords and hashtags related to their industry. This allows entrepreneurs to address customer feedback, respond to inquiries, and manage any potential negative sentiment effectively. By actively managing their brand's online reputation, startups can enhance customer trust and loyalty, which is crucial for long-term success. Lastly, social media marketing tools provide opportunities for social media advertising. Startups can leverage these tools to create and manage targeted ad campaigns on platforms such as Facebook, Instagram, and LinkedIn. With features that allow for audience segmentation and ad performance tracking, entrepreneurs can optimize their advertising efforts, ensuring that they reach the right audience at the right time. In conclusion, social media marketing tools empower startups and entrepreneurs to effectively manage and optimize their presence on social media platforms. These tools offer functionalities such as post scheduling, engagement metrics analysis, brand monitoring, and social media advertising, all of which contribute to building a strong online brand presence and driving business growth.

Social Proof

Social proof, in the context of startup and entrepreneurship, refers to the psychological phenomenon where people assume the actions or decisions of others in an attempt to reflect the correct behavior for a given situation. For startups and entrepreneurs, social proof can play a vital role in attracting customers, investors, and partners. It serves as a form of validation or evidence that others have already found value in a product, service, or venture. By leveraging social proof effectively, startups can build trust and credibility, which are crucial for establishing a strong foothold in the market. Social proof can manifest in various forms, including customer testimonials, case studies, endorsements from industry experts or influencers, user reviews, social media likes and shares, and metrics such as user counts or revenue figures. These different types of social proof can be displayed on websites, social media profiles, marketing materials, and pitch decks. When potential customers see positive feedback from satisfied customers or reputable individuals or organizations, they are more likely to trust the startup and feel more confident in making a purchase or using the product or service. Social proof can also help overcome skepticism or doubts potential customers may have and increase conversion rates. Furthermore, social proof can also influence potential investors and partners. When they see that others have already invested in or partnered with a startup, it signals that the venture is worth considering and reduces the perceived risks associated with investing or collaborating. Startups can actively cultivate social proof by proactively collecting and showcasing testimonials, encouraging happy customers to leave reviews, seeking endorsements from influential figures, and leveraging social media to amplify positive feedback. However, it's important for startups to ensure that the social proof they use is authentic and genuine, as people are increasingly becoming wary of fake or manipulated testimonials and endorsements. In conclusion, social proof is a powerful psychological concept that plays a critical role in startup and entrepreneurship. By leveraging social proof effectively, startups can build trust and credibility, which are essential for attracting customers, investors, and partners and establishing a solid foundation for growth and success.

Solo Entrepreneur

A solo entrepreneur, in the context of startup and entrepreneurship, refers to an individual who starts and manages a business venture on their own, without any additional partners or employees. This means that a solo entrepreneur takes on the responsibility of all aspects of the business, including planning, financing, marketing, and operations. Starting a business as a solo entrepreneur can be a challenging but rewarding endeavor. It requires a high level of dedication, self-motivation, and a diverse set of skills. Solo entrepreneurs often have to wear multiple hats and be proficient in various areas of business, such as sales, accounting, and customer service. One of the advantages of being a solo entrepreneur is the complete control and autonomy over decision-making. Without the need to consult with other partners or employees, solo entrepreneurs have the freedom to make quick decisions and implement changes as needed. This flexibility allows for faster innovation and adaptation to market trends. However, being a solo entrepreneur also comes with its own set of challenges. Limited resources, such as time, capital, and expertise, can pose constraints on the growth and success of the venture. Without a team to rely on, solo entrepreneurs may experience difficulty in scaling the business or handling increased workloads. To overcome these challenges, solo entrepreneurs often leverage technology and automation to streamline processes and enhance productivity. They may also seek support from networks, mentors, or consultants to gain valuable insights and guidance. In conclusion, a solo entrepreneur is an individual who single-handedly launches and operates a business venture. They possess a wide range of skills and must take on all aspects of the business. While they enjoy complete control over decision-making, they may face resource limitations and scalability challenges. By leveraging technology and seeking support from others, solo entrepreneurs can navigate the entrepreneurial journey successfully.

Solopreneur

A solopreneur is an individual who starts and runs their own business single-handedly, taking on all the responsibilities and tasks involved in the venture. Solopreneurs are often experts in their field and have a strong passion for their work, which motivates them to pursue their business goals independently. Unlike traditional entrepreneurs who typically build a team and delegate tasks, solopreneurs prefer to maintain full control and handle every aspect of their business. This includes product development, marketing, customer service, accounting, and more. They are self-reliant and take on all the risk and reward associated with their business.

Special Purpose Acquisition Company (SPAC)

A Special Purpose Acquisition Company (SPAC) is a type of investment vehicle that is specifically designed for entrepreneurs and startup companies to go public and raise capital. SPACs have become increasingly popular in recent years because they offer a unique alternative to the traditional initial public offering (IPO) process. Unlike traditional IPOs, where a company goes through extensive roadshows and regulatory processes to raise capital, SPACs provide a more streamlined and cost-effective way for startups to access public markets. A SPAC is formed by a group of individuals, often experienced investors or industry experts, who establish a shell company with the sole purpose of raising money from public investors. Once the SPAC is formed and listed on a stock exchange, it starts looking for a private company to acquire and merge with. This target company is typically a startup or an early-stage company looking for additional funding and a faster route to the public markets. The SPAC's management team, or the sponsors, takes the responsibility of identifying and evaluating potential target companies that are a good fit for the SPAC's investment strategy. When a target company is chosen, the SPAC uses the funds raised from its initial public offering to acquire a majority stake in the target company. This transaction transforms the target company into a publicly traded entity, bypassing the long and costly IPO process. The shareholders of the target company receive shares in the merged entity, and the SPAC's sponsors typically receive a percentage of the shares as well. SPACs offer several advantages for startups and entrepreneurs. Firstly, they provide a faster route to liquidity compared to traditional IPOs, allowing founders and existing investors to monetize their investments sooner. They also offer greater flexibility in terms of valuation, as the merger negotiations between the SPAC and the target company can be conducted privately. Additionally, SPACs provide access to a broader investor base, including institutional investors and retail investors, who may not have been accessible through a traditional IPO.

Special Purpose Vehicle (SPV)

A Special Purpose Vehicle (SPV) is a legal entity that is created by startups and entrepreneurs to isolate certain risks and assets from the main business. It is commonly used in startup and entrepreneurial ventures to achieve specific objectives, such as raising capital, managing risks, and protecting intellectual property. An SPV is typically a separate company or a subsidiary that is established to undertake a specific project or business activity. It functions as a standalone entity with its own legal identity and financial structure. By setting up an SPV, startups and entrepreneurs can mitigate various risks and enhance the overall efficiency of their operations. One primary purpose of an SPV in the context of startups and entrepreneurship is to raise capital. Startups often require funding from external sources to support their growth and expansion. However, investors may be reluctant to invest directly in the startup's main business due to various reasons, such as increased risks or conflicts of interest. In such cases, startups can establish an SPV to attract investments solely dedicated to a specific project or asset. This allows investors to participate in the venture while limiting their exposure to the risks associated with the startup's core business. Another important role of an SPV is to manage risks. Startups and entrepreneurs often face uncertainties and potential liabilities associated with their business activities. By creating an SPV, they can isolate these risks and protect their main business from potential financial losses. This is especially relevant in industries where large-scale projects or investments are involved, such as real estate development or infrastructure projects. Additionally, an SPV can be used for intellectual property protection. Startups and entrepreneurs may develop innovative technologies or proprietary knowledge that need to be safeguarded from infringement or misappropriation. By transferring these intellectual property assets to an SPV, they can be protected and commercialized separately from the main business. This provides startups with greater control over their intellectual property rights and potential licensing or partnership opportunities. In conclusion, a Special Purpose Vehicle (SPV) is a legal entity used by startups and entrepreneurs to achieve specific objectives, such as raising capital, managing risks, and protecting intellectual property. By setting up an SPV, startups can attract investments, isolate risks, and safeguard their intellectual property assets, thereby enhancing their overall business efficiency and growth prospects.

Stakeholder Mapping

Stakeholder mapping refers to the process of identifying and analyzing the individuals or groups that have a direct or indirect interest in a startup or entrepreneurial venture. These stakeholders can significantly impact the success or failure of the venture, making it essential for entrepreneurs to understand and manage their expectations and relationships. In the context of startup and entrepreneurship, stakeholder mapping involves visually representing the different stakeholders and their relationships with the venture. This mapping helps entrepreneurs to identify the key players and their roles, as well as the level of influence or power they hold. Stakeholders can be categorized into various groups, including investors, customers, employees, suppliers, partners, government authorities, and local communities. Each group has its own set of interests, needs, and expectations that entrepreneurs must acknowledge and address. For instance, investors are often interested in the financial returns and long-term growth potential of the venture. They may expect a certain level of transparency and regular updates on the financial performance and strategic direction of the startup. Similarly, customers expect high-quality products or services that fulfill their needs and provide value for their money. By identifying and understanding the different stakeholder groups, entrepreneurs can develop tailored strategies to engage and manage their relationships effectively. This may involve establishing open lines of communication, maintaining good rapport, and addressing any concerns or issues promptly. Effective stakeholder management can lead to increased support, trust, and collaboration, which are crucial for the long-term success of the venture. Furthermore, stakeholder mapping also helps entrepreneurs in understanding potential conflicts or tensions that may arise among different stakeholder groups. For example, employees may demand higher wages, while investors may prioritize cost-cutting measures. By recognizing these potential conflicts, entrepreneurs can find ways to minimize or resolve them, ensuring alignment and harmony among the stakeholders. Overall, stakeholder mapping provides a valuable framework for entrepreneurs to identify, analyze, and manage the various individuals and groups that have a vested interest in their startup or entrepreneurial venture. By actively engaging and addressing the needs and expectations of these stakeholders, entrepreneurs can foster a

221

supportive and collaborative environment, ultimately increasing the likelihood of success.

Startup Acceleration

Startup acceleration refers to a process that helps early-stage companies and entrepreneurs achieve rapid growth and success. It involves providing guidance, resources, and support to startups to enhance their development, marketability, and sustainability. The primary goal of startup acceleration is to maximize a startup's potential to scale quickly and become a sustainable business entity. Accelerators focus on helping startups refine their business models, develop their products or services, and acquire customers or users rapidly. They typically work in cohorts or batches, where groups of startups go through an intensive program together, learning from experts, mentors, and each other. Startup accelerators offer a range of services to support startups. These services often include mentorship, where experienced entrepreneurs and industry experts provide guidance and act as sounding boards for startup founders. They also offer access to valuable networks, connecting startups with potential investors, partners, and customers. Additionally, accelerators provide educational programs, workshops, and training sessions to help startups improve their skills and knowledge in various areas of business development, such as marketing, finance, and operations. In exchange for their support, startup accelerators typically take an equity stake in the startups they work with. This means that the accelerator becomes a shareholder in the company and participates in its future success. This alignment of interests encourages the accelerator to provide ongoing support and guidance to help the startup thrive. Startup acceleration plays a crucial role in the startup ecosystem. It helps to bridge the gap between idea conception and market entry, providing startups with the necessary tools and resources to navigate the challenging early stages of business development. By offering a structured and supportive environment, accelerators help startups minimize risks, avoid common pitfalls, and increase their chances of success in the competitive startup landscape.

Startup Accelerator Program

A startup accelerator program is a structured and time-limited initiative designed to support the growth of early-stage companies and entrepreneurs. It provides a combination of resources, mentorship, and networking opportunities to help startups scale their operations and achieve their business goals. Accelerator programs typically operate on a cohort-based model, where a group of selected startups go through a defined program together. The program duration can vary, but it is typically around three to six months. During this time, the startups receive intensive guidance and support from a network of industry experts, mentors, and investors. The program curriculum of a startup accelerator is tailored to address the specific needs and challenges faced by early-stage companies. It covers various aspects of entrepreneurship, such as refining the startup's business model, developing a viable product or service, understanding target markets and customer needs, building a strong team, and navigating the funding landscape. One of the key benefits of participating in an accelerator program is access to a wide network of industry connections. Startups get the opportunity to interact with successful entrepreneurs, potential customers, strategic partners, and investors during various events and networking sessions organized by the accelerator. This exposure helps startups in validating their ideas, getting valuable feedback, and building crucial relationships that can accelerate their growth. Another crucial aspect of accelerator programs is the provision of financial support. Accelerators typically offer seed funding to the participating startups in exchange for an equity stake. This financial support enables startups to cover their operational expenses, invest in product development, and reach important milestones that can attract additional investment later on. At the end of the accelerator program, startups usually have the opportunity to pitch their businesses to a group of investors during a demo day. This event serves as a platform for startups to showcase their progress, generate investor interest, and secure further funding to fuel their growth. In summary, a startup accelerator program provides early-stage companies with the necessary resources, mentorship, and networking opportunities to accelerate their growth. It offers a structured curriculum, access to industry connections, financial support, and a platform for fundraising. By participating in an accelerator program, startups can gain a competitive edge, increase their chances of success, and expedite their journey towards becoming sustainable and scalable businesses.

Startup Accelerator

A startup accelerator is a program that helps early-stage startups to grow and scale their businesses. It provides resources, mentorship, and funding to enable founders to accelerate their companies' development and increase their chance of success. The primary goal of a startup accelerator is to support entrepreneurs in refining their business models, validating their ideas, and acquiring the necessary skills and knowledge to navigate the complex startup ecosystem. It aims to provide a structured framework for startups to speed up their growth and reduce the risks associated with starting a new business. Typically, startup accelerators select a cohort of promising startups to participate in their programs for a fixed period, usually ranging from three to six months. During this time, startups work intensively on various aspects of their business, including product development, market research, customer acquisition, and fundraising. One of the key features of a startup accelerator is the provision of mentorship from experienced entrepreneurs, industry experts, and investors. Mentors play a crucial role in guiding founders through the challenges they face and providing actionable advice based on their own past experiences. They help startups identify potential pitfalls, make strategic decisions, and build a strong network of contacts in the industry. In addition to mentorship, startup accelerators often offer access to a wide range of resources and services. These may include coworking spaces, legal and accounting support, marketing and branding assistance, and access to a network of potential customers and investors. Another important aspect of startup accelerators is the opportunity for startups to secure funding. Accelerators typically invest a certain amount of capital in each startup in exchange for equity. This not only provides startups with the financial resources to pursue their growth plans but also serves as a validation of their potential for future investors. Overall, startup accelerators play a vital role in the startup ecosystem by providing critical support and guidance to early-stage companies. They help startups overcome challenges, build a solid foundation, and increase their chances of long-term success in the competitive world of entrepreneurship.

Startup Advisory Board

A startup advisory board is a group of experienced individuals who provide guidance and strategic advice to startup founders and entrepreneurs. The board is typically comprised of experts from various fields, including finance, marketing, technology, and industry-specific knowledge. The purpose of a startup advisory board is to offer objective insights and opinions on critical business decisions and to support the growth and development of the startup. Members of the advisory board bring their wealth of knowledge and expertise to help startups navigate challenges, identify opportunities, and make informed decisions. The composition of a startup advisory board varies depending on the specific needs and goals of the startup. The ideal board members are individuals who have successful track records in entrepreneurship, have expertise in the startup's industry, and possess extensive networks that can be leveraged for the startup's benefit. Each board member should bring a unique perspective and skill set that complements the startup's team and fills any skill gaps. Startups benefit from having an advisory board in several ways. Firstly, the board provides an external perspective and acts as a sounding board for founders. This helps to validate ideas and provides a fresh take on the startup's strategies. Secondly, the board members offer their networks, introductions, and connections that can open doors to potential customers, partners, investors, and talent. Thirdly, the advisory board can provide guidance on important matters such as fundraising, business development, market entry strategies, and talent acquisition. Their experience and insights can prevent startups from making costly mistakes and help them seize opportunities more effectively. It is important for startup founders to establish clear expectations and goals for their advisory board. Communication and regular meetings are crucial for maintaining a productive relationship with the board members. Founders should be open to feedback and actively seek the advice and expertise of the board members. In return, the board members should be committed to the startup's success and provide honest, objective advice in the best interest of the company.

Startup Bootcamp

A Startup Bootcamp is a focused and intensive program designed to support and accelerate the growth of early-stage startups. It is typically run by experienced mentors and industry experts who provide guidance, mentorship, and resources to help entrepreneurs refine their business ideas and transform them into viable and scalable businesses. The primary objective of a Startup Bootcamp is to equip entrepreneurs with the necessary skills, knowledge, and network to navigate the challenges and complexities of starting and growing a successful startup. The program usually lasts for a fixed duration, ranging from a few weeks to a few months, during which participants go through a structured curriculum and participate in various workshops, seminars, and mentoring sessions. The curriculum of a Startup Bootcamp covers various aspects of startup development, including business model validation, product development, market research, customer acquisition, marketing and sales, financial planning, and investor relations. Through a combination of interactive sessions, hands-on exercises, and real-world case studies, participants gain practical insights and develop critical thinking skills that are essential for building and scaling a startup successfully. In addition to training and education, a Startup Bootcamp also provides access to a valuable network of mentors, investors, industry experts, and fellow entrepreneurs. This network is crucial for startups as it offers opportunities for partnerships, collaborations, and funding. The bootcamp also often ends with a demo day or a pitching event, where participants can showcase their progress and attract potential investors. Startup Bootcamps are a highly effective way for entrepreneurs to accelerate their startup journey. By participating in such a program, entrepreneurs can benefit from the expertise and guidance of experienced professionals, gain crucial skills and knowledge, and build a network of valuable contacts. Moreover, the structured and intensive nature of a Startup Bootcamp helps entrepreneurs stay focused, motivated, and accountable, increasing their chances of success.

Startup Capital

Startup capital refers to the initial funding or investment required to launch a new business venture. It is the financial resources that an entrepreneur or startup needs to cover essential expenses such as product development, marketing, hiring employees, and acquiring necessary equipment or resources. Startups often require a significant amount of capital in order to develop their product or service, build a customer base, and establish their brand in the market. This capital is typically sourced from various channels, including personal savings, family and friends, angel investors, venture capitalists, or through crowdfunding platforms.

Startup Culture

The culture of a startup refers to the values, beliefs, attitudes, and behaviors that are shared and lived by the members of the organization. It encompasses the way people interact with each other, the way decisions are made, and the overall atmosphere of the workplace. Startup culture is often characterized by its emphasis on innovation, risk-taking, adaptability, and a fast-paced work environment. One key aspect of startup culture is its focus on innovation. Startups are typically founded on a unique idea or solution to a problem, and fostering a culture of innovation is essential for their success. This means encouraging employees to think outside the box, take risks, and challenge the status quo. Experimentation and failure are both seen as valuable learning opportunities, and employees are encouraged to continuously iterate and improve upon their ideas. In addition to innovation, startup culture also places a strong emphasis on taking risks. Startups operate in a highly competitive and volatile environment, and taking calculated risks is often necessary for growth and success. This can involve anything from entering new markets, trying out new strategies, or even pivoting the entire business model. Consequently, startup culture values individuals who are comfortable with uncertainty, adaptable to change, and willing to take bold actions. A fast-paced work environment is another defining characteristic of startup culture. Startups typically have limited resources and tight timelines, which often result in a sense of urgency and a need for quick decision-making. This fast-paced environment requires employees to be highly motivated, proactive, and efficient in their work. It also fosters a sense of camaraderie and teamwork, as everyone needs to collaborate closely to meet deadlines and achieve goals. Overall, startup culture is an integral part of the entrepreneurial ecosystem. It sets the tone for how work is done, how ideas are generated, and how employees interact with each other. By fostering a culture of innovation, risk-taking, and adaptability, startups can create an environment that nurtures creativity, drives growth, and attracts talented individuals with an entrepreneurial mindset.

Startup Ecosystem Development

A startup ecosystem refers to the interconnected network of resources, support systems, and stakeholders that contribute to the success and growth of startups and entrepreneurship within a particular geographical region or industry. It encompasses both tangible and intangible factors that enable and foster innovation, collaboration, and economic development. Within a startup ecosystem, startups and entrepreneurs can access a wide range of support and resources, including funding opportunities, mentorship programs, incubators and accelerators, networking events, educational initiatives, and regulatory frameworks. These components are essential for startups to thrive and overcome the challenges they face during their early stages of development. Investors also play a crucial role in a startup ecosystem by providing the necessary financial capital to fuel startups' growth and expansion plans. By investing in startups, venture capitalists and angel investors contribute to job creation, technological advancements, and economic growth within the ecosystem. Their investments also attract other investors, creating a positive cycle of funding and support for startups. Collaboration and networking are key characteristics of a vibrant startup ecosystem. By connecting with other entrepreneurs, startups can share knowledge, resources, and experiences, fostering a culture of innovation and learning. The presence of established companies, research institutions, and universities further enhances the ecosystem by offering partnerships, research opportunities, and access to specialized expertise. A favorable regulatory environment is crucial for startups to thrive within an ecosystem. Policies that support entrepreneurship, ease of doing business, and intellectual property protection are essential for attracting and retaining startups. Governments and policymakers can also create initiatives that encourage and foster innovation, such as tax incentives, grants, and public-private partnerships. In summary, a startup ecosystem encompasses the various components that contribute to the growth and success of startups and entrepreneurship. It involves the availability of financial capital, support networks, resources, collaboration opportunities, and a favorable regulatory environment. By nurturing and developing a robust ecosystem, regions and industries can foster a culture of innovation, attract investment, create jobs, and drive economic growth.

Startup Ecosystem

A startup ecosystem is a network of interconnected organizations, institutions, and individuals that work collaboratively to support and nurture the growth of startups and entrepreneurship in a specific geographical area or industry. At its core, a startup ecosystem provides the necessary resources, support, and infrastructure to help startups launch, grow, and thrive. This includes access to funding, mentors, talent, research and development facilities, networking opportunities, government support, and a favorable regulatory environment. In a startup ecosystem, startups are the key players, as they are the innovative and disruptive businesses that are aiming to solve a specific problem or meet a market demand. These startups often have limited resources and face various challenges in their early stages, such as securing funding, developing their product or service, building a customer base, and scaling their operations. However, a startup ecosystem recognizes that the success of startups is dependent on the collaboration and support of various stakeholders. These stakeholders include investors, such as angel investors, venture capitalists, and private equity firms, who provide the necessary capital to fuel the growth of startups. They also include mentors and advisors, who share their expertise and guidance to help startups overcome challenges and make informed decisions. Furthermore, a startup ecosystem involves academic institutions and research organizations, which contribute to the development of new technologies and innovations. These institutions often collaborate with startups to provide access to cutting-edge research, facilities, and talent. Government entities also play a crucial role in creating a conducive environment for startups by implementing policies and regulations that support entrepreneurship, fostering innovation, and providing incentives. Finally, a startup ecosystem includes various support organizations, such as co-working spaces, incubators, and accelerators, that provide physical and virtual spaces for startups to work, collaborate, and access resources. These organizations often offer mentorship programs, networking events, and educational workshops to help startups refine their business models, sharpen their skills, and connect with potential partners or customers.

Startup Failure

A startup failure refers to the cessation of operations by a startup company due to various reasons such as financial insolvency, lack of market demand, management issues, or internal conflicts. In the context of entrepreneurship, a startup failure can be defined as the unfortunate outcome of a venture that is unable to sustain its operations and achieve its intended goals. Startup failures can occur at different stages of a company's lifecycle. Many startups fail within the initial few years of their establishment, during the early stage known as the "valley of death," where they face numerous challenges and uncertainties. These challenges include securing funding, developing a viable business model, building a customer base, and scaling up operations. If a startup fails to overcome these hurdles effectively, it may lead to its eventual failure. Financial insolvency is one of the most common reasons for startup failure. Startups often rely on external funding from investors and other sources to sustain their operations and fuel their growth. If a startup is unable to secure sufficient funding or fails to manage its finances effectively, it can quickly deplete its resources and face bankruptcy, leading to its dissolution. Moreover, inadequate cash flow management, unsustainable cost structures, and failure to generate revenue can contribute to financial insolvency. Another significant factor contributing to startup failures is a lack of market demand for the product or service offered by the startup. Market validation and understanding customer needs are critical for startups to develop products that meet market demand. Failure to identify and address customers' pain points or offering products with limited or niche appeal can lead to a lack of traction in the market. Without sufficient customer adoption and revenue generation, startups may struggle to sustain their operations, leading to failure. Management issues and internal conflicts within a startup can also contribute to its failure. Poor execution of strategy, ineffective leadership, co-founder disputes, and inadequate management of human resources can impede a startup's ability to grow and adapt to market changes. Lack of coordination, misaligned goals, and ineffective decision-making can hinder a startup's progress and lead to its downfall. In conclusion, a startup failure occurs when a startup company is unable to sustain its operations and achieve its intended goals due to reasons such as financial insolvency, lack of market demand, management issues, or internal conflicts. Understanding the factors that contribute to startup failures can help entrepreneurs make informed decisions and improve their chances of success in the highly competitive startup ecosystem.

Startup Funding

Startup funding refers to the financial investment made in a startup company by external individuals or organizations, commonly known as investors, in order to support its early stage growth and development. This funding is crucial for startups as it provides the necessary capital to cover initial expenses, drive innovation, and scale their operations. Startup funding can be obtained from various sources, including venture capitalists, angel investors, crowdfunding platforms, and government grants. Each funding source offers different terms and conditions, such as equity ownership, return on investment, and involvement in decision-making processes.

Startup Growth

Startup growth refers to the strategic and sustainable increase in a startup's size and profitability over time. It is a critical aspect of entrepreneurship, as it determines the long-term success and viability of a startup in the competitive business landscape. Startup growth involves various factors and activities that aim to achieve sustainable and scalable expansion. These include: Funding: Startups often require significant financial resources to support their growth ambitions. This can be achieved through external funding sources such as venture capital, angel investors, or crowdfunding platforms. Adequate funding enables startups to invest in research and development, expand their team, and scale their operations. Product Development: To fuel growth, startups must continuously innovate and develop their products or services. They need to remain customer-centric and adapt to changing market demands. By refining their offerings, startups can attract a wider customer base and generate increased revenue. Marketing and Sales: Effective marketing and sales strategies are crucial for driving customer acquisition and revenue growth. Startups must identify and target their ideal customer segments, develop compelling messaging, and leverage various channels to reach and engage their audience. Building a strong brand presence and developing customer relationships are essential components of startup growth. Team Building: As startups expand, they need to build a talented and motivated team that can execute their growth strategies. Hiring the right individuals, fostering a positive work culture, and providing opportunities for professional development are vital for attracting and retaining top talent. A strong team is essential for sustaining growth and achieving long-term success. Scaling Operations: Startups must develop efficient processes and systems to handle increased demand and scale their operations. This involves optimizing supply chains, improving production efficiency, and leveraging technology solutions to streamline workflows. Scalable operations ensure startups can meet customer demand efficiently and effectively. Risk Management: Managing risks is an integral part of startup growth. Startups must identify potential risks and develop strategies to mitigate them. This includes financial risk management, cybersecurity measures, legal compliance, and strategic planning to anticipate and respond to market fluctuations and uncertainties. Overall, successful startup growth requires a holistic approach, encompassing financial, product, marketing, team, operational, and risk management strategies. By implementing a well-rounded growth strategy, startups can increase their market presence, attract customers, generate revenue, and ultimately position themselves for long-term success and sustainability.

Startup Hub

A startup hub is a centralized physical or virtual space where entrepreneurs, startups, and various stakeholders in the startup ecosystem collaborate, share resources, and seek support for their ventures. It provides an environment that fosters innovation, encourages networking, and facilitates access to a range of essential resources and services for startup success. Startup hubs play a vital role in developing and nurturing entrepreneurial communities. They bring together individuals with diverse skills, experiences, and ideas, promoting collaboration, knowledge sharing, and the exchange of best practices. These hubs often offer various programs, events, and initiatives aimed at empowering entrepreneurs and equipping them with the necessary tools and knowledge to build successful businesses. In a startup hub, entrepreneurs and startups can benefit from the expertise of mentors and advisors who provide guidance and support in key areas such as business strategy, product development, marketing, and fundraising. They can also tap into a network of potential investors, partners, and customers, increasing their chances of securing funding, partnerships, and customers for their ventures. Moreover, startup hubs typically provide access to physical infrastructure and resources that are crucial for startups in their early stages. These may include co-working spaces, well-equipped offices, high-speed internet, and state-of-the-art facilities for prototyping and testing. Access to such resources enables startups to reduce their setup costs, enhance their productivity, and focus on their core business activities. Furthermore, startup hubs often facilitate connections between startups and relevant government agencies, industry associations, research institutions, and other organizations. These connections can open doors for startups to explore opportunities for collaboration, funding, and market access. Additionally, startup hubs may organize events such as pitch competitions, hackathons, and investor demo days, creating platforms for startups to showcase their innovations and attract attention from potential investors, partners, and customers. In summary, a startup hub serves as a vibrant and supportive ecosystem that brings together entrepreneurs, startups, mentors, investors, and other stakeholders. By providing access to resources, networks, and opportunities, it empowers startups to thrive, innovate, and scale their businesses more effectively.

Startup Incubation

A startup incubation is a process that provides support and resources to early-stage entrepreneurs, helping them develop and grow their innovative business ideas. It involves a collaborative environment where startups can access mentorship, infrastructure, and funding to increase their chances of success. The main objective of a startup incubation is to provide guidance and support to entrepreneurs during the critical early stages of their ventures. This includes helping them refine their business plan, develop a product or service, and validate their market potential. Incubation programs often focus on building a strong foundation for startups by addressing various aspects of their business, such as strategy, marketing, finance, and operations. Startups that participate in an incubation program usually benefit from a range of resources and services. These can include physical office space, access to shared facilities and equipment, networking opportunities with other entrepreneurs, and access to a pool of experienced mentors and investors. Incubators also provide business development assistance, helping startups connect with potential customers, partners, and investors. One of the key advantages of incubation programs is the opportunity for startups to receive funding and investment. Incubators often have a network of investors who are interested in supporting early-stage ventures. By participating in an incubation program, startups can gain access to this pool of investors, increasing their chances of securing the necessary funding to scale their business. Furthermore, startup incubation fosters a culture of collaboration and learning. Startups within an incubation program can connect and learn from each other, sharing their experiences, challenges, and knowledge. This collaborative environment helps create a sense of community and allows startups to benefit from the collective expertise of the incubator's network.

227

Startup Incubator

A startup incubator refers to a program that provides support and resources to early-stage startups and entrepreneurs to help them grow and scale their businesses. It typically offers physical workspace, mentorship, access to networks, funding opportunities, and various incubation services. The main goal of a startup incubator is to help startups overcome the initial challenges and increase their chances of success. By offering a supportive environment, expert guidance, and access to essential resources, incubators aim to accelerate the growth of startups and contribute to the overall development of the entrepreneurial ecosystem.

Startup Investment Planning

Startup Investment Planning refers to the process of strategically allocating financial resources in order to support the growth and development of a startup company. It involves making informed decisions about how and when to invest capital in different areas of the business, with the ultimate goal of maximizing return on investment. Entrepreneurs and startup founders engage in investment planning to secure the necessary funding to launch and scale their businesses. This typically includes determining the amount of investment required, identifying potential sources of funding (such as angel investors, venture capitalists, or government grants), and devising a plan for how the funds will be utilized. The first step in startup investment planning is to create a comprehensive business plan that outlines the company's goals, target market, competitive analysis, and financial projections. This document serves as a blueprint for attracting potential investors, as it demonstrates the viability and profitability of the startup. Once the business plan is in place, entrepreneurs can start seeking funding opportunities. During the investment planning process, entrepreneurs need to carefully evaluate the potential risks and rewards associated with different investment options. This involves conducting thorough due diligence on potential investors, assessing their track record and expertise in the industry, and negotiating favorable terms and conditions. It is important for startup founders to strike a balance between attracting sufficient capital and retaining a reasonable level of control over the company's operations. Effective investment planning also involves allocating funds to different areas of the business based on priorities and growth prospects. This may include investing in research and development, marketing and sales, hiring talent, improving infrastructure and technology, or expanding into new markets. Entrepreneurs need to conduct a thorough analysis of their business needs and market trends to determine where to allocate resources for maximum impact. Furthermore, investment planning is an ongoing process that requires regular monitoring and evaluation of the company's financial performance. This allows entrepreneurs to make adjustments and recalibrate their investment strategy as needed to ensure sustainable growth. By effectively managing and deploying their investment capital, startups can increase their chances of success and achieve their long-term goals.

Startup Investment Process Enhancement

Startup Investment Process Enhancement can be defined as the implementation of strategies and improvements aimed at optimizing the process of securing investments for new and emerging startups in the field of entrepreneurship. It involves streamlining various stages of the investment process, such as identifying potential investors, pitching business ideas, presenting financial projections, negotiating terms, and finalizing investment deals. The goal is to enhance the overall efficiency and effectiveness of the fundraising activities, thereby increasing the chances of startup success. The first step in enhancing the startup investment process is to develop a clear and compelling business plan. This document outlines the startup's vision, mission, target market, value proposition, and growth strategies. It should also include a detailed financial forecast that demonstrates the startup's profitability and return on investment potential. A well-prepared business plan is crucial in attracting potential investors and convincing them of the startup's viability. Furthermore, startups can leverage various networking platforms and events to connect with potential investors. These platforms can include entrepreneurship conferences, startup accelerator programs, and online platforms specifically designed for startup-investor matchmaking. By actively participating in these activities, startups can increase their visibility and access a wider pool of potential investors. Another area of improvement lies in refining the pitch deck. This presentation material highlights the startup's value proposition, market opportunity, competitive advantage, and financial projections. It should be concise, visually appealing, and tailored to the target audience. By continuously refining and updating the pitch deck, startups can effectively communicate their key messages and attract investor interest. In addition to these efforts, startups can engage in targeted marketing and communication strategies to raise awareness among potential investors. This can include utilizing social media platforms, writing thought leadership articles, and participating in industry-specific forums. By proactively managing their online presence and generating positive buzz, startups can capture the attention of investors and establish credibility. Lastly, the investment negotiation process can be enhanced by seeking professional assistance. Engaging with experienced legal advisors and financial consultants can help startups navigate complex investment terms, negotiate favorable deals, and ensure legal compliance. This expertise is particularly valuable when dealing with equity investments, convertible notes, and other forms of early-stage financing. In conclusion, Startup Investment Process Enhancement refers to the systematic implementation of strategies and improvements to optimize the fundraising activities of startups. By focusing on areas such as the business plan, networking, pitch deck, marketing, and negotiation, startups can attract potential investors, secure necessary funding, and set the stage for long-term success.

Startup Investment Process

The startup investment process refers to the sequence of steps involved in securing funding for a startup venture from external investors. This process plays a crucial role in the growth and success of a startup, as it provides the necessary capital to fund operations, attract talent, develop products, and scale the business. The first step in the startup investment process is typically to identify potential investors who align with the startup's industry, stage of development, and investment requirements. This involves conducting market research, attending networking events, and leveraging personal connections to create a list of suitable investors. Once the target investors have been identified, the entrepreneur needs to prepare a compelling investment pitch to convince them to invest in the startup. This includes creating a detailed business plan, highlighting the market opportunity, showcasing the startup's unique value proposition, and outlining the financial projections and expected return on investment. After the pitch has been developed, the entrepreneur then approaches the investors to present the opportunity. This can be done through various channels, such as in-person meetings, virtual presentations, or through introductions from mutual connections. The goal is to effectively communicate the startup's vision, convince the investors of its potential, and address any concerns they may have. If the investors express interest in the opportunity, the next step in the process is to negotiate the terms of the investment. This involves determining the amount of funding, the equity stake the investor will receive in return, the valuation of the startup, and any additional terms or conditions that the parties may agree upon. Negotiations may take time and involve multiple iterations before reaching an agreement that satisfies both parties. Once the investment terms have been agreed upon, the final step is the due diligence process. This involves a thorough examination of the startup's financials, legal documents, intellectual property, team, and market potential. The investors may also conduct interviews with key stakeholders and customers to validate the startup's claims. If the due diligence process is successful, the investor and the startup will proceed to finalize the investment deal by signing legal agreements, transferring the funds, and setting up the necessary governance structures. The funds received from the investors will then be used to support the operations and growth of the startup as outlined in the business plan.

Startup Investment Round Planning And Execution

Startup Investment Round Planning and Execution refers to the process of strategically preparing and implementing a funding round for a startup company. Startup companies often require financial resources to support their growth, and one common method of obtaining this capital is through investment rounds. These rounds involve seeking investments from various sources, such as angel investors, venture capitalists, and crowdfunding platforms. The planning phase of an investment round involves careful assessment of the company's financial needs, current valuation, and projected growth. Entrepreneurs need to determine the amount of capital required, as well as the equity or ownership stake they are willing to offer in return for the investment. Additionally, they must identify potential investors who align with their business goals, industry expertise, and network connections. Once the planning phase is completed, the entrepreneur can proceed with the execution of the investment round. This typically involves preparing a comprehensive pitch, which highlights the company's unique selling proposition, market potential, competitive advantage, and financial projections. The pitch is delivered to potential investors through various channels, such as in-person meetings, online presentations, or pitch events. During the execution phase, entrepreneurs engage in negotiations with interested investors, aiming to secure the most favorable terms for their business. This may include negotiating the investment amount, valuation, equity stake, and any additional support or resources the investor can provide, such as mentorship or strategic guidance. At the conclusion of the investment round, the entrepreneur and the investors enter into legally binding agreements, which outline the terms and conditions of the investment. These agreements typically address matters like the rights and responsibilities of the investor, shareholder rights, vesting schedules, and exit strategies. Successful startup investment round planning and execution can enable the entrepreneur to secure the necessary capital to fuel their company's growth and accelerate its path towards becoming a sustainable and successful business.

Startup Investment Round Planning

A startup investment round is a critical phase in the life cycle of a startup, where the founders seek external funding to support their business growth and development. It is a strategic process that involves pitching the startup idea to potential investors in order to secure the necessary financial resources for the company's operations and expansion. During the investment round, entrepreneurs typically approach venture capitalists, angel investors, or crowdfunding platforms with a comprehensive business plan, highlighting the startup's unique value proposition, market potential, and revenue projections. This enables investors to evaluate the startup's feasibility and determine whether it aligns with their investment objectives. Investment rounds are often categorized into different stages, including seed, pre-seed, Series A, Series B, and so on, based on the startup's development stage and funding requirements. Each stage represents a milestone in the startup's progress and typically requires a different level of investment. Seed rounds, for example, are typically the initial funding stage, where an entrepreneur raises funds to validate their concept and build a minimum viable product (MVP) to attract further investment. The investment round planning phase involves several essential steps. First, the entrepreneurs must prepare a compelling pitch deck, which includes a concise overview of the startup's mission, market analysis, competitive landscape, and financial projections. The pitch deck serves as a communication tool to capture the attention of potential investors and convince them of the startup's growth potential. Next, entrepreneurs typically engage in extensive networking and outreach efforts to identify and connect with potential investors. This may involve attending industry events, participating in pitch competitions, or leveraging personal networks to gain introductions to targeted investors. Furthermore, startups often seek the support of mentors or advisors who can provide guidance on the fundraising process and introduce them to relevant investors in their industry. Once the entrepreneur has successfully captured investor interest, they enter the negotiation phase, where the terms and conditions of the investment are discussed and agreed upon. This includes determining the valuation of the startup, the amount of equity to be exchanged for investment, and any specific rights or preferences that investors may have, such as board seats or voting rights. In conclusion, a startup investment round is a crucial step in the entrepreneurial journey, providing the necessary financial capital to fuel growth and drive the startup towards success. It requires careful planning, effective communication, and strategic networking to attract the right investors and secure the funds needed to bring the startup's vision to life.

Startup Investment Rounds

A startup investment round refers to the process of raising capital for a startup company through the sale of equity shares to investors. This capital is typically used to finance the growth and development of the startup, including aspects such as product development, marketing, and hiring. Startup investment rounds are an essential part of the entrepreneurial journey, as it allows startups to secure the necessary funds to fuel their growth and pursue their ambitious goals. These investment rounds typically involve several stages, known as seed, series A, series B, and so on, each representing a different phase of growth and funding needs for the startup.

Startup Investment Strategies

Startup investment strategies refer to the specific plans and actions undertaken by entrepreneurs and investors to secure funding for their startup ventures. These strategies are designed to attract potential investors and convince them to provide financial support to the startup. Startup investment strategies encompass various approaches, techniques, and tactics that aim to maximize the chances of attracting investment. In the competitive world of entrepreneurship, startup investment strategies play a crucial role in the success of new ventures. Entrepreneurs need to develop effective strategies to capture the attention and interest of potential investors. This involves carefully crafting a compelling pitch that clearly communicates the value proposition of the startup, highlighting its unique selling points, market potential, and growth opportunities. One common startup investment strategy is networking and relationship-building. Entrepreneurs often attend industry events, conferences, and meetups to connect with potential investors and build relationships with influential individuals in the startup ecosystem. These interactions provide opportunities to showcase the startup's potential and establish trust and credibility with investors. Another important strategy is conducting thorough market research and analysis. Investors want to see that the startup has a deep understanding of its target market, competition, and customer needs. By conducting market research, entrepreneurs can gather valuable insights that can be used to refine their business model, develop a compelling investment case, and position their startup as a viable investment opportunity. Additionally, startups may adopt a strategic approach to target specific types of investors. For example, some startups may focus on attracting angel investors who provide seed funding and mentorship, while others may target venture capital firms that specialize in early-stage investments. The investment strategy may include identifying the most suitable investors based on their industry expertise, investment criteria, and portfolio compositions. In summary, startup investment strategies involve the deliberate planning and execution of activities that aim to secure funding for new ventures. These strategies encompass networking, market research, relationship-building, and targeted investor outreach. By implementing effective investment strategies, entrepreneurs increase their chances of attracting investment and accelerating the growth and success of their startup.

Startup Investment

Startup investment refers to the provision of financial resources by individuals, organizations, or venture capitalists to support the growth and development of a startup company. It is a crucial element in the life cycle of a startup, as it provides the necessary funding to launch and scale the business. Typically, startup investment involves the exchange of equity ownership in the company for the funding provided. This means that investors become shareholders and have a stake in the success of the startup. The amount of equity given to investors can vary based on factors such as the valuation of the company, the amount of funding required, and the negotiation between the startup and the investor.

Startup Valuation Models

A startup valuation model is a framework used to determine the worth or value of a startup company. It is an essential tool in entrepreneurship that helps investors, founders, and other stakeholders understand the potential value of the company. There are several methods or models used for startup valuation, each with its own set of assumptions, variables, and calculations. Here are some commonly used startup valuation models: 1. Market Approach: This model determines the value of a startup by comparing it to similar companies in the market. It considers factors such as industry trends, growth potential, market size, and competitive landscape. The valuation is based on the assumption that similar companies would have a comparable value. 2. Income Approach: This model focuses on the future income potential of the startup. It calculates the present value of expected future cash flows, taking into account factors such as revenue projections, expenses, profit margins, and growth rate. The valuation is based on the assumption that the value of the startup is driven by its ability to generate profits. 3. Cost approach: This model determines the value of a startup based on the cost to recreate or build a similar company from scratch. It takes into account factors such as development costs, resource requirements, and market demand. The valuation is based on the assumption that the value of the startup is equivalent to the cost of its creation. 4. Scorecard Valuation Method: This model evaluates the startup based on multiple factors or criteria such as the entrepreneur's experience, market size, competitive advantage, traction, and intellectual property. Each factor is assigned a weight or score, and the valuation is determined by aggregating these scores. It is important to note that startup valuation models are not exact science and involve a degree of subjectivity. The chosen model and its calculations depend on various factors, including the stage of the startup, industry dynamics, market conditions, and investor preferences. Additionally, the valuation of a startup is often influenced by negotiation and market forces.

Startup Valuation

Startup valuation refers to the process of determining the worth or value of a startup company. It is an essential aspect of entrepreneurship that allows founders, investors, and stakeholders to assess the potential financial returns and investment opportunities associated with the startup. Valuation is crucial for attracting investors, negotiating funding rounds, and making informed strategic decisions. The valuation of a startup is typically based on various factors, including the company's growth potential, market size, competitive landscape, team expertise, intellectual property, and revenue or profitability projections. However, since startups are often in the early stages of development and may not have consistent revenue streams or established financial statements, the valuation process can be challenging and somewhat subjective. There are several methods commonly used to determine the value of a startup. The most prevalent approaches include the Venture Capital (VC) Method, Discounted Cash Flow (DCF) analysis, Market Multiple analysis, and Comparable Transactions analysis. Each method considers different aspects of the startup's potential and uses various financial indicators to estimate its value. The VC Method is widely used by both investors and entrepreneurs. It involves projecting the startup's future revenues and then discounting them to their present value, taking into account the expected return on investment and the risk associated with the industry or market in which the startup operates. On the other hand, the DCF analysis calculates the present value of the startup's expected future cash flows by discounting them back to the present using a predetermined discount rate. This method is often used when the startup has a more stable and predictable revenue model. Market Multiple analysis compares the startup's financial metrics, such as revenue or earnings, to those of similar publicly traded companies or recent acquisitions in the same industry. This method relies on the assumption that the startup's value is proportional to the performance of comparable companies. Lastly, Comparable Transactions analysis examines the valuations of similar startups that have recently completed funding rounds or been acquired. This approach considers the financial terms and conditions of those transactions to estimate the value of the startup in question.

Startupper

A startupper is an entrepreneur who is involved in the creation and development of a startup company. A startup is a newly established business that aims to bring innovative solutions, products, or services to the market. A startupper plays a key role in the early stages of a startup, taking on various responsibilities to transform an idea into a viable business. This includes identifying market opportunities, conducting market research, developing a business plan, securing funding, building a team, and executing the business strategy. Compared to traditional entrepreneurs, start-uppers face unique challenges due to the high level of uncertainty and risk associated with launching a new business. They need to be highly adaptable, resilient, and willing to take calculated risks to overcome obstacles and drive the success of their startup. In addition to their entrepreneurial skills, start-uppers often possess specific traits that are essential for navigating the startup ecosystem. These traits include a visionary mindset, the ability to think outside the box, a strong passion for their idea, and the determination to persevere amidst setbacks. Start-uppers are also inclined to embrace innovation and leverage technology to disrupt existing industries or create entirely new markets. They are not afraid to challenge traditional business models and are continuously seeking ways to differentiate their startup from competitors. Overall, start-uppers are driven by the desire to bring their vision to life and make a significant impact in their chosen industry. They are constantly seeking growth opportunities, exploring new markets, and evolving their business strategies to achieve sustainable success.

Stealth Mode

A startup operating in stealth mode refers to a company that intentionally maintains a low profile and keeps its activities, products, and plans confidential from the general public, competitors, and potential investors. In the realm of entrepreneurship, stealth mode is a strategic approach employed by startups to minimize external exposure in order to safeguard intellectual property, maintain a competitive advantage, and focus on product development without distractions or

232

undue market pressure. During stealth mode, startup founders and employees typically refrain from actively promoting or disclosing detailed information about their business and offerings through marketing campaigns, public announcements, or media interviews. The primary objective is to avoid attracting attention and maintaining a degree of secrecy to protect their unique ideas, innovative technologies, and potential market disruption.

Stock Options

Stock options are a form of compensation commonly used in the context of startups and entrepreneurship. They are granted to employees or executives as an incentive to drive the company's growth and success and align their interests with those of the shareholders. Stock options give employees the right to buy a certain number of company shares at a predetermined price, called the exercise price or strike price, within a specified period of time, known as the vesting period. The exercise price is typically set at the fair market value of the company's stock at the time the options are granted. During the vesting period, employees earn the right to exercise their options gradually, usually over a number of years. This serves as motivation to stay with the company and contribute to its growth for the long term. Often, a "cliff" is established at the beginning of the vesting period, during which no options can be exercised. After this cliff, options vest gradually on a monthly or quarterly basis. Once the options are vested, employees can choose to exercise them and purchase the underlying shares. If the stock price has increased since the options were granted, employees can buy the shares at the lower exercise price and then sell them at the higher market price, earning a profit (the difference between the two prices). Alternatively, they can hold onto the shares and benefit from any future increase in value. Stock options can be a valuable component of a compensation package, as they provide an opportunity to share in the company's success. They also align the interests of employees with those of the company's shareholders, encouraging employees to work towards increasing the company's value. However, it's important to note that stock options come with certain risks and considerations, such as potential tax implications and the fact that the value of the underlying shares may not always increase or may even decrease.

Storytelling Workshops

Storytelling workshops in the context of startup and entrepreneurship refer to educational sessions or training programs that focus on teaching individuals the art and techniques of effective storytelling for business purposes. These workshops are designed to help entrepreneurs and startup founders learn how to craft and deliver compelling narratives that can captivate audiences, connect with potential investors, engage customers, or inspire employees. During storytelling workshops, participants are introduced to various storytelling concepts, strategies, and tools that can be applied to different aspects of their entrepreneurial journey. They learn how to create a compelling brand story that communicates the vision, mission, and values of their startup. They also explore techniques for weaving personal anecdotes, case studies, and data into their narratives to create a sense of authenticity and credibility. Furthermore, storytelling workshops often provide insights into structuring narratives, using storytelling frameworks, and tailoring narratives to fit different communication channels, such as investor presentations, sales pitches, marketing campaigns, or team meetings. Participants are encouraged to practice storytelling through hands-on exercises, role-playing, and feedback sessions to enhance their storytelling abilities and cultivate their storytelling voice. The benefits of participating in storytelling workshops for entrepreneurs and startup founders are manifold. Firstly, a well-crafted story can effectively capture the attention of potential investors, making it easier to secure funding. Additionally, storytelling helps entrepreneurs build emotional connections with customers, enabling them to differentiate their products or services in a crowded marketplace. Storytelling also plays a crucial role in inspiring and motivating employees, fostering a strong company culture, and attracting top talent. In summary, storytelling workshops in the context of startup and entrepreneurship equip entrepreneurs and startup founders with the necessary skills and knowledge to harness the power of storytelling for business success. These workshops guide individuals in crafting narratives that resonate with their target audience, evoke emotions, and drive action. Through storytelling, entrepreneurs can effectively communicate their vision, connect with stakeholders, and create a compelling brand story that sets them apart in the competitive business landscape.

Strategic Alliances

Strategic Alliances in the context of startup and entrepreneurship refer to collaborations between two or more organizations with the aim of achieving mutual benefits. These alliances are formed to leverage each other's resources, capabilities, and expertise to enhance competitiveness, market reach, and profitability. Such alliances are essential for startups and entrepreneurs as they allow them to access resources and capabilities that may be otherwise difficult to obtain or develop on their own. By partnering with other organizations, startups can benefit from economies of scale, shared knowledge, and reduced costs, enabling them to compete more effectively in the market.

Subscription Agreement

A subscription agreement is a formal contract between a startup company and an individual or entity (subscriber) who wishes to invest in the company in exchange for ownership shares or other financial securities. It is an essential legal document that outlines the terms and conditions of the investment, as well as the rights and obligations of both parties. The main purpose of a subscription agreement is to protect the interests of the startup and the subscribers by establishing clear guidelines and expectations. It typically includes provisions related to the number and price of the shares, the payment terms, the representations and warranties of the startup, the use of funds, and the conditions for the closing of the investment. The subscription agreement plays a crucial role in providing transparency and accountability in startup financing. By clearly defining the terms of the investment, it helps to avoid misunderstandings and disputes between the startup and the subscribers. It also ensures that the investors are well-informed about the risks and opportunities associated with the investment, enabling them to make an informed decision. Additionally, the subscription agreement serves as a legal document that can be enforced in court if any party breaches the agreed-upon terms. It provides a legal framework for resolving disputes and protects the interests of both parties involved. Therefore, it is of vital importance for startups and entrepreneurs to draft and execute a comprehensive subscription agreement with the help of legal professionals. In conclusion, a subscription agreement is a critical legal contract in the context of startup and entrepreneurship. It establishes the terms and conditions of an investment, protects the interests of both the startup and the subscribers, and provides transparency and accountability in startup financing.

Subscription Price

A subscription price, in the context of startups and entrepreneurship, refers to the cost that customers are required to pay on a recurring basis in order to access a product or service provided by the startup. This pricing model enables startups to generate a steady stream of revenue and build a loyal customer base. Subscriptions are commonly used by startups that offer digital products or services, such as software-as-a-service (SaaS) solutions, online memberships, or content streaming platforms. Rather than relying on one-time purchases, subscription pricing allows startups to establish long-term relationships with customers and provide ongoing value.

Sunk Cost Fallacy

The sunk cost fallacy is a psychological bias that occurs when individuals or businesses continue to invest time, money, and resources into a project or decision simply because they have already invested a significant amount in it. The fallacy lies in the belief that the past investments are a justification for further investment, even if it no longer makes logical sense. In the context of startups and entrepreneurship, the sunk cost fallacy can be particularly dangerous. Entrepreneurs often face numerous challenges and obstacles on their path to success. It is not uncommon for startups to encounter setbacks, changes in the market, or unexpected issues that may require a change in strategy or even the complete abandonment of a project. The sunk cost fallacy can lead entrepreneurs to hold on to failing projects or unprofitable ventures in the hope that their previous investments will eventually pay off. This can result in a waste of resources, time, and energy. Moreover, it prevents entrepreneurs from objectively assessing the current situation and making rational decisions based on the potential for future success. Successful entrepreneurs understand that focusing on sunk costs is counterproductive and can hinder progress. They know that in order to thrive, they must be willing to cut their losses and allocate their resources strategically. This means being able to objectively assess the current state of their business and make decisions based on the potential for future returns, rather than being driven solely by past investments. Avoiding the sunk cost fallacy requires a mindset of adaptability and a willingness to take calculated risks. Entrepreneurs should regularly evaluate their projects, using objective data and market research to determine if a change in strategy or a complete pivot is necessary. They should also be willing to let go of projects or ventures that are no longer viable or aligned with their long-term goals. In conclusion, the sunk cost fallacy can hinder the success of startups and entrepreneurs by preventing them from making rational decisions based on future potential. By being aware of this cognitive bias and staying focused on the bigger picture, entrepreneurs can navigate the challenges of entrepreneurship more effectively.

Supply Chain Optimization

Supply Chain Optimization refers to the process of maximizing efficiency and minimizing costs in the movement and transformation of goods and services from production to consumption. It involves strategically managing and improving all aspects of the supply chain, including sourcing, procurement, production, distribution, and customer service. For startups and entrepreneurs, supply chain optimization plays a crucial role in driving competitive advantage and sustainable growth. By optimizing their supply chains, startups can achieve higher levels of operational efficiency, lower production costs, improve customer satisfaction, and increase profitability.

Sustainability Entrepreneurship

Sustainability entrepreneurship refers to the practice of creating and managing a startup business that is focused on addressing social and environmental challenges, while also generating economic profits. It involves developing innovative business models and strategies that aim to create positive impact, and to promote sustainability principles and practices. Sustainability entrepreneurship goes beyond the traditional concept of entrepreneurship, which primarily focuses on profit maximization. Instead, it recognizes that businesses have a responsibility to contribute to sustainable development, by considering the triple bottom line of people, planet, and profit. This means that sustainability entrepreneurs seek to create value not only for their shareholders, but also for society and the environment. Startups that are driven by sustainability entrepreneurship strive to find opportunities to solve societal or environmental problems through their products, services, or business operations. They often pursue disruptive innovations that challenge established norms and practices, and that have the potential to drive systemic change and sustainability improvements. Key characteristics of sustainability entrepreneurship include a strong sense of purpose and mission, a focus on social and environmental impact measurement, and a commitment to transparency and accountability. Sustainability entrepreneurs are often motivated by a desire to create positive change in the world, and they are willing to take risks and overcome obstacles in pursuit of their goals. Sustainability entrepreneurship is closely linked to the concept of sustainable development, which aims to meet the needs of the present without compromising the ability of future generations to meet their own needs. By embedding sustainability principles into their business models, sustainability entrepreneurs contribute to the ongoing transition towards a more sustainable and equitable world.

Sustainability Metrics

Sustainability metrics refer to the quantifiable measures that are used to assess and evaluate the environmental, social, and economic impact of a startup or entrepreneurial venture. These metrics are used to track and monitor the progress and performance of the business in terms of its sustainability practices and goals. Startups and entrepreneurs are increasingly recognizing the importance of incorporating sustainable practices into their business strategies. To ensure long-term success and survive in today's competitive marketplace, startups need to demonstrate their commitment to sustainability. Sustainability metrics enable startups to assess their environmental footprint, social responsibility, and economic viability, thereby helping them to make informed decisions and drive positive change. Environmental sustainability metrics focus on measuring the startup's impact on the environment. This includes metrics such as carbon emissions, water usage, waste generation, and energy consumption. By tracking these metrics, startups can identify areas for improvement and implement strategies to reduce their environmental impact. Social sustainability metrics assess the startup's impact on society and its stakeholders. These metrics may include measures of diversity and inclusion, employee satisfaction and well-being, community engagement, and customer satisfaction. Startups that prioritize social sustainability are more likely to attract and retain talented employees, gain customer loyalty, and foster positive relationships with their local communities. Economic sustainability metrics evaluate the financial performance and viability of the startup. These metrics include key financial indicators such as revenue, profitability, return on investment, and cash flow. By monitoring these metrics, startups can ensure their long-term financial sustainability and make informed decisions regarding resource allocation and investment. In conclusion, sustainability metrics are essential for startups and entrepreneurs to assess and evaluate their environmental, social, and economic impact. By tracking and monitoring these metrics, startups can identify areas for improvement, set goals, and make informed decisions that align with their sustainability objectives. Incorporating sustainable practices into the core business strategy not only enhances the company's reputation and competitiveness but also contributes to a more sustainable and resilient future.

Sustainability Planning

Sustainability planning in the context of startup and entrepreneurship refers to the process of creating and implementing strategies that enable a business to operate in a manner that is financially viable, socially responsible, and environmentally friendly, with the goal of ensuring long-term success and resilience. This type of planning involves considering the impact of the startup's operations, products, and services on various dimensions of sustainability, such as economic, social, and environmental factors. It requires an assessment of the startup's current practices and potential risks and opportunities, as well as the development of goals and action plans to improve its overall sustainability performance.

Sustainability

Sustainability in the context of Startup & Entrepreneurship refers to the ability of a business to achieve long-term success while minimizing its negative environmental, social, and economic impacts. It involves the responsible management of resources and the adoption of practices that contribute to the well-being of present and future generations. Sustainable startups and entrepreneurs strive to create businesses that are resilient and adaptable, capable of thriving in a rapidly changing world. They embrace innovative and eco-friendly approaches to product design, manufacturing, and distribution, aiming to minimize waste, reduce carbon emissions, and conserve natural resources.

Sustainable Business Model

In the context of startups and entrepreneurship, a sustainable business model refers to a method or approach that allows a new venture to generate long-term value while minimizing negative environmental and social impacts. A sustainable business model incorporates strategies and practices that promote economic growth, environmental stewardship, and social responsibility. It aims to create a balance between profitability and sustainable development by considering the triple bottom line: people, planet, and profit.

Sustainable Business Practices

Sustainable business practices in the context of startups and entrepreneurship refer to the adoption of strategies and operations that prioritize long-term environmental, social, and economic sustainability. These practices aim to minimize negative impacts on the environment, promote ethical and responsible behaviors, and ensure the long-term success and competitiveness of the business. Startups and entrepreneurs play a crucial role in driving innovation and disrupting traditional business models. However, they also face unique challenges and opportunities in implementing sustainable practices, such as limited resources, fierce competition, and the need to differentiate themselves in the market. One key aspect of sustainable business practices for startups is the incorporation of environmental considerations into their operations and products. This may involve reducing energy consumption, minimizing waste and pollution, and using eco-friendly materials and technologies. By doing so, startups can not only minimize their ecological footprint but also tap into the growing demand for environmentally friendly products and services. Social sustainability is another essential component of sustainable business practices. Startups should strive to operate in an ethically and socially responsible manner, considering the well-being and interests of their employees, customers, and communities. This may involve fair labor practices, promoting diversity and inclusivity, contributing to local development, and engaging in philanthropic initiatives. Economic sustainability is equally crucial for startups to ensure their long-term success. This involves developing a viable business model that generates profits, while also considering the broader economic impact of their activities. Startups need to consider factors such as fair pricing, responsible financial management, innovation, and adaptability to a changing market landscape. Implementing sustainable business practices requires a proactive and holistic approach. Startups and entrepreneurs need to integrate sustainability into every aspect of their business, from strategic planning and product development to marketing and stakeholder engagement. It also involves building partnerships and collaborations with like-minded organizations, leveraging technological advancements, and staying informed about and compliant with relevant regulations and standards. Overall, sustainable business practices are essential for startups and entrepreneurs, as they not only contribute to the preservation of the planet and society but also enhance the long-term competitiveness and resilience of their business.

Sustainable Business

Sustainable Business in the context of startup and entrepreneurship refers to the establishment, growth, and management of a business that meets the needs of the present without compromising the ability of future generations to meet their own needs. It involves considering the environmental, social, and economic impacts of the business and taking proactive measures to minimize negative effects and maximize positive contributions. In a startup or entrepreneurial setting, sustainable business practices can be integrated into various aspects of the business, including the products or services offered, the supply chain, operations, and stakeholder relationships. It goes beyond simply complying with regulations and aims to create long-term value for the business, society, and the environment.

Sweat Equity

Sweat equity, in the context of startup and entrepreneurship, refers to the contribution of time, effort, and expertise made by founders or team members in order to build and grow their business, in lieu of financial investments. It is an essential concept as it recognizes the value of non-monetary contributions and allows entrepreneurs to bootstrap their ventures. Startups often face limited resources, especially in their early stages, and relying solely on financial investments may not be feasible. Sweat equity allows founders to leverage their skills, knowledge, and hard work to overcome these limitations and build their businesses from the ground up. Sweat equity can be seen in various forms. Firstly, founders may invest their time and effort into developing the product or service, conducting market research, creating a business plan, and executing marketing strategies. This includes long hours, late nights, and intense dedication to the success of the venture. In addition to time and effort, founders may bring in their expertise and industry knowledge, which can be invaluable for the growth of the startup. Their understanding of the market, customer needs, and industry trends can help shape the product or service, refine the business model, and navigate the challenges of entrepreneurship. Sweat equity extends beyond the founders to include team members and early employees. These individuals may join the startup with lower salaries or the promise of future financial benefits in exchange for taking on greater responsibilities and risks. Their commitment and hard work contribute to building the startup's foundation and increasing its chances of success. The value of sweat equity is not only limited to the initial stages of a startup but can continue throughout its journey. As the business grows, founders and team members may continue to invest their time and effort into scaling operations, expanding into new markets, and developing innovative solutions. Overall, sweat equity plays a vital role in the startup ecosystem by allowing entrepreneurs to build their businesses without relying solely on financial investments. It recognizes the value of time, effort, and expertise, and empowers founders and team members to contribute their skills and knowledge to create successful ventures.

Syndicate

A syndicate in the context of startups and entrepreneurship refers to a group of individuals or entities that come together to invest capital or resources into a business venture. This collective

237

investment provides financial backing and support to help the startup achieve its goals and objectives. The members of a syndicate can be individuals, venture capitalists, angel investors, or even other businesses. They pool their resources to provide the necessary funding for the startup, often in exchange for an equity stake in the company. Syndicates can be formed for various stages of a startup's lifecycle, from seed funding to series A, B, and beyond.

Target Audience

A target audience refers to the specific group of individuals or customers that a startup or entrepreneur aims to reach and engage with through its products or services. The target audience is defined by various demographic, psychographic, and behavioral characteristics that set them apart from the general population. In the context of startups and entrepreneurship, identifying a target audience is crucial for several reasons. Firstly, it allows the startup or entrepreneur to understand the needs, preferences, and pain points of their potential customers. This understanding forms the basis for developing products or services that resonate with the target audience and address their specific problems or challenges. Secondly, having a clearly defined target audience helps in crafting effective marketing strategies and messages. By understanding the target audience's motivations, values, and communication preferences, the startup or entrepreneur can tailor their marketing efforts to effectively reach and connect with this specific group of individuals. This can include selecting the most relevant marketing channels, using appropriate language and imagery, and creating compelling content that speaks directly to the target audience's interests and aspirations. Furthermore, defining a target audience enables startups and entrepreneurs to differentiate themselves in the market. By understanding the unique needs and desires of their target audience, they can develop a unique value proposition that sets them apart from competitors. This allows them to position their products or services as the solution of choice for their target audience, gaining a competitive advantage and increasing the likelihood of success. In conclusion, a target audience is a specific group of individuals that a startup or entrepreneur aims to attract and engage with. By understanding the characteristics and preferences of this target audience, startups and entrepreneurs can develop products or services that meet their needs, create effective marketing strategies, and differentiate themselves in the market. Ultimately, identifying and reaching the target audience is essential for the success and growth of a startup or entrepreneurial venture.

Target Market Analysis

A target market analysis is an important component of startup and entrepreneurship, as it helps in identifying and understanding the specific group of customers that a business intends to serve. It involves researching, analyzing, and assessing the characteristics, needs, preferences, and behaviors of the potential customers who are most likely to be interested in the products or services offered by the startup. By conducting a target market analysis, startups and entrepreneurs gain valuable insights into their target audience, enabling them to develop effective strategies for marketing, sales, product development, and customer engagement. This analysis helps in determining the size of the target market, identifying the key demographics (such as age, gender, income, education, occupation, etc.), psychographics (such as interests, lifestyles, beliefs, values, etc.), and behavior patterns (such as buying habits, decision-making processes, preferred channels, etc.) of the target customers. The target market analysis is crucial for startups and entrepreneurs as it assists in identifying the unique selling proposition (USP) of the business, which is essential for differentiation and competitive advantage. It helps in understanding the pain points, challenges, and needs of the target customers, which helps the business to develop tailored solutions and deliver superior value to its customers. Furthermore, the target market analysis assists in setting realistic goals and objectives, creating an effective marketing strategy, and allocating resources efficiently. It helps in defining the positioning of the business in the market and determining the appropriate pricing, distribution, promotion, and communication strategies. By focusing on a specific target market, startups and entrepreneurs can optimize their marketing efforts, minimize costs, and maximize customer satisfaction and profitability.

Target Market

The target market refers to a specific group of individuals or organizations that a startup or entrepreneur plans to sell their products or services to. It represents the segment of the overall market that the startup or entrepreneur wants to focus on in order to maximize their chances of success. Identifying the target market is crucial for startups and entrepreneurs as it enables them to tailor their marketing strategies, product development, and overall business approach to meet the needs and preferences of their intended customers.

Targeted Marketing Campaign

A targeted marketing campaign is a strategic approach used by startups and entrepreneurs to promote their products or services to a specific group of customers who are most likely to be interested in their offerings. This type of marketing campaign focuses on identifying and understanding the characteristics, behaviors, and preferences of a particular target market segment, allowing businesses to tailor their marketing messages and activities to effectively reach and engage this specific audience. Targeted marketing campaigns involve conducting thorough market research and analysis to identify the target market segment that the startup or entrepreneur wants to reach. This includes studying demographic information such as age, gender, location, income level, and education, as well as psychographic factors such as lifestyle, values, interests, and attitudes. By gaining a deep understanding of the target audience, businesses can create marketing strategies that resonate with their specific needs and preferences. Once the target market segment has been identified, startups and entrepreneurs can develop personalized marketing messages and deliver them through various channels, such as social media, email marketing, search engine advertising, and content marketing. The aim is to create highly relevant and compelling content that captures the attention and interest of the target audience, increasing the chances of conversion and customer acquisition. Targeted marketing campaigns offer several benefits for startups and entrepreneurs. Firstly, by focusing their efforts on a specific target market segment, businesses can optimize their marketing budgets and resources, ensuring that they are reaching the right audience with the right message at the right time. This helps to maximize the return on investment and increase the chances of success. Additionally, targeted marketing campaigns allow startups and entrepreneurs to differentiate themselves from competitors by offering a tailored and personalized approach. By understanding the unique needs and preferences of their target audience, businesses can provide customized solutions and experiences that resonate with customers on a deeper level, building trust, loyalty, and long-term relationships.

Tech Entrepreneurship

Tech Entrepreneurship refers to the process of identifying, creating, and scaling innovative technology-based business ventures. It involves applying technology and entrepreneurial principles to develop and bring to market new products, services, or solutions that solve real-world problems and meet customer needs. A tech entrepreneur is an individual or a group of individuals who take the initiative to start and build a tech-based business. This includes identifying opportunities, leveraging technology, and taking calculated risks to turn ideas into successful ventures. A tech entrepreneur plays a vital role in driving innovation, economic growth, and job creation in the technology sector. Startup, in the context of tech entrepreneurship, refers to a newly established business that aims to introduce a disruptive product, service, or business model. Startups typically operate with limited resources, uncertain market conditions, and high growth potential. They are characterized by their agility, flexibility, and focus on innovation. Startups often seek funding from venture capitalists, angel investors, or other sources to fuel their growth and expansion. The key elements of tech entrepreneurship include: 1. Idea Generation: Tech entrepreneurs identify problems or opportunities in the market and generate innovative ideas for products or services that address these challenges. 2. Market Research: They conduct market research to understand customer needs, market dynamics, and the competitive landscape. This helps in validating the potential demand for the proposed solution and refining their business model. 3. Product Development: Tech entrepreneurs develop prototypes or minimum viable products (MVPs) to test and refine their ideas. They leverage technology to create scalable and efficient solutions that offer a competitive advantage. 4. Business Planning: They create a comprehensive business plan that outlines their target market, marketing strategy, operations, and financial projections. This plan serves as a roadmap for the startup's growth and guides decision-making. 5. Financing: Tech entrepreneurs secure funding through various means, such as bootstrapping, crowdfunding, angel investments, or venture capital. This capital infusion helps in hiring talent, scaling operations, and bringing the product or service to market. 6. Execution and Growth: Once the startup is launched, tech entrepreneurs focus on executing their business plan, acquiring customers, and scaling the business. They continually iterate and adapt their strategies based on market feedback and changing dynamics. In summary, tech entrepreneurship involves leveraging technology, innovation, and entrepreneurial principles to start and grow tech-based ventures. It requires a combination of technical expertise, business acumen, and a willingness to take risks. Tech entrepreneurs play a crucial role in driving technological advancements, economic growth, and societal impact.

Tech Incubation

Tech incubation refers to a process where startup companies, particularly those in the technology sector, receive support, resources, and mentorship to foster their growth and development. It is a form of entrepreneurship that promotes innovation, collaboration, and networking within a supportive ecosystem.The primary objective of tech incubation is to accelerate the growth of startup companies by providing them with a nurturing environment and various resources to overcome challenges and achieve success. This support may include access to physical infrastructure, shared office spaces, funding opportunities, business development services, technical expertise, and guidance from experienced mentors and advisors.

Tech Incubator

A tech incubator is a platform or organization that supports the growth and development of startups and entrepreneurs in the technology sector. It provides resources, mentorship, and guidance to help these new businesses flourish and succeed in the competitive market. Incubators typically offer a range of services and benefits to the startups they support. These can include physical office space, access to resources such as computers, software, and hardware, and networking opportunities with industry professionals and potential investors.

Tech Startup

A tech startup refers to a newly established company in the technology sector that is built around innovative ideas and aims to disrupt existing industries or create new ones. Startups are typically founded by entrepreneurs with a vision to solve a specific problem through the use of technology. Unlike traditional businesses, tech startups are characterized by their rapid growth potential and scalability. They often operate in a highly competitive and fast-paced environment, seeking to develop and commercialize cutting-edge technologies or services. The success of a tech startup hinges on its ability to continuously innovate and adapt to changes in the market. In order to thrive, tech startups often rely on attracting venture capital investments to fund their operations and fuel their growth. These investments are provided by venture capital firms, angel investors, or crowdfunding platforms, which seek high returns in exchange for their financial support and guidance. The funding received by startups is typically used to develop their products, expand their customer base, and scale their operations. In addition to financial resources, tech startups also require a skilled and dedicated team to bring their ideas to life. Startup culture often emphasizes agile methodologies, collaboration, and a willingness to take risks. The team members of a tech startup must be passionate, adaptable, and possess the necessary technical skills to develop and maintain the company's products or services. One key characteristic of tech startups is their disruptive nature. These companies strive to challenge existing business models or introduce groundbreaking technologies to create a significant impact in their respective industries. They aim to revolutionize the way people work, communicate, shop, or access services through the use of technology. The potential for disruptive innovation is what attracts investors and drives the growth of the startup ecosystem.

Tech Unicorn

A tech unicorn is a startup company in the technology industry that is valued at over $1 billion. The term "unicorn" was coined in 2013 by venture capitalist Aileen Lee, choosing the mythical animal to represent the statistical rarity of such successful ventures. To be classified as a tech unicorn, a startup must meet certain criteria. Firstly, it must be a private company that is still in its early stages of development. Unlike traditional companies, unicorns have not yet gone public through an initial public offering (IPO) and are not traded on the stock market. This allows them to operate with more flexibility and less regulatory oversight. Secondly, a tech unicorn must have a valuation of at least $1 billion. This valuation is typically derived from funding rounds led by venture capitalists, private equity firms, or other institutional investors. These investors provide funding in exchange for equity, with the expectation of a significant return on their investment when the company eventually goes public or is acquired by a larger corporation. The rapid growth and high valuations of tech unicorns have been facilitated by several factors. The widespread adoption of technology and the internet has created new opportunities for startups to disrupt traditional industries and establish innovative business models. Additionally, the availability of venture capital funding has increased in recent years, enabling startups to secure large investments and fuel their growth. The success of tech unicorns can also be attributed to their ability to leverage technological advancements to rapidly scale their operations. These companies often rely on cloud computing, big data analytics, artificial intelligence, and other emerging technologies to automate processes, improve efficiency, and deliver innovative products and services to their customers. While the term "unicorn" initially carried a sense of excitement and optimism, it has also been subject to criticism. Some argue that high valuations of unicorns are not always justified by their financial performance or long-term sustainability. Additionally, the rapid growth and aggressive expansion strategies pursued by tech unicorns can lead to ethical and regulatory concerns. In conclusion, a tech unicorn is a privately-held startup in the technology industry that has a valuation of over $1 billion. These companies have disrupted traditional industries, achieved rapid growth through technological advancements, and attracted significant investment from venture capitalists. However, the term "unicorn" also carries certain criticisms and challenges associated with high valuations and aggressive expansion strategies.

Technology Entrepreneur

A technology entrepreneur is an individual who starts a company or business in the technology sector with the goal of developing and marketing innovative technological products or services. They combine their expertise in technology with their entrepreneurial skills to create, launch, and grow a successful tech-based venture. As a startup founder, a technology entrepreneur leverages their knowledge, skills, and resources to identify market opportunities and develop solutions that address specific problems or meet the needs of a target audience. They are driven by the desire to disrupt existing industries, solve complex problems, or introduce new and efficient ways of doing things using technology. In the context of entrepreneurship, a technology entrepreneur is someone who takes calculated risks to bring new products or services to the market. They often face challenges such as limited resources, intense competition, technological advancements, and changing market demands. In order to navigate these obstacles and succeed, they need to be creative, adaptable, and possess strong business acumen. A technology entrepreneur typically plays multiple roles within their startup, including but not limited to CEO, product manager, marketer, and strategist. They are responsible for setting the vision and direction of the company, securing funding from investors, building a team of talented professionals, and leading the development and execution of the product or service. Successful technology entrepreneurs understand the importance of continuous learning and staying up-to-date with the latest advancements in their field. They actively seek opportunities to collaborate with other entrepreneurs, industry experts, and investors to expand their network, gain insights, and access resources that can contribute to the growth and success of their startup. In conclusion, a technology entrepreneur is an individual who starts a business in the technology sector, utilizing their expertise in technology and entrepreneurial skills to develop and market innovative products or services. They are risk-takers, problem solvers, and leaders who strive to create impactful solutions that disrupt industries and provide value to their target audience.

Technology Entrepreneurship Development

Technology Entrepreneurship Development refers to the process of creating and growing innovative technology-based startups with the aim of achieving commercial success. It involves identifying opportunities in the market, developing a business model, securing funding, and implementing strategies for growth and sustainability. In the context of startup and entrepreneurship, technology entrepreneurship development focuses specifically on the use of technology to create and deliver new products or services that solve a problem or meet a need in the market. This can include software development, hardware manufacturing, e-commerce platforms, digital services, and other technology-enabled solutions.

Technology Entrepreneurship Ecosystem Development

Technology entrepreneurship ecosystem development refers to the creation and cultivation of an environment that supports the growth and success of startups and entrepreneurs in the technology industry. It involves the establishment of various interconnected elements, programs, and resources, aimed at fostering innovation, collaboration, and sustainable business development. The ecosystem encompasses a range of stakeholders, including entrepreneurs, investors, government agencies, educational institutions, accelerators, incubators, and industry associations. These stakeholders work together to provide a supportive infrastructure, access to funding, mentorship, networking opportunities, and business advisory services to fuel the growth and success of technology startups.

Technology Entrepreneurship Ecosystem

A technology entrepreneurship ecosystem refers to the interconnected network of individuals, organizations, and resources that support the creation, growth, and success of startups and entrepreneurs in the technology sector. This ecosystem is characterized by various components that work together to foster innovation, collaboration, and the development of new technologies. These components include: 1. Entrepreneurs and Startups: The technology entrepreneurship ecosystem revolves around the entrepreneurs and startups themselves. These individuals and teams are driven by a desire to bring new technology solutions to market, disrupt existing industries, and create value. They come up with innovative ideas, build prototypes, and launch new businesses. 2. Mentors and Advisors: Mentors and advisors play a crucial role in the technology entrepreneurship ecosystem by providing guidance, expertise, and support to entrepreneurs and startups. These experienced individuals offer valuable insights, share their industry knowledge, and help entrepreneurs navigate the ups and downs of building a startup. They often have a track record of success in the technology sector and can help startups avoid common pitfalls. 3. Investors: One of the key components of the technology entrepreneurship ecosystem is the presence of investors who are willing to provide funding to startups. These investors, such as venture capitalists and angel investors, invest capital in exchange for equity or other forms of financial return. Their financial resources help startups fund their operations, develop their products or services, and scale their businesses. 4. Support Organizations: Support organizations, such as incubators, accelerators, and co-working spaces, provide dedicated support and resources to startups. These organizations offer physical spaces, mentorship programs, networking opportunities, and access to a wide range of resources, including legal, financial, and marketing support. They help startups overcome early-stage challenges, connect with potential customers and partners, and build a strong foundation for growth. 5. Universities and Research Institutions: Universities and research institutions play a significant role in the technology entrepreneurship ecosystem by fostering innovation and generating intellectual property. They often offer entrepreneurship programs, technology transfer offices, and research collaborations that help facilitate the commercialization of research and development. These institutions provide a knowledge-intensive environment that fuels the creation of technology startups. In summary, a technology entrepreneurship ecosystem encompasses a holistic set of interconnected components and stakeholders that work together to support the creation, growth, and success of startups in the technology sector. By providing a supportive environment, access to resources, and pathways to funding and mentorship, this ecosystem helps drive innovation, economic growth, and technological advancement.

Technology Entrepreneurship Education And Support

Technology entrepreneurship education and support is a multifaceted approach aimed at fostering the development of innovative startups and entrepreneurs in the technology sector. It encompasses a range of educational programs, resources, and mentorship initiatives designed to equip aspiring tech entrepreneurs with the knowledge, skills, and networks necessary to launch and grow successful ventures. One key aspect of technology entrepreneurship education and support is the provision of targeted training and education programs. These programs typically cover a wide range of topics relevant to tech startups, such as ideation and opportunity recognition, business model development, market analysis, financial management, and marketing strategies. Through these programs, aspiring entrepreneurs gain the essential knowledge and competencies needed to transform their technological ideas into viable business opportunities. In addition to formal education, technology entrepreneurship education and support also involves providing startups with access to a variety of supportive resources. These resources can include physical spaces, such as incubators or accelerators, where entrepreneurs can work and collaborate in a supportive environment. They may also include access to research and development facilities, prototyping equipment, or specialized software tools to help entrepreneurs refine their technological innovations and bring them to market. Mentorship and networking also play a crucial role in technology entrepreneurship education and support. Entrepreneurial mentors, often experienced industry professionals or successful entrepreneurs themselves, provide guidance, support, and advice to aspiring tech entrepreneurs. Through mentorship programs, entrepreneurs can tap into the expertise and networks of these mentors, gaining insights into industry trends, access to potential investors or partners, and valuable feedback on their business ideas and strategies. Overall, technology entrepreneurship education and support is a comprehensive framework that aims to foster the growth of innovative startups and entrepreneurs in the technology sector. By providing aspiring tech entrepreneurs with the necessary education, resources, and mentorship, this approach helps to create a vibrant ecosystem where groundbreaking technological ideas can be transformed into successful, sustainable businesses.

Technology Entrepreneurship Education

Technology entrepreneurship education refers to the process of imparting knowledge and skills to individuals in the field of startups and entrepreneurship, with a specific focus on technology-based ventures. It involves teaching and learning activities designed to develop the mindset, competencies, and practical understanding required to successfully launch and grow technology-oriented businesses. The goal of technology entrepreneurship education is to equip aspiring entrepreneurs with the necessary tools and resources to identify, evaluate, and exploit opportunities in the technology sector. It encompasses a range of subjects, including business development, innovation management, market analysis, financing strategies, and intellectual property protection. By providing a comprehensive understanding of the unique challenges and opportunities inherent in technology-based ventures, this education aims to foster an entrepreneurial mindset that can adapt to the rapidly changing landscape of the technology industry. Technology entrepreneurship education is characterized by a hands-on approach that encourages students to put theory into practice. It often involves experiential learning activities such as case studies, simulations, and real-world projects, where students can apply their knowledge and skills in a practical context. This enables them to develop a deep understanding of the complexities involved in launching and growing a technology startup, including the ability to navigate uncertainty, manage risks, and make strategic decisions. Furthermore, technology entrepreneurship education often encourages collaboration and interdisciplinary learning. It recognizes that successful technology startups require diverse skill sets and expertise from multiple domains, such as engineering, design, marketing, and finance. Therefore, it emphasizes the importance of teamwork, communication, and networking skills to foster an environment that nurtures creativity, innovation, and problem-solving. In today's rapidly evolving technology-driven world, technology entrepreneurship education plays a crucial role in cultivating the next generation of innovative entrepreneurs. By providing individuals with the knowledge, skills, and mindset necessary to navigate the complexities of the technology startup ecosystem, it empowers them to create, launch, and scale high-impact ventures that can drive economic growth, create jobs, and address societal challenges.

Technology Entrepreneurship Support And Development

Technology Entrepreneurship Support and Development refers to the process of providing assistance, guidance, and resources to individuals or groups who are starting or running technology-based startups. This support aims to foster the growth and success of these ventures by helping entrepreneurs navigate the challenges and opportunities specific to the technology industry. Technology entrepreneurship involves the creation, development, and commercialization of innovative products or services that are rooted in technology. It requires a unique set of skills and knowledge to identify and seize entrepreneurial opportunities in the fast-paced and ever-changing tech landscape. The support and development of technology entrepreneurship encompass a range of activities and initiatives. These can include providing access to mentorship programs, incubators, and accelerators that offer guidance and resources to entrepreneurs at different stages of their startup journeys. Additionally, technology entrepreneurship support may involve connecting startups with investors and venture capitalists who can provide funding to fuel business growth. This can include facilitating access to networks and platforms where entrepreneurs can pitch their ideas and secure investment to scale their ventures. Furthermore, the development of technology entrepreneurship includes educational and training programs that equip entrepreneurs with the technical skills, business acumen, and industry knowledge necessary to succeed in the highly competitive tech ecosystem. These programs may focus on areas such as product development, marketing strategies, financial management, and intellectual property rights. Overall, technology entrepreneurship support and development play a crucial role in fostering innovation, economic growth, and job creation. By providing the necessary support and resources, stakeholders in the startup and entrepreneurship ecosystem aim to cultivate an environment where technology-based ventures can thrive and contribute to societal progress.

Technology Entrepreneurship Support

Technology Entrepreneurship Support refers to the resources, tools, and guidance provided to individuals or groups who are involved in starting and running technology-based startups. It involves a range of supportive activities that help entrepreneurs navigate the challenges and maximize the potential of their ventures. Startups in the technology sector often face unique obstacles and require specialized support to thrive. Technology Entrepreneurship Support aims to address these challenges by providing various forms of assistance, including mentoring, financing, networking opportunities, and access to relevant infrastructure. Mentoring is a crucial element of Technology Entrepreneurship Support, as it provides entrepreneurs with guidance and expertise from experienced individuals who have successfully navigated the same entrepreneurial journey. Mentors can help startups refine their business models, develop marketing strategies, and overcome hurdles that arise during the early stages of business development. Financing is another vital aspect of Technology Entrepreneurship Support. Startups often require capital to fund their research and development efforts, prototype development, and initial marketing activities. Access to financing options such as venture capital, angel investors, or government grants can significantly enhance the chances of success for technology startups. Networking opportunities play a key role in Technology Entrepreneurship Support as well. By connecting with other entrepreneurs, industry experts, and potential customers, startups can gain valuable insights, partnerships, and customer feedback. Networking events, startup communities, and industry conferences facilitate these connections and provide platforms for startups to showcase their ideas and products. Access to relevant infrastructure is also a critical component of Technology Entrepreneurship Support. This includes physical spaces like co-working spaces, incubators, or maker spaces, as well as access to essential tools and technology. These resources provide startups with the necessary environment to develop their products or services, collaborate with other entrepreneurs, and receive support from industry professionals.

Technology Entrepreneurship

Technology Entrepreneurship refers to the process of creating, developing, and managing a startup that focuses on leveraging technology to bring innovative products, services, or solutions to market. In the context of Startup and Entrepreneurship, technology entrepreneurship involves identifying opportunities where technology can disrupt traditional industries, solve existing problems, or meet unmet customer needs. It requires the ability to recognize and evaluate market gaps, develop a unique technology-based value proposition, and successfully commercialize it. A technology entrepreneur is an individual or a group of individuals who possess a combination of technical skills, business acumen, and a deep understanding of the specific market they aim to enter. They have a passion for innovation, are willing to take risks, and possess the ability to attract and manage resources effectively to bring their vision to reality. The process of technology entrepreneurship typically starts with the identification of a market need or problem that can be addressed using technology. This involves conducting market research, understanding customer pain points, and assessing potential demand for the proposed solution. The entrepreneur then develops a technology-based product or service that provides a unique solution to the identified problem. Once the technology-based solution is developed, the entrepreneur focuses on business model development, which includes defining the target market, identifying revenue streams, and creating a sustainable and scalable business model. This stage also involves securing appropriate funding, either through bootstrapping, angel investors, venture capital, or other funding sources, to support the startup's growth and expansion. After the business model is established, the technology entrepreneur focuses on executing the go-to-market strategy, which involves product launch, marketing, sales, and distribution. This stage requires effective marketing and sales strategies, as well as building partnerships and alliances to gain market traction and reach a broader customer base. Throughout the entire process, technology entrepreneurs need to be adaptable and agile, as the startup landscape is highly dynamic and competitive. They need to continuously innovate, monitor market trends and customer feedback, and be willing to pivot their business strategy if necessary. In conclusion, technology entrepreneurship is the process of creating and managing a startup that leverages technology to develop innovative products or services. It requires a combination of technical expertise, business acumen, and a deep understanding of the market. Successful technology entrepreneurs have the ability to recognize market opportunities, develop unique technology-based solutions, and effectively bring them to market.

Technology Startup

A technology startup is a newly established business that focuses on developing innovative products, services, or platforms using technology as its core foundation. It is characterized by its disruptive nature, agility, and rapid growth potential within a highly competitive market. Within the realm of entrepreneurship, a technology startup typically starts as an idea or a concept that aims to address a specific problem or fill a gap in the market. These startups often leverage emerging technologies, such as artificial intelligence, blockchain, or cloud computing, to create unique and valuable solutions for their target audience.

Techpreneur

A techpreneur, short for "technology entrepreneur," is an individual who initiates, organizes, and manages a startup company in the technology industry. This term specifically refers to entrepreneurs who focus on developing and implementing innovative and disruptive technologies to create new products, services, or business models. Techpreneurs are driven by a passion for technology and the desire to solve real-world problems through technological advancements. Techpreneurs are typically highly skilled individuals with expertise in areas such as software development, artificial intelligence, data analytics, blockchain, internet of things, or other emerging technologies. They often possess a deep understanding of market trends, consumer needs, and technological possibilities, allowing them to identify business opportunities and develop groundbreaking solutions. A key characteristic of a techpreneur is their ability to leverage technology to transform industries and disrupt traditional business models. They are adept at identifying pain points and inefficiencies in existing systems and using technology to create more efficient, scalable, and user-friendly alternatives. Another crucial aspect of being a techpreneur is their entrepreneurial mindset and business acumen. They have a strong drive to succeed and are willing to take risks and overcome challenges along the way. Techpreneurs are skilled at raising capital, managing finances, forming strategic partnerships, and marketing their products or services to gain a competitive edge in the market. Overall, techpreneurs play a vital role in driving innovation and economic growth in the technology sector. Their ability to combine technical expertise with entrepreneurial skills allows them to bring groundbreaking ideas to life and create successful startups that have the potential to disrupt industries and shape the future of technology.

Techpreneurship

Techpreneurship refers to the practice of combining technology and entrepreneurship to create and launch innovative products or services. It involves the identification of business opportunities in the technology sector, the development of a strategic plan, and the execution of that plan to build a successful startup. In today's digital age, technology has become a driving force for economic growth and innovation. Techpreneurs leverage emerging technologies such as artificial intelligence, machine learning, blockchain, and the Internet of Things to develop groundbreaking solutions that disrupt traditional industries and address unmet needs in the market. The process of techpreneurship begins with the identification of a problem or a gap in the market that can be solved or filled using technology. This requires a deep understanding of the target audience, their pain points, and the current market dynamics. With this knowledge, techpreneurs develop a unique value proposition that sets them apart from their competitors. Once the problem and the solution are defined, techpreneurs create a business model that outlines their revenue streams, cost structure, and target market. They also develop a minimum viable product (MVP) that serves as a prototype to validate their idea and gather feedback from potential customers. Furthermore, techpreneurs focus on building a strong team with diverse skill sets and expertise to support the development and growth of their startup. They also seek external funding from venture capitalists, angel investors, or crowdfunding platforms to finance their operations and scale their business. To be successful, techpreneurs need to continuously adapt to the rapidly changing technology landscape, stay updated with the latest trends and advancements, and foster a culture of innovation within their organization. They should also be prepared to overcome challenges such as market competition, regulatory hurdles, and technological limitations. In summary, techpreneurship involves the integration of technology and entrepreneurship to create innovative and scalable startups. It requires a unique blend of technical and business skills, a deep understanding of the market, and the ability to navigate the challenges of running a startup in the technology sector.

Term Sheet Negotiation

A term sheet negotiation is a critical step in the startup and entrepreneurship process where founders and investors outline the key terms and conditions for a potential investment deal. It serves as a preliminary agreement or roadmap that establishes the foundation for the investment relationship and lays out the basic terms that will be further refined and expanded upon in a final legal document, such as a stock purchase agreement or a convertible note purchase agreement. The term sheet negotiation encompasses various aspects of the investment deal, including valuation, investment amount, ownership percentage, liquidation preference, anti-dilution provisions, board composition, voting rights, rights of first refusal, drag-along and tag-along rights, and other important clauses and provisions. Both parties engage in a give-and-take negotiation process to reach mutually acceptable terms that align with their respective interests and goals. During the negotiation, the startup and the investor may have diverging objectives and priorities. Startups typically seek higher valuations, larger investment amounts, minimal dilution of their equity, and favorable control and governance provisions. On the other hand, investors aim for lower valuations, stronger protective provisions, and increased potential for future returns. The negotiation process involves understanding, compromise, and trade-offs to strike the right balance and create a win-win situation for both parties. The negotiation is typically carried out by the startup's founders, their legal counsel, and the investor or their representatives. It requires a thorough understanding of industry norms, market conditions, and legal implications to effectively navigate through the negotiation process. Both parties may engage in multiple rounds of negotiation, exchanging term sheets with revised terms until a final agreement is reached. Once the term sheet negotiation is completed and both parties have agreed on the basic terms, it serves as a basis for drafting the final legal documents. The agreed-upon terms in the term sheet provide guidance and direction for the legal teams to create the necessary legal documents that solidify the investment deal.

Term Sheet

A term sheet in the context of startup and entrepreneurship refers to a document that outlines the key terms and conditions of a potential investment. It serves as a summary or initial agreement between the startup and the investor, providing a framework for negotiating the final investment agreement. The purpose of a term sheet is to establish the basic terms of the investment, such as the amount of investment, valuation of the startup, ownership percentage, rights and preferences of the investor, and any conditions or milestones attached to the investment. It acts as a blueprint for the legal and financial aspects of the investment deal. The term sheet typically includes details about the type of investment being made, which can be equity, convertible debt, or a combination of both. It outlines the specific terms of the investment, such as the liquidation preference, anti-dilution provisions, board seat allocation, and any other special rights or protections that the investor may have. In addition to the investment terms, a term sheet may also include clauses related to the governance and control of the startup. This can include provisions on how major decisions will be made, restrictions on the transfer of shares, and details about any protective rights or veto powers that the investor may have. While a term sheet is not legally binding, it is an important step in the investment process as it outlines the key terms that will be included in the final legal agreement. It helps both parties to understand and negotiate the terms of the investment before committing to a formal agreement.

Token Sale

A token sale, in the context of startup and entrepreneurship, refers to a fundraising method implemented by startups in which they sell digital assets called tokens to investors or the general public. These tokens are typically built upon a blockchain technology, such as Ethereum, and are often used to represent a specific asset or utility within the startup's ecosystem. The purpose of a token sale is to raise capital for the development and operation of the startup's project or platform. It provides a way for entrepreneurs to finance their ventures without relying solely on traditional funding sources such as venture capitalists or banks, which may have stringent eligibility criteria or require equity ownership in return. During a token sale, the startup typically creates a document called a "whitepaper" that outlines the details of their project, including the purpose and functionality of the token, the roadmap of the project, the team behind it, and the terms of the sale. Interested investors can then participate in the sale by purchasing these tokens using cryptocurrency, such as Bitcoin or Ethereum, or in some cases, fiat currency. Token sales offer several benefits to both startups and investors. For startups, it provides a way to secure funding without giving up equity and to build a community of early adopters and supporters who have a vested interest in the success of the project. It also allows them to tap into a global pool of potential investors and overcome geographical limitations. On the other hand, token sales provide investors with the opportunity to gain early access to a promising project and potentially benefit from the appreciation in the value of the tokens they acquire. Depending on the nature of the token, investors may also have certain rights or privileges within the startup's ecosystem, such as voting rights or discounted access to products or services.

Tokenization

Tokenization in the context of Startup & Entrepreneurship refers to the process of dividing ownership of a company or venture into smaller units known as tokens. These tokens represent an investor's share or stake in the company and can typically be bought, sold, or traded on a blockchain platform. Tokenization has gained popularity in recent years, particularly with the rise of blockchain technology and the introduction of Initial Coin Offerings (ICOs) as a fundraising method for startups. Instead of traditional equity or debt financing, startups can issue tokens that provide various rights and benefits to the holders. One key advantage of tokenization is that it allows for fractional ownership, enabling investors to purchase smaller units of a company's equity. This opens up investment opportunities to a wider range of individuals who may not have the means to invest in traditional securities. Additionally, tokenization provides liquidity as tokens can be easily bought, sold, or traded on online platforms, providing investors with the ability to exit their investment more easily compared to traditional equity investments. Furthermore, tokenization offers startups a new way to raise capital. By issuing tokens through an ICO, startups can tap into a global pool of potential investors and raise funds more quickly and efficiently compared to traditional fundraising methods. This can be particularly beneficial for early-stage startups that may struggle to attract traditional investors or secure sufficient funding. However, it is important to note that tokenization also presents certain challenges and risks. Regulatory compliance is a critical consideration, as the legal framework governing token issuance and trading varies across jurisdictions. Startups need to ensure they adhere to applicable securities laws and regulations to avoid legal issues or potential investor harm. Moreover, the volatility of token prices and the lack of investor protections can make token investments risky. In conclusion, tokenization in the context of Startup & Entrepreneurship refers to the process of dividing ownership into smaller units known as tokens. It offers advantages such as fractional ownership and increased liquidity, while also posing challenges related to regulatory compliance and investor risk.

Trademark

A trademark is a legal means for identifying and distinguishing a business, brand, or product from others in the marketplace. In the context of startups and entrepreneurship, trademarks play a critical role in establishing and protecting a company's brand identity and reputation. Trademarks typically consist of logos, slogans, names, or any combination thereof that are directly associated with a particular business. They serve as an exclusive mark that sets a business apart from competitors and allows consumers to easily recognize and differentiate the products or services offered by that business.

Unicorn Company

A unicorn company is a term used in the context of startup and entrepreneurship to refer to a privately held startup company that has reached a valuation of one billion dollars or more. The term was coined in 2013 by venture capitalist Aileen Lee, choosing the mythical animal to represent the statistical rarity of such successful ventures. Unicorn companies are often highly disruptive in nature, introducing innovative products or services that have the potential to fundamentally change industries or create entirely new ones. They are characterized by their rapid growth and ability to attract significant investment from venture capitalists and other institutional investors.

Unicorn Startup Company

A unicorn startup company, in the context of startup and entrepreneurship, refers to a privately held startup company with a valuation of over $1 billion. The term was coined by venture capitalist Aileen Lee in 2013, drawing inspiration from the rarity and mythical nature of unicorns. Unicorn startups have garnered significant attention and excitement in the startup ecosystem. They are often seen as the epitome of success and innovation. These companies demonstrate exceptional growth potential, disruptive business models, and the ability to scale rapidly while maintaining high valuations. Attaining unicorn status is no easy feat. It requires a combination of factors, including a unique and innovative product or service, a solid business model, and a proficient and visionary team. Unicorn companies often leverage technological advancements to develop solutions that address unmet market needs or reinvent existing industries. Unicorn startups, being private companies, are not publicly traded on stock exchanges. Therefore, valuations are based on funding rounds and investments from venture capitalists, private equity firms, or other institutional investors. These funding rounds often occur in stages, beginning with early-stage funding from angel investors and escalating to later-stage funding from larger investors. The allure of unicorn startups lies in their potential for significant returns on investment. Investors, particularly venture capitalists, usually seek out such startups for their high growth potential and the possibility of achieving substantial returns if the startup goes public or is acquired at a later stage. While unicorn status can be an indicator of success, it is important to note that not all startups aim to become unicorns, nor does unicorn status guarantee long-term sustainability. Many startups focus on building strong businesses with steady growth and profitability rather than pursuing rapid expansion at all costs. In conclusion, a unicorn startup company represents a privately held startup with a valuation exceeding $1 billion. These companies are known for their extraordinary growth potential, disruptive business models, and ability to scale rapidly. However, while unicorn status can be an indicator of success, it does not guarantee long-term sustainability or profitability.

Unicorn (Startup)

A unicorn is a term commonly used in the startup and entrepreneurship world to describe a privately held company that has reached a valuation of over $1 billion. It is a rare and highly coveted achievement, hence the term "unicorn." Such companies are often fast-growing and disruptive, with the potential to change entire industries. Unicorns are typically founded by ambitious and visionary entrepreneurs who identify a gap in the market and develop an innovative product or service to fill it. These companies often leverage technology, such as software platforms or advanced algorithms, to create scalable solutions. Their ability to disrupt traditional markets and meet the rapidly changing needs of consumers is what sets them apart. Unicorns are characterized by their ability to attract substantial venture capital funding. Investors are drawn to unicorns because they recognize the potential for significant returns on their investment. The high valuation of unicorns also reflects the market's confidence in the company's growth prospects and ability to generate revenue in the future. Unicorns are not without their challenges. Rapid growth can present operational and scaling issues, including hiring and retaining top talent, managing resources, and expanding into new markets. Additionally, increased scrutiny and expectations from investors and the public can add pressure and create a demanding environment for unicorn founders and their teams. Many unicorns go on to become publicly traded companies through an initial public offering (IPO) or get acquired by larger corporations. However, not all unicorns achieve long-term success. Some may struggle to maintain their high valuations or fail to translate their growth into sustainable profits.

Unicorn

In the context of startup and entrepreneurship, a unicorn refers to a privately-held company that has reached a valuation of $1 billion or more. This term was coined in 2013 by venture capitalist Aileen Lee, choosing the mythical creature as a representation of the rarity of such companies. Unicorns are often associated with technology startups, particularly those in the software and internet industries, although they can exist in other sectors as well. These companies are typically characterized by rapid growth and disruption in their respective markets. They often leverage innovative technology, business models, or both to achieve their exceptional valuations.

Unique Selling Proposition (USP)

A Unique Selling Proposition (USP) refers to a distinctive feature or characteristic that sets a startup or entrepreneur apart from its competitors in the marketplace. It represents the unique value proposition that the startup offers to its target customers or audience. The USP serves as the primary reason why customers should choose a particular startup's product or service over those of its competitors. The USP is crucial for startups and entrepreneurs as it helps differentiate their offerings from others in a crowded market. It highlights the unique benefits or advantages that the startup provides to solve a specific problem or meet a particular need of its target market. Having a clear and compelling USP is vital for distinguishing oneself in a highly competitive landscape and attracting customers.

User Acquisition

User Acquisition in the context of startup and entrepreneurship refers to the process of attracting and converting new users or customers to a particular product or service. It involves various marketing strategies and tactics aimed at increasing the user base and ultimately driving growth and revenue for the startup. The goal of user acquisition is to effectively reach and engage with potential customers, create awareness about the product or service, and compel them to take action, such as signing up, downloading an app, or making a purchase. It is an essential aspect of building a successful startup as it directly impacts the company's ability to scale, generate revenue, and ultimately, succeed in the market.

User Flow Diagrams

A user flow diagram is a visual representation that illustrates the path a user takes when interacting with a website, app, or digital service. It outlines the different screens, pages, or steps a user will encounter and the sequence they will follow to accomplish a specific goal or task. In the context of startups and entrepreneurship, user flow diagrams are an essential tool for designing and optimizing user experiences. They help entrepreneurs understand how users navigate their products or services, identify potential bottlenecks or pain points, and make informed decisions to improve the overall user journey.

User Growth

User growth refers to the increase in the number of users or customers that a startup or entrepreneurial venture acquires over a specific timeframe. It is a key metric that businesses use to measure the success and scalability of their products or services. For startups and entrepreneurs, user growth is vital for several reasons. Firstly, increasing the user base allows for a wider market reach and potential revenue generation. The more users a startup has, the more chances there are of attracting investors and securing funding for further growth and development. User growth is also a reflection of customer satisfaction and loyalty towards the product or service being offered. Achieving user growth requires the implementation of effective strategies and tactics. Startups often employ various marketing and advertising techniques to increase brand awareness and attract new users. This could involve digital marketing campaigns, social media promotions, partnerships with influencers or industry leaders, and search engine optimization (SEO) to improve online visibility. User growth can be further enhanced by providing a seamless and user-friendly experience to existing users. By continuously improving the product or service, addressing user feedback, and implementing new features and updates, startups can increase user retention and attract more users through positive word-of-mouth recommendations. Furthermore, startups may also leverage data analytics to gain insights into user behavior and preferences. By analyzing user data, entrepreneurs can optimize their marketing strategies, personalize user experiences, and identify potential areas for growth and improvement. It is worth noting that user growth should not be pursued at the expense of user quality. While acquiring a large number of users may seem attractive, it is important for startups to ensure that the acquired user base aligns with their target audience and retains value for the business. A strong focus on user acquisition and retention strategies should be balanced with measures to assess the quality and engagement of users. In conclusion, user growth is a crucial metric for startups and entrepreneurs to measure the success and scalability of their ventures. By implementing effective marketing strategies, providing a seamless user experience, leveraging data analytics, and prioritizing user quality, startups can achieve sustainable user growth and drive their businesses towards long-term success.

User Onboarding

User onboarding refers to the process of familiarizing and integrating new users into a startup or entrepreneurship venture. It encompasses all the activities and strategies employed to ensure that new users have a smooth and effective experience when using the startup's products or services. The primary objective of user onboarding is to enable new users to quickly understand the value proposition of the startup's offering and to ensure they can effortlessly navigate through the platform or application. This process plays a critical role in driving user adoption, engagement, and retention, which are vital for the success and growth of startups in highly competitive markets. Effective user onboarding typically involves several key components. First and foremost, it requires designing a seamless and intuitive user interface that allows users to easily navigate and access the startup's features. Clear and concise instructions and prompts should be provided to guide users through the initial setup and configuration process, enabling them to complete necessary tasks without confusion or frustration. Additionally, user onboarding often incorporates educational materials and resources to help users become proficient in using the startup's products or services. These materials can take the form of user guides, tutorials, videos, or tooltips, providing users with step-by-step instructions and explanations of the platform's features and functionalities. Offering support and assistance through online chat or email can also enhance the user onboarding experience by promptly addressing any questions or concerns. Furthermore, startups often employ user onboarding to establish a strong emotional connection with new users. This can be achieved through personalized onboarding experiences, such as tailoring the startup's messaging and interactions based on user preferences or demographics. By demonstrating genuine care and understanding, startups can cultivate a sense of trust and loyalty among their users, fostering long-term relationships. In summary, user onboarding is a critical process in startup and entrepreneurship ventures, essential for helping new users become familiar with the offering and maximizing their engagement and retention. By providing a seamless user experience, clear instructions, educational resources, and personalized interactions, startups can enhance the onboarding process and establish lasting relationships with their users.

User Personas

A user persona is a fictional representation of a target user or customer that helps startups and entrepreneurs understand and empathize with their users' needs, goals, behaviors, and motivations. It is created based on research, data, and insights about the target audience, and is used as a tool for product development, marketing, and decision-making. The purpose of developing user personas in the context of startup and entrepreneurship is to gain a deep understanding of the target audience in order to design and develop products and services that meet their specific needs. User personas help startups and entrepreneurs go beyond demographic information and surface-level preferences by providing an in-depth understanding of their users' pain points, desires, and motivations. By creating user personas, startups and entrepreneurs can effectively prioritize features, design intuitive user experiences, and tailor their marketing strategies to resonate with their target audience. Personas serve as a reference point throughout the development process, enabling startups to make user-centric decisions and minimize the risk of building products that do not meet user expectations. When creating user personas, startups and entrepreneurs typically gather data through various research methods, such as surveys, interviews, and observation. This data is then analyzed and synthesized to identify patterns and common characteristics among the target audience. From there, fictional personas are developed to represent different user types, each with their own distinct goals, behaviors, and needs. Startups and entrepreneurs can give their user personas names, roles, and even include stock photos to make them more relatable and tangible. User personas are often accompanied by narratives or stories that illustrate their motivations, frustrations, and goals. This helps teams develop a deep empathy for their users and ensure that their products and services address their pain points effectively.

User Retention

User retention refers to the ability of a startup or entrepreneurial venture to retain customers or users over a specific period of time. It measures the success of a company in keeping its existing users engaged and interested in its products or services, rather than losing them to competitors or other alternatives. In the context of startups and entrepreneurship, user retention is a critical metric for evaluating the sustainability and growth potential of a business. Acquiring new customers is important, but retaining existing customers is equally, if not more, significant. Building a loyal customer base is crucial for long-term success and profitability. Startup founders and entrepreneurs often invest significant time, effort, and resources in acquiring new customers through marketing and sales strategies. However, without a focus on user retention, these efforts can be futile if customers churn quickly and do not remain engaged with the company's offerings. User retention strategies typically involve understanding and addressing the needs, motivations, and behaviors of existing customers. This may include regular communication, personalized experiences, ongoing support, and continuously improving the product or service based on feedback and user insights. By prioritizing user retention, startups and entrepreneurs can achieve several benefits. Firstly, it can lead to increased customer lifetime value, as retained customers are more likely to make repeat purchases and generate revenue over an extended period. Secondly, satisfied and loyal customers can become brand ambassadors, spreading positive word-of-mouth and referring new customers to the company. Thirdly, user retention can provide valuable data and insights to guide product development and business decisions. In conclusion, user retention is a crucial metric for startups and entrepreneurs to measure their ability to retain customers over time. By focusing on user retention strategies, businesses can enhance customer lifetime value, generate positive word-of-mouth, and gain valuable insights for future growth and success.

User Segmentation

User segmentation is the process of dividing a startup's target market into distinct groups or segments based on specific characteristics and behaviors. This strategic approach allows entrepreneurs to tailor their marketing and product strategies to meet the unique needs and preferences of each segment, ultimately increasing customer satisfaction and business success. In the context of startup and entrepreneurship, user segmentation plays a crucial role in identifying and understanding different customer groups within a target market. By segmenting users, startups can gain valuable insights into the specific needs, behaviors, and preferences of their customers, enabling them to develop targeted marketing campaigns, design personalized products, and deliver exceptional customer experiences. Startups often face several challenges when entering a competitive market. Without a clear understanding of their target customers, they may struggle to efficiently allocate their limited resources and fail to resonate with their audience. User segmentation provides a solution to these challenges by helping startups identify distinct user groups and tailor their marketing efforts to reach and engage each segment more effectively. When segmenting users, startups can consider various criteria such as demographics (age, gender, income), psychographics (personality, interests, values), geographics (location, climate), and behavior (usage patterns, buying habits). By analyzing and categorizing users based on these factors, startups gain insights into different user groups' distinct characteristics and preferences, enabling them to adapt their marketing strategies accordingly. Once the user segments have been identified, startups can develop customized marketing campaigns that resonate with each group's specific needs. By crafting targeted messages and promotions, startups can increase customer engagement, conversion rates, and ultimately, sales. Additionally, user segmentation enables startups to create personalized product offerings that cater to the unique demands of different segments, fostering customer loyalty and satisfaction.

User-Centered Design Best Practices

User-Centered Design (UCD) is a set of best practices in the field of startup and entrepreneurship, focused on creating products or services that meet the needs and desires of the target users. It involves understanding the target users, their behaviors, motivations, and goals, and using that knowledge to inform every stage of the design process. In the context of startups and entrepreneurship, UCD helps companies develop products or services that are user-friendly, intuitive, and enjoyable to use. It involves close collaboration with the target users throughout the design process, ensuring their voices are heard and their feedback is incorporated. UCD also takes into account the business goals and constraints, aiming to create solutions that not only satisfy the users but also align with the company's objectives.

User-Centered Design Framework Development And Implementation

User-Centered Design (UCD) Framework Development and Implementation in the context of Startup & Entrepreneurship refers to the process of creating and integrating a systematic approach that puts the needs, preferences, and behaviors of the target users at the forefront of product or service development. This framework aims to ensure that the end product or service aligns with the requirements and expectations of the users, ultimately enhancing satisfaction, usability, and overall success. Within the startup and entrepreneurial context, UCD framework development involves various stages and considerations. It begins with conducting thorough user research and analysis to gain a deep understanding of the target audience, their pain points, and their preferences. This research helps in identifying key user personas and defining their characteristics, needs, and goals. This information serves as a foundation for designing an effective user experience that meets these requirements. Following the research phase, the next step involves the creation of conceptual designs and prototypes. This allows early testing and validation of user interactions, iteratively refining the product or service based on user feedback. The UCD framework emphasizes the involvement of users in the design and development process through methods such as usability testing, interviews, surveys, and observations. These activities aim to ensure that the user interface, features, and functionality are intuitive, enjoyable, and serve the intended purpose. Once the design is iteratively refined and validated, the UCD framework also considers factors such as accessibility and inclusivity, ensuring that the product or service can be easily accessed and used by a diverse range of users. Additionally, UCD framework implementation involves continuous evaluation and improvement through data-driven analysis and user feedback, allowing for ongoing enhancements and optimizations. In summary, the User-Centered Design (UCD) Framework Development and Implementation in the context of Startup & Entrepreneurship places a strong focus on understanding the needs and preferences of the target users. By integrating user research, prototyping, testing, and iterative refinement, this framework ensures the development of products and services that meet user expectations, leading to increased user satisfaction and business success.

User-Centered Design Framework Development

A User-Centered Design (UCD) framework is a systematic approach used in startup and entrepreneurship to develop products or services that are tailored to meet the needs and preferences of the target users. This framework puts the users at the center of the design process, ensuring that their goals, tasks, and expectations are thoroughly understood and considered throughout the development cycle. In the context of startup and entrepreneurship, a UCD framework involves several key steps. The first step is conducting thorough user research to gain a deep understanding of the target users, their characteristics, behaviors, and needs. This research helps in identifying any pain points or unmet needs that can be addressed through the development of a new product or service. The next step is to create user personas, which are fictional but realistic representations of different user groups. These personas are based on the data collected during user research and help to define and articulate the various user needs, goals, and behaviors that the product or service should address. Once the user personas are defined, the design team can proceed to the next step, which is creating wireframes and prototypes. Wireframes are simplified visuals that outline the structure and functionality of the product, while prototypes are interactive mock-ups that allow users to experience and provide feedback on the product's features and usability. The UCD framework also emphasizes the importance of iterative design and testing. This means that the design team should continuously gather user feedback, make necessary improvements, and repeat the design and testing process until the product meets the users' needs and expectations. Overall, a User-Centered Design framework in startup and entrepreneurship is a user-centric approach that prioritizes user needs and preferences throughout the entire product development process. By understanding and addressing the users' concerns, pain points, and goals, startups and entrepreneurs can increase the chances of creating successful products and services that resonate with their target audience.

User-Centered Design Framework

The User-Centered Design (UCD) framework is a methodology used in startup and entrepreneurship to develop products and services that meet the needs, goals, and preferences of the target users. This approach involves incorporating user feedback and input throughout the design process, ensuring that the final product or service is intuitive, effective, and enjoyable for the users. In UCD, the focus is on understanding the users' behaviors, motivations, and pain points to create a solution that solves a real problem for them. This approach recognizes that the success of a startup or entrepreneurial venture depends on how well it fulfills the needs and expectations of its customers.

User-Centered Design Guidelines

User-Centered Design Guidelines, in the context of Startup and Entrepreneurship, refer to a set of principles and best practices that prioritize the needs, preferences, and experiences of users when developing products or services. This approach places the end-user at the center of the design process to ensure that the final solution meets their requirements and goals effectively. The primary objective of implementing user-centered design guidelines is to create user-friendly and intuitive solutions that align with the target audience's expectations and enhance their overall experience. By following user-centered design guidelines, startups and entrepreneurs can gain valuable insights into their target market, identify pain points and opportunities, and develop solutions that address these in a meaningful way. It involves an iterative design process, where user feedback and testing play a crucial role in shaping and refining the product, resulting in a more successful and marketable offering. Implementing user-centered design guidelines involves several key principles. Understanding the target users' needs, goals, and expectations is paramount, and this can be achieved through various research methods such as surveys, interviews, and usability testing. This research enables startups and entrepreneurs to empathize with their target audience and design solutions that truly resonate with them. Effective communication and collaboration with users throughout the design process is another crucial aspect of user-centered design. By involving users in concept validation, wireframe testing, and prototype evaluation, startups can gather valuable feedback and make informed design decisions. This iterative process ensures that the final product or service meets the users' expectations and requirements. Furthermore, startups and entrepreneurs need to pay attention to usability, accessibility, and visual design. These aspects play a significant role in enhancing the overall user experience. Solutions should be easy to learn, efficient to use, and visually pleasing, taking into account factors such as readability, color contrast, and intuitive navigation. Overall, user-centered design guidelines serve as a compass for startups and entrepreneurs during the product development process, ensuring that their solutions are truly user-centric. By placing the end-users at the forefront of their design strategies, startups can gain a competitive edge by creating solutions that deliver value and enable user satisfaction, leading to increased adoption and customer loyalty.

User-Centered Design Methodology

User-Centered Design (UCD) methodology is a systematic approach that places the needs, preferences, and limitations of the target users at the forefront of the design and development process in the context of startups and entrepreneurship. UCD aims to create user-friendly and intuitive products or services by involving users throughout the entire design journey. This methodology starts with understanding the target users, their goals, and the context in which they will be using the product or service. It involves conducting extensive research, such as market analysis, user interviews, surveys, and usability testing, to gain insights into user needs, pain points, and expectations. By gathering this information, startups can identify user preferences and identify opportunities to differentiate their product or service from competitors. Once the research phase is complete, startups use the collected data to inform the design phase. UCD encourages collaboration and iteration, where entrepreneurs work closely with designers, developers, and other stakeholders to create prototypes. These prototypes are then validated by users through usability testing and feedback sessions. The feedback received during the testing phase is critically analyzed and implemented in subsequent iterations of the product or service. This iterative process allows startups to refine and improve their design based on user insights, ultimately leading to a user-centric end result. By incorporating UCD methodology into their startup culture, entrepreneurs prioritize the satisfaction, efficiency, and usability of their products or services. This approach assists in reducing the risk of developing solutions that do not meet user needs and enables startups to remain agile in responding to user feedback. UCD methodology helps entrepreneurs continuously learn, evolve, and innovate, ensuring that their products or services provide exceptional user experiences and seize market opportunities.

User-Centered Design Principles

User-Centered Design Principles refer to a set of guidelines and principles that focus on creating products and services that meet the needs and preferences of the target users. In the context of startups and entrepreneurship, these principles play a crucial role in ensuring the success and sustainability of the business. The first principle is to understand the users and their needs. This involves conducting thorough research and gathering insights about the target audience, their behaviors, motivations, and pain points. By gaining a deep understanding of the users, entrepreneurs can identify opportunities and design solutions that effectively address their needs. The second principle is to involve users throughout the design process. This means actively seeking feedback and input from users at various stages of product development. By involving users, entrepreneurs can validate their assumptions, uncover potential issues, and make informed design decisions. This iterative and collaborative approach increases the chances of creating a user-centric solution that resonates with the target audience. The third principle is to prioritize simplicity and ease of use. Startups often operate in highly competitive markets, and having a simple and intuitive product can be a significant advantage. By minimizing complexity and ensuring a seamless user experience, entrepreneurs can attract and retain customers, leading to higher user satisfaction and increased loyalty. The fourth principle is to provide relevant and personalized experiences. Tailoring the product or service to individual user needs and preferences enhances the overall user experience and increases engagement. Startups can leverage technologies like artificial intelligence and machine learning to gather insights and deliver personalized recommendations, creating a unique and valuable experience for each user. The fifth principle is to continuously test and iterate. Startups operate in a dynamic and rapidly changing environment, and it is essential to constantly evaluate and improve the product based on user feedback and market trends. By adopting agile and iterative design practices, entrepreneurs can quickly adapt and pivot, ensuring that their offerings remain relevant and competitive. Overall, integrating user-centered design principles into the startup journey is crucial for creating successful products and services. By understanding users, involving them throughout the design process, prioritizing simplicity, providing personalized experiences, and continuously testing and iterating, entrepreneurs can build user-centric solutions that delight customers and drive business growth.

User-Centered Design Process Implementation And Optimization

User-Centered Design Process Implementation and Optimization is a methodological approach followed by startups and entrepreneurs to develop products and services that effectively meet the needs and preferences of their target users. It is a customer-centric design process that focuses on understanding user behaviors, motivations, and goals, and integrating this knowledge into every stage of product development. The implementation of the user-centered design process involves several key steps. Firstly, startups and entrepreneurs collect user data through market research, user surveys, and feedback sessions. This helps in gaining insights into user expectations, pain points, and their overall experience with similar existing products or services. This data forms the foundation for designing user personas, which are fictional representations of target users. These personas help in creating user-centric solutions that align with specific user needs. The next step involves the creation of prototypes or mockups of the product or service. This allows for early testing and validation of design concepts, helping to identify any potential usability issues or user experience challenges. Feedback from users is gathered and incorporated into further iterations of the design, ensuring continuous improvement. Once the prototype is refined, startups proceed with the development of the final product, keeping the user-centered design principles at the forefront. Throughout this process, user testing is conducted to validate the functionality, usability, and user experience of the product. This iterative testing and optimization cycle ensures that the final product is tailored to the needs and preferences of the target users. User-Centered Design Process Implementation and Optimization not only enhances user satisfaction but also contributes to the success and profitability of startups and entrepreneurial ventures. By placing the users at the center of the design process, these companies are able to develop products and services that effectively address pain points, solve problems, and exceed customer expectations. This increases user engagement, loyalty, and ultimately, drives business growth. In conclusion, the user-centered design process is a fundamental approach followed by startups and entrepreneurs to develop innovative products and services that cater to the needs and preferences of their target users. By prioritizing user research, testing, and iterative design, these companies can optimize their solutions, enhance user satisfaction, and achieve business success in a competitive market.

User-Centered Design Process Implementation

A user-centered design process is a systematic approach used by startups and entrepreneurs to develop products or services that are tailored to the needs and preferences of their target users. It involves understanding the users' goals, motivations, and behaviors, and designing products that meet their needs in a seamless and intuitive way. The process focuses on putting the user at the center of the design process, ensuring that their perspectives and experiences are prioritized and considered throughout all stages of development. The implementation of a user-centered design process typically follows several key steps. The first step is to conduct user research, which involves gathering data about the target users through observation, interviews, surveys, or other research methods. This research helps entrepreneurs gain insights into user needs, pain points, and opportunities. The second step is to analyze and synthesize the research findings to identify common themes and patterns, and to develop user personas or profiles that represent different types of users. These personas serve as a reference point throughout the design process, helping entrepreneurs empathize with and understand the needs of their users. Once the user research is complete, the next step is to ideate and generate design concepts. This involves brainstorming ideas for potential solutions and envisioning how the product or service could address the identified user needs. The concepts are then evaluated and refined based on user feedback and usability testing. The process continues with prototyping and iterative design, where low-fidelity prototypes are created and tested with users, and feedback is used to refine and improve the design. This iterative process allows entrepreneurs to validate design decisions and make necessary adjustments before investing in full-scale development. The final step in the user-centered design process is the implementation and launch of the product or service. However, the process does not end here. Continuous evaluation and user feedback is sought after the launch, enabling entrepreneurs to gather insights into the product's performance and make further improvements. This feedback loop is crucial for continuous innovation and for ensuring that the product or service remains aligned with user needs and expectations.

User-Centered Design Process

The user-centered design process is a systematic approach used in startups and entrepreneurship to develop products and services that meet the needs and preferences of the target users. It involves understanding the users' goals, behaviors, and motivations, and using this knowledge to inform the design and development process. At the heart of the user-centered design process is empathy for the end user. By putting the user at the center of the design process, entrepreneurs can create solutions that truly address their pain points and improve their overall experience. This customer-centric approach not only increases the chances of success for startups but also fosters customer loyalty and satisfaction.

User-Centered Design

User-Centered Design (UCD) is an approach that places the needs and preferences of the target users at the forefront of the design and development process. It is a key concept in the fields of startup and entrepreneurship, as it emphasizes creating products or services that are tailored to meet the specific requirements of the end-users. In a startup or entrepreneurial context, UCD involves conducting extensive research to gain an in-depth understanding of the target market and its user base. This research may encompass interviews, surveys, observations, and other forms of data collection to gather insights into the users' goals, behaviors, and preferences. By obtaining this user-centric data, entrepreneurs can make informed decisions about product features, functionality, and user interface design. The UCD process typically begins with defining clear user personas and scenarios to represent different user groups and their specific goals. This helps entrepreneurs empathize with and understand the needs of the target users. Through iterative design and testing, entrepreneurs can refine their product or service prototypes based on user feedback, enabling them to create a user-friendly and intuitive experience. Implementing UCD in a startup or entrepreneurial venture can yield numerous advantages. By prioritizing user needs, entrepreneurs can ensure that their product or service solves a genuine problem and provides value to the target market. This, in turn, increases the chances of gaining customer acceptance and loyalty. Moreover, UCD reduces the risk of investing time, effort, and resources in developing a product or service that fails to meet user expectations. Overall, user-centered design places the user at the center of the design and development process, driving the creation of products and services that are highly attuned to user preferences. By incorporating UCD principles, startups and entrepreneurs can increase their chances of success by creating offerings that resonate with their target market.

User-Centered Innovation

User-Centered Innovation refers to the practice of designing and developing products, services, and solutions based on the specific needs, desires, and preferences of the end-users. It involves placing the user at the center of the innovation process, and ensuring that their input and feedback guide every stage of development. In the context of startups and entrepreneurship, user-centered innovation is crucial for creating successful and sustainable businesses. By focusing on the needs and wants of the target market, startups can develop innovative solutions that effectively address real problems and provide value to customers. This approach allows entrepreneurs to differentiate their offerings from competitors and increase their chances of success in the market.

User-Centered Research

User-Centered Research is a method of gathering insights and feedback from target users in order to inform the design and development of products or services in the context of startup and entrepreneurship. It involves conducting interviews, surveys, observations, and usability tests to understand the needs, preferences, and behaviors of users. The goal of user-centered research is to ensure that startups and entrepreneurs create products and services that meet user expectations, solve their problems, and provide value. By involving users from the early stages of the development process, startups can reduce the risks of building products or services that are not aligned with user needs and expectations.

User-Centric Design

User-Centric Design is a concept in Startup and Entrepreneurship that places the needs, preferences, and experiences of the target users at the forefront of the design process. It involves creating products or services that are directly aligned with the users' goals and expectations in order to deliver a superior customer experience. This design approach aims to enhance customer satisfaction, increase user engagement, and ultimately drive business growth. In a startup or entrepreneurial context, user-centric design involves conducting thorough research and understanding the target audience's demographics, behaviors, and pain points. By empathizing with the users and gaining deep insights into their needs, the entrepreneur can identify opportunities for creating innovative solutions that address their specific requirements. The user-centric design process typically involves several key steps. Firstly, gathering user feedback and conducting surveys, interviews, and observations to gain a comprehensive understanding of the target audience. This allows entrepreneurs to identify common patterns, preferences, and pain points among users and inform the design direction. Following this research phase, entrepreneurs can create user personas, which are fictional representations of

256

the different types of users that may interact with the product or service. These personas help entrepreneurs to better understand the users and align the design to their unique needs and circumstances. Once the personas are established, entrepreneurs can embark on the process of ideation and prototyping. This involves brainstorming innovative ideas and conceptualizing potential solutions to the identified user pain points. Prototypes are then created to test the viability and usability of these solutions, allowing entrepreneurs to gather user feedback and make iterative improvements. User-centric design also emphasizes the importance of continuous testing and iteration. Entrepreneurs should engage with users at every stage of the design process to gather feedback, analyze user behaviors, and refine the product or service accordingly. This iterative approach ensures that the final product or service is tailored to the users' expectations, ultimately leading to higher customer satisfaction, loyalty, and increased chances of business success. In conclusion, user-centric design is a critical concept in the startup and entrepreneurship landscape. By focusing on the needs and experiences of the target users throughout the design process, entrepreneurs can create products or services that resonate with their customers, foster engagement, and drive business growth.

Validation Board

Validation Board is a tool used in the context of Startup and Entrepreneurship to assess the viability and potential success of a business idea. It is a visual representation of the hypothesis or assumptions made about the idea, allowing entrepreneurs to systematically test, validate, and refine their concepts. The Validation Board typically consists of several key sections that guide entrepreneurs through the validation process. These sections include Problem, Solution, Key Metrics, Unique Value Proposition, Channels, Customer Segments, Cost Structure, Revenue Streams, and Unfair Advantage.

Valuation Cap

A valuation cap is a term commonly used in the context of startup and entrepreneurship, specifically in relation to equity financing and angel investments. It is a mechanism used to establish the maximum value at which a convertible note or a convertible security can convert into equity in a future financing round. When a startup raises funding through convertible notes or convertible securities, the valuation cap acts as a limit on the company's valuation at the time of conversion. It addresses the concern of early-stage investors, typically angel investors, who want to protect their investment from being diluted in subsequent rounds at a significantly higher valuation.

Valuation

Valuation in the context of startups and entrepreneurship refers to the process of determining the financial worth or value of a startup company. It is an essential component in the early stages of a startup as it helps determine the amount of funding required, the equity to be given to investors, and the overall potential of the business. Valuation is typically influenced by various factors including market conditions, financial performance, growth potential, competitive landscape, and the team behind the startup. Startups often have unique characteristics that can make traditional valuation methods challenging to apply. Therefore, alternative methods such as discounted cash flow, scoring models, or comparables approach may be used to estimate the value of a startup.

Value Chain Analysis

A value chain analysis is a strategic tool that helps startups and entrepreneurs understand the series of activities and processes that bring a product or service from its conception to its delivery to the customer. It involves examining each step in the value creation process to identify sources of competitive advantage and potential areas for improvement. The value chain is divided into two main categories: primary activities and support activities. Primary activities are directly involved in the creation, production, marketing, and delivery of the product or service. These activities include inbound logistics (sourcing and receiving materials), operations (transforming inputs into finished products), outbound logistics (storing and distributing products), marketing and sales (promoting and selling the product), and service (providing after-sales support). Support activities, on the other hand, are not directly involved in the value creation process but provide support and infrastructure to enable the primary activities to function effectively. These activities include procurement (purchasing raw materials), technology development (research and development, innovation), human resource management (recruitment, training, and development), and firm infrastructure (administration, finance, and planning). Through value chain analysis, startups and entrepreneurs can identify their competitive advantages at each step of the value creation process. This may include cost advantages, differentiation strategies, or unique capabilities that set them apart from competitors. By understanding their strengths and weaknesses, they can make informed decisions on where to focus resources and efforts to create maximum value for their customers. Furthermore, value chain analysis allows startups and entrepreneurs to identify opportunities for improvement and innovation. By examining each activity in the value chain, they can streamline processes, reduce costs, enhance quality, and increase efficiency. This analysis can also help identify potential risks and challenges that may impact the overall value creation process.

Value Chain

A value chain in the context of startup and entrepreneurship refers to the series of activities that an organization undertakes in order to create and deliver a product or service to its customers. It encompasses all the processes involved in transforming inputs into valuable outputs, and includes activities such as product design, production, marketing, sales, and after-sales service. The value chain concept was introduced by Michael Porter, a renowned business strategist, in his book "Competitive Advantage: Creating and Sustaining Superior Performance." According to Porter, understanding and analyzing the value chain is crucial for businesses as it helps them identify the activities that add value to their products and differentiate them from competitors. The value chain consists of two primary types of activities: primary activities and support activities. Primary activities are directly involved in the creation and delivery of the product or service, while support activities provide the necessary infrastructure and resources to facilitate the primary activities. The primary activities in the value chain include inbound logistics, operations, outbound logistics, marketing and sales, and customer service. Inbound logistics involve receiving and storing raw materials or inputs for production. Operations encompass all the activities necessary for transforming these inputs into the final product. Outbound logistics involve the storage and distribution of the finished product to customers. Marketing and sales activities focus on promoting the product and attracting customers. Customer service activities aim to provide post-purchase support and ensure customer satisfaction. Support activities, on the other hand, include procurement, technology development, human resource management, and firm infrastructure. Procurement involves sourcing and managing the inputs necessary for production. Technology development refers to activities aimed at improving products or processes through innovation and research. Human resource management encompasses activities related to hiring, training, and retaining employees. Firm infrastructure refers to the overall organizational structure, planning, and control systems that support the value chain activities. By analyzing the value chain, startups and entrepreneurs can identify areas where they can create competitive advantage and add value to their products or services. This analysis helps in optimizing processes, improving efficiency, and ultimately increasing customer value. It enables businesses to understand their cost structure and identify opportunities for cost reduction or differentiation. Additionally, a thorough understanding of the value chain allows startups to identify potential partnerships or collaborations that can further enhance their competitive position in the market.

Value Proposition Canvas

The Value Proposition Canvas is a strategic tool used in the context of startup and entrepreneurship to articulate and analyze the value that a product or service provides to its customers. It helps entrepreneurs understand their customers' needs and define a unique value proposition that effectively addresses those needs. The canvas consists of two main sections: the customer profile and the value map. The customer profile illustrates the target customers and their characteristics, such as demographics, behaviors, and goals. It helps entrepreneurs identify the specific customer segments they are targeting and gain a better understanding of their needs and desires. The value map, on the other hand, outlines the product or service features, benefits, and attributes that create value for the customers. It helps entrepreneurs identify and define their value proposition, which is the unique combination of features and benefits that differentiate their offering from competitors in the market. The Value Proposition

Canvas is typically used as a visual tool, allowing entrepreneurs to map out their understanding of their customers and their value proposition. By analyzing the canvas, entrepreneurs can identify potential gaps or mismatches between customer needs and the value their product or service provides. It helps entrepreneurs develop new solutions that better align with customer requirements or adapt their existing offering to better address customer pain points. The canvas can also be used to explore and develop value propositions for different customer segments, enabling entrepreneurs to tailor their offering to different market niches. Additionally, it helps entrepreneurs communicate and validate their value proposition with stakeholders, such as investors, partners, and customers, as it provides a clear and concise representation of the product or service's unique value.

Value Proposition Statement

A Value Proposition Statement is a concise and clear outline of the unique benefits and advantages that a startup or entrepreneurial venture offers to its target customers or market segment. It is a powerful tool used to communicate the value and differentiate a product or service from competitors. A well-crafted Value Proposition Statement not only captures the attention of potential customers but also effectively portrays the core essence of the startup or entrepreneurial venture. It serves as the foundation for the marketing strategy and helps in shaping the overall business direction.

Value Proposition

A value proposition in the context of startup and entrepreneurship refers to a statement that clearly communicates the unique benefits and value that a product or service provides to its target customers. It is a concise and compelling summary of why a customer should choose a particular product or service over the alternatives available in the market. A strong value proposition helps a startup differentiate itself from its competitors and effectively communicate the unique selling points that set it apart. It answers the fundamental question of "Why should a customer choose us?" and provides a clear and compelling reason to buy from the startup.

Vendor Evaluation

A vendor evaluation, in the context of startup and entrepreneurship, refers to the systematic assessment and analysis of potential suppliers or service providers to determine their suitability and viability for meeting the organization's procurement needs. Startup businesses often rely heavily on external vendors for various products or services that are essential for their operations. These vendors can range from suppliers of raw materials, manufacturing equipment, software systems, marketing agencies, logistics providers, and other specialized services. The vendor evaluation process typically involves several steps that aim to evaluate the vendor's capabilities, reliability, quality of products or services, pricing, and overall compatibility with the startup's goals and requirements. This process helps startups make well-informed decisions when selecting vendors, ensuring that they choose the most appropriate and reliable partners for their specific needs. During the evaluation, the startup may collect and review information about various vendors, such as their financial stability, industry reputation, past performance, client references, certifications, and compliance with legal and ethical standards. They may also assess the vendor's ability to meet deadlines and provide ongoing support or maintenance when required. By conducting a thorough vendor evaluation, startups can mitigate potential risks and avoid costly mistakes, as they can identify and address any weaknesses or concerns before entering into formal agreements or partnerships. Additionally, this evaluation process allows startups to compare multiple vendors and negotiate favorable terms, such as pricing, delivery schedules, and contractual obligations. In conclusion, a vendor evaluation is an essential process for startups and entrepreneurs to assess and select suitable vendors that align with their business objectives. This evaluation ensures that the chosen vendors can provide the necessary products or services reliably, efficiently, and satisfactorily, contributing to the overall success and growth of the startup.

Venture Capital Financing

Venture capital financing is a form of funding that is typically provided to early-stage startups and entrepreneurs by specialized investors known as venture capitalists. It involves the exchange of capital in return for an ownership stake or equity in the company. Unlike traditional sources of financing, such as bank loans or personal savings, venture capital financing is specifically tailored for startups that have high growth potential but may not have sufficient capital or track record to attract traditional forms of investment. Entrepreneurs seeking venture capital financing usually go through a rigorous selection process that involves pitching their business ideas and potential to venture capitalists. This is known as the venture capital pitch, and it typically includes detailed business plans, financial projections, and presentations to demonstrate the market opportunity and growth potential of the startup. If the venture capitalist sees promise in the startup, they may decide to invest. The amount of investment can vary widely and is dependent on various factors such as the stage of the startup, the industry it operates in, and the growth potential. In addition to capital, venture capitalists often bring industry knowledge, experience, and networks that can help the startup grow and succeed. Venture capital financing is characterized by its high level of risk and potential for high returns. Venture capitalists understand that a significant percentage of the startups they invest in may fail, but they are willing to take the risk in order to identify the few companies that will achieve extraordinary success. In return for their investment, venture capitalists often expect a substantial return on investment, which can be realized through the sale or initial public offering (IPO) of the company. Overall, venture capital financing plays a crucial role in the startup ecosystem by providing early-stage entrepreneurs with the necessary capital and support to grow their businesses. It helps bridge the funding gap between traditional forms of financing and the unique needs of startups, enabling them to pursue ambitious growth strategies and disrupt industries.

Venture Capital Fund

A venture capital fund is a type of investment fund that provides financing to startup companies and small businesses that have high growth potential. The fund typically consists of money pooled together from various investors, such as wealthy individuals, institutions, and corporate entities. The primary objective of a venture capital fund is to generate long-term capital appreciation by investing in early-stage and high-potential businesses. Unlike traditional financing methods, venture capital funds are focused on startups and entrepreneurial ventures that are in the early stages of development and have a high-risk, high-reward profile. When a startup or entrepreneur seeks funding from a venture capital fund, they typically go through an extensive evaluation process. This process involves thorough due diligence on various aspects of the business, including the management team, market potential, competitive landscape, and growth strategy. If a venture capital fund decides to invest in a startup, it typically takes an equity stake in the company in exchange for its investment. This means that the fund becomes a part-owner of the startup and shares in its future success. In addition to providing funding, venture capital funds often provide guidance and mentorship to help the startup grow and succeed. Once a venture capital fund has invested in a startup, it typically works closely with the management team to help the business achieve its growth objectives. This may involve providing strategic advice, connecting the startup with potential customers or partners, and assisting with subsequent rounds of funding. At a later stage, when the startup reaches a certain level of maturity and has achieved significant growth, the venture capital fund may exit its investment through various means, such as selling its stake to another investor or through an initial public offering (IPO). The fund then distributes the returns generated from its investments to its investors.

Venture Capital Funding Cycle

Venture Capital Funding Rounds

Venture capital funding rounds are a crucial aspect of startup and entrepreneurship. These rounds refer to the stages in which a startup seeks funding from venture capital firms or investors to accelerate its growth, expand operations, or launch new products or services. There are typically different types of venture capital funding rounds, each serving a specific purpose in the startup's lifecycle: 1. Seed Round: This is the initial funding stage where startups seek capital to develop their idea or prototype. Entrepreneurs often approach friends, family, or angel investors to secure seed funding. This round helps prove the concept's viability and attract more significant investment in subsequent rounds. 2. Series A Round: Once a startup has a working prototype or a minimum viable product (MVP), it may raise a series A funding round. At this stage, the focus is on refining the product, building a customer base, and scaling up operations. Venture capitalists typically lead series A rounds and provide larger funding compared to seed rounds. 3. Series B Round: In the series B funding round, the startup has usually achieved significant milestones, such as generating solid revenue or acquiring a substantial user base. The objective is to further scale the business, expand into new markets, or develop additional features. Venture capital firms and institutional investors often participate in series B rounds. 4. Series C Round and Beyond: Series C, D, and subsequent rounds are aimed at fueling the startup's rapid growth, acquisitions, or international expansion. These rounds involve substantial investments from venture capital funds, private equity firms, and sometimes even corporate investors. The goal of venture capital funding rounds is to provide startups with the necessary funding to achieve their growth objectives. Besides the funding itself, these rounds often bring expertise, mentorship, and networking opportunities as venture capitalists become stakeholders in the company. Successful funding rounds not only help startups to accelerate growth but also enhance their credibility, making it easier to attract customers, partners, and additional funding in the future.

Venture Capital Funding

Venture capital funding is a type of financing that is provided by investors to early-stage and high-potential startup companies. It is an essential component of the entrepreneurial ecosystem, enabling startups to grow and scale their businesses. In this funding model, venture capitalists (VCs) invest capital in promising startups in exchange for equity ownership. Unlike traditional bank loans, venture capital funding is a high-risk, high-reward form of investment. VCs typically focus on innovative and disruptive startups that show significant growth potential. Startups seeking venture capital funding often have limited financial resources, making it challenging for them to develop and bring their products or services to market. Venture capital funding provides the financial support needed for startups to hire talent, develop their products, conduct research, and expand into new markets. Venture capitalists play a crucial role in the success of startups by providing not only capital but also expertise, industry connections, and guidance. They often take an active role in the management and strategic decision-making of the startups they invest in, helping them navigate the challenges of scaling a business. For startups, venture capital funding is a highly competitive process. Startups need to demonstrate their potential for growth, market opportunity, competitive advantage, and a strong management team to attract investment. VCs conduct thorough due diligence before making an investment decision, evaluating factors such as the startup's business model, market fit, intellectual property, and financial projections. Successful venture capital funding can significantly accelerate a startup's growth trajectory. It can help startups acquire customers, establish strategic partnerships, develop new products, expand into new markets, and ultimately increase their valuation. However, it also entails giving up a certain degree of ownership and control as VCs become stakeholders in the company.

Venture Capital Investment Timeline

Venture capital investment is a crucial process in the context of startups and entrepreneurship. It refers to the provision of funds and support by venture capital firms or investors to early-stage and high-potential startups. These investments are usually made in exchange for equity or ownership stakes in the company. The venture capital investment timeline encompasses several key stages, which include sourcing, due diligence, negotiation, investment, and exit. Let's explore each of these stages in more detail: Sourcing: In this stage, venture capitalists actively search for promising startups with high growth potential. They often rely on their networks, relationships with entrepreneurs, and industry knowledge to identify investment opportunities. Due Diligence: Once a potential investment opportunity is identified, the venture capitalists conduct in-depth due diligence to assess the startup's business model, market potential, competitive advantage, leadership team, and financials. This thorough evaluation ensures that the investment aligns with their investment strategy and risk appetite. Negotiation: If the due diligence process yields positive results, the venture capitalists enter into negotiations with the startup's founders to determine the terms of the investment. This involves discussions about the amount of investment, valuation, ownership percentage, and other rights and obligations. Investment: After successful negotiations, the venture capitalists finalize the investment deal. They provide the agreed-upon funds to the startup, typically in multiple rounds, called series. These funds are intended to help the startup scale its operations, develop products, penetrate the market, and achieve rapid growth. Exit: The final stage in the venture capital investment timeline is the exit. Venture capitalists aim to generate substantial returns on their investments by exiting the startup through methods such as initial public offerings (IPOs), acquisitions, or secondary market sales. This allows them to cash in on their equity stakes and generate profits.

Venture Capital Investment

Venture Capital Investment is a form of funding provided by investors, known as venture capitalists, to startup companies and entrepreneurs with high growth potential. In exchange for funding, venture capitalists typically receive equity or ownership stakes in the startup. This type of investment is commonly associated with innovative and technology-driven industries. Venture capitalists take on considerable risk by investing in startups, as they are often in the early stages of development and may not have a proven track record or revenue stream. However, they are attracted to these opportunities because of the potential for high returns on their investment if the startup is successful. When evaluating a startup for venture capital investment, venture capitalists consider several factors. These include the market size and potential for growth, the uniqueness and scalability of the startup's products or services, the strength and experience of the founding team, and the overall business model and competitive advantage. If a startup secures venture capital investment, the funding can be used for various purposes. This may include product or technology development, marketing and sales efforts, hiring key personnel, expanding operations, or entering new markets. In addition to providing financial support, venture capitalists often offer strategic guidance and industry connections to help the startup accelerate its growth and achieve its objectives. Unlike traditional loans, venture capital investment does not require the startup to make regular repayments. Instead, the venture capitalists aim to generate a return on their investment through an eventual exit strategy. This may involve an initial public offering (IPO), where the startup becomes a publicly traded company, or a merger or acquisition by a larger company. The venture capitalists can then sell their equity stake and realize their profits. In conclusion, venture capital investment plays a crucial role in fueling the growth of startups and entrepreneurial ventures. It provides capital, expertise, and support to promising businesses, increasing their chances of success and enabling them to bring innovative products and services to the market.

Venture Capital Partner

A Venture Capital Partner is an individual or firm that provides financial support and expertise to startup companies in the early stages of their development. They typically invest their own funds or raise money from other investors to provide capital to startups in exchange for equity ownership or convertible debt. As a partner, they play a crucial role in supporting and guiding the startups they invest in. They bring extensive experience and industry knowledge, which they use to evaluate potential investment opportunities, assess the viability of the business model, and identify potential risks and challenges. They also offer strategic guidance and operational expertise to help the startups scale and grow.

Venture Capital-Backed Company

A venture capital-backed company refers to a startup or early-stage business that has received financial support from venture capitalists. Venture capital is a form of private equity funding provided by professional investors to high-potential companies with the aim of generating significant returns on their investment. Entrepreneurs often seek venture capital funding to scale their businesses rapidly and take advantage of emerging market opportunities. In exchange for their financial investment, venture capitalists typically receive equity in the company, allowing them to share in the company's success.

Venture Capital-Backed Growth Strategies

Venture capital-backed growth strategies refer to the specific tactics and approaches that startups and entrepreneurs employ with the financial support of venture capital firms to scale and expand their businesses rapidly. Venture capital is a form of private equity financing provided by investors or firms to early-stage and high-potential startups in exchange for an ownership stake in the company. The goal of these growth strategies is to accelerate the startup's growth trajectory, enhance market share, and achieve sustainable competitive advantages. These strategies typically include a combination of the following elements: - Product Development: Venture capital enables startups to invest in research and development activities to refine and enhance their products or services. This may involve developing new features, improving usability, or incorporating customer feedback. - Marketing and Sales: With venture capital funding, startups can allocate resources to build brand awareness, design marketing campaigns, and execute sales strategies to acquire and retain customers. This may include digital marketing, content creation, social media advertising, and hiring a sales team. - Talent Acquisition and Development: Startups need skilled teams to drive growth and execute their strategies effectively. Venture capital funding enables entrepreneurs to attract top talent by offering competitive salaries, benefits, and career advancement opportunities. Additionally, startups can invest in training and professional development programs to enhance employee skills and capabilities. - Scale Operations: As startups expand their customer base and sales, they need to scale their operations efficiently. Venture capital funding allows entrepreneurs to invest in infrastructure, technology systems, and supply chain optimization to support the growing demand. - Geographic Expansion: Venture capital-backed growth strategies often involve expanding into new markets or geographic regions. This may include opening new offices, entering partnerships with local distributors, or adapting products to suit specific market preferences. - Strategic Partnerships: Startups can leverage venture capital relationships to form strategic partnerships with established companies in their industry. These partnerships can provide access to new customers, distribution channels, technology, or expertise that accelerate growth and enhance market positioning. - Acquisitions: Venture capital funding can enable startups to acquire complementary companies or technologies that enhance their product offerings or remove competitors from the market. This growth strategy allows the startup to quickly expand its market share and consolidate its position in the industry.

Venture Capital-Backed Growth

Venture capital-backed growth refers to the process of funding and supporting the growth of a startup or entrepreneurial venture by a venture capital firm. Venture capital firms are investment institutions that provide capital to startups and high-potential ventures in exchange for equity ownership or a stake in the company. These firms take on high risk in investing in early-stage companies, with the expectation of high returns on their investment if the venture is successful. When a startup or entrepreneurial venture receives venture capital funding, it means that the firm or investment group believes in the potential and growth prospects of the company. The funding is typically used to fuel the expansion of the business, finance product development, enhance marketing and sales efforts, hire additional talent, or scale operations. Unlike traditional sources of funding such as bank loans or personal savings, venture capital provides startups with the necessary capital to pursue aggressive growth strategies. It allows entrepreneurs to focus on building and scaling their business without the financial constraints that often come with early-stage companies. However, venture capital financing comes with certain conditions and expectations. Investors typically take an active role in the company and may require a seat on the board of directors or participation in key decisions. They also expect a significant return on their investment within a specific period, usually through an initial public offering (IPO) or acquisition of the company. For startups and entrepreneurs, venture capital-backed growth can be a game-changer. It provides access to not only the necessary funding but also the expertise and network of the venture capital firm. These resources can help the company navigate challenges, accelerate growth, and gain a competitive advantage in the market. In summary, venture capital-backed growth is a funding and support mechanism for startups and entrepreneurial ventures. It enables companies to secure the necessary capital for growth while leveraging the knowledge and experience of venture capital investors to maximize their chances of success.

Venture Capital-Backed Startup Growth And Scaling

Venture Capital-Backed Startup Growth and Scaling Venture Capital-Backed Startup Growth and Scaling refers to the process by which a startup company, with the financial backing and support of venture capital firms, achieves rapid and sustainable expansion in a short period of time. This growth is typically fueled by a combination of financial investments, strategic guidance, and networking opportunities provided by the venture capitalists. When a startup company secures venture capital funding, it gains access to a pool of capital that can be used to fuel its growth and expansion. This funding can be used for various purposes, such as hiring additional staff, investing in research and development, expanding marketing efforts, or acquiring necessary resources or technology. The main goal of this financial investment is to accelerate the startup's growth and increase its market share. However, venture capital-backed growth goes beyond just financial support. Venture capitalists often bring valuable industry expertise and connections to the table that can help the startup navigate challenges and seize growth opportunities. They can provide strategic guidance, mentorship, and networking opportunities to help the startup scale its operations, enter new markets, or form strategic partnerships. This additional support can significantly enhance the startup's chances of success and accelerate its growth rate. Successful growth and scaling of a venture capital-backed startup requires careful planning, effective execution, and continuous adaptation. The startup needs to have a clear growth strategy that outlines its target markets, revenue streams, and competitive advantages. It must execute this strategy efficiently and effectively to achieve the desired growth outcomes. The startup must also be agile and adaptable, continuously monitoring market conditions, customer needs, and competitive landscape to adjust its strategies and tactics. In conclusion, venture capital-backed startup growth and scaling refers to the process of leveraging financial investments, strategic guidance, and networking opportunities provided by venture capitalists to achieve rapid and sustainable expansion. This process requires careful planning, effective execution, and continuous adaptation to seize growth opportunities and maximize the startup's chances of success.

Venture Capital-Backed Startup Growth

Venture capital-backed startup growth refers to the expansion and development of a startup company that is supported by venture capital funding. This type of funding comes from investors who provide capital to early-stage, high-potential companies in exchange for equity or ownership stake in the company. Startup growth is essential for the success and sustainability of a venture capital-backed company. It typically involves increasing the company's market presence, scaling its operations, and achieving significant revenue growth. This growth is fueled by the infusion of capital from venture capitalists, which enables the startup to invest in key areas such as research and development, marketing, and talent acquisition.

Venture Capital-Backed Startups

Venture Capital-Backed Startups are young and innovative companies that receive financial backing and support from venture capital firms. These firms are specialized investment entities that pool funds from various sources such as high net worth individuals, institutional investors, and corporations, and then invest the money in promising startups with high growth potential. When a startup receives venture capital funding, it means that the venture capital firm believes in its business model, technology, or concept, and is willing to invest a significant amount of money to help the company grow and succeed. Typically, venture capital funding is provided in exchange for equity in the startup, meaning that the venture capital firm becomes a shareholder and obtains a stake in the company. Venture capital firms bring more than just money to the table. They also offer expertise, experience, industry connections, and guidance to the startups they invest in. These firms often have a team of professionals with extensive knowledge in entrepreneurship, business management, and specific industries. They provide valuable mentorship and support to help startups navigate the challenges they face and make strategic decisions. Furthermore, venture capital-backed startups receive not only financial support but also access to a vast network of potential partners, customers, and resources. Venture capital firms leverage their connections and relationships to open doors for startups and facilitate business development opportunities. This network effect can significantly accelerate the growth and success of a startup. However, venture capital funding is not easy to obtain. Venture capitalists carefully evaluate startups before deciding to invest, considering factors such as market potential, team capabilities, competitive advantage, scalability, and return on investment. Startups need to present a compelling business plan, demonstrate their value proposition, and prove their ability to execute their strategies. In conclusion, venture capital-backed startups are innovative companies that receive financial backing and support from venture capital firms. They benefit from not only the capital investment but also the expertise, guidance, and network that venture capitalists provide. This support can help startups overcome challenges, seize opportunities, and ultimately achieve rapid growth and success.

Venture Capital-Backed

A venture capital-backed startup refers to a young and innovative company that has raised funds from venture capital firms or investors, who provide financial backing and support in exchange for equity or ownership in the company. These startups typically have high growth potential and are working on disruptive ideas or technologies that have the potential to create a significant impact in the market. Venture capital firms are investment companies that specialize in funding early-stage and high-risk startups. They typically invest in startups that are in the early stages of development, as these companies often lack the access to traditional forms of financing, such as bank loans or public offerings. In addition to providing financial support, venture capital firms also bring their expertise, networks, and industry knowledge to the table, helping the entrepreneur and the startup succeed.

Venture Capital

Venture capital is a form of financing that is provided to startups and early-stage companies by individuals or firms called venture capitalists. It involves investing in promising businesses with high growth potential in exchange for equity ownership. Unlike traditional forms of financing such as bank loans or issuing bonds, venture capital is more suitable for startups as they typically have limited operating history and lack the collateral required for securing loans. Venture capitalists take on higher risks by investing in these nascent companies, in exchange for the potential for high returns on their investment if the business succeeds. Startup entrepreneurs often seek venture capital funding to finance their businesses due to the various benefits it offers. Firstly, venture capitalists provide not only financial capital but also valuable expertise, industry connections, and guidance to the entrepreneurs. They typically have extensive experience in the startup ecosystem and can contribute to the strategic decision-making process, mentor the management team, and assist with networking opportunities. Secondly, venture capital can help startups overcome the funding gap that occurs in the early stages of a business when traditional financing options are limited. This injection of capital allows startups to hire new talent, invest in research and development, scale their operations, and bring their products or services to market more quickly, giving them a competitive advantage. Additionally, venture capital funding can act as a catalyst for attracting additional sources of capital. By securing an investment from reputable venture capitalists, startups can enhance their credibility and attract follow-on funding from other investors, such as angel investors, private equity firms, or even go public through an initial public offering (IPO). In conclusion, venture capital serves as a crucial source of funding, support, and expertise for startups and entrepreneurs. It enables them to accelerate their growth, navigate through the early stages of a business, and achieve their goals.

Venture Capitalist (VC)

A Venture Capitalist (VC) is an individual or firm that provides financial backing, expertise, and resources to startup companies and entrepreneurs in exchange for equity or ownership stakes in the company. VCs typically invest in early-stage or high-growth companies that have the potential for significant returns on investment. When a startup or entrepreneur seeks funding, they may approach venture capitalists to secure the necessary capital to grow and expand their business. Unlike traditional bank loans or other forms of financing, venture capital investments are typically higher risk and require a longer-term commitment from the investor. Venture capitalists play a vital role in the startup ecosystem by identifying promising business ideas and teams, conducting due diligence, and providing guidance and support to help the company succeed. They often have extensive networks and industry knowledge that can help entrepreneurs navigate the challenges of scaling their business. In return for their investment, VCs receive equity in the company, which means they become partial owners and have a stake in the company's success. This equity stake allows them to share in the company's profits and growth when it goes public or is acquired. VCs may also actively participate in the management and decision-making of the company, especially in the early stages. While venture capital funding can provide startups with the necessary resources to accelerate growth and achieve their goals, it also comes with certain considerations. Founders and entrepreneurs must be willing to give up a portion of their ownership and control of the company in exchange for the investment. VCs also typically expect a higher return on their investment compared to traditional lenders, as they take on more risk by investing in early-stage companies with unproven business models.

Venture Capitalist

A venture capitalist is an individual or firm that invests in early-stage or high-growth startups with the goal of earning significant returns on their investment. They provide financial capital, as well as strategic guidance and industry expertise, to help these startups grow and succeed. Venture capitalists typically invest in startups that have the potential for rapid growth and scalability. They look for innovative ideas, strong management teams, and a large addressable market. In return for their investment, they receive equity in the company, allowing them to share in its future success.

Venture Debt

Venture debt is a financing option available to startups and entrepreneurs seeking additional capital to support their growth and expansion. It is a form of debt financing provided by specialized lenders, typically banks or venture debt funds, to companies that have already raised equity funding from venture capitalists or angel investors. Unlike traditional bank loans, venture debt is tailored to the unique needs of startups and entrepreneurs. The main advantage of venture debt is that it allows companies to access capital without diluting their ownership stake or giving up control of important decision-making. This is particularly attractive for startups that want to maintain a higher level of ownership and control as they continue to develop their business. Venture debt can be structured in various ways, but it typically consists of a combination of term loans and revolving lines of credit. The terms and conditions of venture debt financing are generally more favorable compared to traditional bank loans, reflecting the higher risk profile of startups and the potential for significant returns for investors. The funds provided through venture debt can be used for a variety of purposes, including working capital, capital expenditures, business development, and product expansion. It can also be used to bridge the gap between equity funding rounds, allowing startups to extend their runway and reach key milestones without the need for additional dilution. While venture debt can provide startups with access to much-needed capital, it is important to carefully consider the terms and conditions of the financing agreement. Startups should assess the cost of capital, repayment terms, covenants, and potential impact on future equity financing rounds before deciding to pursue venture debt.

Venture Partner

Venture Partner is an individual who works closely with a venture capital firm or investment fund to identify, evaluate, and support potential startup opportunities. The role of a Venture Partner is diverse and multifaceted. They bring their entrepreneurial experience, industry knowledge, and network to help guide and support the startups within the portfolio of the investment firm. Their primary focus is on fostering the growth and success of the startups they work with.

Venture Studio

A venture studio, in the context of startup and entrepreneurship, is a company that focuses on creating and scaling businesses. Unlike traditional incubators or accelerators, a venture studio takes a more hands-on approach to building startups. At its core, a venture studio is driven by a team of experienced entrepreneurs and industry experts who identify and develop business ideas. These ideas are then transformed into viable startup companies through a combination of capital, resources, and expertise.

Venture-Backed Company

A venture-backed company is a type of company that raises capital from external investors in order to grow and expand its business operations. These external investors, known as venture capitalists, provide funding to the company in exchange for equity or ownership in the business. Startups and entrepreneurs often seek venture capital to fund their business ventures because they may not have access to traditional funding sources, such as bank loans or personal savings. Venture capital provides an alternative source of funding that is specifically targeted towards high-growth potential businesses. When a company successfully secures venture capital funding, it typically means that investors believe in the company's growth prospects and are willing to take on the risk associated with early-stage or high-growth companies. In addition to providing financial support, venture capitalists often bring valuable expertise and business connections to help guide the company's growth and development. One of the key characteristics of venture-backed companies is their potential for high returns on investment. Venture capitalists are typically looking for companies that have the potential to achieve rapid growth and generate substantial profits in a relatively short period of time. This is often achieved through innovative business models, disruptive technologies, or unique products or services. However, venture-backed companies also face significant risks and challenges. The high-growth nature of these businesses often means that they require large amounts of capital to fuel their expansion. This can put pressure on the company to continue delivering strong growth and profitability in order to satisfy the expectations of their investors.

Venture-Backed

Venture-backed refers to a type of business or startup that has received funding or investment from external investors, typically known as venture capitalists. These investors provide capital in exchange for a percentage of the company's ownership or equity. Startups and entrepreneurs often rely on venture capital to finance their businesses and help them grow. Venture capitalists are interested in investing in startups that have high growth potential and a unique business idea or product. They provide funding that can be used for various purposes, including product development, marketing, hiring, and operational expenses. When a startup is venture-backed, it means that it has gone through a funding round where venture capitalists have invested in the company. This funding is typically provided in stages or rounds, such as seed funding, Series A, Series B, and so on. Each stage represents a different level of investment and usually corresponds with the startup's growth and milestone achievements. Venture-backed startups often have higher valuations compared to non-venture-backed companies, as the funding from venture capitalists validates the business idea and its potential for success. This can also attract more investors and generate additional funding opportunities in the future. While venture funding provides startups with financial resources, it also comes with certain risks. Venture capitalists expect a return on their investment and usually require a significant equity stake in the company. They may also have a say in the startup's operations and decision-making process. Additionally, venture-backed startups are under pressure to meet growth targets and achieve profitability within a certain timeframe, as venture capitalists often have a specific exit strategy in mind, such as an initial public offering (IPO) or acquisition. In summary, being venture-backed means that a startup or entrepreneur has secured investment from venture capitalists. This funding can provide the necessary resources for growth but also comes with certain expectations and risks. Overall, venture-backed startups are often seen as having high growth potential and attract further investment opportunities.

Venture-Capital-Backed

Venture Capital-Backed startups refer to companies that have received funding from venture capital firms in order to finance their operations and business growth. This type of funding is provided by investors who are looking to invest in high-potential startups with the expectation of generating a significant return on their investment. These investors, known as venture capital firms or VCs, provide funding to startups in exchange for an equity stake in the company. This means that the venture capital firm becomes a shareholder in the startup and is entitled to a share of the company's profits and losses.

Venture-Capital-Financed Startup

A venture-capital-financed startup is a new and innovative business that receives financial support and expert guidance from venture capital firms in order to grow and scale rapidly. Startup companies typically face significant challenges in their early stages, including limited resources, lack of brand recognition, and uncertain market demand. In order to overcome these obstacles and achieve rapid growth, many startups seek external funding from venture capital firms. Venture capital firms are investment firms that specialize in providing funding and support to early-stage and high-potential companies. These firms typically invest in startups in exchange for equity or ownership stakes in the company. In addition to financial investment, venture capital firms also offer strategic advice, industry connections, and mentorship to help startups succeed. When a startup receives venture capital financing, it means that the company has successfully convinced a venture capital firm of its potential for high growth and strong returns on investment. The funding provided by venture capital firms allows startups to invest in product development, marketing, hiring talent, and expanding operations, all of which are crucial for scaling and achieving market success. However, venture capital financing is not without risks. Venture capital firms generally expect a high rate of return on their investment and may put pressure on startups to achieve rapid growth and profitability. Additionally, startups may have to give up a certain degree of control and ownership in exchange for the funding received. In conclusion, a venture-capital-financed startup is a young and ambitious business that receives financial support and strategic guidance from venture capital firms. This funding helps startups overcome early-stage challenges and accelerate growth, but also comes with certain risks and expectations.

Venture-Capital-Financed

Venture Capital-Financed refers to the process of obtaining funding for a startup or entrepreneurial venture from venture capitalists. Venture capitalists are investors who provide financial support to early-stage and high-growth companies that have the potential to achieve significant returns on investment. When a startup or entrepreneur seeks venture capital financing, they typically approach venture capital firms or individual venture capitalists who specialize in funding startups. These investors evaluate the business potential of the startup and, if they find it promising, provide funding in exchange for equity in the company. The process of venture capital financing usually involves several stages, including seed funding, early-stage financing, and later-stage financing. Seed funding is the initial investment that helps the startup get off the ground and develop its product or service. Early-stage financing typically occurs when the startup has proven its concept and needs additional funding to scale its operations. Later-stage financing is provided to companies that have already achieved significant growth and require further investment to expand their market presence or enter new markets. Venture capitalists invest in startups with the expectation of significant returns on their investment. They usually take an active role in the companies they invest in, providing guidance, industry connections, and strategic advice. In exchange for their financial support and expertise, venture capitalists receive equity in the company, which means they become partial owners of the business. Venture capital financing can be crucial for startups and entrepreneurs as it enables them to access the funding needed to develop their product or service, scale their operations, and pursue growth opportunities. Additionally, venture capitalists' involvement can bring valuable industry knowledge and networking opportunities to help the startup succeed.

Venture-Capital-Funded

Venture-Capital-Funded refers to a type of financing that involves investments made by venture capital firms or individual investors (known as venture capitalists) into early-stage startup companies or businesses with high growth potential. This form of funding is typically provided to startups that are considered to have a high risk-reward profile, as they are in the early stages of development and may not have a proven track record or revenue stream. When a startup receives venture-capital funding, it means that the venture capitalist is willing to invest their money in exchange for equity or ownership stake in the company. This enables the startup to access the necessary capital to fuel its growth, expand its operations, develop new products or services, or enter new markets. In addition to providing financial support, venture capitalists often bring their experience, expertise, and industry connections to the table, acting as valuable mentors and advisors to the entrepreneurs.

Vesting Schedule

Vesting Schedule is a contractual agreement that outlines the process by which an employee or founder of a startup earns ownership (equity) in the company over a specific period of time. This agreement is designed to provide incentives and retain talent by giving individuals a sense of ownership and reward for their contributions to the company's growth and success. In the context of startup and entrepreneurship, a vesting schedule is typically used to distribute equity to founders and key employees. It is a way to ensure that individuals who contribute to the company's early stages and long-term success are rewarded accordingly. The vesting schedule is usually structured in terms of time, with a specific period (commonly known as the vesting period) during which the individual must remain with the company to earn their equity. It is common for the vesting period to span over multiple years, with a gradual release of ownership rights over time. For example, a typical vesting schedule for a startup founder could be structured as follows: 4-year vesting period with a 1-year cliff. This means that the founder would not earn any equity until they have completed the first year of employment with the company (the cliff). After the cliff, the founder would begin to earn a portion of their equity (e.g., 25% per year) on a monthly or quarterly basis over the remaining three years. In case an employee or founder decides to leave the company before completing the vesting period, they would usually forfeit the remaining unvested equity. This provision is often included in vesting agreements to serve as a retention mechanism, encouraging individuals to stay with the company and continue contributing their skills and expertise. Vesting schedules are crucial for startups as they align the interests of founders, employees, and investors. By gradually earning equity over time, individuals are motivated to stay with the company and work towards its long-term success. Simultaneously, investors are confident that the individuals who hold equity in the company have a vested interest in its growth and profitability.

Vesting

Vesting is a common practice in startup and entrepreneurship that refers to the process by which an individual earns ownership or control over a specific amount of equity or stock options granted to them by a company. It is typically used as a way to incentivize and retain key employees, founders, or investors over a certain period of time. When a company offers equity or stock options to an individual, they may set certain conditions and requirements that need to be met before the individual can fully own or exercise their rights to those shares. This period of time is often referred to as a vesting period, and it is designed to align the interests of the individual with the long-term success of the company.

Viral Coefficient

The viral coefficient is a metric used in the context of startups and entrepreneurship to measure the growth and potential success of a product or service. It quantifies the rate at which users or customers refer the product to others, leading to its rapid adoption and spread. The viral coefficient is calculated by multiplying the average number of invitations or recommendations sent by an existing user by the conversion rate of those invitations. Mathematically, it can be represented as: Viral Coefficient = Average Number of Invitations per User x Conversion Rate of Invitations In simpler terms, the viral coefficient measures how many new users are generated by each existing user or customer. A viral coefficient greater than 1 indicates exponential growth, as each user is bringing in more than one new user on average. On the other hand, a viral coefficient below 1 signifies that the product or service is not gaining traction and is not being shared widely. The viral coefficient is an important metric in the startup world as it helps in understanding the viral loop or feedback loop of the product. A viral loop refers to the cycle of users referring new users, who then refer even more users, creating a self-sustaining growth mechanism. A higher viral coefficient indicates a stronger viral loop and the potential for significant user acquisition and growth. Startups and entrepreneurs often focus on maximizing the viral coefficient by implementing strategies to encourage users to refer their product or service to others. This can include referral programs, incentives for sharing, and designing the product in a way that encourages sharing and word-of-mouth marketing.

Viral Growth

Viral growth refers to a rapid and exponential increase in the number of users or customers of a startup or entrepreneurial venture through viral marketing or word-of-mouth. It is a phenomenon where the growth of a startup's customer base spreads like a virus, with existing customers or users referring the product or service to others, who in turn refer it to even more people. This type of growth is characterized by a compounding effect, where each user or customer brings in multiple new users or customers. This compounding effect is what sets viral growth apart from other forms of growth, such as linear or organic growth. In a viral growth scenario, the number of users or customers can quickly skyrocket, reaching a large audience in a short amount of time. Viral growth is primarily driven by two factors: the viral coefficient and the viral loop. The viral coefficient measures the average number of new users or customers that each existing user or customer brings in. A viral coefficient greater than 1 indicates exponential growth, while a viral coefficient of less than 1 indicates stagnant or declining growth. The viral loop, on the other hand, refers to the feedback loop created when users or customers refer the product or service to others. This loop typically consists of three steps: awareness, acquisition, and activation.

First, users become aware of the product or service through various marketing channels. Then, they acquire the product or service and begin using it themselves. Finally, they activate the viral loop by referring the product or service to others, who then go through the same awareness, acquisition, and activation process.

Viral Loop

A viral loop is a marketing strategy commonly used by startups and entrepreneurs to drive customer acquisition and retention through word-of-mouth and referrals. It involves creating a product or service that is inherently shareable and encourages users to spread the word to their network, leading to a continuous loop of new users and increased brand awareness. The viral loop begins with the initial customers of a startup or an early adopter of a product/service. These customers are so satisfied with the offering that they voluntarily share it with their friends, family, or colleagues through various channels such as social media, email, or direct communication. By doing so, they act as brand advocates, increasing the visibility and reach of the startup organically. As more users join the platform or purchase the product, they also become potential ambassadors. To further incentivize this behavior, startups often implement referral programs or provide incentives for successful referrals. This not only encourages existing users to refer others but also entices new users to sign up, creating a positive feedback loop. The success of a viral loop heavily relies on the viral coefficient, which measures the rate at which each new user brings in additional users. A viral coefficient greater than one suggests exponential growth, as each user brings in more than one new user on average. By leveraging the power of social sharing and recommendations, startups can tap into the network effect and reach a larger audience without spending extensive resources on traditional marketing campaigns. Additionally, viral loops can help build a strong community around a product or service, as users who are referred by others tend to have a higher level of trust and engagement. In conclusion, a viral loop is a marketing strategy that focuses on creating a product or service that encourages users to voluntarily share it with others, leading to a continuous loop of new user acquisition and increased brand awareness. It is a cost-effective way for startups and entrepreneurs to leverage the network effect and tap into the power of word-of-mouth marketing.

Viral Looping

Viral looping is a phenomenon in startup and entrepreneurship that refers to the process of acquiring new customers through the organic spread of a product or service by existing customers. It involves the creation of a self-perpetuating cycle where customers not only use the product or service themselves, but also share it with others, who in turn become new customers and continue the loop. This process begins with the initial customers who are attracted to the product or service for various reasons, such as its utility, value proposition, or unique features. As these customers start using and benefiting from the product, they naturally become advocates or promoters, recommending it to their friends, family, and wider networks. These recommendations can take various forms, such as word-of-mouth, social media shares, online reviews, or even offline conversations. The key point, however, is that the recommendations lead to new customers who join the loop and continue the cycle. This creates a viral effect, as the network of customers expands exponentially over time. For a startup or entrepreneur, achieving viral looping is highly desirable as it offers several advantages. First, it helps in rapid customer acquisition and growth, without relying heavily on traditional marketing methods and channels. This not only saves costs but also enables the startup to scale more efficiently. Second, viral looping creates a strong and loyal customer base. As new customers join through recommendations, they already have a level of trust and confidence in the product or service, thanks to the endorsement of their friends or acquaintances. This makes them more likely to become long-term customers and potentially advocates themselves. Lastly, viral looping can lead to a network effect, where the value of the product or service increases with each new customer. For example, if the product is a social media platform, having more users means more interactions, content creation, and network effects, making it more attractive to new users. In conclusion, viral looping is a powerful strategy for startups and entrepreneurs to achieve rapid customer acquisition, build a loyal customer base, and create network effects. By leveraging the organic spreading of a product or service through existing customers, viral looping enables startups to grow rapidly and efficiently.

Viral Marketing Campaign

A viral marketing campaign, in the context of startup and entrepreneurship, refers to a strategic marketing approach that aims to create brand awareness and increase customer engagement through the rapid spread and sharing of marketing content by individuals within their social networks. Viral marketing campaigns leverage the power of social media and online platforms to encourage users to voluntarily share promotional content with their friends, family, and followers. Unlike traditional marketing campaigns that rely on paid advertisements and direct promotions, viral marketing relies on word-of-mouth advertising and peer-to-peer recommendations. Successful viral marketing campaigns often have several key elements. Firstly, they focus on creating unique and compelling content that captures the attention and interest of users. Whether it's a catchy video, a funny meme, or a thought-provoking article, the content needs to be highly shareable and resonate with the target audience. Secondly, viral marketing campaigns utilize various online channels and platforms to amplify the reach and visibility of the content. This includes leveraging social media platforms like Facebook, Twitter, and Instagram, as well as online communities, blogs, and forums where users actively engage and share content with their networks. Furthermore, viral marketing campaigns often incorporate incentives or rewards for users to share the content. These can range from discounts, freebies, or exclusive access to additional content. By providing an added value for sharing, it encourages users to actively promote the content and extend its reach beyond the initial target audience. Overall, viral marketing campaigns have become increasingly popular among startups and entrepreneurs due to their cost-effectiveness and potential for exponential growth. When executed successfully, viral marketing can generate significant brand exposure, increase customer engagement, and drive organic traffic to the startup's website or social media profiles. However, it's important to note that not all campaigns will go viral, and careful planning, creativity, and understanding of the target audience are crucial for maximizing the chances of success.

Viral Marketing Campaigns

Viral marketing campaigns are strategies utilized by startups and entrepreneurs to quickly and organically spread information about their product or service through online platforms, resulting in rapid and widespread brand exposure and engagement. Through the use of various viral elements such as compelling content, memorable catchphrases, or controversial themes, these campaigns aim to generate buzz and provoke interest, ultimately encouraging users to share the information with their own networks, thereby creating a viral effect.

Viral Marketing

Viral marketing refers to a marketing strategy employed by startups and entrepreneurs to spread their brand or product rapidly through online platforms and social media. The goal of viral marketing is to create a buzz or a viral effect among the target audience, resulting in a massive and rapid increase in brand visibility, customer engagement, and product adoption. This marketing technique relies on leveraging the power of social networks, word-of-mouth recommendations, and online sharing to reach a wider audience exponentially. The viral nature of this strategy leads to a snowball effect, where each engagement or share from an individual can potentially reach hundreds or thousands of people.

Viral Product Launch

A viral product launch refers to the successful introduction of a new product or service to the market, where the promotion and adoption of the product spread rapidly through word-of-mouth and online sharing. It involves creating such a strong buzz and excitement around the product that it quickly gains widespread attention and attracts a large number of users or customers. In the context of startups and entrepreneurship, a viral product launch is a highly desirable outcome, as it can lead to rapid growth and high market penetration. It helps startups gain visibility, acquire new customers, and establish a strong initial user base. A viral product launch plays a crucial role in creating brand awareness, generating interest, and driving user adoption. To achieve a viral product launch, startups typically focus on creating a product or service that is innovative, unique, and has a high perceived value. The product should offer a solution to a common problem or fulfill a customer need in a way that is different from existing options in the market. Startups also invest time and resources in developing a compelling marketing strategy that leverages social media platforms, influencers, and online communities to generate buzz and traction. In addition to a compelling product and creative marketing, a viral product launch requires effective planning and timing. Startups often choose to launch their product when there is a peak in public interest or when there is a significant event or trend that aligns with their product. This helps in capturing the attention of potential customers and capitalizing on the existing buzz in the market. By achieving a viral product launch, startups can enjoy multiple benefits. Firstly, it can lead to a rapid increase in customer acquisition, allowing the startup to scale quickly. Secondly, it helps in establishing brand recognition and credibility, as a viral product launch often attracts media attention and positive reviews. Lastly, a viral product launch can create a sense of exclusivity and urgency among customers, driving them to try out the product and become early adopters.

Viral Promotion

A viral promotion is a marketing strategy used by startups and entrepreneurs to rapidly increase brand awareness and attract a large audience through the use of viral content, such as videos, memes, or social media challenges. It leverages the power of social sharing and word-of-mouth to generate buzz and create a viral effect, where the content spreads rapidly and organically among users. This type of promotion relies on the psychology of social influence and the concept of social proof. When people see others engaging with and sharing a piece of content, they are more likely to trust it and feel compelled to share it themselves. This leads to exponential growth in exposure and reach, allowing startups and entrepreneurs to gain visibility and reach potential customers at a fraction of the cost of traditional advertising. Viral promotions often tap into emotions or trends that resonate with a wide audience. By creating content that is entertaining, inspiring, or thought-provoking, startups and entrepreneurs can increase the chances of their content being shared and going viral. It is crucial to understand the target audience and tailor the content accordingly to ensure maximum engagement and virality. Successful viral promotions not only generate brand awareness but also drive traffic to a startup's website or social media platforms. This influx of traffic can be converted into leads or sales, increasing the startup's customer base and revenue. Additionally, viral promotions can help establish the startup or entrepreneur as a thought leader or industry expert, enhancing credibility and attracting potential partnerships or investment opportunities. However, it is important to note that viral promotions are not guaranteed to succeed. The virality of content is inherently unpredictable, and what works for one startup may not work for another. It requires a combination of creativity, timing, and a deep understanding of the target audience's preferences and behaviors. In conclusion, viral promotion is a powerful marketing strategy used by startups and entrepreneurs to create widespread brand awareness and attract a large audience. It leverages viral content and social sharing to generate buzz and reach potential customers at a fraction of the cost of traditional advertising. However, success in viral promotion requires careful planning and understanding of the target audience's preferences.

Viral User Acquisition

Viral User Acquisition refers to a marketing strategy employed by startups and entrepreneurs to rapidly grow their user base through word-of-mouth and the sharing of content among existing users. It involves creating a viral loop where users are motivated and incentivized to share the product or service with their networks, resulting in exponential growth and organic user acquisition. This strategy leverages the network effect, which states that the value of a product or service increases as more people use it. By encouraging users to share the product or service with their friends, family, and colleagues, startups aim to tap into their users' social networks and reach a wider audience. Viral user acquisition typically involves the following key steps: 1. Creating a compelling product or service that solves a problem or meets a need in a unique and innovative way. 2. Implementing social sharing features within the product or service to make it easy for users to share with their networks. 3. Designing incentives and rewards that motivate users to share the product or service. These incentives may include discounts, exclusive access, or other benefits for both the referrer and the new user. 4. Monitoring and optimizing the viral loop by analyzing data and feedback from users. This helps in identifying bottlenecks and areas for improvement to ensure continuous growth. Viral user acquisition has numerous advantages for startups and entrepreneurs: 1. Cost-effective: Compared to traditional advertising and marketing strategies, viral user acquisition can be more cost-effective as it relies on organic growth through user-generated content and referrals. 2. Rapid growth: By tapping into users' social networks, startups can potentially experience rapid growth, reaching a large number of users in a short period. 3. Increased brand awareness: Viral user acquisition allows startups to quickly build brand awareness as users share and talk about the product or service with their networks. 4. Higher user engagement: Users who are referred by their peers are more likely to be engaged and stay loyal to the product or service, leading to higher retention rates. In conclusion, viral user acquisition is a valuable strategy for startups and entrepreneurs to scale their user base efficiently and rapidly by leveraging the power of social networks and incentivizing users to share their product or service. By creating a compelling offering and implementing well-designed referral programs, startups can unlock the potential for exponential organic growth.

Viral User Engagement Methods And Strategies

Viral user engagement methods and strategies refer to the techniques employed by startups and entrepreneurs to increase user engagement and promote their products or services in a viral manner. These methods aim to create a buzz and generate interest around the startup and its offerings. By leveraging the power of social media and online platforms, startups can effectively spread their message and attract a large number of users. One common viral user engagement method is the use of social media contests and giveaways. Startups can run contests where users are encouraged to share their products or services with their friends and followers in exchange for a chance to win a prize. This creates a viral loop where the startup's message is amplified as more and more users participate and share the contest with their networks. Another strategy is to create shareable content that resonates with users. Startups can produce informative or entertaining videos, articles, or infographics that are highly shareable on social media platforms. By creating content that is valuable and engaging, startups can increase their reach exponentially as users share the content with their connections. Influencer marketing is also a popular viral user engagement method. Startups can collaborate with influencers who have a large following and engage their audience by promoting the startup's products or services. When influencers endorse a startup, it can significantly increase the startup's visibility and credibility, leading to higher user engagement. Moreover, startups can use referral programs as a viral user engagement strategy. By incentivizing existing users to refer their friends or contacts to the startup's products or services, startups can tap into the power of word-of-mouth marketing. This can help attract new users and create a sense of community around the startup. In conclusion, viral user engagement methods and strategies are essential for startups and entrepreneurs to effectively promote their offerings and attract a large user base. Through the use of social media contests, shareable content, influencer marketing, and referral programs, startups can create a viral loop that amplifies their message and generates organic user engagement.

Viral User Engagement Methods

Viral user engagement methods refer to marketing strategies and techniques used by startups and entrepreneurs to encourage users to engage with their product or service and promote it among their social networks, resulting in a viral growth of the user base. One effective viral user engagement method is referral programs. These programs incentivize current users to refer their friends and contacts to the startup's product or service. This can be done by offering rewards, discounts, or other benefits to both the referrer and the new user. By enticing users to spread the word, referral programs tap into the power of positive word-of-mouth marketing, as people are more likely to trust recommendations from their friends. A second viral user engagement method is creating shareable content. Startups can generate content that is entertaining, informative, or valuable in some way and make it easy for users to share it with their networks. This could be in the form of videos, articles, infographics, or memes that resonate with the target audience. By sharing the content, users are essentially promoting the startup's brand and exposing it to a wider audience. Social media platforms such as Facebook, Twitter, and Instagram are ideal channels for distributing shareable content. Another viral user engagement method is gamification. Startups can use game elements and mechanics to make the user experience more enjoyable and interactive. By incorporating features such as leaderboards, badges, challenges, or rewards, startups can motivate users to stay engaged with their product or service and compete with others. Gamification not only increases user retention but also encourages users to invite their friends to join and compete, thus driving viral growth. Additionally, user-generated content can play a significant role in viral user engagement. Startups can encourage users to create and share their own content related to the product or service. This can be in the form of reviews, testimonials, photos, or videos that showcase their experience. User-generated content adds authenticity and social proof, ultimately attracting new users and expanding the startup's reach. In conclusion, viral user engagement methods are essential for startups and entrepreneurs to attract and retain users in a fast and scalable manner. By leveraging referral programs, shareable content, gamification, and user-generated content, startups can tap into the power of viral growth and effectively promote their brand among their target audience.

Viral User Engagement

Viral User Engagement can be defined as a phenomenon in the context of startups and entrepreneurship where users of a product or service actively engage with it and promote it to others in a viral manner. It refers to the organic and widespread adoption of a product or service by users who are not only satisfied with it but also actively share their positive experiences with others. Viral User Engagement is a crucial measure of a startup's success as it indicates the ability to attract, engage, and retain users. It involves creating a product or service that not only meets the needs and expectations of users but also encourages them to become advocates and promoters. When a startup achieves viral user engagement, it gains significant momentum and growth as users become the primary drivers of its success. This form of engagement is often achieved through user-generated content, social media sharing, word-of-mouth recommendations, and other forms of organic promotion. Startups can foster viral user engagement by focusing on delivering exceptional user experiences, creating a product or service that solves a real problem, and providing value that users cannot find elsewhere. By understanding their target audience and their needs, startups can develop features and functionalities that resonate with users and make them want to actively engage and share their experiences. Furthermore, startups can leverage social media platforms, online communities, and influencers to amplify their viral user engagement. By encouraging and incentivizing users to share their experiences on these platforms, startups can reach a wider audience and create a ripple effect that leads to exponential growth. In conclusion, viral user engagement is a powerful phenomenon in the context of startups and entrepreneurship. It signifies the ability of a startup to create a product or service that not only satisfies users but also encourages them to actively engage and promote it to others. By fostering viral user engagement, startups can achieve significant growth and success in their respective industries.

Viral User Growth Strategies

Viral user growth strategies refer to a set of deliberate and systematic techniques used by startups and entrepreneurs to rapidly acquire users and expand their customer base through viral means. These strategies leverage the power of word-of-mouth, social sharing, and network effects to achieve exponential growth. One common viral user growth strategy is creating a product or service that is inherently shareable or provides value through sharing. By designing a product that users naturally want to recommend to their friends, family, and colleagues, startups can tap into the viral loop and benefit from the multiplier effect. This can be achieved through features like referral programs, invites, or shareable content that users can easily distribute across their social networks. Another approach is leveraging existing platforms or networks to amplify a company's reach and gain access to their established user base. For example, partnering with influencers or popular social media accounts can help extend a startup's reach and expose their product or service to a larger audience. By targeting the right demographics and leveraging the following of influential users, startups can quickly gain visibility and attract new users. Additionally, creating a strong brand that resonates with users and elicits an emotional response can also contribute to viral user growth. Startups that are able to evoke emotions like excitement, surprise, or awe are more likely to be shared by users, leading to increased brand awareness and user acquisition. By crafting compelling stories, visual content, or experiential marketing campaigns, entrepreneurs can tap into the power of virality to propel their growth. To optimize the effectiveness of viral user growth strategies, it is crucial for startups and entrepreneurs to continuously analyze and iterate their approaches. Monitoring user behavior, tracking metrics, and collecting feedback allows them to refine their strategies, identify areas of improvement, and scale their viral growth efforts. By constantly fine-tuning their tactics and adapting to changing user preferences and market dynamics, startups can sustain and maximize their user acquisition rates.

Viral User Growth

Viral User Growth refers to the rapid and exponential increase in the number of users or customers that a startup or entrepreneurial venture experiences as a result of the viral spreading of its product or service. It is a desirable and strategic objective for startups aiming to achieve significant market penetration within a short period of time. Viral User Growth relies on leveraging the power of social networks and word-of-mouth marketing to quickly and organically attract new users. It involves creating a highly shareable product or service that resonates with its target audience and encourages users to share it with their network. As each user shares the product or service with their friends, family, or colleagues, it creates a domino effect where the number of users grows exponentially.

Viral User Onboarding Strategies And Techniques

Viral user onboarding strategies and techniques refer to the methods and approaches used by startups and entrepreneurs to encourage and enable users to quickly and easily adopt and engage with their products or services. These strategies aim to create a seamless and memorable user experience that generates enthusiasm and word-of-mouth promotion, ultimately leading to the viral growth of the startup. The first step in implementing a viral user onboarding strategy is to clearly understand the target audience and their needs. Startups need to identify their ideal users and tailor their onboarding processes to match their preferences and expectations. By thoroughly researching and understanding the target audience, startups can design onboarding experiences that resonate with them and spark their interest. Another important aspect of viral user onboarding is the use of product walkthroughs and tutorials. These interactive guides help users understand how to navigate and use the product effectively. By providing step-by-step instructions, startups can reduce the learning curve and ensure that users can start using the product without any confusion or frustration. Clear and concise explanations, accompanied by visual aids, can significantly enhance user comprehension and engagement. A critical element of viral user onboarding is the creation of a personalized and gamified experience. Startups can leverage the power of personalization by tailoring the onboarding process to each user's individual preferences, goals, and behavior. By collecting user data and applying it to the onboarding process, startups can provide customized recommendations and suggestions, creating a more relevant and engaging experience for the user. Gamification techniques, such as badges, levels, and rewards, can further drive motivation and encourage users to explore and engage with the product. Building social proof and fostering a sense of community are also key components of viral user onboarding. Startups can leverage testimonials, case studies, and user-generated content to showcase the value and benefits of their product. By highlighting the success stories of existing users, startups can instill confidence and trust in new users. Creating an online community or forum where users can interact, ask questions, and share experiences can foster a sense of belonging and encourage users to become brand advocates. In summary, viral user onboarding strategies and techniques involve understanding the target audience, providing clear and interactive product walkthroughs, personalizing the onboarding experience, leveraging gamification techniques, and building social proof and community. By implementing these strategies effectively, startups and entrepreneurs can create a viral loop of user adoption and growth, leading to the success and sustainability of their businesses.

Viral User Onboarding Strategies

Viral User Onboarding Strategies in the context of Startup and Entrepreneurship refer to the tactics and techniques implemented by companies to encourage new users to quickly adopt and use their products or services, and to share their positive experiences with others, thus creating a viral effect. These strategies typically involve creating a seamless and engaging onboarding process that enables users to understand the value and benefits of the product or service within a short span of time. The goal is to provide new users with a positive and memorable experience right from the beginning, enticing them to continue using the product and recommending it to others.

Viral User Onboarding

Viral user onboarding, in the context of startup and entrepreneurship, refers to a strategy or process used by companies to quickly and effectively onboard new users or customers in a way that encourages them to spread the word about the product or service to others. The aim is to create a viral loop or network effect where existing users become advocates and help in acquiring more users, leading to rapid growth and adoption of the product or service. The primary goal of viral user onboarding is to make the onboarding experience as simple, intuitive, and enjoyable as possible to attract and retain users. By providing a seamless and frictionless experience, companies can increase user engagement and conversion rates. This involves understanding the needs and preferences of the target audience and designing a user onboarding process that aligns with those needs.

Viral User Retention

Viral user retention refers to the ability of a startup or entrepreneurial venture to retain and engage their user base through viral growth strategies. It involves the use of innovative tactics to encourage users to keep using the product or service and to share it with others, resulting in exponential user growth. With viral user retention, startups aim to create a self-sustaining cycle where existing users not only continue using the product or service but also bring in new users. This cycle can lead to rapid and organic growth, allowing the startup to scale without relying solely on traditional marketing and advertising methods. Viral user retention typically involves a combination of factors, including a compelling product or service, a seamless user experience, and incentives for users to invite others. Startups often implement features such as referral programs, social sharing options, or exclusive rewards for users who refer their friends or family. By leveraging these strategies, startups can tap into the networks and social circles of their users, facilitating the spread of their product or service to a wider audience. The success of viral user retention depends on several key factors. First and foremost, the product or service must offer real value and solve a problem for users. Without a strong value proposition, users are unlikely to continue using the product or recommend it to others. Additionally, the user experience must be intuitive and seamless, ensuring that users find it easy to navigate the product and understand its benefits. Furthermore, the viral growth strategies implemented by the startup should be carefully designed and tested to maximize their effectiveness and minimize any potential negative impact on user experience. In conclusion, viral user retention is a crucial aspect of startup and entrepreneurial success. By implementing innovative strategies to retain and engage users, startups can leverage their existing user base to drive organic growth and reach a larger audience. However, it is important for startups to balance their growth strategies with the need to provide a valuable and seamless user experience.

Virality Coefficient

The virality coefficient is a metric used in the context of startups and entrepreneurship to measure the potential growth and success of a product or service. It represents the number of new users or customers that each existing user or customer can potentially bring in through referrals or sharing. Essentially, the virality coefficient focuses on the ability of a startup's offering to spread and attract new customers through the existing user base. It measures the network effect and word-of-mouth marketing potential of the product or service.

Vulture Capitalist

A vulture capitalist, in the context of startup and entrepreneurship, refers to an individual or firm that seeks high returns on their investments by providing capital to struggling or distressed companies. They primarily focus on financially distressed startups or businesses that are on the verge of failure. Unlike traditional venture capitalists who invest in early-stage startups with high growth potential, vulture capitalists typically invest in companies facing financial difficulties, hoping to turn them around for a significant profit or to extract as much value as possible before liquidating their assets.

Warrant Agreement

A warrant agreement is a formal legal contract that outlines the terms and conditions of warrants issued by a company to an investor. In the context of startup and entrepreneurship, a warrant agreement is commonly used as a financing tool to raise capital. When a startup company is seeking funding, it may issue warrants to potential investors. A warrant is a financial instrument that provides the holder with the right to purchase a specified number of shares of the company's stock at a predetermined price, called the exercise price, for a certain period of time.

It is essentially an option to buy the company's stock. The warrant agreement sets out the terms that govern the issuance and exercise of the warrants. It typically includes details such as the number and type of warrants being issued, the exercise price, the expiration date, and any conditions or restrictions associated with the warrants. One important aspect of a warrant agreement is the exercise price. This is the price at which the warrant holder can buy the company's stock. The exercise price is usually set at a premium to the current market price of the stock in order to provide an incentive for the warrant holder to exercise the warrants and invest in the company. The higher the exercise price, the greater the potential profit for the warrant holder if the stock price rises above the exercise price. Another key provision of a warrant agreement is the expiration date. This is the date at which the warrants expire and become void if not exercised. The expiration date is typically several years from the date of issuance, giving the warrant holder ample time to decide whether to exercise the warrants. Warrant agreements may also include provisions related to the company's right to call back, or redeem, the warrants before their expiration date. This means that the company has the option to repurchase the warrants from the holder at a specified price. In conclusion, a warrant agreement is a formal contract that specifies the terms and conditions of warrants issued by a company to investors. It plays a crucial role in the financing of startups, allowing them to raise capital by offering investors the opportunity to purchase the company's stock at a later date and predetermined price.

Warrant Coverage

Warrant coverage in the context of startup and entrepreneurship refers to the inclusion of warrants as part of an investment or financing deal. A warrant is a financial instrument that gives the holder the right, but not the obligation, to buy a specific number of shares of a company's stock at a predetermined price within a specified time frame. Warrant coverage is typically offered to investors or lenders as an additional incentive or form of compensation for their investment or loan. Warrants can be a valuable tool for startups and entrepreneurs seeking capital because they provide potential upside for investors or lenders while minimizing the immediate impact on the company's valuation. By including warrants in a financing deal, startups can potentially attract more investors and secure larger investments, as the warrants offer investors the opportunity to participate in the company's future growth at a discounted price. Warrant coverage also benefits startups by aligning the interests of investors or lenders with those of the company's management team. Investors or lenders with warrant coverage have a vested interest in the long-term success of the company and may be more willing to provide ongoing support, guidance, and resources to help the startup achieve its objectives. However, warrant coverage is not without its risks. If the company's stock price fails to meet or exceed the warrant's exercise price within the specified time frame, the warrants may expire worthless, resulting in no additional benefit for the warrant holders. Additionally, warrant coverage can potentially dilute the ownership stake of existing shareholders if the warrants are exercised and new shares are issued.

Warrant

A warrant is a financial instrument issued by a startup or entrepreneurial venture that gives the holder the right, but not the obligation, to purchase a specified number of the company's shares at a predetermined price within a certain period of time. Warrants are commonly used as a tool to attract investors and incentivize early-stage funding in startup and entrepreneurship.When a startup or entrepreneurial venture issues warrants, it allows potential investors to participate in the future success of the company. Warrants are often included as part of a larger offering, such as a convertible note or preferred stock, and are typically sold alongside other securities. They can be attached to debt or equity instruments and are often used as an additional sweetener to entice investors.Warrants have a predetermined exercise price, which is the price at which the holder can purchase the company's shares. This exercise price is often set at a discount to the current market price of the shares, providing the warrant holder with an opportunity to profit if the company's stock price increases. The exercise period of a warrant typically ranges from a few months to a few years, giving the holder ample time to decide when to exercise the warrant.Startup founders and entrepreneurs issue warrants as a means of raising capital and providing an incentive for investors to support the company's growth. By offering the potential for future equity at a discounted price, warrants make an investment in the company more attractive to investors. This can be particularly beneficial for startups and entrepreneurial ventures that may not have a long track record or substantial assets to offer as security. Warrants can also be beneficial for investors, as they provide the opportunity to participate in the future success of a company without requiring an immediate cash outlay. If the company's stock price increases above the exercise price of the warrant, the holder can purchase shares at a discount and potentially realize a profit when selling them in the open market.

Website Heatmapping Tools

A website heatmapping tool is a software tool or service that allows startup entrepreneurs to visually analyze and track user interactions on their website. It provides valuable insights into how visitors engage with the different elements and content on the website, helping entrepreneurs make data-driven decisions to optimize user experience and increase conversions. Heatmaps are generated based on the data collected from user interactions, such as mouse movements, clicks, scrolling behavior, and form submissions. By using this tool, entrepreneurs can identify areas of high and low engagement on their website, understand how users navigate through the pages, and determine which elements attract the most attention.

White Knight

A white knight refers to a true supporter or a company that comes to the rescue of a startup or entrepreneur in distress. This term originates from the idea of a knight in shining armor who swoops in to save the day. In the context of startup and entrepreneurship, a white knight typically refers to an individual or organization that provides capital, resources, or expertise to help a struggling startup overcome financial or operational challenges. They generally invest in or acquire the distressed startup to help it survive and thrive.

Wholesale

Wholesale refers to the business activity of selling goods or products in large quantities to retailers, businesses, or other intermediaries, rather than to individual consumers. It involves the buying of goods in bulk from manufacturers or distributors at a lower cost per unit and then selling them at a higher price to the end consumers or smaller businesses. In the context of startups and entrepreneurship, wholesale can play a vital role in the supply chain and overall business strategy. Startups often rely on wholesale channels to source their products or materials, allowing them to obtain the necessary inventory at a lower cost, enabling better profit margins or competitive pricing in the market.

Zero To One

"Zero to One" refers to the concept and methodology of creating a new company or startup that aims to bring a completely unique and innovative product or service to the market. Coined by entrepreneur and investor Peter Thiel in his book "Zero to One: Notes on Startups, or How to Build the Future," this term emphasizes the importance of venturing into uncharted territory and creating something new rather than merely competing in existing markets. In the context of startups and entrepreneurship, "Zero to One" emphasizes the value of inventiveness and originality. It encourages aspiring entrepreneurs to focus on creating a product or service that has no direct competitors, rather than attempting to emulate or improve upon existing offerings. This approach not only promises greater potential for success but also ensures that the company has a better chance of establishing a monopoly in its market, which can lead to long-term profitability and growth.

Zero-Based Budgeting (ZBB)

Zero-Based Budgeting (ZBB) is a budgeting approach widely used in the context of startup and entrepreneurship. It involves the allocation of financial resources based on a thorough analysis and justification of each expenditure, rather than relying on historical budgets or incremental changes. In ZBB, the budgeting process starts from scratch for each period, requiring entrepreneurs and startup teams to justify every expense and budget request, regardless of whether it was included or approved in previous budgets. This approach ensures that financial resources are allocated in the most efficient and effective manner, prioritizing investments based on their potential to contribute to the company's goals and objectives.